SAP PRESS e-books

Print or e-book, Kindle or iPad, workplace or airplane: Choose where and how to read your SAP PRESS books! You can now get all our titles as e-books, too:

- By download and online access
- For all popular devices
- And, of course, DRM-free

Convinced? Then go to www.sap-press.com and get your e-book today.

Transportation Management with SAP®

 **PRESS**

SAP PRESS is a joint initiative of SAP and Rheinwerk Publishing. The know-how offered by SAP specialists combined with the expertise of Rheinwerk Publishing offers the reader expert books in the field. SAP PRESS features first-hand information and expert advice, and provides useful skills for professional decision-making.

SAP PRESS offers a variety of books on technical and business-related topics for the SAP user. For further information, please visit our website: *www.sap-press.com*.

Namita Sachan, Aman Jain
Warehouse Management with SAP S/4HANA (2nd Edition)
2020, 909 pages, hardcover and e-book
www.sap-press.com/5005

Jawad Akhtar, Martin Murray
Materials Management with SAP S/4HANA:
Business Processes and Configuration (2nd Edition)
2020, 939 pages, hardcover and e-book
www.sap-press.com/5132

Justin Ashlock
Sourcing and Procurement with SAP S/4HANA (2nd Edition)
2020, 716 pages, hardcover and e-book
www.sap-press.com/5003

Jawad Akhtar
Production Planning with SAP S/4HANA (2nd Edition)
2021, 1,092 pages, hardcover and e-book
www.sap-press.com/5373

Bernd Lauterbach, Stefan Sauer, Jens Gottlieb,
Christopher Sürie, Ulrich Benz

Transportation Management with SAP®

Rheinwerk
Publishing

Editor Megan Fuerst
Acquisitions Editor Emily Nicholls
Copyeditor Julie McNamee
Cover Design Graham Geary
Photo Credit Shutterstock.com/1037068009/© Mr. Amarin Jitnathum
Layout Design Vera Brauner
Production Hannah Lane
Typesetting SatzPro, Krefeld (Germany)
Printed and bound in the United States of America, on paper from sustainable sources

ISBN 978-1-4932-1768-7

© 2022 by Rheinwerk Publishing, Inc., Boston (MA)
3rd edition 2019, 1st reprint 2022

Library of Congress Cataloging-in-Publication Data
Names: Lauterbach, Bernd (Industrial engineer), author.
Title: Transportation management with SAP : standalone and embedded TM /
  Bernd Lauterbach, Stefan Sauer, Jens Gottlieb, Christopher Surie, Ulrich Benz.
Other titles: Transporation mananement with SAP TM
Description: 3rd edition. | Boston : Rheinwerk Publishing, 2019. | Revised
  edition of: Transporation mananement with SAP TM / Bernd Lauterbach,
  Domini, Metzger, Stefan Sauer, Jens Kappauf, Jens Gottlieb and Christopher
  Surie. 1st edition. | Includes index.
Identifiers: LCCN 2018051568 (print) | LCCN 2018052177 (ebook) | ISBN
  9781493217694 (ebook) | ISBN 9781493217687 (alk. paper)
Subjects: LCSH: Materials handling--Data processing. | Shipment of
  goods--Data processing. | Shipment of goods. | SAP transportation
  management.
Classification: LCC TS180.6 (ebook) | LCC TS180.6 .L38 2019 (print) | DDC
  658.7/81--dc23
LC record available at https://lccn.loc.gov/2018051568

Contents at a Glance

Dear Reader,

Planes, trains, ships, and trucks—already, there are a lot of ways to get something somewhere. Factor in purchase orders, sales orders, freight orders, freight units, transportation units, and container units. Then consider the abbreviations: OTRs, DTRs, FWQs, FWOs, FWAQs, and more. And what about your deployment options—SAP TM 9.6 or SAP S/4HANA? Embedded or standalone? When it comes to TM, there's a lot to take in.

Luckily, authors Bernd Lauterbach, Stefan Sauer, Jens Gottlieb, Christopher Sürie, and Ulrich Benz have made a daunting topic manageable with this all-in-one SAP TM resource. Transporting your goods may be a bit more complex than simply moving from A to B, but don't worry—this comprehensive guide will walk you through the entire TM alphabet.

What did you think about *Transportation Management with SAP*? Your comments and suggestions are the most useful tools to help us make our books the best they can be. Please feel free to contact me and share any praise or criticism you may have.

Thank you for purchasing a book from SAP PRESS!

Megan Fuerst
Editor, SAP PRESS

meganf@rheinwerk-publishing.com
www.sap-press.com
Rheinwerk Publishing · Boston, MA

Contents

3   Master Data

4 Transportation Requirements and Order Management

5 Transportation Capacity Management

343

6 Transportation Planning

379

7   Carrier Selection and Subcontracting

8 Transportation Execution and Monitoring 627

9 Transportation Compliance 701

10   Transportation Charge Management   731

13 Integration with Other Components 897

Preface

Transportation, as part of logistics, is one of mankind's oldest businesses. It started with the necessity of individuals to live and trade on more than just locally available, daily goods. People soon began to reach out to a wider range of merchandise, which they could consume themselves, use as a status symbol for their urbanity, or simply push to earn higher profits in trading the goods.

The regional, countrywide, or worldwide wishes and demands of people for goods also fueled production adjustments, as decisions on where, how, and what to produce are no longer based on local resources alone but can be made on a foundation of production, labor cost, and legal requirements. This again resulted in higher demand to distribute raw materials, semifinished goods, and finished goods.

From the early beginnings of logistics, it took some time before the terms "logistics" and "supply chain" became hot topics in arranging the form of production, storage, trading, transportation, and customer centricity we see today. Logistics emerged in the early 1800s with a major focus on war supplies. A huge push forward came around and after the middle of the 1900s with process improvements, such as mass production and material requirements planning, and first technological achievements, such as bar coding of goods. Subsequently, legal regulations and councils pushed the definition and adherence to processes, standards, and performance goals, which affected most transportation activities in logistics.

Increasing globalization made it apparent to companies that required or were involved in transportation that related processes can't be managed without the support of software tools for handling the following correlated aspects:

- Cost-effective and service-level-compliant organization of all movements of goods that are necessary to fulfill the supply chain demand
- Availability of affordable transportation capacity for all upcoming movements of goods
- Proper communication with partners and peers in the logistics network
- Subcontracting of transportation requirements and settlement of all related payments
- Legal compliance of all organized movements of goods
- Transparency to the customers of a business on related logistics processes

Those companies that offer and execute logistics and transportation as a service for others (logistics service providers [LSPs]) have an even more widespread set of qualifications to fulfill in addition to those just listed:

- Evaluate, price, and handle requests of other parties to move their cargo in an end-to-end process or as part of the logistics chain.
- Properly bill other parties and companies for delivered logistics and transportation services.
- Operate their own company in a profitable way, so that selling, buying, and executing logistics services yields a profit that allows market expansion.

This book is about SAP Transportation Management (SAP TM in SAP S/4HANA and SAP TM 9.6). The described process and software is in many ways embedded into an overarching planning and handling of a supply chain. Transportation usually can't be a separate topic. Due to the intensive interaction with the precedent and subsequent logistics and financial processes, a proper integration is of utmost importance. This is where the best-of-breed approach of many standalone transportation systems fails and where the integrated platform approach of an SAP system makes a real difference and leads to a multitude of benefits.

The integration aspect, in conjunction with the power and capabilities of SAP TM, is an important part of the end-to-end business of an enterprise or company that must move goods in order to trade, to ship, or to receive, whether it's running a manufacturing or mining business, trading or retailing company, or as a professional LSP. The scope of SAP TM can be advantageously used in any of the supported industries.

For all processes related to the supply chain, collaboration and tight coordination is required for in-house, intercompany, and customer-focused operations and processes. Today's companies need to be extremely flexible, as the speed of change in product development, logistics, and technology opportunities is increasing more than ever before. On top of that, the long-standing "business as usual" is in many cases interrupted by mergers and acquisitions, which brings completely new strategies to procured companies and the burden of efficient logistics integration to the buying enterprise.

A relatively new development in logistics and transportation is the massive transition into the digital world. Sensors, Internet of Things (IoT), and machine learning have long been topics of research that are now quickly evolving to maturity and swarming over the entire logistics area. Enterprise software for logistics must deal with the effect of these digital transformations. SAP S/4HANA and SAP Leonardo as a digital logistics platform are a well-suited foundation for the transition into the digital age.

The SAP components that can solve this puzzle are centered around SAP TM, which is the focus of this book. Its environment is provided based on an integrated platform, which can be classified in three layers, contributing to its overall functionality:

- Logistics core solutions and the supply chain execution platform (SCE) include the following:
  - SAP TM
  - SAP Extended Warehouse Management (SAP EWM)
  - SAP Event Management and SAP Global Track and Trace
- SAP complementing logistics solutions enable flexible and specialized processes around the logistics core, for example, SAP Enterprise Asset Management or Product Safety and Stewardship (PS&S). Although some of these solutions will be highlighted or mentioned within this book in terms of their integration with SAP TM, a deeper functional description can be found in other SAP PRESS books.
- The SAP enterprise solutions, such as SAP S/4HANA Finance, SAP SuccessFactors for human resource management, or SAP Ariba for procurement, form a foundation to run the backbone of an enterprise. Where required, we'll refer to this foundation.

SAP TM is the central enterprise software element of efficient transportation logistics. Its modern architecture provides the ideal platform for future-proof operation. SAP TM is a comprehensive system offering a powerful and comprehensive set of options and functionality to adapt the software to all kinds of logistics businesses. Since September 2017, SAP TM has been part of SAP S/4HANA.

How This Book is Organized

This book is the third edition of a comprehensive work on transportation management in SAP, and it's based on the functionality and integration capabilities of SAP S/4HANA 1809 as released in September 2018. In parallel, SAP also provides SAP TM as a standalone version under the label SAP TM 9.6, which was released in December 2018.

> **Transportation Management Naming and Coverage**
>
> This book will use SAP S/4HANA as its base system; therefore, we'll refer to SAP TM in SAP S/4HANA (subsequently, just *SAP TM*) throughout.
>
> Viewed from a functional perspective, SAP TM in SAP S/4HANA is widely similar (and often the same) as the standalone SAP TM 9.6 solution. Where major instructions, features, or points of interest diverge, we'll provide you with a text box or clarification for SAP TM 9.6.

This book first provides the necessary background information on transportation and logistics in general and then subsequently introduces SAP S/4HANA. In the main part of the book, we take a deep dive into SAP TM and the link into its ecosystem. The goal of this book is to provide a big picture on SAP TM and its components, including how they work and integrate, and how transportation business requirements map to available software functionality. The following chapters are presented:

- **Chapter 1: Transportation Management Foundations**
  The first chapter gives you an overview on the basics of business software, the new SAP S/4HANA architecture, and how SAP TM functionality is structured and can be used in various ways. In addition, you get an overview of the components that enhance the functional scope beyond pure transportation processes.

- **Chapter 2: Solution Architecture and Technological Concepts**
  The second chapter gives an overview of the technical architecture of SAP TM and how integration is done. We explain the business object foundations—business object processing framework (BOPF) and its business object modeling—and describe the important tools of SAP TM, which are referenced often in later chapters. These tools include the Business Rules Framework (BRF+, rules engine), Post Processing Framework (printing/output), and user interface technologies (e.g., Floorplan Manager [FPM] and SAP Fiori) as a central means to provide workflow capabilities. The third section describes technical integration by services and change handling within SAP TM (Process Controller Framework).

- **Chapter 3: Master Data**
  This chapter explains the general master data of SAP S/4HANA as related to SAP TM (e.g., business partners) and transportation-specific master data, such as networks and resources. It also gives an overview of remodeled master data usage, which replaces the transmission-based technology used between SAP Business Suite and SAP TM.

- **Chapter 4: Transportation Requirements and Order Management**
  This chapter explains how to create and manage transportation orders in SAP TM. For shipper scenarios, it focuses on the new direct integration between SAP S/4HANA order/procurement processes and transportation. In forwarder/carrier scenarios, we'll explain the capabilities of the customer order objects and quotations, as well as the provision of their functionality for customer service and sales.

- **Chapter 5: Transportation Capacity Management**
  For shippers and LSPs, management of freight capacities and schedules is an important aspect of moving cargo. In this chapter, the capacity management process is described, including allocations, freight bookings, and their interplay with schedules.

- **Chapter 6: Transportation Planning**
  Transportation planning deals with the activities involved in the assignment of cargo items to vehicles or reserved capacities on trucks, trains, planes, or vessels. This chapter describes freight units as the basis for planning and transportation units for modeling truck, trailer, container, or railcar scenarios. The new package units will also be explained. You'll get an overview of the interactive and optimized planning capabilities of SAP TM with an explanation of how to configure and use the transportation cockpit, the optimizer, transportation proposals, load planning, package building, and planning-related configuration profiles.

- **Chapter 7: Carrier Selection and Subcontracting**
  This chapter explains freight orders and their use as subcontracting documents to carriers or other service providers. Relevant carriers are determined through carrier selection. Subsequently, a tendering process can be executed to determine the best available price, conditions, and availability of the selected carriers. Carrier selection is a part of the optimization process that allows you to propose and select one or multiple carriers for subcontracting.

- **Chapter 8: Transportation Execution and Monitoring**
  Execution and monitoring deal with handling freight and providing visibility of shipments. In this chapter, we explain the different options for managing the cargo status of freight (i.e., freight document functions, discrepancy handling in SAP TM, loading status, and paperwork). In addition, we describe aspects of export and import handling in international supply chains and the corresponding setup in SAP TM. This chapter highlights the features of SAP Event Management and the processes that allow out-of-the-box integration with SAP TM. We'll also give you

an overview of the new SAP Global Track and Trace, which allows you to add cloud and collaboration aspects to track and trace.

- **Chapter 9: Transportation Compliance**
  This chapter deals with compliance issues arising from trade regulations and hazardous cargo. It explains the integration and functionality of SAP Global Trade Services (SAP GTS), which supports various functions from blacklist screening to export and import compliance handling. Furthermore, the integration with external customs, security, and booking services, such as Descartes Global Logistics Network (GLN), is described. Various tasks involved in handling, checking, and documenting hazardous cargo are done using SAP S/4HANA for product compliance. Like SAP GTS, SAP S/4HANA for product compliance is integrated with the SAP TM processes.

- **Chapter 10: Transportation Charge Management**
  This chapter explains the general aspects of Transportation Charge Management within SAP TM and provides details on how to use it for shipper processes, including setting up agreements (contracts) and defining tariffs and rates. Calculation of charges within forwarding and freight orders is described in detail as well. This chapter also describes charge calculation master data with service products, forwarding and freight agreements (contracts), calculation sheets, rate tables, scales, maintenance functions, upload and download, and contract determination.

  Creation of contracts with vendors in many cases is a lengthy and distributed process, especially with strategic business partnerships. In this chapter, we also describe the tools provided by SAP TM to manage vendor request for quotations (RFQs) and to evaluate vendor responses. The tools are the core of strategic freight procurement and allow efficient implementation of new contracts and the extension of existing contracts.

- **Chapter 11: Charge Settlement**
  This chapter deals with the payables process that shippers face with their subcontractors. After the charges of a subcontracted freight order are calculated, the individual characteristics of forwarding and freight orders are provided and generate a list of charge items to be paid in the charge settlement process. This process was initially done as part of the SAP Business Suite and is now available as part of SAP S/4HANA.

- **Chapter 12: Charge Calculation and Settlement for Logistics Service Providers**
  In Chapter 10 and Chapter 11, we explain the foundation and processes around charge calculation and freight settlement, giving you a view on general capabilities

and the usage by shippers, who buy transportation services. In this chapter, we'll look at the specifics of charge calculation from the view of an LSP, which sells transportation services and needs to deal with customer revenue calculation, customer billing, cost distribution, and profitability. We also build a link to the global service product catalog because the service product is used as a core element of agreements. Finally, we describe strategic customer contract management, which allows LSPs to negotiate new contracts and renegotiate contracts with their customers.

- **Chapter 13: Integration with Other Components**
  This chapter describes the integration between SAP TM and analytics applications of SAP S/4HANA, SAP EWM for traditional and transit warehouse management, and SAP Customer Relationship Management (SAP CRM) for opportunity management. In the transportation domain, a set of new components has been brought to market that support the SAP TM processes in terms of equipment management and planning (SAP Transportation Resource Planning), yard management (SAP Yard Logistics), and vendor portals (SAP Logistics Business Network).

- **Chapter 14: Implementation Best Practices**
  This chapter highlights specific topics to keep in mind when you implement an SAP TM process at a customer site. You'll also get some insight into what needs to be considered when moving from SAP TM based on SAP Business Suite to an embedded version of SAP TM in SAP S/4HANA.

- **Chapter 15: Summary and Outlook**
  This chapter concludes the coverage of SAP TM by providing a synopsis of the challenges the industry faces and the future direction of SAP TM.

Who This Book is For

SAP provides in-depth system documentation, solution manager content, release notes, and installation guides at a very granular level. These accompanying documents are publicly available and include scenario descriptions and detailed explanations on how to deploy and configure SAP TM. In this book, we try to avoid repeating this information in favor of explaining how features interrelate.

Therefore, the intention of this book is not to document all necessary configuration steps of SAP TM. Instead, the book mainly focuses on making process and configuration options transparent and acting as a tool to better understand the essential functionality and issues involved. We've written it for the following audiences:

- Everyone looking for a comprehensible introduction to transportation management with SAP TM will find that each chapter describes in detail specific functional areas or business processes and provides an overview of the underlying functionality and its use. We address SAP beginners and employees in departments where SAP TM is to be implemented, as well as students getting an understanding of core processes in transportation management and how they map to SAP software.

- Ambitious users and consultants of SAP systems will get a deeper understanding of process integration and the upstream and downstream functions, as well as their mapping in SAP TM.

- Enterprise management members and IT decision-makers who are considering the implementation of SAP TM will obtain an overview of its functional richness and building blocks.

Acknowledgements

Very special thanks for the contents of this book go to Jens Kappauf and Dominik Metzger, who contributed as coauthors of the previous version on SAP Transportation Management 9.3:

- **Jens Kappauf** for SAP EWM and master data know-how
- **Dominik Metzger** for SAP TM charge calculation and settlement know-how

Their valuable input and expertise is an excellent foundation for preparing and upgrading the corresponding chapters to the SAP S/4HANA world that you find in the later sections of this book.

Numerous other colleagues and friends contributed to the successful completion of this book by providing knowledge and tips, answering questions, and leading valuable discussions. Every one of them deserves a big "thank you" (in alphabetical order): *Andreas Anselmann, Tobias Berger, Stephan Biwer, Christoph Eichin, Thomas Engelmann, Dragos Florescu, Stefan Förster, Sabine Hamlescher, Bernhard Hauser, Stefan Helmbrecht, Ralf Hierzegger, Robin Huang, Olena Iavorska, Jan Kapallo, Mathias Kinder, Anne Kissler, Kathrin Koffler, Shi Ling, Matthias Müller, Christian Reinhardt, Torsten Saige, Marlene Schumacher, Michael Sinibaldi, Peter Wadewitz, and Marcus Zahn.*

We also want to sincerely thank Emily Nicholls and Megan Fuerst at SAP PRESS, who supported this book project all the way from concept to completion. Their effective and great collaboration was a valuable contribution to the realization of this book.

Next, we would like to express our special thanks to our wives, partners, and families for their tolerance and patience while writing this book:

- Yumi Kawahara with Kai and Yuki
- Dr. Isabella Mayer
- Pia Penth
- Martina Bunte-Sürie with Vicky and Charlotte
- Nadine Benz with Jakob

Finally, we would like to thank our readers of the first and second editions. We hope you'll be impressed by this third edition.

Sincerely,

Dr. Bernd Lauterbach, **Stefan Sauer**, **Dr. Jens Gottlieb**, **Dr. Christopher Sürie**, and **Ulrich Benz**

Introduction

Efficiency in cargo transportation is one of the most important factors to move any kind of goods among manufacturers, traders, and final customers. In this chapter, we present the variety of transportation activities and processes as well as the needs of the participating parties.

Transportation is defined as moving people or goods from one place to another, but this general definition doesn't unfold the complexity and importance of the processes and network behind the scenes. Transportation has become a highly significant factor in logistics, as it carries quite a large amount of logistics cost and is a major contributor to the reliable delivery of goods.

Although our initial definition of transportation included the movement of people, this book doesn't take into account passenger transportation. The movement of people has its own complexity and challenges, such as missed schedules, crowded subways, and overbooked flights or trains. Transportation management, as we describe it in this book, deals with the movement of goods, that is, cargo transportation, and the services required to facilitate it.

Transportation is considered the backbone of the global supply chain. Essentially, no daily process works well without the use of transportation services behind the scenes. Whether it's manufacturing goods from procured components, shipping goods from an online store, restocking groceries in our favorite supermarket, getting fuel for our cars, or buying toys for Christmas gifts, if transportation doesn't work in the background, supplies will falter.

Transportation is a process that we often only realize marginally, such as when waiting in a traffic jam caused by trucks or being annoyed by the noise of a passing cargo train. In reality, transportation is a part of the complex network we are all severely dependent on today. What we see with our own eyes is just a small part of that network, which is formed by supply chain processes in the background. To be able to procure our daily goods, some company must ship it to us. However, someone else previously must manufacture these goods and ship them to the store. The manufacturer won't be able to produce the goods without getting a proper supply of required components and semifinished materials from other companies, and that business of course needs some raw materials shipped from, for example, a mining enterprise. Finally holding the goods in our hands comes from this long supply chain, and all intercompany and internal moves tend to require transportation.

In Figure 1, you can see a schematic example of the transportation processes in a supply chain. A vendor delivers materials or goods to a manufacturer or distributor, which then transports the goods to a production plant. The manufacturer/distributor transforms the materials or goods into finished products, which then are transported to the final receiver. However, each company may also have a need for internal logistics, which again can involve transportation. External transportation can be done directly or via transfer facilities. With many supply chain players in a row or network, it becomes clearer that a lot is at stake if the processes aren't properly managed.

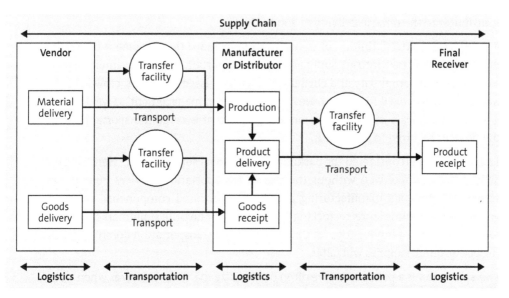

Figure 1 Contributors to Supply Chain, Logistics, and Transportation

Figure 1 also shows the three interrelated terms that will be used throughout this book:

- **Supply chain**
Defines the entire value chain from the first vendor over a sequence of manufacturers or distributors to the final receiver.

- **Logistics**
Defines the operations process of receiving, storing, moving, and shipping of goods from the viewpoint of a supply chain participant.

- **Transportation**
Defines the movement of materials or goods between participants of the supply chain. However, transportation can also happen as part of the logistics functionality within a company and is heavily related to the shipping and receiving processes (e.g., a large chemical plant needs internal transfers of materials).

Transportation Processes in the Industries

Transportation and its management in a company are highly dependent on many influencing factors coming from its ecosystem and integrated business activities in the company itself or in collaborating companies. Transportation management supports the organization of cargo transfers between business partners.

Transportation can be viewed in two general dimensions:

- **Connection type**
The transportation connection type can be either of the following:
  - Domestic (inland): Cargo is moved within a country and doesn't cross its border. Cargo moves aren't relevant for any trade compliance processes (export and import).
  - International: Cargo is moved across borders and may be relevant for trade compliance processes.

- **Transportation mode**
The transportation mode defines the types of transport used for the cargo move, which can be executed with one or multiple modes of transport. Transportation modes include the following:
  - Road transportation: Transportation takes place on public or private roads. Means of transport for road modes are, for example, trucks, trailers, semitrailers, and chassis.
  - Rail transportation: Transportation takes place on public or private rail tracks. Means of transport for rail modes are trains with different kinds of railcars, such

as flatbed, hopper cars, container stack cars, and so on. In some regions (e.g., Europe), rail cargo is sometimes actually moved on the road.

- Sea transportation: Transportation takes place on oceangoing vessels. Means of transport are container vessels, bulk vessels, or tramp ships. Although feeder vessels service smaller ports that aren't on the main lines, they are also considered sea transportation.

- Barge transportation: Transportation is usually done on river barges and often carried out either as domestic moves (e.g., in China on the Yangtze River) or within economic unions (e.g., Germany to Netherlands).

- Air transportation: Transportation occurs via aircraft, which are either pure cargo aircraft or passenger aircraft that also provide cargo capacity. The latter are controlled very strictly concerning cargo security. In some regions (e.g., Europe), air cargo is sometimes actually moved on the road for shorter trips.

- Intermodal transportation: If cargo in containers is moved from a road-based chassis to a rail-based stack car, the term *intermodal* is used. An intermodal move is usually considered to be a rail move with roads at its ends. In some cases, container lines doing sea-based moves with rail or road at its ends use the term for nonocean moves.

Transportation Mode: Unimodal versus Multimodal

Unimodal transportation means that cargo is moved on a single mode of transport, for example, on the road only, but it doesn't mean that only one means of transport is used. For example, three consecutive truck moves can occur with a load transfer in between.

Multimodal means the decision to move cargo involves more than one mode of transportation, for example, an initial truck move, a rail move, and a subsequent truck move. Even if the carrier decides to use a truck instead of a railcar (because it's cheaper), the move is still sold as and considered to be multimodal.

Another common term that we'll use throughout the book is *shipment*. A shipment is the movement of a defined quantity of cargo from its origin to its destination. The cargo can be transported as unimodal or multimodal, and it can potentially be split and transported independently; however, in significant locations or for substantial processes, it must be handled together. Further points to consider about cargo are as follows:

- Cargo is only considered shipped if all cargo left the origin site.
- Cargo is only considered received if all cargo arrived properly at the destination site.
- Cargo must be handled as a single unit when executing legal processes, such as the following:
  - Shipment documentation creation (e.g., house waybill printing, which is the legal shipping document)
  - Shipment trade declaration and checks (e.g., export and import handling)
  - Shipment compliance checks (e.g., dangerous goods check)

From an industry perspective, companies can be separated into two large groups that have a joint view of the set of general requirements they need to focus when performing transportation management:

- **Shipping industries**
  Shipping industries or *shippers*, as used quite often throughout this book, refer to a company or a functional unit of a company that organizes the transportation of goods in the following business contexts:
  - Goods that are sold by that company or one of its subsidiaries
  - Goods that are to be distributed by that company
  - Goods that have been purchased by that company if the buyer and the vendor have agreed that the vendor isn't responsible for organizing the transportation

  Shippers typically don't manage logistics and transportation needs as their main business; instead, their profit as a company is achieved by producing or trading goods and materials. For them, transportation is a necessary medium to physically network with their partners. In a general view, shippers are sometimes called first-party logistics providers (1PLs), as they in former times, tended to do their own logistics. Typical industries that you'll see as shippers in transportation management processes are as follows:
  - Consumer products companies that need to procure and receive materials and manufacture and ship finished goods (e.g., body care product companies)
  - Retail and wholesale distribution companies that receive consumer and other goods, repack the goods according to the needs of their stores, and ship them out to replenish stores (e.g., supermarket chains)

- High-tech companies that receive raw and semifinished materials to produce technology goods to be shipped out to distributors (e.g., computer companies)
- Oil and gas companies that extract fossil energy sources, transport the material to refineries (upstream), and produce finished fuels to be distributed to storage tanks or gas stations (downstream) (e.g., gasoline corporations)
- Mining industry companies that excavate or produce minerals and ship it to raw material handling facilities (e.g., rare earth element mining companies)
- Other industries with transportation needs (e.g., the mill products industry, chemical industry, aerospace and defense industry, agribusiness industry, military organizations, and fashion industry)

- **Logistics service providing industries**

The term *logistic service provider* (LSP) encompasses all companies that provide management and execution capabilities to shippers and other LSPs. This is regarding the flow of goods and materials between origin and destination points, which may be end or intermediate points. Besides pure shipping or its organization, the provider will often handle inventory, warehousing, packaging, and security functions for shipments. The main difference from shippers is that transportation is the main business for LSPs that need to be profitable by selling, buying, organizing, and executing logistics services.

LSPs can be categorized into the following different groups:

- Carriers or second-party logistics providers (2PL): These companies directly execute transportation and logistics processes for others using their own capabilities, that is, their own fleet and storage capacities. In many cases, carriers focus on a single transportation mode (e.g., railway, container shipping line [CSL], trucking company, airline), but multimodal capabilities can also be found.
- Freight forwarders, third-party logistics providers (3PL), and fourth-party logistics providers (4PL): These companies usually don't operate their own fleet; that is, they are much less asset-focused than carriers. Their profession is more to organize end-to-end shipments for shippers, offer them the best way to execute complex moves (e.g., international and multimodal transports), and with this subcontract to carriers who are specialized to execute a specific part of a shipment. A 4PL usually takes this a step higher and offers services not only to execute complex shipments but also to redesign and consult for a supply chain of a shipper, so that it best fits his or her business requirements.

- Contract LSPs: These companies focus on providing sales, storage, maintenance, and transportation-oriented services to shippers so that they can concentrate on their main business goal (e.g., manufacture products). The contract LSP operates general or customized warehouses for a shipper, stores and moves his goods, and may also provide services around the sales cycle, such as ordering hotlines.

- Courier, express, and parcel (CEP) service providers: These companies usually concentrate on the movement of small freight items, such as packages. Their processes are organized to ship standardized freight items in large quantities through their own network of facilities (stations, sorting centers) by making use of a pattern of how to ship freight for a service (e.g., 24-hour delivery). CEP providers can be associated either with transportation or postal industries.

Looking at the various industries and modes involved in transportation, there is unfortunately also a multitude of terms around what commonly is regarded as an order for a shipment. Keeping this in mind, Table 1, provides a list of the different terms used for the same things (an order to move cargo) in different industry contexts.

Order Term	Industry Context
Transport order	General term, but used to sell and buy freight
Forwarding order	Sales order for forwarding service used in SAP TM
Booking	Term used for ocean carriers and air carriers
Waybill	Term used for railways
Customer order	General term, but doesn't indicate transportation relation
Shipment	Term used in courier business or from a shipper view

Table 1 Different Terms for an Order to Move Cargo

The different levels of LSPs are shown in Figure 2 in an aggregated form. A 1PL (shipper) traditionally uses either a 2PL (carrier) to provide transportation on single moves or contracts with a 3PL to orchestrate the end-to-end transportation movement. The 3PL may then contract various 2PLs to move the cargo. The 4PL aims to orchestrate and optimize the whole supply chain of the shipper.

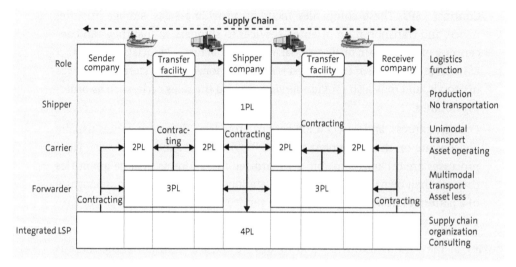

Figure 2 Level of Logistics Providers and Capabilities

Following is a set of operational requirements that all companies—shippers as well as LSPs—should follow when attempting to manage their transportation processes efficiently:

- Transportation processes should be organized in a way that minimizes transportation costs.
- Service-level agreements (SLAs) with business partners should be complied with.
- Available vendors providing transportation services need to be subcontracted in a cost-efficient and contract-conforming manner.
- All cargo needs to be moved in a legally compliant way under recognition of, for example, dangerous goods or trade compliance rules.
- If a company doing transportation manages its own fleet, the available vehicles need to be used in an optimal way, meaning a high percentage of efficiently consolidated loads should be placed on the company's own vehicles while reducing empty vehicle moves.
- When deploying its own fleet, a company also may have to attend to driver and fuel cost efficiency.

These criteria are valid for any company involved in transportation. However, if an LSP owns the process, its major business goal is to provide transportation services successfully and profitably. As you may have noticed, the preceding criteria did not include sales-oriented goals. These come into focus when they are the business of the LSP, as he or she needs to balance and consider the following aspects when doing business:

- Achievable price settings, market requirements, and long-term contracting commitments when selling transportation services to customers (shippers and other LSPs)
- Cost of operating and maintaining a fleet as part of the offered transportation services
- Cost of subcontracting transportation services to other vendors (typically carriers)
- Cost of subcontracting additional services (e.g., customs clearance, transshipment of cargo in port terminals) to other vendors
- Internal cost and profit sharing among organizational units of an LSP leading to a lack of transparency (e.g., a US LSP ships to Europe and orders the vessel transport, but the European LSP should pay for the vessel price to the US organization and get this money from the European recipient)

The preceding considerations are of tremendous importance for LSPs to work profitably and achieve overall growth. As the logistics market can change seasonally, issues around nonavailability of shipment space and options, overcapacity of carriers due to missing transport orders, and long-term commitments to investments and the related risks (e.g., already ordered large vessels) are quite common, and the related price fluctuation can easily lead to bankruptcy. Therefore, a good overview is necessary of the targeted market, the company's and the network's capabilities, and the situations of competitors.

In addition to the operational requirements for all transporting companies mentioned previously, LSPs can also manage the following essential functions:

- Negotiate prices and contracts with customers and manifest these agreements in a price and contract database.
- Capture quotes and orders for transportation services based on established customer contracts and prices. The orders are the foundation for price calculation, routing of shipments, compliance checks, transportation documents, and customer invoice creation, as well as internal collaboration of organizational units.
- Validate prices derived for transportation orders against the overall cost of executing a shipment to guarantee profitable operation.

Discussing transportation modes, shippers, LSPs, and their contracting relations and requirements shows the complexity of transportation. Regarding LSPs, Figure 3 shows the categorization into their different transportation mode priorities and modes of operation. The companies considered to be freight forwarders, 3PL, and 4PL are grouped together as they typically work with fewer of their own assets but potentially move goods end-to-end across transportation modes. On the other hand, those operating their own fleets and concentrating on a mode are grouped as carriers or 2PL. Today, many carriers have a strategy to extend their footprint into end-to-end logistics by starting/buying a new business unit or better integrating a logistics company they are already running today by separating it from a process perspective (i.e., the rail, ocean, and air logistics companies).

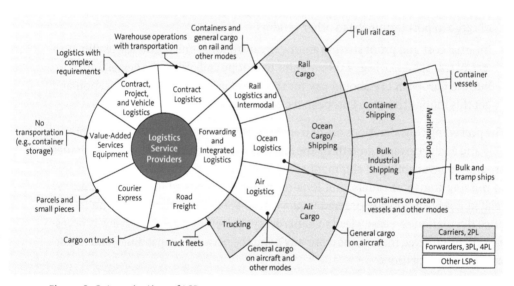

Figure 3 Categorization of LSPs

Transportation Processes, Movements, and Roles

Looking at transportation processes and their variety, steps, and participants, we can say that LSPs usually implement a superset of what shippers do. LSPs are confronted with a large diversification of ways to ship cargo and optimize according to a multitude of different goals driven by the requirements of shipper customers and by the need to operate profitably. Therefore, many of the process variances are explained based on LSP processes, which in the end are, of course, driven by the shippers.

The first variable in shipping is the type of cargo that needs to be moved. Following are the typical cargo categories:

- **General cargo (also packaged goods or break-bulk cargo)**
  Refers to individual cargo items that need to be shipped and individually handled. General cargo usually doesn't contain materials requiring special handling, such as dangerous goods, but complies to general shipping rules. Examples for general cargo are crates with televisions, pallets with cereal boxes, or cartons with screws. In some cases, general cargo items may be shipped together or broken apart into their individual items (hence, the term "break-bulk").

- **Bulk cargo**
  Refers to any kind of solid materials or goods that are shipped in a loose form. For transportation purposes, bulk cargo can be loaded into a vehicle, such as a suitable railcar or compartment vessel (bulker), or it can be prepackaged in containers. Examples for bulk cargo are grain or iron ore. Bulk cargo can easily change weight and volume during transportation (discrepancy) as it never can be loaded or unloaded with the same quantity.

- **Fluid bulk cargo**
  Refers to cargo that is like solid bulk but requires special tank resources or containers to be transported. Some of the fluid bulk transports can also be done via pipeline, which won't be part of this book. Especially for fluid bulk, weight and volume changes due to temperature or vaporization need to be considered as they directly relate to changes in value.

- **Containerized cargo or prepackaged cargo**
  Usually refers to general cargo items that are already loaded into a container or other transportation equipment when being handed over by the shipper. The container is then moved along the whole transportation chain and delivered to the final receiver in an unbroken manner.

- **Piece cargo**
  Refers to cargo made of individual pieces or packages of small size as handled by postal or express services. Piece cargo transportation is usually a mass business that may need millions of individual deliveries per day. Transportation and load transfer of piece cargo in transfer facilities happens along predefined patterns. Individual planning for each piece, as often done for general cargo, isn't common practice.

- **Out-of-gauge (OOG) cargo**
  Refers to any kind of large shipped items that don't fit into standardized sizes of containments or compartments. OOG cargo requires special handling in load transfer and shipping, and it may need special equipment and vehicles. Examples are huge chemical factory components or large mechanical diggers.

When transporting some of these cargo categories (general cargo, containerized cargo, or piece cargo), specific shipping types may be used. In Figure 4, you can see four very common shipping types:

- **Less than truckload (LTL)**
  General cargo or pieces are moved on a truck together with cargo from other shippers.

- **Full truckload (FTL)**
  A complete truck is filled with the cargo of a single shipper.

- **Less than container load (LCL)**
  General cargo or pieces are moved in a container together with cargo from other shippers. This shipping type is usually related to sea shipments and sometimes to rail shipments.

- **Full container load (FCL)**
  A complete container is filled with cargo of a single shipper. This shipping type is usually related to sea shipments.

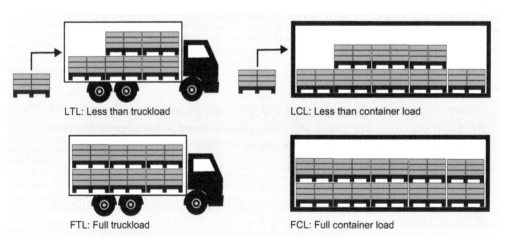

Figure 4 Some Transportation Shipping Types

In some cases, other shipping types are used, for example, wagon load is often used for full railcar shipments with bulk commodities.

Cargo is usually moved as a single shipment when it's either shipped by the shipper as a full truck or container, so that no further consolidation happens. On the contrary, consolidated shipments can either be driven by a shipper who intentionally transports multiple individual shipments together in a containment or can be initiated by a carrier or forwarder that moves cargo for a part of its journey in a joint containment. This is usually the case with LTL or LCL shipments.

Consolidation of shipments in LTL or LCL cases is sometimes driven by a shipper, but it's done intentionally in most cases by an LSP as part of its service. Shippers often explicitly declare their shipments to be consolidated. An LSP uses consolidation as a service offering to their customers to ship smaller quantities without exclusively providing containment. In addition, LSPs will reduce the offered rate to a reasonable level, as the price to be paid by a forwarder to a carrier for shipping a container from Europe to the United States can be split, for example, by weight when recharging the rates plus a profit to each single shipper.

Figure 5 illustrates the consolidation of shipments from a forwarders perspective. Multiple shippers (A, B) need to move cargo from Europe to the United States. The forwarder consolidates the cargo in an LCL container and subcontracts the move to a container shipping line (CSL). The carrier has a cost of $800 to move the container and charges $1,000 to the forwarder (for a $200 profit). The forwarder, which sold the container space to its customers, adds its own profit (again $200) and then splits the resulting container rate of $1200, for example, by weight to his or her shippers, so that shipper A pays $480, and shipper B pays $720. Other split criteria are also applicable.

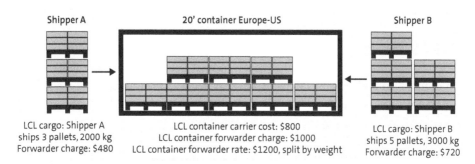

Shipper A | 20' container Europe-US | Shipper B

LCL cargo: Shipper A
ships 3 pallets, 2000 kg
Forwarder charge: $480

LCL container carrier cost: $800
LCL container forwarder charge: $1000
LCL container forwarder rate: $1200, split by weight

LCL cargo: Shipper B
ships 5 pallets, 3000 kg
Forwarder charge: $720

Figure 5 Consolidation of Shipments

Besides consolidation, shipments can be moved in many ways from their origin to destination. In Figure 6, you can see a variety of options for how the movement can be organized, although many more options are also possible. The way a shipment is moved is defined by its movement type, which is related to the transport order, that is, specified by the shipper.

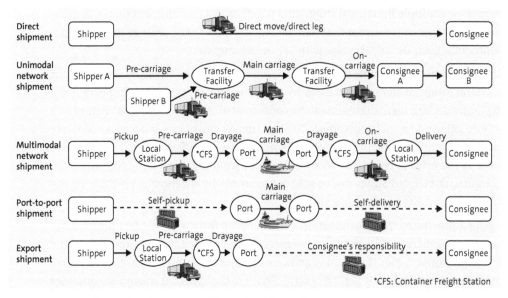

Figure 6 Examples of Movement Types in Shipments

In Figure 6, all moves next to the continuous arrows are related to the movement type, that is, part of the responsibility to fulfill the shipper's order. The dashed arrows aren't part of the order and should either be organized by the shipper or the consignee apart from the order. The movement types shown in Figure 6 are as follows:

- **Direct shipment**
  The shipment is an order for cargo that is moved directly from an origin to a destination with a single means of transport (e.g., truck). This movement type is common for full truckloads but also for smaller shipments in a local geographical context (e.g., courier shipments in the same city).

- **Unimodal network shipments**
  These shipments are moved using a single mode of transport (usually road), but they are routed via the transfer facilities of the LSP. The shipments may be moved to or from the transfer facility in a single or consolidated way. The trip between the transfer facilities is often executed on a scheduled or regular basis (e.g., a scheduled truck the morning and afternoon between Atlanta and Boston).

- **Multimodal network shipment**
  In this very common movement type, cargo is often moved in a consolidated way;

for example, cargo is locally picked up by truck and then transferred in a local station into a consolidated truck that runs to the container freight station (CFS) close to a vessel port or to an airport (ground holding facility [GHF]). In such a consolidation facility, cargo items are packed into ocean containers, air containers, or pallets, and then they become part of a consolidated shipment, which first is delivered to the port or airport facility for handover to the main carrier (CSL or airline). Most of these means of transport run on a regular, that is, scheduled, basis (e.g., daily flights, weekly vessel port calls), but individual operation is possible as well. The carrier then moves the consolidated cargo to its destination, where it's unloaded from the main means of transport and moved to the related CFS/GHF for deconsolidation. The single shipments are then moved on in trucks, for example, to their local destination stations, where they finally are distributed to be delivered to the consignees.

- **Port-to-port shipments**

  When getting an order for a port-to-port shipment, the forwarder or carrier only takes of receiving FCL cargo (ocean) or a prepacked air cargo container in its port facility (terminal) or airport facility and moves the complete unit to its destination facility. The shipper should take care to hand in the cargo at the origin. Upon arrival, the carrier then sends release information to the recipient (consignee) in the form of a delivery note. The recipient uses this document to release the cargo unit from the port facility and move it to its destination on the recipient's own behalf.

- **Export shipments/import shipments**

  This movement type is often used in international trade when the shipper only is responsible to move cargo to a county border, for example, a port terminal. The shipper asks the forwarder to execute and organize all steps to get the cargo safely loaded on board the vessel or airplane (shipped on board). From this point on, the responsibility of organizing further cargo movement belongs to the recipient. The export forwarder informs the receiving forwarder of the cargo, so that the receiving forwarder can arrange further transport. Similar processes apply when importing shipments.

Figure 6 also shows the related stage types, which are the types of segments that cargo is moved along during its transport. The following stage types are found in end-to-end movements:

- **Pickup**
  Pickup refers to a local stage from the shipper's origin to a local transfer facility or station.

- **Pre-carriage**
  Pre-carriage has a larger scope in that it can be used to pick up shipments at a shipper or at a local station and move them—often in a consolidated way—to a more remote transfer facility.

- **Main carriage**
  Main carriage defines the stage on which cargo is moved on its long haul, which can include one or multiple stages and a change of transport mode. A main carriage can, for example, be by vessel from Singapore to Dubai and subsequently by air cargo to Frankfurt (sea-air shipment). The main carriage mode of transport usually takes over as the relevant mode for the whole shipment.

- **On-carriage**
  On-carriage is like pre-carriage but it refers to moving from the destination facility of the main carriage to a local station in the consignee's area or to the consignee itself.

- **Delivery**
  Delivery is related to a local distribution of cargo from a local station to its destination.

- **Drayage**
  Drayage refers to the move of consolidated or containerized cargo from the consolidation facility of a forwarder (CFS/GHF) to a port terminal/airline facility or vice versa. Drayage usually has a local context.

- **Haulage**
  Haulage is also often referred to in transportation. Long-haul transportation implies going over one or more main carriages, and short-haul transportation is done on pre-carriage or on-carriage.

Another characteristic is the responsibility for cargo and its movement. As shown in Figure 6, a shipper isn't always responsible for the whole move, which means the shipper may not pay for every aspect of the end-to-end move nor be responsible for insurance and ownership of the cargo the whole way. The *incoterm* regulation on payment, insurance, and ownership of cargo, as described in the Incoterms 2010 standard, is quite important for international transportation. (Further details can be found in the corresponding documents at *https://iccwbo.org/resources-for-business/*

incoterms-rules/incoterms-rules-2010/.) Here, we'll highlight just a couple of examples:

- **Free on board (FOB) Hamburg**
  FOB means that the shipper includes the freight up to a location (here, Hamburg) in the sales price and is responsible to hand it over on board a vessel in the Hamburg port.

- **Delivered, duty paid (DDP)**
  DDP means the shipper/seller must pay all transportation costs, including import duties, so that the consignee/buyer receives cargo without being responsible for any transport issues.

In all transportation processes, contributing parties play some typical roles. In some cases, roles may be collectively assigned to a single party, but, in general, they can be assigned to individual participants. The most common roles are as follows:

- **Ordering party**
  The party who orders the movement of the cargo and is the contracting party for the move.

- **Shipper or sender**
  The party who ships the cargo. In many cases, the shipper is also the seller of the goods and the ordering party of the shipment.

- **Consignee or recipient**
  The party who receives the cargo. In many cases, the consignee is also the buyer of the goods.

- **Invoicing party**
  The party to whom the invoice for the shipment is sent. In many cases, a single party isn't assigned, but the overall charges are split to multiple invoices to individual participants, which may be driven by the incoterms of the shipment.

- **Payment party**
  The party who pays the invoice for a shipment, which can be the ordering party, the invoicing party, or another clearing company.

- **Beneficial cargo owner**
  The party that holds ownership for the cargo to be transported. This is especially valid if neither shipper not consignee owns the goods.

- **Notifying party**
  The party that needs to be notified on certain shipment milestones, for example, on arrival in the destination country.

- **Contracting or agreement party**
  The party under whose contract the cargo is shipped. In many cases, it's the same as the ordering party, but for a larger enterprise, a subsidiary company may ship under the contract of the head branch.

- **Importer or exporter**
  The agents who take care of trade compliance for a shipment.

- **Forwarder or carrier**
  The LSPs that provide the complete service or parts of it to the shipper.

The parties related to a transportation process need to be properly involved and need to receive the correct legal documentation for handling and as proof or ownership or processing. The following documents are important and are used in many versions throughout the transportation process:

- **House bill of lading (HBL)**
  This document is the legal proof and shipment definition between a shipper and the commissioned LSP. It defines what is moved for this shipper, from where and to where, and who is the main contractor. HBLs are usually the basis for customs declaration—if one part fails, the whole shipment stays in customs until clarification. The HBL is common for ocean shipping.

  On the other hand, house air way bills (HAWB) are used for air shipments, road waybills are used for road shipments, and waybills are used for rail shipments. However, the significance and content of these documents are very similar.

- **Master bill of lading (MBL)**
  The MBL document is usually issued by carriers or forwarders to define the consolidation of multiple shipments into a unit (e.g., container), which is then physically handled. As such, it's a legal document between forwarder and carrier. Security measures are driven by the MBL, and vessels and aircrafts take MBLs as proof of their loaded cargo. For air shipments, it's defined as a master air waybill (MAWB) and may be issued by an authorized forwarder. A forwarder may have multiple MBLs with a carrier on a single voyage or flight.

- **Manifests**
  Manifests declare the load composition of a means of transport from the carrier's perspective. It can also be provided with respect to certain load and unload ports, for example, all cargo items to be loaded onto a vessel in a port. Manifests overarch multiple MBLs.

- **Delivery notes**

  Delivery notes are legal documents provided by carriers that are sent to the recipients of cargo. These recipients then use the document to identify themselves and their cargo when picking it up in the port of arrival.

Besides the previously mentioned movement types that define how a shipment must be organized and moved physically, a forwarder usually offers a variety of commercial transportation forms to customers. Customers may differ depending on what kind of commercial service is addressed: it may be a shipper, a consignee, or a third party. Figure 7 shows examples of buyer's consolidation, purchase order (PO) management, and triangular trades.

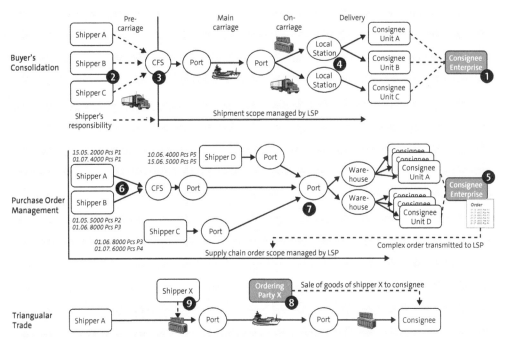

Figure 7 Examples of Complex Commercial Forms in Transportation

The commercial forms of transportation shown in Figure 7 are examples of the complex processes forwarders face in the daily business of logistics that they must resolve with a TMS. Let's explore each a bit further:

- **Buyer's consolidation**

  The buyer of the cargo, which is also the ordering party and legal receiver (e.g., a large toy store chain), instructs the LSP to consolidate goods from multiple shippers in joint containers to be distributed to different warehouses ❶. The LSP is responsible for shipping from its CFS in the country of origin; therefore, each shipper must deliver to the CFS according to that shipper's received order ❷. The LSP consolidates multiple shipments of the various shippers in containers and creates HBLs according to the instruction of the ordering party ❸. The cargo is then moved and distributed into the advised consignee's destination locations ❹. The LSP is responsible for correct consolidation, HBL creation, import, and inland distribution.

Buyer's consolidations can also be handled as seller's consolidations, where a single seller instructs the LSP to consolidate the load and distribute it to various consignees.

- **PO management**

This process is a more complex variant of a buyer's consolidation. The LSP not only ships consolidated cargo for a buyer but also handles the logistics for a complete procurement cycle, for example, the seasonal fashion campaign logistics of an apparel company. The middle part of the scenarios in Figure 7 visualizes PO management.

The consignee instructs the LSP to handle a complex procurement process ❺. This process may not only contain the arrangement of shipments but also negotiation, tracking, and reporting of proper delivery times, quantities, and qualities from each shipper, so that the overall requirement of the ordering party for the campaign can be fulfilled ❻. After calling off and arranging these partial shipments, the LSP takes care that all shipments are moved according to the plan ❼ and arrive on time and on quality in the consignee's warehouses.

- **Triangular trade**

In the triangular trade scenario, also known as cross trade, the ordering party, which sells goods to the consignee, needs to arrange transportation from the shipper to the consignee; in other words, the ordering party doesn't touch the cargo ❽. As an additional step, the ordering party needs to conceal the real origin of the goods and act as the owner of the sold goods ❾. In some cases, specific documents are created that support this obfuscation (switched bill of lading).

Other scenarios include project shipments, where an LSP arranges the transportation for an entire sequence of project deliveries that need to be on time (e.g., rail tracks, locomotives, and railcars from China to Brazil to build a new metro), or charter shipments, where a whole vessel is chartered to a company for a set of voyages.

No matter the level of complexity of a shipment scenario, it always needs to be broken down into its components, which then need to be coordinated. These pickups, pre-carriages, main carriages, on-carriages, deliveries, load transfers, consolidations, shipment documents, and so on need to be planned, created, and used as the basis for operation, which is the focus of a transportation management system (TMS).

Transportation Management System Functional Areas

A TMS fulfills the main tasks to coordinate transportation demand with the available and achievable resources and produces a solution to the transportation scenarios to fulfill customer requirements and—in the case of an LSP—also profitability goals. The main support and solution areas of an TMS are as follows:

- Selling shipment processes to customers
- Planning, optimization, and decision-making to achieve a cost-efficient and well-executable solution for any transportation and transit storage demand fulfillment
- Transportation execution, including provision of all necessary documents and information required to physically perform the movements and all legally required activities
- Efficient subcontracting of transportation services
- Transport tracking with the capability of disclosing and visualizing of the required information to all customers, partners, event management with the capability to mitigate any situation that endangers the initial plan and commitment
- Ability to get instantaneous insight into analytics information on transportation processes, cost, sales, and profitability by providing real-time visibility on logistics and financial key performance indicators (KPIs)

In Figure 8, you can see a component view of such a TMS. The major components are used in a process flow from the left to the right side. The dark boxes will be addressed in the following chapters of this book. The medium gray boxes are also part of the functionality covered in this book, however, as they refer to major independent components, more in-depth information can be found in specialized publications. The light gray boxes can be an important element in the ecosystem of a TMS, but we won't go into details on these topics in the later chapters. Figure 8 lists the chapter numbers of each addressed component via the small number in the bottom-right corner of each box.

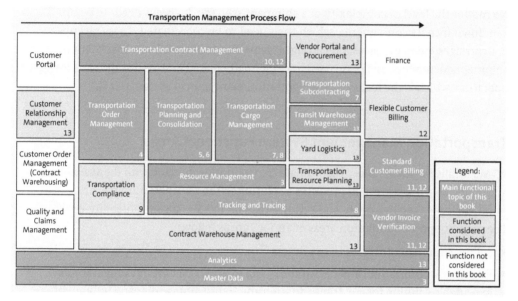

Figure 8 Components of a TMS and Coverage in This Book

The content and functional scope of a TMS can be separated into three areas, which will be addressed in the chapters of this book:

- Foundational data stored and processed in a TMS:
  - Business partner master data, for example, customers, vendors, shippers, consignees
  - Network master data, for example, customer and transfer locations, network connections, schedules, carrier availability
  - Resources to move cargo, which may be either a definition of the company's own fleet objects (truck, vessels, railcars, containers, etc.) or capabilities a partner can provide
  - Cargo master data, for example, dangerous goods or trade compliance characteristics
  - Pricing and rating rules and tariffs
- Processes and business objects handled in a TMS:
  - Order and quote management process with business objects to store and process order and quote data, for example, validity and completeness checks, route determination, price calculation, profitability calculation

- Planning and consolidation with capability to store characteristics of cargo objects to be moved and planned, as well as cargo consolidation
- Cargo management processes with definition of master files as business objects, which represent voyages and tours as well as processes to manage these master files and handle their execution and progress
- Transit warehouse management processes to receive, deconsolidate, store, cross-dock, consolidate, and dispatch cargo in transfer facilities
- Subcontracting of master files to carriers and other partners with the ability to calculate and settle the expected cost
- Billing to customers and settlement of invoices with carriers/vendors with the corresponding invoice business objects
- Engines and automatisms to support processing of TMS data and objects:
  - Planning and optimization engines to do scheduling, route planning, carrier selection, and load optimization in the transportation network
  - Charge calculation engines to do computation of prices and costs based on customer and vendor orders, the contracts they are based on, and the rules and tariffs referred in these contracts
  - Condition evaluation rules to be used in a variety of decision tools everywhere in the TMS processes

Transportation in the Digital Age

The digital age in transportation brings changes to all companies involved in logistics processes. The availability of digital technology and its maturity for transportation and other supply chain processes has made a big leap forward within recent years. On the other hand, integration of various technologies into business processes and the TMS can be difficult if the system isn't flexible enough or enabled to work with these devices and technologies. Many companies are trying to achieve improvements with digital technologies, for example:

- Productivity improvements with lower maintenance and operations cost, such as higher asset availability through better maintenance
- New business models to reach markets that allow more growth
- People and process optimizations with productivity increases

- Risk reduction through improved supply chain control, resulting in fewer claims and charges

Whichever area of business improvement is targeted by a logistics company, several foundational technologies can be used to advance capabilities:

- Machine learning and artificial intelligence (AI) can improve a company's decision and planning algorithms. These technologies learn from past decisions and successes to include factors such as weather patterns, traffic congestion data, and historical traffic reaction patterns into a planning cycle and to achieve better results through optimization.

- Innovative production technologies can completely change a shipment move, for example, by enabling local production of specialized goods with 3D printing, so that many items can be manufactured on demand close to the consignee and only require short-haul shipping.

- Predictive processes allow better detection of risk of failure for a company's own assets and enable the scheduling of required maintenance to avoid unnecessary parts replacement.

- Real-time data availability enables users to make faster decisions and to respond more quickly to changed environments.

- Products are generally smarter due to their own sensors that allow them to report on individual situations and needs, for example, temperature requirements and history or shock sensors for sensible cargo.

- New transparency and communication technologies, such as blockchain, change the pattern of interaction between the players in a logistics process. Selected documents can be made accessible and immutable so that trust between all parties is improved.

All of these new opportunities require a company to be able to adapt their processes and systems to this new world. SAP TM is an open, flexible, and powerful platform to solve today's transportation challenges and leap into the digital age of logistics.

Next, in Chapter 1, we'll provide an overview of the foundations of SAP TM. You'll learn how SAP provides the infrastructure to run transportation business processes and how SAP TM is used and integrated to handle offering, selling, assigning, planning, subcontracting, controlling, tracking, and settling transportation services.

Chapter 1

SAP Transportation Management Foundation

*SAP S/4HANA is a comprehensive and integrated set of business soft-
ware applications that enables enterprises to manage their business
processes. SAP Transportation Management is an essential part of
SAP S/4HANA. In this chapter, we give you an overview of SAP TM in
SAP S/4HANA and how it revolutionizes the potential of business IT.*

SAP S/4HANA comprises all products and applications that an enterprise needs to support its full scope of IT processes, ranging from human resource management to procurement and sales, logistics and manufacturing, and financials. From the perspective of this book, SAP TM is the SAP S/4HANA logistics component that allows you to manage all transportation processes.

Enterprise suite software such as SAP S/4HANA enables companies to plan and execute processes within and between enterprises, to achieve cost efficiency and transparency, to be flexible enough to easily move into new business areas, and to enter the digital world. The applications are built on SAP NetWeaver for SAP S/4HANA, which provides a powerful foundation to smoothly run all technical operations required by the various business areas.

SAP TM in SAP S/4HANA consists of business processes that drive the offering, selling, assignment, planning, procurement, subcontracting, steering, documenting, and settling of transportation services. To help you become familiar with the core concepts of the system and the role of SAP TM in the SAP S/4HANA supply chain execution (SCE) platform, this chapter is divided into the following sections:

- Section 1.1 explains the benefits of using standard software systems. It also clarifies how and why the move from SAP Business Suite to SAP S/4HANA happened.

- Section 1.2 describes how SAP S/4HANA, as a future-proof platform, supports and enables all foundational features to run the required transportation business processes with high flexibility. Within this area, we'll also explain the digital integration with SAP Leonardo.

- Section 1.3 introduces important SAP TM principles and business objects, explains how SAP TM works on a high level, and shows how it interacts with various SAP S/4HANA products and components. At the end of the section, we'll give you a preview of the content of the following chapters.

1.1 Standard Software for Transportation

Looking at the logistics service provider (LSP) market and its IT foundation, specifically designed transportation software is still widespread. In general, software used for transportation management can be assigned to one of the following categories:

- **Legacy**
  Legacy systems are specialized IT systems that are either developed by a company's IT department for its own purposes or tailor-made to the company's needs by a consulting firm. Depending on the system's age, the software can be based on client-server or mainframe technology and thus often can be a dead-end, as either the technology is old and gets out of maintenance, or the knowledgeable people for such a system retire and nobody dares to touch it any more.

- **Best-of-breed**
  Best-of-breed software is produced by companies specializing in transportation or logistics applications. They are often created to cover very specific market requirements, such as truck transportation in North America only or air cargo transportation, but are targeted to a larger user group in that segment. Creating synergies between different business units (BUs) of an enterprise (e.g., usage of one software for an integrated process for air, ocean, and road transport) or simple integration into backend processes (e.g., financials) may be challenging as it can become a continuous change process due to the various software packages and their releases and interfaces.

- **Standard**
  Standard software is often part of an enterprise suite that not only covers transportation or logistics processes but also allows integration into other enterprise areas such as sales, production, or finance. Transportation coverage targets a wider scope than best-of-breed software.

While LSPs often still use legacy or best-of-breed software, shippers usually tend to use standard software, as they already run many integrated processes in their enterprise via such a system.

In this section, we'll take a closer look at standard software and the transition to SAP S/4HANA.

1.1.1   Standard Software as a Foundation of Enterprise IT

The term *standard software* describes a group of programs and applications (e.g., SAP S/4HANA) used to solve or process many similar tasks in an enterprise. In most cases, the programs can be configured. Configuration of the software means that process chains, process steps, and individual functions can be adjusted to meet company-specific and user-specific requirements by setting control parameters, tables, and values to meet specified characteristics and program flows. The SAP terminology for the configuration process is called *Customizing*.

By using standard software, companies can avoid covering common processes, such as transportation management or controlling, by individually developed applications, as these often lead to fragmented or hard to maintain system landscapes. In addition, individual software solutions often indicate that integration efforts and the complexity of data exchange and data consistency increase. Even the use of best-of-breed software bears the risk that different areas of an enterprise using different software solutions split further apart and lead to increased effort and cost as the release development of those tools is completely independent with no guarantee that they will always fit together. Large companies may end up with 500+ systems in their landscape that need to be maintained and integrated in terms of master data consistency, release levels, interfaces, and cross-application processes.

In the long term, standard software can be implemented and integrated in an enterprise much more efficiently than multiple self-developed or independently designed best-of-breed tools. The expensive, error-prone, and cost-pushing software development process is done by an experienced standard software company so that the procured solution can be implemented directly. In many cases, the implementation project can concentrate on process definition, system configuration, master data maintenance, migration from the previous software tool, and user training. As many other companies—especially shippers—already use, for example, SAP standard software, a lot of solution expertise is available in the market for customers to profit from. This can be further optimized by using a template-based approach. Maintenance services and special support activities are available for SAP customers on a 24/7 basis.

Enterprises need to consider whether to use standard software versus individual software. The flexibility of standard software and its regular road map developments by the vendor entails a lot of advantages without losing the option of company-specific enhancements and configurations. A disadvantage, however, may be that only 60%–80% of the required individual processes are covered by the standard, while the rest needs to be provided by enhancements, additional software products, or business process redesign.

The existence of an old legacy system within a company that will no longer be maintained in the near future is a risk that can be mitigated by the use of standard software as a joint platform for IT.

In addition, the recent market developments in digitalization are a strong hint toward standard platforms, as digitalization brings an additional level of complication into the processes and IT. These complications can be handled reliably by a well-integrated and open technology, such as SAP S/4HANA and SAP Leonardo offer out of the box.

1.1.2   The Move from SAP Business Suite to SAP S/4HANA

Standard software is a very important contribution and foundation to successful and well-integrated enterprise processes. It prevents unnecessary data duplication and guarantees cross-application data integrity.

Such benefits have been reason enough for companies to choose an SAP system as foundation, although those advantages are no longer a guarantee for long-term success as, unlike in the 1960s where an S&P 500 company had a 60-year success record, this period is now only 12 years. Company success is very much related to the ability of an enterprise to adjust, merge, and adapt. Digitalization and the ongoing changes in logistics processes require companies to be highly flexible, which is directly mirrored by the IT specification and landscape.

These process changes resulted in SAP rethinking the foundations of the enterprise suite and launching SAP S/4HANA and SAP Leonardo as the long-term successor of the well-known SAP Business Suite.

The name SAP S/4HANA has been defined following the well-known SAP R/3, the predecessor of SAP Business Suite:

- S represents *simplicity* and the *suite*.
- 4 represents the successor of "3" in SAP R/3.

- HANA indicates operation on the in-memory technology of SAP HANA.

Simplicity is one of the major topics of SAP S/4HANA:

- **Simple usage with best usability**
  The system and its processes are easy to use, and you can integrate people, devices, technologies, and networks.

- **Simple business processes**
  Easy execution of business processes allows users to concentrate on changes without being confronted with distracting data.

- **Simple decisions**
  Insight is provided into significant data, trends, and business processes in order to make decisions.

- **Simple process optimization**
  By using machine learning and artificial intelligence (AI) on an in-memory system, processes can be improved compared to slow SAP ERP instances.

- **Simple configuration**
  The system is easy to configure, providing a guided implementation process.

- **Simple data models**
  Based on in-memory technology and very fast data access, technical auxiliaries, such as indexes, aggregation, and redundancy, aren't required any more.

- **Simple access**
  Many centralized processes don't have to be on-premise any more but are available via a cloud service.

SAP S/4HANA is based on the in-memory platform SAP HANA, which went through a step-wise transition starting as a database and development platform via analytics, then a foundation for the SAP Business Suite and implementation of finance processes, and finally as the successor of SAP Business Suite with an integrated in-memory processing and digitalization technology. Figure 1.1 shows the steps of this journey.

In addition to the on-premise version of SAP S/4HANA, SAP S/4HANA Cloud was established as a public cloud service offering comparable functionality. However, looking at SAP S/4HANA version 1809, there are still components that aren't offered in the public cloud yet, including SAP TM, which is planned to follow as a public cloud service in 2019 with limited scope compared to SAP TM on-premise.

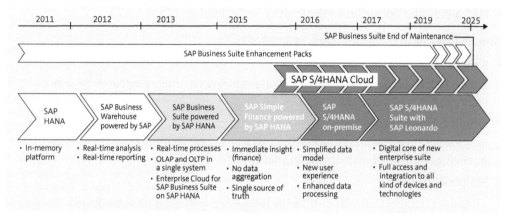

Figure 1.1 History and Development of SAP S/4HANA

Another essential aspect besides the convenience of SAP S/4HANA is its capability to integrate all areas and influences of modern business life, including traditional and digital. Different types of devices, Internet of Things (IoT) technologies, business networks and social networks, people, and big data sources can be joined smoothly with existing processes. Figure 1.2 shows this capability as an overview.

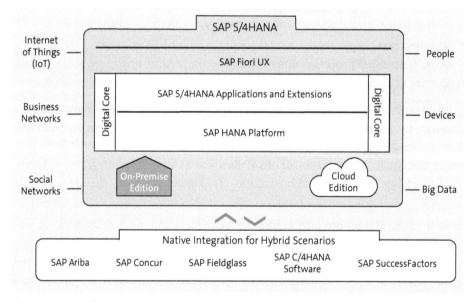

Figure 1.2 SAP S/4HANA's Digital Core: Integrating Processes and Digital Technologies across All Lines of Business and Industries

1.2   SAP S/4HANA as a Future-Proof Platform

The innovative in-memory technology of SAP S/4HANA enables a variety of new process and transaction concepts. Because the SAP HANA database is an integral part of the suite, the availability of all relevant data in the main memory allows for processing benefits that come without previous data replication or aggregation. SAP S/4HANA is built on some guiding principles:

- **Modern architecture**
  The architecture is robust and scalable. The simple data structures deliver high speed because they are working on primary data. Data forms a single source of truth, and consumption of data can be flexibly managed.

- **Role-based design**
  All functions are designed to be people centric and should run on any browser-based device. Flexible workflows allow for better collaboration and decision support.

- **Smart business**
  The suite is built for scalability, automation, and integration of digital technologies. Cockpits provide an exception-based style of working with embedded analytics, prediction analytics, and simulation capabilities.

This section will dive into SAP S/4HANA and its SAP NetWeaver foundation. We'll also explore SAP S/4HANA's intersection with SAP Leonardo technologies, as well as the cloud versus on-premise deployment options.

1.2.1   Features and Concepts of an SAP S/4HANA System

SAP S/4HANA is a comprehensive and fully integrated family of business software applications that allows large and small organizations to perform transactional planning, execution, and documentation of end-to-end business processes. Safe and flawless process execution makes it possible to achieve cost savings and ensure a seamless audit trail. The built-in configurability and flexibility of SAP S/4HANA enables easy adoption of business processes and development of new business portfolios.

Built on SAP NetWeaver, the SAP S/4HANA applications support the best practices of various industries. The integrated components for financials, controlling, production, procurement, marketing, sales, service, supply chain management, and risk and compliance management interact in a powerful way to facilitate transportation management processes in the manufacturing and shipper-focused industries (e.g., consumer products, retail, mill, and chemicals), as well as in the logistics services industry (e.g., freight-forwarding and carriers). LSPs are especially dependent on the robustness and completeness of the transportation management-related applications because the software is used to manage their core business.

Business Objects

The term *business object* is used in many places and contexts throughout this book. Business objects such as purchase orders (POs), sales orders (SOs), invoices, business partners, and equipment are representations of real-world business documents or processes in an IT system. They enclose and structure data belonging to a business-related context and provide a set of methods to create, update, and delete the object or parts of it and to exchange the data via interfaces. No activities ever breach the integrity of the business object.

The whole application suite and its components are based on a configurable interaction of business objects, which can be used in the context of the necessary business processes to represent the logical flow of work tasks and data required to manage the business successfully.

In-Memory Database

The in-memory technology of SAP HANA enables completely new process concepts and transactional processing. Data is available in the main memory of the system. Due to data models largely abstaining from replication or aggregation of data, processes can operate faster and increase data consistency. Memory space can be saved by avoiding data replication and using efficient compression techniques.

Transactional processing of data (online transaction processing [OLTP]) is done in main memory with SAP S/4HANA, instead of retrieving information from a database and writing it back after the transaction. Using in-memory technology, data is retained in direct access, and later evaluations don't have to retrieve and load data again. An analytical system (online analytical processing [OLAP]) can directly work on real-time data instead of relying on hours-old or days-old extracts.

Access to in-memory data also allows much faster and better algorithms for calculations, simulations, forecasts and machine learning, which would be quite difficult with conventional ERP systems. Where a traditional ERP system has the status of being a system of record, an SAP S/4HANA system stands out as a system of intelligence.

SAP Fiori and SAP Fiori Launchpad

Simplifications of SAP S/4HANA include the user interface (UI) and user experience (UX). With SAP Business Suite, the intelligence and expertise was with the user. Even though the use of the system was simple, the user must have a good understanding of how to operate the system and which fields were important.

The philosophy of SAP S/4HANA goes further in that intelligence is now an intrinsic part of the system, and the expertise stays with the user who can concentrate fully on his actual task via the SAP Fiori UX. The system supports the user with important, relevant information in a suitable representation without requiring technical background knowledge.

The SAP S/4HANA UI provides four levels of working (see also Figure 1.3):

❶ The SAP Fiori launchpad provides a role-specific and configurable overview of user activities, delivering important key performance indicators (KPIs) as part of the tiles that guide the user's attention.

❷ The overview page of a tile provides the user with additional details and relationships of a selected business unit or process.

❸ By selecting details on the overview page, the user can view, update, delete, or analyze data more deeply or in a classic way. The user still gets full system support in terms of machine intelligence or process integration.

❹ From the SAP Fiori launchpad, the user can also directly open various analytics views of real-time data.

SAP TM in SAP S/4HANA still has some UIs and screens presented in a conventional way, as the logistics industry has a high demand for dense screens with lots of information.

SAP Fiori Launchpad: Tiles, Links, and Menu Paths

In Figure 1.3 screen ❶, you can see that the UIs of the SAP Fiori launchpad allow you to configure the appearance of menu items either as tiles with or without KPIs or as links in a menu box. In this book, we'll always refer to them in functional descriptions as tiles, even if they can be set as links or are part of a standard role as link definitions.

As we'll describe later in this chapter in detail (Section 1.3), SAP TM can be a part of SAP S/4HANA or can be based on SAP Business Suite (SAP TM 9.6). Due to this fact, there might be slight differences in configuration or menu paths. We'll mention these differences if significant, but to keep it simple, in most cases, we'll list the SAP S/4HANA path.

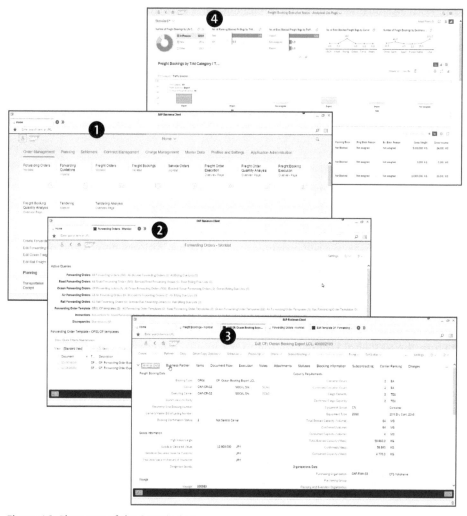

Figure 1.3 Elements of the SAP Fiori UI

1.2.2   SAP NetWeaver for SAP S/4HANA

Sitting on one of the multiple possible operating systems, SAP NetWeaver for SAP S/4HANA is equipped with an operating system–dependent kernel that shields the applications above from the specific behavior and requirements of the hardware and operating system. This architecture allows unified operation of the application and harmonized access to system and hardware functions, such as database and printer access. Supported database systems include SAP HANA and any other database supported by the SAP environment (AnyDB).

In this section, we'll further discuss programming, functions, and business concepts for SAP NetWeaver.

The SAP ABAP Kernel

The ABAP and Java runtime systems of SAP NetWeaver form the foundation of most applications that are executed in a homogenous and stable environment. ABAP is very important to SAP because most application functions are implemented in this proprietary programming language. From its beginnings as a COBOL-like reporting language, ABAP has evolved into a powerful object-oriented programming tool whose language constructs provide excellent support for building business applications. Embedded in the ABAP runtime environment, processes executed by a user can be shielded very well from those of other users so that problems in one executed program don't impact other running processes (this is sometimes a disadvantage in Java application servers).

Access to SAP Program Source Code

ABAP isn't considered flashy, but SAP did develop the language to be a best-fitting, reliable, and fast platform for business applications. ABAP is, so to speak, the "workhorse" of business application programming. SAP views it as very important and fundamental. In addition, the complete source code for the business applications is visible and delivered with the system. With a little programming knowledge, you can start the ABAP Workbench (Transaction SE80) and look around in the coding (e.g., in SAP TM) to find out how it works. The code availability also allows you to enhance and reuse program coding by implementing enhancement spots, for example.

SAP NetWeaver Functions to Support Business Applications

The SAP NetWeaver ABAP runtime environment offers a wide range of system and support functions to all applications running on application servers. These services deal with harmonized access to the application environment (e.g., printing or communication) or with security support and are provided consistently, independent of the database and operating system. You can see an overview of many of the support functions in Figure 1.4. The following support functions are the most important basic system features:

- **Transaction control**
  Transaction control implemented in SAP NetWeaver and well-designed applications guarantees consistency of related business data. If, for example, an invoice for an order is created, then transaction management ensures that the invoice is created correctly, and the invoicing status and data in the related order are updated within the same transaction. Either you accomplish everything consistently or, in the case of a partial inconsistency, all stored data is rolled back to the state it was in when the transaction was started.

- **Work process control (work processes and load balancing)**
  By means of process control, the system balances the workload of the currently running processes and transactions so that each user gets an allocation of processing time to finalize his transaction. Newly started processes are automatically allocated to the least-loaded application server in the system environment.

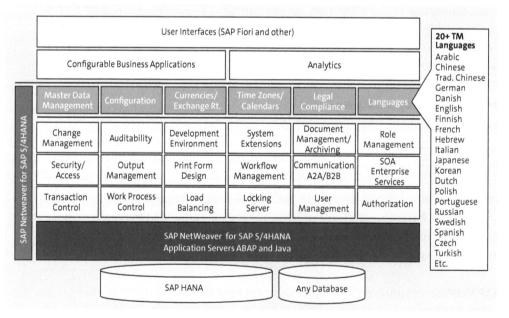

Figure 1.4 Support Functions of SAP NetWeaver for SAP S/4HANA

- **Multilanguage support**
  SAP TM is delivered with more than 20 pretranslated languages; other applications can even offer more. Additional translations can be made as well because the tools are provided with SAP NetWeaver. All language operations are fully based on Unicode. Technically, hundreds of different languages are possible.

- **Locking server**
  The locking server ensures that only one user or transaction at a time can alter a single business object (e.g., user A updates order 123 by adding a new item even as user B deletes order 123). In SAP TM, an extended concept is implemented that works with optimistic locks, which allow multiple users to work in change mode on separate, more independent parts of the same object. Additionally, locking can be implemented at the subobject level, meaning that multiple users can concurrently work on one object, each having their own work set of object data.

- **User management and authorization**
  To manage access rights to applications, you can define user roles with a comprehensive list of authorizations. The user roles can be assigned to named users who can log on to the system. After logon, the authorizations linked to the roles assigned to the user control each activity that the user can carry out with a transaction or object. For example, a call center service agent may create new orders and create invoices but may not be allowed to correct disputed invoices. All these settings can be very specific to each company, so the definition and setup are usually part of the implementation phase of the SAP software.

- **Output management for printing and other channels**
  SAP NetWeaver allows you to manage all printers centrally in the system. In addition to technical integration of printing devices, printing queues and integration of printing activities into the application layer are provided. In newer installations, Adobe Document Server is often used to actively manage the document output. SAP also offers the capability to use the Adobe Forms Designer and interactive PDF forms.

  In the context of output management, SAP NetWeaver offers options for sending created documents by fax or as email attachments instead of printing them. The output management services allow you to automatically create an archived version of the document in a document management system.

- **Communication and services**
  Communication management in SAP NetWeaver supports internal communication processes (application to application [A2A]) as well as external processes

(business to business [B2B]). For all applications, there are plenty of enterprise services (web services with Web Service Definition Language [WSDL] definitions).

- **Workflow management**
  SAP NetWeaver includes a complete workflow management system that can be integrated with all applications, the office functionality of SAP S/4HANA, and business process management.

- **Development workbench**
  SAP NetWeaver contains a complete development environment for development coordination (i.e., packaging of objects), all dictionary objects (e.g., database tables, structures, data elements, etc.), ABAP objects (e.g., programs, function modules, classes, etc.), UIs (e.g., Web Dynpro, Business Server Pages [BSPs], etc.), enterprise services, and other objects, such as authorizations, transactions, and message classes. The development workbench allows you to test all objects instantaneously and has very strong drilldown capabilities, such as a call-to method, referenced structures, and data elements. Figure 1.4 shows an overview of the development workbench. Alternatively, development can be accessed via an Eclipse-based environment.

- **Change and transport organizer**
  Change and transport organizer is a tool for managing centralized and decentralized ABAP Workbench development projects and Customizing projects (i.e., system and process configuration). Development objects and Customizing settings can be clustered in transport requests to achieve a structured release of consistent development and configuration content and to allow export from a development system and import into a test or production system.

Important Business Concepts in SAP Systems

Three essential concepts realized in SAP systems make adoption of business requirements easier and more flexible. These concepts affect SAP NetWeaver as well as the business applications and components built on top:

- **System and client concept**
  The organizational layers (system and client) of an SAP system can be used to implement an enterprise's processes with multiple companies. The client of an SAP system is a concept involving a logical separation of data and work areas within one technical system installation. Using the client, multiple independent organizations can work in a single system in completely separated work spaces with data being shielded from access by unauthorized users.

- **Organizational units**
  The subordinate organizational units allow you to assign users in the same company to work in different areas of responsibility (e.g., purchase organization in the United States and sales organization in China). Organizational units are always related to one client in one system. In terms of multisystem usage, a master data management process must be in place to consistently allow usage of organizational structures.

- **Customizing and Implementation Guide**
  The Implementation Guide (IMG) is a tool for organizing a project implementation, that is, setting up business processes in a project or at a customer's site. You can create multiple projects, each holding Customizing tasks for specific business areas. Customizing tasks allow you to set up the configuration in the SAP system client. The configuration controls which process can be executed in what way, which consistency checks are executed, and which data determinations are done. Figure 1.5 shows part of the reference IMG and a Customizing task in an SAP TM in SAP S/4HANA system.

Examples of typical Customizing tasks are as follows:

- Defining the countries where you do business and which currencies you use within the processes
- Defining order types and their functional details
- Defining price calculation rules and document printing rules

The IMG can also work on an overall task assignment as the Reference IMG, giving you access to all Customizing tasks in the whole system. The structure of the IMG reflects the different business areas to be configured. There are always joint SAP NetWeaver-related tasks such as country and communication settings. In addition, and depending on the installed components, you'll find application-specific tasks. In an SAP S/4HANA system instance, there are settings for procurement, finance, sales, logistics, transportation, production, and so on. In a pure SAP TM instance, you'll find configurations for master data, forwarding order management, planning, and others.

Customizing allows you to define very detailed settings. In fact, in SAP TM, there are more than 500 different mandatory or optional configuration tasks. You can get a system up and running with a minimum settings; however, a high level of configurable flexibility is available if you need it.

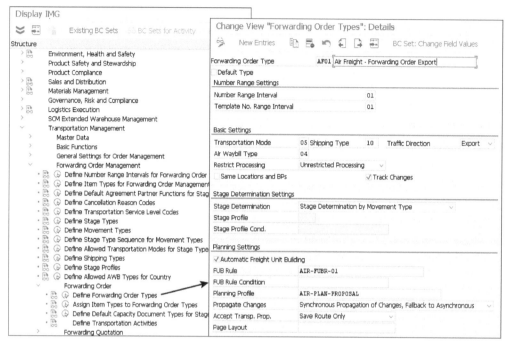

Figure 1.5 Customizing IMG and Configuration of a Forwarding Order Type for Air Freight in an SAP TM System as Part of SAP S/4HANA

1.2.3   SAP Leonardo

SAP Leonardo is a new bundle of components and services that enables SAP S/4HANA to be fully integrated into the processes, data streams, and data algorithms of the new digital world. Figure 1.6 provides an overview of the SAP Leonardo innovation portfolio, including the following key components:

- The SAP Leonardo Bridge links the devices and external services, such as IoT devices and scanners, sensors, business networks, or social networks, into the application layer.

- SAP Leonardo applications provide specific implementations of functionalities enabling the use of linked devices and foundation services for data evaluation and processing to provide the requested output.

- A growing set of SAP S/4HANA applications and software components make use of the SAP Leonardo services, such as logistics networks or asset insight applications. An example for asset insight is collection and evaluation of vehicle, driver, weather, and traffic data to evaluate driving behavior or support driving decisions based on a set of criteria.

- The SAP Leonardo Foundation provides computing, evaluation, and decision mechanisms to support applications with various algorithms.

- SAP Edge Services allows you to support external computation algorithms in the place where data is taken—that is, to have data evaluations already close to the sensor or device—before evaluated data or results are sent to the SAP Leonardo platform.

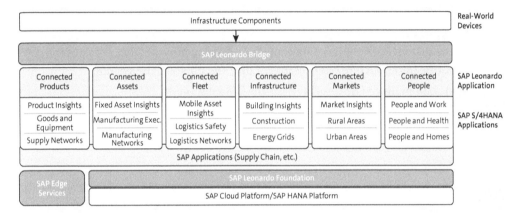

Figure 1.6 SAP Leonardo Innovation Portfolio

SAP Leonardo is a consolidation of technologies, algorithms, and processing guidelines that improves the flexibility of many functional areas, including transportation and logistics. It consists of the following ingredients:

- SAP Cloud Platform for easy development of new digital technologies and applications using SAP Leonardo features

- IoT technologies to integrate outside devices

- Machine learning, AI, and deep learning algorithms with neural networks and other techniques to help machines see, read, listen, understand, and interact via applications with users, devices, and data

- Data intelligence and analytics algorithms, evaluations, and representations to highlight aspects of processed information

- Blockchain support to improve secure and immutable information exchange

- Design thinking workshops to help customers explore and work out new use cases for their digital enterprise

1.2.4   On-Premise and Cloud Deployment

The digital core, products, and suite components of SAP S/4HANA can basically be operated in four different deployment options:

- **On-premise deployment**
  The system is used, operated, and maintained by the customer in the customer's own data center.
- **Application hosting**
  The system operates in a data center of a hosting provider that operates the computing infrastructure but uses, maintains, and operates the system.
- **Private-managed or single-tenant cloud deployment**
  The infrastructure and the system are built, operated, and maintained by a cloud service provider. The customer uses the system exclusively and can make changes to it that go beyond mere configuration.
- **Public-managed or multitenant cloud deployment**
  The cloud service provider provides the infrastructure and a system that operates and maintains it. The customer can log on to the system, configure its own processes, and use them with its private data, but the company can't make any special changes to the system.

In this book, we don't explain the public cloud option of SAP TM, as this is only available with a very limited functional footprint from SAP S/4HANA Cloud version 1811 as compared to the on-premise and single-tenant cloud versions described in the following chapters. However, this may change in the coming years.

1.3   SAP TM as Part of SAP S/4HANA

As the main component used to coordinate both shipper-focused and LSP-focused transportation processes, SAP TM started as a standalone SAP Business Suite application that was then integrated to one or multiple separate SAP ERP systems. In addition, other related components, such as compliance tools, could become part of the SAP TM instance or run side by side.

With the availability of SAP S/4HANA, the market required SAP TM as an integral part of the SAP S/4HANA products to achieve a tighter integration into the master data, processes, and digital core. In addition, SAP S/4HANA is the long-term strategic enterprise software of SAP, which means that all components need to be available as embedded parts of the suite or as integrated products to comply with maintenance regulations. As of today, SAP Business Suite products in logistics are guaranteed to be maintained until 2025. Afterwards, logistics products and components of SAP S/4HANA will receive further release upgrades and feature packs.

Based on these strategic decisions, SAP TM is now available on two platforms:

- **SAP TM in SAP S/4HANA 1809**
  SAP TM was initially released as part of SAP S/4HANA 1709 with a scope limited to shipper-related processes; that is, LSP functionalities such as customer ordering and charging weren't available. This has changed now with SAP S/4HANA 1809, which has functional parity with SAP TM 9.6 to a large extent.

- **SAP TM 9.6**
  SAP TM in SAP Business Suite has been functionally enhanced since SAP TM 8.0 and is now released in version SAP TM 9.6.

In this section, both SAP TM and SAP S/4HANA features are introduced. We'll also discuss relevant components from both SAP S/4HANA and SAP Business Suite that can be integrated with SAP TM in SAP S/4HANA. We'll conclude with a functional overview of SAP TM.

SAP TM in SAP S/4HANA versus SAP TM 9.6

As we've discussed, SAP TM can be used either as part of SAP S/4HANA or standalone for SAP Business Suite. In this book, we'll use SAP S/4HANA as our base system. However, because SAP TM works in nearly the same way for both systems, SAP TM 9.6 users will be able to follow along as well. When there are differences between the systems, we'll highlight them as either for only SAP TM in SAP S/4HANA or for only SAP TM 9.6.

1.3.1   SAP Transportation Management

As a functional component, SAP TM already has a long history within SAP logistics systems and components. Shipper-focused solutions have been provided to large, worldwide operating customers since 1987, when the mainframe system SAP R/2 was released with a module called RT, which allowed the organization of multimodal transports. Its successor on the well-established ERP system SAP R/3 was the Transportation component of Logistics Execution (LE-TRA), which was started in 1993 and released with SAP R/3 3.0 in 1995. Functionally enhanced in the following releases, it grew into a comprehensive solution for shippers to manage their transportation requirements, including cost calculation and settlement. Although still widely used in a large community of manufacturing and trading companies, LE-TRA has been overtaken in functional richness and integration capabilities by SAP TM. Figure 1.7 displays the history of SAP's transportation software.

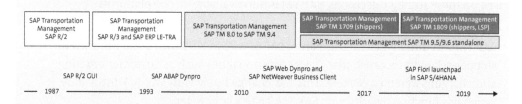

Figure 1.7 History of SAP Transportation Components

After a first start in 2007, which showed that the overall architecture of SAP TM needed to be simplified, the software was redesigned and launched in 2010 as SAP TM 8.0. It was mainly focused on shipper processes but also allowed forwarding by road transportation. In SAP TM 8.1, functionality for ocean freight forwarding (full container load [FCL] and less than container load [LCL]) was added, opening the door into the LSP market. This was extended with SAP TM 9.0 into air freight forwarding. SAP TM 9.1 was further developed to focus on rail quote-to-cash processes, providing many railway-specific features and master data entities. With the success and availability of SAP S/4HANA, SAP TM was integrated into this innovative platform in 2017. First, the shipper functionalities were released with SAP S/4HANA 1709, followed by the LSP-specific process features in 2018 with release 1809. In parallel, SAP TM 9.5 and later 9.6 were provided as standalone releases based on SAP Business Suite.

Scope Overview

When it comes to transportation, cargo, and freight, SAP TM is the main component of the business suite. It delivers the foundation for all mainstream processes and activities in that area. As outlined in the introduction chapter, transportation management functionalities can be used in various business situations:

- Transportation and logistics for shippers is tightly integrated to their sales, procurement, production, and logistics processes.

- Transportation management for freight forwarders enables them to process and manage end-to-end customer transportation orders and with support of multiple partners.

- Transportation management for carriers allows them to efficiently make use of their capacities and manage its use by shipper and forwarder bookings.

- Transportation management for contract LSPs, allows them to offer transportation services in close collaboration with warehousing and sales-related services.

We provide a more in-depth functional overview of SAP TM in Section 1.3.5. As a high-level overview, you can see the functional building blocks of SAP TM in Figure 1.8. To give you more orientation, we added the numbers of the related chapters inside the figure.

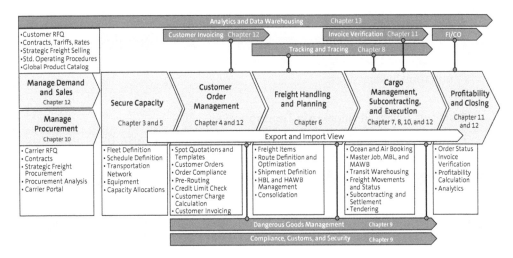

Figure 1.8 Scope Overview of SAP TM

Following are the main functional building blocks of SAP TM:

- Demand and sales deals are managed with the creation of customer sales prices, contracts, product catalogs, and standard operating procedures. This is mainly an LSP functional block.

- Managing procurement allows you to handle carrier contracts and price definitions.

- Securing capacity allows you to define the network and its resources/equipment, including availability and allocations.

- Customer order management is a functional block mainly used by LSP to handle transportation orders from external customers. This includes early routing decisions, compliance checks, and charge calculations for customer invoices.
- Freight handling and planning allows you to define units of freight that are planned to be moved through your network and consolidate it into logical groups (house bills).
- Cargo management, subcontracting, and execution supports handling of master jobs and master freight bills, transit warehousing, subcontracting of trips, execution activities, and supplier charge calculation.
- Dangerous goods management and compliance management handle the integration of SAP TM processes with legal regulations.
- Customer invoicing and invoice verification allow you to execute settlement activities with customers and vendors.
- Tracking and tracing support automated checking of the execution status of cargo.
- Analytics and data warehousing give you information on all aspects of the transportation business.

Basic and Advanced Shipping in Transportation

As transportation functionality has be moved into SAP S/4HANA, there needs to be a synchronization with the scope of transportation that was provided to customers using the traditional LE-TRA (the SAP ERP transportation management for shippers). Therefore, the decision was made to define a two-level scope for functionality:

- **Basic shipping**
  Basic shipping contains all functions that have been part of LE-TRA and are now available in a comparable way to be used by customers as part of SAP TM in SAP S/4HANA. The basic shipping scope is part of the SAP S/4HANA license.

- **Advanced shipping**
  Advanced shipping describes the full scope of SAP TM either for an extended utilization by shippers or an LSP operation. The advanced shipping scope requires a specific license and isn't included in the standard SAP S/4HANA license.

Table 1.1 lists the specific features of SAP TM with the leftmost column showing the SAP TM functions. In the relevance column, you find the applicability of the function for a shipper or an LSP running a transportation management system (TMS). The availability column marks whether a function is part of LE-TRA in SAP TM 9.6 or SAP TM in SAP S/4HANA. The legend for Table 1.1 is as follows: ● function is used or available (SAP S/4HANA: part of basic shipping scope), ○ function is part of SAP S/4HANA advanced shipping scope. "LBN" references the availability as part of the SAP Logistics Business Network (see Chapter 13, Section 13.5).

SAP TM Function	Relevance		Availability	
	Shipper	LSP	SAP TM 9.6	SAP TM in SAP S/4HANA 1809
Organizational master data	●	●	●	●
Business partner master data (customers, vendors, carriers, etc.)	●	●	●	●
Network master data	●	●	●	●
Resource master data		●	●	○
Commodity master data	●	●	●	●
Service product catalog		●	●	○
Customer contract definition		●	●	○
Sales rate and tariff definition		●	●	○
Customer contract negotiation		●	●	○
Carrier/vendor contract definition	●	●	●	●
Buying rate and tariff definition	●	●	●	●
Carrier/vendor contract negotiation	●	●	●	●
Customer quoting (forwarding quotation)		●	●	○
Customer orders (forwarding order)		●	●	○
SO and delivery integration (SAP ERP)	●		●	●
Complex sales and distribution processes (e.g., schedule lines, rescheduling, split, goods receipt [GR]/ goods issue [GI])	●		●	○

Table 1.1 TMS Functions Used by Shippers and LSPs and Their Availability in SAP TM 9.6 and SAP TM in SAP S/4HANA

SAP TM Function	Relevance		Availability	
	Shipper	LSP	SAP TM 9.6	SAP TM in SAP S/4HANA 1809
Global trade integration	●	●	●	●
Dangerous goods management integration	●	●	●	●
Customer/SO routing	●	●	●	●
Customer order pricing	●	●	●	○
Customer invoicing	●	●	●	○
Freight unit and shipment definition	●	●	●	●
Capacity and schedule definition	●	●	●	○
Transportation dispatching for SOs and deliveries	●	●	●	●
Transportation planning for customer orders	●	●	●	○
Consolidation of inbound and outbound load	●	●	●	○
Transportation cockpit and transportation proposal	●	●	●	○
Transportation optimization	●	●	●	○
Load planning and automated pallet building	●	●	●	○
Driver management		●	●	○
Service order management		●	●	○
Freight management for SOs	●		●	●
Freight management for customer orders		●	●	○

Table 1.1 TMS Functions Used by Shippers and LSPs and Their Availability in SAP TM 9.6 and SAP TM in SAP S/4HANA (Cont.)

SAP TM Function	Relevance		Availability	
	Shipper	LSP	SAP TM 9.6	SAP TM in SAP S/4HANA 1809
Automatic carrier selection and ranking	●	●	●	○
Carrier tendering	●	●	●	●
Carrier collaboration portal	●	●	●/LBN	LBN
Freight management costing for carriers	●	●	●	●
Freight management invoice verification	●	●	●	●
Profitability calculation		●	●	○
Track and trace of shipments	●	●	●	●
Warehouse management	●	●	●	●
Transit warehousing		●	●	○

Table 1.1 TMS Functions Used by Shippers and LSPs and Their Availability in SAP TM 9.6 and SAP TM in SAP S/4HANA (Cont.)

Deployment and Integration Options

As mentioned in previous sections, SAP TM is available either in SAP S/4HANA (1809) or on top of SAP Business Suite (SAP TM 9.6). Therefore, you have several options to deploy the system. In Figure 1.9, you can see the resulting deployment options for the two platform versions of SAP:

❶ SAP TM in SAP S/4HANA 1809 can run as an integral part together with other embedded components (logistics, finance) on a single instance. This option has the most benefits in terms of common master data and processes.

❷ SAP TM in SAP S/4HANA 1809 can run as an independent instance connected to another SAP S/4HANA instance for logistics, sales, and finance, for example. This could be the preferred option if a business needs to have transportation up and running independent of other processes (for example, finance).

❸ SAP TM in SAP S/4HANA 1809 can run as an independent instance connected to an SAP Business Suite instance for logistics, sales, and finance, for example.

❹ SAP TM 9.x runs standalone on SAP Business Suite connected to another SAP Business Suite instance for logistics, sales, and finance, for example.

❺ SAP TM 9.x runs standalone on SAP Business Suite connected to an SAP S/4HANA instance for logistics, sales, and finance. This option can be considered temporary, occurring during an upgrade from SAP Business Suite to SAP S/4HANA.

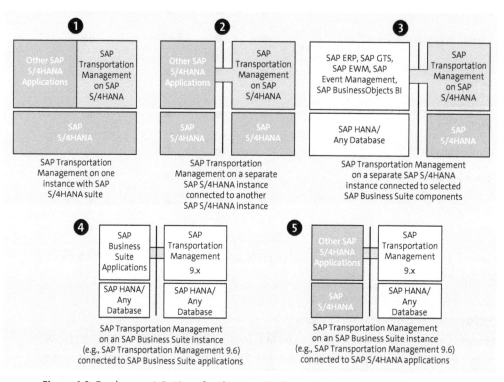

Figure 1.9 Deployment Options for the Two Platform Versions of SAP TM

In Figure 1.10, you can see the available integration paths between components of both platforms. An overview of those components will be highlighted in Section 1.3.3 and Section 1.3.4.

If SAP TM is used as an integral part of SAP S/4HANA, it's fully integrated with the internal components for sales, procurement, shipping, billing, inventory, product safety, and warehousing. In addition, an external integration is available to SAP Global Trade Services (SAP GTS), SAP BusinessObjects Business Intelligence (SAP BusinessObjects BI), SAP Event Management, and SAP Business Warehouse (SAP BW). However, integration to an external SAP S/4HANA or SAP ERP system requires the use of Feature Pack Stack (FPS) levels for SAP S/4HANA or Enhancement Packs (EHPs) for SAP ERP, as shown in Figure 1.10. SAP Customer Relationship Management (SAP CRM) won't be connected to SAP TM in SAP S/4HANA. SAP TM 9.6 keeps its current integration path but isn't planned for integration with an SAP S/4HANA system.

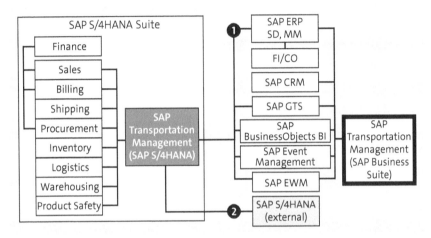

Figure 1.10 Integration Paths between the SAP TM Versions and Other Components

❶ SAP S/4HANA Transportation Management side-by-side to SAP ERP requires SAP S/4HANA 1709 FPS02 with SAP ERP ECC 6.0 EHP 7 or 8

❷ SAP S/4HANA Transportation Management side-by-side to SAP S/4HANA Enterprise Management requires SAP S/4HANA 1709 FPS02

The integration of SAP TM into the SAP S/4HANA stack allows joint data to be directly processed with some fundamental business applications, such as sales, shipping, and procurement. By removing the cross-system data exchange, workload for communication, monitoring, and data synchronization can be significantly reduced. Beyond making full use of SAP S/4HANA features, there are some architectural simplifications to consider, as a lot of process synchronizations now can be omitted:

- In settlement, no A2A messages are required because the charge calculation/settlement and billing/invoicing happens in one system.

- The billing processes now have direct access to required logistics context data.

- Replication of organizational master data is no longer required. SAP TM uses the SAP S/4HANA business partner instead of receiving a copy of customer and vendor via the Core Interface (CIF).

- Product data is no longer replicated because SAP TM uses the SAP S/4HANA product definitions.

- Joint master data can also be used for integration with other modules, such as dangerous goods management.

- SO, POs, and deliveries don't need to be replicated into SAP TM but can be used directly for the transportation process.

- Joint use of different application areas for data retrieval in Core Data Services (CDS) for business logic, analytics, search processes, and so on.

1.3.2   SAP S/4HANA Enterprise Management

The Enterprise Management layer of SAP S/4HANA incorporates a variety of components that are directly or indirectly related to logistics and transportation processes. Note that many of these processes are also available as part of SAP ERP.

Sales

The sales components encompass a range of functions dealing with pricing and selling tangible goods and services. These components are used a lot in manufacturing and trading industries to manage the complete sales process of goods to customers. The following are typical tasks handled in the sales process:

- Managing quotations and SOs
- Conducting availability checks for goods and materials managed in SOs
- Creating scheduling agreements
- Managing credit limit and risk management in association with SOs
- Determining sales price and creating invoices (billing document)
- Managing trade compliance for shippers

The SO is typically the source of transportation demand for shippers, which is processed in SAP TM components either at the shipper's premises (transportation department) or at an LSP. In combination with SAP TM, you can collectively do transportation planning for SOs, allowing you to consolidate one or multiple orders in one shipment or split an order into multiple shipments. You also can jointly plan orders from different systems or clients. Tendering, subcontracting, and executing in SAP TM are possible based on orders prior to delivery creation. You can find further details on order integration with SAP TM in Chapter 4, Section 4.1.

Order management is also used in combination with SAP TM to do customer invoicing. Because SAP TM can create draft or pro forma invoices but doesn't have invoice settlement functionality, the SAP S/4HANA functions for billing and integration into financials are used. You can find details about this integration in Chapter 11 and Chapter 12.

Supply Chain

Supply chain in SAP S/4HANA comprises deliveries, warehousing, and basic/advanced transportation management. The transportation demand generated by these processes is already well scheduled and detailed. Supply chain functionality is typically used to handle the following tasks:

- Centralized and decentralized warehouse management that includes task and resource management and Yard Management
- Delivery preparation and documentation
- GI processing
- Transport organization and documentation
- Direct store delivery management
- Handling unit (HU) management
- Handling of inbound deliveries, including GR processes
- Returns management for deliveries and orders

The former shipping and transportation functionality of SAP ERP, which was provided in the LE-TRA component, stays in SAP S/4HANA only for compatibility reasons. It's not SAP S/4HANA-enabled and will be running out of maintenance. It's completely replaced by the basic shipping scope of SAP TM.

Materials Management

The focus of this component is procurement and inventory management of tangible goods, services, and materials for sale or for use in production processes. The following are typical processes handled with materials management (MM):

- Purchasing requests and PO processing
- Inventory management of materials and products, including material evaluation for accounting and material price management
- Invoice verification for invoices related to goods and service delivery
- Self-billing process support (evaluated receipts settlement [ERS])

- Stock taking and stock correction
- Management of material master data
- Supplier returns management

The processes for purchasing, inbound delivery handling, and returns management provide a PO and inbound delivery-based integration to SAP TM. As described, SAP TM creates only draft invoices. For settling supplier invoices, MM provides invoice verification and self-billing capabilities, which also integrate into the financial components. You can find details about SAP TM supplier draft invoice integration in Chapter 11, Section 11.1.3.

Asset Management

Asset management is used to manage master data for equipment and to plan, organize, and monitor maintenance of all equipment required to sustain a company's operations (in many cases, production machinery and equipment). For transportation, this includes active and inactive transportation equipment, such as trucks, trailers, containers, and railcars. SAP TM provides integration for transportation equipment. SAP S/4HANA is responsible for managing the master data and maintenance plan of the equipment, whereas SAP TM is responsible for its active planning and utilization within the transportation processes. When equipment needs maintenance, it must be removed from transportation plans. Otherwise, if maintenance is approaching, and the equipment isn't at the right location, you need to organize transportation to the repair shop.

1.3.3   SAP S/4HANA Products

Besides the SAP Enterprise Management components mentioned previously, SAP S/4HANA offers a lot of additional functionality via SAP S/4HANA products discussed in the following sections.

SAP S/4HANA for Product Compliance

SAP S/4HANA for product compliance allows you to manage dangerous goods compliance in connection with logistics processes running in SAP S/4HANA, SAP TM, or SAP Extended Warehouse Management (SAP EWM). It consists of a rules engine and documentation and phrase management. The rules engine allows you to load predefined content corresponding to the various Dangerous Goods Regulations (DGR) for different situations, modes of transport, and countries (e.g., ADR and IMDG regulations). Documentation and phrase management support the creation and output of legally required dangerous goods documentation and safety data sheets for dangerous goods transports. We explain SAP S/4HANA for product compliance and its use in connection with SAP TM in more detail in Chapter 9, Section 9.2.

SAP Global Trade Services

SAP GTS is part of SAP governance, risk, and compliance (GRC) solutions. It covers a wide range of trade compliance checks and processes that must be handled in transportation. Due to increasing legal regulation and security checks, transportation has gotten more and more complex from the view of exporting from and importing into countries. Because trade compliance is mostly handled under the responsibility of local governments or groups of countries, the processes and requirements for proper export and import declarations are highly diverse.

SAP GTS supports SAP TM in the order management area, where functionality for general trade compliance and blacklist screening are provided. Furthermore, the shipment process is supported with export and import compliance. You can find more details on SAP GTS in Chapter 9, Section 9.1.

Extended Warehouse Management

Warehouse Management (WM) is a very common functionality for both shippers and LSPs. Many shippers operate a warehouse to store production supplies and finished goods to be shipped to their customers. In the logistics service industry, warehouses can be used in various ways:

- A contract logistics warehouse to keep the inventory for a business partner for whom the LSP takes over the logistics processes
- A transit warehouse (hub) to cross-dock cargo between different vehicles or means of transport without intermediate storage
- A consolidation warehouse (e.g., container freight station [CFS]) where cargo is collected and then consolidated into a transportation unit (TU), which is then moved to a destination

SAP EWM is a WM system with a rich spectrum of warehouse and material handling functionality. It's available based on SAP S/4HANA and SAP Business Suite and can be implemented in an embedded way as well as standalone. Besides pure warehouse inventory management, there is plenty of support for the following functional areas:

- Yard Management
- Unloading and GR handling
- Quality management and dangerous goods handling
- Consolidation of goods into HUs and TUs
- Deconsolidation of TUs and HUs
- Picking and putaway
- Shift and workforce planning
- Value-added services and kitting
- Provisioning and loading

SAP EWM is fully integrated into the logistics processes of SAP S/4HANA, SAP ERP, and SAP TM. In Chapter 13, you can find more details on the integration of SAP EWM, SAP S/4HANA, and SAP TM.

SAP Quality Issue Management

SAP Quality Issue Management (SAP QIM) is a component that allows you to centrally manage compliance and quality issues arising from any kind of business processes. This includes documentation, handling, delegation, and resolution of issues from internal processes, as well as issues reported by customers or identified while collaborating with subcontractors. In addition to the management of the quality process, SAP QIM provides audit trail capabilities, analytical tools, and defect and root cause analysis. SAP QIM is part of SAP S/4HANA (manufacturing). However, integration with SAP TM still must be done on a project basis.

SAP Billing and Revenue Innovation Management

SAP Billing and Revenue Innovation Management has been consolidated out of multiple components that were previously promoted separately:

- **Convergent Charging (CC)**
  A high-speed price calculation engine that allows event-based pricing (formerly known as Highdeal software).

- **Convergent Invoicing (CI)**
  An extremely flexible billing solution that offers billing control by multiple customer profiles (contract accounts). Billing can be driven by events, and grouping of billing items into final invoices is rule based.

- **Financial Contract Accounting (FI-CA)**
  A subledger accounting system that offers very flexible accounting implementations and the ability to integrate into accounts receivable (FI-AR) as a General Ledger (G/L).

- **Financial Customer Care (FCC)**
  Allows you to dispute parts of invoices. It also helps you manage your receivables and collections and do cashiering (in logistics businesses, many orders still must be prepaid in cash before the cargo is moved).

SAP Billing and Revenue Innovation Management has been integrated with SAP TM based on custom development projects. We explain SAP Billing and Revenue Innovation Management in more detail in Chapter 12, Section 12.4.

1.3.4 SAP Business Suite–Related Components

SAP Business Suite is the predecessor of SAP S/4HANA. Based on traditional SAP ERP technology, it's a comprehensive and fully integrated family of business software applications for large, medium, and small enterprises.

SAP TM can be operated side-by-side with components and subcomponents of the SAP Business Suite. For a comprehensive installation, SAP TM is typically connected to the following components:

- SAP ERP with Financial Accounting and Controlling (FI-CO), Logistics General (LO), Sales and Distribution (SD), Logistics Execution (LE), Materials Management (MM), and Plant Maintenance (PM)
- SAP Event Management
- SAP Environment, Health, and Safety (EHS) Management as an integral part of the SAP Supply Chain Management (SAP SCM) Basis layer
- SAP GTS as part of the SAP GRC solutions
- SAP EWM
- SAP CRM
- SAP QIM

Due to the installation requirements, sales and logistics processes and transportation processes always happen in two different environments, which leads to additional master and transactional data exchange. Based on SAP ERP SO data, an *order-based transportation requirement* (OTR) represents the demand in SAP TM. SAP ERP deliveries are integrated with SAP TM *delivery-based transportation requirements* (DTR).

OTRs and DTRs are used in SAP TM to reflect demand (for details, see Chapter 4, Section 4.1).

Drawback of Older SAP ERP Transportation Solutions

Of the multiple (older) transportation solutions in SAP Business Suite, the shipment component in LE was created as an integral part of a shipper's outbound or inbound process and has been used intensively by thousands of SAP ERP customers for more than 15 years. Although it offers comprehensive functionality, it has limitations that make it too inflexible to address general transportation needs or to be the foundation of a complete transportation suite and platform:

- Shipped goods are dependent on material master data, which you need to create deliveries (an LSP usually doesn't have this master data of shipped goods).
- No joint inbound and outbound moves can be handled (either outbound delivery or inbound pickup shipments).
- Shipment demands from multiple SAP ERP systems or clients can't be managed in a centralized way based on LE-TRA because reference documents (e.g., deliveries) from other systems aren't available.
- There is no order management to support selling and billing of transportation services (i.e., LE-TRA isn't easily usable for LSPs).

SAP Event Management

SAP Event Management is a versatile tracking and tracing tool that connects to multiple SAP Business Suite components to provide visibility of business processes and object status. Furthermore, SAP Event Management allows automated process control for intentional reactions to events and status messages or responses for unexpected events or missing milestone reporting.

SAP Event Management provides process tracking and control information that matches the processes in SAP TM for shipment status tracking, consolidation status tracking, equipment tracking, and operational instruction tracking. Bidirectional integration between SAP TM and SAP Event Management means that SAP TM sends process and milestone information to SAP Event Management, which then tracks the process execution and compliance based on information and reporting received from inside or outside the company. Then SAP Event Management posts information back to SAP TM to update the transportation processes. You can find details on SAP Event Management and its integration with SAP TM in Chapter 8, Section 8.2.

SAP Customer Relationship Management

Staying close to customers and providing them with excellent service that meets their requirements has become one of the main differentiators in the transportation and logistics service industry. For freight forwarders and carriers whose core business is logistics services, sales price increases need to have a tangible upside. Therefore, customer intimacy—the art of staying close to customers—has become an attractive driver of rising market share.

SAP CRM can be the platform that bundles all the tools needed for powerful customer service. Especially with the components of the new cloud-based SAP C/4HANA, which includes marketing, commerce, sales, and service cloud functionality, you can achieve proactive customer information and 360-degree insight into all aspects of the customer relationship. Innovative technologies can be implemented, such as chatbots for managing customer requests or machine learning for guidance of chat results into the right channels.

1.3.5   Functional Overview of SAP TM

Let's take a closer look at the overall mode of operation of SAP TM, without going into too much detail yet. In a first step, we introduce the main business objects of SAP TM, as their name will appear throughout all following descriptions. Table 1.2 lists the business object naming, abbreviations, and definitions.

Business Object	Abbreviation	Definition/Description
Order-based transportation requirement	OTR	An order object representing the transportation demand from sales, purchasing, or stock transfer.
Sales order, purchase order, stock transfer order	SO, PO, STO	SAP S/4HANA order objects representing sales, procurement or transfer of goods and the related transportation demand (shipper scenarios only)
Delivery-based transportation requirement	DTR	An order object representing the transportation demand from an inbound or outbound delivery.
Inbound delivery, outbound delivery	IDL, ODL	SAP S/4HANA objects representing inbound or outbound deliveries and the related transportation demand (shipper scenarios only).

Table 1.2 Main Business Objects of SAP TM

Business Object	Abbreviation	Definition/Description
Forwarding quotation	FWQ	An offer from a carrier or LSP to an ordering party for the transportation of goods, which contains information about the price and other conditions related to the transportation services.
Forwarding order	FWO	An order from an ordering party to a carrier or LSP to transport goods from a shipper to a consignee in accordance with agreed terms and conditions.
Freight unit	FU	A set of goods that are transported together across the entire transportation chain. A FU can include constraints for transportation planning.
Transportation unit Trailer unit Railcar unit	TU	A set of goods with an assigned resource that are transported together across a part of the transportation chain. A TU can, for example, be a railcar or a trailer.
Container unit	CU	A set of goods with an assigned container resource that are transported together across a part of the transportation chain.
Transportation resource	RES	A machine, means of transportation, or other asset with a limited capacity that fulfills a function in the supply chain (e.g., truck, container, crane).
Schedule	SCHED	A sequence of stops with related recurring departure and arrival times that is valid for a specified period. Cargo associated with the schedule may move along the sequence or any part of it.
Freight booking	FB	An order providing transportation capacity whose execution is planned by a carrier, for example, a ship owner. The freight booking contains the plan for the logistical processing (e.g., fixed departure times of the ship).

Table 1.2 Main Business Objects of SAP TM (Cont.)

Business Object	Abbreviation	Definition/Description
Freight order	FO	An order whose execution is planned by a carrier or the shipper. The order contains the plan for the logistical processing (e.g., when and onto which vehicle FUs are to be loaded and planned departure times for the vehicle), and execution data.
Forwarding agreement quotation	FWAQ	A quotation object representing a customer request for quotation (RFQ) or a response to such request. Forwarding agreements (FWAs) can be created from the FWAQ.
Forwarding agreement	FWA	A long-term contract that represents the contractual relationship with a customer to whom you're selling transportation services.
Freight agreement	RFQ	An individual business document a shipper or LSP sends to a carrier asking the carrier to bid for the provision of future transportation services in a trade lane for a defined period.
Freight agreement	FA	A long-term contract that represents the contractual relationship with a carrier from whom you're buying transportation services.
Forwarding settlement document	FWSD	A document that is sent to SAP ERP to request the creation of an invoice for logistic services to be sent to a customer.
Freight settlement document	FSD	A document that is sent to SAP ERP requesting the verification of an invoice for logistic services received from a supplier or carrier.

Table 1.2 Main Business Objects of SAP TM (Cont.)

The business objects described in Table 1.2 are used in combination with various processing tools and engines to run transportation management operations. Figure 1.11 shows a typical process flow and the interaction of objects, engines, and master data.

The following descriptions and numbering refer to Figure 1.11. The requirements management component comprises all functions involving SAP TM integration with the shipper's logistics processes (i.e. SOs, POs, STOs, and deliveries). It's frequently used in shipper transportation management, where a company needs to manage transportation for its own distribution and procurement tasks but may also be applied in a tight collaboration in contract logistics.

Starting with SAP S/4HANA 1709, there are two different ways of handling requirements from shipper systems in SAP TM (refer to Section 1.3, Figure 1.9):

- Sales and delivery processes are handled in an SAP ERP system (SAP Business Suite), and SAP TM is operated on a separate instance (either SAP TM 9.6 or SAP TM in SAP S/4HANA). This refers to the light gray boxes in Figure 1.11 and bullets ⒶA1, ⒶA3, and ⒶA4.

- Sales and delivery processes as well as transportation management are handled inside the same SAP S/4HANA instance. This refers to bullets ⒶA6 and ⒶA7.

Requirements Management

In the first case in Figure 1.11, OTRs are created from SAP ERP SOs, POs, or STOs ⒶA1. By means of the transportation planning component (see description later in this section), FUs and freight orders are created ⒶA2, which are used to create delivery proposals ⒶA3 that are sent back to SAP ERP to create deliveries according to the transportation plan. The deliveries may be altered in SAP ERP and, once released, are transferred to SAP TM, resulting in the creation of DTRs that consume the planning result based on the previously used OTRs ⒶA4. In this way, the initial planning result is reused and adjusted without starting from scratch. Based on the freight orders or freight bookings of the planning result (which are the same objects as those described later in this section under "Subcontracting and Tendering"), you can subsequently create shipments in SAP ERP, which allows execution within the SAP ERP logistics context.

If the sales and logistics process is handled on the same SAP S/4HANA instance as SAP TM, the interaction is simplified. The SAP S/4HANA SO ⒶA6 is directly linked to transport planning and freight unit building (FUB), which creates an SAP S/4HANA delivery and manages SO consumption. The cross-system communication for building deliveries is avoided.

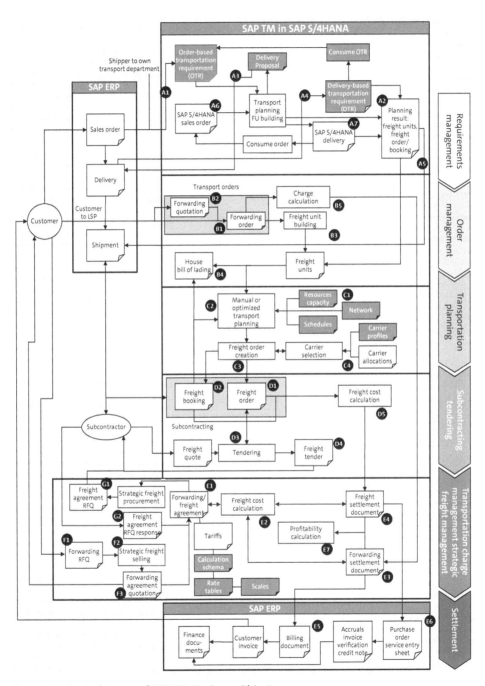

Figure 1.11 Typical Usage of SAP TM Business Objects

Order Management

Order management is the main component for LSPs, where they start the sales processes for their customers. Transportation demand from customers is received as a customer order that creates a forwarding order in SAP TM (❶ in Figure 1.11). Even if the name of the object is closely related to freight forwarding, the same object is also used for carriers to handle customer orders (e.g., *booking* for air and ocean cargo or a *waybill* for rail cargo). In the context of forwarding orders, a variety of processing and check functionality can be used:

- Transportation proposals to get routing options
- Credit limit checks for the order against SAP Credit Management
- Blacklist and denied party screening against SAP GTS Compliance Management
- Dangerous goods check against mode- and country-specific rules defined in SAP S/4HANA for product compliance

A forwarding order can be based on a previously created forwarding quotation, which is a spot quote for a transportation service given to a customer (❷ in Figure 1.11).

Forwarding orders are used to create FUs from the items of the order ❸. FUB is a planning service used to break large orders down into pieces that can be physically handled separately (e.g., on pallets or in truckloads) and that also can go different ways based on logistical or regulatory considerations. At a later stage, house bills of lading (HBL) are generated based on the FUs and assigned freight bookings ❹ to comply with legal documentation regulations.

Forwarding orders integrate with Transportation Charge Management in SAP TM where they use services such as charge calculation to determine the price components of a customer order ❺.

Transportation Planning

Transportation planning provides manual and optimizer-supported planning capabilities to SAP TM and allows multimodal end-to-end planning with consideration of real and virtual transportation costs. It can be used to create a release-ready transportation plan and to determine a list of transportation proposals for possible routings of an order. Transportation planning involves owning and making use of a variety of network and resource master data (used to define the network), resources with their capacity, and schedules for recurring multistop connections (❻ in Figure 1.11).

Operational planning is done in the transportation cockpit as a UI that allows manually performing activities such as assigning FUs to a means of transport and running a parameterized optimization over the whole or a selected subset of the transportation demand. For this activity, the FUs, network, capacity, resources, and schedules—as well as existing and new freight orders and freight bookings—are considered **C2**. Based on the planning result, freight orders are created or FUs are assigned to freight bookings **C3**. During or after this step, carrier selection can be executed, which allows the assignment of one or multiple carriers to a freight order according to carrier profiles, allocation rules, and selection rules **C4**.

Subcontracting and Tendering

The subcontracting component provides order objects representing the relation to service vendors or carriers. Freight orders can be created manually or because of a planning run (**D1** in Figure 1.11). They provide an individually planned definition of a consolidated or unconsolidated freight move to be executed with a means of transport (e.g., a milk run in a city or an FTL move across a country). Freight bookings are used to represent a capacity allocation prebooked on a means of transport, which is often run on a schedule and operated by a carrier within its network **D2**. Examples are air freight capacity reservations for a master air waybill (MAWB) or booked container capacity on a container vessel. For freight bookings, SAP TM offers comprehensive capacity management that allows you to plan and allocate the capacity required to execute transportation services as a forwarder or carrier (e.g., maintenance of master flight plans and four-week flight plans).

Freight bookings usually have an assigned carrier (airline, ocean liner, or railway). For freight orders, individual tendering can be done based on a list of preferred vendors **D3**. Tendering can be executed as peer-to-peer, broadcast, or open. The partners may be integrated either via B2B messaging or through access by a vendor portal. Freight tender and freight quote objects make it possible to keep track of the process and provide the decision basis for carrier selection **D4**. The same way order management is integrated into Transportation Charge Management in SAP TM, subcontracting uses this component to determine the costs of a move, including apportionment to the single FUs of a consolidated shipment **D5**.

The freight order and freight booking business objects used in subcontracting are also the foundation of the execution process and cargo management. SAP TM tools support a variety of processes for these two objects:

- Loading and unloading of consolidated TUs and loose cargo
- Discrepancy handling in hubs and stations
- Consolidation of cargo to and deconsolidation from TUs (e.g., containers and pallets)
- Status management for cargo and shipments
- Creation of legal, regulatory, and operational documentation, such as manifests and bills of lading

Transportation Charge Management

When it comes to cost, revenue, and profitability in transportation, Transportation Charge Management in SAP TM is the component of choice. It integrates into order and subcontracting processes and provides structured contract, tariff, and rate data for all calculations.

In SAP TM, agreements are the main contract objects that can be used as forwarding agreements to represent a customer contract as well as freight agreements to embody a supplier contract (❶ in Figure 1.11). From a structural perspective, these contract types are similar because they contain tariffs referring to calculation schemas that hold a list of charge elements that are applicable for charge calculation either as prices for a customer or costs for a supplier. Each charge element typifies a certain kind of rate, fee, or surcharge (e.g., basic sea freight or port congestion surcharge). To efficiently negotiate a supplier contract or close a customer contract, SAP TM comes with a component called strategic freight management, which allows the creation of contract quotes to suppliers and has analytical tools to analyze and compare bids. From a selected bid, a freight agreement can be assigned to the corresponding supplier.

The freight cost calculation engine analyzes the charge elements of a calculation sheet and calculates the correct amounts in the correct currencies and with the appropriate exchange rates ❷. The calculation results are stored in the charge substructures of the forwarding order (customer invoice) or the freight order and freight booking (supplier invoice).

Settlement

From the forwarding order, freight order, and freight booking business objects, you can create draft invoices for settlement integration to SAP ERP. To create customer invoices, one or more forwarding settlement documents are created from the forwarding order and then are sent to SAP ERP to create billing documents (❸, ❹ in Figure 1.11). For supplier invoice settlement, freight settlement documents are created from the freight order or freight booking; then they are transferred to SAP ERP to create accruals and later to create a PO and service entry sheet (SES) for invoice verification or self-billing (❺, ❻). Based on the two installation options as described in the "Requirements Management" section earlier, SAP TM either has a cross-system integration between SAP TM and SAP ERP or both components are run within the same SAP S/4HANA instance.

Based on the charges calculated on the cost and revenue side, SAP TM produces a profitability calculation for either standard or real costs ❼.

Strategic Freight Management

As proper contract negotiations with customers and subcontractors are a very important prerequisite to profitable operations, the area of strategic freight management provides tools to work out and implement commercial agreements. For freight procurement, freight agreement RFQs (❶ in Figure 1.11) can be created from existing vendor contracts using analytical and simulation tools in strategic freight procurement. The responses from the subcontractors ❷ can subsequently be evaluated, and assignments of business shares can be worked out and finally manifested in freight agreements ❸.

In terms of selling freight services, customers send out RFQs for the freight they intend to ship, for example, within the next quarter, lining out volumes on origin-destination-commodity-equipment combinations of their shipments. These RFQs may be received as Excel sheets and are converted and stores as forwarding agreement quotations ❶. Using strategic freight selling ❷, offers can be worked out in a distributed way (e.g., per trade lane) based on existing tariffs and contracts or from scratch. The resulting forwarding agreement quotation ❸ is then converted back into the customer's format and sent back to the customer. Upon customer request, the forwarding agreement quotations can be converted into forwarding agreements.

1.3.6   Mode of Operation of SAP TM

The organizational capabilities and functional abundance of SAP TM enable its use for a variety of shipper- and LSP-related transportation and logistics processes, such as direct, multistop and multistage, full truckload (FTL), less than truckload (LTL), and ocean carriage door-to-door or port-to-port for FCL or LCL. Consolidated air freight scenarios, rail carriage, and intermodal processes are supported as well.

Air Freight Example

To give you an example of a typical logistics process, Figure 1.12 shows a door-to-door air freight scenario from Bremen, Germany, to Bangkok, Thailand, that uses local processes, such as pickup in Bremen and delivery in Bangkok, and consolidated long-haul truck moves for pre-carriage as well as capacity reservation and schedule-based movements, such as the air freight main leg from Frankfurt to Bangkok. Different flight options must be evaluated to find the most cost-efficient way and to guarantee compliance with customer service-level agreements (SLAs).

Looking at an example like the air freight scenario, you can imagine that the geographical and mode-specific aspects imply that the operational and transactional execution must be handled by different people in different roles. Various employees of LSPs, such as customer service representatives, local station operators, documentation teams, gateway teams, and long-haul dispatchers, are actively involved in various tasks. This "handshake" is organized in SAP's transportation solution, where, with appropriate authorization, each participating person or group gets access to role-specific functionality and the related business objects.

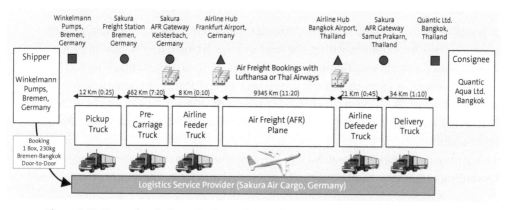

Figure 1.12 Example of a Door-to-Door Air Freight Scenario

Figure 1.13 breaks the air freight process down into example transactional tasks required for an air freight transport with the involvement of six groups and the corresponding task assignments.

Customer service	Export station	Export gateway	Import gateway	Import station	Settlement
• Create customer order • Propose E2E routing • Create work order • Provide visibility • Tracking and tracing • Manage customer exceptions • Manage claims • Basic compliance check • Service catalog • Standard operating procedures	• HAWB/MAWB worklists • Prebook airline capacity • Manage pickups, feeding • Create, manage, close, and print MAWB • Change bookings and routing • Consolidate HAWB to MAWB • Warehouse communication	• Work order and HAWB worklists • Book/manage air cargo capacity, four week flight plan • Create MAWB • Track and trace • Create truck manifests • Manage customs and documents • Consolidation • Compliance checks • MAWB stocks	• Import management • MAWB/HAWB worklists • Break bulk handling • Customs clearance • Plan and manage direct deliveries • Plan and manage defeeding/line haul • Create truck manifest • Customs management	• HAWB worklists • Customs clearance • Transit handling • Break bulk handling • Plan and manage deliveries • Create truck manifest • Create consignee invoice	• Vendor settlement • Carrier invoice creation • Carrier invoice settlement • CASS integration

Figure 1.13 Air Freight Process Tasks in Different Organizations

Connection Capabilities

SAP TM provides powerful workflow and connection capabilities that easily allow assigning and controlling the flow of information and tasks within and between areas of responsibility in a company. Beyond that, SAP TM can integrate processes between several SAP TM instances (e.g., a shipper using SAP TM as its local transportation planning system in combination with SAP ERP, an LSP managing its customer orders with SAP TM, or a carrier managing cargo with SAP TM).

The shipper, the LSP, and the carrier can all be running their own SAP TM instances. For the shipper, SAP TM in SAP S/4HANA is used to arrange transportation. For the LSP and the carrier, SAP TM is used to handle their core business, that is, selling, arranging, buying, and executing freight and cargo moves for their customers. The process flow across the systems is as follows:

1. The shipper receives an order for goods from the customer and starts a sales and delivery process in its SAP S/4HANA system.

2. To arrange transportation, the shipper uses SAP TM to plan shipments based on SOs and deliveries.

3. The planned transportation orders for subcontracting are now communicated as door-to-door service orders to the LSP, which receives them as forwarding orders for transportation services.

4. The LSP uses planning tools in its own SAP TM instance to create freight orders that might be subcontracted to one or more external carriers (e.g., a local truck provider) or that the LSP might execute.

5. In subcontracting, the carrier receives the freight orders from the LSP as forwarding orders in its own SAP TM system and executes them.

6. As the middleman, the LSP now needs to settle customer receivables and vendor payables.

7. The customer receives an invoice from the LSP for the services ordered.

8. The carrier receives a payment for the services executed for the LSP.

SAP TM also is a very efficient platform to drive the collaboration between multiple BUs of an enterprise that have the focus on transportation but view the challenge from their specific domain. LSPs often tend to grow their business into multiple area of logistics that are distinct operations but, in the end, can be a part of an end-to-end process. You can find examples of companies that originally were, for example, a railway or a container shipping line, but decided at certain stages to create a forwarding BU or a trucking BU that operate as independent entities. Although they can take their own external orders, the idea is to gain more share of the operation by using them as part of the end-to-end business.

In the traditional IT world, the BUs act independently in determining their best-of-breed TMS. With higher pressure from the market, companies noticed that running independent TMSs leads to difficulty in identifying synergies in the shared end-to-end processes and executing according to that information. Therefore, the tendency of today's companies is to move their BUs to a joint platform for transportation, which allows them to run the end-to-end order and plan as well as the detailed parts to be managed and executed by the BUs. In Figure 1.14, you can see such an example.

The LSP organization, which originally was a railway, founded a logistics unit (forwarder) and a trucking unit. All three units are running clearly separated parts of a joint platform, which allows them to operate independently but share important data and aspects to achieve synergies.

For relevant parts of the end-to-end process (truck leg, rail leg), information is shared that allows each unit to achieve better results as if they were operating on distinct systems.

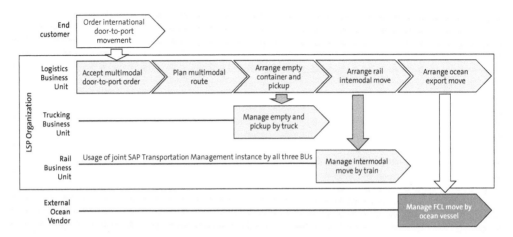

Figure 1.14 SAP TM Instances of Integrating Different Usage Levels

1.4   Summary

In this chapter, we provided you with an overview of the business software, SAP S/4HANA's functional scope, and SAP software provided for transportation management. We established the basic SAP TM business objects and processes that we'll further examine throughout the book, and we discussed the SAP TM mode of operations.

In the next chapter, we'll introduce the SAP TM solution architecture, technical concepts, frameworks, and integration technologies, which can give you a deeper understanding of SAP TM functional principles.

Chapter 2
Solution Architecture and Technological Concepts

When you get started with SAP Transportation Management in SAP S/4HANA, you'll quickly notice two important technological concepts that are different from the traditional SAP ERP technology: The user interface (UI) now uses current web technology, which enables the user to customize the UI easily, and data is now modeled in an object-oriented way.

As you read this book, you'll notice that we rarely use transaction codes and ABAP programs. The reason for this is that SAP TM doesn't use the SAP GUI; it uses web UIs instead.

This means SAP TM's web-based UI can be used without the user having to install any frontend software on his computer. This is especially helpful for users who don't use the application frequently or only execute one business transaction in the system. This chapter will give consultants and technical experts insight into how to customize the UI to adjust the terminology and screen layout to customers' needs.

In SAP S/4HANA, we'll see a different setup of systems compared to what we've known in the SAP ERP era. SAP S/4HANA always consists of two systems: a *backend system* and a *frontend system*. You'll be familiar with the backend system from having already dealt with SAP ERP or previous editions of SAP TM. This is where the business logic resides and where the UIs are built. The frontend system is used to display the UI to the user, and the SAP Fiori launchpad is run on this server. The separation of backend and frontend systems is done to separate hardware capacity between running business logic and rendering the UI. Furthermore, multiple backend systems can be accessed via the same frontend system. This resembles the architecture from approximately a decade ago when the SAP Portal consolidated multiple systems in one UI.

Like other SAP applications developed after the year 2000, SAP TM has moved away from the traditional framework of retrieving both master data and transactional data directly from database tables. The new framework, called the Business Object

Processing Framework (BOPF), encompasses both data storage and data processing. It's the framework of choice not only in SAP TM but also in other functionalities within SAP S/4HANA as well as other SAP applications, such as SAP Business ByDesign. We delve deeper into the contents of data storage and data processing in Section 2.1.

Don't Get Confused about Names!

As part of refactoring many SAP ERP modules in the course of migrating them to SAP S/4HANA, the business object model was also used to model the functionality in other functional areas. However, the tools and frameworks we describe in this section will concentrate on the SAP TM functionality. As the SAP TM application was developed previously as a standalone product and moved into SAP S/4HANA, the technological concepts used in previous versions of SAP TM are taken over into SAP S/4HANA. Therefore, the frameworks and tools used to build object-oriented data modeling for other functional areas in SAP S/4HANA can be different from the ones described in this chapter.

In addition to how data is stored and processed, SAP TM uses a different UI technology, which we examine in Section 2.2 in combination with delving into how SAP TM screens are now displayed in the SAP Fiori launchpad. Furthermore, as we discuss in Section 2.3, SAP TM uses various tools and frameworks that allow a consultant or even the user to customize and personalize the application without having to consult a programmer. These features come in very handy because they reduce the number of modifications—which is a big advantage when it comes to support and troubleshooting. The coding itself is still standard, and customizing of the system is done in a different layer. If customizing has a negative effect on system behavior, you can undo it; removing the customizing layer quickly resets the functionality to standard. No programming is involved in this process.

Finally, we explore the various integration technologies that SAP TM, when used as a standalone application, uses to communicate with other applications in Section 2.4.

2.1   Technological Foundation of SAP TM

If you've ever dealt with software architecture, you've probably heard the term *service-oriented architecture* (SOA) countless times. SOA is not only an architecture for exchanging data between different business partners or systems but also a new way of data modeling within a system itself.

The BOPF is the central technological foundation of SAP TM and incorporates the idea of modeling data in a SOA-compliant way. As a consultant or application expert, you won't find a way around eventually dealing with this framework.

The BOPF models the storage of data in an object-oriented way but also merges the processing of data into the same framework. Therefore, data storage and data processing are closely linked.

If you've already dealt with the traditional technological concepts of SAP applications, the BOPF may seem cumbersome at first glance. However, many developers agree that this framework simplifies how you design a process in a program. In this chapter, you learn that the link between different pieces of information is much closer than with the traditional framework; getting information and understanding how information is related is more tangible because the different pieces of information now follow a hierarchical structure that can also be illustrated by technical drawings.

Although this chapter isn't designed to make you a development expert who knows all the tricks and terms of the BOPF, we do want to give you a basic understanding of how you can interact with the BOPF so you understand where to find data and where to get started if you're looking for the root cause of a problem.

When you access Transaction /BOBF/CONF_UI, you'll find an overview of all business objects used in SAP TM. Figure 2.1 shows how these business objects are grouped into different types. From a technological point of view, these objects are all alike, but from a business point of view, this grouping makes sense.

Let's look at a few of these types. *Business process objects* store transactional data such as customers' transportation requests or transportation orders. As the name suggests, you can find master data stored in *master data objects*, such as vehicle resources or locations. Especially when you're performing transportation planning in SAP TM, you'll enter various profiles and settings that are used for optimizer planning, carrier selection, and so on. This data is stored in *metadata objects*.

Figure 2.1 Business Object Types

2.1.1   Storing Data in the Business Object Processing Framework

Because the BOPF stores data in an object-oriented way, each document or master data item is stored as an object instance in the database. Throughout this chapter, we use a freight order (the order of a transportation service) as an example to illustrate how data is stored.

The freight order has some unique header data such as the order number and the assigned carrier. The special characteristic of this information is that it can occur only once per freight order—with good reason. A freight order with two numbers doesn't make sense.

However, the freight order also has information that can have a different cardinality in any order. If you look at the items in the order, you'll see that some freight orders carry only one item, while others have multiple items. All items, however, are always linked to unique information, such as the order number. We could say that the item information is assigned to the header information.

The BOPF reflects the information structure in its business object structure. When you access Transaction /BOBF/CONF_UI, take a look at the freight order's technical setup by double-clicking the business process object **/SCMTMS/TOR**. A business object consists of different nodes, each with its own purpose. All business objects have one characteristic in common: the superordinate *root node*, which contains the header information we just introduced. The subordinate nodes contain information assigned to the header information, such as the items. Subordinate nodes can have multiple instances within one instance of a business object.

Instances

When we look at the technical setup of a freight order, we're talking about an *instance* of a business object. The business object itself is the definition of the structure. An instance uses this structure and is filled with data.

As you see in Figure 2.2, the item information (**Items of the Transportation Order**) is stored in node **ITEM_TR**, while other information (optional for a freight order) is stored in other nodes.

Figure 2.2 Nodes of the Business Object /SCMTMS/TOR

All information is stored in the nodes in a structured way. If you double-click on a business object node, you can zoom in and take a detailed look at the structure definition of the node.

As you can see on the right side of Figure 2.3, a simple Data Dictionary (DDIC) structure is assigned to each node, in this case, the root node. This *data structure* contains all fields that can be filled with information, such as the freight order number, carrier, and so on. Double-clicking the data structure takes you to the DDIC (Transaction SE11) so you can see the structure.

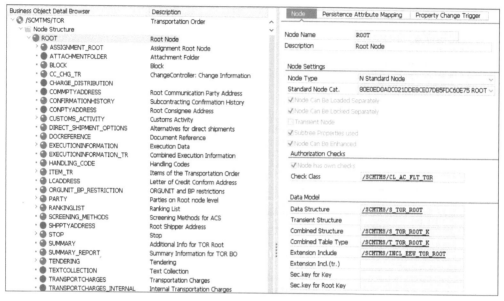

Figure 2.3 Details of a Business Object Node

Figure 2.3 also shows that a combined structure (shown in Figure 2.4) is assigned in addition to a data structure. The combined structure looks exactly like the data structure except that it has three additional fields at the start of the structure:

- **KEY**

  Each node instance can be identified in the database with a unique, 32-digit hexadecimal *key*, such as 005056AC01921ED1BEE25DC2FC88401C.

- **PARENT_KEY**

  In order not to lose the link to its direct superordinate node, each node carries the *parent key* of its superordinate node.

- **ROOT_KEY**

  The *root key* field contains the key of the root node instance that this node instance is part of.

The "Family" in Object-Oriented Modeling

In object-oriented modeling, "family" terms are used instead of the lengthy terms *superordinate* or *subordinate*. (IT people tend to find short terms if abbreviations don't do the trick.) Therefore, the terms *parent node* and *child node* are more often used here.

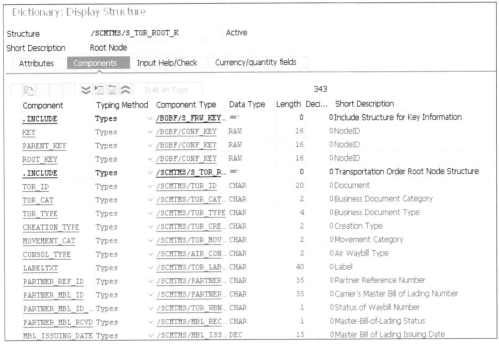

Figure 2.4 Combined Structure of the Root Node of a Business Object

We've talked about *how* data is stored, but we've not yet talked about *where* data is stored. And, even though we're introducing new ways to model data in nodes and objects, at the end of the day, we're back in the world of database tables.

SAP TM 9.6 Data Modeling with SAP HANA

When installing SAP TM 9.6 as a standalone system, you can choose whether you want to install it using a traditional database or a database based on SAP HANA.

We've already mentioned that SAP HANA uses object-oriented data modeling and data processing. However, for the BOPF in SAP TM, there is no difference between using a traditional database or an SAP HANA database. All concepts discussed in this chapter apply to SAP HANA databases, as well as traditional databases.

If you use the SAP TM functionality as part of SAP S/4HANA, the system will always be based on an SAP HANA database.

The BOPF introduces new means only for data *modeling*; data *storage* is done with database table technology that you already know about from SAP products such as SAP ERP. However, the database tables contain the 32-digit keys of the node instances with which you can easily find node instances on the database tables. The details of a node like the one in Figure 2.5 give you information about where data is stored. The structure of the database table is defined with a DDIC table type that can also be found in the node information. The table type is the *combined table type* that you can also see in Figure 2.3, just below the entry for the combined data structure. It usually has the combined structure type as line type.

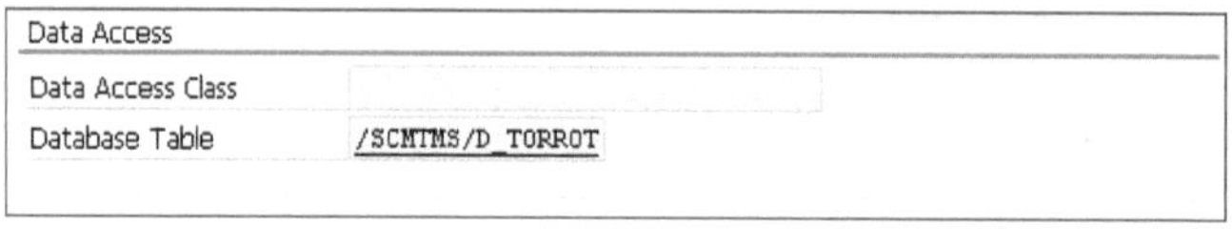

Data Access	
Data Access Class	
Database Table	/SCMTMS/D_TORROT

Figure 2.5 Database Table Assigned to a Business Object Node

Node Associations

One of the goals of the BOPF is for users and developers not to need to connect directly to database tables any more. Therefore, the link between nodes should be established with more than the parent keys and root keys that we've talked about in the previous section—that would be too technical. Another, more general way needs to be established.

Nodes are connected with a special element, called an *association*, provided by the BOPF. An association is a logical link between two node instances. In Figure 2.6, there are associations from the root node to other nodes (**/SCMTMS/TOR • Node Elements • Root • Associations**). When you're retrieving data from a business object instance, follow the path from node to node using the association as a kind of bridge to get required information. For example, if we have only the number of a special freight order and want to know what items are on it, we start at the root node and then use the association between the root node and the item node to get to the information in the item node. After we're on the item node instance, we can look for the field in the DDIC structure assigned to the node.

To take a closer look at an association's setup, you can use Transaction /BOBF/CONF_ UI to access the business object; however, instead of opening the node structure, open the node elements and expand any node. There, you'll find a folder called **Associations**, as shown in Figure 2.6.

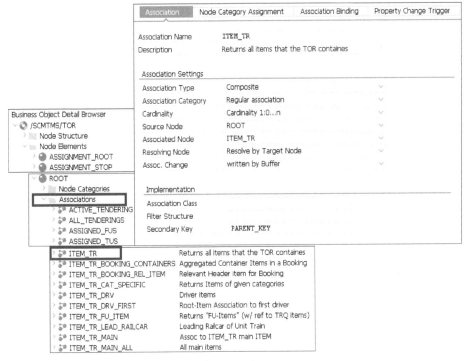

Figure 2.6 Associations of a Business Object Node

Recall that a freight order can contain several items and therefore several instances of the item node. The association defines whether several nodes can be assigned or only one. As you can see in the **Cardinality** field on the right side of Figure 2.6, several item nodes can be assigned to the root node because the cardinality of the association is 1:0...n.

Keep It Nice and Tidy

When you browse through the associations, you'll find some associations from the root node to another node with the cardinality 1:1. You might be wondering why, in this case, another node is needed at all and why the information from the associated node isn't put into the root node.

From a technical point of view, there's really no reason to do this. But from a logical point of view, there *is* a good reason: to keep the model nice and tidy.

Let's consider an example from real life. Your kitchen has a drawer for cutlery, a drawer for pans, and a drawer for herbs and spices. (Hopefully you have more than three drawers in your kitchen, but for this example, three is enough.) Now, instead of using separate drawers, you *could* put everything onto a big shelf—but you would probably have a problem finding anything easily and quickly.

The same applies to the business object model. The more fields a node contains, the bigger the database table will be. A business object node can, in this example, be compared with a drawer; the fields can be compared with the items in your kitchen.

The performance of database accesses depends on the number of fields in one line. Therefore, the number of fields in one line should be kept slim. For this reason, there are some node associations with the cardinality 1:1; the information of the associated node is stored in a different database to improve database reading performance.

Displaying Data Stored in a Database

Let's return to the goal of preventing users and developers from having to connect to databases. This also applies to consultants and technical experts. When working with SAP TM, you should no longer use Transaction SE16 to display data in the background. Instead, stick to the business object model and display data in the object-oriented way.

To do this, you can use Transaction BOBT. Enter the business object in the corresponding field, and then select a query, as shown in Figure 2.7.

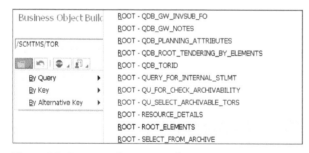

Figure 2.7 Query on the Root Node

Query

A *query* is a predefined search for business object node instances. Developers use queries to find node instances that carry certain information. Although we don't delve deeper into queries in this chapter, you should know that you can use queries in Transaction BOBT to find node instances.

The node instances are displayed in a table view. In the example in which you want to get information about an item in a freight order but you only know the number, you can use a query to display the root node first. Then, you can use the association to the items to get to the item information, as shown in Figure 2.8.

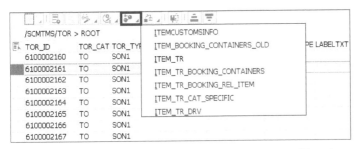

Figure 2.8 Executing an Association in the BOPF Test Workbench

2.1.2   Data Processing with the Business Object Processing Framework

As already mentioned, the BOPF is not only a way of modeling the storage of data but also of handling data processing. If you used Transaction /BOBF/CONF_UI and browsed through the different node elements, you probably noticed that many node elements are assigned to a node:

- Node categories
- Associations
- Determinations
- Validations
- Actions
- Queries
- Alternative keys
- Status variables
- Status derivators
- Status schemas
- Attribute value sets
- Authorization objects
- Authorization field mapping

Don't worry—we won't go through all the node elements in this chapter. However, it's worth taking the time to look at the most important node elements. Associations help to establish a link between two business object nodes and, therefore, mainly support the consistent modeling of data storage; however, the node elements we want to deal with now are used for the data processing part of the BOPF methodology.

The three node elements responsible for built-in data processing are determinations, actions, and validations. You can browse through these elements the same way you browsed through the associations earlier.

Determinations

If you know a little bit about how SAP ERP was coded, you know that even when performing the most elementary changes to data, you need to establish the links to all follow-up activities in the coding. If a user wanted to add some custom logic to the follow-up activities, then the coding needed to be enhanced. In other words, to add custom logic, a developer had to know exactly where in the code certain things happen. With the BOPF, this problem has been solved with determinations. The framework itself calls *determinations* after one of the *create*, *read*, *update*, or *delete* (CRUD) data methods is called. To define when a certain determination should run, all you have to do is select a checkbox.

Let's take a look at an example involving the determination for number drawing for our freight order. As you can imagine, the logic of number drawing needs to be executed only upon creation of the freight order.

When you look at the details of the determination **DET_DRAW_NUMBER** shown in Figure 2.9 (or when you double-click the determination and then go to the **Request, Read & Write Nodes** tab), the following is defined: that the coding to draw a number for the freight order is only called when the root node instance is created. This is defined with the request node depicted in Figure 2.9.

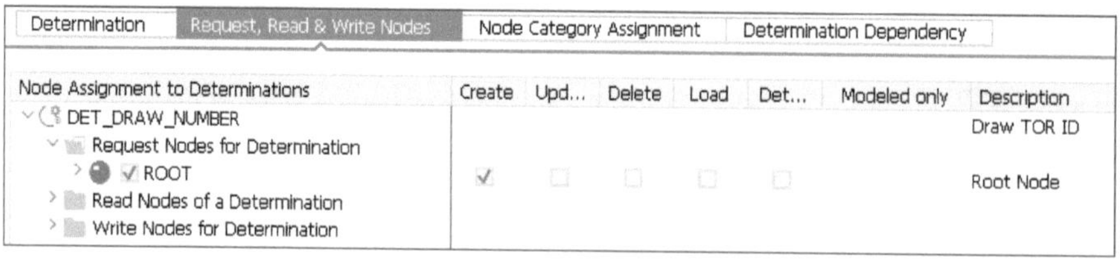

Determination	Request, Read & Write Nodes	Node Category Assignment		Determination Dependency		

Node Assignment to Determinations	Create	Upd...	Delete	Load	Det...	Modeled only	Description
⌄ DET_DRAW_NUMBER							Draw TOR ID
⌄ Request Nodes for Determination							
› ● ✓ ROOT	✓	☐	☐	☐	☐		Root Node
› Read Nodes of a Determination							
› Write Nodes for Determination							

Figure 2.9 Triggering a Determination

Now that we know *when* the determination is called, we can take a look at *how* it's called and how the coding to be processed is found.

When you go back to the **Determination** tab, which is shown in Figure 2.10, you'll find that a class is assigned to the determination. This class is called whenever the determination has to be executed.

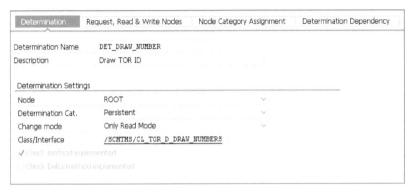

Determination	Request, Read & Write Nodes	Node Category Assignment	Determination Dependency

Determination Name   DET_DRAW_NUMBER

Description   Draw TOR ID

Determination Settings

Node	ROOT
Determination Cat.	Persistent
Change mode	Only Read Mode
Class/Interface	/SCMTMS/CL_TOR_D_DRAW_NUMBERS

✓ Check method implemented

Check Delta method implemented

Figure 2.10 Details of the Determination

Naming Conventions

Whenever you find a class with the name /SCMTMS/CL_TOR_D_*, you can assume that it's a class designed for a determination of the business object TOR.

The naming convention is that after the namespace /SCMTMS/ and the usual identifier CL, there is an abbreviation of the business object that is being dealt with and one letter to determine whether the class is for a determination (D), action (A), validation (V), or query (Q).

Each class assigned to node elements uses an interface that provides three methods, as you can see in Figure 2.11. When a determination is executed, the framework calls the EXECUTE method of the interface. Further methods can be added to the class, but they won't be considered by the framework; instead, they need to be called by the EXECUTE method.

In addition to the EXECUTE method, there are also two more methods provided by the framework: CHECK and CHECK_DELTA. Both methods are optional to be implemented and will serve as a precondition regarding whether the logic of this determination should be executed, that is, whether the EXECUTE method should actually be called.

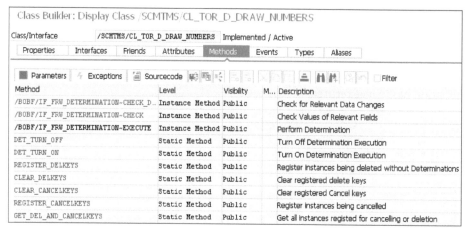

Figure 2.11 Class of a Determination

Actions

Although determinations are always called by the framework, they don't influence the business process in greater terms. Because the course of a business process can't always be foreseen and is often influenced by people, program logic also needs to react to user interaction.

Processing a business object node according to a user's input is done via actions. An *action* is program logic called externally, usually by a button on the UI.

Say, for example, we have put together a full truckload of various cargo items. We want to check whether the combination of goods on the truck is feasible or whether some goods can't be transported together. To execute this incompatibility check on the freight order, we use the corresponding button on the freight order UI.

Incompatibility

This section discusses only what happens to the data. We cover how to set up an incompatibility check in Section 2.3.2.

The UI action is linked to an action of the business object node, and the corresponding program logic is processed. Each action, like the action of the incompatibility check in Figure 2.12, has a class assigned to it that contains an interface with an EXE-CUTE method that is called by the framework. As you can see, the BOPF uses exactly the same approach for linking program logic with the BOPF entities as with determinations.

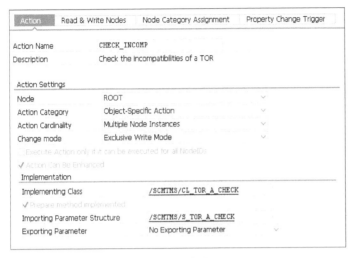

Figure 2.12 Details of an Action in BOPF

Validations

As with determinations and actions, a *validation* is also a piece of coding called and executed by the BOPF. The BOPF offers two different types of validations: the action validation and the consistency validation.

Action validations are associated with an action of the business object node and are called *before* the action is called. The action validation checks whether the action may be executed. For example, if we call the action that sends a transportation order to a carrier, an action validation checks beforehand whether a carrier is already assigned to the transportation order. If not, the action validation fails, and the action won't be executed.

Consistency validations, on the other hand, are called after a change has been made to a business object node. Consistency validations, therefore, aren't directly linked to an action but monitor the change of a node instance, just like the determinations. However, while determinations may change some data on the node instance, the validations don't change anything on the node instance. Instead, they validate the consistency and create warning or error messages to notify the user. In fact, validations don't lock the node instance while the validation is performed. Therefore, validations can't change any data on the node.

For example, when you create a freight order, you save the freight order. A consistency validation is always called when saving the freight order to check whether the locations and dates of the freight order are in a logical order, the vehicle resource isn't used on any other transport at the same time, and so on. If, for example, the vehicle resource used on this freight order is already assigned to another transport at the same time, the validation generates an error message to be shown on the UI. It doesn't, however, remove the vehicle resource from the freight order because that would be a change of the freight order document, which a validation isn't able to do.

As mentioned earlier, without built-in program logic, the developer has to know exactly where the custom enhancement must be inserted. With the BOPF, this is often no longer necessary. Now the developer can simply add program logic using guided procedures that are provided when a business object is enhanced. Standard and custom logic are then displayed next to each other, making it look like one final product in the end (which, in fact, it is).

2.1.3   Business Add-Ins

Rest assured, supporters of the "good old" SAP techniques—there are still some relics from the SAP applications we all know, such as the business add-ins (BAdIs).

BAdIs are enhancements to the standard program logic without any modifications. SAP provides *enhancement spots*, which are specific places in ABAP coding where you can insert special program logic and alter data that needs to be processed.

A very popular example of an enhancement in SAP TM is the BAdI for optimizer preprocessing. Before handing over data to the optimizer, the user can add or change information that was previously gathered by the SAP TM functionality.

To create this BAdI, you need to go to Transaction SE18, as shown in Figure 2.13, and enter the name of the BAdI or enhancement spot. The SAP TM-specific BAdIs start with /SCMTMS/, following the naming convention. When you do an F4 search on the BAdIs, you'll see that SAP TM offers more than 100 BAdIs.

Figure 2.13 Choosing an Enhancement Spot to Enhance Standard Business Logic

In an enhancement spot, there is usually a sample implementation to help the developer get started with the custom enhancements.

You can forward-navigate to the enhancement implementation (like the one shown in Figure 2.14) and to the enhancement's implementing class. The implementing class uses an interface that provides the developer with a data structure that is passed on from the standard coding and, after execution of the custom logic, back to the standard program flow again.

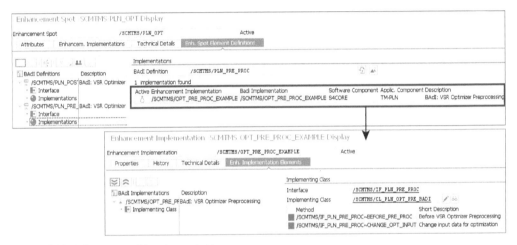

Figure 2.14 Enhancement Implementations

ABAP Development

Because this book aims to give you insight about what you can do with SAP TM as a technical expert, we won't delve deeper into how to implement BAdIs or any ABAP coding at this stage.

2.2   User Interface Technologies

As we mentioned in the introduction to this chapter, SAP S/4HANA requires two systems to display a UI to the user. In this section, we'll first look at how UIs are built and then delve into how they make their way onto the business user's screen.

In addition to the new way of storing and processing data, SAP TM uses a new UI technology. Where former SAP applications relied on SAP GUIs, the new applications use web UI technology.

The shift to web UI technology is accomplished by implementing UIs with Web Dynpro for ABAP—that is, using ABAP coding designed to be transformed into markup language that can be rendered by browsers. While new UIs that were exclusively developed for SAP S/4HANA already use an SAP Fiori technology, the UIs of SAP TM still use the Web Dynpro for ABAP technology, which is then rendered in a way that looks similar to the native SAP Fiori UIs.

SAP TM can't exist *completely* without SAP GUI transactions, but the border between the usage of SAP GUI and web UI technology is clearly marked. While technical experts and consultants can continue to use SAP GUI for Customizing and system monitoring, business users rely on the SAP Business Client to call the SAP Fiori launchpad from which they can perform all business transactions.

Using Two Applications or Only One

We said that for Customizing and system monitoring, SAP GUI transactions are still used, and, therefore, SAP GUI can be used for this.

However, SAP Business Client is also able to display and call all SAP GUI transactions from the SAP Business Client application when logged on to the backend system. In SAP Business Client, you can also see all SAP GUI system connections in your connection list. With this, you could completely renounce using SAP GUI and only use SAP Business Client now.

2.2.1 SAP Fiori Launchpad versus SAP Business Client

Figure 2.15 shows the difference between what the user sees when logging on to SAP S/4HANA in the SAP Fiori launchpad ❶, and the SAP Business Client home screen that is used in SAP TM 9.6 ❷. The SAP Fiori launchpad works with tiles that are clustered in different tabs. We'll explain in more detail how the tiles and tabs are configured when talking about user roles in Section 2.2.3. There is a maximum number of tiles per tab. As you can see in Figure 2.15, all other tiles will be displayed as a text menu below the tile section. Because the SAP Fiori launchpad doesn't offer hierarchical structuring, apps such as **Create Forwarding Order** and **Display Forwarding Order** need to be displayed as two separate tiles on the SAP Fiori launchpad.

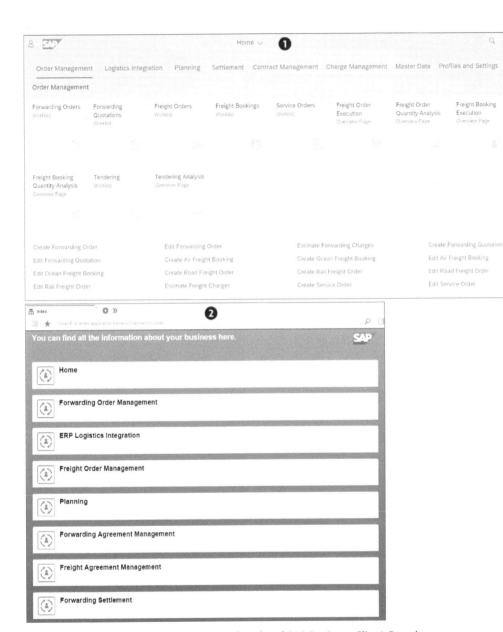

Figure 2.15 Comparison of SAP Fiori Launchpad and SAP Business Client-Based
SAP TM Menu

In contrast to the SAP Fiori launchpad, the SAP Business Client-based home screen is
structured in a hierarchical menu, of which an example is depicted in Figure 2.16.

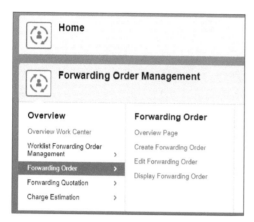

Figure 2.16 Hierarchical Menu in SAP Business Client

You'll also notice in Figure 2.15 ❷ that there is an input bar above the menu. This input bar can be used to search for applications or to call transactions such as Customizing. It's therefore possible to use the business applications as well as the configuration screens from the same UI. Because the frontend system and backend system are separate in SAP S/4HANA, calling Customizing from the SAP Fiori launchpad isn't possible.

SAP Business Client is client software that can be used to access systems that are displayed in the SAP Fiori launchpad or the Web Dynpro menu. However, there are different ways of opening business applications in SAP TM, and each one has a specific purpose:

- **Zero-footprint client**
  The zero-footprint client is used by users such as Basis experts and system administrators who perform most of their activities in SAP GUI.

  Start the zero-footprint client via Transaction NWBC, which can be called in SAP GUI when logged on to the backend system. Calling this transaction opens your standard browser, displaying a list of roles that are assigned to the user. When you choose a role, the browser displays the menu defined in the role.

Menu Functionality

Even though the SAP Business Client UI are displayed in a browser, you should use the menu functionality only within the UI and refrain from using browser functionalities such as the **Back** button or browser favorites.

As you'll learn in Chapter 7, business partners such as carriers can log on to your SAP TM system and respond to tenders or requests for quotations (RFQs) (only available in SAP TM 9.6 and not in SAP S/4HANA 1809). When doing so, they use a hyperlink that takes them to the SAP TM system in their standard browser. The advantage is that carriers don't have to install additional software to access your system with their user name because the standard browser is used with the zero-footprint client approach.

- **Client-installed SAP Business Client**
  The preferred way of using SAP TM is the client-installed SAP Business Client because it offers many advantages. Compared to the zero-footprint client, users don't have to track which roles are assigned to them (information business users shouldn't be concerned with anyway). Additionally, you can decide how many sessions you want to open. If you want to open a new transaction in a new tab, simply click a menu entry in SAP Business Client while pressing `Shift` to open a new tab.

Unlimited Modes

SAP GUI is restricted to six sessions opened in parallel, but there is no such restriction in SAP Business Client. Be aware, though, that opening several sessions in parallel consumes more resources on the application server.

Furthermore, with many sessions open, it's likely that you're locking data in a session that you may not need any more. For that reason, SAP Business Client has an automatic timeout functionality that releases lock entries after a certain time of inactivity. If this happens, you get an error message and must return to your transaction or refresh the page by pressing `F5`.

- **SAP Fiori launchpad**
  The SAP Fiori launchpad is the one-stop shop to open all your SAP systems in one window. It's more of a UI technology than a client application. The tiles depicted on the SAP Fiori launchpad will redirect you to the application chosen and the UI technology within that application (e.g., when opening an SAP TM 9.6 system from the SAP Fiori launchpad, the zero-footprint client opens in a browser as discussed previously). It works in a similar way as the SAP Enterprise Portal and can also be opened from the SAP Business Client that we just described. The SAP Fiori launchpad can also be opened in a browser when opening it from the desktop directly, as shown in Figure 2.17.

Figure 2.17 The SAP Fiori Launchpad on a Windows Desktop

The Importance of the Browser

Whether you're using the zero-footprint approach or the client-installed SAP Business Client, the standard browser installed on your computer is always important.

You may not notice that the standard browser's rendering functionality is in place, even when you're using the installed version of SAP Business Client, but the browser takes over the rendering activities when you're using SAP TM.

Keep your browser version up to date to ensure optimum rendering performance.

2.2.2   Floorplan Manager and Floorplan Manager BOPF Integration

We've talked about the BOPF already in Section 2.1 as the first major technological pillar of SAP TM. We'll now talk about the UI technology, which is the second major technological pillar of SAP TM. The UI technology is supported by the Floorplan Manager (FPM) framework. The FPM is a tool that helps the developer build UIs with different building blocks.

Each UI consists of an FPM application that defines one use case in the SAP TM system. The forwarding order, for example, is one FPM application. As you'll see in Chapter 4, several FPM *application configurations* are designed for the forwarding order, each for different use cases (e.g., ocean forwarding order, air forwarding order, etc.).

Apart from the FPM application, the developer can now use different *UI building blocks* (UIBBs) to build a UI. The FPM framework provides predefined components called *generic UI building blocks* (GUIBBs) for this. For SAP TM, we use the following components:

- **Overview page**
  The overview page defines the general layout of the screen. It provides a global toolbar at the top of the screen and can embed several other components.

- **Form**

  The form GUIBB gives you the opportunity to assemble several text and display fields of a flat structure (e.g., the root node) on the screen. The **General Data** tab on any business document is a typical example of a form GUIBB.

- **List**

  The list GUIBB displays the content of a table. For example, the table in the **Execution** tab of the forwarding order is made of a list GUIBB.

- **Tree**

  Hierarchical relations can be shown in a tree GUIBB. Very common examples of tree GUIBBs are the items in the forwarding order.

- **Tab**

  As you've seen in most UIs, in SAP TM, the information in a document is divided into different tabs. These tabs are also built on a provided GUIBB.

- **FBI view**

  The Floorplan Manager BOPF Integration (FBI) view defines the link between the UIBB and the data in the BOPF. We'll talk about the FBI view later in this section. The FBI view is also a GUIBB in FPM.

Each FPM application configuration must have an overview page to provide the global toolbar. On the overview page, you can assign several UIBBs that can be built based on the listed GUIBBs. This assignment is depicted in Figure 2.18.

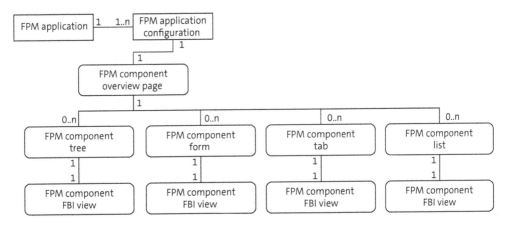

Figure 2.18 Assignment Hierarchy of Components in FPM

As you can see by the shape of the boxes, the overview page and assigned UIBBs are all FPM components, only of different types. The type of FPM component (meaning GUIBB) is described in the second line of the corresponding boxes.

So far, we've defined only the general look of the UI, but we haven't done anything about the link between the data in the system and how it can be put onto the screen. This link is established in the FPM framework using *feeder classes*, which provide the UIBBs with both data and a field catalog. The *field catalog* provides metadata about the data (e.g., which columns are available in a list). In the SAP TM system, the feeder classes are also where the *Floorplan Manager BOPF Integration* (FBI) framework comes into play.

The FBI framework provides generic feeder classes that developers can reuse and assign to the UIBBs they have chosen on the overview page. FBI provides one feeder class per GUIBB; this is necessary because every GUIBB requires its own feeder class that delivers information specific to and specifically structured for the GUIBB.

Apart from the feeder class, the FBI also provides an FBI-specific GUIBB, which is the *FBI view*. The FBI view establishes the link between the BOPF node and the UIBB. Each UIBB has one FBI view. You can see this assignment in the component configuration or component Customizing. As you can see in Figure 2.19, especially in the lower screen, the FBI view contains the business object and business object node of the data that should be displayed in this UIBB. Furthermore, the FBI view contains a UI structure that consists of all fields that should be available on the UI.

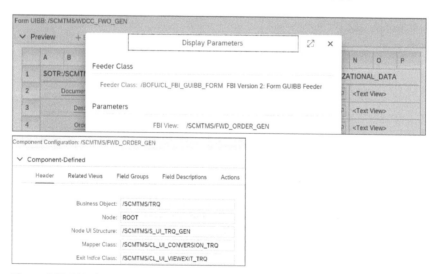

Figure 2.19 FBI View

Node Structure versus UI Structure

We can't use the actual node structure as the structure providing fields to the UI because the concept of the UI structure differentiates between data stored on the database and data to be read by a user.

For example, the creation date of a document is stored as a time stamp in one field of the node structure, but this time stamp isn't readable to any user. Therefore, the UI structure contains three fields for the creation date: date, time, and time zone.

If the UI structure contains fields that aren't part of the UI structure, the *mapper class*, also depicted in Figure 2.19, is responsible for passing the data from the BOPF to the UI structure.

At runtime, the FBI view fills the fields of the UI structure and passes it to the feeder class that passes the data on to the FPM-based UI. All communication between the BOPF and FPM is therefore channeled through the FBI-specific feeder class and the FBI view.

2.2.3   Defining User-Specific Roles, Catalogs, and Menus

Recall that the SAP Fiori launchpad displays tiles grouped in tabs. The user role will eventually define what tiles and tabs the user is able to see. SAP has predefined some roles according to the tasks different users may have in their daily business.

For the SAP Fiori launchpad, all tiles are collected in *catalogs* that are configured on the frontend system. We differentiate between *technical catalogs* and *business catalogs*. Technical catalogs are a collection of tiles that technically are related. As you can see in Figure 2.20, the SAP TM functionality provides two technical catalogs: one technical catalog is generated out of the replication of the Web Dynpro applications that were designed in the backend system. The second catalog is the one containing new SAP Fiori apps that were explicitly designed for SAP S/4HANA.

However, the technical catalogs aren't used to display tiles on the SAP Fiori launchpad when a business user logs on. Instead, business catalogs subdivide the applications into logical groups. These groups should reflect the different divisions within a company.

However, it's only the SAP Fiori launchpad group that eventually defines which applications are represented as tiles and which ones as text links. As you can see in Figure 2.21, the tiles are put into a layout that will be reflected on the SAP Fiori launchpad when a business user logs on. The tiles in the group, however, will have to reference tiles from the business catalogs.

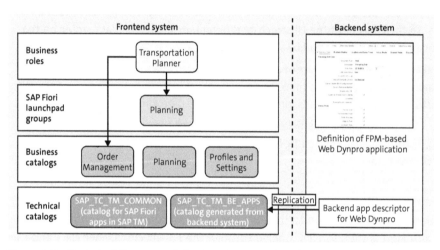

Figure 2.20 Technical Structure of the SAP Fiori Launchpad

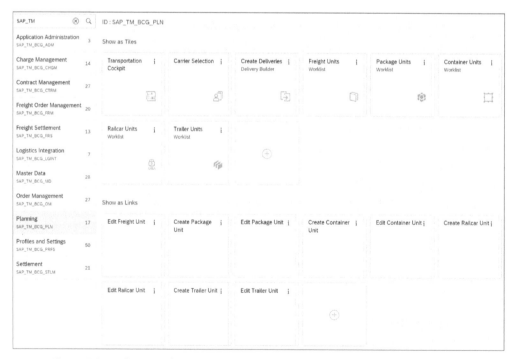

Figure 2.21 Definition of SAP Fiori Launchpad Groups

To define which user role will be able to access which apps, the SAP Fiori launchpad groups need to be assigned to a user role in Transaction PFCG of the frontend system. When defining the role, both the SAP Fiori launchpad group (which defines how the tiles and text links should be displayed) and the corresponding business catalogs (which define what Web Dynpro applications to access) are assigned to the role. If a user is assigned numerous roles, all of the tiles and links defined in the respective roles are displayed in the SAP Fiori launchpad.

User Roles in SAP TM 9.6

When using SAP TM 9.6, the SAP Fiori launchpad and the concept of a frontend system aren't applicable. Therefore, the Web Dynpro applications can directly be assigned to a user role. The hierarchical menu structure can be defined by creating folders that define the hierarchical structure.

To alter the menu of a role, go to Transaction PFCG, and copy a provided role into your namespace. Access your newly created role, and go to the **Menu** tab, which has a folder structure like the SAP Easy Access menu in SAP GUI. The first folder always represents a workspace that is displayed in the workspace area of SAP Business Client. The subfolders and applications are displayed in the menu area of SAP Business Client.

Drag and drop transactions from folder to folder. Right-click the application to display its details or add parameters.

In the details, you can define the application and application configuration you would like to render available. Furthermore, the parameters define how an application is opened, for example, in create mode or display mode.

2.2.4 Customizing Screen Areas

Compared to SAP GUI transactions, one big advantage of Web Dynpro for ABAP applications is the ability to customize screens. As a technical expert or consultant, you can now perform changes to the UI in Customizing mode without touching any lines of code or making modifications to the system.

When browsing through a business transaction, you might come across some fields that you either don't need or that you want to rename. With SAP Business Client and Web Dynpro ABAP, you can change the UI in Customizing mode. From the business transaction, right-click on the screen area you want to customize, and choose **Technical Help**, as shown in Figure 2.22. A new popup opens, and you can navigate to the UI Customizing by clicking on the link of the component Customizing of the current view.

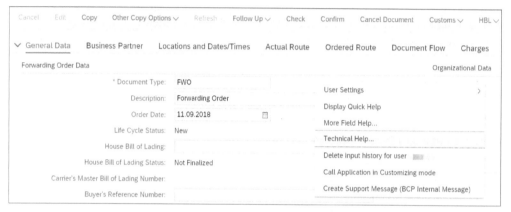

Figure 2.22 Opening Technical Help for a Web Dynpro Application

---

Creating a Customizing for a UIBB

In a new SAP TM system, you won't see the link for the component Customizing in the technical view popup. If this is the case, choose the link for the component configuration.

In the component configuration (which is SAP standard and should therefore not be changed), you can choose **Other Functions • Create Customizing**.

Note that both the component configuration as well as the component Customizing are located in the backend system.

In the UI Customizing, you can add and remove fields, change labels, and change the way fields are displayed, as shown in Figure 2.23. Your changes can be seen directly in the preview screen of the Customizing application.

Figure 2.23 Customizing a Web Dynpro Application

2.3   Frameworks and Tools Used throughout SAP TM

Business process execution in SAP TM is based not only on new SAP TM-specific developments but also on various tools that enhance SAP TM functionality and support business process execution:

- Business Rules Framework plus (BRF+)
- Incompatibilities
- Post Processing Framework (PPF)
- Document creation and adaption
- Optimizer server
- Process Controller Framework

Some of these are third-party tools that require a license independent of the SAP license for SAP S/4HANA. If you've worked with other SAP applications before, you've probably come across some of these tools already.

In general, the purpose of using these tools is to enable the user to configure the system in more detail with no modifications or coding.

2.3.1   Condition Framework Using the Business Rules Framework

The most prominent framework you'll come across when using SAP TM is the *Business Rules Framework plus* (BRF+), which provides conditions to aid in automatic decision-making in SAP TM business process execution.

Conditions are tools that determine an input value based on master data or transactional data and derive an output value from the determined input value. Their use is widespread throughout the SAP TM functionality; you'll find possible action areas for them in all process areas.

The following are the most common functions:

- Document type determination
- Determination of organizational units
- Determination of the applicant rate tables in Transportation Charge Management
- Incompatibilities
- Determination of loading/unloading time of a freight unit
- Determination of delivery time windows for a freight unit

Take the determination of the organizational units of a freight order as an example. In this case, the condition is processed upon creation of the freight order.

The condition type used for this process step is /SCMTMS/TOR_ORGUNIT. In Customizing, you can see this condition type by following the IMG path **Transportation Management • Basic Functions • Conditions • Define Condition Types**. The definition of the condition type includes three important details that you might need for your condition creation, as shown in the boxes in Figure 2.24.

The first checkbox indicates whether more than one instance of this condition type is allowed in the system. Some condition types, called *singleton conditions*, may have only one condition defined in a system. Note that their point of call can't be influenced by Customizing. For example, when sending a sales order (SO) to a standalone SAP TM system, there is one condition type in the SAP TM system that determines the document type of the document created by the transferred SAP S/4HANA SO. In Customizing, there is no means of determining which one of these condition types should be called.

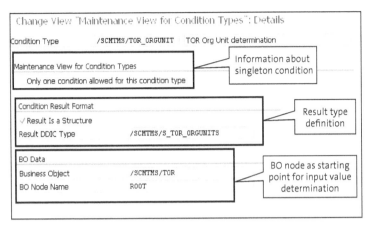

Figure 2.24 Definition of a Condition Type

If there can be more than one condition of a condition type, as in our example, then there is a field where this condition has to be entered to be processed, for example, in Customizing for the freight order type.

The second crucial piece of information is the DDIC type of the result. In Customizing, you can enter a data element, structure, or table type that is used as the output of the condition. If a structure is used, the corresponding flag in Customizing must be set.

If you're building more complex infrastructures, then the last piece of information in Figure 2.24 is the most important. In the **BO Data** section, you can see where the condition starts searching for an input value. The business object and business object node are displayed here.

You'll create a lot of conditions to automate business decisions when you're setting up your SAP TM functionality. In our example, we want to determine the planning and execution organization based on the source and destination location of the freight order. Our formula is pretty easy: If the source location of the freight order is Istanbul, and the destination location of the freight order is Berlin, then the planning and execution organization is Turkey. If the freight order goes the other way around, the planning and execution organization is Germany.

We start creating our condition by choosing the **Create Condition** tile in the **Profiles and Settings** tab of the SAP Fiori launchpad. We choose the corresponding condition type (which in our case is **/SCMTMS/TOR_ORGUNITS**) and specify that we want to create a condition based on a *decision table*, which is also the example in Figure 2.25.

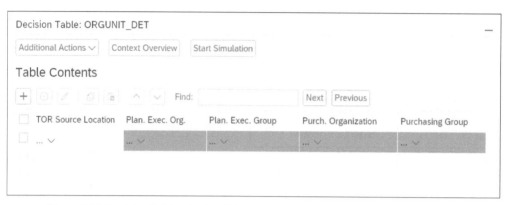

Figure 2.25 Decision Table of a Condition

Creating Conditions in SAP TM 9.6

The menu path for creating conditions in SAP TM 9.6 is different from the path just described. In SAP TM 9.6, choose menu path **Application Administration • General Settings • Conditions • Create Condition**.

This is the most commonly used type of condition. With the decision table, you can map a combination of input data to explicit output data, as you'll see later.

In some cases, you might want to use a condition with direct business object access. This condition determines the input data (which, in this case, is also the output data). Direct business object access is commonly used when defining incompatibilities, which we deal with in Section 2.3.2.

When we define the condition, we see a decision table. Input columns have a gray background, and output columns have a green background. You can see that, by default, the source location of the freight order is taken as an input value. You can change the input data by clicking the **Data Access Definition** button at the top of the screen.

In Figure 2.26, you can see that there is one predefined *data access definition*: the source location of the freight order. You can add more input values by adding a line to the table. With ⌑F4⌑ help, you can see what data access definitions are offered for this condition type. If you know that your input value can be found on the root node of the business object /SCMTMS/TOR, which represents the freight order, you can leave the **Data Access Definition** field empty and enter the business object, business object node, and field directly in the corresponding fields.

Figure 2.26 Data Access Definition of a Condition

Note that you can enter only the business object and node that were defined as the starting point in Customizing or a node that is directly associated with this node.

For example, we want to add the destination location of the freight order as a second input value. Because this data access definition isn't predefined, and the information isn't stored on the root node of the TOR business object, we need to build our own data access definition.

Because the information we want to retrieve isn't stored on the root node, we need to use a *data crawler* to use associations to navigate to the node where our field is. To do so, we need to define or find a data crawler profile via the Customizing menu path **Transportation Management · Basic Functions · Conditions · Define Data-Crawler Profile.**

In this Customizing activity, we want to look at an already existing data crawler profile that provides the last location of a freight order (**/SCMTMS/TOR_LAST_LOC**). On the first screen, it's defined where the data crawler should start "crawling" the data on the business object. The data crawler has to start at the starting point of the condition; in our case, this is the business object **/SCMTMS/TOR** and the node **ROOT** (refer to Figure 2.24). In the upper part of Figure 2.27, you can see how this starting point is defined.

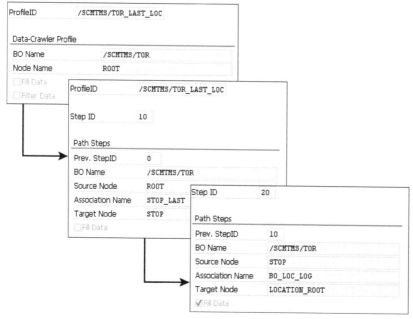

Figure 2.27 Data Crawler

Now we need to define where we want to go. To do this, we define a step for the data crawler, which we do using the **Path Steps** in the dialog structure. The lower two screens of Figure 2.27 show how these path steps are maintained.

The data crawler step represents our use of an association. When we enter a step number and press ⌷Enter⌷, the starting point of this step is automatically updated. The only thing we have to maintain is the association we want to use. Fortunately, the business object /SCMTMS/TOR offers an association that not only returns data of the node STOP (where all stops of the freight order are stored) but also offers an association that filters out all stops except the destination location.

Therefore, we use the association STOP_LAST. To retrieve the location ID and further details of this location, however, we decide to add another step by moving to the root node of the business object representing the location (refer to **Step ID 20** in Figure 2.27). Because we've now reached the point where we want to be with our data crawler to retrieve data, we select the **Fill Data** checkbox shown at the bottom of Figure 2.27.

Notice that, in the lower area of Figure 2.26, you can enter the data crawler profile directly on the screen where you define your data access definitions for your conditions. However, to enable reuse of the data crawler, we want to assign the data crawler profile to a new global data access definition.

To do so, we create a new data access definition in Customizing, following the menu path **Transportation Management • Basic Functions • Conditions • Data Access Definition**. Here, we create a new data access definition and assign the data crawler profile, define the step in which we want to retrieve data, and enter the field we want to read. The field is the component name of the DDIC structure assigned to the node that we've navigated to with our data crawler.

To help your users enter the right input data, enter the data type of the field in **Data Element for F4 Helps**. If you don't know the data type of your input, you can look it up in the DDIC structure of the business object node.

Because condition types can start at different business object nodes, not all data access definitions created in Customizing may be used in a condition of a certain type. Therefore, data access definitions are assigned to condition types in Customizing. When you follow the Customizing path **Transportation Management • Basic Functions • Conditions • Assign Condition Type to Data Access Definition**, you can maintain a corresponding entry to assign the data access definition we just created to the condition type /SCMTMS/TOR_ORGUNIT. If you set the **Dflt DAD** field to **Data Access Definition is Default for Condition Type (X)**, your data access definition is displayed in every new condition of this type.

In our new condition, we can now enter our data access definition in the corresponding field. The information concerning data crawler profile and input help is entered automatically.

If you click **Back**, you go back to the decision table and maintain values by clicking the link. We can now enter the data in the decision table, as shown in Figure 2.28.

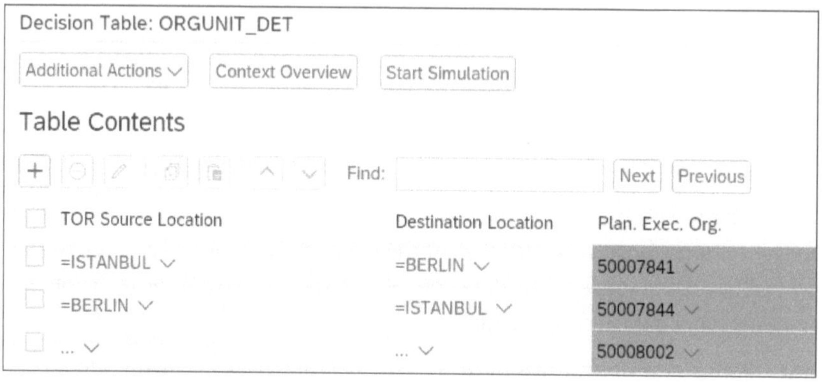

Figure 2.28 Decision Table

When maintaining more complex decision tables, note that the system always reads decision tables from top to bottom. If a corresponding combination of input values is found, the system stops looking through the table and continues the business process with the output values found.

In our example, we now have a third planning and execution organization: Europe. This organizational unit is responsible for all other freight orders except for the ones between Istanbul and Berlin. We therefore enter a third line in the decision table, leaving the input values empty (which acts as a wildcard) and enter the planning and execution organization. In this case, it's very important to enter this line as the last line in the decision table because if it's the first, all freight orders get the planning and execution organization Europe.

Organizational Units in Decision Tables

Organizational units have an ID and organizational unit number. In decision tables, only the number is displayed. Therefore, you don't see the IDs **Germany, Turkey**, and **Europe**, which we've used in our example in Figure 2.28, but only the organizational unit numbers.

After saving the condition, you can assign your condition to a freight order type, as shown in Figure 2.29. The planning and execution organization is always determined using your condition when you create a freight order of this type.

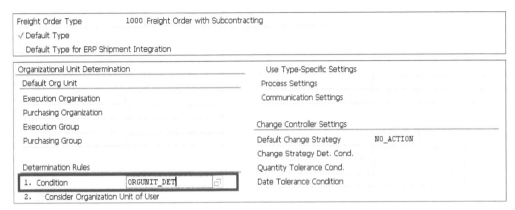

Figure 2.29 Organizational Unit Determination in Freight Order Type Customizing

---

Transporting Conditions

If you set up the system so that Customizing can be transported when you enter a condition in edit mode, you're asked to record your changes to the condition in a software Customizing transport request.

Conditions can be transported to other systems. Be aware that this makes sense in some circumstances but not all; in our example, using organizational unit numbers doesn't make sense because the organizational unit numbers would be different in another system. However, conditions can also be created and edited in systems where normal Customizing in Transaction SPRO isn't permitted.

2.3.2   Incompatibilities

Incompatibilities are used to implement loading constraints and routing constraints. Loading constraints identify goods as incompatible with other goods, vehicles, or compartments. Routing constraints identify goods or vehicles as incompatible with locations.

Incompatibilities

This section about incompatibilities aims to give you an overview of the functionality incompatibilities provide and how they work. We take a more detailed look at the use of incompatibilities in the corresponding sections of this book, especially in Chapter 6, Section 6.7.4.

You can create incompatibilities by choosing the **Create Incompatibility** tile in the **Profiles and Settings** tab of the SAP Fiori launchpad.

Creating Incompatibilities in SAP TM 9.6

When creating incompatibilities in SAP TM 9.6, the menu path is different from the menu path described later in this section. Please follow **Application Administration · Planning · General Settings · Incompatibility Definitions · Create Incompatibility** to create an incompatibility.

You'll follow a similar menu path to create incompatibility settings, which we'll discuss later in this section.

An incompatibility has two main settings: incompatibility area and incompatibility type. You can find both at the top-right corner of Figure 2.30. The **Incompatibility Area** field defines where this incompatibility can be used—that is, in the entire optimizer run or only in carrier selection, and so on.

The **Incompatibility Type** field defines what should be made incompatible with what. You define incompatibilities by setting up two conditions. Depending on the incompatibility type you've chosen, the condition type of both conditions is predefined.

For example, say we want to define that a certain truck can't carry fruit and vegetables, so we choose the incompatibility type **Freight Unit – Vehicle Resource**. Incompatibilities make use of conditions to determine values that are then validated based on whether they are incompatible to each other. The condition types of the two conditions being compared are now predefined. By clicking **Create Condition**, you can create a new condition from the **Incompatibility Definition** screen.

On the left side of Figure 2.30, we create the first condition: **FRUIT INCOMPATIBILITY**. Because the freight unit itself doesn't carry any unique information that identifies it as a fruit or vegetable, we need to fine-tune the condition.

We know that the products **APPLE**, **PEAR**, and **ORANGE** are fruits. Therefore, we define the decision table in such a way that if the input (the data access definition looks at the product ID of the freight unit's product item) is one of these, then the output is **FRUIT**, as illustrated in Figure 2.31.

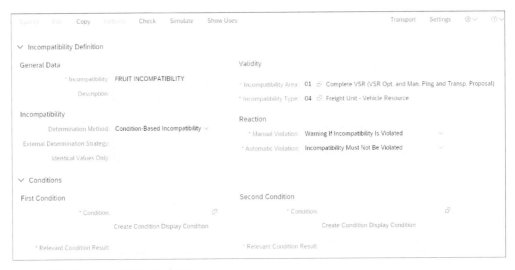

Figure 2.30 Incompatibility Definition

Figure 2.31 Grouping Multiple Input Options to One Value for Incompatibilities

The first condition is automatically entered into the corresponding field in the **Incompatibility Definition** screen when you save it. We now enter the value "FRUIT" in the **Condition Result** field.

Now we need to create the second condition: the condition determining the resource name. In this condition, we can use the direct business object access condition because we only need the name of the truck. Set the condition access type to direct business object access, and define a corresponding data access definition.

In the incompatibility definition screen, we now set the condition result of the second condition to **TRUCK1**. Now the truck is incompatible with all freight units that are defined as **FRUIT** in the first condition.

Grouping Products for Transportation Purposes

This example doesn't have any grouping information on the transportation quality of the freight unit. In general, we recommend storing that information in the product's *transportation group*.

After we've saved our incompatibility definition, we can group it together with others in *incompatibility settings*, which are shown in Figure 2.32. In these incompatibility settings, we can define whether we want equal behavior in manual and optimizer planning.

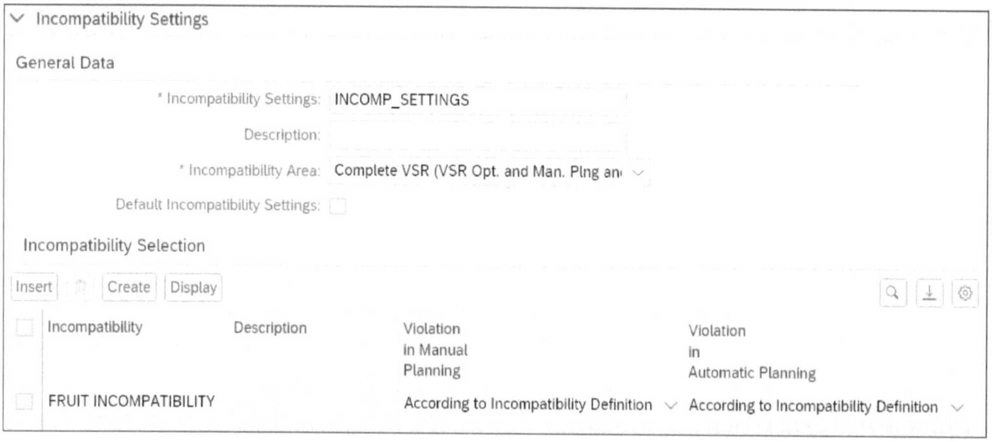

Figure 2.32 Incompatibility Settings

We delve deeper into the use of the different incompatibility types when we talk about planning with the SAP TM functionality later on.

2.3.3   Post Processing Framework

The Post Processing Framework (PPF) is a tool in SAP TM used to execute program logic that is considered a follow-up action to a certain business process step.

The PPF is used for the following tasks, or *actions* (to name a few):

- Document printing
- Sending messages, such as email, fax, or electronic data interchange (EDI)
- Workflow triggers

All actions are defined in the PPF with a *schedule condition* that defines whether the action needs to be executed and a *processing time* that defines when to execute the action.

In general, it's important to note that PPF actions can only process information that is already saved to the database. This prevents you from accidentally sending preliminary transportation orders to a carrier, for example.

The transaction for configuring the PPF isn't part of any SAP TM role. Instead, you must enter Transaction SPPFCADM in the backend system. On the initial screen of this transaction, you can see various PPF applications. Select **/SCMTMS/TRANSPOR-TATION**, and choose **Define Actions Profiles and Actions**.

An action profile like the one shown in Figure 2.33 bundles all actions concerning a specific business process area (e.g., the action profile /SCMTMS/TOR bundles all actions important for the freight order).

Let's briefly consider the most important settings of the PPF. In Figure 2.34, you can see in the **Action Settings** area, where we can define the processing time of the action and whether the action should be scheduled automatically or by a batch job.

The processing type of the action can be one of the following:

- Trigger alert
- Method call
- Workflow
- Smart Forms actions
- External communication

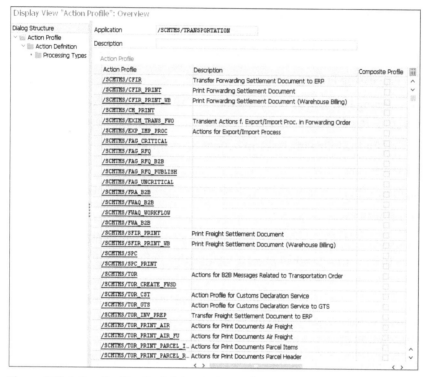

Figure 2.33 Action Profiles Containing Action Definitions

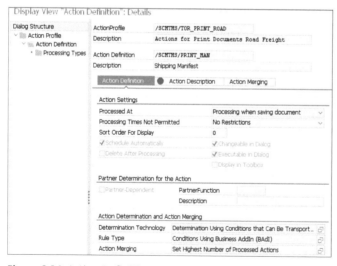

Figure 2.34 Action Definition

The type you choose determines the required information for the detailed processing.

Schedule conditions define whether an action should be processed at all. The most common way of defining a schedule condition is to implement the BAdI EVAL_START-COND_PPF.

You can also define start and scheduling conditions in Transaction SPPFCADM by choosing the application **/SCMTMS/TRANSPORTATION** and selecting **Condition Configuration (Transportable Conditions)**.

2.3.4   Document Creation

The previous section mentions that you can accomplish document printing with PPF. However, SAP TM is also capable of designing print forms to a certain extent. SAP TM integrates with Adobe Document Server, a tool that can be run within SAP GUI in the backend system.

Start Transaction SFP, and choose the print form you want to alter. Then add new fields to the print form or alter the layout on the **Layout** tab as illustrated in Figure 2.35.

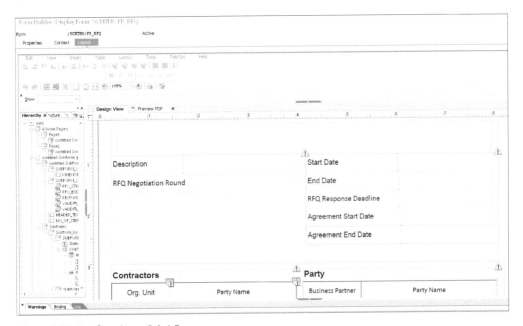

Figure 2.35 Configuring a Print Form

Adobe Document Server

Adobe Document Server requires its own license and its own plug-in for you to use it within SAP GUI.

We won't go deeper into altering print forms in this chapter. For more information, consult resources that cover the Adobe Document Server.

2.3.5   Optimizer

SAP has already used optimization programs in various supply chain management applications, such as SAP Advanced Planning and Optimization (SAP APO)-Transportation Planning/Vehicle Scheduling (TP/VS), a predecessor of SAP TM. The optimizer is a C++-based application designed to solve transportation problems in a mathematical way. (Bear in mind that transportation problems might not be solved completely but can be handled with a best approach. This applies to the optimizer, too.)

The optimizer can be run on hardware different from the application servers running SAP TM. In fact, we recommend this because the system requirements of SAP TM and the optimizer differ.

Optimization runs can be performed in parallel. To provide enough optimizer resources, either the optimizer should provide a sufficient number of slots or you should connect several optimizer engines to the backend system running the SAP TM functionality, as shown in Figure 2.36.

RCCF: Destinations for Engines							
Dest. ID	Appl.	Short Text	Status	M...	P...	Comm. Type	Communication Connection
TSFM01	TSFM	Strategic Freight Management Optimizer	Active	⌄ 10	1	RFC	⌄ OPTSERVER_TSFM01
TSPS01	TSPS	Transportation Service Provider	Active	⌄ 10	1	RFC	⌄ OPTSERVER_TSPS01
TVRG01	TVRG	Transportation Proposal	Active	⌄ 10	1	RFC	⌄ OPTSERVER_TVRG01
TVSO01	TVSO	Load Optimization	Active	⌄ 10	1	RFC	⌄ OPTSERVER_TVSO01
TVSR01	TVSR	Vehicle Scheduling and Routing engine	Active	⌄ 10	1	RFC	⌄ OPTSERVER_TVSR01
TVSS01	TVSS	Vehicle Scheduling engine	Active	⌄ 10	1	RFC	⌄ OPTSERVER_TVSS01

Figure 2.36 Optimizer Connections

You can monitor the optimizer connections in Transaction RCC_CUST. As you can see in Figure 2.36, the optimizer provides six applications:

- **TSFM** for strategic freight management
- **TSPS** for carrier selection

- **TVRG** for transportation proposals
- **TVSO** for load optimization
- **TVSR** for optimizer routing and scheduling
- **TVSS** for scheduling of existing freight orders

It's important to know that these six applications are only executable files on the optimizer server. No master data or transactional data is stored on the optimizer engine except for log files.

If you want to update your optimizer program, simply download the newest version of the executable files for the SAP Supply Chain Management (SAP SCM) optimizer from the SAP Software Center (*https://launchpad.support.sap.com/#/softwarecenter*), and replace the existing files on the server with the new ones.

2.3.6   Process Controller Framework

Another tool in SAP TM that simplifies enhancements of the standard logic is the Process Controller Framework. In many functional areas of SAP TM, strategies provided by the Process Controller Framework are performed. A *strategy* is an order of methods being performed one after another. Because all methods included in a strategy contain the same signature, it's very easy for developers to add their own methods to a strategy.

For example, you can define the strategy for performing manual planning in the planning profile. As you can see in Figure 2.37, there are several strategies to choose from.

If you compare these strategies in Customizing (follow the IMG path **Transportation Management • Basic Functions • Process Controller • Assign Methods to a Strategy**), you can see that they all have common methods (e.g., VSRI_PRE or VSRI), but some strategies also offer additional methods (e.g., VSRI_SCHED).

If you want to enhance the logic of manual planning, add your own methods to the strategy or create a completely new strategy.

Services define which strategies may be used in which context. In SAP TM, a service is linked strictly to a use case. A strategy containing several methods can then be assigned to a service. This establishes the hierarchy shown in Figure 2.38.

Change View "Method assignment to Strategy": Overview

Method assignment to Strategy

Strategy	Method	Sequence	Description
VSRI_1STEP	VSRI_PRE	10	Interactive planning and Carrier Selection
VSRI_1STEP	VSRI	20	Interactive planning and Carrier Selection
VSRI_1STEP	VSRI_POST	30	Interactive planning and Carrier Selection
VSRI_1STEP	VSRI_TSPS	40	Interactive planning and Carrier Selection
VSRI_ALP	VSRI_PRE	10	Interactive Planning and Automatic Load Planning
VSRI_ALP	VSRI	20	Interactive Planning and Automatic Load Planning
VSRI_ALP	VSRI_POST	30	Interactive Planning and Automatic Load Planning
VSRI_ALP	VSRI_ALP	40	Interactive Planning and Automatic Load Planning
VSRI_CHK	VSRI_PRE	10	Interactive Planning Strategy + check
VSRI_CHK	VSRI	20	Interactive Planning Strategy + check
VSRI_CHK	VSRI_POST	30	Interactive Planning Strategy + check
VSRI_CHK	VSRI_CHECK	40	Interactive Planning Strategy + check
VSRI_DEF	VSRI_PRE	10	Default Interactive Planning Strategy
VSRI_DEF	VSRI	20	Default Interactive Planning Strategy
VSRI_DEF	VSRI_POST	30	Default Interactive Planning Strategy
VSRI_SCH	VSRI_PRE	10	Interactive planning and scheduling
VSRI_SCH	VSRI	20	Interactive planning and scheduling
VSRI_SCH	VSRI_POST	30	Interactive planning and scheduling
VSRI_SCH	VSRI_SCHED	40	Interactive planning and scheduling

Figure 2.37 Method Assignment to Strategies

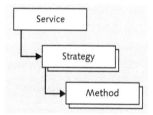

Figure 2.38 Process Controller Hierarchy

2.4   Integration Technology with SAP TM

So far in this chapter, we've talked about the technologies that enable business logic within SAP TM. In Chapter 1, Section 1.3, we saw that the SAP TM functionality is embedded in SAP S/4HANA, but it can also be run as part of SAP Business Suite and SAP SCM. If we run an SAP TM system that isn't embedded in an SAP S/4HANA system or whenever communicating with internal or external systems outside of the system the SAP TM functionality runs in, technologies that enable business logic *within* SAP TM aren't sufficient without integration with other SAP or non-SAP applications.

Integration Scenarios with SAP TM in SAP S/4HANA

As you've learned in Chapter 1, most integration scenarios have been eliminated with embedding SAP TM in SAP S/4HANA. In this section, we'll therefore focus on integration scenarios when SAP TM is run separately as part of SAP Business Suite.

Figure 2.39 shows that SAP TM 9.6 uses various integration technologies to communicate with other applications. We'll take a look at these integration technologies in this section.

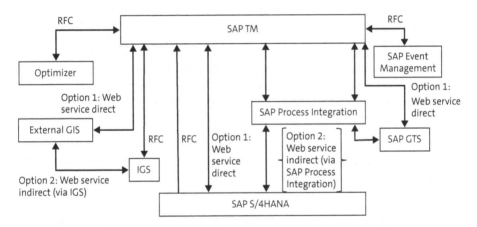

Figure 2.39 Overview of SAP TM Integration When Not Embedded in SAP S/4HANA

2.4.1   SOA-Based Integration with SAP Process Integration

When you look at the early stage of SAP R/3, you can see that the entire business logic was meant to run on one system. All the data gathered in business transactions was supposed to be stored on a central database from which it could be retrieved by different application modules.

Nowadays, with the big increase in data volume and the high level of interconnectivity of business partners (both internally and externally), system landscapes have become heterogeneous. Not only is data spread throughout different systems, but business logic is also run in several applications. With the introduction of SAP S/4HANA, SAP has taken a step toward reversing this trend and reintegrating functionality that has grown in a heterogeneous solution landscape into one centralized system. However, we still see a large number of enterprises running on a heterogeneous system landscape, which is why we want to spend some time discussing how SAP TM can work in such environments.

To orchestrate both the supply of data and the business logic for the entire system landscape, you need to establish a central instance that is aware of all systems in the system landscape and knows where data can be provided. In the SAP system landscape, this central instance is SAP Process Integration.

SAP Process Integration provides a platform that allows different interfaces to communicate with each other. The communication is established using a uniform technology: web services. SAP Process Integration not only acts as a directory for systems and applications in a landscape but also supports and monitors communication among systems.

The concept of SOA was established after it became clear that the entire business logic of an enterprise could not be executed in one system alone. SOA is supposed to enable interaction between systems regardless of their respective system architectures or programming languages.

Web services are essential helpers of SOA that implement the concept of the interaction of systems. Web services contain a data structure, usually in XML format, that shows what data can be passed from or to a system in the system landscape. In the respective applications, *proxies* interpret the web service and execute business logic in the application.

The system applications offer their web services to a service broker (in our case, SAP Process Integration). The service broker acts as a web service directory; you could also say the service broker is like a dating agency for business systems. All systems in the system landscape can now access the directory of web services in SAP Process Integration and download the web services descriptions into their applications. At that point, they can start implementing business logic that either fills the XML data structure to send data to other systems (this system is the *service consumer*) or implements logic to interpret the XML to use the data (this system is the *service provider*). After it executes the business logic, the service provider can respond with another XML file to the service consumer.

We could look at more theory to understand the integration of systems with SOA and web services, but it might be best to examine it using a concrete example. Let's look at the solution architecture for the integration of an SAP S/4HANA sales and distribution SO into SAP TM.

Let's assume that the system landscape we have is an SAP TM 9.6 application that wants to interact with SAP S/4HANA. The first step is to register both SAP TM and SAP S/4HANA in the System Landscape Directory (SLD) of SAP Process Integration so that it's aware of both systems and their application purposes. (The content of SAP Process Integration is constantly updated, which means it knows what an SAP TM application is for.)

After the systems are registered in the SLD, the web services can be published to the respective systems. A web service consists of two service interfaces—one interface for each application. The service interface can be loaded into the application system.

Let's look at the service interface on the SAP TM side. The service interface for SAP S/4HANA order integration is called `IntracompanyTransportationRequestRequest_In`, and you can find it in the SAP TM system using Transaction SPROXY. If you pay close attention, you'll see that after you've confirmed the transaction code, there is a notification in the message area that the Enterprise Services Repository (ESR) is started. Because the ESR is situated in the SAP Process Integration system, the information we see in Transaction SPROXY is actually loaded from the connected SAP Process Integration system.

SAP S/4HANA versus SAP ERP

Although we're referring to SAP S/4HANA as our base system here, all integration steps through the next four sections apply to SAP ERP as well.

Figure 2.40 shows the numerous service interfaces available for SAP TM. The service interfaces enable not only communication between SAP systems within a company (application-to-application [A2A] communication) but also the communication between SAP systems and legacy systems or systems of external business partners (business-to-business [B2B] communication).

There are a few important things to consider about how the web service works when you're selecting the service interface for integrating SAP S/4HANA orders into SAP TM.

On the detailed view of the service interface, you can see a number of different tabs. Get familiar with the data structure that is passed to the SAP TM system. If you go to the **External View** tab and expand one node after another, as depicted in Figure 2.41, you'll see that the XML message's data structure consists of two parts: the message header and the transportation request itself. The message header contains metadata about the message, especially stating from which system this message was sent and which system was supposed to be the recipient.

Figure 2.40 Service Interfaces in Transaction SPROXY

The important information for us is in the transportation request, which indicates what data can be passed to the SAP TM system. Notice that the data structure is somewhat similar to the data structure of the business object /SCMTMS/TRQ, of which an instance will be created with this web service.

When data is exchanged between two systems, both systems need to be able to interpret the data that is passed. Therefore, if the service consumer sends a date to the service provider, the service provider needs to know that the field will be no longer than eight digits. This can't be taken for granted because the SAP S/4HANA system has its own data types that aren't communicated to SAP TM. *Global data types* are used for this reason.

Global data types are defined in SAP Process Integration. Here, we can create a global data type for a delivery date. Although global data types are based on core data types, such as string, integer, and so on, you can also encounter aggregated data types, meaning a structure containing several global data types. These global data types within an aggregated data type are again based on core data types.

The entire XML message format consists of fields using global data types. After the service interface is loaded into the application system, the proxy generation performs the necessary next steps.

So far, we've only looked at the data structure of the service interface's message. Remember, however, that the SAP TM system can't yet work with the data types contained in the message, so we need to perform a proxy generation. A proxy is an application system–owned interpreter of the web service's service interface; it converts the global data types of the message into data types the SAP TM system can work with. Let's look at what the proxy generation achieved with the city name of the shipper party.

The city name was based on a global data type (upper box), but as you can see in Figure 2.41, the proxy has generated its own data element in the SAP TM system (lower box).

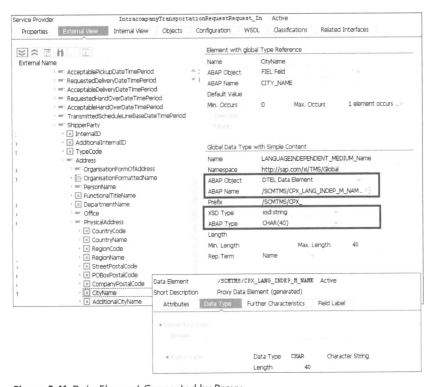

Figure 2.41 Data Element Generated by Proxy

The global data type defined that the city name should be based on the core data type string and should not be longer than 40 characters. If you look at the generated data type in Transaction SE11, you can see that this setup has been taken over in the new data element in SAP TM.

If aggregated global data types are used, the proxy generates a structure type.

So far, we've only looked at the data structure of the service interface in SAP TM. However, the OTR or DTR won't be created unless some business logic is executed. As we've said, a web service consists of a common data structure and business logic on the service consumer's side as well as on the service provider's side. In communication between the service consumer and the service provider, neither knows exactly what is happening on the other side of the communication channel. The business logic of the communication partner is supposed to be a black box. This makes sense especially if communication via web services has been established between two systems with different programming languages.

The proxy not only generates the data elements in the system but also creates a *provider class* (see Figure 2.42).

Figure 2.42 Proxy Provider Class

Use of the provider classes is comparable to the use of the classes assigned to actions, validations, and determinations that we discussed earlier. The provider class consists of a constructor and an executing method that is called after a message of this service interface is received in the system.

When you display the service interface in Transaction SPROXY, go to the **Properties** tab shown in Figure 2.42. Here, you'll find the provider class that was also generated by the proxy (lower part of the upper screen). When delving deeper into the implementation of this class (the middle screen shows methods provided by the class), you'll see that, in our example, the instance of the business object TRQ will be created. The lower screen shows an excerpt from the actual coding implemented in the method.

This Isn't the Entire SOA Story

Communication between two SAP systems using SOA is a very complex topic for which many resources are available. This section provides just a quick glimpse at how the integration of transactional data between SAP S/4HANA and SAP TM works.

Recall from Figure 2.39 that you have two options for transferring an SAP S/4HANA order from SAP S/4HANA to SAP TM: either using SAP Process Integration as middleware or using a direct web service–based communication channel. Both options have advantages and disadvantages, and the choice is yours.

The web services for the standard integration are delivered with the SAP TM-specific content for SAP Process Integration. In both application systems, you need to activate some business functions to use the service interfaces. We describe these in further detail in Chapter 4, Section 4.1.

We've now looked at the service interface for receiving information from an SAP S/4HANA document to create a corresponding document in SAP TM. The same settings can be observed in the SAP S/4HANA system, where the service interfaces for the service consumer's side are present. You can get a detailed look at the SAP S/4HANA service interfaces in Transaction SPROXY in the SAP S/4HANA system.

As outlined in Table 2.1, SAP TM offers several web services for A2A communication that can be clustered into different functional areas of SAP TM.

Service	Service Consumer	Service Provider
Transportation Requirements (OTRs and DTRs)		
Create transportation requirements	SAP S/4HANA	SAP TM
Cancel transportation requirements	SAP S/4HANA	SAP TM
Provide document flow	SAP S/4HANA	SAP TM
Freight Settlement		
Transfer freight settlement document to SAP S/4HANA	SAP TM	SAP S/4HANA
Cancel freight settlement document	SAP TM	SAP S/4HANA
Delivery Proposals		
Propose inbound delivery creation	SAP TM	SAP S/4HANA
Propose outbound delivery creation	SAP TM	SAP S/4HANA

Table 2.1 Overview of A2A Services in SAP TM

Update of Transferred Documents

In most cases, the web services that create documents in the other system are also used for updates. The proxy provider class evaluates whether a document has already been created and updates the corresponding document. Therefore, no duplicate documents are created in the service provider's system.

2.4.2   Integration with SAP Process Integration without Predefined Content

If you take a closer look at the capabilities of SAP Process Integration, you'll see that this middleware application is used not only as a service broker and system landscape directory but also for supporting message mapping in B2B communication. B2B communication takes place when two companies exchange data with their respective systems.

Let's walk through another example. We're a carrier, and our customer (a fashion company) wants to order transportation services. The fashion manufacturer uses an SAP TM system and has implemented various shipper scenarios. After the fashion manufacturer has finished transportation planning, an order for transportation execution is placed. To do this, the shipper sends out an RFQ to us, the carrier. As a carrier, we're also using an SAP TM system. As you'll see in more detail in the next chapters, the document flow is as follows: the shipper has created a freight order and now sends us an RFQ. Because we're a carrier, and the shipper's freight order is a transportation request, we then create a forwarding quotation or forwarding order for the shipper's freight order (depending on the exact process).

This B2B communication can be established using SAP Process Integration. After the shipper's RFQ has arrived in our system landscape, SAP Process Integration determines which inbound service interface needs to be triggered to which recipient based on the sender's system information and the message type. If the data structures of the RFQ and the forwarding order's service interface don't match, SAP Process Integration can also perform field mapping. The service interface on our SAP TM side then automatically creates a forwarding quotation or forwarding order.

Table 2.2 lists all available B2B service interfaces that SAP TM provides.

Service	Service Consumer	Service Provider
Transportation Requirements (Forwarding Order and Forwarding Quotation)		
Create transportation requirements	External	SAP TM
Cancel transportation requirements	External	SAP TM
Confirm transportation requirements	SAP TM	External
Tendering		
Send transportation order	SAP TM	External
Cancel transportation order	SAP TM	External
Send RFQ	SAP TM	External
Receive RFQ response	External	SAP TM
Freight Booking		
Send freight booking	SAP TM	External
Cancel freight booking	SAP TM	External

Table 2.2 Overview of B2B Services in SAP TM

Service	Service Consumer	Service Provider
Confirm freight booking	External	SAP TM
Send transportation waybill	SAP TM	External

Table 2.2 Overview of B2B Services in SAP TM (Cont.)

Using SAP TM and Other Systems

In this example, we assumed that both business partners use SAP TM applications. Unfortunately, this can't be taken for granted.

Note, however, that the mapping of messages in SAP Process Integration can be much more sophisticated than in this example. SAP Process Integration can also map incoming IDocs to service interfaces.

Synchronous or Asynchronous?

Web services can be performed synchronously or asynchronously. All A2A and B2B web services in SAP TM are performed asynchronously. This makes sense because, in most cases, a user has to validate information that was entered using a service interface. For example, if a freight booking is sent to a carrier, the carrier needs to evaluate whether the requested space is still available. In the case of a synchronous communication, the shipper can't work until the carrier has responded with at least a technical confirmation of the message receipt.

If you're still using an SAP ERP system, SOA-based communication between SAP ERP and SAP TM for order integration works only if an SAP ERP 6.04 SP 9 system or higher is in place. Older versions of SAP ERP don't offer the business functions and service interfaces needed to use the predefined content for communication as explained in this chapter.

To integrate SAP ERP without predefined SAP Process Integration content, you have to establish IDoc communication out of SAP ERP that is sent to SAP Process Integration, where the IDoc needs to be mapped to the predefined service interface for OTR and DTR creation. Furthermore, direct communication between SAP ERP and SAP TM that bypasses SAP Process Integration is no longer possible.

2.4.3   Monitoring Integration Messages with Service Interfaces

As you've seen, communication with SAP TM is usually established using service interfaces with or without SAP Process Integration as middleware. In implementation projects, you might encounter situations when the communication setup is finished, but the incoming messages don't yet achieve the desired result. To troubleshoot, we recommend monitoring the incoming and outgoing messages in SAP TM to see which fields were filled incorrectly or what error messages occurred during processing of the message.

The monitoring of service messages isn't specific to SAP TM but is common to many SAP applications. However, it's worth looking at it now because it rounds out the topic of communication between different systems.

With Transaction SXMB_MONI, you can display all messages that have arrived in your SAP TM application or left the SAP TM system. After you enter the transaction, select **Monitor for Processed XML Messages**, and then define further selection criteria, such as the name of the interface or the time frame.

The first column of the list of messages shows the message status and whether it was processed correctly. Consider a few common examples:

- **Checkered flag**
  The message was processed successfully.

- **Green flag**
  The message has been recorded, but the queue needs to be started manually.

- **White flash on red button**
  An error has occurred.

- **Green arrow**
  The message wasn't processed successfully but can be restarted in Transaction /SAPPO/PPO2.

By double-clicking the **Status Details** field, you can view the XML message that was sent or received. If an error has occurred, you can see the error message on the right side. If you want to view the content of the message, navigate to **XML Message · Inbound Message · Payload · MainDocument,** and the message content is displayed in the lower window on the right side of Figure 2.43. This is **Window 2.**

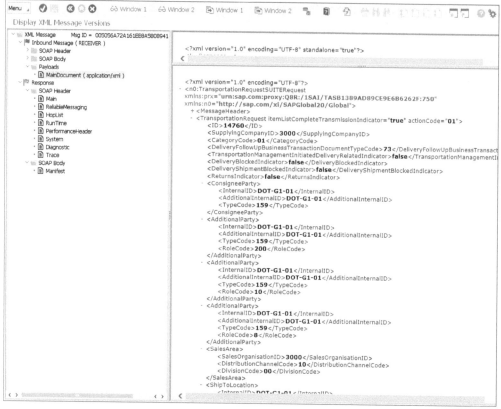

Figure 2.43 Monitoring the XML Message

Sometimes, the message isn't processed correctly because a field wasn't filled in or was filled in incorrectly. In this case, if you want to test whether this is the only issue with the message, you don't need to resend data from SAP S/4HANA; instead, you can simulate the message entry. When displaying the message content as explained, download this XML file to your computer by clicking the **Download Window 2** button at the top of the message display screen (see Figure 2.43).

After that, go to Transaction SPROXY, and enter the service interface you used. Notice the **Test** button in the menu bar as in Transaction SE80. If you enter the test mode, you'll be able to upload your XML file again, manually alter data in the XML editor, and then process the service interface using your manipulated message. Keep in mind that you need to trigger COMMIT WORK manually to write data to the database. You can do this in the general menu of this transaction by following the menu path **Extras · Trigger COMMIT WORK** (shown in Figure 2.44).

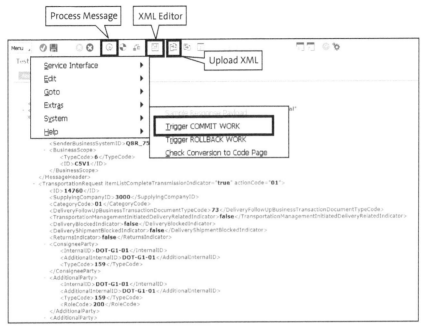

Figure 2.44 Simulating Data Entry for an XML Message

2.4.4   Remote Function Call–Based Communication

Figure 2.39 shows that SAP S/4HANA communicates with SAP TM not only using web services via SAP Process Integration but also using *remote function calls* (RFCs).

RFC-based communication is used to integrate master data from SAP S/4HANA to SAP TM. Because we aren't dealing with individual transactional data here, but instead with mass data, RFC communication is used instead of web services because web services are usually designed for communication concerning transactional data.

Integrating master data from SAP S/4HANA to the SAP TM functionality that resides within another SAP S/4HANA system is done using technology provided by the master data governance framework: the Data Replication Framework (DRF). When transferring master data from an SAP S/4HANA system to a standalone SAP TM system, we use the Core Interface (CIF).

While the DRF also uses service interfaces, master data integration with CIF is established using RFC communication, as is the integration of SAP TM and SAP Event Management. SAP Event Management can be installed on the same system as SAP TM. However, you need to use Transaction SM59 to define an RFC connection to the SAP Event Management system, even if it's installed on the same system as SAP TM. We cover the setup of SAP Event Management integration in Chapter 8, Section 8.2.

2.5   Summary

This chapter introduced you to the technological foundation of SAP TM, showing its two major technological pillars: the BOPF, which takes over the tasks of data modeling, storage, and processing, and the UI technology built on the FPM framework. We also covered how the data stored in the BOPF is transferred to the UI technology using FBI.

While talking about UI technologies, we explored how the SAP Fiori launchpad interacts with the user and how catalogs decide what tiles are shown to the user in the SAP Fiori launchpad. SAP TM screens can be customized without any coding or modifications.

Next, we looked at other tools and frameworks used in SAP TM, such as the BRF+, the PPF, and the Process Controller Framework. These tools facilitate Customizing and adapting SAP TM to the business use case.

The final part of this chapter covered the technical integration of an SAP TM stand-alone system with other business applications. In general, we've differentiated between an A2A communication using predefined content on both application systems and B2B communication, where only predefined content in SAP Process Integration is available for SAP TM. This technical information about SAP TM is meant to build a foundation for the SAP TM business processes described in Chapter 3 through Chapter 12.

Now that we've looked at the technological foundation of the SAP TM system, we'll introduce the SAP TM–specific master data before starting to delve into the processes run with the SAP TM functionality.

Chapter 3
Master Data

Master data serves as a cornerstone for any business process. All central business objects and procedures, such as order management, planning, subcontracting, and shipment costing, are based on master data. In addition, it maps both the internal organization and partner business relationships and is essential for specifying the transportation network and available resources.

In the previous chapter, we gave you an overview of the solution architecture and technological concepts of SAP TM. Before we take a closer look at transportation requirements, planning, and execution, we dedicate this chapter to explaining the mandatory and optional master data, while making you familiar with the most important terminology and configurations.

Master data is an integral part of any planning system and the cornerstone of any business process. All central business objects and processes that are key to transportation management are based on logistical master data. This data, apart from general master data such as organizational structures and business partners, typically includes the transportation network and resources, which together describe how transportation orders can be executed. Therefore, whether you work with SAP TM 9.6 or SAP TM in SAP S/4HANA, master data is important because it supports both planning and execution activities.

One of the key features of SAP TM is that it allows logistical processes to be executed independently of master data relating to business partners and transported goods. For third-party logistics providers (3PLs) who mainly provide transportation services, it's essential that the transaction data can be created with minimal existing master data.

In this chapter, we explain both logistics master data representing the transportation network and general master data and resources used to execute the transportation of goods. All other master data and transportation mode-specific settings are explained in the relevant context. To support end-to-end transportation scenarios for shippers and logistics service providers (LSPs) and to ensure consistency with the execution process, a set of general master data is required, for example, to model your organizational structure and avoid the recurring maintenance of addresses or product attributes. We look at this general master data in Section 3.1. For scenarios that use SAP TM in a side-by-side deployment, we explain master data integration that can be based on the Core Interface (CIF) for SAP TM 9.6 or the Data Replication Framework (DRF) for standalone instances of SAP TM in SAP S/4HANA integration. By seamlessly integrating with SAP ERP or SAP S/4HANA and avoiding master data maintenance, SAP TM can use and reuse existing customer and product master data.

Several master data elements are needed to support proper transportation planning and execution. In Section 3.2, we explain how these elements are created and combined to outline a transportation network.

For transportation execution and to represent the capacity needed to perform the transportation activity, resource master data such as vehicles and trailers are used. To reflect availability and operating times and to handle transportation orders, you can set up calendar and handling resources. The configuration and maintenance of resources is explained in Section 3.3.

Let's begin by exploring the use of general master data in SAP TM.

3.1   General Master Data

All corporate departments use general master data. Because it maps both the internal organization and the partner and business relationships, general master data serves as a cornerstone for any business process. Clearly defined master data is of central importance for well-regulated financial processing in particular. In this section, starting with the definition of the organizational structure, we present a thorough overview of the most important general master data, its significance for transportation processes, and, if applicable, its integration and distribution.

3.1.1   Organizational Structure

The individual elements of an organizational structure are used to map an enterprise in an SAP system. These organizational structures determine the operational framework in which all sequences and functions of logistics and financial processes occur. They also reflect the legal and organizational structure of a company. Organizational master data allows you to create organizational models, which are the legal, geographic, or organizational boundaries for the organizations that take part in the transportation process. By representing the structure of a company and being used to determine responsibilities, the organizational units build a framework in which all relevant business processes occur.

In this section, we'll dive into the internal organizational structure, its creation, and how to merge organizational hierarchies originating from different source systems.

Internal Organizational Structure

An organizational structure can be set up as a combination of organizational elements. The simplest structure may consist of a single employee who is responsible for various tasks. However, in a larger enterprise, or in the case of an LSP, the structure may be divided into various organizational areas. Figure 3.1 shows the structure, cardinality, and relationships between the organizational elements in the enterprise resource planning (ERP) system (SAP ERP or SAP S/4HANA) and SAP TM.

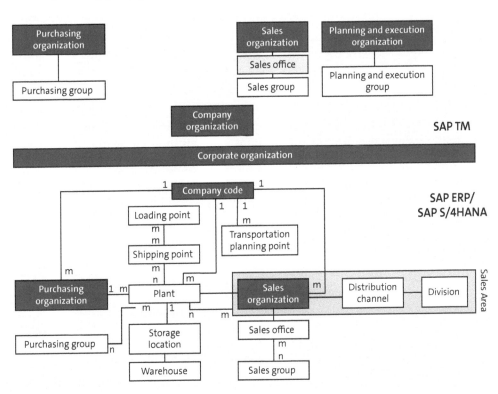

Figure 3.1 Organizational Structures in SAP ERP or SAP S/4HANA and SAP TM

In SAP TM, organizational units can be modeled independently from the SAP ERP or SAP S/4HANA system. They are categorized in three basic types:

- Sales (sales organization)
- Purchasing (purchasing organization)
- Planning and execution

These organizations can be further divided into groups and offices; employees acting on different roles are typically assigned to organizational groups.

The optional corporate organization usually serves as the highest node and entry point in the organizational structure. The company organization corresponds to the company code. Like the company code, the company organization defines the local currency and usually represents the legal entity of the company.

The sales organization organizes and structures the sale of logistics services and executes these services. It can consist of a hierarchy of suborganizations (e.g., for each country), sales offices (e.g., East Coast, West Coast, etc.), and sales groups (e.g., air freight, sea freight, etc.).

In SAP ERP and SAP S/4HANA, the sales organization is combined with two additional organizational elements to define sales areas. These two elements, the division and distribution channel, don't exist in SAP TM. Because certain master data in SAP S/4HANA builds on these two organizational elements, they can be defaulted in Customizing (**Transportation Management · Master Data · Basic Functions · General Settings · Define General Settings for SAP TM**), which is shown in Figure 3.2.

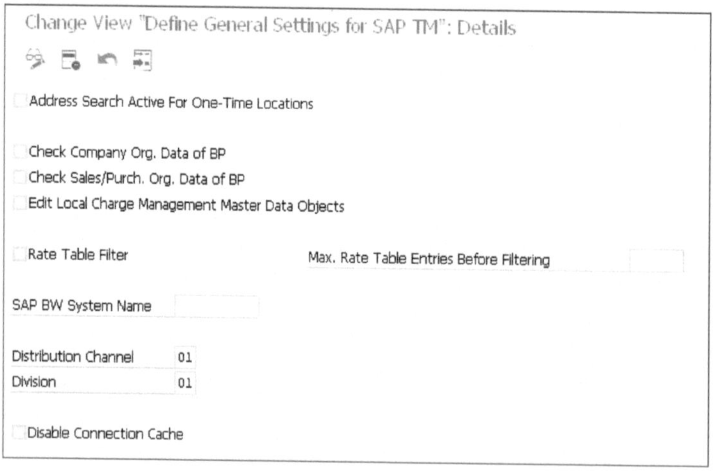

Figure 3.2 General Settings for SAP TM

These default values are used to access business partner master data stored on the sales area level by adding these as defaults.

The sales organization is relevant in the following documents:

- Forwarding quotations
- Forwarding orders
- Customer contracts for the sale of freight-handling services
- Forwarding settlements

The next basic type of organizational unit is the purchasing organization. The actual procurement of materials and services always takes place in relation to a purchasing organization. You need purchasing organizations and purchasing groups for subcontracting. The purchasing organization arranges and executes all purchasing transactions relating to the logistics services provided by carriers and freight forwarders.

Several purchasing organizations can be defined, for example, one for each country or each transportation mode. Several purchasing groups (e.g., for each shipment type, region, etc.) can be assigned to each purchasing organization. The following types of documents are generally associated with the purchasing organization:

- Freight orders
- Freight bookings
- Service orders
- Freight agreements
- Freight settlements

For transportation planning and execution, which is the final organizational unit type, you can define planning and execution organizations. These represent the different organizational units that are responsible for freight by land, sea, and air in different geographical regions. In this context, the planning and execution organization organizes the dispatching of accepted transportation orders and planning of loads to be shipped, and then either executes the activities required or oversees their execution if they are outsourced.

Similar to purchasing organizations, planning and execution organizations can be subdivided into several planning and execution groups. They are used in the following documents and objects:

- Freight unit
- Package unit

- Transportation unit (TU)
- Freight orders
- Freight bookings
- Resources

While sales organizations, purchasing organizations, and planning and execution organizations are limited to their specific tasks according to their definition, in some LSP scenarios, it's required that the same organizational unit performs several tasks, such as selling transportation services to a customer and purchasing transportation services from a vendor. For this purpose, you can define a generic organizational unit of type forwarding house. A *forwarding house* is an organizational unit that can perform sales activities, purchasing activities, and planning and execution activities and can therefore be assigned to any of the mentioned documents and objects.

Creating the Organizational Structure

Because a direct relationship with financial grouping objects (e.g., company codes, accounts, internal orders, etc.) is deliberately *not* established in SAP TM, the organizational data needs to be mapped to SAP ERP or SAP S/4HANA or the connected external billing system for settlement and used there for financial assignment.

The organizational structure in SAP TM can be defined independently, or the same organizational structures can be used in SAP TM and SAP ERP or SAP S/4HANA to enable a meaningful assignment of the sales and purchasing processes to the subsequent settlement processes. An example of this kind of structure was provided earlier in Figure 3.1, which compares organizational structures in SAP TM and SAP ERP or SAP S/4HANA.

In this context, the company organization corresponds to the SAP ERP or SAP S/4HANA company code and is used by Transportation Charge Management for invoicing and charging. When we create organizational units and staff assignments, we can distinguish between two elements:

- Organizational units
- Positions

An organizational unit is an object that is used to map the corporate structure of a company in an organizational model in an SAP system via various organizational elements and attributes. When you create the organizational element, you assign two things to it:

- **Organizational unit function**
  The organizational unit function describes the purpose of an organizational unit. Functions include purchasing, sales, planning and execution, company, corporate, and forwarding house.

- **Organizational unit role**
  The organizational unit role defines the organizational element's level within the hierarchy. The following roles can be selected: organization, office, and group.

The hierarchical relationship of organizational elements, based on the roles and functions, is fixed. For organizational units with a sales function, you can only assign organizational elements with unit role group to the organizational elements with unit role office. The element with the office unit role can only be assigned to an organizational unit with an organization unit role. For organizational units with a purchasing or planning and execution unit function, you can only assign organizational units with a group unit role to organizational units with an organization unit role. You can also assign employees to the organizational unit, which you need to do to use the workflow capabilities.

Organizational structures are created in Customizing by following menu path **Transportation Management · Master Data · Organizational Management · Organizational Model · Create Organizational Model** or using Transaction PPOCE. Changes to these structures are made in Customizing by following the menu path **Transportation Management · Master Data · Organizational Management · Organizational Model · Change Organizational Model**. Alternatively, you can use Transaction PPOME (see Figure 3.3).

Business Partners

When an organizational unit is created, the system automatically creates a business partner in the background. This business partner is used in transactional documents to represent the assigned organizational unit. For that purpose, you need to configure the internal number assignment in the Customizing for SAP TM by following the menu path **Cross-Application Components · SAP Business Partner · Business Partner · Basic Settings · Number Ranges and Groupings**.

The *position* (e.g., purchasing team lead in Figure 3.3) organizational unit is used mainly to cascade and represent a hierarchy for workflow processing. If a process requires the involvement of several users in a specific sequence, and users should respond to errors and exceptions or approve a business document (e.g., to check whether a freight agreement meets specific commercial conditions), workflows are used.

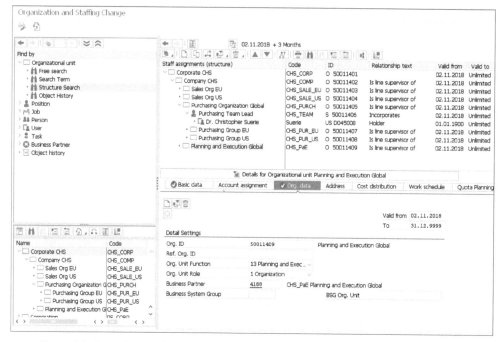

Figure 3.3 Organizational Hierarchy of an LSP

In this context, you can define the organization's hierarchical structure and assign employees with specific tasks to individual organizational elements. Consider the following employees:

- The tendering manager, who is responsible for freight tendering in a purchasing organization

- The sales manager, who is responsible for credit limit checks in a sales organization and is the recipient of the relevant workflow tasks

- A purchasing agent, who is responsible for invoice verification

- Transportation planners, truck drivers, loading clerks, and warehouse personnel, who are assigned to an organizational element categorized as planning and execution

Creating and Merging the Organizational Hierarchy

While organizational structures can be created as just described, you can also upload definitions of organizational hierarchies from SAP ERP, SAP Supply Chain Management (SAP SCM), an internal SAP S/4HANA component, or an external SAP S/4HANA system using a report shown in Figure 3.4. You can find this report in Customizing by following the menu path **Transportation Management · Master Data · Organizational Management · Organizational Model · Create and Merge Organizational Hierarchy** or launching report /SCMTMS/TRANS_ORG_MODEL directly.

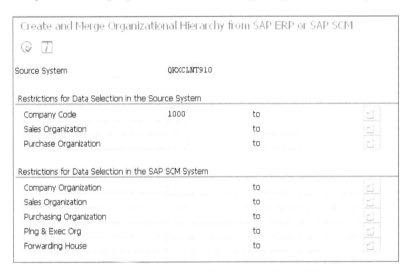

Figure 3.4 Report to Create and Merge the Organizational Hierarchy

The report reads the existing structure in the source system, displays the organizational hierarchy, and then creates and saves the corresponding elements in the SAP TM organizational model.

To refine the selection of existing definitions of organizational hierarchies from the source system, you can enter the relevant company code, sales organization, and purchasing organization. To transfer the selected elements to the transportation system, you can either drag the selection to the SAP TM organizational hierarchy or use the buttons. You can remove the transferred elements before the organizational hierarchy has been saved. After the data has been saved, though, you have to make adjustments in the organizational model itself.

3.1.2   Business Partner

Business partners are typically persons or organizations in which a company has a business interest. Whether it's a single entity or a group of business partners, this master data object is used for a variety of business transactions. In general, *business partners* are all legal entities or individuals with whom a company maintains business contacts. SAP systems usually differentiate between *customers* and *vendors*. From an accounting point of view, all customers with whom a company is in contact are *debtors*. Suppliers (or vendors) who provide deliveries or services are called *creditors*. A business partner can be a debtor and a creditor at the same time and therefore have different business partner roles.

Business partners, as well as the roles they assume for your company, are managed centrally. According to this *role concept*, the business partner is defined as a general business partner first, and afterwards its business partner roles are assigned. Each role might contain specific data that is relevant for the role. This way, there is no need to store redundant data because the general business partner data is independent of a business partner's function- or application-specific extensions. Therefore, when a business partner is first created in an SAP system, the general business partner role is automatically assigned and populated with general data such as name, search terms, and so on.

Business partners are all organizations, enterprises, and individuals with a fixed or loose working or order-based relationship with a shipper or LSP. This relationship may be defined by long-term contracts that are negotiated between the parties involved or by ad hoc activities (e.g., quotations and orders). On the other hand, business partners may also be employees of the company, such as drivers. In the context of SAP TM, the following business partner roles are relevant:

- Business partner (general) (000000)
- Customer (FLCUO1)
- FI customer (FLCUO0)
- Vendor (FLVNO1)
- FI vendor (FLVNO0)
- Carrier (CRMO10)
- Global trade services: Customs office (SLLCOF)
- Driver (TMO001)
- Organizational unit (BUPO04)

- Contact person (BUP001)
- Prospect (BUP002)
- Employee (BUP003)
- Internet user (BUP005)

The role carrier (CRM010) contains the role vendor (FLVN01). Both roles allow maintenance of data on the level of a purchasing organization. Roles FI customer (FLCU00) and FI vendor (FLVN00) allow maintenance of data on the company code level.

As mentioned at the beginning of this chapter, SAP TM allows logistics processes to be executed largely without the existence of business partner master data. However, a business partner master record is virtually indispensable when it comes to settlement and billing.

In the following sections, we'll unpack business partner master data further.

Defining Business Partners

As mentioned before, business partners can be centrally maintained and defined using the SAP role concept. You find the relevant maintenance transaction in **Master Data • Define Business Partner**, by launching Transaction BP, or by using specific apps **Sales • Create Customer** for customers or **Purchasing • Create Vendor** for vendors or carriers. In the Define Business Partner app, you can create new business partners or assign additional roles to existing business partners. Figure 3.5 shows the definition of a carrier created in the roles of business partner (general), financial services business partner, and carrier. You can maintain the following information for all general business partners using the provided tabs:

- **Address**
  The business partner's main address.

- **Address Overview**
  Additional addresses with a note on usage (e.g., mailing address or delivery address).

- **Identification**
  Additional ID numbers to identify the business partner for communication (e.g., the IATA agent code of an air freight service provider, Standard Carrier Alpha Code, or commercial register number).

- **Control**
  Business hours and texts.
- **Payment Transactions**
  Details for payment transactions, including bank details and payment card details.
- **Status**
  Status information and lock flags.

Additional texts from the **Additional Texts** tab (e.g., addresses or signatures) can be used for printing addresses or signatures on documents such as air waybills. To support printing in several languages, define the language of the texts and enter additional texts for one text type in different languages for one business partner instance.

Depending on the business partner role, additional information or special tab pages are available. For business partners with the role carrier, the **Transportation Data** tab shows transportation-relevant information, such as the standard carrier alpha code assigned to the (road) carrier, in Figure 3.5.

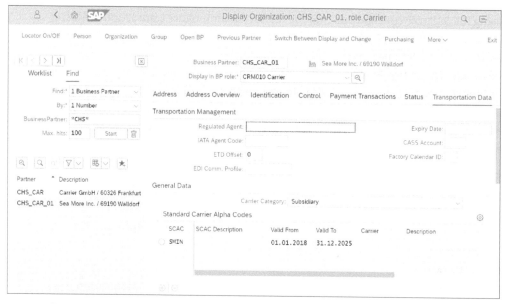

Figure 3.5 Business Partner Master Record for a Carrier

Carrier Profile

Additional carrier-specific information is stored in the carrier profile, which can be created for business partners with role carrier in Transaction /SCMTMS/TSPP or on the classical user interface (UI) from menu path **Logistics • Transportation Management • Master Data • Transportation Network • Define Carrier Profile**.

The carrier profile is used to define carrier- and transportation lane-specific parameters and attributes to define the service provider's range of responsibilities, transportation capabilities, and service level. These parameters typically include the following:

- Routes operated in the transportation network, as shown in Figure 3.6
- Freight codes, product freight groups, and transportation groups
- Transport equipment used or available (refer to Section 3.1.3)
- Fixed and dimension-based transportation costs for carrier selection

These profiles are used in subcontracting processes such as carrier selection to determine the carrier. In this context, carrier determination can take into account internal costs, as well as parameters specific to the transportation lane, such as whether transportation allocations or business shares should be used or whether the carrier is eligible for continuous moves. More details about carrier selection will be provided in Chapter 7.

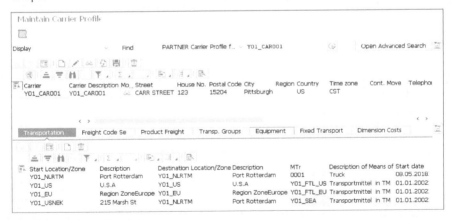

Figure 3.6 Carrier Profile

Employees and Internal Organizational Units

When you define the organization of an enterprise, business partners are automatically created for the individual organizational units (Section 3.1.1). These are created with the organizational unit role and can be used directly to map business transactions *within* the enterprise.

It's also possible to define a business partner's employees as business partners themselves if they occupy a dedicated role in your business partner's enterprise (e.g., the carrier's dispatcher who is personally responsible for your enterprise). These employees are defined in the role of employee (see Figure 3.7). Because of the option to create hierarchies and relationships between business partners, you can then assign the employee as a subordinate business partner of the carrier and assign a relevant function description to the employee to clarify his role. Figure 3.7 shows the definition of a business partner employee and the relationship between this employee and the main business partner (carrier).

Figure 3.7 Business Partner and Relationship Definition for Employees

For transportation execution, a driver is a person who can operate vehicles (see also Section 3.3) and perform transportation-related tasks. Drivers are defined as business partners with role driver.

Figure 3.8 illustrates that this role not only provides additional parameters such as qualifications but also allows you to specify the driver's availability and create shift sequences and absences, similar to the resource availability mentioned in Section 3.3.5. Although the system doesn't check the consistency of required or offered qualifications (e.g., to handle dangerous goods or operate a specific vehicle), these qualifications held by the driver typically include licenses or certain permissions. The configuration of qualifications can be found in Customizing via menu path **Transportation Management · Master Data · Resources · Resource Attributes · Define Settings for Qualifications**. Drivers are assigned to freight orders on the **Driver** tab.

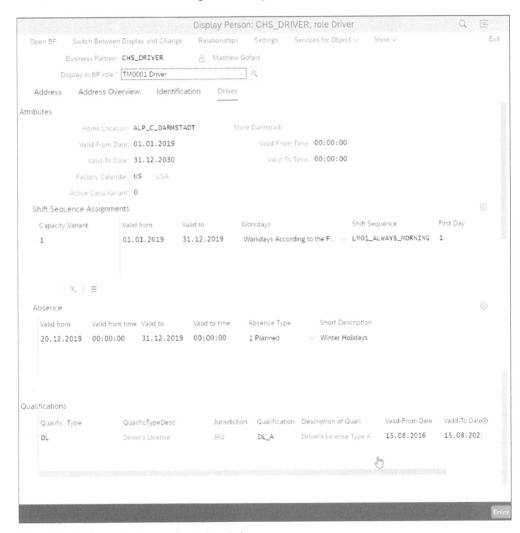

Figure 3.8 Business Partner with a Driver Role

Business Partner Determination

Business partners are assigned to transactional documents, such as forwarding orders, freight orders, or freight bookings, either manually or automatically. During the assignment to a transactional document, it is checked that for the assigned business partner, an appropriate business partner role has been defined. The automatic assignment of business partner is controlled by a business partner determination profile, which can be assigned to the corresponding document type in Customizing (e.g., **Transportation Management** · **Freight Order Management** · **Freight Order** · **Define Freight Order Types**).

The business partner determination profile in Figure 3.9 is defined in Customizing via menu path **Transportation Management** · **Master Data** · **Business Partner** · **Define Partner Determination Profiles**. You can specify relationships between partner functions and how these relationships are used to automatically determine business partners for partner functions. The following relationships are available to determine a business partner:

- **Partner function and source partner function**
  The business partner associated with the source partner function is copied to the partner function.

- **Business add-in (BAdI)**
  A customer-specific logic can be implemented in a BAdI to determine the business partner.

- **Fixed business partner**
  A business partner is fixed and assigned to a partner function in Customizing.

- **Relationship category**
  The corresponding business partner for a partner function is determined based on the partner relationship specified in the business partner master data (business partner relationships).

- **Partner function and source partner function in business partner master data**
  The business partner is determined based on the relationship between organizations and business partners in the business partner master data (**Customer/Vendor Partner Determination** tab).

In addition to the pure determination, the business partner determination profile defines the set of partner functions available in a document, the sequence in which the business partner functions are displayed on the **Business Partner** tab of the transactional document, and the level of control a user is granted in inserting, editing, and deleting partner functions.

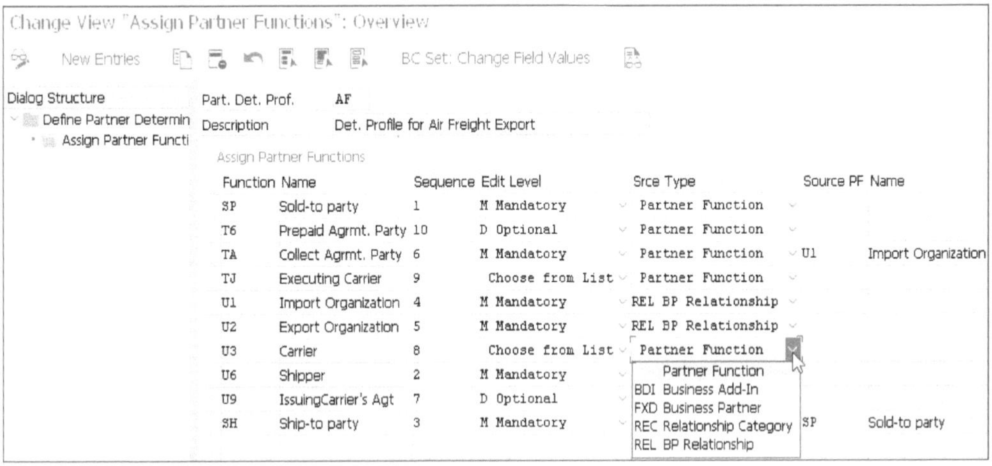

Figure 3.9 Business Partner Determination Profile

3.1.3 Materials

Material master data (or product master data, which is the term used from the transportation perspective and will be used interchangeably in this section) doesn't have a definitive set of semantics in transportation logistics. Instead, it may differ radically depending on the role and perspective of the user. By definition, product master data classifies, identifies, and characterizes materials, articles, and services that are purchased, sold, manufactured, or provided as a service and remain essentially unchanged over a long period.

From the shipper's point of view, the material master data includes the deliverable, producible, and sellable goods. Materials can be maintained with their attributes and various quantities and can then be allocated to organizations. In addition, you can define various types of transport materials and equipment in the material master (e.g., pallets, pallet cages, and cardboard boxes), which can also represent transport demand through their use in packaging one or more other materials.

In addition to the obligatory definition of material number and description, you must define the base unit of measure (e.g., count, box, or kilogram). Via the base unit, you can define additional quantity units with the conversion factors. The indication of the gross and net weights and volume is especially important for logistics processing because these values are taken into account for the capacity calculation of combined shipments. Volume refers to the volume occupied by a material during transport, not the net contents of a unit of material. In the material master, there is a sales view (**Sales: General/Plant**) in which you can define the **Trans. Grp** and **Material freight grp** as transport-relevant attributes (see Figure 3.10).

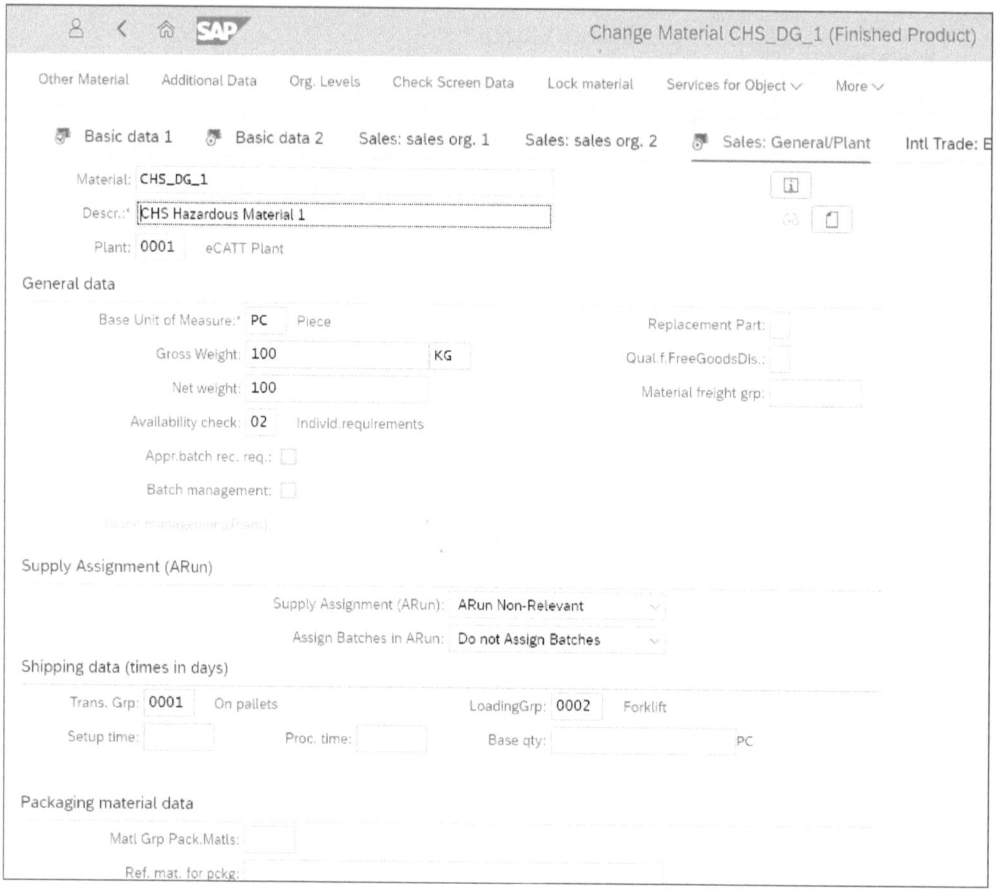

Figure 3.10 Material Master

The transportation group is a categorization criterion that allows you to categorize materials that have the same defined processing conditions. Examples of values in the transportation group include palletized goods, refrigerated goods, and dairy products. If the material is classified as dangerous goods, you need to create a dangerous goods master record for transportation processing. Product Safety and Steward-ship (PS&S) lets you save the necessary identifications and definitions for the various norms and carriers. Here, you can store dangerous goods classes and codes, material characteristics, rules for loading materials together, paper print definitions, and other details for dangerous goods definition. Each material classified as a dangerous good requires its own separate dangerous goods master record.

Transportation services offered by an LSP are often commissioned with reference to standard material types or material groups as product master records. Such grouping can be done in the necessary granularity (with three to eight digits), using elements such as the commodity or harmonized system (HS) code, UN hazardous materials number, or other standards.

In transport processes in which full loads are frequently requested and transported (e.g., in container line operations or railway operations with full railcars), the product master records are usually defined based on transport equipment. The content of the transport equipment is often only roughly specified and not precisely known at the time of the initial order. Therefore, the range of ways in which LSPs can view the product master is much more diverse. In this case, the product master can be used in the following ways:

- Precisely defined products in 3PLs
- Standardized freight codes and material groups
- Roughly defined product categories
- Categories of transport equipment in which products represent only the outer packaging of the materials being transported
- Service products

Standardized or custom freight codes or material groups (e.g., statistical goods numbers) are used to ensure appropriate grouping and classification of products. Standardized freight codes or material groups are often used as product master records if an LSP focuses mainly on the provision of transportation services not bound by a specific contract. Other details (e.g., weight) can be represented only in a generalized way and must be entered individually in the transportation order. Standardized freight codes and material groups are frequently used in rail logistics, for example, where they are used directly to calculate freight charges.

In business processes in which full loads are generally commissioned and transported (e.g., container line haul and rail transportation with full railcars), it's useful to define material master records based on transport equipment. In this case, materials merely represent the outer packaging of the actual material transported. These cases often involve the transportation of large numbers of the same or similar containers or railcars, the contents of which need to be defined only in general terms and, in many instances, can't even be specified when the order is initially created. However, the transport equipment must be defined (e.g., a 20-foot refrigerated container or a 67-foot flatcar). Only the required number of transport equipment products is defined as the load, and more precise details about the goods to be transported are added later.

Product master data is important for packaging and the definition of packaging hierarchies. The relevant product master data for this process will be explained in detail together with its use in Chapter 6, Section 6.3.3.

In SAP TM, an LSP's product represents the services operated by that provider and therefore doesn't refer to the material goods that are transported (as in the case of express service providers). You can create service product catalogs in master data. We describe service products in Chapter 12, Section 12.1.3.

When SAP TM is operated without product-related master data, all goods to be transported are entered only as text in the transportation order. All load-specific and transportation-relevant details are directly maintained in the order itself.

3.1.4 Dangerous Goods

The handling of dangerous materials is regulated by numerous laws and regulations. Essential master data must be managed and maintained with the most up-to-date security regulations. Goods receiving and goods issue processing, warehouse operations, labeling, and printouts must be adapted to meet the requirements for handling dangerous materials and goods. The dangerous goods functions enable you to ensure the safe transportation of dangerous goods in compliance with international regulations.

If a material has been classified as dangerous, you need to create a dangerous goods master record to check this material during transportation processing. The transportation business documents that contain the material are then checked for the relevant regulations and to ensure that all necessary information is included and parameterized in the business document. When you perform dangerous goods checks for your business documents, the system bases the checks on the relevant dangerous goods data. This is typically done in a shipper scenario.

In a nonshipper scenario, if an LSP is supposed to handle dangerous goods, the LSP usually doesn't have dangerous goods master data in its system. Therefore, dangerous goods checks can also be done without dangerous goods master data, using document-based dangerous goods records instead. LSPs can directly maintain dangerous goods-related data in the forwarding order if a dangerous goods profile has been assigned to the corresponding forwarding order type. The document-based dangerous goods records can also be created automatically when a forwarding order based on data sent by the business partner (e.g., the shipper) is created.

Dangerous Goods Content Loader in SAP TM 9.6

The dangerous goods content loader is currently only released for SAP TM 9.6. There, you can use a content loader to import PS&S regulatory content, downloaded from the SAP Service Marketplace, directly into the dangerous goods master data tables in SAP TM 9.6. This functionality is especially useful for LSPs that don't have the dangerous goods master data in their system and usually receive data from their shippers, either in written or electronic form. It helps them to minimize the effort required to maintain and enter relevant data in a forwarding order and can be used as a template for document-based dangerous goods records. The content itself comprises Dangerous Goods Regulations (DGR), the necessary texts (e.g., substance names and phrases), and the required Customizing data.

In this section, we describe both the master data and classification of the dangerous goods master record, as well as the relevant settings and parameters to maintain phrases and text outputs. This master data is typically provided by the shipper, while document-based dangerous goods checks are based on the data in the relevant business documents and the basic configuration of PS&S services in SAP TM. This configuration is part of transportation compliance and is therefore explained in Chapter 9.

Dangerous Goods Master

When you check dangerous goods, you're checking the product you want to transport against the rules you've defined in Customizing. This can be a check of certain aspects of the dangerous goods master data or the combination of the goods you want to transport. The check reflects the national and international regulations regarding the transportation of dangerous goods. The regulations depend on the transportation mode and the countries crossed while transporting the goods, and the check is triggered by material master attributes.

Figure 3.11 shows a material and the relevant settings to define whether hazardous substance data exists for this product and how to perform a dangerous goods check. These attributes can be found in the material master in the **Basic data 2** tab. Here, you can specify whether the material is a hazardous substance or environmentally relevant. The actual execution of the check, as well as the output of dangerous goods documents, is controlled by a **DG indicator profile**. The profile itself contains a combination of indicators that are maintained in the dangerous goods check settings of the PS&S services; in Figure 3.11, this is **GPP** (dangerous goods, relevant for document output and checks). You can find these settings in Customizing by following the menu path **Transportation Management · Basic Functions · Dangerous Goods · PS&S Services · Dangerous Goods Management · Dangerous Goods Checks and Dangerous Goods Documents · Common Settings · Specify Indicator Profiles for the Material Master**.

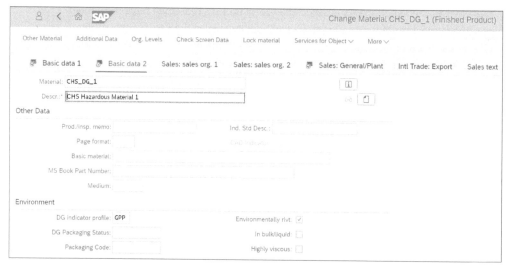

Figure 3.11 Dangerous Goods Indicator Profile in Material Master

The system can perform checks automatically; in addition, you can trigger the checks manually. Due to different risks in transporting dangerous goods, the system carries out checks in different ways and at different process steps to ensure safety during transportation. For example, the system can perform checks during freight unit building (FUB) and vehicle scheduling and routing optimization. This ensures the compliance of the resulting freight unit and freight orders. In addition, you can perform checks on all relevant business documents. If there are dangerous goods errors, you can correct them and perform the check again.

The dangerous goods master contains the data required to perform dangerous goods checks and generate dangerous goods documents and papers according to the applicable DGR and laws. To create a dangerous goods master record, you assign a DGR to an existing product and add other data. After you've created a dangerous goods master record, it becomes available for dangerous goods checks and for creating dangerous goods documents. To create a new dangerous goods master record or display or edit an existing one, you use the transactions in the classical UI via **Logistics • Transportation Management • PS&S Services • Dangerous Goods Management • Dangerous Goods Master** (in SAP TM 9.6, the menu path is **Master Data • Dangerous Goods Management • Dangerous Goods Master**). Figure 3.12 shows the dangerous goods master of the material master from Figure 3.10. To meet national and international regulations for this material, this master record has been created with reference to specific regulations, a validity area (**Val. Area**), and a mode of transport category (**DG Mode**).

Figure 3.12 Dangerous Goods Master

Legal regulations are relevant for the transportation of dangerous goods. You classify the master data by assigning a validity area and mode of transport category to the DGR. The classification assigns classes and codes and therefore specifies how the transportation is restricted or should be executed. The validity areas for dangerous goods data records are defined according to the applicable DGR and specify the countries, regions, jurisdictions, or organizational units in which the parameters of the dangerous goods master are valid. To carry out dangerous goods checks and generate dangerous goods papers, you must ensure that the validity areas for the dangerous goods master records don't overlap. In addition, the mode of transport category specifies the type of transport to which the rule applies—for example, road, rail, inland waterway, sea, or air (cargo and passenger).

Figure 3.13 shows the underlying structure and relationship of some of the most important parameters of the dangerous goods master record and the "handshake" with the PS&S configuration. (To learn more about PS&S service configuration and compliance checks, see Chapter 9.)

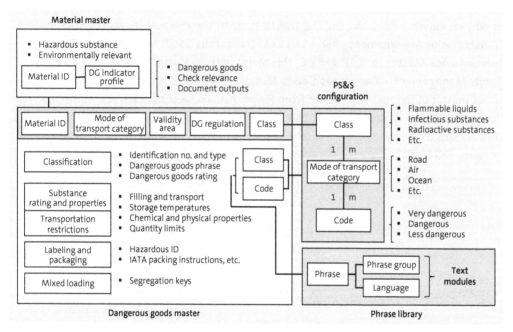

Figure 3.13 Structure of Dangerous Goods Parameters

In addition to the classification data, the dangerous goods master contains information about the dangerous substances themselves (see Figure 3.13). To help you be compliant with legal regulations, hazardous materials are accompanied by detailed information about how they are supposed to be filled and transported, their storage conditions, and what to do in the event of an accident.

The classification of the products and substances that present a danger during transport is based on classes and codes, which are assigned to the DGR specified in the dangerous goods master. The assignment of classification codes to dangerous goods classes and regulations is part of the PS&S configuration shown in Figure 3.14, which you can find in Customizing via **Transportation Management · Basic Functions · Dangerous Goods · PS&S Services · Dangerous Goods Management · Dangerous Goods Master** (in SAP TM 9.6, the menu path is **SAP Transportation Management · SCM Basis · EH&S Services · Dangerous Goods Management · Dangerous Goods Master**).

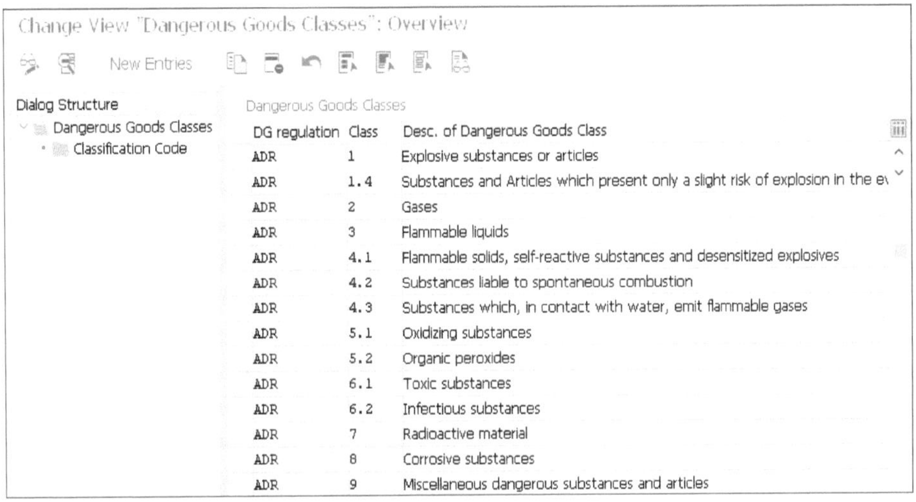

Figure 3.14 Assignment of Classification Codes to Classes

Labels on tanks, trucks, and containers indicate the type of risk of the hazardous or dangerous substance and clearly identify the dangerous goods. For example, toxic substances carry a danger label consisting of a black skull and crossbones on a square white background. The declaration—usually warning placards and alphanumeric keys in the top half of the label—follows internationally agreed-upon symbols and code systems. It provides information about required extinguishing media, required personal protection measures, and possible reactions of the substance.

Phrase Management

Whether the physical execution of a transport occurs by sea, land, or air, it often crosses borders and is handled by people speaking different languages. Therefore, warnings and instructions regarding how to handle dangerous goods can be language-dependent. These texts are usually printed on specifications and first aid measures; they are typically used for document creation, dangerous goods texts on dangerous goods documents, and reporting.

A central tool to manage these texts is available. The language-dependent text modules are called *phrases* and are part of the master data for dangerous goods handling. Phrases are managed in phrase libraries and grouped together in phrase groups. Figure 3.15 shows the **Phrase Library CUST** and **Phrase N03.00700810**, which belongs to **Phrase Group 03.00**.

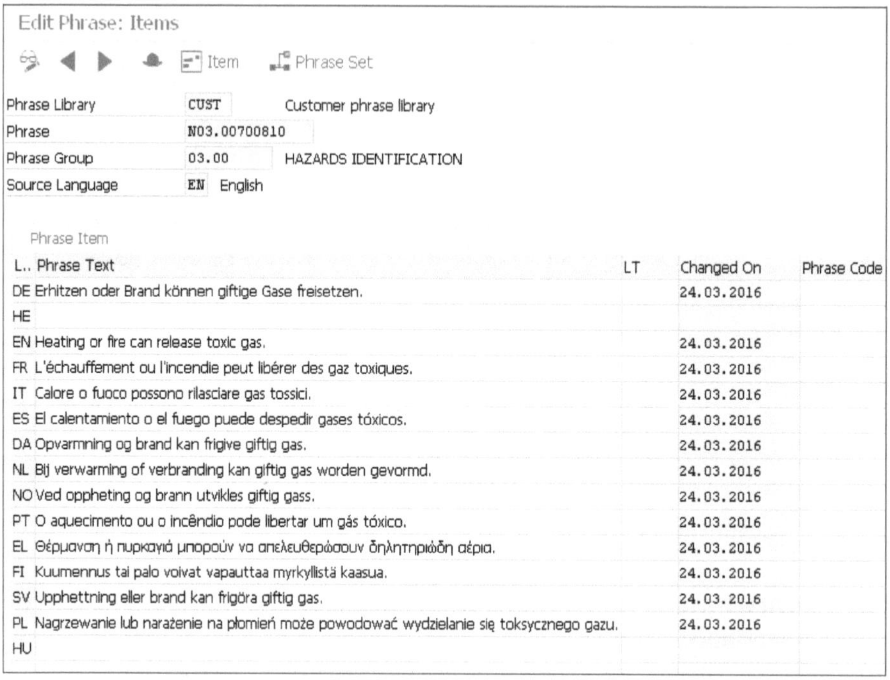

L..	Phrase Text	LT	Changed On	Phrase Code
DE	Erhitzen oder Brand können giftige Gase freisetzen.		24.03.2016	
HE				
EN	Heating or fire can release toxic gas.		24.03.2016	
FR	L'échauffement ou l'incendie peut libérer des gaz toxiques.		24.03.2016	
IT	Calore o fuoco possono rilasciare gas tossici.		24.03.2016	
ES	El calentamiento o el fuego puede despedir gases tóxicos.		24.03.2016	
DA	Opvarmning og brand kan frigive giftig gas.		24.03.2016	
NL	Bij verwarming of verbranding kan giftig gas worden gevormd.		24.03.2016	
NO	Ved oppheting og brann utvikles giftig gass.		24.03.2016	
PT	O aquecimento ou o incêndio pode libertar um gás tóxico.		24.03.2016	
EL	Θέρμανση ή πυρκαγιά μπορούν να απελευθερώσουν δηλητηριώδη αέρια.		24.03.2016	
FI	Kuumennus tai palo voivat vapauttaa myrkyllistä kaasua.		24.03.2016	
SV	Upphettning eller brand kan frigöra giftig gas.		24.03.2016	
PL	Nagrzewanie lub narażenie na płomień może powodować wydzielanie się toksycznego gazu.		24.03.2016	
HU				

Figure 3.15 Editing Dangerous Goods Phrases

The *phrase library* defines the phrase assignment and origin. Using the import functionality provided by PS&S, you can upload purchased or company-specific phrase libraries and merge them with your existing phrase library. You can also update active phrases after importing a new version of the passive library by creating phrase references from the passive phrases to phrases in the active phrase library.

For each library, a *phrase group* is used to classify phrases. Each phrase belongs to a single phrase group and might have different assigned phrase codes. These codes are optional, language-dependent abbreviations for individual phrases.

3.1.5 Master Data Creation and Integration

Depending on the deployment option used for SAP TM, the relevant master data is created based on different strategies and interfaces. If you're using SAP TM in SAP S/4HANA, no integration is required, as shown in Figure 3.16. Material master data and business partner master data are readily available, and location master data is created on the fly or via a report when needed. This is a major difference compared to the classical SAP TM 9.6 deployment, which integrates a SAP TM 9.6 instance with an SAP ERP system (sidecar approach). In this deployment scenario, CIF is used for master data creation in SAP TM based on the corresponding objects in SAP ERP. SAP TM products are created based on SAP ERP material master data and business partners, and locations are created based on the corresponding vendor/customer/plant/shipping point information from SAP ERP.

SAP S/4HANA (no integration required)

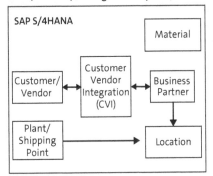

Classical Integration: SAP ERP and sidecar SAP TM

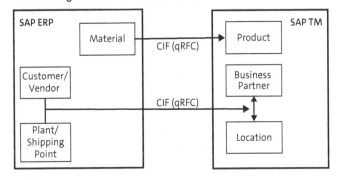

Figure 3.16 Classical Integration and SAP TM in SAP S/4HANA

Two more deployment options are available, if a side-by-side approach has to be used, because SAP TM should be used together with multiple SAP ERP or SAP S/4HANA instances as sources of transportation requirements. These deployment options are shown in Figure 3.17. For these two deployment options, SAP TM in SAP S/4HANA is used as a sidecar, while the transportation requirements originate either from SAP ERP or from SAP S/4HANA. Consequently, the master data (material, business partner, location) needs to be transferred from the source system (SAP ERP, SAP

S/4HANA) to SAP TM in SAP S/4HANA. In these deployment scenarios, the DRF is used as an interface technology.

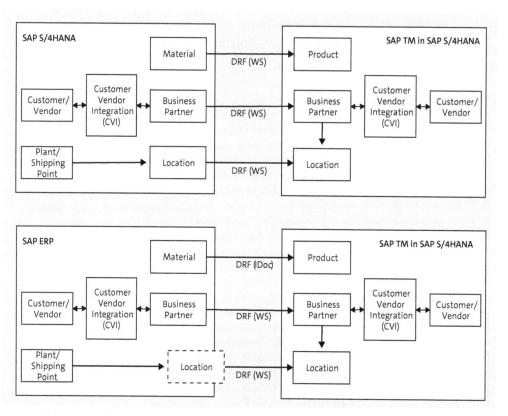

Figure 3.17 Side-by-Side Deployment Options with SAP TM in SAP S/4HANA

How these different interfaces work and how they are configured will be described in the remainder of this section.

Core Interface for SAP TM 9.6

CIF is used in the classical deployment scenario with SAP TM being deployed as a sidecar. Technically, it's based on the SAP SCM Basis component, in which the SAP SCM master data is made available. CIF is a real-time interface that enables both the provision of initial data and data alterations.

The connection between the two systems is achieved via a remote function call (RFC) connection. The special feature of this type of communication between the systems lies in the asynchronous processing of the data transfer. This means that the data from the sending (i.e., SAP ERP) system is first buffered and then transferred, or that it's transferred and subsequently buffered by the receiving (SAP SCM) system, and then processed.

Outbound and inbound processing is performed in sequence in an outbound or inbound queue. In the event of an error caused by a failed network connection, for example, this queue saves all transfers and enables seamless continued processing after the error has been located and eliminated. The queue is a type of waiting line that enables real-time exchange and processing of information, making SAP SCM-based planning in real time possible. This type of RFC invocation is known as a *queued remote function call* (qRFC) (see Figure 3.16).

The key element of the CIF is the integration model. Integration models contain the necessary parameters to indicate which master data in the SAP ERP system is to be selected and transferred. This means that data to be transferred to SAP TM 9.6 is selected via the integration model. The model is activated after its generation. The data involved is generally either material-related or material-independent objects. Material-related objects include materials and plants. Material-independent objects include shipping points and customer and vendor master data.

One-Way Transfer

The transfer of master data is performed in only one direction: from SAP ERP systems to the SAP SCM system. Changes to a master record aren't transferred back to the SAP ERP system.

To create an integration model, you need to define the logical system of SAP TM 9.6 as the target system. In addition, you need to specify the object types (e.g., customer master records) to be transferred and their specific selection criteria (e.g., customer number [ranges]). For the transfer of materials to products, there is a 1:1 relation. However, for customers and vendors, you can create two objects on the SAP TM 9.6 side: locations and business partners. Therefore, you must define whether the integration model should create only locations, only business partners, or both. It depends on the selected data of the integration model, whether you want to create only business partners (e.g., for vendors that are carriers) or both (e.g., vendors from which you receive materials). Depending on the data volume, you can include all relevant data into one integration model or split into several integration models. Common business practice is to create separate integration models for each object type.

Activating an integration model causes an initial transfer of master data from SAP ERP to SAP TM 9.6. The integration models to be activated are compared with the integration models that are already active. In this way, the transfer restricts itself to differences; in other words, the system transfers only data for filter objects that aren't contained in any active integration models. The data transfer between SAP ERP and SAP TM 9.6 is executed automatically based on CIF configuration. Master data changes in SAP ERP are tracked and recorded by change pointers. Activating a generated integration model checks and analyzes these change pointers, determines the changed master data, and finally transfers it to the target system.

Because the selection of the integration model is static, to include newly created materials or customers into the integration model, it must be regenerated and reactivated periodically. This is typically done daily or hourly depending on the frequency of master data changes and the necessity to transfer them in a timely manner to SAP TM 9.6. The generation and activation of the integration models themselves can also be automated and configured as a background job using the selection criteria as variant. Table 3.1 lists the relevant background jobs and transaction codes to execute creation, activation, and deletion of integration models manually or automatically.

Program	Transaction	Description
RIMODDEL	CFM7	Deletes the deactivated integration models.
RIMODGEN	CFM1	Generates a new version of the integration model, taking account of new master data. For example, if a new material master record has been created, and this new master data is within the selection range of the integration model, the system automatically creates a new inactive version of the integration model.
RIMODAC2	CFM3	Deactivates the old version of the integration model and activates a new version including all data that will be transferred to the target system. The report compares the old version of the integration model with the new runtime version and subsequently triggers the delta upload of changed data.

Table 3.1 Background Program and Transactions for CIF

Customer Vendor Integration in SAP TM in SAP S/4HANA

In SAP S/4HANA, the business partner is the central object to store partner data. You can use customer vendor integration (CVI) to create customer master data or vendor master data based on a business partner and vice versa. That means, CVI is bidirectional, and you can both propagate customer/vendor master data to business partners as well as populate data from the business partner to the customer/vendor. One customer and one vendor can be assigned to a business partner simultaneously in a corresponding business partner role so that a business partner is always available for holding customer or vendor data.

In general, master data synchronization synchronizes master data objects in an SAP system that are similar from a business point of view but not from a technical point of view; in this way, you can integrate different SAP applications (e.g., sales and distribution [SD] or materials management [MM] with SAP TM) seamlessly in your business processes. The synchronization of customer and business partner master data allows you to integrate SAP applications that make technical use of the business partner in its UI and use the customer master as a technical basis in subsequent business processes. Master data synchronization is available for the two master data objects business partner and product:

- Synchronization of the business partner with the customer/debtor master
- Synchronization of the business partner with the supplier/creditor master
- Synchronization of the product with the material master

It's important to note that master data synchronization can neither synchronize master data objects across systems nor transfer master data objects from external or legacy systems. It only synchronizes objects within one system (SAP S/4HANA).

Technically, there are two synchronization options available:

- **Synchronization using the synchronization cockpit**
  The synchronization cockpit is used to prepare, perform, and check the initial synchronization of master data objects.

- **Synchronization from the master data maintenance**
  When master data is saved, the synchronization process is carried out for those objects for which it has been activated. This process can be used to create or change existing objects.

CVI takes place in the background while the master data is processed. Customer integration and vendor integration can be used independently from each other, but both may be required in a SAP TM scenario. You can find the relevant activities to control master data synchronization in Customizing with path **Cross-Application Components · Master Data Synchronization · Synchronization Control**. The specific settings for CVI are done in Customizing via path **Cross-Application Components · Master Data Synchronization · Customer/Vendor Integration**. Finally, the synchronization cockpit shown in Figure 3.18 can be executed from Customizing via **Cross-Application Components · Master Data Synchronization · Synchronization of Master Data · Execute Synchronization Cockpit**.

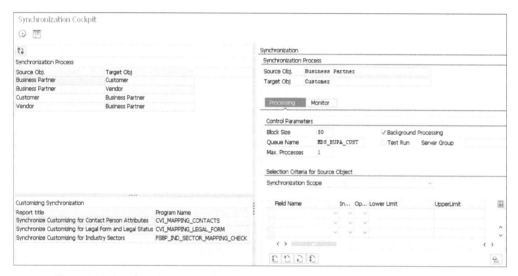

Figure 3.18 Synchronization Cockpit

Data Replication Framework for SAP TM in SAP S/4HANA (Receiving)

The DRF is used to replicate master data such as business partners, products, and locations between source systems (e.g., SAP ERP or SAP S/4HANA) and target systems (SAP TM in SAP S/4HANA), as shown in Figure 3.17. You can use this function to replicate master data to SAP TM in an SAP S/4HANA target system. The DRF uses key mapping to map the IDs of the corresponding objects in the source and the target system to determine the IDs of local master data entities based on the IDs of the master data objects in the source system. Thereby, a replication can be made, even if the object IDs in the two systems aren't identical. This is essential if a target system receives data from several source systems that may contain the same objects with different IDs or where the same key may be used for different entities in different source systems.

The DRF offers to replicate master data by using an object selection or by defining a replication model. The Customizing for the replication model shown in Figure 3.19 is defined in **Logistics General · Merchandise Lifecycle Optimization · Outbound · Data Replication Framework · Define Custom Settings for Data Replication · Define Replication Models**.

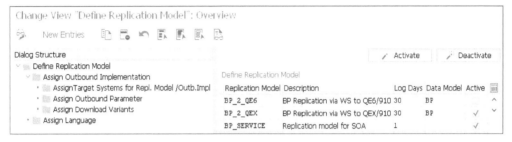

Figure 3.19 Replication Model

For business partners (business object 986 – Business Partner), the outbound implementation `986_3 – Outbound Impl. for BP/REL Services` is used to initiate a web service to create a replication request message, which is answered by a confirmation message upon successful creation of the business partner in the target system. Key mapping can be based on the `Business Partner ID` or on the `Business Partner UUID`. Note that locations aren't automatically created from the DRF with the replication of the business partner but have to be created locally in the target system based on business partner master data. The following business partner roles are transferred with the DRF:

- Business partner (general) (000000)
- Organizational unit (BUP004)
- Carrier (CRM010)
- Customs office (SLLCOF)
- Driver (TM0001)
- Supplier (FLVN01)
- FI supplier (FLVN00)
- Customer (FLCU01)
- FI customer (FLCU00)

For products (business object 194 – Material), you can use outbound implementation `194_3 – Outbound Impl. for Product via Services`, if the source system is SAP S/4HANA or outbound implementation 194_1 – Material through IDoc, if the source system is SAP ERP. Using the DRF allows you to transfer product master data, which doesn't depend on organizational levels such as plant, storage location, or sales organization. The master data replicated in SAP TM in SAP S/4HANA includes client-dependent data, language-dependent material descriptions, and conversion factors for units of measure. For products, key mapping supports both the Material ID Internal Format and Material ID External Format.

As mentioned before, locations are typically created locally from business partner master data in SAP TM in SAP S/4HANA. However, plants and shipping point Customizing data exist in SAP S/4HANA and SAP ERP, which needs to be represented as location master data in SAP TM processes. Therefore, DRF can also be used to create location master data in the source system based on plant and shipping point information and to replicate this location master data to the target system. If the source system is SAP ERP, this option isn't viable because no location object exists there. Therefore, the plant and shipping point Customizing settings are directly replicated to SAP TM in SAP S/4HANA where the locations can then be created in this case.

For locations (business object 189 – Location), you can use outbound implementation 189_1, if the source system is SAP S/4HANA. If the source system is SAP ERP, you can use outbound implementation 464_L for plants and outbound implementation DRF_0045_L for shipping points/receiving points. The key mapping for locations supports the Location Number and the Location UUID.

Instead of a direct integration between SAP S/4HANA and SAP TM in SAP S/4HANA as depicted in Figure 3.17, SAP Master Data Governance (SAP MDG) can be used as a central repository with central master data ownership. This is useful for large companies for governance purposes.

Location Creation

For SAP TM in SAP S/4HANA, DRF is one of two sources for master data creation. The other way to create master data for SAP TM in SAP S/4HANA is internally. Some locations may come from DRF, while some locations may come from local creation.

There are three ways of creating locations, which are required as the nodes in the transportation network as will be described in Section 3.2.1:

- Based on business documents
- Based on business partner master data
- Based on a report

The creation of locations based on business documents guarantees that for each source and destination of a transportation requirement, the corresponding location exists prior to the creation of the freight unit. Whenever a document that is relevant for SAP TM is created or updated, it's checked whether all necessary locations to represent plants, shipping points, or business partners exist. If a location is missing, it will be created immediately. This logic applies to the following SAP TM document categories:

- SD documents: Sales order
- MM documents: Purchase order, stock transfer order
- Deliveries: Outbound delivery, inbound delivery

The creation of locations based on business partner master data can be activated using an implementation of BAdI /SAPAPO/LOC_CREATE. The BAdI implementation allows a location to be created after the creation of a business partner. Subsequent updates of the business partner address are also triggered.

Finally, locations can also be created based on report /SAPAPO/CREATE_LOCATION. This report, shown in Figure 3.20, is used to create locations for plants, shipping points, and business partners. Locations are created for those objects within the selection for which no location already exists. To update locations representing plants and shipping points, you can use report /SAPAPO/UPD_LOC_SP_PL. This report updates the addresses and geo-coordinates of locations and should be triggered on demand or periodically.

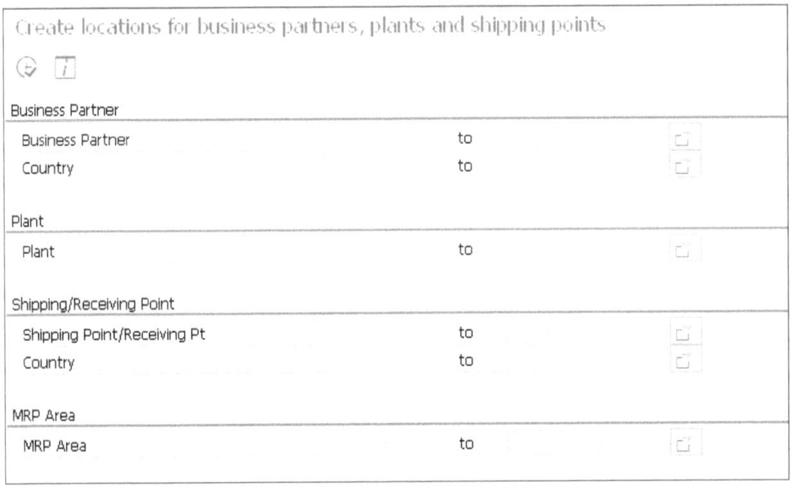

Create locations for business partners, plants and shipping points		
⊙ ⓘ		
Business Partner		
Business Partner	to	▢
Country	to	▢
Plant		
Plant	to	▢
Shipping/Receiving Point		
Shipping Point/Receiving Pt	to	▢
Country	to	▢
MRP Area		
MRP Area	to	▢

Figure 3.20 Creation of Locations by Report

By default, the location details and descriptions are taken from the original entities. In addition, the location names correspond to the names of the original entities (e.g., business partner name), except for shipping points, which are prefixed with *SP_*. If a location with the defaulted name already exists, suffixes (_01, _02, etc.) are appended to the name. The location details, names, and descriptions can be adapted by implementing BAdI /SAPAPO/LOC_DETAILS.

Integration with SAP Enterprise Asset Management

Only the classical deployment option (SAP TM 9.6) shown previously in Figure 3.16 allows integration of downtimes and resource master data between SAP ERP and SAP TM. SAP Enterprise Asset Management can be used to manage a company's own resources (e.g., vehicles, TUs, or handling resources). Double maintenance is avoided by automatically creating and updating resources out of SAP ERP via CIF. In addition, by integrating with the SAP ERP Plant Maintenance (PM) component, maintenance and downtimes are also communicated to SAP TM.

Figure 3.21 shows the principles of the integration. The technical objects in PM that represent the resources for SAP TM are equipment and functional locations.

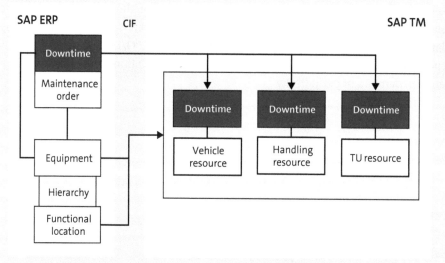

Figure 3.21 Integration with SAP Enterprise Asset Management

A piece of *equipment* is an individual physical object, such as a truck or container. The *functional location* represents an organizational unit in SAP ERP that structures the maintenance objects of a company according to functional, process-oriented, or geographic criteria, and typically represents the place where maintenance tasks are performed. The object in PM representing the downtimes of a resource and the location where the maintenance takes place is the *maintenance order*, which is based on equipment, a functional location, or both.

Attributes not available in SAP ERP are required to create the resource master data in SAP TM 9.6. These attributes include the resource type (e.g., vehicle resource or TU resource), corresponding equipment group and equipment type (e.g., vehicle group/type), resource class, and time zone or factory calendar. These attributes are added using a mapping table in Customizing via menu path **SAP Transportation Management • Transportation Management • Integration • Master Data Integration • integration of Technical Objects with TM Resources**.

This section introduced the general master data, the main characteristics of the organizational structure, the business partners and materials, and the creation and integration of these objects. Before we explain the resources, let's continue with the logistics master data that is used to define and specify the transportation network.

3.2 Transportation Network

The transportation network defines direct reachability between your locations and transshipment locations, which together define how freight can be transported between your locations. Direct reachability between location A and location B means that B can be directly reached from A by a transportation option, such as a vehicle resource or schedule. Transshipment locations allow reloading from one transportation option to another. The network definition is essential for automatic planning, which determines the best path through the network and assigns the most suitable carriers for given transportation demands and for charge calculation considering freight and forwarding agreements that contain rates defined on trade lanes as the geographical basis.

The following sections introduce locations and all other concepts for modeling your transportation network from reachability, transshipment locations, and business partner relation perspectives:

- Locations (Section 3.2.1) form the nodes in the network at which goods are loaded or unloaded. Locations represent the most basic network concept because they define the source and destination of any transportation.

- Transportation zones (Section 3.2.2) allow you to group locations and thereby define reachability and transshipment options in an aggregated fashion.

- Transportation lanes (Section 3.2.3) define reachability between locations and zones on a means of transport and carrier level.

- Schedules (Section 3.2.4) express recurring reachability at fixed dates and times along a predefined location sequence for a given mode or means of transport, as described in Section 3.3.1.

- Transshipment locations (Section 3.2.5) are required for intermodal transportation or any scenario involving consolidation and deconsolidation.

- Default routes (Section 3.2.6) define paths from source to destination through a sequence of transshipment locations. They implicitly define transshipment locations to be used from source to destination and can also predefine schedules or carriers to be used for the stages from source to destination.

- Trade lanes (Section 3.2.7) offer an additional perspective on the network. These are used to define business relationships to your customers (i.e., forwarding agreements) and carriers (i.e., allocations, business shares, and freight agreements).

- The transportation network cockpit (Section 3.2.8) is a powerful tool to visualize all objects of the transportation network on a map, search for specific objects, and maintain objects on the map. Its text-based cousin, the transportation network overview personal object worklist (POWL), is presented as well.

- The integration with geographical information systems (GISs) (Section 3.2.9) is essential to determine the geographical coordinates of locations and distances and durations between locations, as well as providing the geographical map data for a graphical visualization of a map.

3.2.1   Locations

A *location* represents a logical and/or physical location where goods are delivered, picked up, or transshipped, or where trucks and trailers get coupled or uncoupled. To define a location, select the menu path **Master Data • Define Location** (in SAP TM 9.6, the menu path is **Master Data • Transportation Network • Define Location**). Enter the name and location type, which you can select from a list of more than 15 standard location types. These include, for example, production plant (1001), distribution center (1002), customer (1010), port (1100), and airport (1110).

You can maintain additional data in the following tabs (see Figure 3.22):

- **General**

  In the **General** tab, you can maintain identifiers such as the **UN/LOCODE** and the **IATA Code**, which are commonly used in ocean freight and air freight businesses, respectively; the **Geographical Data** specifying longitude, latitude, and altitude; and the **Precision** level that was used to determine the geographical coordinates. You can lock the geographical data, which then won't be affected if the address data are changed. In addition to the time zone and assigned business partner, the tab contains the priority, which can be used to define location-dependent nondelivery costs or earliness and lateness costs to be considered in automatic planning.

- **Address**

  The **Address** tab contains the default address, PO box address, and other contact details. The geographical coordinates are determined automatically as soon as you maintain the country code (see Section 3.2.9 on integration with GIS). By following the menu path **Logistics · Transportation Management · Transportation Network · Geocoding · Mass Geocoding** (in SAP TM 9.6, the menu path is **Application Administration · Master Data · Transportation Network · Location: Mass Geo-Coding**), you can determine geographical coordinates for many locations in one step.

- **Alt. Identifiers**

  Alternative identifiers for the location can be maintained in a dedicated tab. You can predefine the possible types of alternative location identifiers by selecting the IMG menu path **Transportation Management · Master Data · Transportation Network · Location · Configuration for Alternative Location Identifiers.**

- **TM**

  The **TM** tab allows you to maintain the minimum and maximum goods wait times, which are described in more detail in Section 3.2.5. In addition, you can define the trailer handling capability that can enable trailer swap, recoupling, or recoupling for pickup and delivery only. You can also specify air cargo security information; classify the location as unknown shipper, known shipper, account shipper or regulated agent; and set the handover party code and its expiry date. It's also possible to link the location to an SAP Extended Warehouse Management (SAP EWM) target system and specify the SAP EWM warehouse number.

- **Resources**

  You can assign calendar and handling resources in the **Resources** tab. These are described in more detail shortly.

Figure 3.22 Maintaining a Location

You can assign handling or calendar resources (operating times) for inbound and outbound transportation in the **Resources** tab. A calendar resource defines during which time intervals loading and unloading can take place at the location. In addition to this, a handling resource can restrict the number of loading and unloading activities that can be handled in parallel at the location. Thus, both calendar resources and handling resources affect the scheduling of unloading and loading activities at the location. You also have the option of not assigning a calendar or handling resource. In this case, loading activities at the location aren't subject to any time restrictions. See Section 3.3.5 for an introduction to handling resources and calendar resources.

Figure 3.23 shows the maintenance of the inbound and outbound resources for a location in the **Resources** tab. By entering the values for consumption, you can define how much of the capacity offered by the relevant handling resource is consumed by a loading or unloading activity. You can define the same handling resource for inbound and outbound activities.

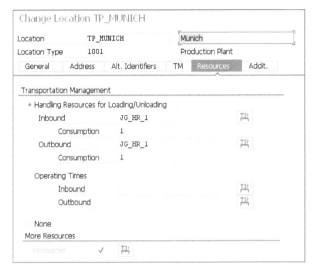

Figure 3.23 Defining Inbound and Outbound Resources for a Location

You can also click the button next to the **More Resources** field to define handling resources or calendar resources that depend on the means of transport. This enables the use of several handling resources at the same location (e.g., different loading ramps for truck and rail transportation). If a vehicle type isn't used in the vehicle-type-dependent settings for a location, the general inbound and outbound resources for the vehicle type apply.

In the example shown in Figure 3.24, unloading activities at location **TP_MUNICH** are scheduled in accordance with calendar resource **TB_CAL** if the means of transport **HH_EU_M** is used, while neither calendar nor handling resource is used for means of transport **HH_EU_S**. Loading activities are scheduled according to handling resources **JG_HR_1** and **JG_HR_2** for means of transport **HH_EU_M** and **HH_EU_S**, respectively. The **Valid** column allows you to determine whether to use the calendar resource (value **1**), the handling resource (value **2**), or neither resource (value **0**) for scheduling for each means of transport.

Central versus Decentral Location-Specific Definition of Calendar and Handling Resources

While you can still use the preceding definition of calendar and handling resources used at a certain location, we recommend using the scheduling settings to define calendar resources and handling resources per location for various reasons. First, you can centrally define these constraints for all locations, which is much easier compared to maintaining them separately in each single location. Second, you can create alternative scheduling settings, enabling easy switching between them for simulation purposes, which would be nearly impossible to achieve when defining directly in each location. Third, you can easily upload and download scheduling settings.

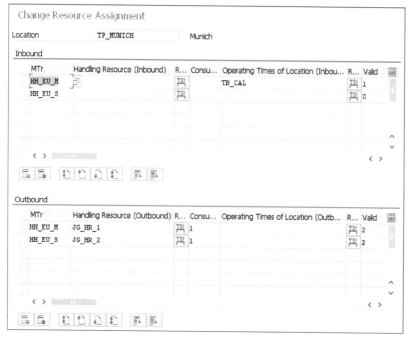

Figure 3.24 Defining Means of Transport-Dependent Inbound and Outbound Resources for a Location

Using a Resource for Inbound and Outbound Transport or for Several Locations

A calendar resource or handling resource can be used for inbound and outbound transportation at a single location or at several locations simultaneously. This means that you only need to maintain representative templates for opening times in calendar resources as a one-time activity, and you can then reuse these same templates for many different locations that have the same opening times.

You can store any locations that you don't want to store permanently in the system as master data as one-time locations. These are used whenever it's necessary to enter location data, such as address details, but a reference to the master data record isn't possible or desirable. A one-time location is defined by the name of the organization, the address or communication data, or a combination of these details. One-time locations are typically used when you create forwarding orders from new ordering parties, and the locations of these parties aren't defined in the master data.

3.2.2   Transportation Zones

A transportation network usually contains a large number of locations. Defining relationships such as transportation lanes or trade lanes between pairs of locations is possible, but it's a time-consuming and error-prone task. A definition on the location-to-location trade lane level for agreements, allocations, and business shares isn't required in many transportation businesses. Instead, these need to be maintained on a more aggregated level.

A *transportation zone* is a group of locations; it allows the transportation network to be represented and maintained in an aggregated form. Relationships such as transportation lanes or trade lanes can be defined on the zone level, which is much more compact, manageable, and less error-prone.

To define a transportation zone, select the menu path **Master Data · Define Transportation Zone** (in SAP TM 9.6, the menu path is **Master Data · Transportation Network · Transportation Zones · Define Transportation Zone**), and click the button for creating a transportation zone. When you enter the name and description of the transportation zone, the screen for maintaining the transportation zone appears. You can also search for existing zones and edit one of them (see Figure 3.25).

In the **Zone – Location** tab, you can explicitly assign locations to the zone and exclude locations from the zone. The **Zone – Postal Code** tab allows you to assign a set of valid postal code ranges of a specific country to the zone, and in the **Zone – Region** tab, you can include a set of countries and regions. The last two tabs result in an implicit assignment of those locations to the zone, which match the postal code ranges, countries, or regions defined for the zone. This implicit assignment is very useful because of its robustness: new locations entering the transportation business are automatically included in the respective zones. If you want to know the locations included in a zone, just select the zone, and click the **Display Included Locations** button.

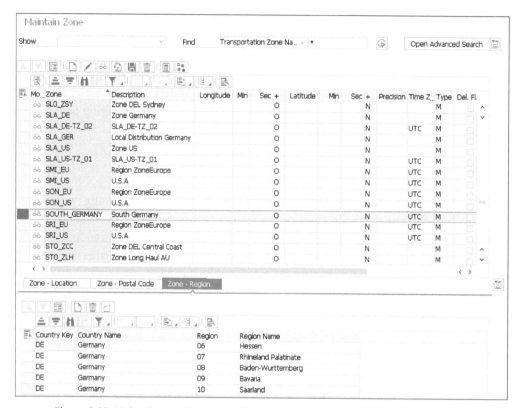

Figure 3.25 Maintaining a Transportation Zone

The zone type is determined automatically and indicates whether the zone contains only direct location assignments (direct zone), only postal code assignments (postal code zone), only region and country assignments (region zone), or a combination of these (mixed zone).

You can define the geographical coordinates of a zone, which are used to display the zone in the transportation network cockpit. Alternatively, you can use the **Calculate Coordinates** button or determine the geographical coordinates for many zones in a single step by selecting the menu path **Logistics · Transportation Management · Master Data · Transportation Network · Transportation Zone · Calculate Transportation Zone Coordinates** (in SAP TM 9.6, the menu path is **Application Administration · Master Data · Transportation Network · Calculate Transportation Zone Coordinates**).

If you need many zones—say, one per country or one per region—you can select the menu button in the top-left corner of the zone maintenance and follow the menu path **Extras • Create Zones** to create all the required zones in a single step by choosing the countries and regions relevant for your business.

The transportation network can be structured to a greater degree using the transportation zone hierarchy, in which zones can be assigned to other, higher-level zones. All locations within a transportation zone automatically also belong to the higher-level transportation zone. The transportation zone hierarchy is used when determining the distance and duration between locations and has a far-reaching impact on many business processes, such as charge calculation, transshipment scenarios, *vehicle scheduling and routing* (VSR) optimization, and carrier selection.

To maintain the transportation zone hierarchy, follow the menu path **Logistics • Transportation Management • Master Data • Transportation Network • Hierarchy • Maintain Hierarchy** (in SAP TM 9.6, the menu path is **Master Data • Transportation Network • Transportation Zones • Define Transportation Zone Hierarchy**). As shown in Figure 3.26, use the **Name RELH_ZONE** for the transportation zone hierarchy and the name **RELHS_ZONE** for the hierarchy structure, and select **Create** or **Change**. The **RELHS_ZONE** hierarchy is delivered as standard. The customer-specific transportation zone hierarchy must be maintained in the **RELH_ZONE** hierarchy.

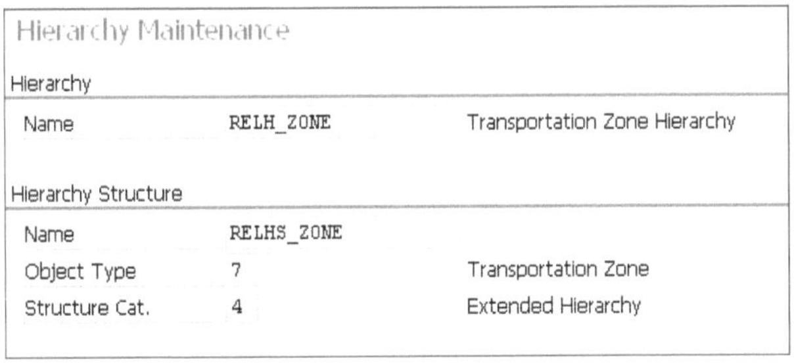

Hierarchy Maintenance		
Hierarchy		
Name	RELH_ZONE	Transportation Zone Hierarchy
Hierarchy Structure		
Name	RELHS_ZONE	
Object Type	7	Transportation Zone
Structure Cat.	4	Extended Hierarchy

Figure 3.26 Choosing the Transportation Zone Hierarchy

Maintenance of the transportation zone hierarchy is shown in Figure 3.27.

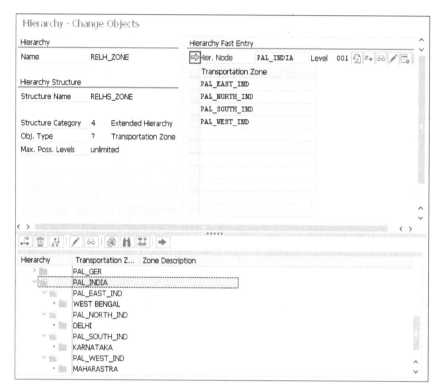

Figure 3.27 Maintaining the Transportation Zone Hierarchy

The maintenance screen is structured around an overview of the existing transportation zone hierarchy displayed as a tree structure and the **Hierarchy Fast Entry** area, where you can enter new hierarchy nodes. The RELH_ZONE hierarchy element is the root node in the hierarchy, which means that all other zones are directly or indirectly subordinate to this element. You can double-click to select a parent node in the tree display, enter one or more zones in the **Hierarchy Fast Entry** screen area, and click the **Copy** button to add these to the hierarchy. To delete zones from the hierarchy, select a hierarchy element in the tree display, and click the **Delete Objects from Hierarchy** button. This deletes all *subordinate* elements from the hierarchy. To remove all objects from the hierarchy, delete the root (note, however, that the RELH_ZONE element is retained to allow you to add new elements to the hierarchy later).

Careful Modeling of Transportation Zones and Zone Hierarchy

Use the transportation zones and transportation zone hierarchies to model your transportation network as compactly as possible and avoid redundancies when defining transportation zones and in the transportation zone hierarchy.

Remember that the same location can be contained in several transportation zones and that transportation zones can overlap in this way. When you're creating a new zone, the system informs you by a message if it overlaps with an existing zone.

Two transportation zones are considered to be overlapping if they have at least one location in common and are considered equivalent if they contain the same set of locations. Equivalent transportation zones are always overlapping, but overlapping transportation zones aren't necessarily equivalent.

We recommend that you avoid defining equivalent zones because a very large number of implicit combination options may arise for automatic planning (transportation proposals and VSR optimization), both during automatic determination of transportation lanes, distance, and duration (Section 3.2.3) between locations and when determining transshipment locations. This may lead to long runtimes in certain cases.

If you've maintained equivalent zones, you should delete all but one of these. In addition, check overlapping transportation zones to determine whether the overlaps are useful from a business perspective or whether they could be eliminated.

Keep your transportation zone hierarchy as flat as possible.

3.2.3   Transportation Lanes

Transportation lanes describe the reachability of locations within the transportation network. They are defined by three elements:

- A start, which may be a location or a transportation zone
- A destination, which also may be a location or a transportation zone
- A means of transport

A valid transportation lane indicates that the destination can be directly reached from the source by resources of the means of transport. When you maintain the start or destination, a transportation zone always represents all of the locations it contains. If a transportation lane is defined between two transportation zones, this means that the means of transport operates between all locations in the start transportation zone and all locations in the destination transportation zone. A transportation lane from a start location to a destination transportation zone indicates that the means of transport operates between that location and all locations in the transportation zone. An intra-zone lane (a transportation lane where the start and destination transportation zones are the same) indicates that the means of transport operates between any two locations within this zone. A location transportation lane (a transportation lane where the start and destination location are the same) has no influence on reachability between locations but can be used for the initialization of allocations.

Compact Maintenance of Transportation Lanes

Check whether the reachability of locations in your transportation network can be modeled by transportation lanes with transportation zones as the start and/or destination. In most cases, fewer transportation lanes are required if you define them using transportation zones rather than using locations directly.

To maintain a transportation lane, follow the menu path **Master Data • Define Transportation Lane** (in SAP TM 9.6, the menu path is **Master Data • Transportation Network • Transportation Lanes • Define Transportation Lane**). You can maintain transportation lanes in the following tabs:

- **Tr. Lane**
  To create or change individual transportation lanes, enter the start and destination, and select **Create** or **Change**.

- **Intra-Zone Lane/Loc. Transp. Lane**
  Enter a location or transportation zone. You can then create or change a transportation lane from the location to the same location (location transportation lane) or from the transportation zone to the same transportation zone (intra-zone lane).

- **Mass Maint. (Create)**
  Use an existing transportation lane as a template for generating new transportation lanes. You can overwrite existing transportation lanes, leave them unchanged, or enhance them with additional information (see Figure 3.28). You can also specify whether the duration and distance are to be copied from the template or recalculated.

- **Mass Maint. (Display/Change)**
  You can define selection criteria for transportation lanes (start, destination, start

location type, destination type, etc.) and then display or change the selected transportation lanes based on these criteria.

The screen for maintaining an individual transportation lane and the mass maintenance screen have similar structures. The mass maintenance screen is shown in Figure 3.28. Here, you can create several transportation lanes at the same time, assign both a means of transport and a carrier to each, and maintain all of the transportation lane parameters.

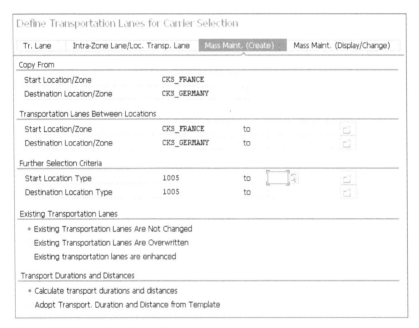

Figure 3.28 Mass Creation of Transportation Lanes

The left side of Figure 3.29 shows the transportation lanes. The means of transport for the transportation lanes are displayed in the **Means of Transport** screen area, with one row representing each means of transport in a transportation lane. You can double-click on a row to select the corresponding means of transport for a transportation lane and maintain the following parameters:

- The validity dates for the means of transport on the transportation lane.
- The distance between the start and destination and the amount of time it will take the means of transport to travel that distance (i.e., the duration). You can generate a proposal using the button provided.

- Two control indicators that indicate whether the specified duration and distance are to be overwritten by an automatic distance and duration determination.

- The **Precision** field that indicates whether the distance was calculated automatically based on the straight-line distance (value: **0000**), with GIS precision (**0100**), or entered manually (**1000**).

- The quantity, distance, and minimum costs, of which the last is only relevant for destination-based distance costs (the use of these costs is controlled in the cost profile, which is discussed in Chapter 6, Section 6.7.3).

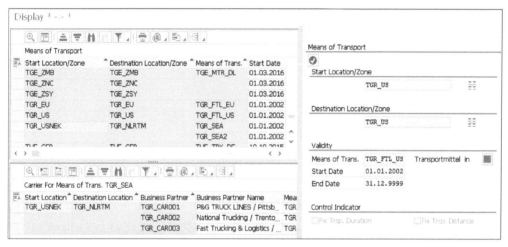

Figure 3.29 Displaying Transportation Lanes

Additional parameters allow you to control the carrier selection (see also Chapter 7, Section 7.1.4):

- You can specify whether business shares are to be taken into account in carrier selection, which tolerances apply when an excess or shortfall occurs, and which penalty costs are to be used in cases that fall short of or exceed the business share.

- You can define a strategy for carrier selection by selecting the **Relevant for Carrier Selection** field and specifying whether costs and/or priorities are to be used, which costs are to be used (e.g., internal costs or costs from SAP TM charge calculation), and whether or which continuous moves are permitted.

- You can decide whether the planning period or the minimum and maximum capacities defined for the carriers are to be used for the initialization of allocations (see Chapter 5, Section 5.2).

- You can also define several means of transport for a transportation lane. To do this, click the **Create** button for a new entry in the **Means of Transport** screen area.

For each means of transport, you have the option of assigning carriers in the **Carrier** area (in the same way you assign a means of transport) and maintaining additional details for each carrier that is relevant for carrier selection:

- Internal costs
- Priority
- Arrival and departure windows for continuous moves
- Maximum distance for continuous moves
- Discounts for continuous moves
- Desired business share for the carrier
- Minimum and maximum capacity for initializing the allocation of the carrier (see Chapter 5, Section 5.2)

You can also define whether the carrier is to be considered for peer-to-peer tendering and broadcast tendering and then define its priority for each tendering mode (see Chapter 7, Section 7.3).

You can control the effects of the parameters maintained for the transportation lane on carrier selection in the carrier selection settings (see Chapter 7, Section 7.1.4). Note that direct shipment option determination (see Chapter 6, Section 6.2.2) uses carrier selection to choose the best option, and thus the carriers on the transportation lane represent the only alternatives considered.

The automatic transportation lane, distance, and duration determination selects the appropriate transportation lane for a means of transport and a specified start and destination location and determines the corresponding distance and duration between the start and destination. This automatic determination is used, for example, by automated planning procedures and VSR optimization or transportation proposals; it enables the integration of a GIS to spare users the laborious task of manually maintaining distances and durations between locations (Section 3.2.9).

The selection of a transportation lane for a start and destination location is necessary because the hierarchies of transportation zones (Section 3.2.2) and means of transport (Section 3.3.1) may give rise to several transportation lanes, which subsume the means of transport, start, and destination location.

You can make settings in Customizing to specify the sequence in which the three hierarchies (start, destination, and means of transport) are to be taken into account when determining the transportation lane. To do this, select the IMG path **Transportation Management · Master Data · Transportation Network · General Settings for Transportation Network Determination**. The **Consider Hierarchical Relationships between Means of Transport First** and **Consider Source Hierarchy First** parameters allow you to select one of the following four access sequences:

- (1) Means of transport, (2) Start, (3) Destination
- (1) Means of transport, (2) Destination, (3) Start
- (1) Start, (2) Destination, (3) Means of transport
- (1) Destination, (2) Start, (3) Means of transport

The access sequence determines which hierarchy is taken into account first when a transportation lane is determined.

Let's consider an example that is based on a scenario with a means of transport T1, a higher-level means of transport T2, locations A and B, zone ZA (which contains location A), and zone ZB (contains location B).

When a transportation lane from A to B is requested, the transportation lane determination function goes through the possible combinations in this sequence, following the access sequence: (1) Means of transport, (2) Destination, (3) Start:

1. Means of transport T1, Start A, Destination B
2. Means of transport T2, Start A, Destination B
3. Means of transport T1, Start A, Destination ZB
4. Means of transport T2, Start A, Destination ZB
5. Means of transport T1, Start ZA, Destination B
6. Means of transport T2, Start ZA, Destination B
7. Means of transport T1, Start ZA, Destination ZB
8. Means of transport T2, Start ZA, Destination ZB

The first combination in this sequence for which a transportation lane exists returns the transportation lane as a result. The underlying principle here is to select more specific transportation lanes first, which allows you to maintain general transportation lanes and refine exceptions with more specific transportation lanes.

The automatic distance and duration determination determines a start location S, a destination location De, a distance Di(S,De), and a duration Du(S,De) for a given means of transport T. Depending on the configuration, the distance from the transportation lane can be used, or, alternatively, it can be calculated on the basis of a straight-line distance or with an external GIS, which takes account of the existing road network, and so on.

When a specific request is submitted for (T,S,De), the system first checks whether a transportation lane exists for (T,S,De). If it finds one, the distance and duration values maintained for the transportation lane (T,S,De) are returned directly as the result for Di(S,De) and Du(S,De).

If a transportation lane (T,S,De) doesn't exist, a transportation lane (T′,S′,De′) is determined in accordance with the configured access sequence. This transportation lane (T′,S′,De′) is a "superior" (higher-level) transportation lane in at least one of the hierarchies (i.e., means of transport, start, or destination). If the GIS quality parameter is set for means for transport T′ (for information about maintaining a means of transport, Section 3.3.1), the GIS calculates the distance Didyn(S′,De′). If GIS quality isn't selected for T′, then Didyn(S′,De′) is calculated as the product of the straight-line distance between S′ and De′ and the distance factor for means of transport T′.

The distance Didyn(S,De) is then determined the same way for means of transport T on the basis of the GIS quality parameter of T. The requested distance Di(S,De) is then calculated as follows: Di(S,De) = Didyn(S,De) × Di(S′,De′)/Didyn(S′,De′). The relationship between the distance Di(S′,De′) maintained for the transportation lane (T′,S′,De′), and the result of the dynamic distance calculation Didyn(S′,De′) is thus also used to determine the specific distance requested. All distance calculations are based on the geographical coordinates of S and De (or S′ and De′).

If the distance of transportation lane (T,S,De) or (T′,S′,De′) isn't maintained, then Di(S,De) = Didyn(S,De), and Di(S′,De′) = Didyn(S′,De′), respectively.

The duration calculation for Du(S,De) is essentially the same as the calculation of Di(S,De). Note, however, that the three speeds of the means of transport are required to call the GIS. If the three speeds aren't maintained, the GIS isn't called, and the duration is calculated using the straight-line distance and the average speed of the means of transport. If two relevant means of transport have identical entries for the three speeds, the GIS would be called only once per source and destination pair, and the determined distance and duration would be used for both means of transport.

If the duration of transportation lane (T,S,De) or (T′,S′,De′) isn't maintained, then Du(S,De) = Dudyn(S,De), and Du(S′,De′) = Dudyn(S′,De′), respectively.

3.2.4   Schedules

A schedule represents a recurring transportation that follows a predefined location sequence. It can be used to model regular ship, air, road, or rail transportation and is valid for a specific period. The schedule contains a set of departure rules defining the pattern of days on which the transportation is possible, the times of departure and arrival among the location sequence, and cutoff and availability times needed for transshipment scenarios. A departure represents one instance of transportation along the whole location sequence, with all arrival times and departure times being determined by the departure time at the first location of the sequence. The departures of a schedule can be generated based on a departure rule of the schedule or maintained manually. A departure defines that goods can be transported along the location sequence, or a subsequence of it, respecting the predetermined departure and arrival times for the locations. Thus, a schedule defines reachability in the transportation network, according to a predefined location sequence and given the departure and arrival times of the stops.

Figure 3.30 shows an example of a carrier flight schedule with location sequence Frankfurt, Chicago, and Los Angeles, and two departure rules, which can be used to generate the departures (called *flights* for the air mode of transport), as shown in Figure 3.31.

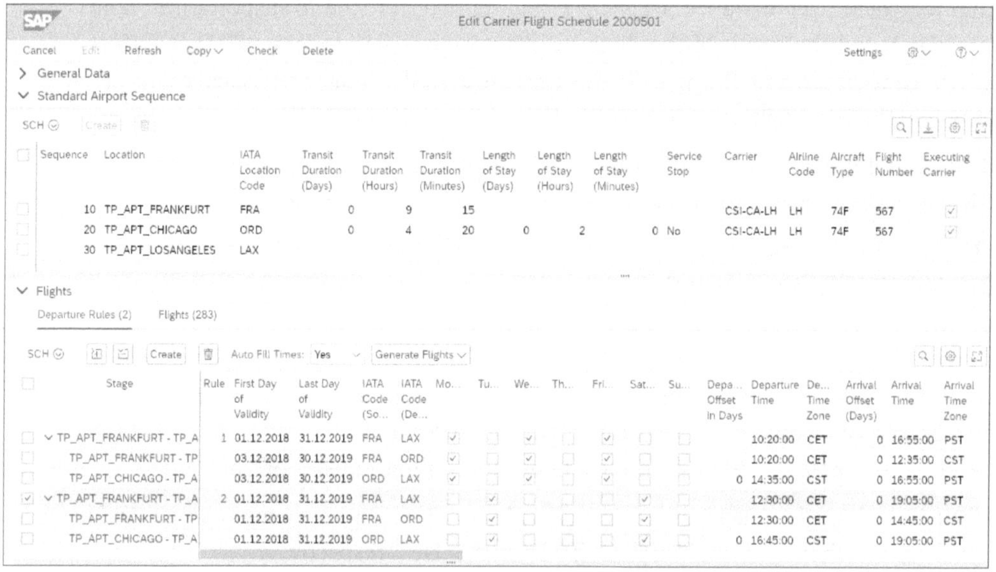

Figure 3.30 Carrier Flight Schedule with Location Sequence and Two Departure Rules

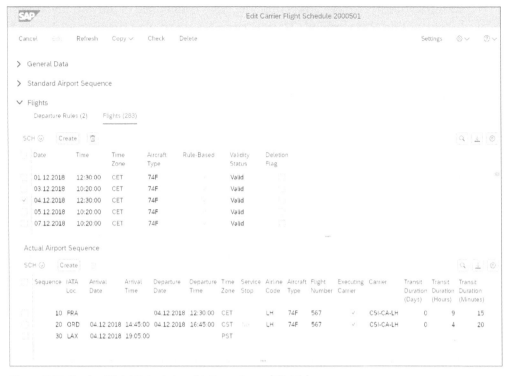

Figure 3.31 Carrier Flight Schedule with Departures (Flights)

Schedules can be consumed by creating a freight document based on a schedule's departure, either by manual (ad hoc) creation (see Chapter 5, Section 5.4.1, and Chapter 7, Section 7.2.1), capacity management (see Chapter 5), or transportation planning (see Chapter 6, Section 6.6.4, Section 6.6.5, and Section 6.7). The schedule-based freight document inherits schedule data from the location sequence; the relevant times for departure, arrival, cutoff, and availability; and any available capacities. Capacity management allows the systematic creation of freight documents for a set of schedules and all their departures in a predefined time period (e.g., for next months). Transportation planning chooses the best departures for a given set of freight units, either by creating new freight documents for the chosen schedule departures or by consuming already existing schedule-based freight documents, which may stem from capacity management or a previous planning step.

Each schedule has a type chosen from the types maintained in the IMG menu path **Transportation Management • Master Data • Transportation Network • Schedule • Define Schedule Types**. The schedule type defines how schedules of this type can be used. You can define the following:

- **Default Type**
  One of all schedule types can be marked as default. If you create a new schedule and don't specify a schedule type, this default type is chosen.

- **Mode of Transport**
  You can choose one of the modes of transport defined in the system (Section 3.3.1), such as road, rail, sea, or air.

- **Gateway**
  This specifies whether the schedule is a gateway schedule or a carrier schedule. The schedule can have a source gateway and a destination gateway, and using the additional parameters **Skip Source GW** and **Skip Destination GW**, you can even omit one gateway. Thus, you can model three kinds of gateway schedules, containing both source and destination gateway, only source gateway, and only destination gateway.

- **Direct**
  For a gateway schedule, you can define whether the two gateways are directly connected or whether other locations, such as ports or airports, are used in between, which is the most common use case. The corresponding schedules are called direct gateway schedules and indirect gateway schedules, respectively.

- **Reference**
  If you've chosen an indirect gateway schedule type, you can define whether it refers to a carrier schedule or is maintained without reference to any carrier schedule.

- **Document Type**
  This specifies the freight document type that is used for creating freight documents out of the schedule.

- **Allocation Type**
  If you maintain an allocation type, you can create allocations of this type out of the schedule (see Chapter 5, Section 5.1). Otherwise, you can't create allocations out of the schedule.

- **Template**
  This defines the schedule to be used as a template only; that is, the freight documents can be changed manually regarding location sequence and departure and

arrival times. If the schedule isn't used as a template, the location sequence and times can't be changed manually, and the freight document keeps a reference to the schedule. Independent of this parameter, automatic planning never changes the location sequence or departure or arrival times.

- **CC Strategy**
  The change controller strategy is called after the schedule has been changed. For example, you can define a change controller strategy for automatic propagation of the schedule changes into the already created freight documents. Note that the standard doesn't propagate any schedule changes into referencing freight documents, allocations, or schedules. However, the reference data status of a referencing instance is updated to allow the user to identify the need for manual adjustments according to the schedule changes.

- **Deletion Strategy**
  The deletion strategy is called after the schedule has been manually deleted by the user or automatically deleted per report. It allows you to insert your own logic to be processed after schedule deletion.

- **Offset Time Type**
  You can choose between two alternatives for defining cutoff and availability times in the schedule. On the one hand, with the **Relative** option, your cutoff and availability entries in the schedule are interpreted relatively. A cutoff of 1 day and 12 hours means that the cutoff time for a departure at 8 a.m. is mapped into a cutoff time of 8 p.m. two days before. Similarly, an availability of 20 hours for an arrival at 5 p.m. is mapped into an availability time of 1 p.m. on the next day.

  On the other hand, with the **Absolute** option, the time is interpreted absolutely, and the date is determined relatively by a minimum offset. A cutoff is defined by an absolute time and an offset in days. For example, a departure at 10:00 a.m. and a cutoff defined by an offset of one day and a time of 11:30 a.m. results in a cutoff time 11:30 a.m. two days before. For a departure at 11:45 a.m. and the same cutoff values, the cutoff time would be 11:30 a.m. one day before.

- **Auto-Fill Times Mode**
  Using this parameter, you can configure whether the automatic filling of dates and times works based on times or durations.

- **One Order**
  If this parameter is active, only one freight document can be created per schedule departure, and this freight document covers the complete location sequence of

the schedule. Thus, all freight units to be transported by this departure are consolidated into the same freight document. The schedule gets locked during planning to ensure that another planning session can't create another freight document. Deactivating this parameter, you can create multiple freight documents for one departure by either manual or automatic planning.

- **Use Capacities**
  You can use this flag to maintain schedules with capacities.

- **Use Transportation Costs**
  This parameter allows you to define internal planning costs for the schedule, such as fixed costs for using a departure and quantity costs.

- **Do Not Propagate Carrier**
  You can specify whether the carrier defined on the schedule header is propagated to referencing schedules or freight bookings when assigning the schedule.

A carrier schedule contains a location sequence along which goods can be transported by a carrier with the given mode of transport. Each intermediate location in the sequence can be used to load and unload goods, whereas the first and last locations allow only loading and unloading, respectively. The following carrier schedule types are delivered as standard: ocean carrier schedule (type 1000), carrier flight schedule (1100), road carrier schedule (1200), and rail carrier schedule (1300). Ocean carrier schedules connect ports, carrier flight schedules connect airports, and the other two types connect locations via road and rail, respectively. The location sequence can model ocean carrier schedules with 20 or more ports, as well as direct flights between two airports and multistop flights along a sequence of airports. Carrier schedules are used mostly to represent transportation capabilities offered by external carriers, such as ocean carriers and road carriers. However, it's not mandatory to assign a carrier. This makes it possible to model a schedule for your own fleet or for an air freight scenario in which an airline offers its schedule but is represented by regional subsidiaries that can all receive air freight bookings for the schedule.

A gateway schedule allows transportation from a source gateway (for consolidation) to a destination gateway (for deconsolidation), or from a source gateway to a destination port, or from a source port to a destination gateway. Gateways usually serve as transshipment locations (Section 3.2.5); for ocean transport of containers, they are commonly called container freight stations (CFSs). The following gateway schedule types are delivered as standard: sailing schedule (type 2000), sailing schedule with reference (2100), master flight schedule (2500), master flight schedule with reference (2600), and road gateway schedule (2200). Indirect gateway schedules, such as sailing schedules and master flight schedules, connect the source gateway to the destination gateway via a source (air-) port and a destination (air-) port. Indirect gateway schedules are used to model scenarios in which the transportation between the (air-) ports is mainly organized by consolidation at the source gateway, and deconsolidation is organized at the destination gateway.

The gateway-to-gateway connection wraps the port-to-port connection details. This allows the users to focus on cutoff times at the source gateway and availability times at the destination gateway, which implicitly consider the cutoff times at the source port and the availability time at the destination port, respectively. The departure rules and departures between the (air-) ports can be defined implicitly by reference to an underlying ocean carrier schedule or carrier flight schedule, respectively, or explicitly without any reference to a carrier schedule.

For an ocean carrier schedule with the port sequence PT_DEHAM (Hamburg), PT_USPNJ (Newark), and PT_USCHS (Charleston)—with these ports having container freight stations CFS_DEHAM, CFS_USPNJ, and CFS_USCHS, respectively—you can define three sailing schedules covering the following locations:

1. CFS_DEHAM → PT_DEHAM → PT_USPNJ → CFS_USPNJ
2. CFS_DEHAM → PT_DEHAM → PT_USCHS → CFS_USCHS
3. CFS_USPNJ → PT_USPNJ → PT_USCHS → CFS_USCHS

While the first and third sailing schedules use a direct port connection out of the underlying ocean carrier schedule, the second sailing schedule uses an indirect port connection with port PT_USPNJ as the intermediate port between the ports PT_DEHAM and PT_USCHS.

Gateway schedules that refer to two or more carrier schedules are called *connection gateway schedules* and can be used by transportation planning and capacity management like any other gateway schedule. A significant portion of air freight forwarding worldwide is handled by connection flights that combine multiple flights offered by one or multiple airlines. If certain connection flights are used frequently in your business, you can create a connection master flight schedule with departure rules that combine departure rules of multiple carrier flight schedules. Figure 3.32 gives an example of a gateway in Frankfurt to an airport in Frankfurt to an airport in Chicago to an airport in Denver to a gateway in Denver. The departure and arrival times for the airport-airport stages stem from two referenced carrier flight schedules.

In ocean freight forwarding, the analogous concept of connection voyages is also used to combine multiple voyages offered by one or multiple ocean carriers.

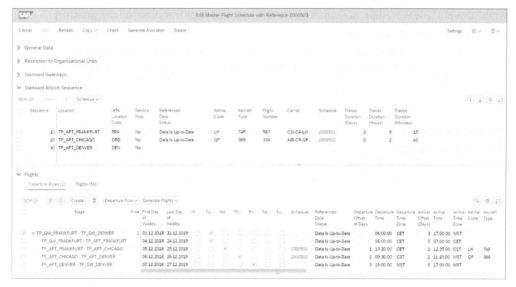

Figure 3.32 Departure Rule for a Connection Master Flight Schedule

Modeling Main Vessels, Feeders, and De-Feeders by Gateway Schedules

Frequently, ocean transportation involves a main vessel that covers big ports, feeder vessels that bring goods from smaller ports to one of the main vessel's ports, and de-feeder vessels transporting goods from the main vessel's ports to smaller ports. Figure 3.33 shows an example with a main vessel visiting the ports Ⓐ, Ⓑ, and Ⓒ. The first feeder connects ports ❶ and ❷ with main port Ⓐ, the second feeder connects ports ❸ and ❹ with main port Ⓑ, the first de-feeder connects main port Ⓑ with ports ❺ and ❻, and the second de-feeder connects main port Ⓒ with ports ❼ and ❽. Usually, the main vessel is the bottleneck as it covers much bigger distances.

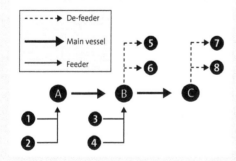

Figure 3.33 Main Vessel with Feeders and De-Feeders

If you want to transport goods between all small ports, you could model this by bringing detailed feeder and de-feeder schedules into the system, and create sailing schedules, one for each pair of source and destination port. Each sailing schedule would combine a feeder schedule, the main vessel schedule, and a de-feeder schedule. In many cases, you don't need that precision level on the feeder and de-feeder level. For example, let's assume that port ❶ serves ❹ within two days and port ❼ gets served from ❸ within five days. Then, you could define a sailing schedule with source gateway ❶, first port ❹, last port ❸, destination gateway ❼. While the main ports get connected by an ocean carrier schedule for the main vessel, the feeding and de-feeding durations can be maintained as pickup transit duration and delivery transit duration for the two gateways, respectively.

If you need de-feeders but no feeders at all, you could use a sailing schedule without source gateway; that is, it starts with the main vessel port but with destination gateway to cover the small port served by a de-feeder.

Create a new schedule by following the menu path **Master Data · Create Schedule** (in SAP TM 9.6, the menu path is **Master Data · Transportation Network · Schedule · Create Schedule**) and choosing the schedule type. When creating a carrier schedule, you first define the **General Data** and the **Standard Stop Sequence**, as shown in Figure 3.34 for a road carrier schedule.

Maintain the validity and the stop sequence by iteratively adding the locations. Optionally, you can define the description, means of transport, and carrier, either explicitly or implicitly, by entering its Standard Carrier Alpha Code (SCAC), which is commonly used in the U.S. transportation industry. Additionally, you can maintain the following general data:

- **Transportation Group**
  The transportation group can be used to determine which freight units can be assigned to the schedule at hand.

- **Capacity**
  You can define weight, volume, and two additional capacity restrictions. These serve as templates for the capacities that are maintainable for departure rules, which themselves also serve as templates for the capacities maintained per departure generated for the departure rule. Note that the capacities can be maintained only if this functionality is activated in the schedule type.

Figure 3.34 Road Carrier Schedule: General Data and Location Sequence

- **Transportation Costs**

  You can define quantity costs and fixed costs, which are considered by automatic planning and apply per schedule departure. In the optimizer cost settings, you can specify whether the quantity costs are multiplied by the distance traveled (see Chapter 6, Section 6.7.3). Like the capacity definition, these costs serve as templates for the departure rules that also serve as templates for the generated departures. This functionality can be used only if it's activated in the schedule type.

- **Mode-specific fields**

  For ocean carrier schedules, you can define the loop to group related schedules along the same rotation. For carrier flight schedules, you can define the airline code, flight number, and aircraft type code, as well as whether the carrier is executing the flight itself, to identify code-shared flights.

The stop sequence serves as a template for the departure rules and allows you to maintain the following data:

- **Transit Duration**
  This represents the transit duration from a stop to its successor.

- **Distance**
  The system automatically determines the distance between two consecutive stops based on the geographical coordinates of the locations. You can manually change the proposed distance.

- **Length of Stay**
  This represents the length of stay at an intermediate stop.

- **Cargo Cut-Off**
  You can define the cutoff time that is considered by automatic planning. This value specifies when freight units must be delivered to the location at hand so that they can be transported by the schedule from this location. Depending on the schedule type, you can define it relatively or absolutely, as described previously. It's also possible to define document cutoff and dangerous goods cutoff times.

- **Availability Time**
  You maintain the availability time considered by automatic planning, which defines when freight units delivered by the schedule to the location at hand can be picked up for further transportation departing from the location.

By clicking the **Create** button in the **Departure Rules** tab, you can maintain multiple departure rules following the location sequence. Figure 3.35 shows an example of two departure rules defined for the road carrier schedule depicted in Figure 3.34. You can define the validity of the rule, which can be a subperiod of the schedule's validity; the pattern of days; the times of departure, arrival, cargo cutoff, document cutoff, dangerous goods cutoff, and availability; and the durations for transit and length of stay.

With the **Auto Fill Times** option, you can change one departure or arrival time and let the system propagate this to the other times. Defining a factor calendar allows you to suppress generation of departures on public holidays according to the calendar.

You can select multiple departure rules and generate departures by clicking the corresponding button for either the whole validity period or an explicitly defined period. The departures are displayed in the **Departures** tab, as shown in Figure 3.36. All the times and durations are derived from the departure rule definitions. By clicking the **Create** button, you can create a new departure. When you select a departure, all these times and durations are displayed in the **Actual Stop Sequence** area. It's possible to manually change times and durations, even if they were generated based on a departure rule.

	Stage	Rule	First Day of Validity	Last Day of Validity	Means of Transport	Monday	Tuesday	Wednes..	Thursday	Friday	Saturday	Sunday	Departure Time	Arrival Time
	∨ TP_MUNICH - TP_BONN	1	01.12.2018	31.12.2019		✓	✓	✓	✓	✓	✓		06:00:00	15:23:39
	TP_MUNICH - TP_STUTTGART		01.12.2018	31.12.2019		✓	✓	✓	✓	✓	✓		06:00:00	09:08:59
	TP_STUTTGART - TP_MANNHEIM		01.12.2018	31.12.2019		✓	✓	✓	✓	✓	✓		09:38:59	11:11:24
	TP_MANNHEIM - TP_FRANKFURT		01.12.2018	31.12.2019		✓	✓	✓	✓	✓	✓		11:41:24	12:53:09
	TP_FRANKFURT - TP_BONN		01.12.2018	31.12.2019		✓	✓	✓	✓	✓	✓		13:23:09	15:23:39
✓	∨ TP_MUNICH - TP_BONN	2	01.12.2018	31.12.2019		✓	✓	✓	✓	✓			18:00:00	03:23:39
	TP_MUNICH - TP_STUTTGART		03.12.2018	31.12.2019		✓	✓	✓	✓	✓			18:00:00	21:08:59
	TP_STUTTGART - TP_MANNHEIM		03.12.2018	31.12.2019		✓	✓	✓	✓	✓			21:38:59	23:11:24
	TP_MANNHEIM - TP_FRANKFURT		03.12.2018	31.12.2019		✓	✓	✓	✓	✓			23:41:24	00:53:09
	TP_FRANKFURT - TP_BONN		04.12.2018	01.01.2020			✓	✓	✓	✓	✓		01:23:09	03:23:39

Figure 3.35 Road Carrier Schedule: Departure Rules

	Date	Time	Time Zone	Rule-Based	Weight	Weight UoM	Volume	Volume UoM	Quantity Costs	Quantity Costs UoM	Fixed Costs	Validity Status	Deletion Flag
✓	01.12.2018	06:00:00	CET	✓	30	TO		86	M3	2	TO	50,000	Valid	
	03.12.2018	06:00:00	CET	✓	30	TO		86	M3	2	TO	50,000	Valid	
	03.12.2018	18:00:00	CET	✓	30	TO		86	M3	2	TO	50,000	Valid	
	04.12.2018	06:00:00	CET	✓	30	TO		86	M3	2	TO	50,000	Valid	
	04.12.2018	18:00:00	CET	✓	30	TO		86	M3	2	TO	50,000	Valid	

Actual Stop Sequence

	Sequence	Location	Arrival Date	Arrival Time	Departure Date	Departure Time	Transit Duration (Hours)	Transit Duration (Minutes)	Distance	Dist. UoM	Cargo Cut-Off Date	Cargo Cut-Off Time	Availability Date	Availability Time
	10	TP_MUNICH			01.12.2018	06:00:00	3	8	251,968	KM	01.12.2018	04:00:00		
	20	TP_STUTTGART	01.12.2018	09:08:59	01.12.2018	09:38:59	1	32	123,216	KM	01.12.2018	07:38:59	01.12.2018	11:08:59
	30	TP_MANNHEIM	01.12.2018	11:11:24	01.12.2018	11:41:24	1	11	95,666	KM	01.12.2018	09:41:24	01.12.2018	13:11:24
	40	TP_FRANKFURT	01.12.2018	12:53:09	01.12.2018	13:23:09	2	0	160,667	KM	01.12.2018	11:23:09	01.12.2018	14:53:09
	50	TP_BONN	01.12.2018	15:23:39									01.12.2018	17:23:39

Figure 3.36 Road Carrier Schedule: Departures and Actual Stop Sequence

For ocean carrier schedules, you can maintain the vessel name and its International Maritime Organization (IMO) ship identification number on the departure rule and departure level. For carrier flight schedules, it's possible to mark intermediate stops as service stops (e.g., for refueling); service stops can't be used for loading or unloading but appear in the air freight bookings created for the schedule. It's also possible to maintain the aircraft type code on the departure rule stage level. Moreover, for multistop flights, you can define per stage whether the carrier is operating this stage itself or whether it's a code-share flight.

Maintaining gateway schedules is similar to maintaining carrier schedules, but some important additional data has to be maintained. First, you maintain the source gateway and the destination gateway, with corresponding cutoff times for the source gateway, transit duration to source port, transit duration from the destination port, and availability time for the destination gateway, as shown in Figure 3.37 for a sailing schedule; if your schedule type skips source or destination gateway, then you just maintain one gateway.

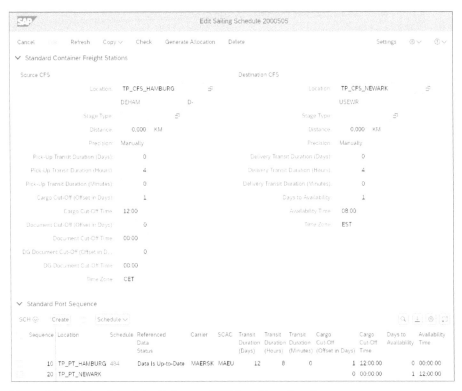

Figure 3.37 Sailing Schedule: Gateways (CFSs) and Location Sequence

Then, you define the standard port sequence by entering the locations. By clicking the **Schedule** button and selecting the **Assign** option, you can let each stage refer to an ocean carrier schedule, from which all times and durations are taken over in the sailing schedule. For a sailing schedule without reference, you have to manually maintain all this data in the sailing schedule itself.

You define the departure rules similarly to carrier schedules. The difference is that you can reference the referenced carrier schedules' departure rules by selecting the created departure rule's stage, clicking the **Departure Rule** button, and selecting the **Assign** option to select a departure rule of the referenced carrier schedule.

With connection gateway schedules, you just maintain more stages and link them to different schedules. Each departure rule stage refers to one departure rule of the referenced carrier schedule.

The **Referenced Data Status** field indicates whether the underlying carrier schedules have changed since the gateway schedule was created. This is quite useful if you want to quickly check whether your gateway schedule is affected by weekly updates of carrier schedules that are uploaded into the system.

Several transportation businesses, such as global shippers and global freight forwarders, make frequent use of the regular schedules of ocean carriers and airlines, which publish their schedules and update them on a regular basis. For any mode of transport, schedules can be uploaded via function module /SCMTMS/BAPI_SCHEDULE_SAVE-MULT, which offers create, update, and delete access to the schedules in the system. This approach requires mapping of the external data into the generic interface of the function module. Alternatively, you can run the report /SCMTMS/SCH_UPLOAD that's available via the menu path **Logistics · Transportation Management · Master Data · Transportation Network · Schedule · Schedule Upload** (in SAP TM 9.6, the menu path is **Application Administration · Master Data · Transportation Network · Schedule Upload**), as shown in Figure 3.38, and use one of the standard-delivered upload strategies or build your own upload strategy.

For example, the carrier flight schedule upload strategy SCHUP_CS_A allows you to upload schedule data from *.xls* and *.csv* files with a specific column signature, which is described in SAP Note 1743069, based on sample files. These files are designed to represent flight schedules in a simple and compact way that is easy to understand and maintain. OAG, one of the leading data providers for flight schedules for most airlines worldwide, offers its data in the file format offered by the standard upload strategy SCHUP_CS_A, which allows a straightforward integration of flight schedules into SAP TM. See SAP Note 1857686 for more details on this efficient schedule integration, which frees the system integrator from building custom interfaces to all relevant airlines in the world.

Ocean carrier schedules can be uploaded analogously by the upload strategy SCHUP_ CS_S. SAP Note 2136548 describes the column signature and sample files.

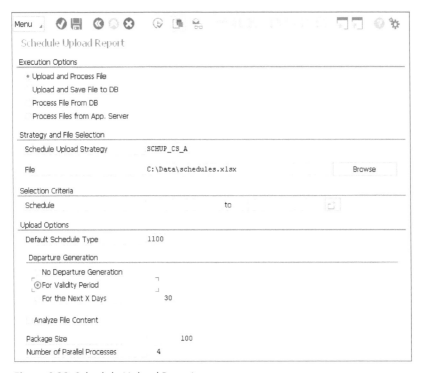

Figure 3.38 Schedule Upload Report

The upload report offers direct processing of a file, which is recommended for small and medium files. If the file is very large or will be uploaded by a background job, it can be uploaded into the database and then processed from the database. You can define an additional selection filter so that only the matching schedules out of the files are uploaded. The schedule type can be predefined; if not predefined, it has to be set in the file. You can trigger an automatic generation of departures for either the whole validity period of the schedule or a relative time period. The latter option is useful if you have departure rules that cover the whole next year, but you're used to creating freight documents for only the next four weeks. You can extract additional data out of the schedule file via the **Analyze File Content** option. In the carrier flight schedule scenario, this would return a list of the contained IATA location codes, airline codes, and aircraft codes; these are useful for verifying the completeness of your corresponding master data. The package size and number of parallel processes make it possible to adapt the schedule upload according to the expected file size, the available hardware, and the desired runtime of the upload.

Although this report can automatically create departures, there are some scenarios in which you'll want to upload schedules but not create departures immediately. If you're handling a lot of schedule data, manually triggering the creation of departures may be a tedious task, so you can use the report /SCMTMS/SCH_CRT_DEP or follow the menu path **Logistics · Transportation Management · Master Data · Transportation Network · Schedule · Creation of Schedule Departures** (in SAP TM 9.6, the menu path is **Application Administration · Master Data · Transportation Network · Creation of Schedule Departures**) and explicitly create departures for a set of schedules. You define a selection of the relevant schedules (based on schedule types, carriers, and schedules), as well as the time period for which the departures will be generated. It's also possible to run this report in a simulation mode first to determine how many departures will be generated. As with the schedule upload report, you can also define package size and number of parallel processes.

If schedules have limited validity (e.g., half a year), and new schedules are regularly created in the system to reflect the corresponding transportation options (here, for the next half a year), then the number of schedules in the system grows continuously. Usually, the outdated schedules aren't used anymore, so we recommend that you remove them from the system to restrict the data volume and prevent users from wasting time with useless schedules.

Of course, you can manually delete schedules (e.g., by selecting them from a query result in the transportation network overview POWL; Section 3.2.8). If you follow the menu path **Logistics · Transportation Management · Master Data · Transportation Network · Schedule · Schedule Deletion** (in SAP TM 9.6, the menu path is **Application Administration · Master Data · Transportation Network · Schedule Deletion**) and run the report located there, you can define a selection of schedules, choose one of the following deletion options, and delete the matching schedules automatically:

- **Complete Schedules**
  The whole schedule is deleted, with all its departure rules and departures.

- **Departures in the Past**
  This deletes only schedule departures in the past. The remaining departures and all departure rules are kept, even if they don't have a departure anymore.

- **Sched w/o Dep & Past**
  This acts like the previous option but also deletes schedules without any departure.

- **Consider Deletion Flag**
  This option deletes all schedules with an active deletion flag.

To avoid undesired deletion of schedules, you can first run a simulation of the found schedules by choosing the **Show Schedules/Departures** option, as shown in Figure 3.39.

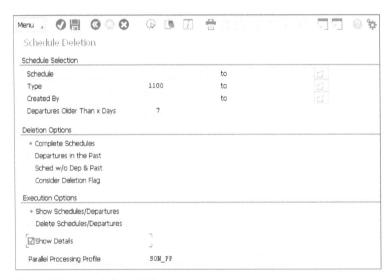

Figure 3.39 Schedule Deletion Report

If a schedule is still referenced by freight documents, allocations, or other schedules, then it's marked for deletion and can't be used for new references by those documents. A schedule is deleted only if there are no references to it. Thus, if you're running the schedule deletion report on a weekly basis, the deletion markers get set immediately, and the schedule is deleted only if the referencing documents have disappeared.

3.2.5   Transshipment Locations

In global transportation networks, an individual transportation order is usually executed using multiple modes of transport in sequence. The mode of transport is changed at transshipment locations, where the goods are unloaded and reloaded.

Let's walk through the steps of an example in which goods are transported from Germany to the United States:

1. A truck transports the goods from the start destination in Germany to the port of Hamburg.

2. At the port, the goods are unloaded from the truck and reloaded onto a ship.

3. The ship carries the goods to the port of Newark.

4. The goods are unloaded and reloaded onto a truck.

5. The truck transports the goods to their destination.

In this scenario, the ports in Hamburg and Newark serve as transshipment locations. Whereas goods are unloaded and reloaded from and onto different modes of transport in this example (truck and ship), there are also transshipment scenarios in which the mode of transport remains the same. This is the case, for example, with collection trips by truck, where the goods collected are unloaded and reloaded onto other trucks at a local depot, and these trucks then carry the goods along a long-haul route to another depot.

To define a location as a transshipment location, select the menu path **Master Data · Assign Transshipment Location** (in SAP TM 9.6, the menu path is **Master Data · Transportation Network · Locations · Assign Transshipment Location**). Define a set of locations or transportation zones and a transshipment location, and then choose **Create/ Update Assignments** to assign the transshipment location to the set of locations or transportation zones, as shown in Figure 3.40.

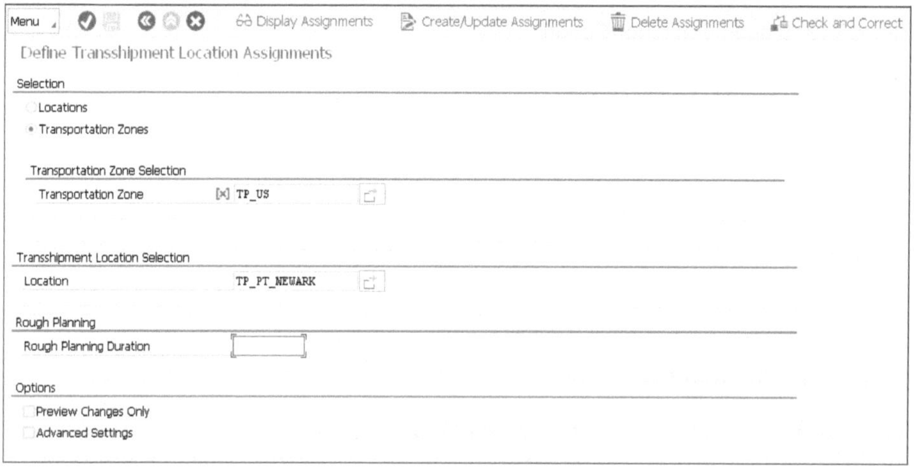

Figure 3.40 Defining Transshipment Location Assignments

You can also display already-defined transshipment location assignments, as shown in Figure 3.41.

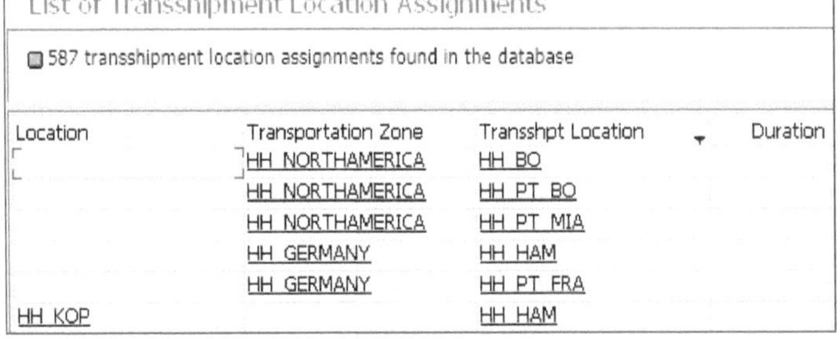
List of Transshipment Location Assignments

587 transshipment location assignments found in the database

Location	Transportation Zone	Transshpt Location	Duration
	HH_NORTHAMERICA	HH_BO	
	HH_NORTHAMERICA	HH_PT_BO	
	HH_NORTHAMERICA	HH_PT_MIA	
	HH_GERMANY	HH_HAM	
	HH_GERMANY	HH_PT_FRA	
HH_KOP		HH_HAM	

Figure 3.41 Transshipment Location Assignments

For each transshipment location assignment, you can also define a duration that is considered by rough planning (see Chapter 6, Section 6.7.2). If rough planning is activated, and the duration is maintained, transportation from the transshipment location to the assigned locations and zones—and vice versa—is possible with the defined duration without definition of a schedule or a transportation lane. This allows the modeling of intermodal scenarios in which, for example, pre-legs and subsequent legs aren't planned in detail but should be planned in a rough way based on the maintained (rough) transportation duration instead. The rough planning concept represents a simple version of reachability for automatic planning, but no freight documents are created for the rough-planned parts of the transportation. Therefore, we don't consider it to be a complete way of expressing reachability.

The transshipment location determination finds the relevant transshipment locations for a given source and destination location in an iterative procedure. The process starts with the given source and determines the transshipment locations that are explicitly assigned to the location and its zones. Each subsequent iteration adds transshipment locations that are explicitly assigned to the locations added in the previous step. Similarly, transshipment locations are determined from the perspective of the destination location. This process determines the transshipment location network connecting the source and destination, and you can define a limit on the number of consecutive transshipment locations leading from source to destination (see Chapter 6, Section 6.7.2). In Customizing, following the menu path **Transportation Management • Master Data • Transportation Network • General Settings for Transportation Network Determination**, you can specify that the transshipment location determination will only consider directly connected transshipment locations.

Note that default routes can also be used to define transshipment locations in an explicit fashion. However, the transshipment locations in a default route apply only if the transportation is planned along the default route. (Section 3.2.6 has more details on default routes.)

In intermodal scenarios, many different schedules may touch one specific port. To allow the port to be used as a transshipment location for connecting two schedules arriving at and departing from the port, respectively, the port has to be defined as a transshipment location for all other locations covered by the schedules. In a global ocean schedule network that connects hundreds of ports, this would be an enormous, error-prone maintenance task. In a global air freight network covering thousands of airports, the task would be even larger. Therefore, SAP TM offers automatic connection determination, which can be activated in the optimizer settings (see Chapter 6, Section 6.7.2). This means that any location covered by two schedules can serve as a transshipment location for all locations covered by the two schedules and therefore represents an implicit transshipment location definition. This significantly reduces the maintenance required for defining transshipment locations. If even the pre-legs and subsequent legs in a global network are served by schedules, no explicit transshipment location assignment is required anymore. Only if pre-legs and subsequent legs are *not* covered by schedules do the transshipment locations entering the schedule network have to be defined explicitly.

Reachability and Transshipment Locations

There are three ways to define that location A can be reached from location B:

- Define a transportation lane from A to B, on either the location level or appropriate zones.
- Define a schedule that goes from A to B, either directly or indirectly via other locations.
- Define a (rough) duration for a transshipment location assignment of A to B or vice versa, and use rough planning.

There are three ways to define B as a transshipment location for location A:

- Define an explicit assignment, as just described.
- Define an explicit assignment along a default route, as described in Section 3.2.6.
- Define an implicit assignment, as just described.

In scenarios that include transshipments (e.g., an intermodal scenario from Asia to Europe), you have to ensure that reachability and transshipment locations are

---

defined appropriately. In scenarios without transshipments (e.g., a local distribution scenario within Bavaria, Germany), you have to ensure that the reachability within Bavaria is defined appropriately.

If you want to transport goods from location A to location C using location B as a transshipment location, you must implicitly or explicitly define B as a transshipment location for A or C and define reachability from A to B and from B to C using any of these possibilities.

From this perspective, the reachability network and the transshipment network together form the transportation network, where the reachability network is the set of all locations and their reachable relations, and the transshipment network is the set of all locations and their transshipment relations.

You can define a minimum goods wait time and a maximum goods wait time for a location to be taken into account in the scheduling of activities during the transshipment of a demand. The goods wait time of a demand is the length of time between the end of unloading and the start of reloading at the transshipment location.

For example, a minimum goods wait time of 1 day ensures that the goods delivered remain at the transshipment location for at least 1 day before they are transported further. With a maximum goods wait time of 72 hours, the goods delivered must not remain at the transshipment location for more than 72 hours before they are picked up.

3.2.6   Default Routes

In complex transportation networks, there may be numerous possible paths from one source to one destination. For many businesses, only a few of these possible paths are reasonable; often, business experience or careful analysis of the network leads an organization to know the most desirable route for a given source and destination. Therefore, many transportation businesses are organized by default routes; these are static rules defining how goods are to be routed geographically through the global transportation network. For intermodal transports, default routes can predefine the sequence of transshipment locations, as mentioned in the last section. For truck and trailer scenarios involving dynamic recoupling, default routes can predefine the sequence of coupling and uncoupling locations for the trailer unit.

A default route defines a location sequence for a given source and destination, which can be locations or zones. For a transport from a source to a destination, the default route serves as a template guiding the transportation through the network.

Given a source location and a destination location, the system determines matching default routes and chooses the most specific one. A default route matches a given source location S and destination location D if the default route's source is location S or a zone containing S and the default route's destination is location D or a zone containing D. If there are multiple matching default routes, the system chooses the most specific one; a direct location match is more specific than a zone match.

The ability to define default routes with a source zone and a destination zone significantly reduces the default route maintenance efforts. Let's consider an ocean scenario in which goods from Germany are transported to the United States via ports in Hamburg and Newark. This could be expressed by maintaining many location-to-location default routes, each having one source location in Germany and one destination location in the United States. Assuming 20 source locations in Germany and 50 destination locations in the United States, this would result in 1,000 default routes. Defining one zone for Germany and one zone for the United States, you can define one default route from Germany to the United States via the transshipment ports Hamburg and Newark. This zone-to-zone default route has the same effect as the 1,000 location-to-location default routes. Another advantage of the zone-to-zone default route is that you don't have to create new default routes if new source or destination locations show up in the source and destination zone.

To define a default route, select the menu path **Master Data • Create Default Route** (in SAP TM 9.6, the menu path is **Master Data • Transportation Network • Default Route • Create Default Route**), and enter the default route type, which you can select from the defined default route types. Besides maintaining the description and the validity period, you can restrict the applicability of a default route by choosing an option for **Dangerous Goods** (only dangerous goods, only nondangerous goods, or all goods) and setting the **Shipping Type** (see Figure 3.42). By maintaining the **Transportation Stops** list, you can define the following per stage: mode of transport, means of transport, stage type, schedule, and carrier, which represent constraints for planning. For example, if a schedule is defined for a specific stage, planning will only create a transportation plan using the given schedule for this stage. Similarly, if a carrier is defined for a specific stage, it will be used by planning.

You can also maintain the transit durations per stage and the lengths of stay per intermediate stop, which all gets aggregated to the transportation duration in the header. Alternatively, you can just maintain the transportation duration on the header level. When you enter a forwarding order, the system determines the matching default route and uses the transit durations and lengths of stay to determine requested pickup and delivery times for the generated freight unit stages and the ordered route of the forwarding order. Thus, the transportation duration isn't used explicitly in planning but only indirectly via the freight units' time windows.

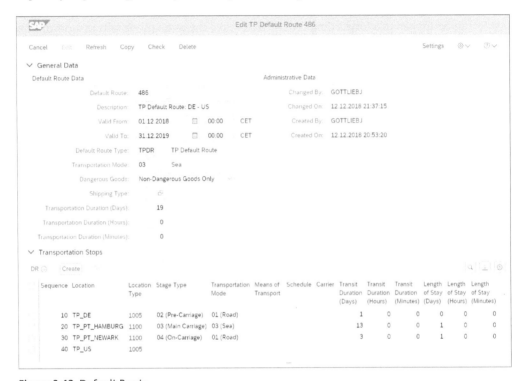

Figure 3.42 Default Route

Analogously to the transit durations, you can also define the distance per stage, which is taken over into a demand document when applying the default route. The main purpose is to provide an indication of the distance of unplanned demand document stages.

Per stage, you can also define the responsible planning and execution organization and whether this organization has to explicitly check any freight unit assignments for freight documents created for this stage. Such definition of your organization interaction model allows you to structure responsibilities for different business units in your company (e.g., for ocean freight bookings on the main legs of your default routes; see Chapter 5, Section 5.4.1).

Default route types can be maintained by selecting the IMG menu path **Transportation Management • Master Data • Transportation Network • Define Default Route Types**. For a default route type, you can define the mode of transport that is passed on to default routes created for this type. Similar to the shipping type, a default route can be applied to a forwarding order if both have the same mode of transport or one mode is undefined. You can also specify whether the default route is mandatory—that is, any freight unit or TU with stages built according to a default route must use the mandatory default route. For example, either the freight unit stages were built by the corresponding FUB option, or they were created out of a forwarding order by the schedule selection functionality using default routes. The default route type also allows defining whether the default route can be used for freight units, trailer units, railcar units, container units, or package units in the VSR optimizer, as described in Chapter 6, Section 6.4.2.

Default routes can be used in various contexts for defining the stages of freight units, TUs, and forwarding orders' actual routes, the latter including the selection of schedules. These use cases are described in the following sections.

Creating Freight Unit Stages

During FUB, freight unit stages can be automatically generated based on a default route. Given a freight unit at hand, the system determines a default route based on the freight unit's source location and destination location. Then the freight unit stages are created according to the default route's location sequence. Thus, the location sequence defines the transshipment locations to be used when moving goods from source to destination.

This functionality is useful if the transportation of goods is to be organized strictly in a rule-based fashion. For example, if goods moving from Germany to the East Coast of the United States will always be transported via the ports in Hamburg and Newark, this can be modeled by a default route with the source zone representing Germany as the first stop, the port in Hamburg as the second stop, the port in Newark as the third stop, and the destination zone representing the East Coast of the United States as the fourth stop.

As an alternative to applying default routes during FUB, the transportation cockpit allows you to apply default routes to selected freight unit stages, too (see Chapter 6, Section 6.6.1). Each selected freight unit stage is replaced by freight unit stages according to the most specific default route. Compared to the previous use case of strictly organizing transports according to default routes, this use case considers default routes as one option to guide the transportation through the network. However, the user can explicitly define any path through the network and use the default routes only on demand (e.g., if the user isn't sure about a good path through the network). Note that the cockpit allows splitting and merging of freight unit stages, so the system always offers the planner the manual choice to change freight unit stages that were already created by default routes.

Creating Transportation Unit Stages

You can also use FUB to create TUs by specifying a TU type as a document type in the freight unit building rule (FUBR). Like freight unit stages, TU stages can be generated automatically based on a default route. Given a particular TU, the system determines a default route based on the TU's source and destination locations. Then, TU stages are created according to the default route's location sequence.

Different TU types can cover different modes of transport, such as the trailer unit for a road and the railcar unit for a railway. For a trailer unit, the location sequence of the determined default route defines the locations where the trailer can be uncoupled from and to a truck; thus, the corresponding trailer unit stages are to be assigned to road freight orders. For a railcar unit, the location sequence of the determined default route defines the locations where the railcar is uncoupled from and to a train, and hence the corresponding railcar unit stages are to be assigned to rail freight orders. For a container unit and package unit, the default route is interpreted analogously to a freight unit (i.e., it defines the stages of the container unit and package unit, respectively).

In certain transportation scenarios, the trailers in the transportation network are moved back and forth along a predefined chain of coupling and uncoupling locations. This scenario can be modeled by a default route applied during FUB to create trailer unit stages. This rule-based approach greatly simplifies manual planning, allowing the planner to start with assigning trailer unit stages to road freight orders and freeing the planner from manually defining trailer unit stages. As with freight units, the planner can also manually apply default routes to selected TU stages in the transportation cockpit.

Creating Forwarding Order Stages and Selecting Schedules

For a forwarding order, the system can determine the available schedules per forwarding order stage, allowing the user to choose from the alternative schedules. After a schedule is chosen, its data (e.g., departure date and time and arrival date and time) is taken into the stages of the forwarding order's actual route.

The schedule determination also considers default routes. If a matching default route is found, new stages are proposed for the forwarding order according to the location sequence of the default route. If the default route considers more specific information for a stage—such as a carrier or schedule to be used—then only schedules for this carrier or only the predefined schedule are offered to the user for the stage.

When the user has chosen one alternative, the proposed forwarding order stages (in the actual route) are created according to the default route, like the creation of freight unit stages and TU stages by a default route. However, additional information, such as carrier and schedule, is also taken from the default route into the forwarding order stages.

The location sequence of the default route defines the transshipment locations to be used for the forwarding order. When the user creates freight units for the forwarding order, the freight unit stages are created according to the forwarding order stages while also considering the carriers and schedules defined by the default route.

This functionality enables scenarios in which the actual routes of forwarding orders are predefined in a rule-based fashion. For example, such scenarios are relevant for ocean freight forwarders in a less than container load (LCL) scenario, in which the transportation is organized by rules guiding freight through the network. In addition to defining the sequence of ports to be used for ocean transportation, even an ocean carrier and its ocean carrier schedule can be predefined per stage in a default route.

3.2.7   Trade Lanes

The relationships of your transportation business to your carriers and customers are usually structured in a geographical fashion. For example, you may have a forwarding agreement with a certain customer from Germany to North America, a freight agreement with an ocean carrier from Germany to the United States, and an allocation with another carrier (airline) from the airport in Frankfurt to the airport in Chicago. You may also have defined a business share between your two favorite road carriers within Germany to be 40% for the first carrier and 60% for the second carrier.

Trade lanes specify the basic geographical relationships that structure all these business objects. A trade lane can have a mode of transport and a means of transport. The trade lane defines a direction for transportation, which is characterized by the orientation and a source and destination (both being either a location or a zone).

You can define a trade lane by selecting the menu path **Master Data · Create Trade Lane** (in SAP TM 9.6, the menu path is **Master Data · Transportation Network · Trade Lane · Create Trade Lane**) and entering a trade lane type. Then you can specify its description, mode of transport, means of transport, and geographical definition, which consists of the orientation, source, and destination (see Figure 3.43).

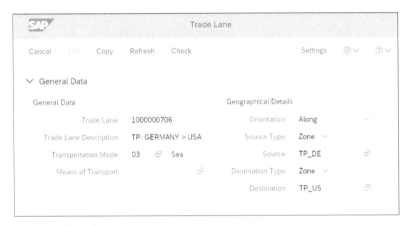

Figure 3.43 Trade Lane

You can maintain the following orientations:

- **From**
  Covers transportation starting from a selected location or zone and reaching any other location.

- **To**
  Covers transportation starting from any location and reaching a selected location or zone.

- **Within**
  Covers transportation within a zone (i.e., starting from a location in the zone and reaching another location in the zone).

- **Along**
  Represents transportation starting from a selected location or zone and reaching another selected location or zone.

- **Inbound**

  Covers transportation within and to the selected zone (i.e., all transportation that ends in the zone and starts inside or outside the zone).

- **Outbound**

  Represents transportation within and from the selected zone (i.e., all transportation that starts in the zone and ends inside or outside the zone).

The trade lane types can be defined via the IMG menu path **Transportation Management · Master Data · Transportation Network · Trade Lane · Define Trade Lane Types**. Here, you can specify the number range interval per trade lane type.

Transportation Lane versus Trade Lane

Although both concepts characterize the direction of transportation between a source and a destination—both being locations or zones—they have different aims.

The transportation lane defines reachability—that is, which means of transport can be used to transport goods from a source to a destination and which carriers are available per means of transport. In addition, it contains many parameters that affect transportation planning, optimization, and carrier selection. Thus, the transportation lane defines how transportation can be planned and executed in your network, so it has a significant impact on transportation processes.

The trade lane is just the geographical basis for multiple business objects that define the relationships to carriers and customers. It can be defined for a means of transport or mode of transport, or even without reference to a mode of transport. Its orientation concept is more generic than the direction in a transportation lane. The trade lane itself doesn't contain any control parameters, so it doesn't influence any transportation processes. However, in conjunction with objects such as forwarding agreements, freight agreements, allocations, and business shares, it's the key element to structure your business from a geographical perspective.

3.2.8   Transportation Network Cockpit and Overview Personal Object Worklist

Let's look at two complementary tools for providing transparency of the transportation network and searching and maintenance capabilities: the transportation network cockpit and the transportation network overview POWL.

Transportation Network Cockpit

The transportation network cockpit allows the display of the transportation network or parts of it on a geographical map, as well as the creation of master data objects, such as locations, transportation zones, and trade lanes, on the map. For objects displayed on the map, you can navigate to the corresponding (text-based) maintenance UIs described in the previous sections. Visualizing the network on a map is probably the best way to understand the network structure and verify its correctness and completeness. Certain transportation network master data inconsistencies can be identified easily on the map, such as incorrect geo-coordinates for locations or missing geo-coordinates, which are frequently shown as a spot with coordinate (0,0) in the Atlantic Ocean, where there is definitely no island.

By following the menu path **Master Data · Transportation Network Cockpit** (in SAP TM 9.6, the path is **Master Data · Transportation Network · Transportation Network Cockpit**), you can define search criteria for locations, transportation zones, transportation lanes, trade lanes, schedules, and default routes. When you click the **Go** button in the search dialog, the resulting objects are displayed on the map, as shown in Figure 3.44, for a set of schedules matching the schedule search criteria.

Figure 3.44 Transportation Network Cockpit

The **Results Overview** area provides a list of the search results. You can iteratively add search results to the map and clear the map to start with a new search. You can focus on the map and the master data selection screen area, respectively, by hiding the other screen area.

If you want to see the complete network offered to you by a carrier, select the **Business Partner Network** tab to show all network master data for the chosen carrier. The set of all transshipment locations can be displayed via the corresponding button.

Use the **Connections** tab to search for paths from a source location to a destination location, which allows you to easily check whether your network definition is complete from a reachability and transshipment location perspective. The found paths are displayed on the map, and, in addition, if there is no direct reachability from source to destination, this is displayed as a red arc. If you expected connections to exist, but none are shown, this helps identify whether a transshipment location, schedule, or transportation lane is missing for the connection. Because the network definition is crucial for automatic planning, we recommend verifying the completeness and correctness of your network definition by the transportation network cockpit in case automatic planning doesn't find the transportation plan you expected.

When you right-click any object on the map, the context menu allows you to do the following:

- Show the details of the object, which opens the maintenance UI of the object and allows editing.
- Hide the object at hand, other objects, or unrelated objects.
- For a location, you can find assigned transshipment locations, related transportation zones, transportation lanes, trade lanes, schedules, default routes, and connections to another location; create a trade lane referring to the location; or move the location on the map.
- For a transportation zone, you can find assigned transshipment locations, related locations, transportation lanes, trade lanes, schedules, and default routes; create a trade lane referring to the transportation zone; or move the zone on the map.
- Display arc-based objects, such as transportation lanes, trade lanes, schedules, and default routes, on the street level or as a straight line.

Right-clicking on the map itself, you can do the following:

- Search for addresses and display them on the map.
- Define whether arcs will be displayed as straight lines or on the street level.
- Show the display profile, which includes a legend for the displayed objects and allows adjusting some aspects of their appearance on the fly, for example, switching labels on or off (see Chapter 6, Section 6.6.4, for more details on configuring the map and using the display profile).
- Remove highlighting from the results of the last search.
- Create a location or a transportation zone at the current position on the map.
- Search locations nearby, within a given distance limit.
- Personalize the map to your needs. For example, specify the initial area shown on the map (the default is the world), and choose among the map types (preconfigured maps from various GIS vendors).

Transportation Network Overview Personal Object Worklist

Whereas the transportation network cockpit represents the geographical view of the network, the transportation network overview POWL provides queries and worklists for all schedule types delivered in standard, default routes, and trade lanes.

As shown in Figure 3.45, you can select the menu path **Master Data · Schedules and Default Routes Worklist** (in SAP TM 9.6, the menu path is **Master Data · Transportation Network · Overview Transportation Network**) and choose the query for master flight schedules, for example. With standard POWL sorting, filtering, and personalization capabilities, you can quickly navigate through master flight schedules that are relevant for you or export the list to a spreadsheet. Many key characteristics are shown here, such as airline code, flight number, source and destination, number of generated departures, number of intermediate stops (to quickly identify multistop flights), and an indicator for connection master flight schedules. The reference data status allows you to identify master flight schedules that refer to updated underlying carrier flight schedules and may need manual adjustments (see Chapter 5, Section 5.1.3). For any set of schedule instances selected in the result list, you can create freight documents and generate departures. You can also display, edit, copy, or delete a selected schedule instance or create a new one.

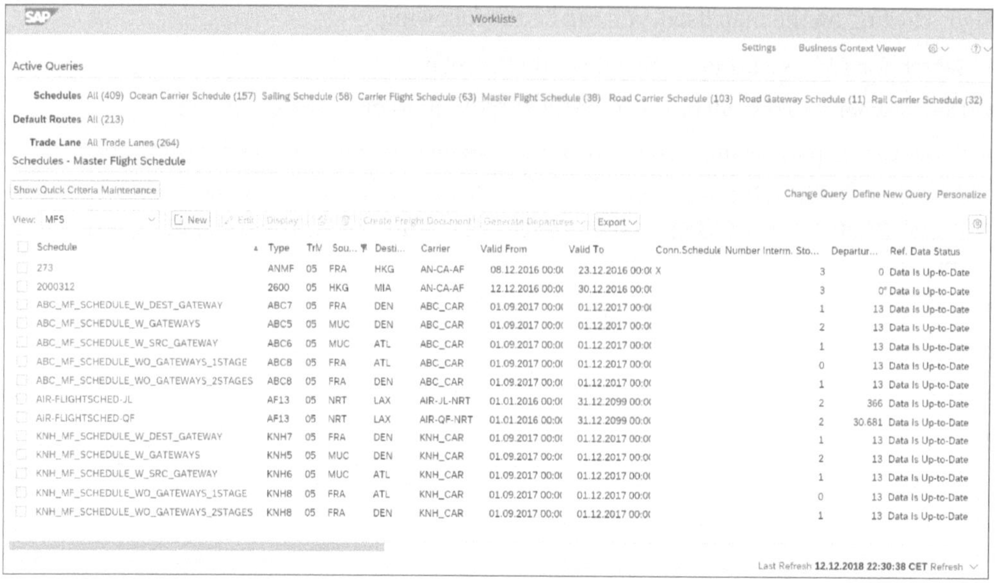

Figure 3.45 Transportation Network Overview with Master Flight Schedule Query

3.2.9   Integration of Geographical Information Systems

A *geographical information system* (GIS) captures and stores geographical data, enabling data analysis and visualization. In the context of transportation, it allows geo-coding, distance and duration determination, routing, and geographic map visualization, which are essential for informed decision-making.

Basic Functionalities

Given an address, the geo-coordinates representing longitude, latitude, and altitude are determined. Geo-coding is the prerequisite for any decision-making based on geographical data. It's required to show locations at their right positions on the map and enable distance and duration determination and routing.

Given a source and destination geo-coordinate, the distance and duration to reach the destination from the source are determined. Most GISs allow you to configure whether to determine the shortest or fastest path.

Distances are required to do optimizer-based planning, minimize the total distance traveled when transporting freight, or adhere to distance-based constraints for trucks. Distances also get shown for demand and capacity documents and their stages in the transportation cockpit, as well as charge calculation and settlement, where the charges are calculated based on the distance of the transportation.

Durations are also required for optimizer-based planning, minimizing the total duration for a transport, or considering constraints on the total duration of a transport. As with distances, durations are also shown in the transportation cockpit for documents and their stages. The system differentiates between net and gross duration, where the former represents the pure travel duration, and the latter includes potentially scheduled idle times between departure and arrival of the travel at hand.

The distance and duration determination is done by shortest-path algorithms in the GIS based on a graph of the transportation network, which usually contains the junctions of streets and highways as nodes and their connections as arcs with distances.

So given a source and destination geo-coordinate, the best route to the destination from the source is determined. Here, a route is represented by a sequence of geo-coordinates, starting with the source and ending with the destination. The routing is required to determine distance and duration, but, in many cases, only distance and duration are required and retrieved from a GIS. The routing information is retrieved from a GIS only if it will be visualized on a geographical map, as in the transportation network cockpit described in Section 3.2.8 or in the transportation cockpit's map described in Chapter 6, Section 6.6.4.

Routing, Default Routes, and Vehicle Scheduling and Routing

The terms *route* and *routing* are used in various contexts. In the GIS context discussed in this section, *routing* means determining a path through the street network, which is frequently called a route and specifies which streets, highways, and paths to use to travel from a source location to a destination location. The path connects the source and destination by very detailed intermediate physical positions (available only in the GIS), such as crossroads, highway exits, and so on, and thus it defines how a driver can execute transportation from source to destination.

A *default route* is a statically defined path through a transportation network consisting of locations maintained in the SAP TM system. Usually, crossroads aren't maintained as locations. Thus, a default route is defined on a higher level of aggregation.

The *vehicle scheduling and routing* (VSR) optimizer solves vehicle routing problems in the transportation network specified by locations in SAP TM. For a given fleet of vehicles and transportation orders, the optimizer decides which orders will be delivered by which vehicle. In addition, the optimizer determines the best possible route for each vehicle. Here, again, a route is a sequence of locations in the network. Like the default route, routes are defined on a higher level than the level of crossroads, and so on.

While a default route is defined manually and statically, usually based on business experience, the routes obtained by the VSR optimizer are determined automatically and dynamically, based on optimization criteria. One of the criteria is the total distance traveled, which is based on pair-wise distances between the locations. Interestingly, these distances can be retrieved out of a connected GIS, which internally performs a routing task between two locations to determine the distance required by the VSR optimizer to make its routing decisions.

The geographical map shows a set of transportation-relevant objects. These objects can be based on position (e.g., locations, zones, and resources) or relation (e.g., freight units, freight orders, trade lanes, and schedules). The relation-based objects can be shown as straight lines connecting two consecutive locations in an idealized way or based on the detailed routing information, which makes it possible to check the actual route along the street level. However, the higher-detail level of an actual route comes with a longer response time because many more details must be retrieved out of the connected GIS to draw the detailed segments on the street level.

Map visualization is extremely helpful to understand, analyze, and explain the transportation network structure, as explained in Section 3.2.8 for the transportation network cockpit. While a list of locations in a tabular representation is hard for anyone not familiar with the locations to interpret, a visualization of the locations on the map allows everybody to understand the relative geographical positions on the map and thereby also assess neighborhood relations and distances between locations.

When planning transports, a map of the freight units and planned freight orders enables the planner to identify geographical consolidation potentials, which are much harder to identify in tabular lists of freight units and freight orders. Moreover, the quality of an actual route of a freight order can easily be judged by checking it on a map. For example, good routes should not contain any crossing stages, which is hard to judge in a tabular stage list but is easily checked on a map. See Chapter 6, Section 6.6.4, for more details on map-based planning, and Chapter 6, Section 6.6.1, for examples of the transportation cockpit including a map.

The routing can be visualized on the map, enabling the user to see which streets and highways are used to reach the destination from the source. This is helpful during execution of the transportation. For example, if information about traffic jams is also shown on the map, it enables the planner to judge whether there is a risk of delays and to trigger replanning if needed.

Integration and Technology

Some GIS vendors offer global data, and others offer only regional data, such as for North America, Europe, Australia, or China. Some SAP TM users are familiar with certain GIS vendors when they start using SAP TM and want to continue using tools from these vendors. Global companies may even use multiple GISs (e.g., one per continent or region). For all these reasons, SAP TM doesn't contain its own GIS but offers an open infrastructure into which any GIS or even multiple GIS tools can be easily integrated. This way, SAP TM users can choose which GIS to integrate into SAP TM.

The integration of services for geo-coding, distance and duration determination, and routing requires ABAP knowledge. More information is contained in SAP Note 1685381, which contains a white paper that explains how to use and configure GIS services and a guide describing how to connect SAP TM to an external web service.

It's state of the art to directly connect to a GIS by web services rather than using middleware between the GIS and SAP TM. Although SAP TM still supports a standard integration via the GIS services contained in the SAP Internet Graphics Server (IGS) for compatibility reasons, its use is not recommended because IGS requires its own server, its interface is tied to one vendor, and it uses only single-distance calls. The result is acceptable performance only for small scenarios.

The visualization of maps within SAP TM is covered by SAP Visual Business, which provides two-dimensional scenes on geographical maps accessible by REST-based web services. You can configure the map content in Customizing by following the menu path **Transportation Management · Basic Functions · Geographical Map · Visual Business · Maintain Application Definitions**. See *http://scn.sap.com/docs/DOC-43251* for configuring or changing a map provider for SAP Visual Business.

While integrating a GIS provides a lot of value for many scenarios, this value has a cost, including GIS license fees and the effort to develop and configure the integration. We recommend that you build up and preserve know-how about the GISs you use because GIS products evolve, and you may want to integrate more GIS services later. Most GIS vendors offer web services and some still offer local installations. Especially for these installations, it's important to have local know-how to keep the system up and running.

We also recommend that you check the accuracy of the integrated GIS by explicitly checking known examples for geo-coding, distances, routing, and map visualization. It's also helpful to monitor the availability of the GIS integration because downtime may have a severe impact on transportation planning or charge calculation. From a performance perspective, we recommend using mass calls for distance and duration determination because determining a whole matrix in one step is an order of magnitude faster than determining a distance matrix by a set of individual calls. This is especially important when running optimization scenarios involving a large number of locations per optimizer run.

Of course, you can run SAP TM without GIS. In this case, geo-coordinates for locations are determined on the region and country level and can be maintained manually to get higher accuracy without a GIS. However, this may be a tedious, error-prone task. Without GIS, the distance determination can be done based on the straight-line distance, which is a reasonable approximation of the street-level distance for some scenarios. Alternatively, the distance can be maintained explicitly on the transportation lane level, which, again, is hard, error-prone work—especially if medium or large transportation networks are modeled. Nevertheless, all these options without GIS are also valid, so it's up to the user to judge the value of a GIS integration for the business, decide whether to integrate a GIS, and choose the right GIS vendor and option.

3.3   Resources

Resources play a central role in planning and execution and are required to physically transport goods within the transportation network and to load and unload goods at the locations in the network. The system offers the following *resource classes*:

- **Vehicle resources**
  These resources represent trucks, trailers, locomotives, and railcars.

- **TU resources**
  These resources model containers or unit load devices.

- **Drivers**
  These resources are required to operate trucks, and they combine the properties of a business partner and a resource (as described in Section 3.1.2).

- **Calendar resources**
  These resources represent opening hours at locations.

- **Handling resources**
  These resources generalize calendar resources, imposing additional time-dependent capacity constraints, for example, to model the number of open doors at a warehouse.

You can get an overview of the maintained resources in a POWL that you can reach by the menu path **Master Data · Resources Worklist** (in SAP TM 9.6, the path is **Master Data · Resources · Overview Resources**).

Section 3.3.1 introduces the mode of transport and the means of transport, which is the key concept to structure vehicle resources. Section 3.3.2 discusses equipment groups and types that also serve structuring purposes for three resource classes. Section 3.3.3 describes vehicle resources and how to define compartments and vehicle combinations. TU resources are explained in Section 3.3.4. Calendar and handling resources are described in Section 3.3.5.

3.3.1 Mode and Means of Transport

Transportation is structured according to the following key concepts:

- **Mode of transport**
  The *mode of transport* defines which mode (e.g., road, rail, sea, and air) is used for transportation.

- **Means of transport**
  The *means of transport* is assigned to a mode of transport and models a class of vehicle resources with the same fundamental properties (e.g., distance and duration determination or planning cost settings).

- **Vehicle resource**
  A *vehicle resource* is assigned to a means of transport and represents a resource such as a truck, trailer, locomotive, or railcar that can be used for planning and execution.

Let's delve into the mode of transport and means of transport.

Mode of Transport

The modes of transport maintained in the system are categorized into four *transportation mode categories*: road, rail, sea, and air. You can use predefined modes of transport or configure new ones (see Figure 3.46) in Customizing using the menu path **Transportation Management • Master Data • Transportation Network • Transportation Lane • Maintain Transportation Mode** (in SAP TM 9.6, the path is **SAP Transportation Management • Transportation Management • SCM Basis • Master Data • Transportation Lane • Maintain Transportation Mode**).

The following parameters are available:

- **MTr**
  The means of transport is used as default for distance and duration determination. This default is only used if no specific means of transport could be determined for a capacity document at hand.
- **Sust. Fctr**
  The sustainability factor can be used to model the carbon dioxide emissions.
- **Main Carr.**
  The mode of transport can be used for main carriage.
- **MTrCat**
  This parameter defines the dangerous mode of transport category.

Change View "Transportation Mode (TM specific)": Overview

Transportation Mode (TM specific)

TranspMode	Transp. Mode descr.	MTrCat	TModCat	Main Carr.	Sust. Fctr	MTr	MTr Descripti
01	Road	1	Road			0001	Truck
02	Rail	2	Rail				
03	Sea	4	Sea	✓			
04	Inland Waterway	3	Sea				
05	Air	5	Air	✓			
06	Parcel	1	Road				

Figure 3.46 Configuration of the Transportation Modes

Means of Transport

Means of transport are essential to group vehicle resources from reachability and planning cost and constraint perspectives. To maintain a means of transport in Customizing, select the menu path **Transportation Management • Master Data • Resources • Means of Transport and Compartment • Define Means of Transport**. Figure 3.47 shows the maintenance screen where, in addition to the name, description, standard code, and mode of transport, the following parameters can be defined:

- The **Superordinate MTr** field assigns the means of transport to another means of transport, which enables defining a means of transport hierarchy as shown in

Figure 3.48. Usually, all trucks have the same reachability properties in your transportation network, but the planning costs of small, big, cooled, and non-cooled trucks differ; and the same holds true for small, big, cooled, and non-cooled trailers. Using the shown means of transport hierarchy, you can assign the root truck means of transport to a transportation lane to define the reachability of this means of transport and all its children in the hierarchy, which simplifies the transportation lane maintenance considerably and makes it less error-prone. The planning costs can be defined on lower levels in the means of transport hierarchy. The middle layer in this hierarchy would not be required from the planning cost perspective but could be used to define allocations for carrier, as explained in Chapter 5, Section 5.2.

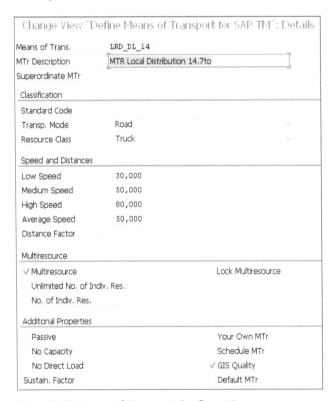

Figure 3.47 Means of Transport Configuration

- The **Speed and Distances** section allows you to define the **Average Speed** and a **Low Speed**, **Medium Speed**, and **High Speed** (which represent the average speeds when traveling in developed areas, on highways, and on motorways). The **Distance**

Factor defines the ratio between the distance to be considered and the straight-line distance.

- The **Multiresource** flag defines whether a resource assigned to the means of transport represents a *single resource* (i.e., it models one physical resource instance, e.g., the truck with license plate HD – DE 567) or a *multiresource* that models a resource type (i.e., a set of resources with equivalent properties). While single resources are used to plan a company's own fleet of trucks and trailers, multiresources are commonly used to represent subcontracted trucks for which you don't care about their license plate but just the fact that you can use a truck of that kind. Using the **Unlimited No. of Indiv. Res.** parameter, you can define that the multiresource represents an infinite number of resource instances. You can limit the number of resource instances modeled by a multiresource by the **No. of Indiv. Res** parameter. While companies without their own fleet would usually only use multiresources, road carriers or shippers with their own fleet would usually use single resources for each owned truck and trailer and multiresources for subcontracting purposes. The **Lock Multiresource** parameter defines whether multiresources get locked during planning. If a multiresource is locked, it can't be used in two parallel planning sessions. If it's not locked, the system enables two or more parallel planning sessions, but it can't guarantee that the defined limit of resource instances is met.

- The **Passive** parameter defines whether the resource is active or passive. While an *active resource* can move alone, a *passive resource* can only be moved by an active resource. In the road mode of transport, trucks and trailers represent active and passive resources, respectively. Analogously, locomotives and railcars represent active and passive resources for the rail mode of transport.

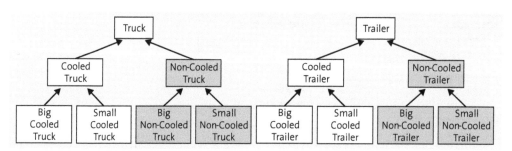

Figure 3.48 Means of Transport Hierarchy

- The **No Direct Load** parameter defines that goods can't be loaded into the resource at hand—neither into the resource nor into any compartments assigned to it. Typically, this flag is used for tractors and locomotives. Similarly, the **No Capacity** parameter can prohibit using compartments for the resource.

- The **Your Own MTr** parameter defines whether resources assigned to this means of transport belong to your own fleet. This is just a descriptive parameter; the main planning-relevant properties are expressed by the multiresource parameters explained previously.

- The **Schedule MTr** parameter allows using the means of transport for schedules.

- The **GIS Quality** option determines whether a GIS is used for the distance and duration determination. If this option is selected, the GIS calculates the distance and duration. The duration determination takes account of the low, medium, and high speeds specified. If a GIS tool isn't used, the distance is calculated as a product of the straight-line distance and the distance factor, while the duration is based on the average speed entered. Refer to Section 3.2.3 for details on distance determination based on a means of transport and to Section 3.2.9 for integration of GIS tools.

- The sustainability factor (**Sustain. Factor**) models the carbon dioxide emissions.

- You can define one means of transport as the default for distance and duration determination (**Default MTr**). This default is only used if no specific means of transport could be determined for a capacity document at hand.

3.3.2 Equipment Groups and Types

The main idea of an *equipment type* is to define certain properties once for a type, which then get copied from the type into a new resource for the type at hand (note that you can also explicitly copy a resource). An *equipment group* is a grouping of multiple equipment types, with the main purpose to structure equipment types.

In Customizing, you can use the menu path **Transportation Management • Master Data • Resources • Define Equipment Groups and Equipment Types** to define the following groups and types, as shown in Figure 3.49:

- Vehicle groups and vehicle types in the **Vehicle Groups** view
- TU groups and TU types in the **Transportation Unit Groups** view
- Handling resource groups and handling resource types in the **Handling Resource Groups** view

Change View "Transportation Unit Types": Overview

Dialog Structure	TU Group	CN

∨ ▓ Transportation Unit Groups
  • ▓ Transportation Unit Types
  • ▓ Transportation Mode Assignment
∨ ▓ Handling Resource Groups
  • ▓ Handling Resource Types
∨ ▓ Vehicle Groups
  • ▓ Vehicle Types

Transportation Unit Types

TU Type	Description	
20B0	20 ft Bulk Cont, 20x8	
20G0	20 ft Dry Cont, 20x8	
20G1	20 ft Dry Cont, passive, 20x8	
20H0	20 ft Insulated Cont, 20x8	
20P1	20 ft Flat Cont, 20x8	
22B0	20 ft Bulk Cont, 20x8.6	
22G0	20 ft Dry Cont, 20x8.6	
22G1	20 ft Dry Cont, passive, 20x8.6	
22H0	20 ft Insulated Cont, 20x8.6	
22P1	20 ft Flat Cont, 20x8.6	
22P3	20 ft Flat Collapsible Cont, 20x8.6	
22P7	20 ft Platform Cont, 20x8.6	
22R1	20 ft Reefer Cont, 20x8.6	

Figure 3.49 Maintaining Equipment Types

A vehicle type is assigned to a means of transport and allows users to define certain properties that can be copied into new vehicle resources. A vehicle group is an abstract grouping of multiple vehicle types into a group.

TU groups and TU types are much more important for TU resources than vehicle groups and vehicle types for vehicle resources because they are the only way to structure TU resources into types and to group the types. Figure 3.50 shows one example with two TU groups consisting of four types each. While the means of transport hierarchy used for vehicle resources can have an arbitrary number of hierarchy levels, this TU hierarchy contains just two levels: the groups and the types. In the maintenance screen, you can also assign mode of transport categories to a TU group; in the preceding example, you would assign road, rail, and sea to containers and air mode of transport category to unit loading devices. We recommend using TU groups and types to structure your TU resources.

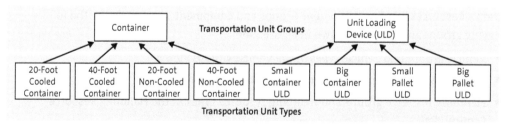

Figure 3.50 TU Groups and Types

In the same way, you can also define handling resource groups and types to structure your handling resources and copy certain properties from a type to a new handling resource.

Note that equipment groups and types can be used in a carrier profile to identify the capabilities of the carrier, as already mentioned in Section 3.1.2. The physical equipment properties are also used for forwarding order or quotation items of the type container. Based on the item type configuration, the equipment group is entered automatically, and equipment types of this group are displayed for selection. Depending on the equipment group and type, the system automatically calculates the tare weight and capacity. This data, together with the physical property data of the equipment type, is relevant for the planner and is then available in the forwarding order and subsequent documents.

Resource Classes

The system contains predefined resource classes. You can find these settings by following the IMG menu path **Transportation Management · Master Data · Resources · General Settings · Define Resource Class**.

3.3.3   Vehicle Resources

Vehicle resources are mainly used to represent trucks, trailers, locomotives and railcars. As the road mode of transport is relevant for almost every company dealing with transportation, we focus our discussion on trucks and trailers. We'll now explain vehicle resources in detail, before introducing compartments, vehicle combinations, and decreasing capacities.

Vehicle Resources

You can display and maintain existing resources or create a new resource via the menu path **Master Data · Resources · Define Resource**. From the initial screen, enter a name and resource type, and then click the **Create Resources** button. This takes you to the main resource maintenance screen shown in Figure 3.51, where you can maintain resources for all classes except for drivers. Alternatively, you can copy a resource from a template resource using the menu path **Master Data · Resources · Copy Resource from Template**. In the resource maintenance screen, the table in the top allows you to maintain some key properties that are included in the detailed tabs.

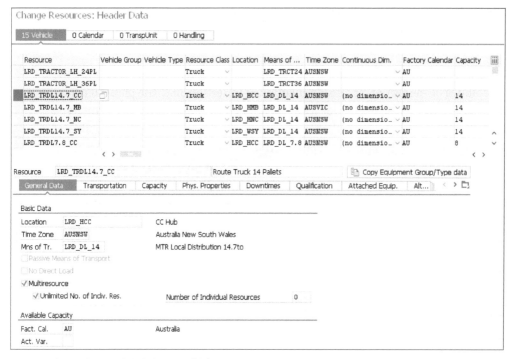

Figure 3.51 Maintaining a Vehicle Resource

The **General Data** tab allows you to define a depot location and a time zone. If a depot location is defined, the time zone is taken from it. You can assign a means of transport, which then determines whether it's a passive resource and allows direct loading, and then define that the resource is a multiresource and limit the number of instances it represents. Additionally, you can specify the factory calendar used for planning. To create or change a factory calendar in Customizing, follow the path **Transportation Management · Master Data · Calendar · Maintain Factory Calendar** (in SAP TM 9.6, the path is **SAP Transportation Management · SCM Basis · Master Data · Calendar · Maintain Factory Calendar**).

The **Transportation** tab defines the resource validity period and its registration number that can cover the license plate for trucks and trailers. You can set a planning block, choosing among predefined reason codes that can be maintained in Customizing, following the path **Transportation Management · Master Data · Resources · General Settings · Define Resource Planning Block Reason Codes**. You can also define a default driver for a truck resource, which gets pulled into a road freight order if a new road freight order is created for the truck resource at hand and the corresponding freight order type requires driver assignment. There are additional pure descriptive fields to define, for example, ownership of the resource or when it was taken into service.

The **Capacity** tab is key to define the loading capacity of the resource at hand. You can define its capacity from a weight and volume perspective as well as additional capacities for definable units of measures. For example, you can define a unit of measure for pallets and define the resource's capacity for it. Additionally, the internal length, width, and height are defined, which are also considered during planning when assigning objects with defined sizes.

The **Phys. Properties** tab specifies more details about the resource at hand, which are considered during load planning and load consolidation, as described in Chapter 6, Sections 6.7.7 and 6.7.8.

Resource Viewer to Verify and Maintain Physical Properties

Load planning and load consolidation use a lot of data maintained here, such as the width, length, height, number of axles, distance between the axles, maximum weight per axle group, and so on. It's crucial to work with correct data because even a single typo may lead to unexpected optimizer results.

Using the menu path **Master Data • Resource Viewer** (in SAP TM 9.6, the menu path is **Master Data • Resources • Resource Viewer**), you can search resources and display them three-dimensionally, as shown in Figure 3.52, which is an example of a truck with fixed double deck position. If you confuse the values for width and length of the truck in the physical properties, you can immediately detect this visually in a very intuitive way. Such a mistake would be hard to find at first glance when just checking the corresponding two data fields.

The resource viewer allows editing the physical properties and saving them in the resource master data, as depicted in Figure 3.53. The **Resource Configurator** section allows users to maintain general properties of the resource at hand, such as the number of axle groups, the type per axle (e.g., single or tandem), and the distances between axles. The **Sections** area enables users to define flexible split decks. In the shown example, the first part of the truck's cargo space offers using beam split decks, which can be positioned in the vertical range of 1 – 2.20 meters and have a height of 0.10 meters; no beam split decks are allowed in the last part of the truck. You can also define the maximum load weight on a split deck, whether it needs to be vertically positioned on a grid or is fully flexible within the specified vertical range, and whether it's removable; that is, it doesn't consume any space if not used.

You can also choose one vehicle type or TU type and visualize it three-dimensionally.

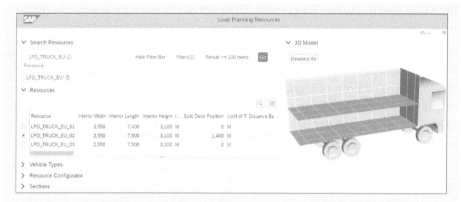

Figure 3.52 Search Criteria and Resource Overview in Resource Viewer

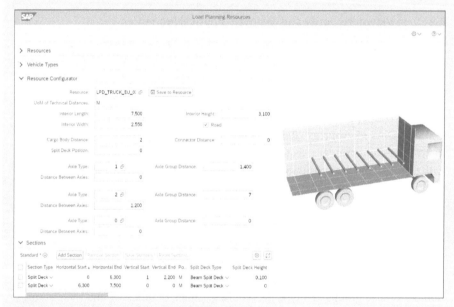

Figure 3.53 Maintaining Properties in the Resource Viewer

The **Downtimes** tab can be used to specify time segments in which resources aren't available. In general, they can be specified for all resource classes, including drivers (here they are maintained as absence times of the corresponding driver business partner). The actual availability of a resource within its validity period depends on the factory calendar, downtimes, and shift and break definitions. You can define a set of downtimes in which each downtime has a start and end date and time, a certain type (planned downtime for inspection in repair shop or resource inactive due to damage), a location, and a short description. For example, if a truck resource is planned for an inspection, you can define a corresponding downtime, including the location where the inspection takes place. Then, the transportation planner can plan the needed empty trips to move the truck to the location before the downtime begins, and any subsequent trip after the downtime would start from that location.

If you try to plan a capacity document overlapping with a downtime, the system will issue a warning message. Downtimes differ from a regular, scheduled nonworking time based on the factory calendar or the shift sequence (e.g., break or holiday) because the resource can still contain loaded goods during the weekend but not during downtime (e.g., because it gets repaired).

Additional tabs allow users to maintain the following mainly descriptive properties, as well as short texts:

- **Qualifications**
  You can choose among qualifications that have been defined in Customizing via menu path **Transportation Management** • **Master Data** • **Resources** • **Resource Attributes** • **Define Settings for Qualifications**. When assigning a default driver to a truck resource, the system checks whether the qualifications are matching.

- **Attached Equip.**
  You can select among the attached equipment items specified in Customizing using menu path **Transportation Management** • **Master Data** • **Resources** • **Resource Attributes** • **Define Settings for Attached Equipment**.

- **Alternative Names**
  You can select among the alternative names defined in Customizing using menu path **Transportation Management** • **Master Data** • **Resources** • **Resource Attributes** • **Define Categories for Alternative Names**.

- **Grouping**
  You can select among the groupings specified in Customizing using menu path **Transportation Management** • **Master Data** • **Resources** • **Resource Attributes** • **Define Settings for Grouping Attributes**.

Compartments

Trucks and trailers frequently have multiple compartments for transportation efficiency reasons. Let's review two examples from different industries:

- **Product incompatibilities**

  Different fuel types must not be mixed when transporting fuel to gas stations. A truck with five compartments can be used to transport up to five different fuel types. Any fuel type could go into any compartment, but each compartment can carry only one fuel type at a time. Serving a gas station demanding five fuel types could be done by one truck with five compartments, which is much more efficient than using five trucks without compartments.

- **Products requiring special conditions**

  Frozen, chilled, and ambient products require transportation with special temperature conditions. A truck with one frozen compartment, one chilled compartment, and one ambient compartment can transport all three product categories together, which is much more efficient than using trucks that offer only one temperature zone and don't have multiple compartments.

The definition of compartments for vehicle resources is structured as shown in Figure 3.54 and can be maintained in Customizing via menu path **Transportation Management · Master Data · Resources · Means of Transport and Compartment · Define Compartment Type**, as shown in Figure 3.55. You can assign a *compartment profile* to a means of transport, and the structure and properties of the compartment profile are used for all vehicle resources assigned to the means of transport. A compartment profile contains a set of *compartment types*, and one compartment type could even be used multiple times in a compartment profile.

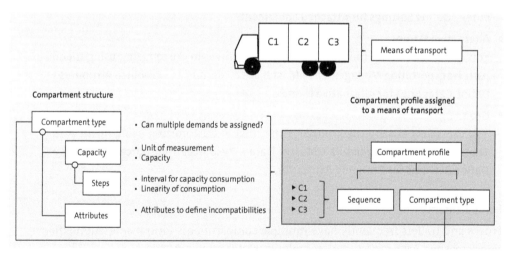

Figure 3.54 Relation between Vehicle Resources and Compartments

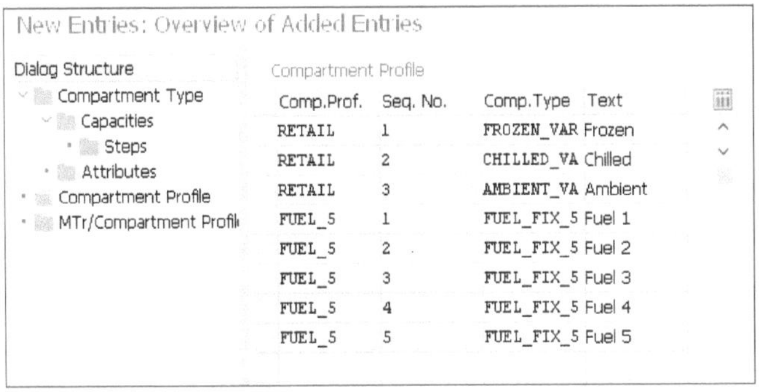

Figure 3.55 Maintaining Compartments

The compartment type defines the properties of one compartment in a vehicle resource, such as its capacity and its attributes, which can, for example, model its temperature-control capabilities to differentiate frozen, chilled, and ambient compartments and be used to define incompatibilities between transportation demands and a compartment with a certain attribute value. You can also define capacity steps modeling a partially step-wise and/or linear consumption of the compartment capacity by the loaded goods. This can be used for palletized goods and when compartment walls can be placed only between pallet rows; you can model that placing one or two pallets in a row that can contain three pallets already blocks the complete row from truck perspective (because these places aren't available for other compartments anymore). Figure 3.55 shows two compartment profiles: the profile RETAIL contains three different compartment types containing different attribute values (not shown), and the profile FUEL_5 contains five identical compartments.

The compartment type capacity allows users to model vehicle resources with *fixed compartments* and *variable compartments*. If the capacities of all assigned compartments add up to exactly the figure specified as the total capacity of the resource, the compartments are called *fixed*. If the capacities of all assigned compartments add up to a figure greater than the capacity of the resource, the compartments are called *variable*.

The compartments in retail scenarios are usually variable, meaning that the vehicle can be fully loaded with frozen goods, fully loaded with chilled goods, fully loaded with ambient goods, or loaded with any combination that doesn't exceed the vehicle resource capacity. In a fuel distribution scenario, by contrast, the compartments are usually fixed; that is, the total vehicle capacity can be fully used only by filling each compartment to its full capacity.

Vehicle Combinations

Trailers get moved by trucks, and a *means of transport combination* specifies which truck and trailer resources are allowed to move together in one combination. We refer to a *vehicle combination* when an actual combination of vehicle resource instances moves together.

Means of transport combinations can only be defined for road means of transport because rail usually offers a much wider range of combinations of locomotives and railcars, which would be quite time-consuming to maintain explicitly.

A means of transport combination represents one active vehicle and one or multiple passive vehicles. Refer to Chapter 6, Section 6.4.2, for more details and background on truck and trailer combinations.

You can define means of transport combinations in Customizing by following the menu path **Transportation Management • Master Data • Resources • Means of Transport and Compartment • Define Means-of-Transport Combinations** (see Figure 3.56). The combination contains a set of means of transport and defines the number of instances per entry. Usually, a means of transport combination can carry more goods than its individual entities. Due to legal restrictions, a vehicle combination may only be allowed to carry fewer goods than the sum of its entities could carry; this can be modeled by defining the capacity of a means of transport combination. You can also assign attribute values, which can be used to model incompatibilities, for example, between a means of transport combination and a location.

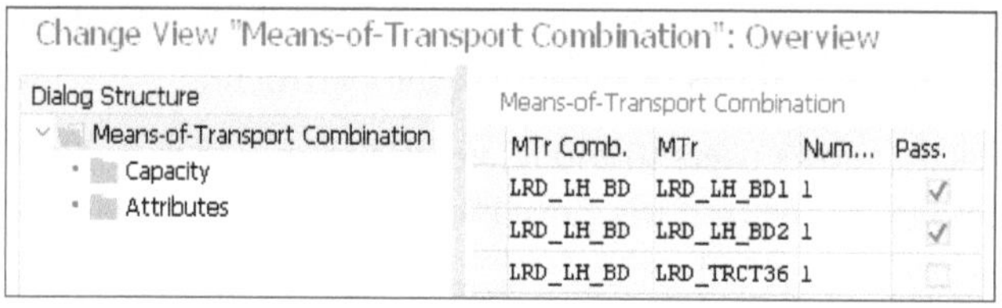

Figure 3.56 Maintaining Means of Transport Combinations

Figure 3.57 shows an example of a vehicle combination consisting of a truck and a trailer, each having three compartments. Capacity constraints can be defined for each compartment, for the truck, for the trailer, and for the vehicle combination that consists of the truck and the trailer.

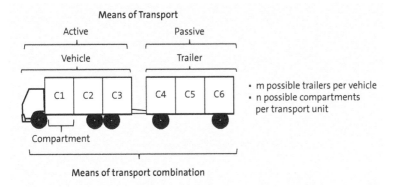

Figure 3.57 Means of Transport Combination with Compartments

Modeling Means of Transport Combinations

The VSR optimizer evaluates a succession of alternative vehicle combinations, beginning with the active vehicle and consecutively adding each of the passive vehicles. It's therefore essential to avoid any gaps in the number of permitted vehicle combinations. Consider the example depicted in Figure 3.56, which contains a tractor, trailer 1, and trailer 2. If you want the VSR optimizer to use this kind of combination, you also have to define a means of transport combination that represents the tractor and trailer 1.

Decreasing Capacities

One special feature is the modeling of decreasing capacities, which can be defined for both active and passive vehicle resources. In some transportation scenarios, goods are transported for several customers simultaneously and are separated by partitions within the vehicle. These partitions reduce the total capacity of the vehicle because a partition itself consumes a certain amount of capacity. The decrease in the capacity of the vehicle or TU resource can be defined based on the number of stops. You can define decreasing capacities independently of compartments using the menu path **Profiles and Settings • Create Decreasing Capacity Settings** (in SAP TM 9.6, the menu path is **Application Administration • Planning • General Settings • Decreasing Capacity settings**). Figure 3.58 shows the decreases for ranges of stops being defined for each means of transport. Each capacity decrease can be maintained absolutely or relatively and is based on the number of stops in the relevant stop range.

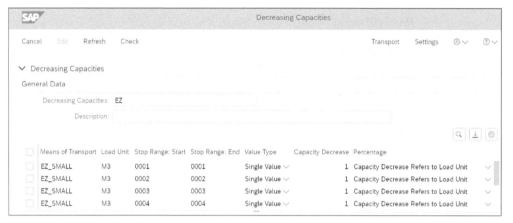

Figure 3.58 Decreasing Capacities

3.3.4   Transportation Unit Resources

TU resources are used to model containers, which are used in road, rail, and sea modes of transport, or unit loading devices commonly used in air freight business. Figure 3.59 shows that you can maintain them in the same maintenance screen as vehicle resources. As the maintenance capabilities have already been described in Section 3.3.3, we just highlight the main differences here.

A TU resource isn't assigned to a means of transport. As consequence, it's also not assigned to a mode of transport, there is no concept to differentiate between single resource and multiresource, and so on.

Like vehicle resources that can be structured by vehicle groups and vehicle types, TU resources can be structured by TU groups and TU types, as explained in Section 3.3.2.

Transportation Units and Transportation Unit Resources

TUs form a class of documents representing transportation by trailers, railcars, containers, and packages. The specific documents—called trailer units, railcar units, container units, and package units—are explained in Chapter 6, Section 6.4. TU resources are used to model container resources for which you can create documents called container units. Trailer resources and railcar resources are represented by passive vehicle resources with means of transport assigned to road and rail mode of transport, respectively. There is no dedicated resource for a package; instead, the packaging material is used to define the relevant properties for a package.

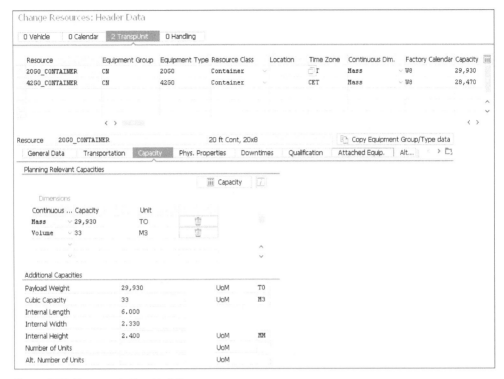

Figure 3.59 Transportation Unit Resource

3.3.5 Calendar and Handling Resources

While vehicle and TU resources model the transportation of goods, calendar and handling resources define when loading and unloading can take place at a location. These resources are considered by scheduling and automated planning (see Chapter 6, Section 6.6 and Section 6.7), and their availability and capacity can be visualized best in the Gantt chart (see Chapter 6, Section 6.6.5), which is much more intuitive than a tabular list of time periods. You can define calendar and handling resources in the same maintenance screen used for vehicle resources and TU resources.

Let's briefly highlight some of the main characteristics of these resources:

- **Calendar Resources**
  Calendar resources model operating times, which define during which time periods loading and unloading can take place. You can assign a calendar resource to a specific location, but you don't have to—that is, you could even reuse the same calendar resource at various locations.

- **Handling Resources**

  Handling resources are used for handling transportation orders at a location—that is, for loading goods onto a truck (outbound) or unloading goods from a trailer (inbound). For example, handling resources can be used to map loading ramps or doors (see Figure 3.60), and they generalize calendar resources.

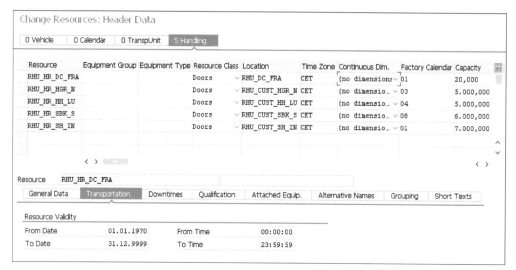

Figure 3.60 Handling Resource

In addition to operating times, they can define restrictions regarding the maximum number of activities that can be executed simultaneously. You can specify time-dependent capacities in the capacity profile and maintain downtimes to restrict the resource availability.

3.4   Summary

In this chapter, we've introduced general master data, such as the organization structure and business partners, and explained how to create and integrate them in the different deployment options of SAP TM.

The transportation network defines how transportation demands can be executed from a geographical perspective, based on concepts such as reachability between locations and usage of transshipment locations.

We described the available resource classes that represent trucks, trailers, containers, and so on that are used to move goods, and we explained calendar and handling resources that impose additional constraints on loading and unloading goods at your locations.

Both the transportation network and the resources are key to defining how to plan and execute your transportation.

The next chapter explains how transportation requirements are represented in SAP TM.

Chapter 4

Transportation Requirements and Order Management

Regardless of whether you're looking from the perspective of a ship-per, a logistics service provider, or a carrier, the transportation process starts with a request for transportation services. This chapter covers the different ways to start the process in SAP Transportation Management and how to record the requests in the system.

When we look at a very simplified, document-driven process flow in SAP Transportation Management (SAP TM), we see that not many documents are used to cover the transportation process. In fact, there are only three process steps (leaving out Transportation Charge Management for the moment) that cover the transportation planning process, as you can see in Figure 4.1. In SAP TM, the starting point of the process is always a *transportation request* (TRQ), followed by freight unit and transportation order.

Figure 4.1 Transportation Planning Process

SAP TM can be used to monitor and execute the transportation processes of many different industries, so transportation process approaches can vary significantly.

These approaches require different ways of starting the transportation process in the system. For example, for a shipper, transportation isn't the core business, so the focus is laid not on the ordering and execution of transportation services, but on manufacturing, materials management, and so on. The shipper will most likely use sales and distribution (SD) or materials management (MM) functionality to cover these processes. Because the transportation process isn't the core business, the leading system in the entire value-generating process should be the core SD or MM functionality because it handles processes that produce the competitive advantage. The SAP TM functionality therefore *receives* information; it's not allowed to alter any information that is important for the manufacturing process.

To work within this scenario, SAP S/4HANA integrates the SD and/or MM functionality with the SAP TM functionality by sharing information across multiple documents. We cover this integration in Section 4.1.1.

However, if we look at the transportation process from the perspective of a logistics service provider (LSP) or carrier, the transportation process *is* the core process. Therefore, more emphasis needs to be placed on the information generated by the transportation process. Because the SD functionality doesn't provide detailed enough information for the LSP's and carrier's needs, the information needs to be generated in the SAP TM functionality, which is now the leading information (i.e., process-driving) functionality.

Because the SD integration doesn't deliver sufficient information for transportation as a core business, the TRQ needs to be created in the SAP TM functionality itself. So how can these different requirements be covered with only one document, as shown in Figure 4.1? The answer is that they can't. Although the main process flow remains the same, we need to take a closer look at the TRQ process step. When zooming in on this step in Figure 4.2, we can see that several documents are necessary.

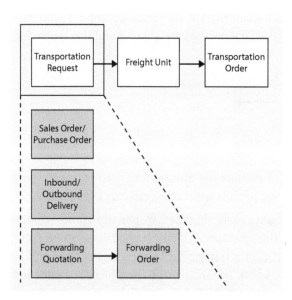

Figure 4.2 Transportation Request Documents

However, it's important to remember that all documents and the respective process variants lead to the common next step: freight unit building (FUB), which will be covered in Chapter 6.

Figure 4.2 shows the different TRQ documents. While the SD sales order (SO), MM purchase order (PO), and inbound and outbound deliveries cater to the shipper's transportation process variant, the forwarding quotation and forwarding order cover the LSP's and carrier's requirements.

Now, let's delve deeper into both process variants and focus on how these documents support the start of the transportation process.

4.1   Triggering the Transportation Management Process

In Chapter 1, we introduced the tight integration across different functionalities as one of the major benefits of SAP S/4HANA. In this section, we take an in-depth look at how that integration can be established. First, it must be said that you don't need to be an SD component expert to establish the integration into the SAP TM functionality, but it *is* advantageous to know a little bit about the standard SD and MM document flow.

Triggering the Process in SAP S/4HANA versus SAP TM 9.6

Section 4.1.1, Section 4.1.2, and Section 4.1.3 will deal with triggering the transportation management process if the SAP TM functionality resides in the same SAP S/4HANA system as the SD and MM functionality.

However, you can also run the SAP TM functionality in a separate SAP S/4HANA system or use SAP TM 9.6 and connect it to an SAP S/4HANA or SAP ERP system. This integration is described in Section 4.1.4. However, in that section, we take for granted you've understood the concepts described in Section 4.1.1 to Section 4.1.3 already.

SAP TM can integrate the following SD and MM documents:

- Sales orders (SOs)
- Purchase orders (POs)
- Stock transfer orders (STOs)
- Inbound deliveries

- Outbound deliveries
- Scheduling agreements (only in SAP TM 9.6 in connection with an SAP ERP system)

As always, you can't immediately begin with integrating orders or deliveries into SAP TM. First, you need to make sure the prerequisites for the integration are fulfilled. In general, there is only one major prerequisite: the master data. With the move of the SAP TM functionality into SAP S/4HANA, this prerequisite is almost met automatically. As described in Chapter 3, the master data defined to create documents in the SD and MM functionality is reused by the SAP TM functionality. However, some basic considerations should be made when defining master data in SAP S/4HANA in case this master data should also be used in the SAP TM functionality:

- **Locations and business partners**
  When defining orders in the SD or MM functionality, we usually deal with business partners and shipping points or plants. However, the SAP TM functionality will require entities called *locations*. If you've dealt with SD and MM functionality in the past, you'll notice that the entity of a location isn't used in SD and MM. However, SAP S/4HANA now provides this kind of entity.

  For SD and MM documents to trigger the transportation management process, the business partners, shipping points, and plants need to be translated to locations. This is done automatically by the SAP S/4HANA system when saving an order or delivery that is integrated with the SAP TM component. The system checks whether locations already exist for the shipping point and business partner of the order or delivery and, if not, creates them.

  Alternatively, this can be done using program /SAPAPO/CREATE_LOCATION in Transaction SE38. The use of this program is a prerequisite to using SAP TM in SAP S/4HANA later on because the SD and MM functionality doesn't use locations but the SAP TM functionality requires them.

- **Organizational data**
  In the transportation process, it's optional to assign a sales organization to a TRQ. However, if you want to represent the sales organization from the SO in the SAP TM TRQ, you need to transfer the organizational model to SAP TM as you can create an independent organizational model in SAP TM.

Integration of Master Data with the Same Names

Although shipping points and plants can use the same number in SD and MM, this becomes an issue when creating locations out of them because the locations require a unique number. Therefore, a business add-in (BAdI) can be implemented to avoid potential duplicates when creating locations for shipping points and plants. The most common way to overcome this issue is to employ prefixes to the location ID that identifies locations as shipping points (e.g., using the prefix **SP**) or plants (when using the prefix **PL**).

In Customizing, you can get to these BAdI implementations by following the IMG menu path **Transportation Management • Business Add-Ins (BAdIs) for Transportation Management • Master Data • Transportation Network • Location • BAdI: Adaptation of Location Details and Descriptions**.

Customizing Paths in SAP S/4HANA

The IMG paths we depict in this section are for an SAP TM component hosted in an SAP S/4HANA system. The IMG paths for an SAP TM system based on SAP NetWeaver, such as SAP TM 9.6, can differ but are largely similar. Where there are significant differences, we'll make a note in the text.

Furthermore, some *business functions* need to be activated for the SAP TM integration. The following business functions are required; some of them are specifically designed for the SAP TM integration:

- LOG_TM_ORD_INT
- LOG_TM_ORD_INT_II
- LOG_TM_ORD_INT_III
- LOG_TM_ORD_INT_IV
- LOG_TM_IV_INT
- SD_01
- OPS_ADVRETURNS_1

These business functions are necessary for the integration with the SAP TM functionality within the same SAP S/4HANA system. For integrating with SAP TM functionality outside of the same system or an SAP TM 9.6 system, see Section 4.1.4.

4.1.1   Sales Order Integration

The most commonly used type of integration between SD and SAP TM is the *SO integration*. With SO integration, shippers use the SAP TM functionality to organize the transport of goods sold to the customer. In this section, we focus on how to trigger the transportation management process from a SO.

We activate the integration of SOs into the SAP TM functionality with the IMG path **Integration with Other SAP Components · Transportation Management · Logistics Integration · Activate Integration of Sales Documents**.

As you can see in Figure 4.3, the activation of a sales document always depends on three things:

- Sales organization plus distribution channel and division
- SO type
- Shipping condition (if not relevant, you can leave **Shp.Cond.** empty)

Change View "Sales Document Integration": Overview

Sales Document Integration

Sales org.	Distr. Chl	Division	Sales doc. type	Shp.Cond.	Control Key	TM No.	Log. Int. Profile	Control Key Description
0001	01	01	LZ		0001			Transfer Sales Order, O. Delivery; Order Scheduling inactive
0001	01	01	RAOR	01	RACC		RAIP	Logistics Integration Control Key
0001	01	01	RARE	01	RACC		RAIP	Logistics Integration Control Key
0001	02	01	ZOR	01	0001			Transfer Sales Order, O. Delivery; Order Scheduling inactive

Figure 4.3 Integration of Sales Documents

The activation of the sales document is done via a *control key*, which defines which document types should be integrated. Figure 4.4 shows the standard control keys. Note that the control keys also define whether the SOs are integrated with the SAP TM functionality within the SAP S/4HANA system or are sent to an external SAP TM system (inside another SAP S/4HANA instance) or SAP TM 9.6. This is defined with the **Integration Mode** as shown in Figure 4.4. In this section, we'll only discuss the integration with the SAP TM functionality within the same SAP S/4HANA instance.

Control Key Parameters

Ctl Key	Integration Mode		SO to TM	PO to TM	Outbd Del.	Inbd Del.	SO Sched.	PO Conf.	Pln. Stat.	Control Key Description
0001	External TM System	∨	✓	☐	✓	☐	☐	☐	✓	Transfer Sales Order, O. Delivery; Order Scheduling inactive
0002	External TM System	∨	✓	☐	☐	☐	☐	☐	☐	Transfer Sales Order; Order Scheduling inactive
0003	External TM System	∨	✓	☐	✓	☐	✓	☐	☐	Transfer Sales Order, O. Delivery; Order Scheduling active
0051	I Internal TM Component	∨	✓	☐	☐	☐	☐	☐	☐	Integrate Sales Order
0052	I Internal TM Component	∨	✓	☐	✓	☐	☐	☐	☐	Integrate Sales Order, Outbound Delivery
0053	I Internal TM Component	∨	☐	☐	✓	☐	☐	☐	☐	Integrate Outbound Delivery
0054	I Internal TM Component	∨	☐	✓	☐	☐	☐	☐	☐	Integrate Purchase Order
0055	I Internal TM Component	∨	☐	✓	☐	✓	☐	☐	☐	Integrate Purchase Order, Inbound Delivery
0056	I Internal TM Component	∨	☐	☐	☐	✓	☐	☐	☐	Integrate Inbound Delivery

Figure 4.4 Control Keys for Order and Delivery Integration

When looking in detail at Figure 4.3, you'll notice that an SAP *TM number* can be entered in some cases and a *logistics integration profile* was maintained in other cases. The SAP TM number is used when integrating with external SAP TM systems, thus we'll come back to this in Section 4.1.4. The logistics integration profile as depicted in Figure 4.5 is crucial to the entire transportation management process because it consolidates all configuration that is required to trigger the transportation management process, such as the freight unit building rule (FUBR) or the decision regarding whether to plan on requested or confirmed quantities.

Logistics Integration Profile							
Profile	Description	Freight Unit Building Rule	FUB Rule Condition	Autom. FU Building	Plan on Requested or Confirmed ...	Actual Qty	Incoterm Loc. Stage Bldng
DIL1	DI1 Log. Profile: Split per 100 kg		DI_FUBR_COND	✓	01 Plan on Requested Quan... ⌄		Two Active Stages – T... ⌄
HD3O	HP Parcel	HP_PARCEL		✓	01 Plan on Requested Quan... ⌄		Two Active Stages – T... ⌄
HKP	HKP Split per 100 kg	CSI-FUB		✓	01 Plan on Requested Quan... ⌄		Two Active Stages – T... ⌄
LJLI	Johnny's Logistics Integration P...	ZLJ_FUBR		✓	01 Plan on Requested Quan... ⌄		Two Active Stages – T... ⌄
MEU1	MEU Log. Profile: Estimate Pack...	MEU_FUBR_PB		✓	01 Plan on Requested Quan... ⌄		Two Active Stages – T... ⌄

Figure 4.5 Logistics Integration Profile

When integrating an SD SO with the SAP TM functionality, a freight unit is created directly from the SO. The logistics integration profile, which we assigned to a SO document type and—optionally—the sales organization and shipping condition in Figure 4.3 defined how the freight unit was built. We'll discuss freight units in further detail in Chapter 6, Section 6.2.

In Figure 4.5, you can see a setting defining the system behavior when dealing with incoterm locations. Usually, the freight unit created out of the order or delivery would only contain one stage, from the source to destination. Potential intermediate stops would be determined during the planning process. However, the incoterm location defined in the order or delivery can have an impact on the routing of the freight unit.

In Figure 4.5, the **Incoterm Loc. Stage Bldng** field defines how the incoterm location of the order should be interpreted.

Depending on the Customizing entry you've chosen, two stages are created in the freight unit. As shown in Figure 4.6, stage 1, represented by the bold line, leads from the source location to the incoterm location. Stage 2, shown as the dashed line, leads from the incoterm location to the destination location.

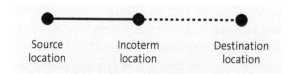

Figure 4.6 Stage Split on Incoterm Location

Depending on the scenario, the stage that is relevant for the shipper's planning can be stage 1 or stage 2. Remember, a freight unit represents an SAP S/4HANA SO as well as an SAP S/4HANA PO and an STO. This means that freight units can be used for both outbound transportation processes and inbound transportation processes.

Therefore, the Customizing entries apply to both outbound and inbound processes. With this Customizing entry, you can define whether the shipper is responsible for stage 1 or stage 2. The Customizing entry also defines whether the stage the shipper isn't responsible for should be created at all. If it should be created, it will be created as a *statistical stage*, meaning it has no influence on the freight unit and therefore on the planning process steps.

If you've integrated an order that represents an internal transfer of goods, such as with an STO, and the shipper is nevertheless responsible for the entire transportation, you can also choose to create two relevant stages. If no incoterm location is entered in the order, no stage splitting is done during FUB.

In orders, you can assign multiple customers and creditors to the order using different partner functions. In the freight unit, you can see on the **Business Partners** tab that the documents in SAP TM also apply to the participation of different business partners in the transportation process.

However, you need to map the defined partner functions of the order to the *business partner roles*. You can define the partner functions in Customizing by following the IMG menu path **Transportation Management • Master Data • Business Partners • Define Partner Functions**. In a standard SAP S/4HANA system, the most common party roles are already predefined. The business partner roles are defined in the master data record of the business partner. This defines what roles the business partner can assume (e.g., vendor, driver, carrier, etc.). To use this information in the SAP TM documents, the business partner role needs to be translated into a partner function. This can be defined in Customizing using the IMG path **Transportation Management • Master Data • Assign BP Roles to Partner Functions**.

If you can't see any freight unit being created or updated in SAP TM in SAP S/4HANA, you can check if an output was triggered. To do so, access the SO you've just saved, and then go to the output overview by following the menu path **Extras · Output · Header**. If you see an output of type TRSO with a green traffic light, the output message was created successfully.

4.1.2   Integration of Materials Management Orders

The integration of MM orders is, in many regards, similar to the integration of SD documents. The most important Customizing activity in SAP S/4HANA for the transfer of MM documents is the specification of the control keys and logistics integration profiles, as just described in the previous section.

The integration of purchasing documents can be activated in Customizing using the IMG path **Integration with Other SAP Components · Transportation Management · Logistics Integration · Activate Integration of Purchasing Documents**. Similar to the activation of sales documents, the logistics integration profile and control key define how the integration with the SAP TM functionality is processed.

4.1.3   Integration Scenarios

If the SAP TM system is the dedicated system leading the transportation process, you would probably set up the integration scenario as shown in Figure 4.7.

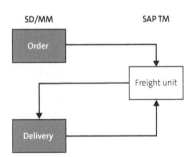

Figure 4.7 Order Integration with Delivery Proposal

The order is created in SD or MM and then integrated into the SAP TM functionality. In SAP TM, the freight units are created automatically. Now the process continues in SAP TM. The freight units are planned on freight orders according to the delivery dates, service levels, incoterms, and so on that were defined on the orders.

After the planning of the freight unit is done, we know a more precise delivery date of the goods that were ordered. This information can then be played back to SD or MM, where delivery documents are created accordingly. This process step is called the *delivery proposal.*

Delivery proposals are used to propagate planning information from SAP TM to SD or MM, where deliveries are then created. The process is called delivery proposal and not delivery creation because, in the end, SD and MM decide how deliveries should be created. The information for the delivery proposal derives from the freight units.

After you've finished planning the freight units, follow the menu path **Logistics Integration · Create Deliveries.** When you enter a selection profile (preferably the same one you've used for planning), your freight units are displayed. Select the freight units you want to create delivery proposals for, and choose **Create Delivery Proposals.** You can review the proposals at the bottom of the screen and then send the proposals to SD or MM by clicking **Create Deliveries.**

The delivery proposals are created using settings and information from the freight units. While the delivery dates are collected from the freight order that is now assigned to the freight units, the quantities are taken from the freight units themselves. SAP TM also tries to consolidate several freight units into one delivery proposal, if possible, for example when they are planned onto the same freight order. However, the consolidation is done only if the order allows order consolidation.

Speaking of quantities, it's also possible to create delivery proposals based on the quantities actually picked up by the carrier. This scenario is especially important for bulk transportation and only applicable if delivery creation can be done only after execution has already started. In this scenario, the freight orders are created based on the freight units and sent to the carrier, and the carrier picks up the goods. As part of the execution process, which we delve deeper into in Chapter 8, Section 8.1, the carrier now reports the actual weight and volume of the goods picked up.

When the **Actual Qty** checkmark is selected in the logistics integration profile (refer to Figure 4.5), the delivery proposal is created based on the actual quantity reported by the carrier and not based on the planned quantity of the freight unit.

After the delivery proposals are released, delivery documents are created. SD and MM might split one SAP TM-based delivery proposal by creating several deliveries, possibly due to additional split criteria maintained in the order and delivery document type Customizing. However, no data (e.g., dates or quantities sent from SAP TM) is changed, and separate delivery proposals created in SAP TM aren't consolidated into one delivery in SD or MM.

The delivery proposal in SAP TM also takes into account that SD and MM consume order schedule lines in chronological order. Therefore, the SAP TM functionality proposes a delivery for a schedule line of an order item only if all schedule lines of the same order item with earlier delivery dates already have an assigned delivery.

In SAP TM, you can also define how delivery proposals should be created. These settings are consolidated in a *delivery profile*. Although the delivery profile is optional, it makes sense to create a profile to reuse the same settings every time you want to create delivery proposals. You can define delivery profiles via the SAP Fiori launchpad menu path **Profiles and Settings • Create Delivery Profile**. The settings you can define here concern how and if freight units can be consolidated into one delivery proposal and which freight units may not be consolidated.

One option of the delivery profile is to "fix" the planning result for freight units and freight orders by selecting the **Fix Planning Results** checkbox, which is shown in Figure 4.8. Fixing the planning means after the planning results are transferred via the delivery proposals, they can no longer be changed in SAP TM. This is a good strategy because you might continue processing the transferred data in the orders and deliveries, as well. You'll learn more about fixing freight orders in Chapter 6. You can define how the delivery proposals should be created (e.g., one proposal per item, one proposal per freight unit, etc.).

Control		
Fix Planning Results:	☐	
Delivery Creation:		⌄
Incompatibility Settings:		⬚ Display
Aggregate Order Items:	☐	
Exclude FUs/FOs blocked for execution:	☐	
Exclude FUs/FOs blocked for planning:	☐	

Figure 4.8 Delivery Profile

The last feature of delivery profiles that we want to mention is incompatibilities, which we introduced in Chapter 2. Incompatibilities in delivery profiles can be used to prevent certain freight units or items from being consolidated into one delivery proposal.

Delivery profiles are optional and especially unnecessary if you've already planned the freight units; in this case, SAP TM considers the freight units consolidated on freight orders. Settings such as incompatibilities are already taken into consideration during the planning process. However, if you want to create delivery proposals *before* the freight units are planned, you can do this as well. In this case, the settings in the delivery profile are crucial to help SAP TM decide which freight units should be consolidated.

In a daily business, you probably won't manually create delivery proposals every time you've finished planning some freight units. Therefore, background report /SCMTMS/ DLV_BATCH was created for you to run as a batch job. You need to define a selection profile by selecting your freight units or freight orders; the background report does exactly what you can do interactively in the SAP Fiori launchpad (skipping your review, of course).

After the delivery proposals have been sent, deliveries are created. SAP TM receives information about the status of the delivery creation. The delivery type being used for the delivery creation is the one defined in the SD or MM setup. If you've activated the transfer of this delivery type to SAP TM as well, then not only is a short message about the delivery creation transferred to SAP TM, but even more happens—the delivery is integrated, and the freight unit, initially created for the order, is updated with information from the delivery. You might be wondering what we can do with the delivery information now because the planning process has already happened. Recall that SD or MM might create deliveries slightly differently from the delivery proposal; this information is then represented in the updated freight unit.

If you look into the document flow of the freight unit now, you can see not only the SAP TM documents but also the order and delivery documents. What you'll also notice is that the order is now a predecessor document of the delivery, and the delivery is again a predecessor document of the freight unit (even though the freight unit was created before the delivery).

In the integration scenario described previously, SAP TM was leading the planning process; it decided not only how the planning should be done, but also whether and how the items of the order were split or consolidated. In some cases, it makes sense to leave that decision in SD or MM. Because the freight unit can be created from the order and the delivery, you can decide whether to leave out the integration of either one.

Figure 4.9 shows how the integration scenario works if SD or MM is still the leading system for delivery creation and item order consolidation. In this case, the order would not trigger the transportation management process and thus the freight unit creation. Only after the delivery is created for the order should freight units be created.

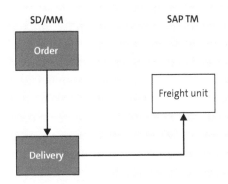

Figure 4.9 Delivery Integration without Delivery Proposals

Those freight units now better represent the splits and consolidations that have been done previously in SD or MM. Planning can now start, although the planning results don't affect the delivery dates of the delivery anymore. Therefore, make sure the dates in the freight unit are considered as hard constraints during planning. (See Chapter 6 for more information about soft and hard constraints in planning.)

So far in this section, we've only delved into the architectural setup of SAP TM as part of the same SAP S/4HANA system instance as the SD and MM functionality. This setup is called *internal SAP TM component integration*. As you can see in Figure 4.10 ❶, the SAP TM component can directly communicate with the SD and MM components without the need of any cross-system messages.

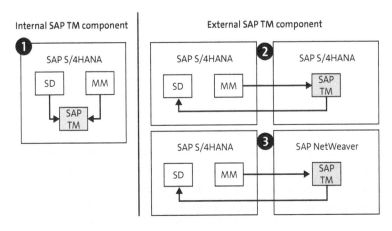

Figure 4.10 Architectural Integration Scenarios

279

However, there are also cases where SAP TM isn't part of the same system instance as the SD or MM components. This case is called *external SAP TM system integration*. The external SAP TM system integration can be subdivided into two scenarios. Scenario ❷ in Figure 4.10 describes the case of several SAP S/4HANA systems being run in parallel, of which one hosts the SAP TM component. This makes sense in large-scale companies that require multiple SAP S/4HANA systems but still want to use a centralized transportation management system. The functionality and user experience in this scenario is exactly the same as in scenario ❶, only the integration path is different.

In scenario ❸, SAP S/4HANA communicates with an SAP TM system that isn't based on the SAP S/4HANA stack (refer to Chapter 2 for more details on the technical foundation of the SAP TM component) but on an SAP NetWeaver stack. This could be an SAP TM 9.6 system that hosts the same functionality as the SAP TM component in SAP S/4HANA or an older release of SAP TM.

When using an external SAP TM system integration, we can no longer create the freight units directly from the orders and deliveries. In this case, we need an intermediary document in SAP TM to reflect the information passed from the order and/or delivery. The document representing the order's information in SAP TM is called *order-based transportation requirement* (OTR) and is a copy of the data maintained in the SO or PO (or scheduling agreement).

The delivery documents is represented in SAP TM by the *delivery-based transportation requirement* (DTR). Both OTR and DTR are read-only documents in SAP TM as they represent the order's and delivery's information in the SAP S/4HANA system that is the information leading system. Any change in order quantity therefore has to be maintained in the order or delivery and propagated to the OTR and DTR document. In the following section, we'll now take a more detailed look at the OTR and DTR document and how the overall process flow differs with these documents in place.

4.1.4   Order-Based and Delivery-Based Transportation Requirements

Let's assume we're using an external SAP TM component, either in a separate (stand-alone) instance of SAP S/4HANA to the SD and MM component or SAP TM 9.6. After an SO is created, a web service will send information from SAP S/4HANA to SAP TM. After the web service is successfully executed, a document is created in the SAP TM system; this is the OTR, which represents the SO data generated in SAP S/4HANA and carries all information relevant for the transportation process.

Orders and Deliveries Originating in SAP ERP

This section mainly covers the process of how data is sent from SD and MM functionality to SAP TM functionality that isn't part of the same SAP S/4HANA instance as SD and MM. We'll discuss the integration with the example of using the SD and MM functionality in SAP S/4HANA. However, the information described in this section also holds true when using SD and MM functionality in an SAP ERP system (IMG paths might be slightly different in an SAP ERP system than described in this section).

In the following sections, we'll look at the technology and configuration involved to transfer information to standalone SAP TM in SAP S/4HANA or SAP TM 9.6 and how it's processed, starting with the integration of order documents and covering delivery documents later on.

Order Documents

Recall Figure 4.3 in which we activated the integration of sales documents. Remember that we mentioned the SAP TM number that can be maintained in this Customizing activity, which is only relevant when communicating with an external SAP TM component. You'll notice when you fill in this field that no F4 help is available. The purpose of this field is to link one SAP S/4HANA system to several SAP TM systems. If several SAP TM systems are linked to one SAP S/4HANA system, and the SAP TM number is filled, SAP S/4HANA decides to which SAP TM system the order should be sent, based on the entries made in the table shown previously in Figure 4.3. However, you can enter anything you like here. The "navigation" of which logical system the message is routed to is done entirely in SAP Process Integration, where the string sent from SAP S/4HANA is interpreted and translated into a logical system. If you encounter such a situation, consult an SAP Process Integration expert to ensure that the routing is performed correctly.

In contrast to the direct creation of freight units upon saving the SO or PO, a message needs to be created that sends information from SAP S/4HANA to SAP TM. Therefore, the SO needs to create an output.

SD has a feature called *output determination* that is used to control the output—meaning follow-up activities, messages, and documents—for sales, shipping, transportation, and billing. It's used to exchange information with external and internal systems that represent business partners when looking at it from a process perspective.

Output determination can automatically propose output for an SD document using the condition technique that we already know from SAP ERP (not to be mistaken with Business Rules Framework plus [BRF+] conditions used in the SAP TM functionality).

As you can see in Figure 4.11, the core of the output determination is the output determination procedure, which consists of steps that are supposed to be executed in the given order. Each step represents a condition of a defined condition type; this condition determines whether an output of the defined output type should be triggered.

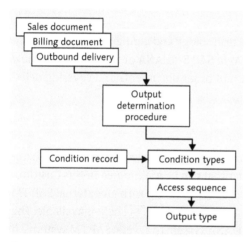

Figure 4.11 Output Determination in SD

The *condition type* is linked to the output type and can contain condition records that define when an output should be triggered. In terms of structure, a *condition record* is a table (like the decision table in conditions used in the SAP TM functionality) that is used to find a value. However, in this condition technique, a condition type can contain several condition records of different structures (e.g., one condition record where the input data is sales organization and customer, and a second condition record where the input data is order type).

With the *access sequence*, you can define in which order the condition records should be processed. Because the condition type is linked to the output type, you don't need to define which output needs to be triggered. This is implicitly done in the output determination procedure, where you define a condition type.

Recall that the output type is linked to the condition type, meaning that after the condition type finds a suitable result, the output of this output type is triggered. In SAP S/4HANA, several output types are available that represent print output, electronic data interchange (EDI) messages, application-to-application (A2A) messages, email, and so on. Some of these are shown in Figure 4.12.

For the integration of the SO, you need to create a new output type (output type TRSO). To do this in your SAP S/4HANA system, follow the IMG menu path **Sales and Distribution • Basic Functions • Output Determination • Output Determination • Output Determination Using the Condition Technique • Maintain Output Determination for Sales Documents • Maintain Output Types**.

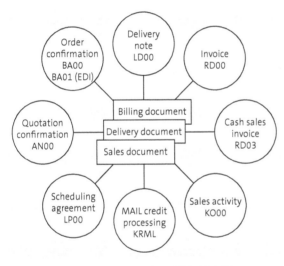

Figure 4.12 Output Types in SAP S/4HANA SD

To maintain the output type TRSO, you need to define general data, processing routines, and partner functions, as shown on Figure 4.13.

After the output type is configured, you can add it to the output determination procedure by following the IMG menu path **Sales and Distribution • Basic Functions • Output Determination • Output Determination • Output Determination Using the Condition Technique • Maintain Output Determination for Sales Documents • Maintain Output Determination Procedure**. Simply add a new step with condition type TRSO and requirement 27 to procedure V10000.

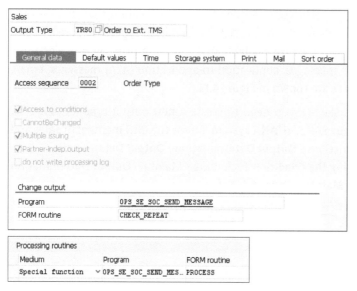

Figure 4.13 Output Type TRSO

Assignment of Output Determination Procedures

This chapter assumes use of the standard output determination procedure and the standard SO type for integration. However, it's clear that this might not always be the case. If you're using a different SO type, you can assign an output determination procedure to the order type by following the IMG menu path **Sales and Distribution · Basic Functions · Output Determination · Output Determination · Output Determination Using the Condition Technique · Maintain Output Determination for Sales Documents · Assign Output Determination Procedures**.

After you've configured these SAP S/4HANA settings (for more details on the configuration steps, consult the guide "Basic Settings and Integration for SAP ERP and SAP S/4HANA" found in the SAP Help Portal for SAP TM), a message according to output type TRSO is always sent when a SO has been created, updated, or deleted.

In contrast to SD documents, MM documents (e.g., POs) use the workflow technology known from previous SAP ERP releases for processing the output. Therefore, error handling as described for the SO isn't possible for POs, STOs, or inbound deliveries.

The OTR is the corresponding SAP TM document that contains all transportation-relevant information from the SAP S/4HANA orders. It can represent four things:

- SOs
- POs
- STOs
- Scheduling agreements

For SAP TM, it doesn't matter whether the predecessor document was an SO, STO, PO, or scheduling agreement. The OTR represents all of these SAP S/4HANA document types.

Remember from Chapter 2, Section 2.3.1, that there is a singleton condition that is used to define the OTR type of integration SAP S/4HANA orders. You can create and define a condition of the condition type /SCMTMS/OTR_TYPE to differentiate OTRs by type. Among other information, you can also use the SO type used in SAP S/4HANA for the condition definition. There is a predefined data access definition that you can use for this. If the condition doesn't find a result, the default type is used. The default type is defined in Customizing for OTR types with a corresponding flag.

Let's take a close look at the OTR document itself. You'll notice that, compared to other SAP TM documents, the amount of information is relatively low. This is because the only information stored on the OTR is transferred from SAP S/4HANA and is crucial for the transportation process.

The most important difference from other documents in SAP TM is that there are no action buttons on the OTR. The document is read only, with no changes allowed because in this scenario, the SAP S/4HANA system is the information leading system, so any updates should come from SAP S/4HANA.

On the **General Data** tab, you'll see the most important information, such as the OTR document type and the total weight and volume of the freight. There is also a field for a sales organization. Recall that you can integrate your sales organization from SAP S/4HANA and put it on the OTR, but it might not serve for the purposes of SAP TM.

Sales Organization in SAP S/4HANA and SAP TM

When first looking at the empty **Sales Organization** field on the OTR document, you might find it strange that the sales organization used in the SAP S/4HANA SO wasn't moved over to the OTR.

However, in most cases, this is correct. Because SAP TM covers the transportation process, the sales organization in this case isn't the organizational unit selling the *products* anymore; the sales organization in the OTR is the organizational unit selling the *transportation services*. In most cases, these are different organizational units, if the shipper even sells the transportation of products at all.

On the bottom of the screen displaying the OTR document, you can see the information area for the items. Because one OTR represents one SO, all items of the SO are displayed and listed here. Here you can also find the delivery date that was assigned to the items on the SAP S/4HANA SO. The delivery date in SAP S/4HANA can be defined in many different ways, such as using a connected available-to-promise (ATP) check or simple route determination in SAP S/4HANA. No matter which way you determine the delivery date in SAP S/4HANA, it's a date the SAP TM system will work with.

On the **Locations and Dates/Times** tab, you can see the locations of the entire transportation. The source location is the shipping point or plant for which the SO was created. The destination location is the location that was created from the customer transferred from SAP S/4HANA. Note that the destination location isn't for the sold-to party maintained in the SO, but for the ship-to party.

You'll notice that in many cases the source and/or destination locations are empty. This is because the source and destination location can vary from item to item, depending on the storage location or shipping point assigned to the items of the SAP S/4HANA order. During FUB, several freight units are created for the OTR because the transportation locations of the items differ. If the source location on the header level of the OTR document is empty, you can assume that it's created for an SAP S/4HANA SO; if the destination location is empty, you can assume it's created for an SAP S/4HANA PO.

In Section 4.2.1, we describe how the transportation order clerk can manually predefine the routing of the transportation requirements by adding stages to the forwarding order. With OTRs, there is no such functionality. The transportation path is simply defined from shipping point to customer for an SO, meaning that the OTR contains only one stage. (We describe one exception concerning incoterm locations later.)

After FUB, the freight unit stage can be split into several stages if the transportation process requires this. This process represents the difference between the *ordered route* and the *actual route*. As its name suggests, the ordered route is the routing that was ordered by the customer (for an integrated SAP S/4HANA order, simply a direct transportation path). The actual route, on the other hand, is the route that was actually used. If the SAP S/4HANA SO was defined from a shipping point in Germany to a customer in the United States, the ordered route is simply from Germany to the United States. However, the actual route looks different—for example, one stage is from Germany to a port in the Netherlands, one stage is from the Dutch port to an American port, and one stage is from the American port to the customer. Therefore, although the ordered route differs from the actual route, the actual route isn't reflected on the OTR; the OTR represents only the transportation *requirement* and therefore the ordered route.

When looking at the Customizing of OTR types as depicted in Figure 4.14, you'll see that, compared to other document types in SAP TM, there isn't much to customize here. You can access the OTR type Customizing by following the IMG menu path **Transportation Management · Integration · Logistics Integration · External SAP TM System Integration · Order-Based Transportation Requirement · Define Order-Based Transportation Requirement Types**.

Rather than going into every detail of the type Customizing, we mention only the most important topics here. Because you can't do anything with the OTR itself, it's mandatory to create freight units to start planning. While we go into detail of FUB later in this book, it's still worth mentioning that we have some options in this area.

The **Automatic Freight Unit Building** checkbox defines whether a freight unit should be built automatically after the OTR is created. This makes sense in many use cases. If you consider consolidation of SOs, however, you might not want to create freight units directly after creation, but instead only trigger FUB via a batch job so you can consolidate several OTRs to one freight unit.

Regardless of whether you want to create freight units automatically or using a batch job, you need to define how the freight units should be created. To do so, you define a FUBR in Customizing. If the method of creating freight units depends on some values of the OTR, you might even want to use a condition to find the right FUBR.

The default units of measurement can be used to have consistent units of measurement in the SAP TM system. If the integrated material master contains unit of measurement conversions, the default units are used on the OTR's header information. The item information will keep the units of measurement from the original SAP S/4HANA order.

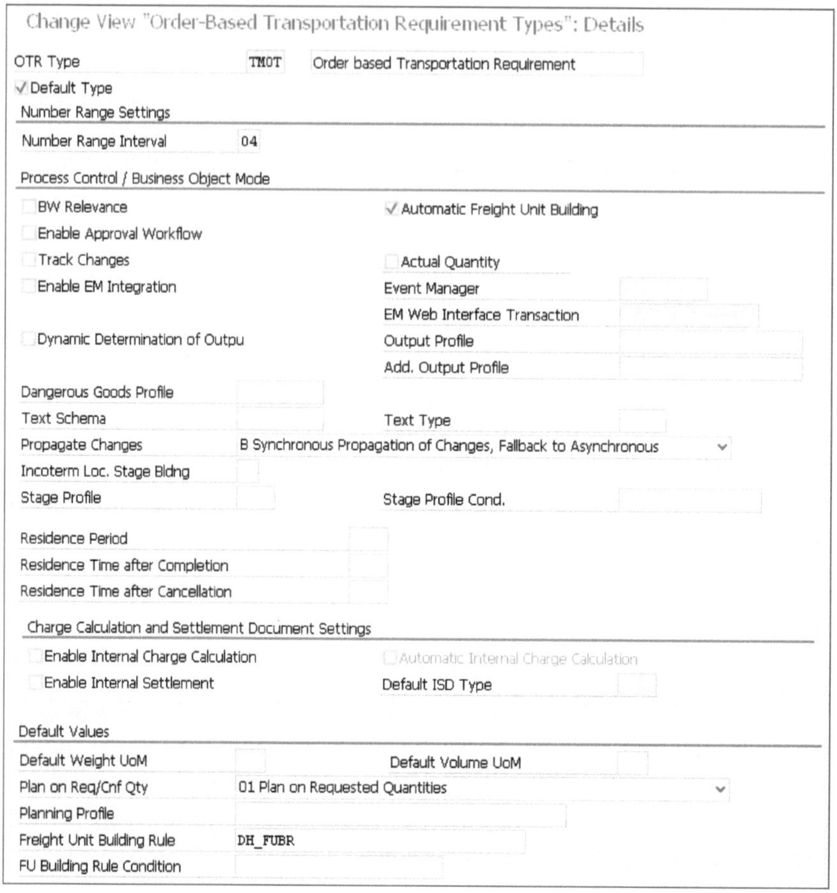

Figure 4.14 OTR Type Customizing

Charge Calculation on OTRs

Recall that there are no buttons or actions a user can use on the OTR, which means that no charge calculation can be executed for the OTR. The reason for this lies in the intended process. Because OTRs are used in the shipper's process, the SAP S/4HANA system is the leading system—for potential surcharges for transportation services, too. Charge calculation in SAP TM is used to calculate selling rates for transportation services and is therefore used only on forwarding orders that are used in the LSP's or carrier's processes. Therefore, the surcharges for transportation must already be imposed on the SAP S/4HANA SO.

The **General Data** tab includes a user interface (UI) section about the incoterms and incoterm location. The incoterm and the corresponding location are assigned to the order in SAP S/4HANA, and that information is transferred to the SAP TM system. The same logic about stage splitting based on incoterm locations that was already discussed in Section 4.1.1 also applies to OTRs.

To recognize the incoterms in SAP TM, you need to maintain them in SAP Supply Chain Management (SAP SCM) Basis Customizing via the IMG menu path **Transportation Management • Basic Functions • General Settings • Incoterms • Define Incoterms**. In this Customizing activity, you can also define whether the incoterm requires an incoterm location.

On the OTR, you'll find three important statuses: the planning status, the execution status, and the consumption status. The planning status shows whether freight units have been created (if so, the planning status is **In Planning**; if not, the planning status is **New**). If the freight units are not only created but also already planned on freight orders, then the planning status changes to **Planned**. If the freight unit is planned on freight orders, the execution status of the OTR shows whether the freight order is already executed, in execution, or not yet executed.

The consumption status of the OTR shows whether DTRs were already created and have *consumed* the freight units of the OTR. Figure 4.15 depicts the integration scenario with both order and delivery being sent from SAP S/4HANA to the SAP TM system. In this case, the freight unit is initially created based on the OTR after the order is sent to the SAP TM system.

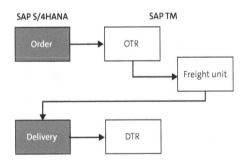

Figure 4.15 Integration Scenario with External SAP TM Component and Freight Unit Consumption

At a later stage, when the delivery is created (either via delivery proposal or internally within the SAP S/4HANA system), the DTR is created for the S/4HANA delivery. The freight unit is then reassigned to the most current S/4HANA document, which is the DTR representing the delivery. We call this process *freight unit consumption* because the document flow is rearranged, and the freight unit is no longer directly associated with the OTR.

Not only statuses but also blocks are kept in sync between the SAP S/4HANA order and the OTR in SAP TM. The mapping of block reasons is done purely on the ID of the block reason codes, meaning that the reason codes in SAP S/4HANA and SAP TM need to be the same.

The OTR document can define two kinds of blocks: a planning block and an execution block. While the planner is still able to plan a freight unit of an OTR that has an execution block defined, the planning block doesn't even allow the planning of the freight unit. When you use the Customizing path **Transportation Management • Integration • Logistics Integration • External SAP TM System Integration • Define Blocking of Transportation Requirements • Define Blocks Based on Delivery Blocks**, you can define whether a block set on the SAP S/4HANA order should automatically set a planning and/or execution block on the corresponding OTR document.

The block can be defined on the SAP S/4HANA order on the header level or each schedule line. Therefore, the blocks on the OTR document are also set on either the header level (i.e., for all items of the OTR) or only a particular item.

If you want to propagate more information from the SAP S/4HANA order to the OTR in SAP TM, you can do this in the **Notes** tab on the OTR document. Because the OTR can't be edited, the notes of the OTR need to come from the SAP S/4HANA order.

Delivery Documents

Recall that both SAP S/4HANA orders and SAP S/4HANA deliveries can be integrated into SAP TM. The integration setup on the SAP S/4HANA side is very close to the integration setup of SAP S/4HANA orders, so we won't go into details about the deliveries again. Make sure you activate the transfer of the delivery documents in the IMG menu path **Integration with Other SAP Components • Transportation Management • Logistics Integration • Activate Integration of Delivery Documents**. Notice that this IMG activity looks very similar to what we've seen when activating the transfer of SAP S/4HANA orders.

Also on the SAP TM side, the technical integration is almost the same as with SAP S/4HANA orders. Another TRQ document is created, which is the DTR. Technically, there is no difference between the OTR and the DTR; they are both instances of the business object /SCMTMS/TRQ and are differentiated only by different document names.

You can also see the similarity between the OTR and DTR when you compare the document type Customizing activities of both business objects. The DTR type Customizing contains exactly the same settings as the OTR, including settings concerning FUB, stage splits based on incoterm locations, and so on.

The DTR is the business document representation of the SAP S/4HANA deliveries, as the OTR was for SAP S/4HANA orders. When you're setting up the integration scenario between SAP S/4HANA and SAP TM, you have different options for which documents you want to integrate and how the interaction of SAP S/4HANA and SAP TM documents should work. The main issue to determine is which system should be the leading system for the transportation process. The correct choice depends on what you want to achieve with the SAP S/4HANA integration.

4.1.5   Integration of Scheduling Agreements in SAP TM 9.6

Scheduling agreements describe recurring deliveries to a customer or to a company's own plant. We can therefore also differentiate between SD scheduling agreements, which represent recurring deliveries to customers, and MM scheduling agreements, which describe recurring deliveries to our plants.

Availability in SAP S/4HANA 1809

The creation of freight units out of scheduling agreements isn't available in SAP S/4HANA 1809. When using SAP TM 9.6, however, OTR documents can be created from the scheduling agreements when using an SAP ERP system instead of an SAP S/4HANA system. This section will therefore only describe the integration between SAP ERP and SAP TM 9.6 because it's the only combination available at the time of writing (winter 2018).

The integration of scheduling agreements uses the same configuration on both sides as the integration on SO documents we discussed in Section 4.1.4. The activation of scheduling agreement transfer is done using the activation table for sales documents depicted in Figure 4.3, for both MM scheduling agreements and SD scheduling agreements.

When a scheduling agreement is sent to SAP TM, it creates one OTR document per scheduling agreement with multiple item lines—one per delivery of the scheduling agreement because the delivery quantity and date differ per item line of the scheduling agreement.

Because the scheduling agreement can be updated or extended in SD or MM or is valid for a very long time, instead of transferring all deliveries of the scheduling agreement to SAP TM, we can consider transferring only the ones in the near future. To do so, you can use IMG path **Integration with Other SAP Components · Transportation Management · Logistics Integration · Define Settings for Sales Scheduling Agreements Integration** (or **Define Settings for MM Scheduling Agreements Integration**). In this Customizing activity, you can define the time horizon that should be transferred to SAP TM. For MM scheduling agreements, you can also define whether just-in-time or forecast delivery schedules should be transferred. (It can only be either just-in-time or forecast, never both.) Because this Customizing activity is optional, just-in-time delivery schedules will be transferred only if nothing was defined.

If you decide to transfer only a certain time horizon, you need to make sure to schedule batch jobs in SAP ERP that transfer the new delivery lines to SAP TM that become relevant in the course of time. There are two batch jobs available:

- TMINT_SAGSD_TRANSFER (for SD scheduling agreements)
- TMINT_SAGMM_TRANSFER (for MM scheduling agreements)

4.2   Forwarding Orders and Forwarding Quotations

In Section 4.1, we talked extensively about the integration of orders and deliveries into the SAP TM functionality. The integration of those documents was introduced to SAP TM with release 8.0 (at that time only in the way described in Section 4.1.4), which was meant to be the release focusing on the shipper's business.

As you've learned so far in this chapter, integrated TRQs only serve the purpose of transferring the transportation-relevant information of orders and deliveries to the SAP TM functionality to execute the transportation process there. SOs and POs in SD and MM aren't sophisticated enough to serve as the TRQ document for LSPs or carriers. In these businesses, more information is required than simply what goods need to be transported from where to where on what date. These businesses often add much more information to the TRQ when transportation service-level codes, Transportation Charge Management, and consolidation come into play. Simply stated, transportation is the core business of LSPs and carriers, which explains why more emphasis is put on the transportation information.

Like SOs, POs, and deliveries, the forwarding orders and quotations generally act as the beginning of the operational process in transportation management. The issuing of a forwarding order creates a business transaction between two companies, or—in more sophisticated scenarios—even among multiple companies.

In this following, we'll discuss the details of the forwarding order document in Section 4.2.1, including what information it can contain and how to process that information. Furthermore, we'll look at quoting processes in Section 4.2.2 and Section 4.2.3 before delving into the functionality that helps users create recurring customer requests more quickly in Section 4.2.4.

4.2.1 Forwarding Order Document

The forwarding order is often called the "typewriter" of SAP TM because most of the data entered into the document is generated at the point of document creation. However, this term undervalues the forwarding order for the transportation process. The forwarding order is the only document in which you can define the data that is used for the entire transportation process of planning, Transportation Charge Management, execution, and so on.

The central business object behind the forwarding order is the TRQ object, which we first discussed in the context of OTRs and DTRs in Section 4.1.4. The forwarding order makes use of the same object used by OTRs and DTRs, which means that comparable data is written into the same database areas.

The forwarding order is the central order business object in SAP TM, and it helps you perform all of the important order-taking processing steps in order management. A forwarding order can be created in different ways:

- **Manual creation**
  This is the most common way of creating TRQs in SAP TM. A customer relations manager of the LSP or carrier talks to the customer and enters all data manually in the SAP Fiori UI.

- **Incoming EDI message**
  Many big LSPs and carrier companies have been using EDI communication for a long time. Therefore, it's only logical that they also prefer EDI communication for the creation of forwarding orders in their systems. SAP TM makes this functionality possible by providing business-to-business (B2B) web services that automatically create a forwarding order. This web service integration can be compared to the integration of orders into an external SAP TM component, but more information can

be transferred, such as transportation stages, dates concerning the transportation, and so on.

- **Use of a template**
  In many cases, customers order the same type of transport on a regular basis. To avoid having to type in the same data every time, the order clerks of the LSP or carrier use templates. A new forwarding order can then be created as a copy from the template. We'll talk about templates later in this chapter.

A fundamental feature of the forwarding order is that the document can be saved at practically any time during the order-taking process. If you want to create freight units from the forwarding order automatically, a few prerequisites need to be met. However, the forwarding order can still be saved in any incomplete state. After the forwarding order contains sufficient information for FUB, the freight units are created. This helps customers and LSPs to enter orders even if some information is missing. At LSPs or carriers, multiple employees are also often involved with the order-taking process. For instance, the customer's contact person enters all the customer's information, but the forwarding order is complete only after a transportation clerk has added data that is relevant for planning and execution.

When you browse the SAP TM system in SAP Fiori launchpad, you'll notice that, like master data or planning, forwarding orders have a dedicated work area called **Order Management.** When you access this tab in the SAP Fiori launchpad, you can see that the **Forwarding Orders Worklists** tile provides a personal object worklist (POWL) with all existing forwarding order documents and their related documents.

As you can see in Figure 4.16, the SAP TM functionality provides you with many pre-configured queries categorizing forwarding orders into the different transportation modes.

At the top of each POWL query are some buttons that you can use to perform actions on the forwarding order documents without opening the documents themselves. For process steps such as collective invoicing and consolidated FUB (explained in detail in other chapters), this feature comes in very handy because the actions can be executed on several documents together.

By clicking **Show Quick Criteria Maintenance**, you can set more filters on the pre-defined queries. A screen area opens where all possible filter values can be defined. The quick criteria are saved so that every time you enter the POWL query again, your last entries are remembered. If you want to avoid this, you can alternatively use the filter of the POWL table itself by clicking a column's header.

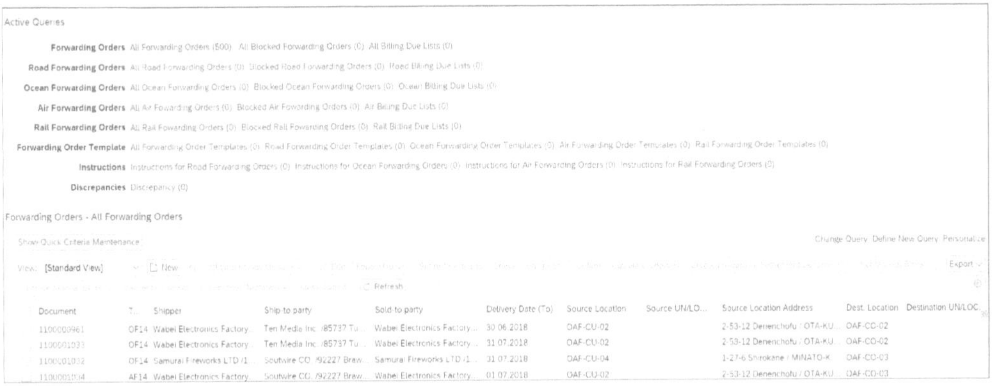

Figure 4.16 POWL for Forwarding Orders

If you have some selections you want to permanently display in the forwarding order POWL, you can use the **Define New Query** link on the top-right corner of the POWL table. In a guided procedure, you can enter your selection criteria, name the POWL query, and assign the query to one of the query categories (the lines on top of the table). Note that this newly created query is available only for your user and can't be used by other users.

Because the forwarding order is a very large and complex business object, this section is the longest section of the chapter. However, you won't find pages explicitly dedicated to the Customizing of the forwarding order type. Instead, we go through the forwarding order document tab by tab and delve deeper into the functionality of the different fields. If Customizing influences the process flow of the fields, we mention this while covering the corresponding section of the forwarding order document. You can find the forwarding order type Customizing via the IMG menu path **Transportation Management • Forwarding Order Management • Forwarding Order • Define Forwarding Order Types**. If other Customizing activities are involved in the forwarding order, they are mentioned when they become relevant.

When starting to create a forwarding order, you'll notice that one piece of information is very crucial to the system: the transportation mode. You can predefine the transportation mode of a forwarding order in the forwarding order type. However, if you want to use one forwarding order type for several transportation modes, you can leave this setting empty. When you access the **Create Forwarding Order** tile in the **Order Management** tab, you'll see that you can enter not only a forwarding order type but also data such as the transportation mode, a template number, or a forwarding agreement to which the forwarding order is related. You'll learn more about Transportation Charge Management for forwarding orders later in this chapter.

If you haven't defined a transportation mode in the forwarding order document type, then you should decide on a mode here. Note that defining the transportation mode as air, for example, doesn't mean you can't create transportation stages of other transportation modes, such as road or rail. The transportation mode decision is relevant only for the naming of fields in the forwarding order and for which fields are displayed or hidden. In fact, you can also change the transportation mode of the forwarding order while creating it (i.e., after you've already entered some data). When doing so, you'll notice that the screen changes, and the availability of tabs and the naming of fields change.

General Data

After you've defined a document type, you're directed to the forwarding order document. If you haven't defined a template, you'll see that the document is almost empty; only some fields are prepopulated. The **General Data** tab shown in Figure 4.17 displays the most important information that is globally relevant for the transportation contract between a customer and an LSP or carrier.

The **Order Date** near the top of the screen is prepopulated with the current date, but you can alter it as necessary. The order date is important not only for reference but also for Transportation Charge Management. Rate tables that are used in Transportation Charge Management can have different validity dates. Depending on the settings you've made for charge calculation, you can calculate charges based on either the actual transportation date or the order date.

In the top-right corner of the **General Data** tab, you can find the fields for the organizational data—the sales organization, office, and group responsible for the forwarding order. In Chapter 3, we discussed the importance of organizational units in SAP TM, so we don't go into detail here again. However, it's important to note that entering a sales organization is one of the prerequisites of creating a freight unit. If no sales organization is entered, neither automatic FUB nor manual FUB will succeed.

Just as we discussed with the integration of orders and deliveries in Section 4.1.1, the incoterm is a very important piece of information for transportation responsibilities. You can enter the same incoterms here that you already defined in Customizing. The incoterm location here is free text because it's agreed upon with the customer. Because you can define your stages in a forwarding order manually, no mapping or stage splitting is done based on the incoterm location entered.

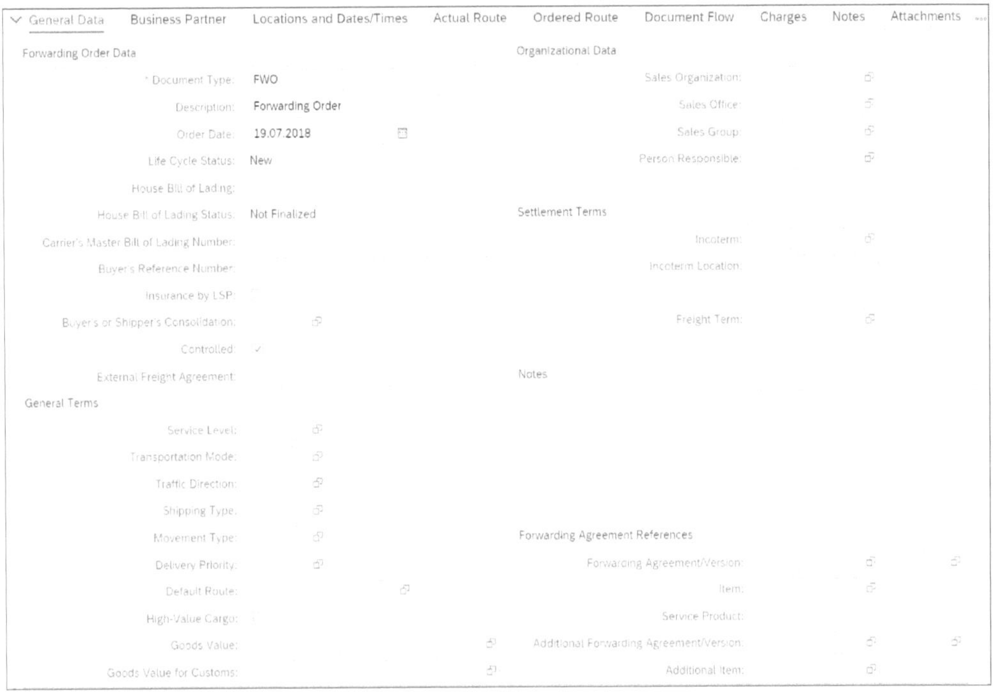

Figure 4.17 General Data of a Forwarding Order

However, the incoterm is considered in charge calculation and settlement. Depending on the incoterm you use, the stages are charged against different partner functions of the forwarding order. You can assign a payer partner function (i.e., which partner function should pay for which stage types) in Customizing by following the IMG menu path **Transportation Management • Forwarding Order Management • Define Default Agreement Partner Functions for Stages**. We look at stage types later in this section.

The **Controlled** checkbox in the **Forwarding Order Data** section on the **General Data** tab (refer to Figure 4.17) defines whether the ordered transportation is a controlled or uncontrolled transport. With uncontrolled transports, the LSP organizes the entire transportation chain, including the main stage; however, the main stage is charged not from the carrier to the LSP but directly to the sold-to party of the entire transport (known as the ordering party in SAP TM 9.6). You can define an uncontrolled transport by deselecting the checkbox. If you deselect the checkbox, the **External Freight Agreement** field becomes editable. You can then enter the freight agreement that exists between the carrier and the sold-to party.

When doing further planning of the freight units belonging to a forwarding order that have been declared uncontrolled transports, you can find the **Controlled** checkbox and the external freight agreement on the **Terms and Conditions** tab of the freight booking that covers the main stage of the freight units. Note that you can consolidate uncontrolled freight units on one freight booking only if they all have been assigned the same external freight agreement. The pre-carriage and on-carriage of an uncontrolled transport are still charged from the carrier to the sold-to party via the LSP. Figure 4.18 illustrates the difference between controlled and uncontrolled transports, which is a scenario that often takes place in sea and air transportation and affects the main carriage only.

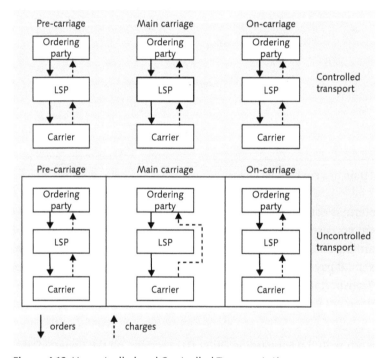

Figure 4.18 Uncontrolled and Controlled Transportation

We cover further details of the different transportation modes and their impact on the forwarding order later in this chapter.

Two more very important pieces of information are the movement type and the shipping type. These settings are crucial for the air and sea transportation processes; they influence the data entry and validation of the forwarding order. Shipping type and movement type are also prerequisites for the creation of freight units from a forwarding order.

The *shipping type* defines what kind of transportation the customer has ordered. In the transportation business, the differentiation is, roughly speaking, between a full container load (FCL) and a less than container load (LCL). In SAP TM, these processes are shipping types. Considering that the terms FCL and LCL are mainly used in sea transportation, the shipping types may depend also on the transportation mode.

You can define shipping types in Customizing by following the IMG menu path **Transportation Management · Forwarding Order Management · Define Shipping Types**. In this Customizing activity, you define all the shipping types you need. The shipping type entered in the forwarding order document determines what items may be defined on the item area of the forwarding order. In Customizing, you therefore need to define your shipping type, whether all cargo items need to be assigned to an equipment item (e.g., a unit load device (ULD) in air, a container in sea, or a railcar in rail), or whether such equipment items are allowed at all.

Unit Load Device

When talking about packaging units in air transportation processes, we use the term *unit load device* (ULD) to represent special types of pallets or containers used in air transportation.

If you enter the shipping type "ULD," depicted in Figure 4.19, you get an error message in the forwarding order if not all of your items are assigned to equipment items. We look at the definition of items in the next section.

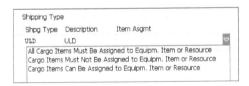

Figure 4.19 Shipping Type Customizing

In this Customizing activity, you can also define for which transportation modes the shipping type is valid. This covers the fact that the terminology is different in different transportation modes.

The shipping type can be entered manually on the forwarding order or be preset in the forwarding order document type Customizing.

The second important feature is the *movement type*. The movement type in the forwarding order determines its routing. It's worth taking a detailed look at the impact of the movement type because you have to deal with it when creating forwarding orders.

In general, movement types can be defined in Customizing in the IMG menu path **Transportation Management · Forwarding Order Management · Define Movement Types**. Here, you can simply define your movement type and whether the location assigned to the shipper should be taken automatically as the source location of the forwarding order. The same setting can be done with the ship-to party and the destination location.

At this point, we've only defined a movement type code. The influence on routing is determined in the Customizing activity that you can find by following the IMG menu path **Transportation Management · Forwarding Order Management · Define Stage Type Sequence for Movement Types**.

Figure 4.20 shows the standard Customizing for the default movement type **DD** (door-to-door). As you can see, you can define a stage type sequence with sequence numbers. As with all sequence-related Customizing activities, the numbers don't have to be exactly sequential, at least in numerical order. For the movement type, you define the stage types that are being used. We talk about stage types later, in the section about the **Stages** tab. For now, we can state that we bring different stage types into a sequential order. In addition, we define whether the occurrence of a particular stage type is optional or mandatory. For the movement type in our example, only the main carriage (stage type **03**) must occur. The **StageProp.** checkbox defines whether some stages on the **Stages** tab should already be created when the corresponding movement type is selected on the **General Data** tab.

Define Stage Type Sequence for Movement Type

Mov. Type	Seq. No.	Stage Type	StgeTpeOcc	StageProp.	Det. Rule	Set. Rule
DD	1	01	Stage type must occur at le... ∨	✓	Always Relevant for Planning ∨	In Execution ∨
DD	2	02	Stage type can occur in any... ∨	☐	Always Relevant for Planning ∨	In Execution ∨
DD	3	03	Stage type can occur in any... ∨	✓	Always Relevant for Planning ∨	Uplift Conf./Shipped on Boa... ∨
DD	4	04	Stage type can occur in any... ∨	☐	Always Relevant for Planning ∨	In Execution ∨
DD	5	05	Stage type must occur at le... ∨	✓	Always Relevant for Planning ∨	In Execution ∨

Figure 4.20 Assigning Stage Type Sequences to a Movement Type

The next column defines whether the stage is relevant for planning or only statistical. On the **Stages** tab, you can manually assign a planning and execution organization to each stage. The decision about whether the stage is relevant for planning is based on the setting in this Customizing activity, which again considers the planning and execution organization. Some of the settings you can choose in the **Det. Rule** column compare the planning and execution organization with the sales organization of the forwarding order. If these two organizations belong to different companies or countries, the stage isn't declared as relevant for planning. However, you can also take the easier route here (if that applies to your business process) and simply state whether this stage is always or never relevant for planning.

The last column in Figure 4.20 (**Set. Rule**) specifies from what point in time an internal settlement of the stage can be created. You can choose different execution statuses here to define in what execution status the corresponding stage of the freight unit must be to start an internal settlement.

Another transportation process that is often used in air and sea transportation is the *shipper's consolidation* in export transportation and the *buyer's consolidation* in import transportation. If your forwarding order has a corresponding transportation mode assigned to it, you can set this information on the **General Data** tab of the forwarding order. The transportation for the LSP is considered like an FCL or ULD transportation because the shipper organizes the transportation to the port, but different house bills of lading (HBLs) need to be issued for each item of the forwarding order, even though only one freight unit was created.

In the transportation business, the HBL number—not the forwarding order number—is the relevant number for identifying the entire transportation. You can find the corresponding field on the **General Data** tab of the forwarding order.

You can manually enter a waybill number or HBL number in this field, which is then propagated to the freight units that belong to this forwarding order. However, the assignment of waybill numbers can also be triggered automatically using *waybill stocks*. To do this, activate the use of waybill stocks in the Customizing of the forwarding order document type by selecting the **Enable Waybill Stock** checkbox and assigning an HBL or house air waybill (HAWB) strategy. The strategy defines how the HBL should be created: per forwarding order, per container, per shipper/ship-to party combination, and so on.

To draw HBL numbers, you need to define waybill stock types in Customizing by following the IMG menu path **Transportation Management · Master Data · Waybill Stock · Define Waybill Stock Types**.

The waybill stock type defines how the HBL number is put together. Figure 4.21 shows how a waybill stock type is assigned to a transportation mode.

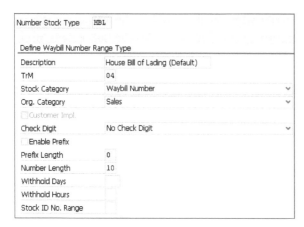

Number Stock Type	HBL	
Define Waybill Number Range Type		
Description	House Bill of Lading (Default)	
TrM	04	
Stock Category	Waybill Number	∨
Org. Category	Sales	∨
☐ Customer Impl.		
Check Digit	No Check Digit	∨
☐ Enable Prefix		
Prefix Length	0	
Number Length	10	
Withhold Days		
Withhold Hours		
Stock ID No. Range		

Figure 4.21 Waybill Stock Type Definition

You can further define whether the number resulting from this stock type should be used as a waybill number or a tracking number. On the bottom of this Customizing screen, you define how the number should be put together, whether a prefix is assigned, the length of the number, and how a potential check digit should look. You can also define how long the number should be withheld after being returned.

After defining a number stock type, we can use it to create a waybill stock. In the SAP Fiori launchpad, go to the **Master Data** tab, and access the **Waybill Number Stocks Worklist** tile to create a new waybill stock based on the number stock type. Here you can define a number range from which a number should be drawn. At the bottom of the screen, you can then define when this waybill stock should be taken into account by defining certain combinations of sales organizations and ordering parties. If the combination of sold-to party and sales organization of the forwarding order matches one of the combinations defined in the waybill stock, a number is drawn from here.

If you choose to assign an HBL number automatically, the **House Bill of Lading** field on the forwarding order isn't editable. Instead, you need to select **HBL · Draw HBL Number** from the action toolbar at the top of the forwarding order screen. This works only after the sales organization, sold-to party, and cargo have been entered.

Waybill Stocks and Numbers

You can find further details about waybill stocks and waybill numbers in Chapter 8, Section 8.1.

On the **General Data** tab of the forwarding order, you can also enter the value of the goods that need to be transported. This information may become relevant for charge calculation or customs. Note that this information is only a manual entry. The values aren't taken from product master data.

We talked about the transportation service-level codes when we discussed order integration. You can manually assign a service level code to the forwarding order. The service level might influence your planning and charge calculation if you've made corresponding entries.

If you want to define your own service-level codes, do this via the IMG menu path **Transportation Management • Forwarding Order Management • Define Transportation Service Level Codes**. If your service-level code applies only to certain transportation modes, then you can define this here, too.

Items

At the bottom of the forwarding order document, you'll find the table of items that are ordered to transport in this forwarding order. You can define several items and create item hierarchies that represent how the packaging was done. Figure 4.22 shows a simple example of an item hierarchy. You can create an item hierarchy like this by choosing **Insert • Container** to insert the first item.

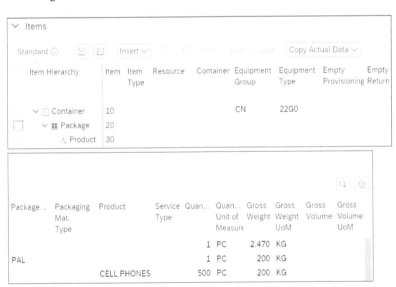

Figure 4.22 Item Area of the Forwarding Order

303

To create a subordinate item, select the superordinate item (in this case, the container), and again choose **Insert • Package**. The new item is created as a subordinate item that is displayed in a hierarchical way. Alternatively, you can enter the data of the items directly into the table and then create a hierarchy by dragging and dropping a subordinate item onto a superordinate item.

For items, the *item type* is a mandatory piece of information. The item type encompasses several settings relevant for the item.

Figure 4.23 shows the information you can define in the Customizing of the item types, following the IMG path **Transportation Management • Forwarding Order Management • Define Item Types for Forwarding Order Management**. The **Item Category** field defines what kind of item this item type describes. It also impacts the way an item hierarchy can be built.

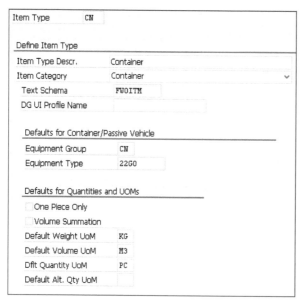

Figure 4.23 Item Type Definition

Item Hierarchy

SAP TM predefines what an item hierarchy can look like. Whether a subordinate-superordinate item relationship is allowed depends on the item category assigned to the item type. In general, SAP TM allows only the following item hierarchies:

- Resource (trailer or railcar)
- Container (may contain a package or product item)
- Package (may contain a package or product item)
- Product (must be the lowest item in the hierarchy)

If you want to define an item type that is relevant for dangerous goods processing, you can assign a dangerous goods UI profile to this item type. You'll find further information about dangerous goods UI profiles and processing in Chapter 9.

If you've defined an item category as a container or passive vehicle, you can assign equipment groups and equipment types to the item type, and all relevant data from the equipment type is then automatically put on the item data in the forwarding order. You can define equipment types via the IMG menu path **Transportation Management • Master Data • Resources • General Settings • Define Equipment Groups and Equipment Types**. The physical properties of the equipment type are used as the tare weight in the forwarding order item. More information about equipment types can be found in Chapter 3, Section 3.2.

Recall that the shipping type you've defined on the forwarding order's general data determines what item categories you may use. If the shipping type defines that no equipment items are allowed, then you get a corresponding error message if you try to insert an equipment item. However, if you've defined a shipping type that requires equipment items, you can't create freight units before all items have been packed into equipment items.

In addition, you can limit the number of item types you can use on a forwarding order by assigning item types to the forwarding order type. You can do this in Customizing by following the IMG menu path **Transportation Management • Forwarding Order Management • Forwarding Order • Assign Item Types to Forwarding Order Types**. After you've assigned some item types to your forwarding order type, no other item types can be selected in your forwarding order. If you've assigned several item types of an item category, you can define a default item type. When you insert a certain item category in the forwarding order, the default item type is automatically used. The default item type is especially important when you're using the B2B integration for automatically creating forwarding orders. Because the web service doesn't carry the information of the item type, this information has to be taken from Customizing.

If you define containers as equipment items in the forwarding order's items, you're working with anonymous entities, if you wish. Containers can be (but don't have to be) defined as master data, such as vehicle resources. If you define a forwarding order for rail or road transportation, however, you can assign a passive vehicle from master data (a railcar or truck trailer) to the forwarding order and use it as an equipment item.

When you define an item hierarchy, the weight of the products of the lowest items in the hierarchy is aggregated up to the highest item level. On each level, the gross weight of the subordinate item is taken over as the net weight of the superordinate item and added with the tare weight to determine the gross weight. This again is taken over as the net weight of the next superordinate item, and so on.

If you've defined default units of measurement on the item level, the quantities of the lower item levels are converted to the default unit of measurement. Note that if you've chosen a product item from product master data, no quantities are moved into the forwarding order item; the quantities need to be inserted manually.

In forwarding orders, you don't necessarily need product master data records for your product items. Even though you can choose product master data for your product items, you can also insert free text into the corresponding field. This is especially handy for LSPs and carriers that transport different materials every day because they don't need to create master data for each material.

If a customer orders the transportation of 300 cell phones, you can enter this in one item line defining a quantity of 300 pieces. However, your transportation process may require you to treat each cell phone individually to enable you to enter specific data for each phone or to simplify freight unit splitting. If so, you can still enter one item line, define pieces and weight for all 300 cell phones, select this line, and click the **Split** button at the top of the item table. The item line is split automatically into 300 individual lines. In addition, the gross weight entered is distributed equally among the new items.

When you select an item line, a new screen area appears below the item table. In this screen area, you can enter several pieces of information specific to the individual item. This information is also propagated to the corresponding freight unit in FUB. The item details contain several tabs.

Let's look at the item details for a product item (the information displayed in the item details section may vary depending on the item category of the item selected) that appear on the following screen tabs:

- **Details**
  You can enter item-specific details here. Some data, such as the product name, is

moved from the item table. Other data you can define only here in this screen area. If you enter a goods value for an individual item, this information is also moved to the corresponding field on the **General Data** tab of the forwarding order. The field is then not editable anymore, but the system expects you to enter this information on every item as necessary. On the **General Data** tab of the document, the values of the individual items are then added up.

- **Quantities**
  The quantities entered in the item table are taken over. In the item details section, you can then define the confirmed quantities; for example, in case of under capacity, you can confirm a lower quantity to the customer if you can't fulfill the entire order volume. Furthermore, this tab also records the feedback from the drivers concerning the actual quantities. Especially in bulk transportation scenarios, the exact quantity can't be provided by customers because it might be dependent on temperature and humidity. However, the actual quantity transported is the basis for charge calculation. Therefore, the measurements performed when loading the truck are recorded and visible on this tab. If multiple measurements are performed, a history of actual quantity records can be accessed via this tab.

- **Locations and Dates/Times** and **Business Partner**
  These tabs are visible in the item details only if it was defined in the forwarding order type Customizing that locations, dates, and business partners can't be globally defined in the forwarding order. The **Same Locations and BPs** flag in Customizing determines whether you're required to enter the transportation locations and business partners on the item level or whether it's sufficient to define them globally on the forwarding order. If the locations and business partners are defined on the item level, this differentiation is also taken into consideration by FUB as a split criterion. The tabs in the **Item Detail** screen area are exactly the same as on the forwarding order, so we don't go into detail about defining business partners and locations here but instead cover it later in this chapter.

- **Document Reference**
  You can add references to the item on the **Document References** tab. In many cases, this tab needs to be filled manually because the document references might be system independent. You can reference a specific item of the referenced document. To differentiate different document types, you need to use *business transaction document types* that you can define in Customizing via the IMG menu path **Transportation Management · General Settings for Order Management · Define Business Transaction Document Type Codes**. As already mentioned, the document type codes can be defined independently of the system if you want to reference a

photo on a server, a phone call protocol, and so on. You can also reference an item from the referenced document. You can also define type codes for items following the IMG menu path **Transportation Management** · **General Settings for Order Management** · **Define Business Transaction Document Item Type Codes**. Document type codes and item type codes aren't linked to each other. For implementation projects, we recommend that you use these type codes as often as the document references are used (i.e., charge calculation or routing decisions).

- **Customs**
  You can define customs-relevant data. You'll find more about customs declarations when we cover SAP Global Trade Services (SAP GTS) integration in Chapter 9.

- **Discrepancies**
  During FUB, the quantities of the forwarding order items are moved into the freight unit. However, if it's discovered in the execution process that the actual quantities of the freight unit differ from the quantity declared in the forwarding order, the quantities are changed in the freight unit. This results in a recorded discrepancy between the freight unit's item and the forwarding order's item. This discrepancy is displayed on the **Discrepancies** tab of the item details. The current status of the discrepancy handling is also recorded here. We'll discuss more details about discrepancy handling in Chapter 8, Section 8.1.

You'll notice that there is one more item category available in the forwarding order that we haven't yet mentioned: the *service item*. A service item defines—as the name suggests—services that should be performed as part of the customer order. Services are anything except the physical movement of the goods or containers (which is handled already in detail with the freight units and subsequent processes, e.g., planning, subcontracting, etc.), such as container cleaning, customs clearance, documentation, and so on.

You can assign *instruction sets* to a service item to track the progress of the service in the forwarding order, which means you can make sure that the service ordered in the forwarding order is also performed. Charge calculation can also consider service items by adding surcharges to the forwarding order's charges.

Service items aren't transferred into the freight unit, which means they can't be seen during the planning phase on the freight unit directly. They can be assigned to any level of the item hierarchy, meaning they can be added to the forwarding order as an independent item or as a subordinate item of a resource item, container item, package item, or product item. They can't, however, be a superordinate item to any other item.

Business Partners

After you define all relevant data on the **General Data** tab and enter the items that need to be transported, you can assign business partners to the transportation contract.

To sketch a very simple example first, only two business partners are assigned to the forwarding order: the shipper where the goods are picked up and the ship-to party where the goods are delivered.

In the forwarding order, the business partners take over different responsibilities. These responsibilities are reflected by *partner functions* (or *party roles* in SAP TM 9.6) that you can see on the **Business Partners** tab. You can add party role codes in Customizing via the IMG menu path **Transportation Management · Master Data · Business Partners · Define Partner Functions**.

As you can see in Figure 4.24, the **Business Partner** tab includes a table where you can assign business partners to the party roles. The partner roles **Sold-to party**, **Shipper**, and **Ship-to party** are mandatory in every forwarding order.

	General Data	Business Partner	Locations and Dates/Times	Actual Route		Ordered Route		Document Flow		Charges		Notes
Standard ⊙		Check Credit Limit										
Actions	Partner Function	Business Partner	Deviat... Address	Name	Street	Ho... Numt	Post...	City		Region	Country
✎ ⊡	Sold-to party	Y17_SHIP1		Chicago Bakeri...	S Clark Street	11...	60605	Chicago			US
✎ ⊡	Shipper	Y17_SHIP1		Chicago Bakeri...	S Clark Street	11...	60605	Chicago			US
✎ ⊡	Ship-to party	Y17_SHIP2		US food Comp...	Mile Road	15...	48235	Detroit			US

Figure 4.24 Business Partners in the Forwarding Order

The business partners you assign to the partner functions need to be maintained as master data. As you can see in the figure, the addresses of the business partners are taken from master data. However, if you want to use a different address than the one defined in the master data, you can do so by selecting the **Deviating Address** checkbox. If you select the row of the party role whose address you want to change in the forwarding order, you can change it in the **Printing Address** field below the table. This field is prepopulated with the address from master data. The address defined here is used for document printing.

Only three partner functions are mandatory in a forwarding order unless you define differently. *Partner determination profiles* define which additional partner functions are mandatory on a forwarding order. You define partner determination profiles in Customizing via the IMG menu path **Transportation Management · Master Data ·**

Business Partners · Define Partner Determination Profiles. In a partner determination profile, you select the partner functions that you want to define as mandatory in the forwarding order. You can also define how business partners are copied from one partner function to another. In the example in Figure 4.24, the sold-to party and the shipper are the same business partner. Therefore, in the partner determination profile, we could define that the business partner of the sold-to party should be copied to the shipper, as shown in Figure 4.25.

Assign Partner Functions							
Function	Name	S...	Edit Level	Srce Type		Source PF	Name
U6	Shipper	1	M Mandatory	∨ Partner Function	∨ SP		Sold-to party

Figure 4.25 Partner Determination Profile

You can use a partner determination profile not only for defining fixed relationships among the party roles of a forwarding order but also for assigning a discrete business partner to a particular partner function. Of course, this is only recommended if the same business partner is relevant in all scenarios.

The partner determination profile can be assigned to the forwarding order type directly in Customizing. However, depending on the transportation scenario, you might not be able to define the mandatory partner functions with only one partner determination profile. Instead, the mandatory partner functions can depend on the incoterms assigned to the forwarding order. Therefore, you can also define the partner determination profile depending on the incoterms and forwarding order type. To do so, follow the Customizing menu path **Transportation Management · Master Data · Business Partners · Assign Partner Determination Profiles Based on Incoterms**.

Although entering business partners in the forwarding order isn't really complicated, we can't understate the importance of the entries. The assignment of a business partner to the sold-to party is crucial for charge calculation, which we describe in Chapter 10.

Recall that business partners can be defined globally on the **Business Partner** tab of the forwarding order or individually for each item, depending on the Customizing of the forwarding order type. The definition is the same; it only has to be done on the item details.

Locations and Dates/Times

Some of the most important information for transportation planning is the definition of locations and times. On the **Locations and Dates/Times** tab, you can define the source and destination location of the entire transportation. Note that the routing isn't defined here but on the **Actual Route** tab. If you've defined that locations and business partners aren't the same for every item, you can still define either a global source location or a global destination location and leave the other location empty on the global level to fill it in on the item level.

The location you choose on this tab needs to be maintained as location master data. If you've chosen location master data, you'll see that the corresponding fields in the address area of the screen are filled with that address.

In the global transportation business, locations are always assigned a global identifier, which depends on the transportation mode. Depending on the transportation mode defined for the forwarding order, the global identifiers are displayed on the **Locations and Dates/Times** tab. Because air transportation uses International Air Transport Association (IATA) codes and sea transportation uses United Nations Code for Trade and Transport Locations (UN/LOCODES), if you use an air forwarding order, you'll see a field **IATA code**, and if you use an ocean forwarding order, you'll see a field **UN/LOCODE**. The codes are assigned in the location master data and prepopulated in the forwarding order when location master data is selected.

If you've followed along with our example, you've defined business partners in the forwarding order. If you go to the **Locations and Dates/Times** tab, you'll see that locations are already entered. If the business partner assigned as the shipper has been assigned a location, this location is automatically taken as the source location of the forwarding order. The same applies to the ship-to party and destination location. It also works the other way around, meaning that if you define locations first, the partner functions of shipper and ship-to party are filled automatically. However, if both partner functions and locations are filled, and you change one of them, no changes are made to the other.

If a customer calls and wants to get a transportation service from a location that you haven't used before, you don't have to define new master data for this location. Instead, you can just leave the **Location** field in the forwarding order empty and type in the address directly, as shown on Figure 4.26. Entering the address creates a *one-time location*. The one-time location is no different from location master data—in fact, a new location master data item was created. The new location is represented by a number that you can use later to add more information in the location master data. Usually the number range for one-time locations starts with 1. If you want to change this, follow the IMG menu path **Transportation Management • Master Data • Transportation Network • Location • Define Number Range Intervals for One-time Locations**.

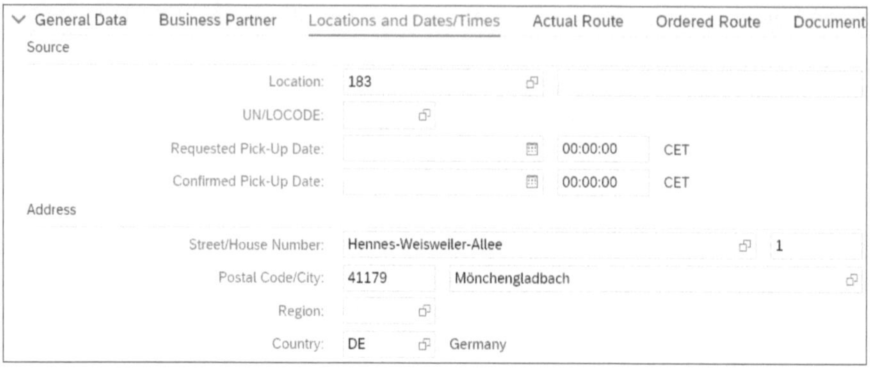

∨ General Data	Business Partner	Locations and Dates/Times	Actual Route	Ordered Route	Document

Source

Location:	183	⊡		
UN/LOCODE:		⊡		
Requested Pick-Up Date:		▦	00:00:00	CET
Confirmed Pick-Up Date:		▦	00:00:00	CET

Address

Street/House Number:	Hennes-Weisweiler-Allee		⊡	1
Postal Code/City:	41179	Mönchengladbach		⊡
Region:		⊡		
Country:	DE	⊡	Germany	

Figure 4.26 Locations with One-Time Location

Take the Term "One-Time Location" Seriously

If you've started thinking that you no longer need to create locations in master data, be aware that one time really should mean one time. Therefore, we recommend that you use one-time locations in exceptional cases only. In other cases, take the time to create a location master first.

However, when entering an address that is already used in a location master data record, the location ID of this master data record is drawn into the forwarding order. With this functionality, you can avoid having several master data records for the same address in the system.

On the same tab as the locations, you can also define the ordered transportation dates for pickup and delivery. Note that the dates entered on this tab are used for the entire cargo transport, meaning that the pickup date is the pickup date of the first stage, and the delivery date is the delivery date of the last stage of the transport. What you define here are the ordered dates; there is no validation of whether the time frame between pickup and delivery date is feasible (there is a validation of whether the delivery date is after the pickup date, in case of typing errors). Pickup and delivery dates aren't both mandatory; one of the dates is sufficient for FUB.

The dates and times are defined in the forwarding order in the time zone that is used by the corresponding location. Transportation planning usually works with a time frame for delivery or pickup, not a single specific time. In FUB, the time defined in the forwarding order is rendered into a time frame, if this is required. You'll find more information about pickup and delivery time windows in Chapter 6.

When you've defined the items of the forwarding order, you'll probably come across some fields concerning confirmation. The LSP can confirm quantities and dates/times to the customer after order-taking. This process step can be automated with the **Automatic Confirmation** flag in the forwarding order type Customizing. In addition, you can define on what data the confirmation should be done. This Customizing mainly concerns the dates to be confirmed. The confirmation can be done based on order data, meaning the ordered dates are simply confirmed. Another option in Customizing allows you to do planning first and then confirm to the sold-to party the dates that result from planning. If you want to confirm manually, you need to enter dates in the corresponding fields of the confirmed dates.

If you don't want automatic confirmation, you can fill in the confirmation fields by clicking the **Confirm** button in the action toolbar of the forwarding order document.

Routing

After creating source and destination locations and dates for the entire process, the LSP usually defines the exact routing, including any potential intermediate stops that are on the forwarding order. Note that in real life, these activities are often done by different employees. The forwarding order can be saved in every state and passed on to the next team, so enriching the forwarding order with more data isn't a problem.

The team responsible for routing the forwarding order uses the **Actual Route** tab to define the route. On that tab, you'll find a table containing all stages that have been created for the forwarding order. In many cases, some stages are predefined here, thanks to the movement type entered on the general data of the forwarding order. Recall that the movement type can be assigned mandatory and optional stage types. In Customizing, you can decide whether some stages should be proposed on the forwarding order when a particular movement type is chosen.

However, there is a second way of automatically assigning stages to the forwarding order. In Customizing of the forwarding order type, you can specify whether stage determination of the forwarding order should be done using the movement type or using a *stage profile*. Stage profiles can be defined in Customizing via the IMG menu path **Transportation Management • Forwarding Order Management • Define Stage Profiles**. This Customizing activity looks very similar to the Customizing activity of assigning stage types to the movement type, which was depicted in Figure 4.20. You can make the same settings here as in the movement type Customizing activity.

You might be wondering why there are two different ways of defining the same thing. With stage determination by movement type, you always get a fixed stage setup—the one you assigned to the movement type. With stage profiles, you can be more flexible.

Figure 4.27 shows an excerpt from Customizing of the forwarding order type. If you decide to use stage determination by stage profile, you can assign a stage profile directly to the forwarding order type. In this case, the stage setup is always the same for the forwarding order, no matter which movement type is chosen. You can also determine the stage profile using a condition. This offers the flexibility to determine the stage profile based on any data from the forwarding order, compared to a 1:1 assignment of a stage profile to a forwarding order type. We recommend that you fill in a stage profile even if you're using a condition. If the condition doesn't return a result, the assigned stage profile is considered as a fallback solution.

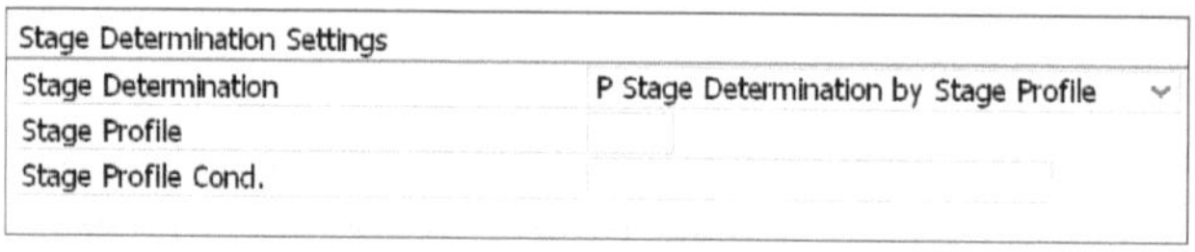

Stage Determination Settings	
Stage Determination	P Stage Determination by Stage Profile ⌄
Stage Profile	
Stage Profile Cond.	

Figure 4.27 Stage Determination by Stage Profile

Stage Determination

Stage determination by movement type is independent of the forwarding order type. No matter which document type is used, the stage setup assigned to the movement type is always considered.

When you use stage determination by stage profile, the stage determination depends more on the forwarding order type.

We've talked a lot about how stage types are assigned to stage profiles or movement types. Now we should take a closer look at what stage types actually are.

Stage types define the characteristic of the transportation stage in the entire transportation. In Customizing, you can create stage types by following the IMG menu path **Transportation Management · Forwarding Order Management · Define Stage Types**.

In Customizing, you simply assign a description to the stage type, as shown on the left in Figure 4.28. You also need to determine the stage category for the stage type. Stage categories are standard categories in the SAP TM functionality that can't be enhanced. Like item categories, stage types are clustered into six groups. Several process steps in the SAP TM functionality use the stage category rather than the stage type. For example, in Transportation Charge Management, you can decide for which stage categories the rate table should be taken into consideration. In addition, the stage category **Main Carriage** has several validations, which we examine later.

Define Stage Types			
Stage Type	Description	Stage Cat.	Ins. Set
01	Pick-Up	Pre-Carriage	⌄
02	Pre-Carriage	Pre-Carriage	⌄
03	Main Carriage	Main Carriage	⌄
04	On-Carriage	On-Carriage	⌄
05	Delivery	On-Carriage	⌄

Figure 4.28 Stage Type Definition

Because instruction sets can be assigned to stage types, it might make sense to restrict stage types to certain transportation modes. You can do this with the Customizing activity found via the IMG menu path **Transportation Management • Forwarding Order Management • Define Allowed Transportation Mode for Stage Types**. Here you can decide which transportation modes are allowed for a certain stage type. You can also define a default transportation mode, which is used for the stage type after the stage type has been assigned to the forwarding order's routing.

Now that we've talked a lot about Customizing and the prerequisites for the forwarding order's routing, we return to the forwarding order document and start with a manual routing of the forwarding order.

When looking at the tabs available in the forwarding order document, you can see that the SAP TM functionality differentiates between the *ordered route* and the *actual route*. As the names suggest, the *ordered route* is the routing that the customer orders or that is agreed upon with the customer in a contract. Therefore, the routing of the ordered route is also considered by Transportation Charge Management.

When you've linked a forwarding agreement item (i.e., an item of a long-term contract with a customer) to your forwarding order, you can also draw in the agreed routing from this item. In this case, the routing is defined as a default route in the agreement item and is pulled into the forwarding order. The stages of the forwarding order are then prepopulated with the stages of the default route.

However, if the LSP wants to do a different routing (e.g., to optimize costs), the LSP can insert a different actual route. The *actual route* is moved to the freight unit so that transportation planning works with the stages and dates defined in the actual route. You can see the actual route definition also in Figure 4.29.

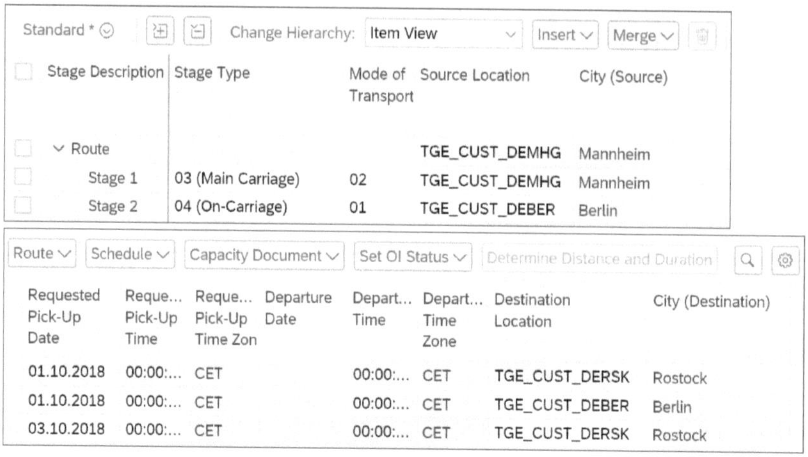

	Stage Description	Stage Type	Mode of Transport	Source Location	City (Source)
	∨ Route			TGE_CUST_DEMHG	Mannheim
	Stage 1	03 (Main Carriage)	02	TGE_CUST_DEMHG	Mannheim
	Stage 2	04 (On-Carriage)	01	TGE_CUST_DEBER	Berlin

Route ∨ Schedule ∨ Capacity Document ∨ Set OI Status ∨ Determine Distance and Duration

Requested Pick-Up Date	Reque... Pick-Up Time	Reque... Pick-Up Time Zon	Departure Date	Depart... Time	Depart... Time Zone	Destination Location	City (Destination)
01.10.2018	00:00:...	CET		00:00:...	CET	TGE_CUST_DERSK	Rostock
01.10.2018	00:00:...	CET		00:00:...	CET	TGE_CUST_DEBER	Berlin
03.10.2018	00:00:...	CET		00:00:...	CET	TGE_CUST_DERSK	Rostock

Figure 4.29 Actual Route of the Forwarding Order

If the movement type or stage profile has already proposed some stages, those stages will be in the ordered route. The actual route will also contain those stages.

The source location and pickup date of the first stage are taken from the **Locations and Dates/Times** tab, and so are the destination location and delivery date of the last stage. If more than one stage is proposed, you need to enter the other locations and dates manually, except that the routing was drawn from a default route of the associated agreement item.

If you want to add stages, select a stage and insert another stage either before or after it. Alternatively, you can split the selected stage into two stages and enter new intermediate stops in the forwarding order.

If you've defined schedules in your transportation network, you can directly assign a schedule instance (meaning a voyage or flight) to a stage in the forwarding order. To do so, click the **Schedule** button at the top of the stage table, and then click **Assign**. A search help appears that looks for schedules that run between the locations of the stage. After a schedule is assigned, a booking for this schedule is created. The dates from the schedule are also propagated into the forwarding order's stage. The delivery date of a stage is always the earliest pickup date of the next stage unless you define a different pickup date. When you select the stage that you've chosen a schedule for, more information from the schedule (e.g., cutoff dates) is available below the stage table.

If you don't want to assign schedules (e.g., because you're planning a road transport), you can create a freight document directly from the stage by choosing **Capacity Document • Create One per Stage**. The dates defined in the stage then serve as dates for the freight document. Alternatively, you can select an already-created freight booking for your stage.

To do all of this, you need to define in Customizing what document types should be used for the freight documents and whether the features just described should be available on the forwarding order type. You can find all of these settings by following the IMG menu path **Transportation Management • Forwarding Order Management • Forwarding Order • Define Default Capacity Document Types for Stages**.

You can choose a freight document type based on the following information:

- Forwarding order type
- Shipping type
- Stage type
- Transportation mode
- Sales organization

The freight document type can be either a freight order type or a freight booking type.

It's also possible to create one freight document for several consecutive stages, but make sure that all stages for which you want to create a common freight document have been assigned the same freight document type.

As you learned earlier in this book, SAP TM comes with an optimizer engine that you can use for routing and scheduling instead of manually creating stages with locations and dates. As a prerequisite, you need to assign a planning profile to your forwarding order type in Customizing, and then select **Route • Transportation Proposal** on the **Actual Route** tab to start the optimizer.

The optimizer returns one or several results that you can choose from. If you accept one of the results, it's moved into the routing of the forwarding order. In the Customizing of the forwarding order type, you can choose how the transportation proposal's result should be considered in the forwarding order. If only the routing is supposed to be copied into the forwarding order, the stages are filled accordingly with dates and locations. Alternatively, freight documents may already have been created from the transportation proposal, and they are then assigned to the forwarding order's stages.

In some cases, the actual routing differs from the ordered route. If the LSP has agreed with the customer that the actual route should be the basis for charge calculation, you can copy the actual route into the ordered route. To do so, navigate to the **Ordered Route** tab, and choose **Copy from Actual Route**. When you look at the stage table on the **Ordered Route** tab, you can see that, except for copying the actual route into the ordered route and splitting stages, there isn't much you can do here. This is because all other functions for routing would affect the routing for planning and execution and are therefore available only on the actual route. You might also have noticed that it's not possible to copy the ordered route into the actual route. This is because the actual route is always kept in sync with the ordered route automatically until any changes are done to the actual route directly.

Let's return to the **Actual Route** tab again. If the employee taking the order is also responsible for the transportation planning, he can directly access the transportation cockpit from the forwarding order. Select **Follow-Up • Start Transportation Cockpit** in the action toolbar at the top of the document. The transportation cockpit is filled with the selection criteria that were assigned to the planning profile that is supposed to be used by the forwarding order (planning profiles can be assigned to forwarding order document types in Customizing).

Because a forwarding order can contain items with different source and destination locations, the stages displayed on the **Actual Route** tab (and on the **Ordered Route** tab, as well) sometimes need to be on the item level.

SAP TM offers an item view and a stage view for the stage table. You can switch between the stages by choosing the hierarchy in the **Change Hierarchy** dropdown list at the top of the stage table.

In our example, two items in the forwarding order have the same destination location but different source locations. We want to define a routing that sends item 1 from its source location to the source location of item 2, from where both items are transported together to their common destination location.

Figure 4.30 shows the **Item View** before the insertion of the additional stage for item 10. After we split the stage of item 10, item 10 contains two stages, whereas item 20 still contains only one stage.

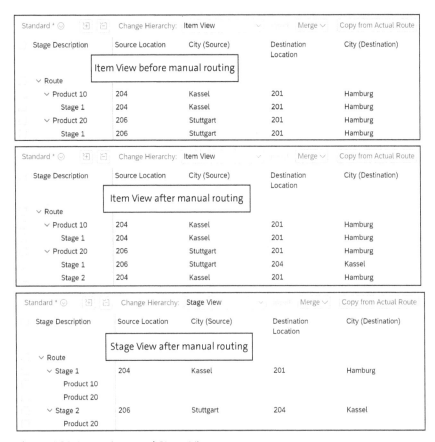

Figure 4.30 Item Views and Stage View

When we switch to the **Stage View**, we can clearly see which stages have to be planned separately for the two items and which stages can be planned together.

Some validations are performed when you do the routing of the forwarding order. Most validations concern whether all mandatory stage types have been used and whether the transportation modes assigned to the stage types are allowed. Validations also check whether the stage type representing the main carriage uses the transportation mode for which the forwarding order was created.

The sales organization is responsible for entering the order, for example, but isn't allowed to create freight bookings for specific transportation stages or send them to a carrier. Therefore, it can propose how to transport the goods (by specifying a route and schedule and assigning a freight order or freight booking) and set the organization interaction status to **To Be Checked** to transfer the affected stages to the planning and execution organization. You can set the interaction status on the stage table by selecting **Set OI Status • To Be Checked**. The planning and execution organization checks the proposal and transportation stage details in the transportation cockpit. It can then confirm the data exactly as proposed in the forwarding order, change data such as the departure, and then confirm the proposal or reject it outright. The status for the stage in the forwarding order then changes to **Confirmed, Confirmed with Deviations**, or **Rejected**, respectively.

The prerequisite for this process step is that you've defined a planning and execution organization for the stage. You can directly assign an organizational unit in the stage table.

Charges and Internal Charges

The **Charges** and **Internal Charges** tabs show the result of charge calculation. Even though charge calculation is a very important topic in forwarding order management, we don't go into great detail about Transportation Charge Management until Chapter 10. In general, these two tabs show the result of a performed charge calculation.

In the Customizing of the forwarding order type, you can enable both internal and external charge calculation. Whether internal or external charge calculation is triggered depends on the combination of sales organization and sold-to party in the forwarding order. The sold-to party can also be an organizational unit from your own company.

In this Customizing activity, you can also specify whether charge calculation should be triggered manually or automatically when the document is saved. If you want to trigger charge calculation manually, select **Charges/Settlement • Calculate Charges** or **Charges/Settlement • Calculate Internal Charges** from the action toolbar at the top of the document.

Profitability

The read-only **Profitability** tab contains valuable information for the LSP business. This tab compares the expected revenue as determined by the charge calculation performed on the forwarding order and the expected costs that derive from the charge calculation on the freight documents related to the forwarding order.

On this tab, you can differentiate between *planned profitability* and *expected profitability*. Although the two terms sound very similar, they are different because the data source for the profitability analysis is different. For planned profitability, the charges from the forwarding order's charge calculation are compared to the charge calculation that is done on the related freight documents.

Cost Distribution

Often, several forwarding orders are consolidated on one freight document. However, when you perform a profitability analysis, the costs imposed on the freight document need to be distributed to the related forwarding order.

SAP TM offers a cost distribution functionality, which we discuss in Chapter 11, Section 11.2.

To calculate profitability on the forwarding order, you need to enable and configure cost distribution, no matter whether consolidation on freight orders took place.

Expected profitability, however, considers the data from the settlement documents—both the forwarding settlement document and the freight orders' or freight bookings' settlement documents.

Output Management

Like every business document in SAP TM, you can also trigger output for the forwarding order. We don't want to go into the details of setting up output here; we discuss only how to assign output-related Customizing to the forwarding order and how to see the output on the forwarding order document.

In Customizing, you assign output profiles to the forwarding order type. The output profile is defined in the Post Processing Framework (PPF) (see Chapter 2, Section 2.3.3).

After an output profile is assigned or dynamically determined, you can go to the **Output Management** tab on the forwarding order document. You'll see an empty table. When you select **Generate · Actions Including Condition Checks**, all output actions that meet the schedule conditions defined in the PPF are triggered.

The table is filled with the actions that meet the schedule conditions. You can see whether the actions have been processed and what kind of actions they are.

As you can see in Figure 4.31, we have only print actions in our example. This means the forwarding order document is supposed to be printed. When you select a line, more details about the action are listed below the table. When you select the **Document Preview** tab in the actions details view, you get a print preview of the document, filled with all the information that we filled in during this chapter or that was derived automatically.

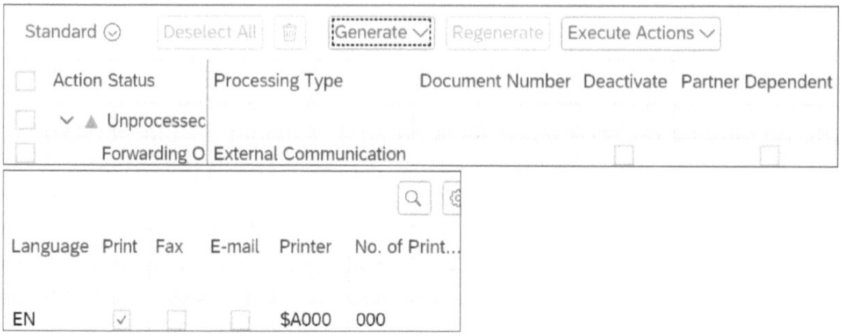

Figure 4.31 Output Management

Global Functions on the Forwarding Order

At this point, we've systematically browsed through the forwarding order tab by tab. However, there are some functionalities of the forwarding order that can't be directly assigned to tabs. We discuss these next.

Recall from Figure 4.1 that the transportation process starts with a transportation requirement and then continues with planning using the freight unit document. Consequently, the forwarding order has to build freight units to continue the transportation process.

We discuss the FUB step in Chapter 6, Section 6.1, but for now, we need to take a closer look at how to trigger it from the forwarding order either manually or automatically. You can define this in Customizing of the forwarding order type. If you choose to use automatic FUB, the freight unit is created the first time the forwarding order is saved. If you make any planning-relevant changes to the forwarding order later, the freight unit is updated accordingly.

> **Prerequisites for Freight Unit Building**
>
> Whether you're using automatic or manual FUB, some fields in the forwarding order need to be filled in to create a freight unit:
> - **Sales Organization**
> - **Source and Destination Location**

- **Items with Quantities**
- **Dates and Times**
- **Movement Type**
- **Shipping Type**
- **Transportation Mode**
- **Business Partners for Mandatory Partner Functions**

In some cases, even more fields are required. You can check whether you've filled all required fields for FUB by clicking the **Check** button in the action toolbar of the forwarding order.

You can also manually create freight units by selecting **Follow-Up • Create Freight Units** from the action toolbar, but this is only enabled if automatic FUB is disabled in Customizing of the forwarding order document type. Manual FUB is often used if freight units might be built for several forwarding orders. In this case, you can select several forwarding orders from the POWL and then create freight units from the POWL. If dates, locations, sales organization, and so on are the same on several forwarding orders, the freight unit consolidates these forwarding orders into one freight unit.

To create freight units, you need to assign an FUBR to the forwarding order type in Customizing. If the way freight units should be built depends on data in the forwarding order, you can also assign a condition to determine the FUBR. As with stage type profiles, you can specify an FUBR in addition to a condition in Customizing to have a fallback scenario in case the condition doesn't return any result.

When a customer company orders a cargo transport from its own premises to another customer, the originating customer also often needs to be provided with a container to load prior to the actual cargo transport. You can also define in the forwarding order document that an empty container should be provided to the shipper before the cargo transport happens. The transportation activities ordered with the forwarding order can then include the actual cargo movement as well as the movement of empty containers, as shown in Figure 4.32.

To do so, you can define in the item detail that this container item should be provided to the shipper and/or returned from the ship-to party to a container yard after it's unloaded. After it's defined that the container item is subject to empty provisioning and/or empty return, new tabs appear in the item detail area where you can define the container yard where the empty container is supposed to be picked up from or returned to. Along with this information, you can also define when the container should be picked up and brought to the shipper (for empty provisioning, when it should be picked up at the ship-to party; for empty return, when it should be returned to the container yard).

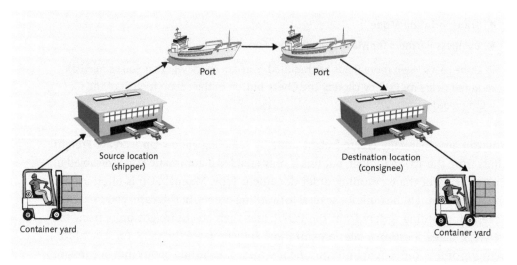

Figure 4.32 Empty Container Provisioning and Return

Note that even though empty provision and empty return are now also part of the forwarding order, the source and destination locations of the forwarding order remain the shipper and the ship-to party. The empty provisioning and empty return information remains on the container item.

When you create freight units for forwarding orders that include empty provisioning and/or empty return, FUB is triggered separately for the actual cargo movement (between shipper and ship-to party) and the empty container movements. This means that the freight unit for the cargo movement can be of a different document type than the empty container movement. Furthermore, you get a separate freight unit or container unit document for the empty container movement.

In an LSP business, there are multiple empty container movements that need to be organized. For the LSP, it's therefore often beneficial to transport an empty container directly from a ship-to party to a shipper instead of transporting the empty container back to a container yard and subsequently picking it up from there to transport it to the next shipper.

As you can see in Figure 4.33, the container travels directly from the ship-to party of one forwarding order to the shipper of another forwarding order. This process is called *triangulation*. You can triangulate empty container units on the container unit POWL. When you select all container units or a subset of them and choose **Triangulation • Create Triangulation**, the system automatically finds container units that can be triangulated based on the following information:

- Involved container yards
- Pickup and delivery dates
- Container types or container numbers

If applicable container units are found, the container unit from the container yard to the shipper of a forwarding order is merged into the container unit from the ship-to party to the container yard. This means the container yard location is no longer part of the container unit, and one of the two container units is deleted because it's now also represented with the other container unit.

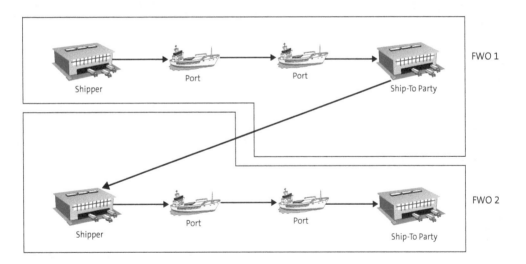

Figure 4.33 Container Triangulation

Empty Provision and Empty Return

While we've talked about empty provisioning and empty return of containers only, it's important to note that it's also possible to use the same functionality for railcar items in the forwarding orders.

However, if you have an item hierarchy that includes a railcar item containing one or several container items, empty provisioning or empty return is possible only for the railcar item (i.e., the highest level of the item hierarchy).

Sometimes, forwarding orders are created only for charge calculation and business administration reasons. In this circumstance, avoid passing these forwarding orders onto transportation planning by choosing restricted processing of the forwarding order in Customizing of the forwarding order type. This way, the forwarding order is always blocked for planning and execution.

SAP TM in SAP S/4HANA provides the credit limit check feature. You can activate the credit limit check in Customizing of the forwarding order type. The activation of the credit limit check is allowed only if forwarding settlement is also allowed; this way, the credit limit check is performed when the forwarding order is created.

In Customizing of the forwarding order type, you can decide what happens if the credit limit check fails. The negative check result can either be only informative and have no impact on the forwarding order or cause a planning and execution block until the credit limit check is successful.

A credit limit check is always performed again if any of the following information of the forwarding order has changed:

- Sales organization
- Credit limit check amount (usually the result of the charge calculation)
- Business partners
- Logistics data with influence on charge calculation

If you need to cancel a forwarding order, you can do this either from the action provided in the POWL or directly from the document. If you cancel a forwarding order, and freight units have already been created for this document, those freight units are canceled and withdrawn from the freight documents on which they might have been planned.

Canceling Freight Units from Freight Documents

If freight units are canceled (e.g., because the related forwarding order was canceled), then the planning is withdrawn, which means the freight units are taken off the freight order or freight booking. If you want to notify the planner automatically about this change, you need to set up your freight documents accordingly by using a change controller strategy that handles this situation.

You can find more information on the setup of freight documents and change controller strategies in Chapter 7.

When you cancel the forwarding order by clicking the **Cancel Document** button either on the document itself or on the POWL, you're asked to define a cancellation reason code. The code you choose can be used for analysis and is displayed on the **General Data** tab of the forwarding order below **Life Cycle Status**, which is changed to **Canceled**.

You can define cancellation reason codes in **Transportation Management • Transportation Management • Forwarding Order Management • Define Cancellation Reason Codes**. You don't need to specify a cancellation reason code when canceling a forwarding order. Canceled forwarding orders can still be used for charge calculation, for example, when the cancelation reason code indicates that the cancelations were caused by the customer only.

As you've seen, the forwarding order contains a lot of information for business administration, transportation planning, charge calculation, and organizational interaction. In many LSP processes, these different process areas are usually performed by different areas within the company.

For the person who takes the order, it would be cumbersome to navigate through all the tabs we've mentioned to enter relevant data. Therefore, he can use the page selector, which is located in the action toolbar in the top-right corner of the forwarding order document.

Recall from Chapter 2, Section 2.2.4, that you can customize the forwarding order screen according to your needs. However, it might be useful to switch between a **Fast Order Entry** screen and the full-blown forwarding order document. SAP TM provides **Fast Order Entry** screens for the air, land, and sea transportation modes because the required information depends on the transportation mode.

Figure 4.34 shows a **Fast Order Entry** screen for land transportation. It displays only the data needed for order entry, including the business partners, sales organization, general terms, locations, dates, and items.

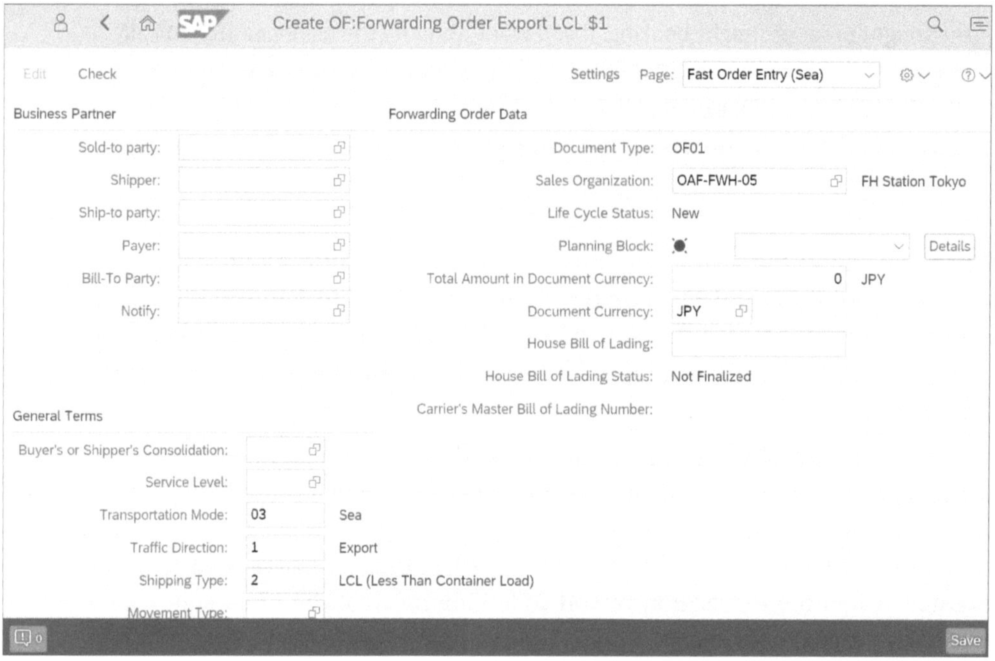

Figure 4.34 Fast Order Entry Screen

If you need more information on the **Fast Order Entry** screen, you can add more fields in screen Customizing.

Notice that there is no action toolbar in Figure 4.34. The **Fast Order Entry** screen works only for order entry. You need to switch back to the conventional forwarding order screen for processing the forwarding order.

As already mentioned, the sold-to party can send an order via EDI messages to make the LSP or carrier create a forwarding order. This process can be automated with SAP TM because the service interface TransportationRequestRequest_In works for all fields that might be relevant for creating a forwarding order. Make sure you've done the setup of the field and service mapping in SAP Process Integration properly. The forwarding order is created automatically if this service interface is triggered.

If you want to confirm data back to the sold-to party, you can also use EDI communication with the service interface `TransportationRequestConfirmation_Out`. For more information about the automatic creation of documents using service interfaces and communication with web services, return to Chapter 2, Section 2.4.

4.2.2   Charge Estimation

Customers often call the LSP to request a price for a transportation service. Although you can enter and perform charge calculation on the forwarding order, it takes a lot of time, and with the customer waiting on the phone, you might require a quicker way of calculating charges.

For this reason, the **Estimate Freight Charges** tile in the **Order Management** tab of the SAP Fiori launchpad takes you to a screen where you can quickly estimate the charges for the customer's order.

Charge Estimation

To use the charge estimation, you need to have set up the Transportation Charge Management component. You can find more information on Transportation Charge Management in Chapter 10 and Chapter 12.

Notice that because the charge calculation itself usually works independently of the document type, no forwarding order type is necessary to start the charge estimation; only the transportation mode needs to be entered. The charge estimation screen in Figure 4.35 looks a little like the **Fast Order Entry** screen of a forwarding order. On this screen, you're asked to enter all data that is relevant for charge calculation. The following fields are mandatory:

- **Purchasing Organization**
- **Source Location**
- **Destination Location**
- **Sold-to Party**

Other fields may not be mandatory for system validation but are often required to perform charge calculation (e.g., **Item**).

If no pickup date is entered, the current system date is used as the pickup date for the charge calculation.

Charge Estimation Application

As described in Chapter 2, Section 2.2.1, SAP TM applications can be displayed in a browser using a hyperlink. Because this also applies to the charge estimation, think about providing the customer with the link to the charge estimation application. This allows the customer to use SAP TM's capability without contacting the LSP.

If you do this, make sure you thoroughly check your authorization setup so that the customer can only estimate its own charges.

The charge estimation is read-only information; that is, the estimated charges can't be saved or turned into a forwarding order.

Figure 4.35 Charge Estimation Screen

4.2.3   Forwarding Quotations

We've spent a long time talking about the forwarding order, which is the document that represents the actual order or contract between a sold-to party and an LSP or carrier. However, before you can create an order in the transportation process, you often need to create a quotation, which is covered by SAP TM with the *forwarding quotation* document. This business document helps the sold-to party send the data of a potential forwarding order with the quotation price. When the quotation is success-ful, the forwarding order can be created in relation to the quotation.

Notice that the forwarding quotation looks very similar to the forwarding order. In fact, you can do most of the things we talked about in Section 4.2.1 in the forwarding quotation. You can create forwarding quotations via the **Create Forwarding Quota-tion** tile in the **Order Management** tab of the SAP Fiori launchpad. Just as you did with the forwarding order, when creating a forwarding quotation, you need to define a for-warding quotation document type. You can specify a forwarding quotation docu-ment type in Customizing by following the IMG menu path **Transportation Management • Forwarding Order Management • Forwarding Quotation • Define For-warding Quotation Types**.

When looking at the forwarding quotation itself and customizing its type, you'll find many similarities between the forwarding quotation and the forwarding order. The following features and processes are handled exactly the same way as in the forward-ing order:

- Item definition
- Item definition with different source or destination locations
- Item type assignment to document types
- Stage determination by either movement type or stage profile
- Automatic charge calculation when saving the document
- Partner determination by partner determination profile
- Transportation proposals
- Creation of one-time locations
- Cancellation of the forwarding quotation with a reason code

---

Note

You can find the corresponding Customizing activity via the IMG menu path **Trans-portation Management • Forwarding Order Management • Forwarding Quotation • Assign Item Types to Forwarding Quotation Types**. Make sure that when you create a forwarding order out of a forwarding quotation, the same item types are assigned to the forwarding order type that are used for the forwarding order creation.

Not everything is the same, though. Figure 4.36 shows the most important differ-ences between a forwarding quotation and a forwarding order. In the quotation, you can specify a valid-to date, which is the deadline by which the quotation must be accepted or rejected.

Just like with charge calculation on the forwarding order, SAP TM can calculate the quotation price. This takes place, for example, if the customer calls the LSP or carrier and asks for a price. The price is calculated, and you can submit it to the sold-to party by selecting **Response · Submit** from the action toolbar at the top of the screen.

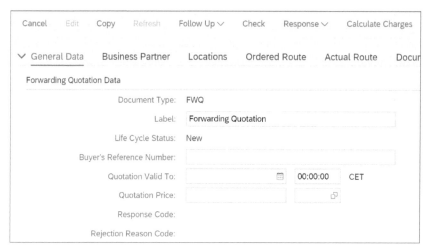

Figure 4.36 Forwarding Quotation Fields and Actions

The communication that takes place during the quotation process can vary from customer to customer. When communication occurs by phone, you can simply update the status of the quotation manually using the actions provided by the **Response** button. Below the quotation price, as depicted in Figure 4.36, you can see your response to the customer—whether you've accepted the quotation or rejected the quotation. When rejecting a quotation, you can specify a rejection reason, which can also be communicated to the sold-to party. The forwarding quotation document is canceled after the quotation has been rejected.

The forwarding quotation also supports the communication between sold-to party and LSP via EDI communication. In this case, the forwarding quotation can be created via the corresponding web service TransportationRequestQuotationCreateRequest_In. This service interface provides all the necessary fields to create a forwarding quotation in SAP TM, just like manual creation of a forwarding quotation. The response of the carrier or LSP is then sent out to the sold-to party with the service interface TransportationRequestQuotationConfirmation_Out.

4

Service Interface

Even though the name of the service interface `TransportationRequestQuotation-Confirmation_Out` suggests that you can use it only to confirm or accept quotations, you can also use it to reject quotations.

A quotation can also be made in the course of a tendering process. Imagine that the sold-to party also uses SAP TM and starts a tendering for a freight order in its system (learn more about triggering the tendering process in Chapter 7, Section 7.3). A request for quotation (RFQ) is sent out to the LSP or carrier, and a forwarding quotation is created for the customer's RFQ.

EDI Messaging from SAP TM to SAP TM

It's possible to start a tendering process and communication between a sold-to party's SAP TM system and a carrier's SAP TM system. However, you need to make sure you have the correct SAP Process Integration setup in place so that the outgoing B2B messages of the RFQ are matched to the correct incoming B2B service interfaces.

If you want to use your forwarding quotation as part of the tendering process, you need to define this in Customizing of the forwarding quotation type. In the Customizing activity, change the setting **Quotation Mode** to **With Request for Quotation**. The forwarding quotation document UI changes slightly. You get additional fields showing the response due date and a potential price limit.

As shown in the top-right corner of Figure 4.37, the response options are now restricted to **Accept** and **Reject** because you can only accept or reject an RFQ and communicate a price.

Whether you're using a forwarding quotation with or without RFQ, the processing of a forwarding quotation is mostly the same. Processing a forwarding quotation isn't much different from processing a forwarding order.

When the forwarding quotation has come in, you can do the routing of the quotation manually on the **Actual Route** or **Ordered Route** tab. (Return to Section 4.2.1 for more information on how to do manual routing on this tab.) Alternatively, you can use a transportation proposal for the route determination of the forwarding quotation by specifying an FUBR in Customizing of the forwarding quotation type, similar to Customizing of the forwarding order type. No freight units are built based on the forwarding quotation; the FUBR is used only for the simulation of the FUB and optimizer planning in the transportation proposal.

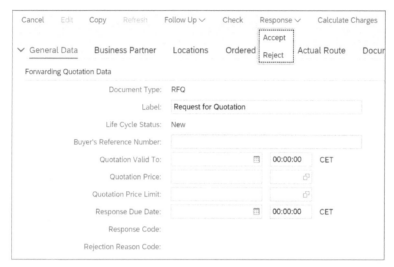

Figure 4.37 Forwarding Quotation with Request for Quotation

After you route the forwarding quotation, you can calculate charges for the document in exactly the same way as on the forwarding order. The prerequisite is again the correct combination of sales organization, sold-to party, and existing master data in Transportation Charge Management. As before, the calculated price is displayed on the **General Data** tab, as shown in the preceding figures. You can also manually overwrite the quotation price later. Only this value is communicated to the customer.

As with the forwarding order, you can view the detailed result of charge calculation on the **Charges** tab. Because the quotation doesn't serve as an actual order or contract, settlement isn't possible based on the forwarding quotation document.

If the customer has accepted the quoted price, you can now create an actual order for the quotation. But don't worry—you don't need to create a new forwarding order from scratch; you can create the forwarding order directly from the forwarding quotation by selecting **Follow Up · Create Forwarding Order** in the action toolbar of the forwarding quotation.

The forwarding order type that is used for creation must be defined in Customizing of the forwarding quotation type in the **Default Forwarding Order Type** field. In Customizing of the forwarding quotation type, you can specify how many forwarding orders may be created out of the forwarding order. Additionally, a forwarding order can be created out of a forwarding quotation only if the quotation was already submitted.

All relevant data is copied from the quotation to the order. The most important data copying is probably the calculated charges. Because master data in Transportation Charge Management might change during the quotation and order-taking process, you want to avoid calculating charges again on the forwarding order when a different result could occur. Therefore, the charge calculation results are copied to the forwarding order, and the status for charge calculation indicates that no further charge calculation is necessary. If you need to do a charge calculation on the forwarding order again, you can do so using the functionality covered in Section 4.2.1.

The assignment of the forwarding quotation to the forwarding order is displayed in the document flow if you've created a forwarding order from a forwarding quotation. Later, the document flow of the freight unit and freight orders will document that the process has started with a forwarding quotation.

However, in some cases, you create a forwarding order independently of the forwarding quotation even though a quotation exists for this workflow. In this case, you can subsequently assign a forwarding quotation to a forwarding order.

On the forwarding order, actions are available in the action toolbar that enable the retroactive assignment of the forwarding quotation to the forwarding order, as shown in Figure 4.38. When you want to assign a forwarding quotation to the forwarding order, click the **Forwarding Quotation** • **Assign FWQ** button. A new popup appears in which you can enter the document number of the forwarding quotation. However, checks are performed to determine that the selected forwarding quotation aligns with the current forwarding order. The standard checks include whether the locations and dates in both documents match and whether the combination of sold-to party and sales organization is the same.

Figure 4.38 Assignment of Forwarding Quotation to Forwarding Order

> **Enhancing the Standard Check**
>
> You can enhance these checks with a BAdI found via the IMG menu path **Transportation Management • Business Add-Ins (BAdIs) for Transportation Management • Forwarding Order Management • Assignment of Forwarding Quotation to Forwarding Order • BAdI: Extension of Checks for Assignment of Forwarding Quotation to FWO.**

When you're creating documents for an import/export process, you can also assign an import forwarding quotation to an export forwarding order. You'll find more information on import/export processes in Chapter 8.

4.2.4   Creating Orders and Quotations with Reference

In the transportation business, LSPs and carriers often have a stock of regular customers who frequently order transportation services for the same route or with similar items. If you don't want to create new orders or quotations from scratch, you can use existing documents and create new ones from them.

One option is to copy an existing forwarding order (e.g., from a transportation service performed in the past) and update certain information, such as dates. When you copy the forwarding order, no link is established between the existing forwarding order and the copy. A forwarding order can also be copied with a new type, meaning the new forwarding order takes over most of the data from the existing forwarding order but is assigned a different forwarding order type. This method is used in import/export processes where an import forwarding order is created from the export forwarding order. (Again, Chapter 8 offers more information about import and export forwarding orders.) When you display a forwarding order, click the **Other Copy Options • Copy with New Document Type** button in the action toolbar to open a new tab in SAP Fiori. In this tab, you can specify the new document type and, if necessary, a new transportation mode.

You can get to this screen shown in Figure 4.39 by opening the **Create Forwarding Order** tile in the **Order Management** tab of the SAP Fiori launchpad.

In the **Basic Data** upper screen area, you define information that should be assigned to the new document you want to create. In the **Create with Reference to** lower screen area, you assign references to existing documents. We revisit this screen in a few pages, so keep it in mind.

You can use this initial screen to create a forwarding order as a copy from an existing forwarding order. Enter the **Forwarding Order Type** in the upper screen area and specify a forwarding order document number in the **Create with Reference to** area. The new document acquires all the data from the reference forwarding order. However, as already mentioned, no reference is shown in the document flow.

The risk with copying an existing forwarding order is that you have to be very careful with the already-existing data. Discrepancies might result if you accidentally copy item quantities that the customer did not order.

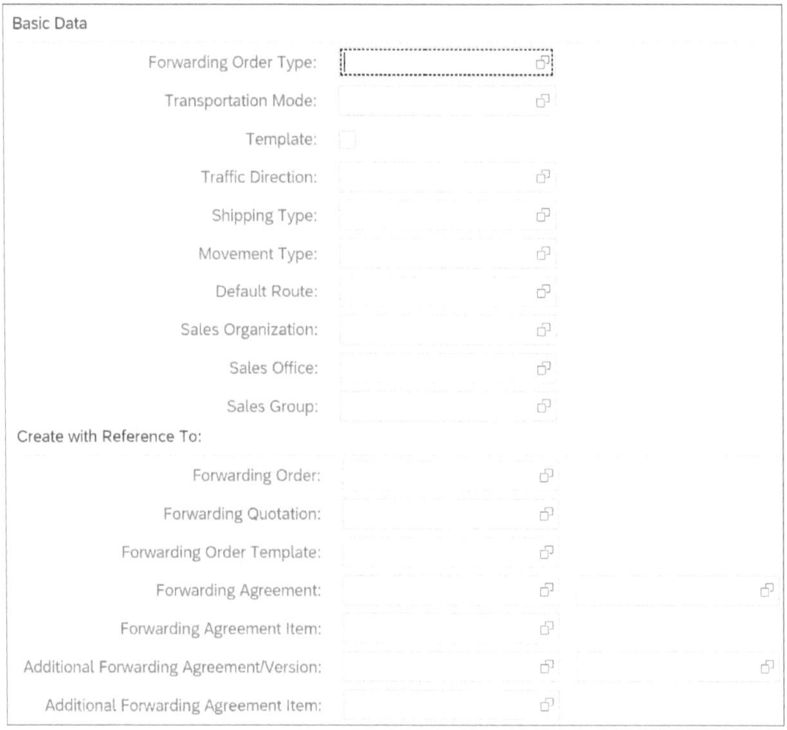

Figure 4.39 Forwarding Order Creation Initial Screen

To avoid this risk, you can create templates for forwarding orders. To create a template, you use the same tile as when creating forwarding orders. On the initial screen, as shown in Figure 4.39, select the **Template** checkbox in the **Basic Data** area. You don't need to customize any separate forwarding order template types, but you can use the forwarding order types.

If you look at the template document, you'll see that it closely resembles the forwarding order (which is no surprise, because it's a template for creating forwarding orders). Note that you can't trigger charge calculation or FUB from forwarding order templates because these functionalities are reserved for the forwarding order document itself.

The template document is missing some tabs that appear on the actual forwarding order document: **Profitability**, **Attachments**, **Internal Charges**, **Output Management**, and **HBL or HAWB**. These forwarding order tabs are concerned with the actual execution of the transportation service. Because the template isn't meant to have anything to do with process steps that trigger transportation execution, FUB and charge calculation are disabled.

The biggest difference is that you can't define any dates in the **Locations and Dates/Times** tab. This is because templates should be timeless, meaning that, in most cases, it's the dates that differ from order to order.

After you save the template, a document number is assigned. We recommend that you use a different number range for templates and actual forwarding orders to differentiate between the two document categories. You can assign the number range of both the forwarding order documents and the forwarding order templates in Customizing of the forwarding order type.

Now when you want to create a forwarding order from a template, you have different options. One option is to use the POWL that was shown earlier in Figure 4.16 for forwarding orders. This POWL includes queries to find template documents. For example, you can search template documents for a certain combination of sales organization and sold-to party or a specific routing. When you've found the right template, you can select it in the POWL and click the **Create Forwarding Order from Template** button at the top of the screen.

Alternatively, you can display the template by using the **Display Forwarding Order** tile. If you know the document number of the template, you can insert it. The system automatically recognizes that you've chosen a template. If you don't know your document number, you can select the **Template** checkbox on the initial screen. If this checkbox is selected, the F4 help displays only forwarding order template documents.

When displaying the template document, you can also click the **Create Forwarding Order from Template** button from the action toolbar. If you want to copy the template with a new document type, as explained previously, the new document is also a template document.

The third option is to use the initial screen of the forwarding order creation. In the **Create with Reference to** area, you can specify a template document number. All data from the template is then copied into the forwarding order. Like when you copy existing forwarding orders, no relationship between the template and order is displayed.

Creating forwarding orders from the forwarding quotation is possible not only with the features described in Section 4.2.3. If you look at Figure 4.39 again, you'll see that you can also define a forwarding quotation in the **Create with Reference to** area.

Creating a forwarding order with *reference* to a forwarding quotation is the same process as creating a forwarding order from the forwarding quotation—meaning that the prerequisites for creating a forwarding order from a forwarding quotation must be met. In this case, the forwarding quotation is added to the forwarding order's document flow as a predecessor document.

In the **Create with Reference to** area of Figure 4.39, you can assign forwarding agreements as a reference for the forwarding order that is being created. This referencing has a slightly different effect than the referencing of quotations, templates, and other orders.

No data is copied into the new forwarding order. The referencing here is used to avoid the system-based agreement determination, which is explained in detail in Chapter 10, Section 10.2. If you assign agreements as reference, these agreements are considered when calculating charges on the forwarding order.

Although we've primarily concentrated on forwarding orders during our discussion of the template, templates can also be used for forwarding quotations. The following features are also applicable for quotations:

- Defining different number ranges for templates
- Creating forwarding quotation templates
- Using the reference area on the initial screen of the forwarding quotation creation
  - Referencing forwarding quotations
  - Referencing forwarding quotation templates
  - Referencing forwarding agreements
- Disabling charge calculation of forwarding quotation template

Because the transportation requirement document marks the beginning of the transportation planning, charging, and execution process, it's a very important document for the whole process. The information entered in the transportation requirement is passed on to the next process steps. The transportation requirement document is the only document in which information about the goods to be transported is entered into the system.

Consider Figure 4.40, which was shown at the beginning of this chapter in relation to which transportation requirement documents exist and how they are used. You should be able to explain the differences between the documents and give details about each of the documents depicted by the bottom-left boxes.

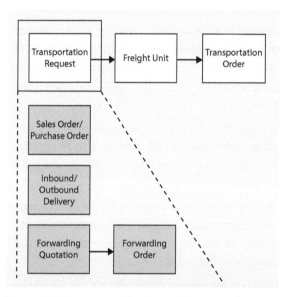

Figure 4.40 Transportation Request Documents

4.3   Summary

We've walked through quite a lot of steps in this chapter; now, let's review the process as a whole.

There are two ways of creating transportation requirement documents in SAP TM. The first option is the integration of MM or SD order and delivery documents into the SAP TM functionality, which was explained in detail in Section 4.1.1. This option is used by the shipper industry that uses SAP TM for the transportation of its own manufactured and sold or purchased materials.

You can integrate the following SAP orders:

- SOs
- POs
- STOs
- Scheduling agreements

The order integration described in Section 4.1.1 and Section 4.1.2 works using the output determination procedure. You need to do some configuration concerning the output management and the activation of the transfer of the orders to the SAP TM functionality. If you want to integrate orders created in the MM component (POs or STOs), use the output processing workflow.

After the order has been transferred to the SAP TM functionality, a freight unit is created. The freight unit doesn't differentiate between SD and MM orders.

After the freight units have been planned, the SAP TM functionality can send a delivery proposal to the orders in SD and MM. Deliveries can then be created based on the planning results in SAP TM, but the leading functionality that determines how deliveries are created is still SD or MM. The integration of created deliveries is configured like the integration of orders.

If you're using a separate instance to run SAP TM, the integration needs to be set up slightly differently. In this case, the SD or MM order or delivery is sent to the SAP TM instance via web service, and a document representing this order—the OTR—is created in SAP TM. The delivery is represented by SAP TM with the DTR document. If both order and delivery are sent to the separate SAP TM instance, an OTR consumption can take place. The integration with an external SAP TM system is described in Section 4.1.4.

The second option for creating transportation requirement documents in SAP TM is creating forwarding orders and forwarding quotations. These documents are used by LSPs and carriers who need more information about the requested transportation process than what is integrated from SAP S/4HANA orders.

Forwarding orders can be created via EDI messages or manually. The forwarding order document combines various pieces of information:

- Information relevant for business administration
- Data relevant to charge calculations
- Data crucial for transportation planning

This information is displayed in the document in different tabs. The most important tabs of the forwarding order are explained in Section 4.2.1.

If customers inquire about the price of a transportation service based on existing agreements, no order has to be created. The charge estimation, covered in Section 4.2.2, calculates the charges of transportation services without creating any documents in SAP TM. This application could possibly also be provided to the customer directly if a customer requests charge estimations very often.

In a tendering process, the customer's inquiry doesn't necessarily result in the creation of an order. Therefore, the first step of the customer engagement is to create a forwarding quotation, as described in Section 4.2.3. With the help of the forwarding quotation, the customer's inquiry can be communicated to and registered by the LSP or carrier, which then communicates a price to the customer. This communication can also be done electronically using web services.

After the customer agrees to the quoted price and terms, a forwarding order can be created from the forwarding quotation.

If forwarding orders or quotations are often created for the same routing or material, the person who takes orders can make the task easier by creating template documents up front. When an order needs to be created, the data can be reused via templates, and the employee can add data specific to the individual order. Templates are covered in Section 4.2.4.

After the transportation requirement is completely entered and confirmed, and freight units have been built, the transportation planning process can start. Let's continue in Chapter 5 with the capacity management process before going into the details of transportation planning in Chapter 6. In that chapter, you'll recognize much of the information that we've entered in either the SAP S/4HANA order/delivery or forwarding order.

Chapter 5
Transportation Capacity Management

Transportation capacity management allows you to plan consumption of your carriers' transportation capacities on a long-term, mid-term, and short-term basis. This helps you secure the capacities you need to run your transportation business and reduces transportation costs by early reservation and avoidance of ad hoc subcontracting.

Transportation capacity management is the process of defining and using your carriers' transportation capacities on different time horizons and geographies. It starts with the long-term contractual part covered by freight agreements and associated capacities, which are represented by freight agreement allocations. Based on carrier schedules, mid-term capacity planning considers gateway schedules based on the carrier schedules and schedule-based allocations to plan the capacities for these gateway schedules. The short-term, operative part is the creation of freight documents according to the previously defined mid-term capacities. These operative freight documents are used in daily business, which assigns incoming new freight to the freight documents.

In this chapter, Section 5.1 presents the capacity management process, including the interplay of the business documents covering the strategic, tactical, and operative aspects; systematic creation of freight documents; and change management that enables you to react to changes in carrier schedules, which are the basis of your business.

Section 5.2 presents allocations, which are used to plan your consumption of your carriers' capacities on various geographical and time levels. The geographical levels range from location-to-location to zone-to-zone levels, and the time levels contain schedule departures as well as daily, monthly, and yearly perspectives. Allocations can be used to create freight documents with corresponding capacities. They are also used by automatic carrier selection to avoid exceeding planned capacities.

Section 5.3 introduces business shares, which manage the distribution of freight to your carriers according to predefined target shares among the carriers for a specific trade lane and are considered during automatic carrier selection.

Section 5.4 presents freight bookings, which are the freight documents that cover ocean freight and air freight transportation. Basically, these freight bookings can be used to reserve capacity from your carriers. After the carrier has confirmed the booking, you can add freight to it. When you've completed your planning and want to execute the booking, you can send the content of the booking to your carrier, representing the legal document accompanying the execution of the transportation.

5.1   Capacity Management

Capacity management involves planning the transportation capacities your carriers offer to you. The capacity management process involves various business documents that represent the long-term contractual aspect, mid-term capacity planning perspective, and short-term view on capacities that can be used in daily business.

Let's begin in Section 5.1.1 with an overview of the capacity management process and interplay of the involved business documents that reflect these perspectives. Section 5.1.2 describes how the (operative) freight documents can be systematically created based on the mid-term capacity planning. Section 5.1.3 presents the change management capabilities that help you to react to changes in your carriers' schedules.

5.1.1   Overview

The capacity management process aims to define and plan the transportation capacities that carriers offer you and that you want to use for your transportation demands. We present the process from the perspective of a global air forwarding company, but the process or parts of it can also be used for ocean forwarding or shippers that systematically reserve and use their carriers' capacities for any mode of transport. Capacity management has the following main goals:

- To secure sufficient transportation capacity and avoid bottleneck situations in which you can't transport what you need to transport

- To reduce transportation costs by using planned capacity to negotiate good long-term contracts and by avoiding expensive ad hoc bookings
- To ensure stable, reliable, and long-term relationships with your carriers

Capacity management involves the objects and logical sequence of creating these objects as depicted in Figure 5.1, shown here using an air freight perspective. Negotiations with your carriers result in freight agreements, which specify the freight rates per trade lane and are explained in detail in Chapter 10, Section 10.1.1. You can define freight agreement allocations, which are assigned in the freight agreements and represent long-term capacity reservations per trade lane. The freight agreement and assigned allocations resemble the contractual perspective on capacity management.

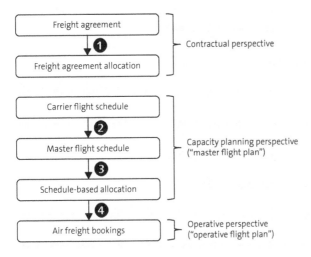

Figure 5.1 Overview of the Capacity Management Process

Carrier flight schedules can be uploaded automatically into the system, as described in Chapter 3, Section 3.2.4; they represent the regular departures that you may want to use in your daily transportation business. You can define master flight schedules, which connect a source gateway with a destination gateway and can refer to one carrier flight schedule or, in the case of a connection flight, multiple carrier flight schedules offered by different airlines. In the master flight schedule, you can trigger creation of schedule-based allocations with buckets referencing the departures of the master flight schedule. This allows you to define capacities for the departures.

In the air freight business, it's common to define the schedule-based allocations for the next 6 to 12 months, and this plan is frequently called a *master flight plan*. In SAP

TM, the master flight plan is represented by three objects: the carrier flight schedule to define the departures offered by the carrier; the master flight schedule to define cutoff times, source, and destination gateway; and the schedule-based allocation to define the capacities among the departures.

When you reach the operative management of capacities, it's important to firmly reserve the planned capacities from the carriers; otherwise, the carrier may use them for other customers. These reservations are made by creating air freight bookings based on the master flight plan; for example, the departure date, time, and capacity are taken out of the master flight plan and put into the newly created booking. The air freight bookings are sent to the carrier and, once confirmed by the carrier, represent the operative flight plan that secures the short-term capacities. Usually, the air freight bookings are systematically created each week for the next six weeks. Whereas the master flight plan is used mainly internally and usually not communicated to the carrier, the operative flight plan is the basis for daily business and is therefore aligned with your carrier.

Planning freight is done based on the operational flight plan. New freight units can be assigned to the air freight bookings, iteratively consuming the capacity reserved by the bookings. If bookings were created only when the required freight units appear, there would be a high risk of not getting the carrier's confirmations or having to change the bookings' quantities each time new freight shows up.

You can manually perform the steps ❶, ❷, and ❸ in Figure 5.1. Step ❹ can also be done manually but is usually performed automatically by the report to systematically create freight documents out of schedules, which we describe in Section 5.1.2.

The capacity management process secures capacities on the long-term level with the freight agreement allocations and allows capacity planning on the mid-term level with the master flight plan, which is then used to secure capacities on the short-term level with the operative flight plan. This kind of hierarchical planning is common in business areas other than transportation (e.g., in supply chain management and production planning), where planning can take place on strategic, tactical, and operative levels.

Let's illustrate the capacity management process with typical examples for direct flights, multistop flights, and connection flights.

Figure 5.2 shows an example of a direct flight from Frankfurt (FRA) to New York (JFK). The carrier flight schedule with flight number LH-400 offers weekly departures, starting on Monday, June 1, 2018, at 9:00. The master flight schedule connects gateways in Frankfurt and New York and references the carrier flight schedule's departures. The schedule-based allocation references the master flight schedule's departures and assigns a capacity to each departure. The air freight bookings have been created based on the master flight schedule and schedule-based allocation, with one booking per departure and taking the capacity of the allocation and departure date from the master flight schedule.

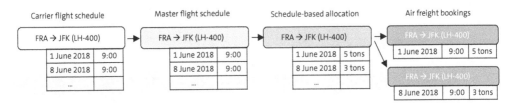

Figure 5.2 Example of Direct Flight

Figure 5.3 shows an example of a multistop flight from Addis Ababa (ADD) to Kilimanjaro (JRO) and then to Mombasa (MBA). The carrier flight schedule with flight number LH-9664 offers weekly departures, starting on Monday, June 1, 2018, at 10:20 in ADD and 13:40 in JRO. Assuming there are gateways in ADD, JRO, and MBA, you can create three master flight schedules: the first from ADD via intermediate airport JRO to MBA, the second from ADD to JRO, and the third from JRO to MBA. These master flight schedules reference the carrier flight schedule's departures and consume both stages—the first stage and the last stage, respectively—of the underlying carrier flight schedule. Each master flight schedule is referenced by one schedule-based allocation that assigns capacities to each departure.

The air freight bookings are created based on the master flight schedules and their schedule-based allocations. Although the three bookings on June 1 refer to the same physical flight from ADD to JRO to MBA, they are treated as independent bookings from the capacity perspective. The bookings from ADD to MBA, from ADD to JRO, and from JRO to MBA contain 2 tons, 1 ton, and 2 tons, respectively. Thus, the carrier receives two bookings that cover the first stage and have a joint capacity of 3 tons, and two bookings that cover the second stage and have a joint capacity of 4 tons.

Figure 5.4 shows an example of a connection flight from Frankfurt (FRA) to Caracas (CCS) to Bogota (BOG).

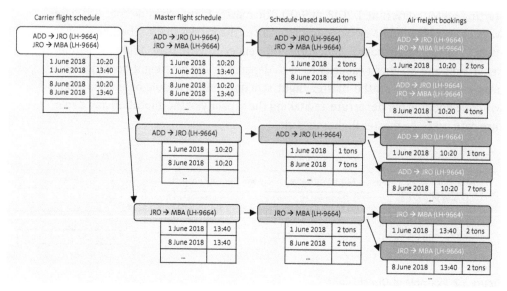

Figure 5.3 Example of a Multistop Flight

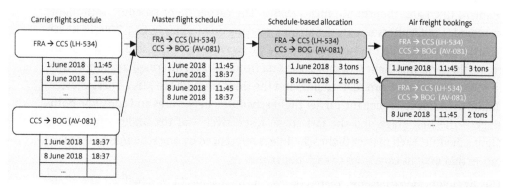

Figure 5.4 Example of Connection Flight

There are two direct carrier flight schedules from FRA to CCS and from CCS to BOG, offered by two different carriers. Assuming there are gateways in FRA and BOG, you can create a master flight schedule connecting the departures of the first carrier flight schedule with the departures of the second carrier flight schedule. In the master flight schedule, you can define the carrier who will receive freight bookings created for the schedule. The (connection) master flight schedule is referenced by one schedule-based allocation to assign capacities to each departure. The air freight bookings are created based on the master flight schedule and their schedule-based allocations.

For a specific trade lane and carrier, the freight agreement allocation defines the planned capacity per time bucket. Allocations allow different bucket types, such as daily, weekly, monthly, quarterly, yearly, and schedule-based, which we explain in Section 5.2. Each allocation stores the available capacity per bucket and provides the already-consumed capacity per bucket, which can be determined automatically.

You can define the trade lanes in the freight agreements and, hence, the freight agreement allocations on the location-to-location level, but these are frequently defined on the zone-to-zone level to define rates and capacities on a more aggregated level. A zone can represent a set of regions or countries, and you can easily create zones for all regions and countries in the world, as described in Chapter 3, Section 3.2.2.

For example, you may have a freight agreement allocation from Frankfurt to the United States and schedule-based allocations from Frankfurt (FRA) to New York (JFK) and from Frankfurt to Chicago (ORD). Then, air freight bookings from Frankfurt to New York would match both allocations and consume their capacities (as shown in Figure 5.5), with air freight bookings being identified by their master air waybill (MAWB) number.

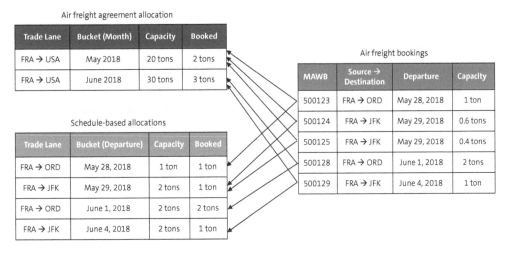

Figure 5.5 Air Freight Bookings Consuming Freight Agreement Allocation and Schedule-Based Allocation

To model the whole capacity management process, you have to define the following:

- Freight agreement allocation type in the freight agreement type
- Schedule-based allocation type in the master flight schedule type that enables references

It's possible to use only a subprocess with a subset of these objects or variants of the process. For example, you can omit the master flight schedule and the schedule-based allocation and directly create an air freight booking with reference to a carrier flight schedule or, in case of a connection flight, multiple carrier flight schedules. In this case, you explicitly maintain the booking's capacity.

5.1.2   Systematically Creating Schedule-Based Freight Documents

You can systematically create schedule-based freight documents by executing report /SCMTMS/MP_SCHED_CREATE_TOR, which you can also reach via menu path **Logistics · Transportation Management · Administration · Background Processing · Creation of Schedule-Based Documents** (in SAP TM 9.6, the path is **Application Administration · Background Processing · Creation of Schedule-Based Documents**). In the **Planning Operation** tab, you can choose which freight documents are created: air freight bookings, ocean freight bookings, road freight orders, or rail freight orders. For each selected freight document category, an individual tab allows you to define selection criteria (see Figure 5.6), where you can see the schedule selection criteria to be used for creating air freight bookings.

Besides defining the criteria, you also set the time period for which freight documents are created based on the determined schedules' departures. If the report was run twice or with overlapping selection criteria, you may not want to create duplicate freight documents, so you should set the corresponding parameter accordingly. Some air freight-specific parameters are available, such as the default contract basis, which allows the creation of allotment, blocked space, charter, and ad hoc air freight bookings, and the trigger for MAWB creation.

The **Technical Settings** tab allows you to define the following system behavior:

- Cancel processing if a selection error occurs.
- Cancel processing if a freight document creation error occurs.
- Display the selected departures of the determined schedules.
- Save or show the freight documents in simulation mode without saving.

- The package size allows parallelization.
- A log is written as shown in Figure 5.7. You can define whether message details are added and how long the log files are available in the system.

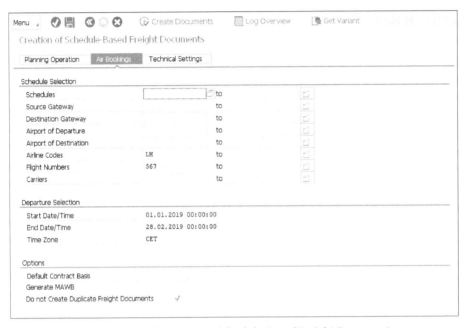

Figure 5.6 Selection Criteria for Creating Schedule-Based Freight Documents

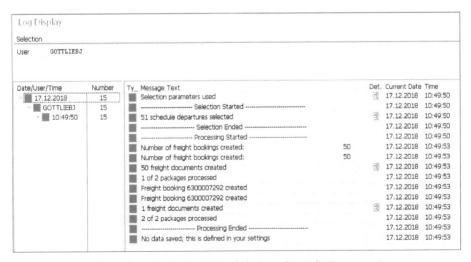

Figure 5.7 Log Information for Created Schedule-Based Freight Documents

5.1.3   Schedule Change Management

If you uploaded or manually created your carriers' schedules, defined schedule-based allocations, and created air freight bookings, then your operative flight plan is up to date. Frequently, the carrier alters the schedule by changing the departure date or time, omitting complete departures, or offering new departures. You can upload the changed schedule data as carrier flight schedules, and the system adjusts the previous versions accordingly. Alternatively, you can manually change the carrier flight schedule. This change has an impact on the subsequent business documents in the capacity management process.

In the event of a delay of the first flight by 10 minutes in a connection master flight schedule that has a connection time of 3 hours, you can accept this delay because 2 hours and 50 minutes is still sufficient to bring the freight from the first to the second airplane. However, if the delay of the first flight is 3 hours, you can't keep the connection and must decide whether to take a later departure of the second flight, choose a different carrier flight schedule for the connection, or, in the worst case, give up this connection master flight schedule and create an alternative master flight schedule with a different connection airport.

For connection flights, in particular, a delay of the first flight may invalidate the complete connection. For this reason, there is no automatic propagation of the changes into the subsequent business documents. Instead, the master flight schedule, schedule-based allocation, and air freight booking have a reference data status that indicates whether the underlying carrier flight schedule has changed. This status field is shown in the corresponding POWL queries for these objects so that you can easily identify the affected objects and manually react to the changes. Within these objects, the reference data status is shown on the header level and on the detail level:

- In a master flight schedule, the stages of the departure rules indicate whether the underlying carrier flight schedule's departure rule has changed.
- In a schedule-based allocation, the departure buckets indicate whether the underlying departure has changed.
- In an air freight booking, the stages of the carrier routing indicate whether the underlying departure has changed.

The user interfaces (UIs) of these three objects allow you to copy the most recent information from the underlying carrier flight schedule or change the reference and take the data out of another carrier flight schedule. Thus, you can manually change the master flight schedule, schedule-based allocation, and air freight bookings so that they consider the changed carrier flight schedule. This is intended to be a manual step because the reaction to the change may require interaction with the involved carriers (e.g., via phone or email). However, by implementing the appropriate change controller strategies, you can automate this change process according to your needs.

Although explained in the context of air freight, the reference data status and capabilities for manual reactions to changes in carrier schedules are available for gateway schedules, schedule-based allocations, and freight documents in general—that is, for all modes of transport.

5.2   Allocations

An allocation represents the planned capacities for a carrier and a trade lane during a validity period. The capacities can be defined for multiple dimensions, such as volume, weight, and 20-foot equivalent units (TEUs), as well as a sequence of time periods of the same granularity, which are frequently called (time) *buckets*. For each dimension and time period, the allocation captures the already-consumed portion of the maintained capacity. All freight documents matching the carrier, trade lane, and validity period consume the corresponding buckets of the allocation. As soon as a freight document is created, the matching allocations are determined asynchronously and updated according to the freight document's capacity. The consumed quantities are visible in the allocations and allow tracking of the capacities and their utilizations. Recall from Section 5.1.1 that one freight document can consume buckets of multiple allocations.

Figure 5.8 shows a schedule-based allocation for carrier **CSI-CA-LH**, a trade lane from a gateway in Frankfurt to a gateway in Chicago with the mode of transport air and validity from November 30, 2018, to December 30, 2019. The buckets represent departures of the underlying schedule 2000506 and the shown departures start on December 3, 2018. For each departure bucket, you can maintain the maximum gross weight and maximum gross volume. The corresponding consumption is shown as well. In this example, the allocation was newly created with no recorded consumptions yet.

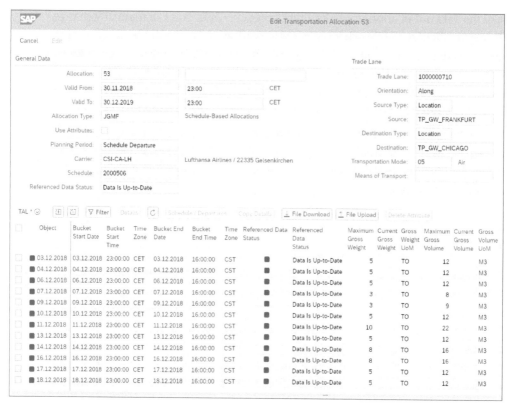

Figure 5.8 Schedule-Based Allocation for Air Freight

Figure 5.9 shows an allocation with monthly buckets covering transportation from Germany to the United States in 2019 by one ocean carrier. Here, the capacity is defined by the number of 20-foot containers per month, measured in TEUs. Consumed weight and volume can also be tracked, although no capacity was defined.

Schedule-based allocations can be created only from a schedule, as mentioned in Chapter 3, Section 3.2.4. You can create other allocations by following the menu path **Master Data · Create Transportation Allocation** (in SAP TM 9.6, the path is **Planning · Allocation · Create Allocation**) and specifying the allocation type. An allocation created out of a freight agreement is called a *freight agreement allocation*, and its only difference from other allocations is that it's contained in the freight agreement.

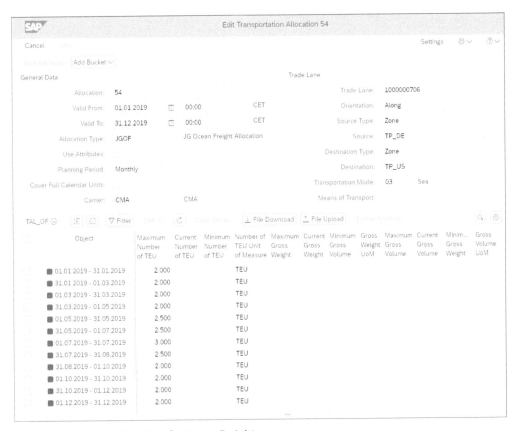

Figure 5.9 Monthly Allocation for Ocean Freight

Alternatively, you can select **Master Data · Transportation Allocations Worklist** (in SAP TM 9.6, the path is **Planning · Allocation · Overview Allocations**) for the POWL and choose the query for allocations to maintain allocations. It's possible to select multiple allocations and maintain them in the same UI, as shown in Figure 5.10. At the top, you can see general information about the allocations and choose which of them is shown in detail at the bottom, where the buckets are displayed.

The POWL allows uploading allocations from a file and downloading selected allocations into a file. Alternatively, you can upload allocations by report /SCMTMS/TAL_IMPORT, which is reachable via menu path **Logistics · Transportation Management · Administration · Background Processing · Allocation Upload** (in SAP TM 9.6, the path is **Application Administration · Background Processing · Allocation Upload**), as well.

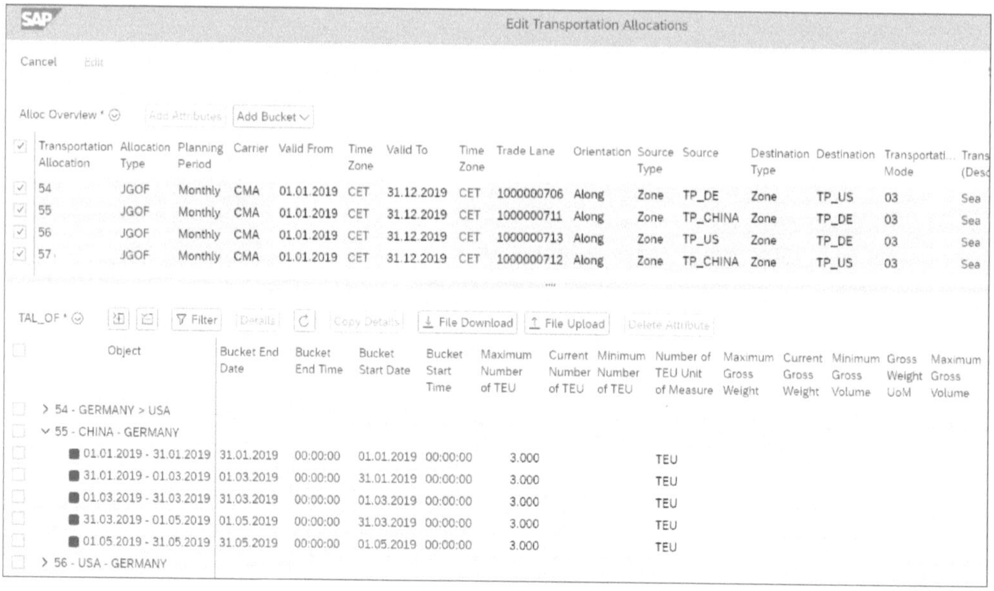

Figure 5.10 Maintaining Multiple Allocations in One UI

In the allocation maintenance UI, you can filter allocations and buckets, for example, according to a start and end time, reference data status being out of date, or their consumed quantity being above the maximum quantity. Whereas automatic carrier selection respects the allocations' capacities, it's possible to manually create freight documents that result in the capacity being exceeded. The user is informed about such a capacity violation via a warning message in the freight document and by the allocations' buckets showing higher consumption than capacity. Click the **Schedules/ Departures** button to compare the current allocation's departure dates and times with those from the underlying schedule and decide which schedule data should be transferred into the allocation's buckets.

In Customizing, you can follow the menu path **Transportation Management · Planning · General Settings · Define Transportation Allocation Types** and define allocation types by specifying the following parameters:

- **Default Type**
  If you created an allocation from scratch and didn't choose an allocation type, the default allocation type is chosen; it's set by this parameter.

- **Mode of Transport**
  You can define the mode of transport or omit this field.

- **Planning Period**
  You can choose among daily, weekly, monthly, quarterly, yearly, and schedule departure. Whereas the first considers all freight documents in the specified time period—also called (time) buckets—the last option refers to departures of an underlying schedule. This means that all freight documents created for that departure are covered by the bucket.

- **Schedule-Based Allocation**
  This specifies that the allocation depends on a schedule—that is, you can create the allocation only out of a schedule, for which the allocation type has been defined in the schedule type, as mentioned in Chapter 3, Section 3.2.4. The schedule determines the validity and trade lane of a schedule-based allocation.

- **Full Calendar Units**
  You can define whether the bucket fully covers a calendar unit or if it can start at any time but has a duration according to the planning period. If you use a daily planning period and don't use full calendar units, you can have a planning period from Monday at 8:00 until Tuesday at 8:00. If you use a monthly planning period and full calendar units, the bucket starts at 0:00 on the first day of the month and lasts until 0:00 on the first day of the next month.

- **Use Attributes**
  This allows you to create multiple buckets for the same period of time. The buckets consider different attribute combinations based on shipping type, contract basis, or handling code. Using handling codes for the upper deck and lower deck of an airplane, you can define two buckets with individual capacities, one for the upper deck and one for the lower deck. The concept of attributes is described shortly in more detail.

- **Use Carrier Selection**
  This defines whether allocations of this type are considered by carrier selection.

- **Carrier Selection Unit of Measure**
  If carrier selection is activated, you can specify the allocation's unit of measure that is considered for carrier selection. You may define allocations with volume, weight, and TEU quantities and choose carrier selection considering the TEU capacities.

- **Update Quantity Automatically**

  This defines whether a newly created allocation or bucket gets an automatic update of its consumed quantities.

- **Bucket Overlapping**

  A freight document may cover multiple buckets of the allocation. Using this parameter, you can define whether all covered buckets get consumed by the freight document or only the first covered bucket gets consumed. This parameter should not be changed if allocations already exist in your productive system because the buckets will contain data according to both consumption modes, which makes the quantities hard to interpret.

- **Allocation BW Relevance**

  This specifies whether the allocation type is relevant for analytics based on SAP Business Warehouse (SAP BW).

It's possible to define multiple buckets for one time period based on different attribute combinations. The prerequisite is that you've selected the **Attributes** option in the allocation type Customizing. Now you can maintain an allocation and introduce attribute nodes by clicking the **Add Attributes** button, as shown in Figure 5.11, where two attribute nodes have already been created. The departure buckets are shown hierarchically below the attribute level. Each departure appears under each attribute node, which allows you to define the capacity for each attribute combination and departure.

Standard attributes are the contract basis (which can be allotment, blocked space, charter, or ad hoc), service level, and shipping type. In addition, you can click the **Details** button to add one or multiple handling codes, which characterize the goods that can be transported and the required equipment, such as three unit load devices (ULDs) (as shown in Figure 5.11).

If you enter quantities in the attribute row, they are propagated into the departures' fields below. If you create freight documents for this allocation, one air freight booking is generated per attribute and departure combination, and the additional information, such as the handling codes and equipment, is copied into the bookings.

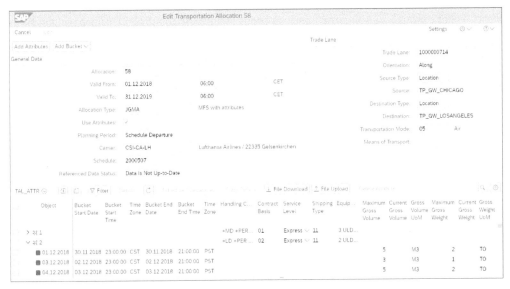

Figure 5.11 Schedule-Based Air Freight Allocation with Attributes

Handling Codes

Handling codes can classify goods and characterize how they are to be transported. You can define handling codes in Customizing by following the menu path **Transportation Management • Basic Functions • General Settings • Define Handling Codes**. For each handling code, you can add a description and specify whether it's to be used in external communication or serves internal purposes only.

When adding handling codes in the attribute node of an allocation, you can choose among the following handling code constraint modes relevant for the freight documents created for the allocation:

- **Handling Code Must Be Identical**
  Only freight units with the same handling code can be assigned to the freight document. This constraint mode is shown in the allocation with the prefix **+**.

- **Exclude Objects with This Handling Code**
  Only freight units that don't have this handling code can be assigned to the freight document. This constraint mode is shown in the allocation with the prefix **-**.

- **Not Relevant for Planning**
  No constraints are imposed, and this handling code is used only for informational purposes. The handling code is shown directly in the allocation without prefix.

For example, defining the handling codes PER (perishables) and FRO (frozen goods) as external and C23 (special code 23) as internal, you can force the system to include perishables, exclude frozen goods, and mention special code 23 as a handling code for information purposes only. This combination is displayed as +PER − FRO C23.

If you want to use handling codes without allocations, you can select the menu path **Transportation Management • Basic Functions • General Settings • Define Handling Code Constraint Profile** in Customizing, capture a combination of handling codes and corresponding constraint modes in a handling code constraint profile, and assign it to a means of transport. When you create freight orders with that means of transport, the handling codes and their constraint modes are copied from the profile into the freight order.

Handling codes can be entered in air forwarding orders, are propagated into the corresponding freight units, can be defined for freight documents as just described, and are considered by automatic and manual planning, where the handling codes can be displayed in the transportation cockpit. If marked as external, they are contained in the air freight booking messages sent to the carriers.

5.3   Business Shares

Although you may have your preferred carrier for a certain trade lane, you also collaborate with other carriers, perhaps to resolve bottleneck situations, peak demands, or other issues with your preferred carriers. Giving freight orders to other carriers only when you have severe problems may not be a good basis for a solid relationship.

To protect your relationship with the other carriers, you may decide to grant them a certain percentage of your transportation business each month. In this way, you can establish a stable relationship but still give most of your transportation business to your preferred carrier. In other scenarios, you may have an agreement with your two major carriers that each of them gets 50% of your transportation business in a certain region. This helps your relationship with the two carriers because they can rely on getting the agreed-upon amount of your business.

With SAP TM, you can define such target shares per carrier as a business share for a trade lane and means of transport or mode of transport on a daily, weekly, monthly, quarterly, or yearly basis. The business shares are used by carrier selection, as described in Chapter 7, Section 7.1.

Via the menu path **Master Data · Create Business Share** (in SAP TM 9.6, the path is **Planning · Business Share · Create Business Shares**), you can create business shares, as shown in Figure 5.12.

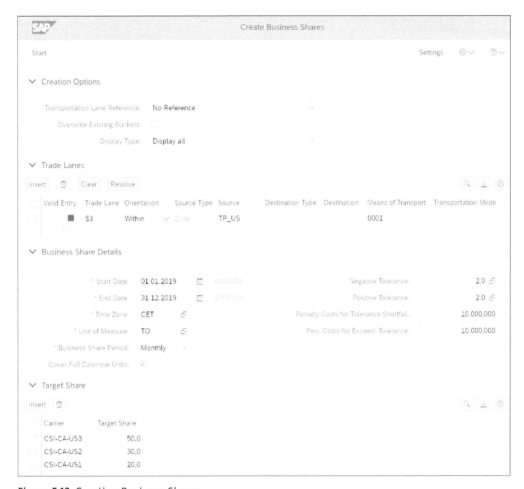

Figure 5.12 Creating Business Shares

In the **Trade Lanes** area, you can define the trade lanes for which you want to define business shares. For each trade lane, you can define the means of transport or mode of transport. In this example, the trade lane represents all transports within the transportation zone USA, and the business share is defined for means of transport **0001**. In the **Target Share** area, you can insert the relevant carriers and assign a percentage for each. The **Business Share Details** area specifies the validity period of the business share, business share period (which can be daily, weekly, monthly, quarterly, or yearly), and unit of measure that is used to determine the percentages among the freight documents that match the trade lane and the (time) buckets. As in the allocation type Customizing, you can also define whether the business shares refer to full calendar units.

Automatic carrier selection takes into consideration the negative and positive tolerances and corresponding penalty costs for violating the tolerances; these are explained in detail in Chapter 7, Section 7.1.2.

The **Creation Options** area specifies how the business share is created:

- Without reference to a transportation lane
- Only if a corresponding transportation lane exists
- Only if a corresponding transportation lane exists with the data copied from the transportation lane

You can define whether existing buckets are overwritten. The display type determines whether only newly created business shares or all business shares are shown.

After you've maintained the data in all the areas, click the **Start** button to create the business shares. Then the created business shares are displayed and can be edited, as depicted in Figure 5.13. You can also edit business shares by selecting the menu path **Master Data · Business Shares Worklist** (in SAP TM 9.6, the menu path is **Planning · Business Shares · Overview Business Shares**), selecting multiple business shares and editing them in one UI, similar to the process for allocations described in Section 5.2.

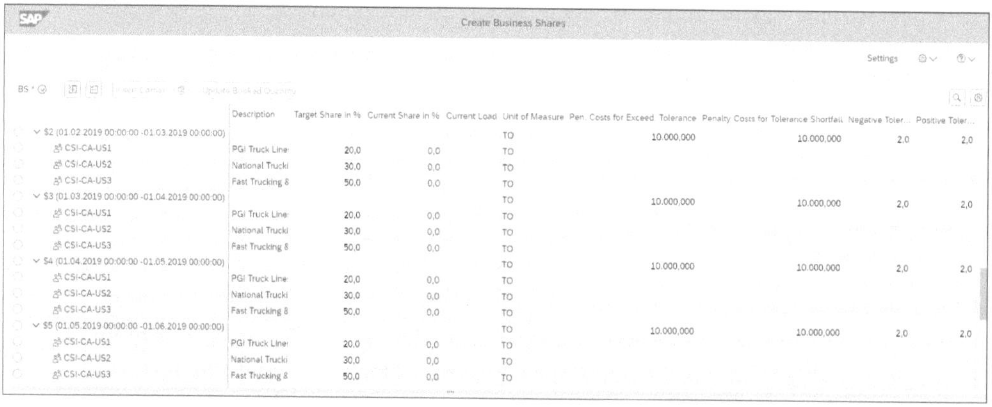

Figure 5.13 Maintaining Business Shares

The current values of the business shares are updated automatically when new freight documents are created, analogously to the allocations' consumption values. In the previous example, the business shares have just been created, so all carriers have a share of 0%. The shares are calculated per bucket.

5.4   Freight Bookings

Freight bookings are used to reserve freight space on a vessel or in an airplane. The corresponding mode-specific freight documents—called ocean freight bookings and air freight bookings, respectively—provide mode-specific information, such as the vessel name or flight number, on their UIs. The space reserved by freight bookings is consumed by assigning freight units or container units to the bookings.

An ocean freight booking represents ocean transportation from a port of loading to a port of discharge, and an air freight booking represents air transportation from an airport of departure to an airport of destination. Freight bookings can cover a consolidation location before the source (air-) port and a deconsolidation location after the destination (air-) port, as illustrated in Figure 5.14. These consolidation and deconsolidation locations are called container freight stations (CFSs) in the ocean case and gateways for the air case. Because the term *gateway* is also used in ocean scenarios, we also use the term *gateway* in the general sense. It's possible to omit the source gateway, the destination gateway, or both gateways, analogously as for schedules as described in Chapter 3, Section 3.2.4. Note that the main leg can consist of multiple stages to model connection flights or multistop voyages.

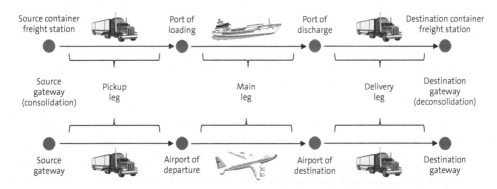

Figure 5.14 Structure of Locations and Stages of Ocean Freight Bookings and Air Freight Bookings

Bookings can be generated based on schedules, can capture the results of planning (e.g., the assigned freight units), and are subcontracted to your carrier. As we cover in Chapter 7, you can directly define a carrier or use carrier selection to determine the carrier of a booking. You can send the freight booking to your carrier and explicitly set the response by the carrier, which can confirm the booking, confirm with deviations, or reject the booking.

Charges can be calculated, freight settlement documents can be created, and costs can be distributed among the involved parties. Freight bookings also serve for transportation execution processes, such as printing, tracking, and tracing the progress of transportation.

Let's examine both kinds of freight bookings. Section 5.4.1 presents ocean freight bookings, reviewing the different functional areas in the UI. Section 5.4.2 describes air freight bookings, focusing on how they differ from ocean freight bookings and additional air freight specifics.

5.4.1   Ocean Freight Bookings

There are many ways to create ocean freight bookings. You can follow the menu path **Order Management • Create Ocean Freight Booking** (in SAP TM 9.6, the menu path is **Freight Order Management • Ocean • Create Ocean Freight Booking**) and manually create an ocean freight booking. You can also create ocean freight bookings from the corresponding POWL query, which is available via the menu path **Order Management • Freight Bookings Worklist** (in SAP TM 9.6, the menu path is **Freight Order Management • Ocean • Overview Ocean Freight Bookings**). Alternatively, it's possible to copy ocean freight bookings, which means that the header and logistical data of the original booking but no assignments (e.g., to freight units) are copied.

You can also create ocean freight bookings by manual planning (see Chapter 6, Section 6.6), automatic planning (see Chapter 6, Section 6.7), or capacity management, using the report to create schedule-based freight documents, as explained in Section 5.1.2. Manual and automatic planning can also change the freight unit assignments to freight bookings. It's also possible to create freight bookings from an ocean forwarding order for the stages of the actual route, as described in Chapter 4, Section 4.2.

Ocean freight bookings contain a lot of information that is structured on the UI in multiple areas, which are described in the following list:

- **Business Partner**
  Here, you can define the carrier, executing carrier, shipper, consignee, and many more business partner roles. The carrier confirms the booking and charges for it, although the executing carrier may be a different carrier.

- **General Data**
  The **General Data** area in Figure 5.15 displays information about carriers, goods, capacity requirements, organizational data, and data about the voyage, vessel, underlying schedule, transportation distance, and duration. It's possible to maintain a booking without reference to a schedule.

Figure 5.15 General Data of an Ocean Freight Booking

- **Terms and Conditions**
  The **Terms and Conditions** area specifies the incoterm, the incoterm location, and whether it's a controlled or uncontrolled transport. You can also define the freight term, which can be prepaid or collect and, together with the traffic direction (import or export), determines how freight settlement documents are created. Additionally, it's possible to define the movement type, the shipping type used for subcontracting, and whether consolidation at the source CFS and destination CFS is intended. If no consolidation is chosen, the corresponding CFS is skipped.

- **Document Flow**

  The **Document Flow** area shows the relationships with the involved business documents, as depicted in Figure 5.16 for an ocean freight booking. You can find documents for the pre-leg or subsequent leg, which is helpful for analyzing time conflicts or assessing the effects of potential delays in the transportation chain. By clicking the hyperlinks, you can navigate directly to the involved documents.

Figure 5.16 Document Flow

- **Transportation Dependencies**

  The **Transportation Dependencies** area is available only for ocean freight bookings and displays the dependencies to other freight documents, such as road or rail freight orders for the pre-leg or subsequent leg. This is helpful for analyzing time conflicts or assessing the effects of potential delays in the transportation chain.

- **Items**

  The **Items** area allows you to display and maintain information about the loaded cargo and its structure consisting of containers or ULDs, freight units, packages, and products, as shown in Figure 5.17.

  You can insert new containers, packages, and products and assign freight units to containers by dragging and dropping them. It's also possible to insert new freight units selected according to their identifiers, forwarding orders, or arbitrary attributes. You can also distribute the items of an already-assigned freight unit over several containers, ULDs, or compartments of the ocean freight booking, air freight booking, or freight order, respectively. The freight unit's quantities can be split and distributed over multiple ULDs. You can also report discrepancies if the actually loaded goods differ from the planned and expected freight. This process is described in detail in Chapter 8, Section 8.1.2.

You can define your own hierarchical view to display the cargo structure according to your needs, as explained in Chapter 6, Section 6.6.3. As in the transportation cockpit, you can dynamically switch between alternative hierarchical views.

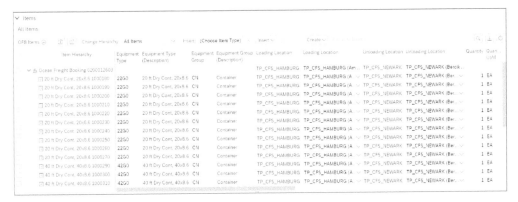

Figure 5.17 Items

- **Location and Dates/Times**

  The **Location and Dates/Times** area contains all relevant data about the pickup location, port of loading, port of discharge, and delivery location, as well as the corresponding departure date and time, cutoff dates and times for cargo, customs, dangerous goods, documents, and expected arrival date and time, as shown together with the stages in Figure 5.18.

- **Stages**

  The **Stages** area shows the same information from the stage perspective, which is particularly helpful if the booking refers to schedules for which the references are displayed or contains more than three stages. More than three stages appear in ocean connection bookings that refer to multiple underlying ocean carrier schedules or in multistop bookings, which we discuss later. By clicking the **Schedule** button, you can assign a schedule to the stage, unassign a schedule, or update the stage's data per the schedule's data, as mentioned in Section 5.1.3. If you manually create an ocean freight booking for a connection voyage without reference to a connection sailing schedule, you create multiple stages and assign a different ocean carrier schedule to each stage.

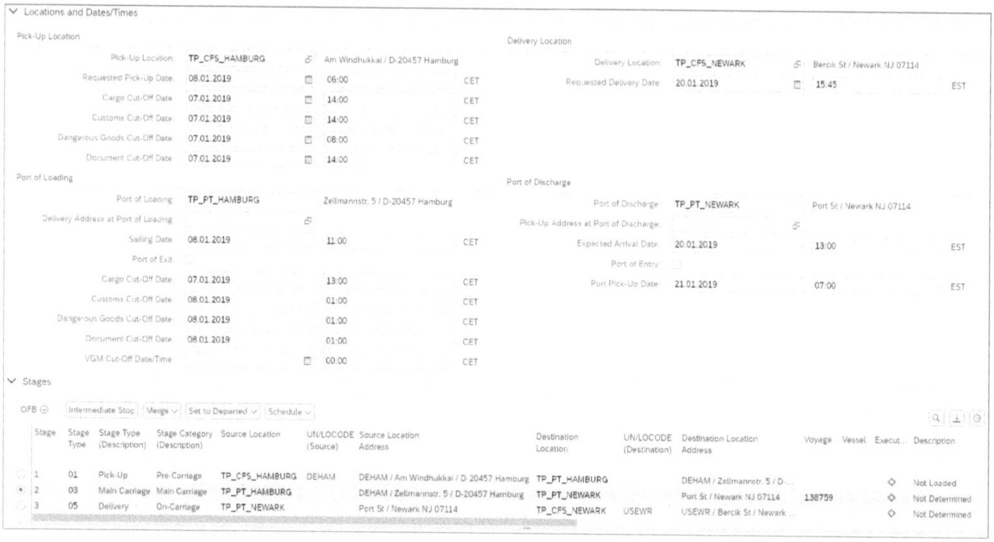

Figure 5.18 Locations, Dates and Times, and Stages

- **Capacity Requirements**

  The **Capacity Requirements** area lists the required and confirmed capacities and determines the corresponding cargo capacity, as shown in Figure 5.19. In this example, two equipment types refer to a 20-foot container, and the last two equipment types refers to a 40-foot container, which is reflected in the corresponding cargo capacity that is measured in TEUs.

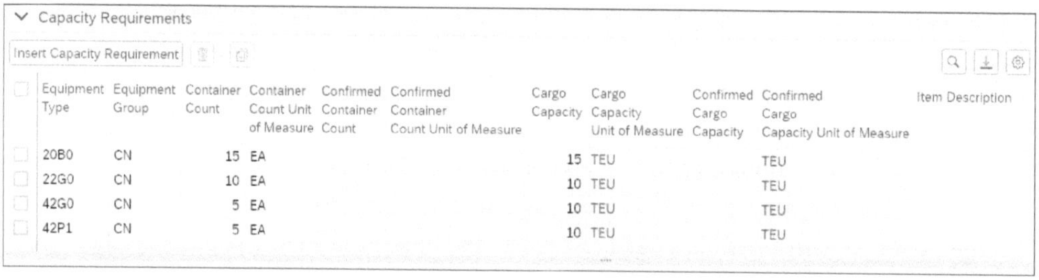

Figure 5.19 Capacity Requirements

- **Overview**

  The **Overview** area provides a quick overview of the stages and items in a hierarchical view, as depicted in Figure 5.20. You can expand the stages and see the items below, including the substructure of the involved containers. The planned start and end times for each stage are also shown. This area is useful if you want to see the most important information at a glance without having to gather the details that are spread over multiple areas.

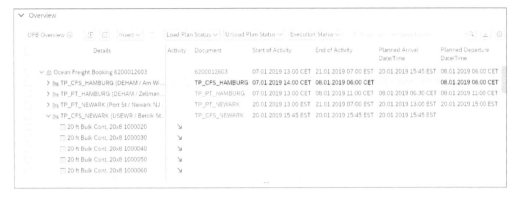

Figure 5.20 Overview of Ocean Freight Booking

- **Carrier Ranking**

  The **Carrier Ranking** area shows the results of carrier selection, which is a ranked list of the available carriers. Automatic carrier selection chooses the best carrier according to the criteria you've specified. If, for some reason, you want an alternative carrier, you can check the other available carriers in the ranking list and select another carrier. See Chapter 7, Section 7.1, for more details on carrier selection.

- **Subcontracting**

  The **Subcontracting** area provides an overview on the subcontracting aspects, including the carrier, the partner reference number, and information of the freight agreement reference.

- **Service Orders**

  The **Service Orders** area covers the service orders defined for the freight booking and its items. A service order can capture tasks such as customs clearance of the document or cleaning and fumigating containers. It's possible to calculate charges for the covered services and create settlement documents for the services. See Chapter 7, Section 7.2.4 , for more details on service orders.

- **Statuses**

  The **Statuses** area captures all kinds of status values, including lifecycle status; fixing status; fixing status of requirement assignment; archiving status; and more values for subcontracting, confirmation, invoicing, dispute cases, execution, customs, transmission to SAP ERP, and consistency. The document status and item status can be set by the corresponding buttons in the booking's toolbar. Refer to Chapter 7, Section 7.2.1, for a discussion of status values in the context of freight orders, which behave similarly to freight bookings, and to Chapter 8, Section 8.1.4, for a detailed description of execution-related status management.

- **Blocking Information**
  The **Blocking Information** area provides the planning block, execution block, and invoicing block status as well as detailed information about blocked elements.

- **Output Management**
  The **Output Management** area allows you to print documents and send messages. See Chapter 2, Section 2.3.3, for more details on the underlying technology.

- **Communication History**
  The **Communication History** area provides an overview of the communicated documents, including partner reference numbers and relevant business partners.

- **Execution**
  The **Execution** area collects data about planned events, their expected date and time, and their actual date and time, which can be reported by SAP Event Management, as explained in Chapter 8, Section 8.2.

- **Charges**
  The **Charges** area provides details about the determined charges for the freight booking. You can trigger charge calculation by clicking the corresponding button in the toolbar of the freight booking. See Chapter 10 for more details on charge calculation.

- **Cost Distribution**
  The **Cost Distribution** area shows details about cost distribution, which is relevant if multiple parties are involved and the charges of the freight booking should be distributed among these parties. More details on cost distribution are presented in Chapter 11, Section 11.2.

- **Customs**
  The **Customs** area displays information relevant for customs handling, such as the customs status, border crossing information, a list of customs activities, and item groups. You can trigger creation of export declaration, request security filing, and perform other customs-related activities. Refer to Chapter 9, Section 9.1, for more details on customs handling.

- **Administrative Data**
  The **Administrative Data** area displays when the freight booking has been created and last changed, and by whom.

- **Change Documents**

  The **Change Documents** area shows, on a rather technical level, the changes that were made in the ocean freight booking, if that option was activated in the freight booking type. The **Attachments** area allows you to store attachments, such as documents and URLs, in the freight document. References to other documents can be captured in the **Document References** area, and notes can be added in the **Notes** area.

You can define the booking types via the Customizing menu path **Transportation Management • Freight Order Management • Freight Booking • Define Freight Booking Types**.

The booking type contains standard sections such as **Basic Settings**; **Number Range Settings**; **Planning Settings**; **Execution Settings** that include **Event Management Settings**; **Output Options**; **Organizational Unit Determination** containing **Default Organizational Unit Entries** and **Determination Rules**; **Charge Calculation and Settlement Document Settings**; **Residence Periods** relevant for archiving; **Integration Settings**; **Checks and Blocks**; **Service Definition**; **Default Units of Measure** for volume, weight, and quantity; **Default Types** for documents created out of the booking; **Predecessor Document Handling**; **Change Controller Settings**; **Additional Strategies**; **Partner-Related Settings**; and **Additional Settings**. All of these are also available for freight order types (see Chapter 7, Section 7.2.1), except for the predecessor handling that can enable organizational interaction.

Let's consider how freight bookings differ from freight orders:

- All booking types can be subcontracted, in contrast to freight order types, which can forbid subcontracting to cover transportation businesses fully relying on their own fleets. Although carrier selection and tendering are offered for freight orders, only carrier selection is possible for freight bookings. In most scenarios, the carrier is already known at the time of booking creation.

- Whereas freight orders allow star-shaped, unrelated, and other stage structures, freight bookings allow only sequential stages.

- Freight orders cover self-delivery and self-pickup scenarios, which aren't relevant for freight bookings.

- You can create pickup and delivery freight orders for the stages from consolidation location to source (air-) port and from destination (air-) port to deconsolidation location, respectively. The freight booking type can define the pickup freight order type and delivery freight order type.

- Usually, an ocean freight booking transports goods along a port-to-port connection. In some ocean transportation businesses, it's common to have ocean freight bookings transporting goods along a port sequence. Freight can be loaded in all but the last port, and freight can be unloaded in all but the first port. Using the **Freight Booking with Multiple Ports of Loading and Ports of Discharge** flag, you can enable ocean freight bookings with a port sequence that has more than two stops. Such ocean freight bookings can only be created manually, and this functionality is offered only for ocean scenarios.

- Service orders can be created from freight bookings, and you can specify the default service order type.

- You can choose between manually entering the value of goods on the header level and automatically aggregating it via the values of the items' goods.

- You can't assign drivers to bookings.

- The container item source determines whether container items are taken from the forwarding order or manually defined in the freight booking. In the first case, the item structure of the forwarding order is copied directly into the freight booking. In the second case, if you enter a number of containers, an equipment group and an equipment type in the **Capacity Requirements** area of the freight booking, corresponding container items are created automatically in the **Items** area. The assigned freight units become subitems of these container items.

- Freight bookings can be fixed when capacity planning is finished. As for freight orders, you can fix the document when it's created or choose not to fix it at all.

- Within the **Service Definition** section, in addition to the default service level, service level condition, and traffic direction, you can define the shipping type, the movement type, and whether a consolidation location and a deconsolidation location, respectively, are involved. Using the last two parameters regarding consolidation and deconsolidation locations, you can create port-to-port, port-to-gateway, gateway-to-port, and gateway-to-gateway ocean freight bookings and their air freight booking counterparts.

- Within the **Predecessor Document Handling** section, the sales organization in a forwarding company can access freight bookings and assign forwarding orders and their freight units, but the final decision about the assignment is made in the planning and execution organization. The organization interaction status of the corresponding freight unit stages can request confirmation from the planning and execution organization where the capacity manager works. After a forwarding order is assigned to the booking, the capacity manager has to check and confirm the assignment. He may accept or reject the assignment; in the second case, an alternative freight booking needs to be identified to ensure that the sold forwarding order can be executed. In the transportation cockpit, the fields for the organization interaction model aren't visible in the standard lists, so you have to activate them in the corresponding views. Refer to Chapter 6, Section 6.2.2, which discusses the organization interaction model from the freight unit stage perspective.

The **Organization Interaction** parameter activates the organization interaction processing for freight bookings. If active, you have to define an auto-confirmation profile.

The auto-confirmation profile allows you to confirm freight unit stages automatically, which means that they don't have to be checked manually by the planning and execution organization. Define these profiles using the Customizing menu path **Application Administration · General Settings · Organization Interaction · Auto-Confirmation Profiles · Create Auto-Confirmation Profile**. For example, you can define that all assignments of quantities below 50 kg are confirmed automatically, which means that all assignments above 50 kg have to be confirmed manually by the planning and execution organization. The **Update from Predecessor** parameter specifies whether the assignment of freight unit stages to a freight booking is processed asynchronously or synchronously. If you use the organizational interaction process, we recommend the asynchronous processing, which doesn't lock the freight booking and may therefore lead to exceeding the booking capacity. The assignment of the freight unit stage can then be confirmed automatically or manually.

- For **Execution Settings**, the same settings are offered as for freight orders. In addition, you can specify whether the carrier confirmation is a prerequisite for reaching the **Ready for Execution** status.

- The **Co-load and Air Cargo Security Check** parameters and the corresponding authorization check are described next in the context of air freight bookings.

5.4.2   Air Freight Bookings

Air freight bookings have many functional similarities to ocean freight bookings. The following screen areas are identical to ocean freight bookings: **Overview, Blocking Information, Customs, Cost Distribution, Service Orders, Output Management, Communication History, Document Flow, Attachments, Notes, Document References, Execution**, and **Administrative Data**.

You'll notice some differences in the following screen areas:

- **Business Partner**

  The **Business Partner** area is also identical to ocean freight bookings. Frequently, the carrier is different from the executing carrier due to code-shared flights. For example, one carrier executes the flight under its flight code LH-577, and one or multiple other carriers offer it as their own flights (e.g., UA-344 and AC-349).

- **Locations**

  The **Locations** area is more compact than for ocean freight bookings and provides information about the airports of departure and destination and the expected departure and arrival dates and times. The cargo cutoff and availability times are also shown.

- **Booking**

  The **Booking** area shown in Figure 5.21 contains a lot of general data, such as the issuing carrier, MAWB stock, and drawn number (see Chapter 8, Section 8.1.1, for more details), source and destination airport, and expected departure and arrival dates and times.

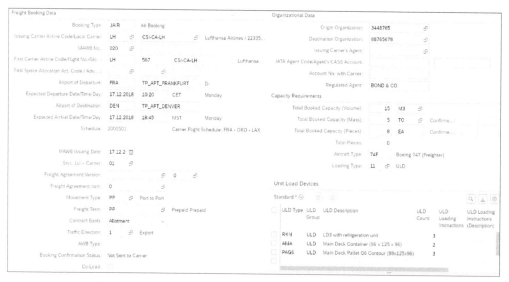

Figure 5.21 Booking Area of Air Freight Booking

Source and destination gateway information and the corresponding cutoff dates and times are displayed, too. Organizational data, such as the source organization and the destination organization, can be maintained. The capacity requirements,

ULD information, and handling codes with their constraint modes are shown as well. We refer to Section 5.2 for more details on the use of handling codes.

The contract basis is contained in the **Booking** area and can be selected from the values defined in Customizing. To do so, follow the menu path **Transportation Management • Freight Order Management • Freight Booking • Define Contract Basis**. The contract basis entries allotment, blocked space, charter, and ad hoc are delivered by default and reflect different levels of contractual commitment to the carrier of the air freight booking. The higher the commitment is, the higher the cost of the cancellation. For example, if you cancel an allotment, only low costs, if any, are incurred. If you cancel a blocked space booking, however, you usually have to pay the full freight amount to the carrier.

The **Booking** area also contains the **Carrier Routing** section, shown in Figure 5.22, which provides the stages' information, similar to the **Stages** area of ocean freight bookings. The example in the figure shows two stages of a connection flight from Frankfurt (**FRA**) to Chicago (**ORD**) by **LH** and from Chicago to Denver (**DEN**) by **QF**. For each stage, you see the referenced schedule and reference data status, which are explained in Section 5.1.3:

- Charges
  The **Charges** area contains the same settlement content as ocean freight bookings but adds some air waybill-specific information. It's also possible to activate printing of other charges in the house air waybill (HAWB) and the MAWB.

- Capacity and Cargo
  The **Capacity and Cargo** area contains cargo management, just as for the ocean freight bookings' **Items** area, and provides capacity information, such as the booked volume and weight, remaining capacity for volume and weight, and utilization as a percentage. For air freight bookings, the cost efficiency is determined mainly by the density factor, which characterizes the ratio of volume to weight and is shown as well.

- Operations
  The **Operations** area contains general data, such as the air waybill type and issuing date of the MAWB, as well as additional goods information about declared value, insurable value, and handling instructions.

- Statuses
  The **Statuses** area collects various statuses concerning lifecycle, fixing, archiving, subcontracting, execution, customs, transmission to SAP ERP, and consistency.

■ **Booking EDI Data**

The **Booking EDI Data** area contains information to be communicated to the airline like a high-level description of the cargo, special service requests, and other service information.

Figure 5.22 Carrier Routing

Usually, a special department is responsible for creating air freight bookings. The capacity managers in this department may already create bookings, but the bookings should become visible to planners and sales agents only after they have explicitly been published. To do so, the capacity manager can set the status to **Published**. The **Intermediate Processing** parameter in the **Execution Settings** section of the Customizing allows you to define whether newly created bookings get the status **Unpublished** or **Published**. Unpublished bookings get a planning block status and therefore can't be consumed or seen by other departments. Publishing removes this planning block status. A published booking can be unpublished.

It's also possible to restrict further the visibility of the air freight bookings to certain organizational units within your company. The capacity manager can maintain several organizational units, together with their functions (sales, company, or forwarding house) in the **Restriction to Organizational Units** area. With the **Set to Published with Restrictions** button, the capacity manager can publish the booking to the maintained organizational units. Authority checks for display and changing the air freight booking are also executed, according to the user's role and organization. Note that the organizational units can already be maintained in a master flight schedule and are then copied into the air freight bookings created for the master flight schedule.

Together, the publish concept, restricted visibility concept, and organization interaction model described in Section 5.4.1 enable fine-grained access control for the air freight bookings in your company.

Special security requirements arise for air cargo and are covered by air cargo security (ACS) checks and statuses. These can be activated in the forwarding order type Customizing with the **Enable Air Cargo Security Check** parameter and in the booking type Customizing by the **ACS Check** and **ACS Authority Check** parameters in the **Additional Settings** section. The required ACS status is captured in forwarding orders and propagated to freight units. The available ACS status can be maintained in air freight bookings. It can also be defined in a master flight schedule and is copied into air freight bookings created from the master flight schedule.

The following standard ACS status values are available, ordered from highest to lowest security: *secure for passenger aircraft* (SPX), *secure for cargo aircraft* (SCO), and *not secure* (NSC). The ACS check determines whether the ACS status of a freight unit is compatible with the assigned air freight booking. Freight units with the status SPX can be assigned to air freight bookings with the status SPX or SCO, and freight units with the status SCO can be assigned to bookings with the status SCO. A freight unit with the status NSC gets the planning block status and therefore can't be assigned at all. In this case, the corresponding forwarding order has to be processed according to security guidelines until it becomes secure. Then the status can be changed, and the document can be planned.

Automatic planning ensures that only compatible assignments are made. Depending on your user's authority, manual planning yields either a warning or an error message for an incompatible assignment.

You can maintain country-specific ACS status values in Customizing by following the menu path **Transportation Management • Basic Functions • Security • Define Air Cargo Security Statuses** and assigning the country-specific values to the standard ACS status values (SPX, SCO, and NSC).

In some countries, such as the United States, the air forwarder must have known the shipper for a certain period of time, which can be defined in Customizing via the menu path **Transportation Management • Basic Functions • Security • Define Offsets for Calculating Known Shipper Status**. If the forwarder knows the shipper for more than half a year, for example, the shipper's goods can be shipped via air freight. Otherwise, the forwarding order gets the status NSC, which means that the forwarder has to check the goods very carefully before transporting them by airplane. The known shipper status can be maintained in the business partner or the corresponding location, and it's automatically copied into a newly created forwarding order if the **Copy Air Cargo Security Data** parameter is active in the forwarding order type.

In the co-load process, you transport goods on a flight and use the air waybill stock and contract of another forwarder, the consolidator. This scenario is relevant if you don't have a contract with a carrier for a certain destination or if you don't have enough freight for the destination. Co-loading is a purely manual process, in which you maintain the consolidator and the MAWB number received from the consolidator in your air freight booking. This process is enabled by the **Co-load** parameter in the air freight booking type.

5.5 Summary

This chapter has introduced the capacity management process and its building blocks for planning capacities from long-term, mid-term, and short-term perspectives.

We've discussed schedules as the basis for systematically creating freight documents and scheduling change management capabilities. Allocations are used to allocate capacities for a carrier on a trade lane to certain (time) buckets, which can refer to a planning period (e.g., a week or a month) or to a schedule departure. Business shares allow defining the desired distribution of your transportation business on a trade lane across multiple carriers, again per bucket. Ocean freight and air freight bookings represent the booked capacity for a carrier on the operational level.

The next chapter explains transportation planning, which makes use of the planned capacities by assigning freight units and other demand documents to schedules and freight documents.

Chapter 6
Transportation Planning

Planning transportation activities are a key component of any transportation management solution. A proper transportation plan can help save money if it reasonably addresses the constraints present during its execution.

In previous chapters, we introduced business documents that represent a transportation need in SAP Transportation Management (SAP TM), such as sales orders (SOs), deliveries, order-based transportation requirements (OTRs), delivery-based transportation requirements (DTRs), and forwarding orders. On the other hand, vehicle resources, container resources, schedules, and freight bookings were introduced as a means to represent transportation capacity. The key objective of transportation planning is to create a transportation plan that brings together transportation needs and transportation capacity in the most efficient manner.

The first step that can be attributed to planning upon the creation of a transportation need is the creation of freight units. Freight units represent transportation requirements for planning and are obtained from their predecessor business documents via freight unit building rules (FUBRs). Freight units represent transportable objects that are kept together from their source to their destination (e.g., pallets and containers).

In the planning process, freight units can be assigned to multiple freight orders in a transportation chain or consolidated into one freight order, as is done in a local delivery tour. Essentially, the planning step covers the assignment of freight units to freight orders; these freight orders are the result of planning.

This planning step can be performed manually or automatically. A purely manual planning step can assign freight units to a vehicle resource using drag-and-drop functionality in the transportation cockpit to create a freight order; it can make the same assignment using the optimizer called by a background job.

The main objective of planning is to support the user with reasonable guidance for manual planning, as well as with powerful automation capabilities. The transition between both planning alternatives is smooth because automatically created plans can be adapted manually, and manual planning processes can make use of automation. For example, you can start the optimizer interactively in the transportation cockpit.

The planning process is configured mainly by two profiles: the selection profile and the planning profile. The *selection profile* is responsible for the decision about *what* needs to be planned, and it basically selects the freight unit (stages). The *planning profile* determines *how* to plan—that is, which transportation capacities are available for planning and which constraints (e.g., incompatibilities) need to be considered.

The transportation cockpit is the central user interface (UI) for planning. It's very flexible and configurable by the definition of various layouts so that it can process many structurally different planning scenarios (e.g., from planning a local road transport to planning overseas transportation chains).

This chapter is structured in the following way. First, Section 6.1 provides an overview of the documents involved in the planning process and the decisions that may need to be taken. In Section 6.2, we examine freight units and address the different properties of freight units defined by the freight unit type, their relationship to predecessor and successor business documents, and rules for their creation. Section 6.3 describes package building and the process of converting products and quantities into a package hierarchy. Thereafter, Section 6.4 introduces transportation units (TUs), which can be used to represent the transportation plan for scenarios involving trailers, railcars, containers, and packages. Section 6.5 presents the planning process configuration, including details on planning strategies, selection profiles, and planning profiles. Section 6.6 deals with manual planning by covering the transportation cockpit and its rich configuration capabilities based on page layouts as well as user-centric decision-making based on the transportation proposal functionality. Section 6.7 deals with automated planning. In contrast to Section 6.6, the focus here is on processes and functionality that aren't primarily interactive and user driven. Background planning and detailed insight into the optimization capabilities are in the scope of this section. The last section concludes with a description of load consolidation and load planning processes.

6.1   Documents and Decisions

Planning means assigning demands to capacities, resulting in a plan that optimizes the given business objectives and meets desired constraints. Transportation planning involves various business documents and different decision levels beyond the pure assignment of demands to capacities.

Figure 6.1 shows the business documents relevant for planning and their assignment options. Demand documents and their stages can be assigned to capacity documents. A capacity document can represent the transportation of one or more demands' stages. While a freight unit only represents a pure demand and freight orders and freight bookings represent pure capacities, TUs can represent both demand and capacity at the same time. Note that freight units, package units, and container units can be assigned to any capacity document shown in the box above them, which is symbolized by the gray box around the six capacity documents, including road freight order and trailer unit.

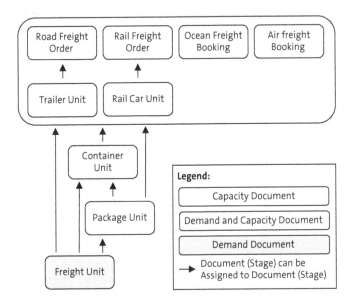

Figure 6.1 Documents and Assignment Decisions

The documents serve the following business purposes:

- **Freight unit**
  A freight unit represents an original transportation demand abstracting from forwarding orders, SOs, or deliveries, which is transported through the complete transportation chain without splitting it on any transportation stage. As a pure demand, a freight unit consumes capacity. See Section 6.2 for details on freight units.

- **Road freight order**

  Road freight orders represent transportation by road, which can be subcontracted or executed by a company's own fleet. This document represents a capacity and can consolidate multiple demands that consume the capacity. See Chapter 7.

- **Rail freight order**

  In the same way as the road freight order, a rail freight order represents transportation by rail.

- **Ocean freight booking**

  Ocean freight bookings represent subcontracted ocean transports. Like freight orders, a booking can consolidate multiple demands. See Chapter 5, Section 5.4.1.

- **Airfreight booking**

  Like ocean freight bookings, an air freight booking represents transportation by an airplane. See Chapter 5, Section 5.4.2.

- **Trailer unit**

  A trailer unit represents demands in a trailer that get transported by a road freight order. See Section 6.4.2 for details.

- **Rail carunit**

  Railcar units represent demands in a railcar that get transported by a rail freight order. Section 6.4.3 provides details on railcar units.

- **Container unit**

  A container unit models a demand transported in a container, as described in Section 6.4.4.

- **Package unit**

  Package units represent demands that are transported together in the same packages, for example, a pallet or carton. See Section 6.4.5 for details.

While trailer units and railcar units are dedicated to the road and rail mode of transport, container units frequently involve multiple modes of transport on the container unit stages. Package units may also get shipped in multiple modes of transport, directly or indirectly via container units.

Freight orders represent the movements of trucks and locomotives. Freight bookings represent the subcontracted movement of vessels or airplanes. Without freight orders and freight bookings, neither freight units nor TUs can be transported. However, freight orders can represent transportation without TUs and freight units; these represent empty moves, which may make sense, although you usually attempt to avoid them.

We use the term *freight document* as abstraction from road freight orders, rail freight orders, ocean freight bookings and air freight bookings. Freight documents can get subcontracted and form the basis for execution. They may be created in advance to reserve a carrier's transportation capacity, which is then consumed by assigning demands.

You can consolidate multiple freight units into a container unit, which serves as capacity from the freight unit viewpoint. However, the container itself also represents a demand that needs to be transported. In an intermodal container transportation scenario from China to Europe, the container may have three stages that are assigned to a road freight order for pre-carriage within China, an ocean freight booking for main carriage, and another road freight order for the subsequent carriage in Europe.

Note that all documents created by freight unit building (FUB) don't allow consolidation; that is, you can't assign other demand documents. See Section 6.2.3 for details on FUB.

Planning means decision-making, and creating a transportation plan can involve the following decisions:

- **Demand document stage sequence decision**
  For any demand document, the stage sequence defines the flow through the transportation chain. For example, for a freight unit, the stage sequence defines the hub sequence used to transport from source to destination location. Thus, the freight unit stage sequence defines the path through the hub network.

- **Consolidation decision**
  Each demand document stage can be assigned to a different capacity document. In many scenarios, many demands get transported by many capacity documents, and the consolidation decision defines which demands get transported together by the same capacity document. Another low-level consolidation decision is involved when different products get consolidated into mixed pallets.

- **Routing decision**
  As freight orders may consolidate many demands with different sources and destinations, the stop sequence defines the routing across all involved locations, which is essential as its total distance and duration mainly impacts transportation efficiency.

- **Scheduling decision**
  The scheduling decisions for a freight order involve assigning start and end times

to all activities, such as loading, unloading, and transporting. Ocean freight bookings are frequently based on predefined schedules and their departures. Both scheduling and the choice of the right schedule departure are essential for the desired service level to deliver on time.

- **Resource assignment decision**
  Road freight orders and trailer units get executed by certain truck and trailer resources. Similarly, rail freight orders and railcar units are assigned to certain locomotive and railcar resources, and container units get assigned to container resources. Thus, for any capacity document, which resource or resource type will be used is determined.

- **Driver assignment decision**
  Companies running their own truck fleet need to assign the right drivers to the road freight orders at hand. Decisions need to be made regarding whether a single driver or a team of two drivers is needed, as well as whether the driver assignment decision is made on the document or document stage level.

- **Carrier assignment decision**
  Companies without their own fleet subcontract their road freight orders to road carriers. Usually, several alternative carriers are available from which to choose for execution.

- **Packaging decision**
  If transportation demands contain product quantities, decisions need to be made regarding how the products get packaged for transportation. For example, different products may get consolidated into pick cartons, and both stock cartons (of one product) and pick cartons get consolidated into a mixed pallet.

- **Physical positioning decision**
  Road freight orders may involve transportation of pallets, each containing multiple cartons. Physical positioning can be relevant on two levels: positioning cartons in a pallet and positioning pallets in the truck. Positioning is important to maximize the utilization of pallets and trucks, optimize transportation efficiency, and ensure transportation safety, for example, considering axle weight constraints.

Due to the huge diversity of different transportation businesses, not every business will involve each decision type. But each transportation business requires one or multiple decisions, which can be made manually, automatically, or by a combination thereof, as described in Section 6.6 (manual planning) and Section 6.7 (automatic planning). Obviously, many decisions depend on each other.

The decisions are made based on the available transportation network (described in Chapter 3, Section 3.2), resources (see Chapter 3, Section 3.3), and various constraints imposed by the planning profile and additional settings (Section 6.5.2).

6.2 Freight Units

Freight units are an important element in the planning process because they provide the link between transportation requirements—for example, a forwarding order and the transportation document (i.e., the freight order). They can be omitted only in special circumstances if the transportation requirement exactly matches the to-be-created transportation document (called a *shortcut planning process*). This process is described in more detail in Section 6.2.3.

Let's start with the definition of a freight unit and then move into properties of the freight units defined in Customizing and the information stored in the freight unit. The third subsection of Section 6.2 deals with the process of creating freight units. How to integrate package information into this process will be the topic of Section 6.3.

6.2.1 Freight Unit Definition

The *freight unit* is a set of goods transported together through the entire transportation chain. The freight unit is the smallest unit that can be transported. This means that everything included in one freight unit stays together from its source to its ultimate destination—that is, it's always transported together.

The granularity of freight units required for transportation planning depends greatly on your business scenario. For example, if you're an electronics manufacturer, a freight unit can be one of the following:

- One USB stick if you want to send this USB stick from your distribution center directly to the final consumer (e.g., as a parcel shipment)
- A container full of USB sticks if you want to replenish your distribution center in the United States from your factory in China

Freight Unit Granularity

The more freight units are formed, the more detailed and individually you can plan. However, this makes planning more complex and requires higher processing capacity, leading to longer runtimes. Just imagine the system load and number of objects created if you had created freight units for each USB stick in a replenishment scenario. Therefore, we strongly recommend that you define the granularity of freight units only to the detail level required for your business scenario.

Given the dependency of the "optimal" freight unit granularity on the business scenario, there is no general rule for how freight units should be created. However, the following uses cases can be distinguished:

- For general cargo, freight units may be created based on handling units (e.g., pallets) or a group thereof.
- For full container freight, a freight unit usually represents the container.
- For bulk products, a freight unit may represent a quantity that corresponds to the capacity available for the transportation of the product. For example, a forwarding order for 5,000 tons of fertilizer to be transported with railcars with a capacity of 50 tons each should yield 100 freight units of 50 tons each.

Figure 6.2 shows how freight units relate to other objects in SAP TM. They are created based on transportation requirements (n:m relationship).

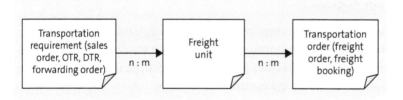

Figure 6.2 Relationship of Freight Units to Other Objects

One freight unit can have one or more transportation requirements as predecessor documents. This means that freight units can be used to consolidate transportation requirements from several forwarding orders by considering the restriction that the freight unit stays together on the complete transportation chain (i.e., predecessor documents must have the same origin, destination, dates, etc.). On the other hand, one transportation requirement can yield several freight units. This is probably the more important case because there are many good reasons that one transportation requirement is split over several freight units:

- An SO that consists of several items that have different transportation characteristics (e.g., frozen pizza and fresh ravioli require different temperature conditions during transportation)
- An SO with an item that has different schedule lines (e.g., transportation should be in weekly quantities and not together)
- An SO with an item representing a large quantity of a bulk product (e.g., the full quantity needs to be split into quantities that fit with the capacity of transportation resources)

In the planning process, freight units are assigned to transportation orders (n:m relationship). Any type of assignment is allowed (1:1, 1:n, n:1, n:m) and depends on the business scenario:

- **1:1**
  A 1:1 assignment can occur if a customer orders a full truckload directly from the plant to his warehouse.

- **1:n**
  A 1:n assignment can occur for a container that is shipped across several stages. This container is then assigned to one freight order (e.g., by truck) for the pre-carriage, another freight order or freight booking (e.g., by sea or air) to represent the main carriage, and a third freight order (e.g., by rail) to represent the on-carriage.

- **n:1**
  An n:1 assignment typically occurs in distribution scenarios (e.g., if the freight order represents a truck transport that delivers the load to multiple customers [unloading locations]).

- **n:m**
  An n:m assignment can occur as a result of any combination of these scenarios.

6.2.2   Properties of Freight Units

Freight units are created based on a certain freight unit type. The freight unit type defines the properties of a freight unit and can be defined in Customizing via the menu path **Transportation Management · Planning · Freight Unit · Define Freight Unit Types**.

You should use different freight unit types based on your business requirements; that is, the electronics manufacturer may have different tracking and tracing requirements for freight units that represent final customer orders compared to freight units that represent stock replenishments for the distribution center. Thus, two different freight unit types can be used that are customized differently with respect to their execution tracking relevance and event management settings that govern integration with SAP Event Management.

In addition, you can influence the following properties of a freight unit in freight unit type Customizing:

- Number range settings
- Change controller settings
- Planning settings
- Execution settings
- Integration settings
- Direct shipment options
- Output options
- Organizational unit determination
- Additional settings

Because the freight unit represents the transportation demand in planning, it has to answer the following questions:

- **What needs to be transported?**
  This answers the question about the set of goods being transported. Relevant information is quantities and units of measure, as well as characteristics (e.g., temperature conditions to be met during transport).
- **Where to transport?**
  This answers the question about the source and destination location and potentially predefined transshipment locations defined as stages in the freight unit.
- **When to transport?**
  This deals with the temporal aspect of transportation (e.g., when the freight unit should be picked up at the source and delivered at the destination location).

To represent the dates and times of pickup and delivery in the freight unit, four time stamps are defined in the freight unit for both pickup and delivery. Figure 6.3 shows how these time stamps are obtained based on the requested dates and times defined in the freight unit's predecessor document.

A condition with condition type /SCMTMS/TOR_TIMEWIND can be assigned to the freight unit type in freight unit type Customizing. Based on this condition, SAP TM calculates four time stamps for pickup and delivery, which have the following interpretation later in automated planning:

- **Acceptable date—start**
  No pickup/delivery is allowed prior to this date (e.g., because the product hasn't been produced yet).

- **Requested date—start**
  This is the start of the desired pickup/delivery period. A pickup/delivery between the acceptable and requested start date is allowed but can be penalized in planning as an earliness cost.

- **Requested date—end**
  This is the end of the desired pickup delivery period. A pickup/delivery within the requested start and end date doesn't incur any penalty costs in planning. This period can be used to represent the appointment time window agreed on between the supplier and customer at the source/destination location.

- **Acceptable date—end**
  No pickup/delivery is allowed after this date. Any pickup/delivery between the requested and acceptable end date is allowed but can be penalized in planning as a lateness cost.

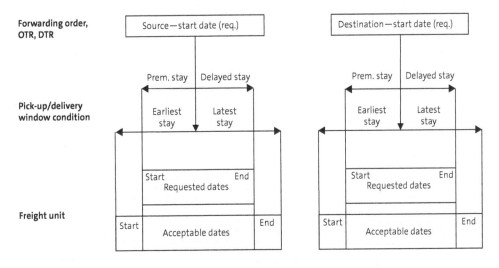

Figure 6.3 Schematic Description of Pickup and Delivery Windows

Not all of these dates have to be defined. For example, if the customer accepts all deliveries no matter how early they are, then no acceptable start date for the delivery needs to be defined.

Using the concept of conditions in the freight unit type Customizing to define pickup and delivery time windows allows for a lot of flexibility in setting up business scenarios. If the requested or acceptable dates shouldn't be the same for all freight units of the same freight unit type, the time window condition can be used to define different dates based on the destination location (customer) or goods included or any other relevant criteria of the freight unit. Thus, to increase the service level for important customers, these can be assigned a much tighter time window than less important customers.

Freight units can be scheduled automatically in the FUB process (if **Distance/Duration Determination: Enable Automatic Determination** is selected in freight unit type Customizing) by clicking the **Scheduling** button in the transportation cockpit or by applying a default route to the freight unit. This allows for better information and visibility for unplanned freight units, as it will directly show realistic transportation durations calculated based on geo-coordinates.

In the SAP TM UI, you can access freight units from different origins: by using the Edit Freight Unit app via the **Planning** menu option, via the link in the document flow of other documents such as forwarding orders or freight orders, or via personal worklists (POWLs) (e.g., **Planning • Freight Units (Worklist)**). Figure 6.4 shows the standard freight unit UI.

The information contained in the freight unit is structured into different tabs. The following are the most relevant:

- **General Data**

  The **General Data** tab contains an overview of the freight unit:

  - **Source Location** (address and pickup window)
  - **Destination Location** (address and delivery window)
  - **Required Capacity** (quantities and unit of measure)
  - **Organizational Data**
  - **Freight Unit Type**
  - **Freight Unit Building Rule** (Section 6.2.3)

  Thus, the **General Data** tab answers questions related to what, where, and when.

- **Items**

  The **Items** tab displays the information related to the content of the freight unit. It shows you the hierarchy of items (container, package, and product) contained in the freight unit, as well as the individual products with their quantities and units of measure.

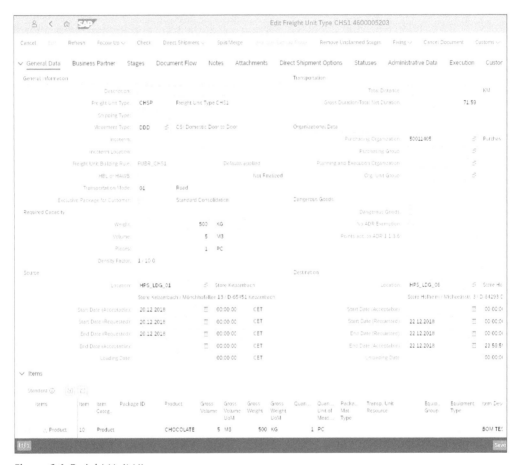

Figure 6.4 Freight Unit UI

- **Business Partner**

  On the **Business Partner** tab, you can find information about the relevant business partners (e.g., shipper and consignee).

- **Stages**

  The **Stages** tab can contain one or more entries. In the simplest scenario, only one stage is present—the stage from the source of the freight unit to its destination. This implies no constraints for planning; that is, the freight unit can later be transported directly from its source to its destination or indirectly via transshipment locations—whatever is the most effective way for the business scenario.

However, additional stages can be added to the freight unit manually in the **Stages** tab by applying a default route or by using the transportation proposal functionality (Section 6.6.9 and Chapter 3, Section 3.2). If the transportation network allows sea transports from Europe to North America to originate from Hamburg or Rotterdam, these options may be offered to a customer based on a transportation proposal in the forwarding order, and the customer's choice is represented as stages to or from Hamburg or Rotterdam in the freight unit. This stage information is considered to be a constraint in planning.

Freight Units in Stages

The freight unit, which exists only once, appears in several virtual instances (stages) in planning. These instances can be planned independently from each other (e.g., pre-carriage, main carriage, and on-carriage). That is, different users can plan the individual stages at different times.

This is common business practice because the user responsible for US domestic transport (e.g., on-carriage from port to customer) often isn't familiar with domestic transport in Europe (pre-carriage from source to port) or ocean transport (main carriage from port to port). Furthermore, the individual stages are frequently not planned in the same sequence in which they occur; rather, the main carriage ocean is planned first based on the sailing calendar of the ocean vessel, while pre-carriage and on-carriage are planned later.

- **Document Flow**
  The document flow shows all related (predecessor and successor) documents for the freight unit.

- **Notes**
  Notes can be used to add texts to the freight unit.

- **Attachments**
  Attachments can be any electronic documents (e.g., PDF files) or URLs. Files and URLs can be organized in a folder structure.

- **Direct Shipment Options**
  The direct shipment options can be generated automatically when the freight unit

is created via a process controller strategy (default: **Dso_Def**) based on the freight unit type Customizing settings, or the options can be manually triggered from the freight unit UI.

Direct shipment options are generated for each carrier-service level combination based on a freight agreement. Thus, they represent "real" costs. They can be used if freight units aren't consolidated during planning but rather are assigned directly to a carrier. In planning using the optimizer, the most cost-effective price (direct shipment option) can be used as a reference cost to decide whether a consolidated solution for multiple freight units is more cost efficient than the sum of direct shipment options for the individual freight units. If the direct shipment option is chosen, the freight unit needs to be converted to a freight order either manually or via a background report.

The full parcel process using direct shipment options is explained in detail in Chapter 7.

- **Statuses**
  The freight unit has several statuses. Let's take a look at the most relevant:
  - The lifecycle status shows whether the freight unit is **New**, **In Process**, **Completed**, or **Canceled**.
  - The **Fixing** status determines whether the business document can be changed or not. Fixing prevents the change of only existing planning results.
  - Possible planning statuses are **Not Planned**, **Partially Planned**, and **Planned**, depending on whether none, some, or all stages of the freight unit have been planned.
  - The **Execution** status of the freight unit is changed when any of the freight orders or bookings that the freight unit is assigned to are executed.

    Freight units can be blocked separately for planning and execution. Use cases for planning blocks include when not all planning-relevant information is available or approvals are missing. Use cases for execution blocks can be missing approvals or required prepayment.

- **Execution**
  The **Execution** tab provides the interface to SAP Event Management (see Chapter 8, Section 8.2). All events reported for a freight unit are displayed in this tab, including planned and actual dates and times. Expected events can be reported on the **Execution** tab, and unexpected events can also be inserted there.

Finally, an organizational interaction status can be maintained in the stages of the freight unit. The organizational interaction status relates to an internal business process between different organizational units (e.g., the sales organization and planning and execution organization) of a logistics service provider (LSP). The sales organization may be allowed to create stages in a forwarding order, but the planning and execution organization is responsible for assigning the stages to schedules, freight bookings, or freight orders. The organizational interaction status that is maintained independently for each stage determines which organization is tasked with the next activity. Figure 6.5 shows how the different organizational units interact and how this is represented in the organizational interaction status of the freight unit stage.

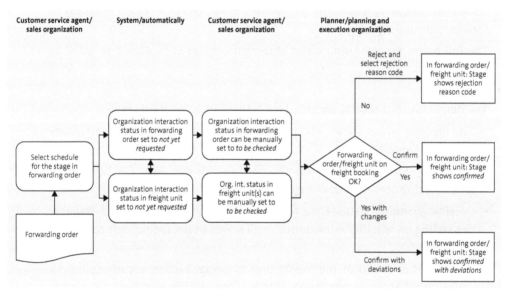

Figure 6.5 Organizational Interaction Process

6.2.3   Creating Freight Units

Figure 6.6 displays the triggers that start the creation of a freight unit from its predecessor documents (i.e., SOs purchase order [POs], deliveries, OTRs, DTRs, or forwarding orders). FUB is either triggered automatically or done manually. If freight units shouldn't consolidate items from different predecessor documents, which is the most common case, then automatic FUB can be activated for the relevant document order type in Customizing:

- For forwarding orders: **Transportation Management · Forwarding Order Management · Forwarding Order · Define Forwarding Order Types**

- For OTRs: **Transportation Management · Integration · Logistics Integration · External TM System Integration · Order-based Transportation Requirement · Define Order-based Transportation Requirement Types**

- For DTRs: **Transportation Management · Integration · Logistics Integration · External TM System Integration · Delivery-based Transportation Requirement · Define Delivery-based Transportation Requirement Types**

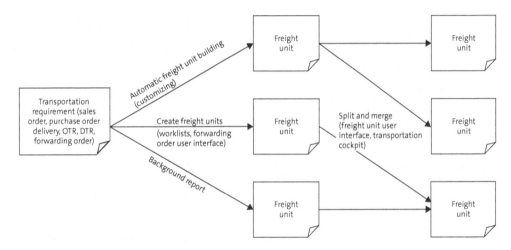

Figure 6.6 Trigger for Freight Unit Creation

For the use of SAP TM in an embedded scenario (internal SAP TM component integration), automatic FUB is mandatory and must be selected in the logistics integration profile (**Transportation Management · Integration · Logistics Integration · Internal TM Component Integration · Define Logistics Integration Profile**). In this scenario, freight units can't be created across business documents automatically, but only using the manual merge activity.

In addition, freight unit creation can be triggered by a background report for transportation planning preparation (report /SCMTMS/TRQ_PREP_PLNG_BATCH) shown in Figure 6.7. There are also manual options for triggering the creation of freight units either directly from the forwarding order UI or via worklists for any of the possible predecessor documents (i.e., OTR, DTR, and forwarding order).

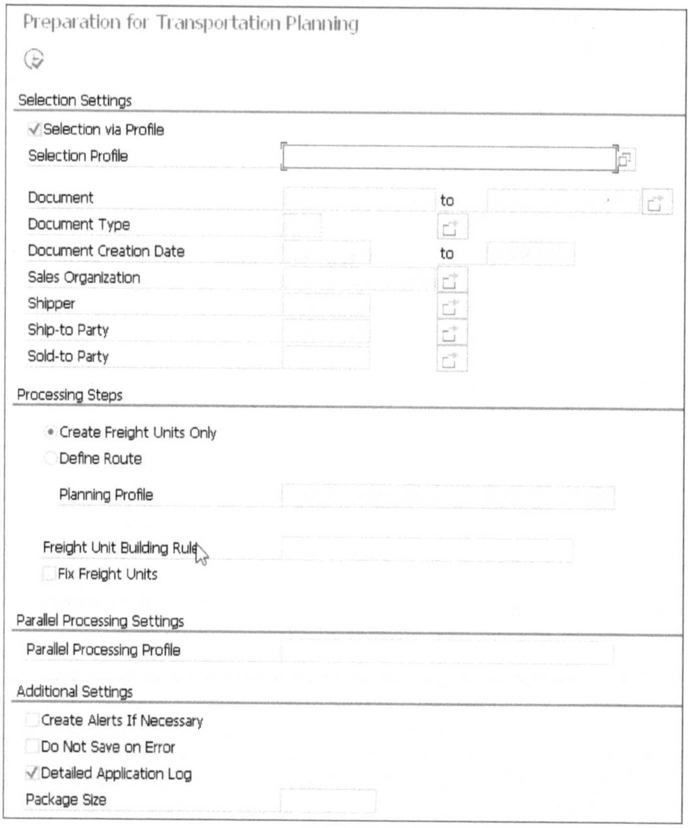

Figure 6.7 Background Report for Freight Unit Creation

After freight units have been created, you might have to change them. Changes from preceding business documents are propagated automatically to the freight unit, and change controller strategies assigned in freight unit type Customizing (**Transportation Management · Planning · Freight Unit · Define Freight Unit Types**) govern the behavior of the reaction to a change. However, manual changes also may be needed (e.g., if a freight unit needs to be split into two parts because its full quantity can't be assigned to a vehicle resource due to a capacity limitation). For this purpose, a split and merge transaction allows you to execute the required changes directly in the freight unit UI or from the transportation cockpit. FUBRs are defined in **Profiles and Settings · Create Freight Unit Building Rule** (in SAP TM 9.6, the menu path is **Application Administration · Planning · General Settings · Freight Unit Building Rule**).

In the FUBR shown in Figure 6.8, you can control the strategy used during freight unit creation. The **Consolidate as Much as Possible** option in the **Freight Unit Building Strategy** field allows you to consolidate items from one or more different predecessor business documents into one freight unit. **Consolidate per Request (Compatible Parts)** allows you to consolidate several items of the same predecessor business document, and **Consolidate per Item** creates one freight unit per item of the predecessor business document.

Additionally, you can maintain whether the FUBR is allowed to split items into several freight units. This is generally allowed by all three strategies but may not be reasonable in certain planning scenarios.

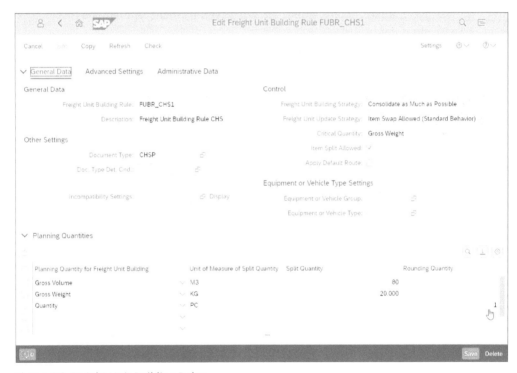

Figure 6.8 Freight Unit Building Rules

The resultant business document type of the freight unit is another important setting in the FUBR. Although the name FUBR may indicate that the resultant business document is always a freight unit, this isn't the case; in fact, the result of an FUBR can be a freight unit, package unit, TU document, or freight order. Which object is created is specified in either the **Document Type** field or the **Doc. Type Det. Cnd.** (document type determination condition) field with a condition of type /SCMTMS/TOR_TYPE.

Creating a freight order directly from the FUBR is called the *shortcut planning process* because, in this case, freight units as separate business documents are omitted, and additional planning steps aren't required because the freight order is created right away. A typical planning scenario that uses this feature is the zero-click scenario, which can be configured in the following way:

1. The transportation requirement (SO, OTR, etc.) triggers freight unit creation automatically because **Automatic Freight Unit Building** is activated in its document type Customizing or the corresponding logistics integration profile.

2. The determined FUBR has a resultant business document type defined that creates a freight order.

3. A background job or the creation strategy of the business document type triggers carrier selection and tendering for the freight order.

In this process, no user activity is required after saving the transportation requirement. A freight order is automatically created, tendered, and awarded to a carrier.

The FUBR also needs to consider incompatibilities, which we discuss in Section 6.7.4 in more detail. Assume that certain products aren't allowed to be transported together; for example, ice cream and ketchup can't be shipped together because they have different temperature requirements. Thus, these two items of the transportation requirement need to be kept apart in FUB, although other items of the same transportation requirement (e.g., chocolate ice cream and strawberry ice cream) can be consolidated into one freight unit. Incompatibilities can be used to express such a planning constraint, so incompatibility settings can be assigned in the FUBR.

You can also use freight unit creation to consolidate items of a business document into a container and display the freight unit as a container. To be able to do this, you need to define **Equipment Group** and **Equipment Type** in the FUBR. In this scenario, SAP TM takes the physical properties defined in Customizing for the equipment into account (**Transportation Management** • **Master Data** • **Resources** • **General Settings** • **Define Equipment Groups and Equipment Types**) (see also Chapter 3, Section 3.3).

Last, you have to define planning quantities. Planning quantities are an integral part of the FUBR because only planning quantities are copied into the freight unit from predecessor business documents. For each planning quantity, a split quantity and a rounding quantity can be defined. The split quantity defines the maximum value a freight unit can take in any of the planning quantities. If the gross weight in the transportation requirement is 9 tons, and the split value for gross weight is defined as 4 tons, three freight units with gross weight 4 tons, 4 tons, and 1 ton would be created. If the rounding quantity is defined as one piece, and the 9 tons from the previous example corresponded to six pieces of 1.5 tons each, then the result would be three freight units of 3 tons (two pieces) each.

Critical Quantity

Finding the best possible assignment of items to freight units is a knapsack problem. Because of the combinatorial nature of this task, it's too computationally expensive to solve this kind of optimization problem during FUB.

Therefore, a heuristic is applied that can be influenced by maintaining the *critical quantity* in the FUBR. In this heuristic, all items are sorted in descending order based on their critical quantity and assigned to freight units in this sequence. This heuristic provides the optimal result unless the items are very heterogeneous; that is, some items are very small but heavy compared to large but light items.

Figure 6.9 provides an example in which the optimal and heuristic solutions deviate from each other, assuming that the critical quantity is gross weight and the split quantity for gross weight is 10 tons and 10 cubic meters for gross volume.

OTR items			Heuristic assignment				Optimal assignment		
Item	Gross weight [to]	Gross volume [m3]	FU 1	FU 2	FU 3	FU 4	FU 1	FU 2	FU 3
10	8	2	X				X		
20	6	4		X				X	
30	4	6		X				X	
40	2	1	X						X
50	2	1			X				X
60	2	1			X				X
70	2	1			X				X
80	1	8				X	X		
Total	27	24	10 / 3	10 / 10	6 / 3	1 / 8	9 / 10	10 / 10	8 / 4

Figure 6.9 Assignment of Items to Freight Units

Considering that FUBRs are so important, how does SAP TM determine which one to use? The first attempt is to read a condition of type /SCMTMS/FUBR from the predecessor business document type Customizing or the logistics integration profile:

- For forwarding orders: **Transportation Management • Forwarding Order Management • Forwarding Order • Define Forwarding Order Types**

- For OTRs: **Transportation Management • Integration • Logistics Integration • External TM System Integration • Order-Based Transportation Requirement • Define Order-Based Transportation Requirement Types**

- For DTRs: **Transportation Management • Integration • Logistics Integration • External TM System Integration • Delivery-Based Transportation Requirement • Define Delivery-Based Transportation Requirement Types**

- For internal SAP TM component: **Transportation Management • Integration • Logistics Integration • Internal TM Component Integration • Define Logistics Integration Profile**

The next step is to determine the FUBR based on this condition. If there is no condition defined, or the determination fails, the FUBR is determined directly from the predecessor business document type Customizing. If nothing is maintained there, default settings are applied.

You can see which FUBR has been applied for any freight unit in the freight unit UI on the **General Settings** tab.

In some transportation processes, freight unit information is also required to show packaging information (e.g., number and size of pallets). Next, we'll explain how to create packaging information within the items of the freight unit (i.e., package building) during freight unit creation.

6.3   Package Building

Given a set of products and quantities, package building determines the packaging hierarchy to be used for transportation. The packaging hierarchy mainly determines the utilization of cartons and pallets but also of containers, trailers, and trucks. It can be communicated to a warehouse system, so that cartons and pallets can be built in the warehouse before the truck picks them up. Besides the packaging hierarchy, package building also determines the size (length, width, height) of the package and whether another package can be stacked on it. These properties and the package's weight are essential input for load planning, which determines physical positions of packages in a truck, trailer, or container.

Usually, package building is performed automatically, but it's also possible to manually change the packaging hierarchy within a capacity document. Figure 6.10 illustrates unpackaged product items within a road freight order (left) and the packaging hierarchy determined by package building (right), which includes pallet items, carton items, and product items. The term package is used as abstraction from pallet and carton. Although there is no explicit concept for pallets and cartons in SAP TM, we'll consequently use these terms for illustrative purposes because they are more intuitive as the technical, abstract concepts of top-level package and bottom-level package. While the shown example contains at most two packaging levels—pallets on level 1 and cartons on level 2—using the appropriate package type assignment, you can configure the system to build even more than two packaging levels.

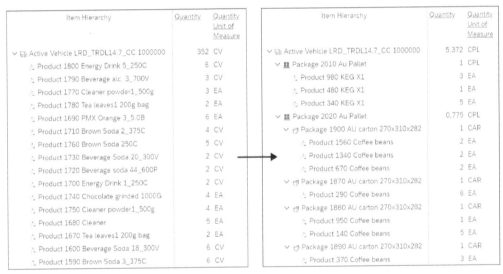

Figure 6.10 Packaging Hierarchy before (Left) and after Package Building (Right)

In this section, we'll discuss package building in three parts: integration into the planning process, algorithmic approach, and configuration.

6.3.1   Integration into the Planning Process

Package building can be used at different steps in the planning process. During FUB, it can be used to determine the packaging hierarchy of the transportation demand at hand. This usage can be activated by defining the **Package Building Profile** in the advanced settings of the FUBR depicted in Figure 6.11. Using the **Package Building Result** field, you can define whether the determined complete packaging hierarchy or only the determined number of packages is stored as an estimate. Defining a **Maximum Number of Packages per FU** greater than zero lets FUB split the transportation demand into multiple freight units that contain at most the specified number of packages, as described in Section 6.2.2.

Figure 6.11 Package Building Settings in the Advanced Settings of the FUBR

Package building can also be triggered for capacity documents, such as road freight orders, trailer units, container units or package units, either explicitly in the capacity document UI or in the transportation cockpit. This process is only supported in SAP TM 9.6 and not in SAP S/4HANA 1809.

In the cockpit, you can use the **Create Packages** button or trigger package creation automatically during a manual planning operation, such as assigning a freight unit to a road freight order, by using a manual planning strategy that includes package building (see Section 6.5.1). You need to maintain the package building profile in the planning profile. To use package building for the capacity document type at hand, this functionality has to be activated by the **Enable Pkg Building** parameter in the **Planning Settings** section of the document type Customizing, as shown in Figure 6.12 for a road freight order type. The **Update Load Plan** option defines whether package building and/or load planning will be triggered automatically by item changes in the original transportation demand.

Figure 6.12 Freight Order Type Customizing to Activate Package Building and Define Update Behavior for Item Changes

The main reason for using package building is that the original transportation demands contain product quantities but no packaging information. In addition, the packaging information is needed to enable more accurate planning or to define the packaging to be executed in the warehouse. The parameters described previously enable the following two main business scenarios:

- A package will only contain goods of one original transportation demand. In this case, package building should be triggered already during FUB, and the determined packaging hierarchy should be stored. This approach prevents pallets containing goods from different customers and transportation demands. In execution, this means that one customer can be served by unloading all its pallets from a truck; therefore, there is no need to touch goods to be delivered to other customers. This scenario is commonly used when serving a few customers by one truck, and each customer orders goods covering multiple pallets. Moreover, this usually assumes unloading pallets by forklifts at the customers' locations.

- A package can contain goods of multiple original transportation demands, for transportation efficiency reasons. This may lead to goods for different customers getting consolidated into the same pallet or carton. In this approach, you would first do consolidation decisions, that is, consolidate multiple customers' demands into a capacity document, such as a road freight order. Then, package building is triggered for the capacity document, storing the determined packaging hierarchy in the capacity document. In this approach, it's recommended also to call package building already during FUB by using the option to store the package number estimate because this allows making consolidation decisions based not just on volume or weight information but also considering the expected number of packages. This approach yields mixed pallets containing goods to multiple customers. Therefore, in execution, the goods for one customer get pulled out of the relevant mixed packages during the stop at the customer. This scenario is commonly used when many customers can be served by one truck because each customer orders only a few products and quantities.

Figure 6.13 shows the planning process for the first business scenario in a local distribution example. The initial situation contains a set of unplanned freight unit stages from one distribution center displayed as square on the map to multiple customers shown as triangles on the map. Package building has been used within FUB, storing the determined packaging hierarchy in the freight units. Therefore, the freight units represent a set of packages shown in the 3D view and colored by customer. As the first planning step, the vehicle scheduling and routing (VSR) optimizer (Section 6.7.1) consolidates the freight units into two road freight orders shown on the map, assigning a truck resource and defining the stop sequence for each freight order. Each road freight order contains the packages of the assigned freight units, as shown for one of the freight orders that consolidates three customers. The packages are shown as unplanned objects in the 3D load plan view because they aren't yet positioned in the truck. Load planning (Section 6.7.8) is the second planning step that determines a load plan for the packages in the truck; that is, they get positioned in the truck's cargo space. This finishes the planning process, and the road freight orders can be executed.

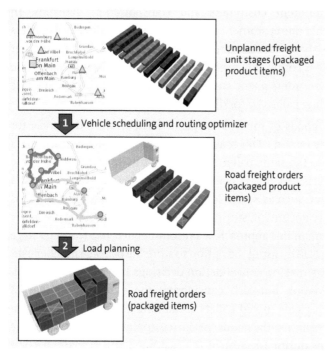

Figure 6.13 Planning Process Based on Storing the Complete Packaging Hierarchy during FUB

Figure 6.14 displays the planning process for the second business scenario, again in a local distribution example. The initial situation contains a set of unplanned freight unit stages with unpackaged goods from one distribution center to multiple customers. Package building has been used within FUB to determine the expected number of pallets, depicted as the quantity dimension in the shown freight unit stage list. Using the VSR optimizer (Section 6.7.1) as the first planning step, the system consolidates the unplanned freight units into one road freight order, assigns it to a truck resource, and defines its stop sequence. The road freight order contains the unpackaged products from the assigned freight unit stages, displayed as unplanned objects besides the truck in the 3D load plan view. Package building is used as the second planning step, resulting in a packaging hierarchy with six pallets containing the individual products. Because the pallets haven't yet been positioned on the truck, they are still shown as unplanned objects in the 3D load plan view. Load planning (Section 6.7.8) represents the third planning step that positions the pallets in the truck's cargo space. Planning is now completed, and the road freight order can be given to execution.

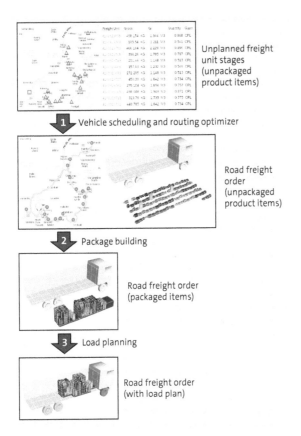

Figure 6.14 Planning Process Based on Estimated Number of Packages and Triggering Package Building for Road Freight Orders

Of course, there are transportation businesses in which package building isn't required at all. The most obvious example is transportation of unpackaged products.

In another example, the original transportation demand (e.g., forwarding order, SO, or delivery) already contains a predefined packaging hierarchy that must not be changed in SAP TM.

6.3.2   Rule-Based and Detailed Package Building

Package building can create the following different kinds of pallets:

- Single product or mixed, that is, containing multiple products
- Full or incomplete, meaning there is still space left
- Stackable (i.e., another pallet can be stacked on it) or nonstackable

First, the system builds single product pallets and then mixed pallets. A mixed pallet can be built by a rule-based approach or detailed package building that uses an optimization algorithm to determine physical positions (x, y, z) and orientations of products and cartons in it.

Rule-based package building can build mixed pallets in a layer-based and volume-based style, where the layer definition stems from the product master, and volume-based means that individual product quantities get consolidated until the sum of their volumes or weights hits the corresponding capacity of the pallet. The system can build different kinds of layers:

- Single product or mixed, that is, containing multiple products.
- Full or incomplete.
- Flat (i.e., all items in the layer have same height) or nonflat.

    A nonflat layer doesn't allow stacking, that is, neither another layer nor another pallet can be stacked on it. A pallet is stackable if it's either a full single product pallet or a mixed pallet consisting only of full and flat layers. Thus, a volume-based mixed pallet doesn't allow stacking.

Figure 6.15 shows 11 examples for rule-based pallets:

- The pallet ❶ represents a full single product pallet; that is, it only contains one product P1 and the maximum number of pieces defined in the corresponding product master data. This pallet is stackable.
- An incomplete single product pallet ❷ is defined by the system as nonstackable.
- The mixed pallet ❸ contains two full layers, 1 and 2, of product P1 and three complete layers, 3–5, of product P2. This pallet is stackable because it only contains full single product layers.

- Example ❹ is similar to ❸, but its topmost layer is mixed, containing two products P2 and P3. As the topmost layer is full and flat, this pallet is stackable.
- The mixed pallet ❺ contains an incomplete layer and is therefore nonstackable.
- Example ❻ shows a mixed pallet containing a mixed layer that is flat but incomplete. Therefore, this pallet is nonstackable.
- Although the mixed pallet ❼ contains a mixed layer that covers the full footprint of the pallet, it's nevertheless nonstackable because the mixed layer is nonflat.

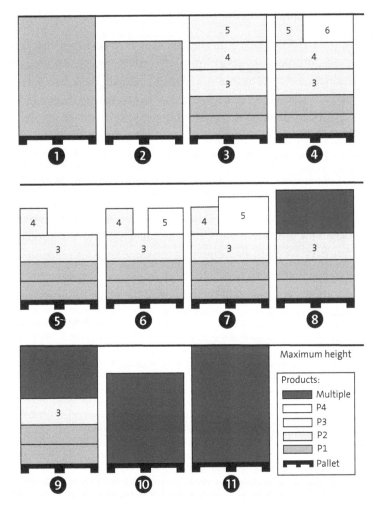

Figure 6.15 Examples of Single Product and Mixed Pallets Built in Layer-Based and/or Volume-Based Fashion

- The mixed pallet ❽ shows a combination of layer-based and volume-based package building. It contains three full single-product layers and multiple products on top, which causes this pallet to be nonstackable.

- Example ❾ is similar to ❽, but the volume-based portion has reached the maximum height of the pallet. Although this pallet is full, it isn't stackable because it contains a volume-based portion.

- Example ❿ doesn't contain any layers, but it's built purely in volume-based style, thus it's nonstackable.

- The mixed pallet ⓫ is full but nonstackable.

While the rule-based approach only assigns product quantities to packages, detailed package building uses an optimization algorithm to determine physical positions and orientations of products and cartons in a mixed pallet. All pallets created in this approach are considered nonstackable. Figure 6.16 shows the following three examples for mixed pallets created by detailed package building (objects positioned on the mixed pallets are colored by product):

- Example ❶ shows a mixed pallet with high diversity of different products and sizes. Some products are turned by 90 degrees to maximize the volume utilization.

- Pallet ❷ contains two different products that have same size. Again, some boxes are turned by 90 degrees for utilization purposes. The pallet has been constructed by towers, which gives easy access to all products at the same time for unloading.

- Example ❸ shows a mixed pallet with two cylindrical products of different height and diameter. The goods are positioned in the middle of the pallet for safety reasons; the center of gravity of the load is centered as much as possible.

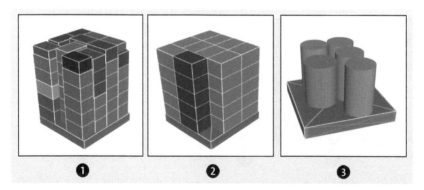

Figure 6.16 Examples for Mixed Pallets Created by Detailed Package Building

6.3.3 Configuration

As different packaging businesses may require the consideration of very different rules during package building, the system offers a rich set of configuration capabilities:

- **Product (master data)**
  Defines product-specific parameters considered during package building.

- **Package type assignment**
  Determines the packaging materials to be used and defines additional constraints and parameters depending on products, business partners, locations, equipment groups, equipment types, and packaging materials.

- **Package building profile**
  Determines algorithmic parameters for rule-based and detailed package building. It includes references to other profiles, such as the *product relationship profile* or the *profile for package building optimizer*.

Let's take a closer look at each.

Product Master Data

Using the menu path **Logistics · Transportation Management · Master Data · Material · Create** (in SAP TM 9.6, the menu path is **Master Data · General · Define Product**), you can maintain the product master data that is essential for package building. Figure 6.17 shows the definition of relevant units of measures for a product.

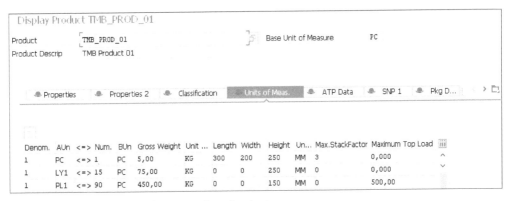

Figure 6.17 Defining Units of Measure for a Product

In this example, the base unit of measure is **PC** (pieces). The table defines its relation to other units of measures. The first row specifies the weight and size of one individual piece (**PC**). The second and third row define how many pieces fit into one full layer (unit of measure **LY1**) and one full pallet (**PL1**). You can also maintain additional constraints:

- The **Max.StackFactor** is considered during detailed package building and defines how many pieces of the product at hand can be stacked on top of each other.

- Load planning considers the **Maximum Top Load** of a full pallet, which defines how much weight of other pallets can be stacked on top.

The **Pkg Data** tab allows you to define additional parameters for package building. The **Capacities** section specifies the following properties of a packaging material:

- The **Maximum Weight** defines how much load can be put into a package using the packaging material at hand.

- The **Closed Packaging** parameter defines whether the packaging material is open or closed. While a pallet is the most typical example for an open packaging material, cartons, pallet cages, and cool packs are examples of closed packaging materials. The main difference is that the outer volume of a closed package is independent of the load in it. In case of an open package, the outer volume depends on the tare volume of the package and the goods loaded.

- The **Filling Level** is considered by volume-based package building to determine when to stop further consolidation into the package at hand.

The **Package Building Settings** section defines the following parameters for products to be packaged:

- The **Reference Product for Package Building** allows structuring products by reference products, resulting in a reference product hierarchy. This concept allows products to be grouped in a hierarchical fashion for package building and certain parameters and constraints to be defined on the reference product level, which reduces master data maintenance efforts greatly and is much less error-prone than maintaining all properties on the real product level. Figure 6.18 shows an example that could be used in the beverage industry. The **Ambient** reference product contains four reference products that differ in the beverage's product packaging class (**CAN**, **PET**, **GLASS**, **KEG**). The level below represents the size within the packaging class, except for kegs that don't vary in size. The real products represent the leaves in this hierarchy. Using this hierarchy, you can maintain stacking factors on the lowest reference product level, and you can define incompatibilities for packing on the levels **CAN**, **PET**, **GLASS**, and **KEG**. The reference product **Ambient** can be used to differentiate from other product areas, such as chilled and raw materials (not depicted in Figure 6.18).

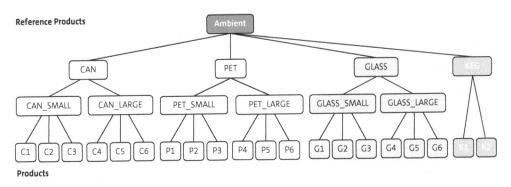

Figure 6.18 Example for Reference Product Hierarchy

- The **Product Shape** can be defined as cuboid or cylindrical with axis along the length, width, or height. The shape is used for visualization purposes in the 3D load plan view for pallets and products to be loaded into trucks, trailers, or containers.

- The **Product Orientation Profile** defines how the product can be oriented during detailed package building. You can maintain a *product orientation profile* in Customizing by following the menu path **Transportation Management • Master Data • Product • Define Product Orientation Profile** (in SAP TM 9.6, the menu path is **SAP Transportation Management • SCM Basis • Master Data • Product • Define Product Orientation Profile**). Figure 6.19 shows an orientation profile that enables all six orientations to be used during detailed package building. The maintenance is based on six flags arranged in a matrix, in which the columns define which side of the object can be put on the ground (**Bottom Side**), and the rows define the allowed **Rotation** angles.

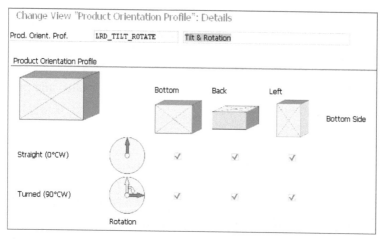

Figure 6.19 Orientation Profile Allowing All Possible Orientations

- The **Overhang Threshold [%]** is considered in detailed package building and defines how much of the bottom surface of the product must directly touch the products below.

- The **Absolute Height Threshold** defines the allowed height difference of other products on which the product at hand is stacked. This parameter is considered by detailed package building and allows stacking on nonflat surfaces.

Package Type Assignment

Following the menu path **Master Data – Product · Change Package Type Assignment** (in SAP TM 9.6, the menu path is **Master Data · General · Define Package Type Assignment**), you can define various rules and constraints for package building. The package type assignment is composed of three views, as shown in Figure 6.20:

- **BP**
  Defines parameters specific to business partners.

- **BP-Location**
  Defines product-independent parameters.

- **Product-BP-Location**
  Defines product-dependent parameters.

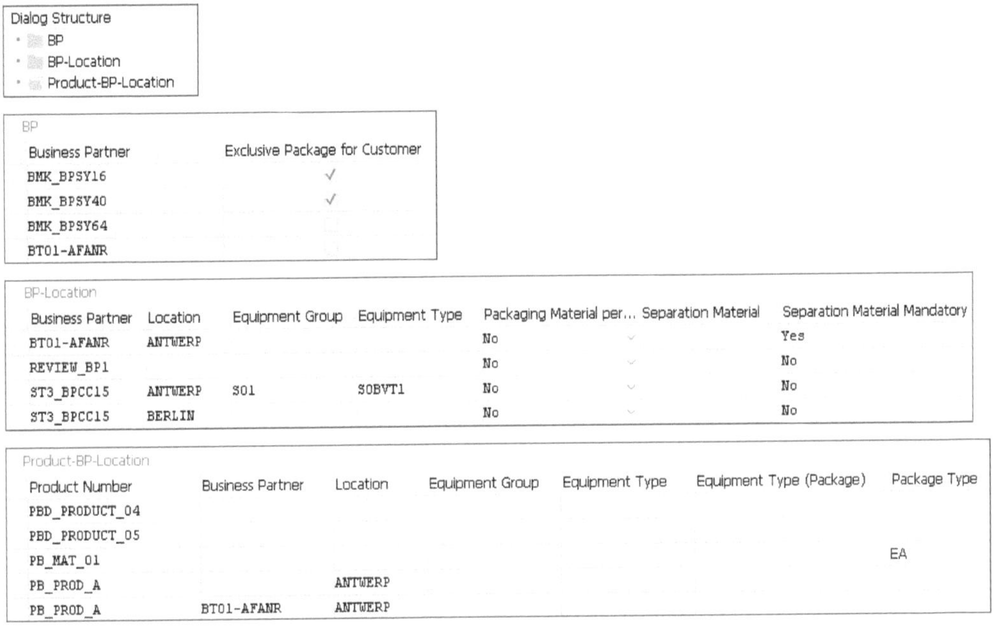

Dialog Structure
- BP
- BP-Location
- Product-BP-Location

BP

Business Partner	Exclusive Package for Customer
BMK_BPSY16	✓
BMK_BPSY40	✓
BMK_BPSY64	
BT01-AFANR	

BP-Location

Business Partner	Location	Equipment Group	Equipment Type	Packaging Material per...	Separation Material	Separation Material Mandatory
BT01-AFANR	ANTWERP			No	⌄	Yes
REVIEW_BP1				No	⌄	No
ST3_BPCC15	ANTWERP	301	SOBVT1	No	⌄	No
ST3_BPCC15	BERLIN			No	⌄	No

Product-BP-Location

Product Number	Business Partner	Location	Equipment Group	Equipment Type	Equipment Type (Package)	Package Type
PBD_PRODUCT_04						
PBD_PRODUCT_05						
PB_MAT_01						EA
PB_PROD_A		ANTWERP				
PB_PROD_A	BT01-AFANR	ANTWERP				

Figure 6.20 Product Package Type Assignment Composed of Three Views

The **Product-BP-Location** view allows you to define the packaging materials and other parameters for a given combination of the key fields **Product Number**, **Business Partner**, **Location**, **Equipment Group**, and **Equipment Type**. You can use explicit entries and patterns in these key fields or leave some initial. The system will choose the most specific entry in case of a tie. You can define the following parameters:

- **Packaging Material** is used for full packages.
- You can specify the **Package Type** into which the product at hand needs to be packed. The package type is represented by a unit of measure and applies to both single product and mixed packages. Rule-based package building will use the conversion rules in the product master to determine how many pieces fit into the package type. For example, you can introduce package types for pallets and cartons, and then define some products to be put into cartons, some products to be put into pallets, and the cartons to be put into pallets. See Figure 6.21 for such an example involving stock cartons (packaging material **LRD_CSTO_0**) and pick cartons (**LRD_CPICK_1**) put into pallets (**LRD_CHEP_PALLET**). Here, the package types are represented by the units of measure **CPL** and **CAR** for pallets and cartons, respectively.

˅ 🚚 Active Vehicle LRD_TRVAN1.8_SY	1,307 CPL	
˅ ▦ Package 40 Chep Pallet	1 CPL	LRD_CHEP_PALLET
⌂ Product 10 Water	48 CV	LRD_WATR7_1.25P
˅ ▦ Package 80 Chep Pallet	0,307 CPL	LRD_CHEP_PALLET
˃ ⌂ Product 90 Water	1 CV	LRD_WATR7_1.25P
˅ ▦ Package 50 AU CARTON 270x310x...	1 CAR	LRD_CSTO_0
⌂ Product 20 Coffee beans1 1kg bag	6 EA	LRD_COFB1_1.0B
˅ ▦ Package 60 AU CARTON 270x310x...	1 CAR	LRD_CSTO_0
⌂ Product 30 Tea leaves1 200g bag	33 EA	LRD_TEAL1_200B
˅ ▦ Package 70 Pick carton 1	1 CAR	LRD_CPICK_1
˃ ⌂ Product 110 Tea leaves1 200g bag	1 EA	LRD_TEAL1_200B
˃ ⌂ Product 100 Coffee beans1 1kg bag	1 EA	LRD_COFB1_1.0B

Figure 6.21 Packaging Hierarchy with Two Nesting Levels

- **Maximum Height of Package** and **Maximum Weight of Package** represent the limits for a single product package that consists of the packaging material and the products in the package.

- **Packaging Material (Mixed)** defines the packaging material to be used for mixed packages.

- **Maximum Height of Mixed Package** and **Maximum Weight of Mixed Package** represent the limits for a mixed package, including both packaging material and assigned products.

- **Ignore Limits for Full Packages** specifies whether the weight and height limits defined in this row are applied to build full single product pallets.

- **Packaging Material per Layer** defines whether the packaging material will be put below a full single product layer. If there are multiple layers of the same product, the packaging material is only considered once. Although this extra usage of the packaging material adds to the volume and weight of a layered mixed pallet, it can increase warehouse efficiency as it enables the use of forklifts to decompose layered mixed pallets.

- If the **Separation Material** is defined, it's used on top of a full single product layer as soon as other products get stacked on it. If there are multiple layers of the same product, the separation material is only considered once. **Separation Material Mandatory** can be used to enforce usage of the separation material even if nothing is to be stacked on top. Figure 6.22 illustrates four examples regarding separation materials and packaging material per layer. In case ❶, the separation material has been defined, and its usage is enforced for product 1. Example ❷ shows that the separation material has been defined for product 2. In example ❸, separation materials have been defined for both products, and their usage has been enforced. Example ❹ is similar to ❸, but, in addition, the packaging material will be put below product 1, triggered by the previously described parameter **Packaging Material per Layer** parameter.

- You can forbid the building of mixed packages using the **No Mixed Packages** parameter.
- Similarly, **No Mixed Layers** can be used to suppress building mixed layers.
- **Single Mixed Package** is used to forbid a product being spread over multiple mixed packages.
- In the same way, **Single Mixed Layer** can suppress a product being spread over multiple mixed layers.
- **Max Number of Products** defines the maximum number of products in a mixed package.

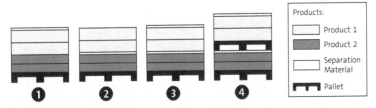

Figure 6.22 Layered Mixed Pallets and Usage of Separation Material and Packaging Material

The **BP-Location** view offers the very same parameters as the previous view for a given combination of business partner, location, equipment group, and equipment type. In the same way, you can use patterns and explicit entries or leave some key fields empty. This view offers one additional parameter—**Product Arrangement**—that specifies whether detailed package building arranges products in layers or towers.

The **BP** view allows you to define that certain customers require an exclusive package; that is, consolidation with goods for other customers isn't allowed for packages to the customer at hand. This can be useful to model that some customers are capable to unload pallets by a forklift, while other customers get served by manually pulling goods from a mixed pallet that may contain goods for other customers, too.

Package Building Profile

The package building profile (see Figure 6.23) mainly determines how packages will be built. It can be defined in Customizing using the path **Transportation Management** ·

Planning • **Package Building** • **Define Package Building Profile** (in SAP TM 9.6, the menu path is **SAP Transportation Management** • **SCM Basis** • **Pack** • **Package Building** • **Define Package Building Profile**).

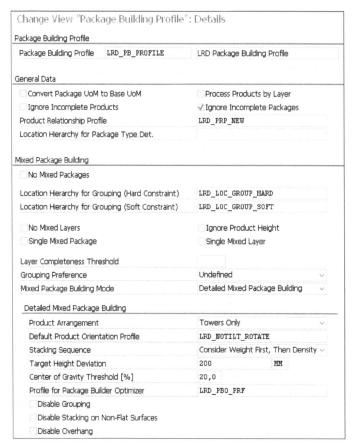

Figure 6.23 Package Building Profile

It offers the following parameters in the **General Data** section:

- **Convert Package Unit UoM to Base UoM** enables conversion of the created package item's unit of measure to the base unit of measure of the packaging material.

- **Process Products by Layer** can be used to suppress creation of full single product pallets as the first step in package building. Instead, the system builds layer-based pallets first.

- You can assign a **Product Relationship Profile** to define stacking constraints and incompatibilities. Using the menu path **Master Data – Product** · **Change Product Relationship Profile** (in SAP TM 9.6, the menu path is **Master Data** · **General** · **Define Product Relationship Profile**), you can maintain its stacking settings and consolidation settings, as shown in Figure 6.24 and Figure 6.25, respectively. The stacking settings define for a combination of two products whether the first can be stacked on the second and vice versa. The consolidation settings specify whether two given products are incompatible for consolidation on the first or last level in the consolidation process. In an example with pallets and cartons, the system first consolidates into cartons, and then—as the last step—into pallets. The consolidation sequence number controls the processing sequence if multiple product combinations are candidates for being consolidated. The example in Figure 6.25 shows that coffee and tea must not be consolidated into the same carton but can be put into the same pallet. Dry and ambient products can't be consolidated at all, nor can kegs be consolidated with any other products, such as bags, cans, and PETs. Cans, PETs, and bags can be consolidated, but the consolidation sequence defines that cans are first consolidated with PETs and then with bags.

Prod. Rel. Prof.	LRD_PRP		
Stacking Settings			
Product 1	Product 2	Stack Product 1 on 2	Stack Product 2 on 1
LRD_BAG	LRD_CPICK	Disallow	Allow
LRD_CAN	LRD_BAG	Disallow	Allow
LRD_CAN	LRD_CPICK	Disallow	Allow
LRD_PET	LRD_BAG	Disallow	Allow
LRD_PET	LRD_CPICK	Disallow	Allow
LRD_VTR	LRD_BAG	Disallow	Allow
LRD_VTR	LRD_CPICK	Disallow	Allow

Figure 6.24 Product Relationship Profile Defining Stacking Settings

Consolidation Settings			
Product 1	Product 2	Incompatible	Consolidation Seq.
LRD_RM_CAN	LRD_RM_BAG	No	20
LRD_RM_CAN	LRD_RM_PET	No	10
LRD_RM_CP_COFFEE	LRD_RM_CP_TEA	Yes (On First Level Only)	
LRD_RM_DRY	LRD_RM_AMBIENT	Yes	
LRD_RM_KEG	LRD_PM_CPICK	Yes	
LRD_RM_KEG	LRD_RM_BAG	Yes	
LRD_RM_KEG	LRD_RM_CAN	Yes	
LRD_RM_KEG	LRD_RM_PET	Yes	

Figure 6.25 Product Relationship Profile Defining Consolidation Settings

- You can use **Location Hierarchy for Package Type Det.** to let the package type assignment be determined based on a location hierarchy instead of just locations. This is particularly useful if many locations have the same properties and constraints from the package type assignment viewpoint. You can define such a hierarchy in Customizing by following the menu path **Transportation Management · Master Data · Hierarchy · Define Hierarchy Structure** (in SAP TM 9.6, the menu path is **SAP Transportation Management · SCM Basis · Master Data · Hierarchy · Define Hierarchy Structure**) and using the hierarchy structure **PB_LOC_HIERARCHY.**

The **Mixed Package Building** section (refer to Figure 6.23) specifies whether and how mixed packages will be built:

- **No Mixed Packages** can be used to forbid creation of any mixed package.

- **Location Hierarchy for Grouping (Hard Constraint)** allows you to define location groups by hierarchy. Package building ensures that products to customers of one group aren't consolidated into a package together with customers outside the group. You can use this to ensure transportation safety when serving multiple towns connected by highways and avoid carrying partially unloaded mixed pallets on the highway. Another use case is to forbid consolidation of products to customers that require serving from the right side of the truck with customers that get served from the left.

- **Location Hierarchy for Grouping (Soft Constraint)** is very similar to the previous one, but it just defines a soft instead of a hard constraint. Thus, the system tries to consider it but is allowed to violate the constraint if unavoidable. For example, in a business serving many customers in a shopping mall, the driver can unload more efficiently if all products for the shopping mall are located in the same mixed packages. However, it's acceptable that some leftovers are contained in mixed packages serving other customers.

- **No Mixed Layers** is used to suppress creating any mixed layers.

- Similar to the corresponding parameters in the package type assignment views, **Single Mixed Package** and **Single Mixed Layer** can be used to avoid a product being distributed among multiple mixed packages and layers, respectively. If these parameters are active, they overrule the corresponding parameters in the package type assignment.

- **Ignore Product Height** defines whether mixed layers can contain products of different heights. If a mixed layer contains products of different heights, it's nonflat, and therefore nothing can be stacked on it.

- **Layer Completeness Threshold** can be used to define layers as full already if the defined percentage of the footprint is covered. If not maintained, a layer is only full if 100% of its footprint is occupied. Recall that stacking goods on a layer is only allowed if it's full. This parameter enables stacking on layers that are defined as virtually full although they are actually not full.

- **Grouping Preference** guides package building to keep either products of the same customer or the same product together.

- Using **Mixed Package Building Mode**, you can choose between volume-based and detailed mixed package building. The selection of volume-based package building includes layer-based package building if activated in the package type assignment.

If detailed mixed package building is activated, you can maintain additional parameters in the **Detailed Mixed Package Building** section (refer to Figure 6.23):

- **Product Arrangement** defines whether mixed packages will be arranged by towers or layers. Layers are usually easier to handle in the warehouse but hard to unload by a driver if many different products are contained in the pallet. This parameter defines the default for package building, which can be overruled by more specific product arrangement definitions from the **BP-Location** package type assignment view.

- **Default Product Orientation Profile** is applied to all products for which no orientation profile is defined for the product itself nor for any of its reference products.

- **Stacking Sequence** can enforce a strict ordering of products stacked on each other. The ordering can be by weight first, then density; by density first, then weight; or undefined. Note that all stacking constraints apply together: the stacking sequence, the stacking settings defined in the product relationship profile, and the stacking factor defined in product master.

- Detailed package building minimizes the height differences of the surface of the package to build a stable package with a surface that is as flat as possible. This objective is defined as standard deviation of the heights of the different cartonized or noncartonized products that form the surface of the package, weighted by the sizes of these individual product surfaces. **Target Height Deviation** allows you to define the target deviation from the standard deviation.

- Detailed package building aims at putting the center of gravity into the middle of the pallet (with respect to length and width). This objective is modeled as a soft constraint, and the **Center of Gravity Threshold [%]** defines a rectangular area in the middle of the pallet that doesn't cause penalty costs for violating the soft constraint. For example, if the pallet has width 80 cm and length 120 cm, the threshold 10% would define a rectangle with 8 cm width and 12 cm length.

- You can assign a **Profile for Package Builder Optimizer** that determines the maximum optimizer runtime and whether the run will be finished after a certain time without improved results. As shown in Figure 6.26, you can also define the **Optimization Emphasis** that controls the trade-off between exploration and exploitation, that is, searching for different solutions and fine-tuning already found solutions. Moreover, the **Optimizer Dump Level** and **Optimizer Trace Level** can be set, which are relevant for support and analysis purposes.

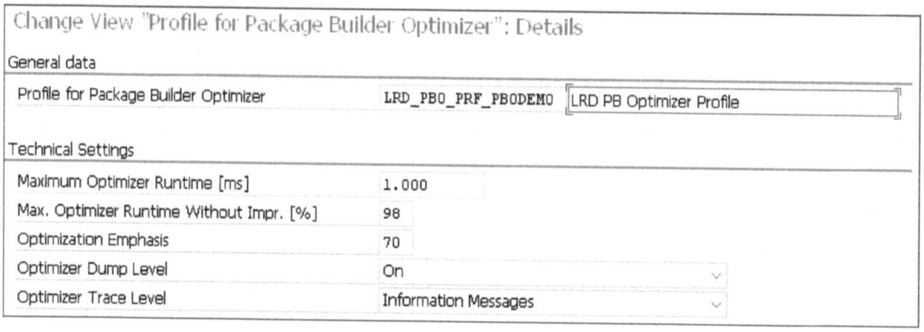

Change View "Profile for Package Builder Optimizer": Details		
General data		
Profile for Package Builder Optimizer	LRD_PBO_PRF_PBODEMO	LRD PB Optimizer Profile
Technical Settings		
Maximum Optimizer Runtime [ms]	1.000	
Max. Optimizer Runtime Without Impr. [%]	98	
Optimization Emphasis	70	
Optimizer Dump Level	On	
Optimizer Trace Level	Information Messages	

Figure 6.26 Package Building Optimizer Profile

- For product handling efficiency reasons, a grouping heuristic is used to consolidate similar products together on mixed pallets. Here, similarity is defined by the reference product hierarchy. In an example based on the reference product hierarchy shown earlier in Figure 6.18, it's desirable to keep all can products together on a mixed pallet, and the same holds for PET, glass, and keg products. Cans will be mixed with PET or glass only if this reduces the number of mixed pallets. You can skip the grouping heuristic by selecting **Disable Grouping**.

- **Disable Stacking on Non-Flat Surfaces** can be used to forbid stacking on nonflat surfaces.

- If you want to avoid any overhangs, but you have still some overhang parameters defined, for example, in the product master, you can use the **Disable Overhang** parameter.

Refer to SAP Note 2581421 for more details and examples on package building.

Package Building Test Report

Package building depends heavily on master data quality, and it may be difficult and time-consuming to identify the root cause of an unexpected result within a freight unit or a freight order. You can use the test report /SCMB/TEST_PB to browse through the reference product hierarchy in bottom-up or top-down fashion or to run package building without the need to create demand or capacity documents in SAP TM. For example, you can define a set of products and quantities and review the resulting packaging hierarchy. Within this result, you can also review the reference hierarchy for the products at hand, including relevant parameters and constraints defined on each level in the reference product hierarchy. You can review the determined package type assignment relevant for the products at hand. We recommend using this report when setting up your master data. The bigger and more complex the scenario, the harder it is to identify the root cause for unexpected results. Therefore, growing your scenario iteratively and verifying the obtained package building results will save you a lot of time.

6.4   Transportation Units

TUs can represent both demand and capacity. They share some similarities with freight units and others with freight orders, but they also differ from both freight units and freight orders. From the viewpoint of the possible document assignments shown earlier in Figure 6.1, TUs are located between freight units and freight documents.

Scenarios involving trailers, railcars, containers, and packages can be modeled by TUs, abstracting from the specific documents called *trailer units*, *railcar units*, *container units*, and *package units*.

Section 6.4.1 explains TUs' similarities and differences to freight units and freight documents. Trailer units and relevant scenarios involving trucks and trailers are described in Section 6.4.2, followed by Section 6.4.3 and Section 6.4.4 discussing railcar units and container units, respectively. Finally, package units are introduced in Section 6.4.5.

6.4.1   Transportation Units versus Freight Units and Freight Documents

Like freight documents, TUs have stages defining their paths through the network. While trailer, railcar, and container resources can be assigned to the corresponding TUs, package units represent one or multiple packages, each having an assigned packaging material.

On the one hand, TUs can't move themselves; instead, they require being moved by a truck, locomotive, vessel, or airplane and thus need to be assigned to a freight document. Therefore, they represent a demand for transportation, like freight units.

The assignment of a TU to a freight document can be done directly—for example, trailer unit to road freight order—or indirectly, such as container unit to trailer unit, which is then assigned to a road freight order.

While a freight document can't be assigned to another freight document, TUs allow nested assignments within this document category. For example, consider the following assignment chain: freight unit → package unit → container unit → trailer unit → road freight order. In this case, the TUs represent three consolidation levels between freight unit and road freight order. It isn't possible to consolidate a trailer unit into another trailer unit, and this holds true analogously for railcar units, container units, and package units.

Freight documents can be subcontracted, but TUs and freight units can't be subcontracted. To be transported and subcontracted, they have to be assigned to freight documents.

On the other hand, TUs can consolidate other demands. Therefore, they also represent a capacity for transportation, like freight documents.

While a freight unit represents a single transportation demand, the TU can represent a set of transportation demands that may even have different source and destination locations. For example, a trailer is moved from location A to B to C, delivering three freight units: the first from A to B, the second from A to C, and the third from B to C.

In general, TUs provide a lot of modeling capabilities but that requires additional planning decisions and adds planning complexity. Therefore, we recommend avoiding using TUs if your business can be modeled without them. Of course, for many transportation scenarios, using TUs is mandatory because it's the only feasible way to model your business.

Like freight units, TUs can be created by FUB, as described in Section 6.2.3. However, such TUs don't allow consolidation of other demands, so they represent pure demand documents. Therefore, we focus the following discussion of TUs on the more interesting case of TUs allowing consolidation of demands.

Each TU has a specific type, which you can maintain in Customizing by following the menu path **Transportation Management • Planning • Transportation Unit • Define Transportation Unit**. The similarity of TUs to freight units and freight orders is reflected directly in the TU type, so we won't describe it in detail; instead, refer to Section 6.2.2 for freight unit types and Chapter 7, Section 7.2.1, for freight order types. It's important to mention that you can assign item types to the TU type, which is useful for multi-items in railcar units, as mentioned in Section 6.4.3.

There are many ways to create TUs:

- Manual planning can be done in the transportation cockpit, as described in Section 6.6.8.
- The VSR optimizer can create trailer units and railcar units based on freight units, container units, and package units.
- Load consolidation can create trailer units and container units based on freight units and package units. See Section 6.7.7.
- Package units of linear distribution type can be extracted out of road freight orders, as described in Section 6.4.5.
- FUB can create trailer units, railcar units, container units, and package units, but these TUs represent pure demand documents and don't allow consolidation.
- Explicit creation can be done via the menu paths **Planning • Create Trailer Unit**, **Planning • Create Railcar Unit**, **Planning • Create Container Unit**, and **Planning • Create Package Unit** (in SAP TM 9.6, the paths are **Planning • Trailer Unit • Create Trailer Unit**, **Planning • Railcar Unit • Create Railcar Unit**, **Planning • Container Unit • Create Container Unit**, and **Planning • Package Unit • Create Package Unit**).

You can go to **Planning** (in SAP TM 9.6, the menu path is **Planning • Worklist Planning • Overview Planning**) to get an overview of trailer units, railcar units, container units, or package units in the system. From here, you can edit, create, and cancel trailer units, railcar units, container units, and package units.

6.4.2   Trailer Units

Many road transportation businesses involve trailers, but not all them require being modeled by trailer units. Let's first review a few examples to define our terminology. Figure 6.27 shows different trucks and trailers. Box trucks have their own loading capacity, while tractors don't have their own capacity. Full trailers can be coupled to box trucks, and semitrailers can be coupled to tractors. From a planning perspective, full trailers and semitrailers are handled identically, so from now on, we refer only to *trailers*. We also don't differentiate between box trucks and tractors and simply use the term *trucks* for both. Only where required do we explicitly refer to tractors.

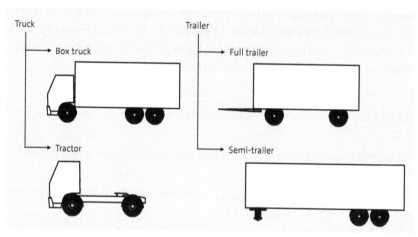

Figure 6.27 Truck and Trailer Examples

The combination of a truck and trailer moving together is also called *vehicle combination*. While the preceding examples represent vehicle combinations with one truck and one trailer, in some regions of North America and Australia, tractors can carry two or three trailers—such a combination is called a *road train*.

Transporting a trailer requires it being coupled to a truck. Although the last trailer in a road train is physically coupled to its predecessor trailer, this is simplified and abstracted from the planning viewpoint to coupling all trailers to the truck. For example, for a road train with one tractor and three trailers, all trailers get directly coupled to the tractor.

Trailers can get loaded and unloaded even when not being coupled to a truck, and they can be moved consecutively by multiple trucks. Thus, trailers bring more flexibility and cost efficiency, but this may also lead to more planning decisions to be made and hence planning complexity.

A trailer unit can consolidate multiple demands, such as freight units, package units, or container units. The stages of the trailer unit define the trailer's planned movements in the transportation network. Each trailer unit stage needs to be assigned to a road freight order, providing flexibility to assign each trailer unit stage to a different road freight order and truck resource. However, this flexibility results in complexity, and we recommend carefully checking whether you can model your scenario without trailer units.

Trailer units are required in the following cases:

- Trailers get loaded or unloaded while not being coupled to the truck.
- The truck is operating in different vehicle combinations across the stages in its freight order.
- You want to plan on an individual trailer resource level or to use load planning considering the trailer's axle weights.

Let's review some examples, in order of increasing planning complexity, and how they can be modeled:

- **All tours of a trailer always done by the same tractor**
  If a trailer resource is always attached to the same tractor resource, the scenario can be modeled by a vehicle resource resembling a box truck. All transportation demands are assigned to the road freight order, and there is no need for trailer units.

- **All tours of a trailer are always done by the same box truck**
  If a trailer resource is always attached to the same box truck resource, the scenario can be modeled by a vehicle resource with two compartments—one for the box truck and one for the trailer. Like the previous case, using trailer units isn't required. However, if the box truck or the trailer contain compartments relevant for planning, the simplification by compartments modeling truck and trailer isn't applicable, and you have to use trailer units.

- **Each trailer tour done by the same truck, but trailer resource used with multiple trucks**
  If a complete trailer tour is done by the same truck but different tours of the same trailer resource can be done by different truck resources, you can use trailer units to enable dynamic assignment of truck resources to trailer resources. Here, planning needs to decide which vehicle resource moves the trailer unit at hand.

- **Trailer tour done by multiple trucks (dynamic recoupling)**
  The trailer is consecutively carried by two or more trucks. This requires a trailer unit with at least two stages, and the stages are assigned to different vehicles. For example, the trailer unit is moved along locations A, B, and C; the movement from A to B is done by vehicle V1, and the movement from B to C is done by vehicle V2.

Thus, the trailer is coupled to V1 at location A, moved to B, uncoupled from V1, coupled to V2, moved to C, and then uncoupled from V2.

- **Road train with the same tractor and trailer resources**
  A road train permanently operated with the same tractor and trailer resources can be modeled analogously to case 2, with one compartment per trailer. If the trailers have compartments relevant for planning, you have to use trailer units.

- **Road train with dynamic recoupling**
  This represents the highest planning complexity. Multiple trailer units can be moved by one road freight order, and one trailer unit can be moved by multiple road freight orders, one per trailer unit stage.

If you use trailer units, the transportation plan is represented by trailer units and road freight orders, which resemble the perspectives of the trailer and of the truck. Due to the stage-wise assignments of trailer units to road freight orders, you can't change the stages of the trailer unit without changing the stages of the corresponding road freight order, and vice versa. The planner has to think from the trailer perspective and from the truck perspective, which requires quickly changing the perspective or, ideally, having both perspectives at the same time—a function that is offered by the transportation cockpit, as described in Section 6.6.1.

Dynamic recoupling is frequently used in scenarios where the distance from source to destination is so large that the driver of the truck can't make the trip in one shift. Trailer swaps are introduced to maximize utilization of the trailer fleet. Suppose one trailer has to be moved from Hamburg to Munich, and another trailer has to be moved from Munich to Hamburg. The first truck may take the first trailer from Hamburg to Fulda, which is located roughly halfway between Hamburg and Munich. The second truck may take the second trailer from Munich to Fulda. In Fulda, both trailers are uncoupled and then coupled to the other truck. Then the first truck takes the second trailer from Fulda to Hamburg, and the second truck moves the first trailer from Fulda to Munich.

This plan allows each of the drivers to be back at home at the end of their shifts. The first trailer unit has stages from Hamburg to Fulda to Munich, and the second trailer unit has stages from Munich to Fulda to Hamburg. The first road freight order has stages from Hamburg to Fulda to Hamburg, and the second road freight order has stages from Munich to Fulda to Munich. Figure 6.28 shows such a scenario in the Gantt chart, both from truck view (upper part) and trailer view (bottom part). You can see that loading and unloading of the trailers takes place while not being coupled to the corresponding tractor.

Figure 6.28 Trailer Swap Depicted in a Gantt Chart

In Australia, road trains may consist of tractors carrying two trailers in urban areas and three trailers elsewhere. Suppose that the trailers are systematically moved from A to B to C and then back from C to B to A. Two trailers can be carried between A and B, and three trailers between B and C. Here, the planning decision involves defining the road trains—in other words, which trailers are moved together by which tractor. Using two default routes for the systematic movements from A to C and back, the trailer units' stages can be determined in a rule-based fashion, and then planning only has to decide about the tractor assignment to the trailer units' stages.

6.4.3   Railcar Units

Rail transportation is done by trains, which may consist of one locomotive resource and a set of railcars. There are scenarios in which the whole train is subcontracted, and demands such as freight units, package units, or container units are assigned directly to rail freight orders. In other scenarios, planning is required on the individual railcar level, which is supported by railcar units that can play a role similar to that of trailer units in truck and trailer scenarios.

Manual planning supports the same functionality as for truck and trailer scenarios; that is, you can assign a locomotive to rail freight orders, create railcar units with assigned railcar resources and freight units, and assign a railcar stage to one rail freight order.

While trailer units and road freight orders have the same stages during their joint movement, railcar units and rail freight orders have only the stops in common, where the railcar is loaded, unloaded, coupled, or uncoupled. The main motivation for this modeling is the reduction of data volume because usually a rail freight order contains many more railcars than a road freight order contains trailers.

Some companies ship a lot of cargo by railcars. If 25 complete railcars full of a certain product are to be shipped, this would create an enormous number of railcar units. To reduce the number of documents, you can use the concept of multi-items to have one railcar unit that represents the load of 25 railcars. Via the menu path **Transportation Management • Forwarding Order Management • Define Item Types for Forwarding Order Management** in Customizing, you can define an item category as a passive vehicle resource and enable multi-items. The multi-item can represent multiple subitems without explicitly generating the subitems. Alternatively, the multiple subitems can be generated automatically by expansion. For the subitems, you have to specify an item type that can be a subitem of a multi-item.

6.4.4   Container Units

A container unit can be assigned directly to any freight document, but it can also add one nesting level. Multiple freight units can be consolidated into a container unit, and multiple container units can be put into a trailer unit or railcar unit. In this case, container units involve four object layers relevant for assignment decision-making: Which freight units are transported in which container units, which container units are carried by which trailer unit or railcar unit, and how are these trailer units and railcar units moved? While the freight unit has the same volume and weight along all its stages, both the TU and the freight order may have different (loaded) volumes and weights per stage. If package units are involved, too, even five object layers are relevant for assignment decision-making.

Companies that don't own container resources may order empty containers and return the empties after delivery, as described in Chapter 4, Section 4.2.1, and they care mainly about the container movements of the cargo. They don't care about the choice of the physical container instance; instead, they just consider the required container type, for example, 20-foot versus 40-foot.

Companies that receive such forwarding orders (including empty provisioning and empty returning for containers) have to plan these empty movements and can do so by container units covering the empty stages.

Companies that own and provide container resources with special properties, such as cooling capability or special construction to carry dangerous liquids, face the challenge that the container resources may be spread in the network of container yards and customer locations. If a customer requires a container transport from a source location to a destination location, an empty container resource has to be identified and transported from its current location to the required source. In the chemical industry, product-dependent cleaning activities may be required in advance. Suppose that a previous product has been delivered with a container resource that is now empty at a container yard. If the next product to be delivered isn't compatible with the previous one, an additional movement from the yard to a cleaning station is required.

Figure 6.29 illustrates the complexity of container planning with a real-world example from a road carrier with its own truck, trailer, and container equipment to demonstrate how the required business documents relate to each other:

- **Freight unit**
  Freight is to be transported from location D to G.

- **Container unit**
  The planner decides to use a container resource located at B, clean it at C, bring it to D to load the freight unit, transport it to rail hub E, transport it to rail hub F, and then deliver it to destination G.

- **Trailer unit**
  The planner has decided to use the company's own trailer resource located at A to transport the container from B via C and D to E.

- **Road freight order 1**
  The company's own truck carries the empty trailer from A to B, where the empty container is loaded to the trailer, moves to cleaning station C, and subsequently moves to D and E.

- **Rail freight order**
  This represents the rail transportation from rail hub E to rail hub F. This is done by subcontracting to a rail carrier.

- **Road freight order 2**
  The final transportation from rail hub F to the destination location G is done by subcontracting to a road carrier.

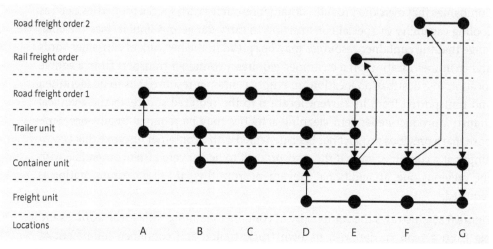

Figure 6.29 Container Unit Stages and Involved Business Documents

The stages of the involved business documents are shown in Figure 6.29. The up arrows show that a demand is assigned to a capacity, and the down arrows indicate that the demand is unassigned from the capacity.

You can see that the freight unit is the only pure demand document, the three freight orders are pure capacity documents, and both trailer unit and container unit represent both demand and capacity documents at the same time. From the container unit perspective, the freight unit is a demand document and the trailer unit, rail freight order, and second road freight order are capacity documents. From the trailer unit perspective, the container unit is a demand document, and the first road freight order is a capacity document.

We just described the plan, but how does it come together? The planner has to make many decisions to create this plan in the following sequence:

1. Select the container resource, based on its current location.
2. Choose the cleaning location.
3. Define the container's route through rail hubs E and F.
4. Create the rail freight order based on available rail carrier schedules' departures.
5. Choose the trailer resource and truck resource.
6. Choose the road carrier for last stage.

All these decisions can be made in the transportation cockpit by creating the relevant business documents, defining their stages, and assigning demand documents to capacity documents. Most of these decisions can even be made automatically.

6.4.5   Package Units

A package unit can represent one or multiple packages to be transported together. Pallets, pallet cages, and cartons represent typical examples for packages. Like a freight document, a package unit contains a packaging hierarchy that may include multiple top-level packages. Each stage of a package unit represents a transportation demand that needs to be assigned to freight documents, either directly or indirectly, as already discussed in Section 6.4.1.

From a planning viewpoint, the package unit is very similar to the container unit. It can be assigned to any freight document, trailer unit, and railcar unit, and you can assign multiple freight units to a package unit. In addition, you can assign a package unit to a container unit. As already mentioned, the package unit can't be assigned to a resource dedicated to packaging.

It isn't possible to assign a package unit to another package unit. If a deep packaging hierarchy is required, the package unit can model the top-level package(s), and the packaging substructure is represented by the package unit's packaging hierarchy.

Specific Parameters for Package Units

The package unit offers some special concepts and features that aren't available for container units and enable specific planning processes such as *integrated delivery and line-haul planning*. We'll now give an overview of the specific package unit type parameters and then describe how they can be used for integrated delivery and line-haul planning:

- **Seq. Type of Stages**
  This parameter allows differentiating between the **Defined and Linear** and **Linear with Distribution** types. The first type represents a linear stage sequence as in freight units or container units; that is, the stages must be executed in a strictly linear fashion. The **Linear with Distribution** type allows one or more "normal" linear stages followed by one distribution stage, which represents distribution to multiple customers by the same truck. The sequence of the customers is undefined in the package unit, but when assigned to a road freight order, the stop

431

sequence of the freight order determines the sequence of the customers contained in the package unit's distribution stage. Figure 6.30 shows a package unit with a linear stage from warehouse to hub and a distribution stage from hub to multiple customers, which is displayed on the map in a star-like fashion because the customer sequence is undefined. Note that SAP TM in SAP S/4HANA 1809 only supports the **Defined and Linear** type.

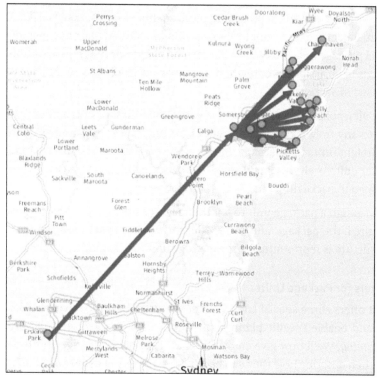

Figure 6.30 Package Unit with One Linear Stage and One Distribution Stage

- **Assignment of Pred. Docs**

  You can define whether freight units must be fully assigned to the package unit at hand or whether you allow a *multi-assignment*; that is, the product quantities of a freight unit stage are distributed across multiple package units. Figure 6.31 illustrates the multi-assignment concept in an example with three freight units, two package units, and one road freight order. The quantities of each freight unit are distributed across the two package units, which both are assigned to the same freight order. A multi-assignment is only allowed if all quantities of a freight unit stage are (indirectly) assigned to the same freight order. If you assign one of the package units to a different road freight order, this would trigger a freight unit split to reach a consistent status; that is, the product quantities of a freight unit stage are fully assigned to one freight order. Note that SAP TM in SAP S/4HANA 1809 doesn't support multi-assignment.

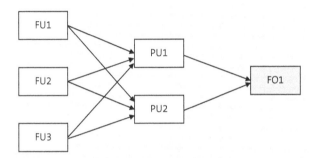

Figure 6.31 Package Units with Multi-Assignment of Freight Units

- **Package Unit Creation Rule**
  This parameter allows defining whether all packages at hand get assigned to one package unit or each package gets assigned to an individual package unit. The first option bundles multiple packages, ensuring that they are always planned together. While this option considerably reduces the number of package units relevant for planning, it also reduces flexibility for assignment decisions. The second option results in more package units and maximum flexibility for assignment decisions, as each package unit could be assigned to a different capacity document. The second option is the most natural one, but, in some cases, the first option might be useful as well.

Integrated Delivery and Line-Haul Planning Based on Package Units

Let's now discuss the integrated delivery and line-haul planning process, in which the package unit with distribution and multi-assignment plays the key role to link delivery planning with line-haul planning. The business scenario is sketched in Figure 6.32. Products are transported from the warehouse to customers. The warehouse is located in a metropolis, and delivery trucks can directly serve customers from the warehouse by metropolitan tours. Customers in remote regions get served by delivery trucks from regional hubs, which get served from the warehouse by line-haul trucks. As there are many customers in each region, and customers usually order many different products but with small quantities, mixed pallets must be built containing goods for many different customers. For example, you may have a delivery truck containing 12 pallets that serve 50 customers—which means that the driver has to pull the ordered product quantities out of the mixed pallets for each customer.

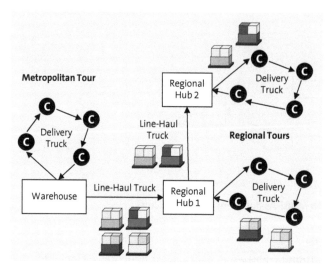

Figure 6.32 Integrated Delivery and Line-Haul Tour Scenario with Mixed Pallets

For warehouse efficiency reasons, the mixed pallets for the delivery tours are already built in the warehouse to avoid any rebuilding of pallets in the regional hubs. This leads to the main challenge in this scenario: the mixed pallets are built in the warehouse, but their structure depends on the customers that are consolidated into the same delivery tour. The solution of this challenge is to decompose the planning process as follows:

1. Plan delivery tours, build the mixed pallets for the delivery tours, and create the load plan for the delivery tours.

2. Plan line-haul tours based on the mixed pallets originating from the delivery tours, and determine the load plan for the line-haul tours.

Package units represent the mixed pallets that form the result of delivery planning and serve as input for line-haul planning. Roughly speaking, package units represent the document that links delivery planning with line-haul planning. One subtle aspect of the process is that delivery planning is done before line-haul planning, while line-haul tours get executed before the corresponding delivery tours.

Let's review the process steps in detail. As the transportation of each freight unit to a regional customer will cross the hub, we define default routes from the warehouse via regional hub to the customers in the regions. Applying the default route already during FUB results in two freight unit stages: one from warehouse to hub, and one from hub to customer. Based on these freight units, the integrated delivery and line-haul planning process is composed of the following steps, which are depicted in Figure 6.14, Figure 6.33, and Figure 6.34:

1. The VSR optimizer is run for each regional delivery planning scenario, which consists of the unplanned freight unit stages from the regional hub to the customers and the available delivery trucks. The freight units contain estimates of the number of pallets but no detailed packaging structure yet. As a result, unplanned freight unit stages get planned and consolidated into road freight orders.

2. Package building is run for all road freight orders. As a result, the freight orders contain a packaging hierarchy.

3. Load planning is applied to all road freight orders, resulting in a load plan attached to each freight order.

4. The packages in the freight orders need to be finalized first, expressing that the planner doesn't expect any more changes. Then, package units are created for all top-level packages in the freight orders' packaging hierarchies. Before this step, freight units are directly assigned to freight orders. After this step, freight units are assigned to package units that are assigned to the freight order. One prerequisite for this step is to use the **Linear with Distribution** package unit type, and we strongly recommend activating multi-assignment in the package unit type, as this step otherwise could blow up the number of freight units significantly (due to freight unit splits needed to ensure that each freight unit is completely assigned to one package unit). One key functionality to link delivery with line-haul planning is that the creation of package units also considers preceding freight unit stages. If a package only contains freight unit stages that all have the same preceding stages—which is the case in our scenario because they all have one common line-haul stage from warehouse to hub—the system will also plan these freight unit stages and assign them to the package unit created. As a result, the freights units are completely planned, that is, not just the delivery stage but also the line-haul stage. The package units contain an unplanned linear stage that represents the line-haul stage to be planned next and a planned linear with distribution stage assigned to the delivery road freight order.

6

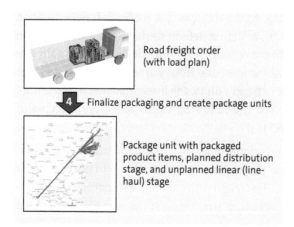

Figure 6.33 Creation of Package Units after Delivery Planning

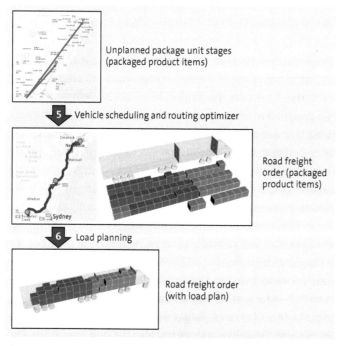

Figure 6.34 Line-Haul Planning Process

5. After the preceding steps have been completed for all delivery regions, line-haul planning starts by running the VSR optimizer for all unplanned package unit

stages from the warehouse to the regional hub and considering the available line-haul trucks, which are usually much bigger than the delivery trucks serving the customers. As a result, the package unit stages get planned, and the line-haul freight orders get created. In the example shown in Figure 6.34, the line-haul freight order is assigned to a tractor carrying two trailers, represented by two trailer units. Thus, each package unit has been assigned to one of the two trailer units that are both assigned to the road freight order.

6. As the last step, load planning is triggered for the road freight order, resulting in a load plan for each trailer that considers all axle weight constraints across the whole vehicle combination.

Delivery planning (steps 1–4) is performed for all regions. Line-haul planning (steps 5–6) is started only after delivery planning has been finished for all regions, and all required package units have been created based on the delivery freight orders.

The preceding process contains many automatic components, such as VSR optimizer, package building, and load planning. In practice, we recommend automating as much as possible and reworking manually only where required. Of course, all process steps can also be performed in a pure manual fashion.

6.5   Planning Strategies, Profiles, and Settings

Planning strategies define the different steps performed in manual and automatic planning. You can use standard planning strategies and incorporate your own enhanced strategies, too. Section 6.5.1 reviews the available planning strategies.

Section 6.5.2 presents planning and selection profiles that—together with additional settings—define the planning scenario and configure planning parameters.

6.5.1   Planning Strategies

Planning contains many different decision levels, as described in Section 6.1. When performing a certain manual or automatic planning step, you may want to define which additional decisions will be made automatically by the system. In one example, you may want to trigger load planning after each manual planning step to see the effect of the decision on the load plan immediately. In another example, you want to run carrier selection immediately after the VSR optimizer.

A *planning strategy* defines the system behavior for different planning steps in manual planning and automatic planning. The system offers the following standard planning strategies for manual planning:

- VSRI_DEF for manual planning
- VSRI_SCH for manual planning with subsequent scheduling
- VSRI_CHK for manual planning with subsequent checking
- VSRI_ALP for manual planning with subsequent load planning
- VSRI_CPB for manual planning with subsequent package building
- VSRI_PBLP for manual planning with subsequent package building and load planning
- VSRI_1STEP for manual planning with subsequent carrier selection

The following standard strategies are available for automated planning, specifically vehicle scheduling and routing (VSR):

- VSR_DEF for VSR optimization
- VSR_1STEP for one-step optimization (which calls VSR optimization and then carrier selection optimization) and for transportation proposals (carrier selection is called for each determined transportation proposal)
- VSR_ALP for VSR optimization with subsequent load planning
- VSR_CPB for VSR optimization and consecutive package building
- VSR_CPBALP for VSR optimization with consecutive package building and load planning

Additional strategies are available for the following purposes:

- VSS_DEF for scheduling
- VSR_CHECK for checking the plan
- TSPS_DEF for carrier selection optimization
- ALP_DEF for load planning
- ALC_DEF for load consolidation

Each strategy consists of a sequence of methods. If you want to refine the standard behavior, you can build your own strategies, which can reuse the standard methods. After these are defined, you can use your own strategies in the profiles to replace the default standard strategies. Refer to Chapter 2, Section 2.3.6, for more details on defining strategies and methods.

6.5.2   Profiles and Settings

Besides the configurability of the UI, which we'll describe in Section 6.6, many additional parameters define the planning scenario and how planning can be performed. The selection of objects relevant for planning can be handled by selection profiles, and planning parameters are covered by planning profiles. We'll cover both in the following sections.

Selection Profiles and Selection Attributes

The selection profile defines which documents are considered for planning and can be created via the menu path **Profiles and Settings • Create Selection Profile** (in SAP TM 9.6, the menu path is **Application Administration • Planning • Selection Profiles • Create Selection Profile**). The selection profile consists of three building blocks: time-related selection attributes, geographical selection attributes, and additional selection attributes, as shown in Figure 6.35.

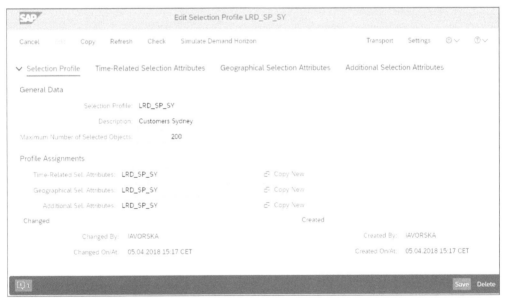

Figure 6.35 Selection Profile

You can create the three attribute objects independently of each other and the selection profile by going to **Profiles and Settings** (in SAP TM 9.6, the menu path **Application Administration • Planning • Selection Profile Attributes**). The building block principle allows reuse of the same attribute definitions in different selection profiles.

Selection according to the selection profile returns objects that meet the criteria of the time-related selection attributes, geographical selection attributes, and additional selection attributes. The selection profile allows you to define a limit for the number of selected objects.

The time-related selection attributes use two horizons—one for the pickup time windows and one for the delivery time windows—as shown in Figure 6.36. You can define the horizons as relatively, relatively with fixed start time, or absolutely. The **Simulate Demand Horizon** button allows you to simulate the effect of the chosen parameters in a popup, which displays the determined date and time of pickup start, pickup end, delivery start, and delivery end for a defined anchor time that is defaulted with the current date and time but can be changed arbitrarily.

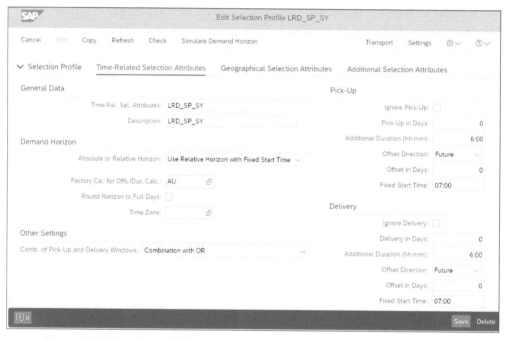

Figure 6.36 Time-Related Selection Attributes

Using the **Absolute** option, you can explicitly maintain the pickup horizon and the delivery horizon, which is quite useful if you want to reproduce one planning session.

The **Use Relative Horizon with Fixed Start Time** option shown in Figure 6.36 enables defining a time period by a fixed start time and a relative duration. In the example, the start time is fixed at 7:00 and the duration is 6:00, so the resulting horizon is 7:00–13:00. Such a scenario is useful if you plan the morning tours first and then the afternoon tours.

In the relative option, you can define a range by specifying the number of days and an additional duration in hours and minutes. Additionally, you can define an offset in days, hours, and minutes, as well as an offset direction that points into the past or into the future. The system takes the current time and adjusts it by the offset to determine the start of the horizon. Adding the range to this yields the end of the horizon.

For both relative options, you can specify a factory calendar, which enables the system to consider nonworking days when determining the start of the relative horizons. If the determined start day is a nonworking day, the horizon's start is moved to the next working day, and the range remains the same. The relative horizon is useful if you always plan objects in advance (e.g., for the next three days).

You can round the horizon to full days and define the time zone to be used for this rounding. Using the **Ignore Pick-Up** and **Ignore Delivery** flags, you can focus selection on the dates of only pickup or delivery. If both are marked as relevant, you can define whether both pickup and delivery or only one of them must be within its horizon.

Alternatively, you can enforce a combination of pickup time window with a source location and delivery time window with a destination location. This option selects objects with a source location matching the geographical source selection attribute and the pickup time window falling into the pickup horizon, along with objects with a destination location contained in the geographical destination selection attributes and the delivery time window in the delivery horizon. This allows scenarios to consider all inbound and outbound objects in the same horizon at a certain location.

Transportations within different countries or regions can often be planned independently of one another, enabling a geographical decomposition of the global transportation planning scenario into multiple local and independent planning parts. Geographical selection attributes allow you to select objects based on geographical criteria, which you can maintain in the **Source Locations**, **Source Zones**, **Destination Locations**, and **Destination Zones** tabs, as shown in Figure 6.37.

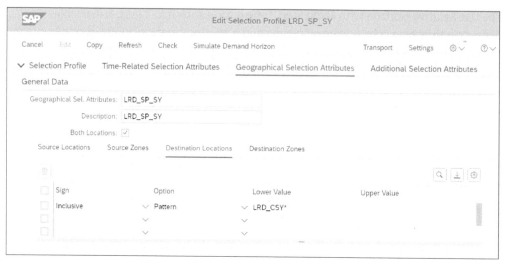

Figure 6.37 Geographical Selection Attributes

You can enter several criteria for each tab. All source locations and locations in source zones marked as **Inclusive** are relevant, but the corresponding locations marked as **Exclusive** aren't. The destination locations are determined the same way. The **Both Locations** checkbox defines whether the selected objects must meet the criteria for their source and destination or whether it's sufficient if only their source or destination matches its criterion.

You can use the additional selection attributes to define more selection criteria specified the same way as the location selection in the geographical selection attributes, but here you can refer to any other fields available in the queries for freight units, capacity documents, and original transportation demands, such as forwarding orders. Multiple criteria for the same object and field are combined with the logical OR, and the criteria for different fields are combined with the logical AND. Additionally, you can specify the following:

- Planned objects are included or excluded.
- Objects blocked for planning are included or excluded.
- All or only selected container unit stages are selected.
- All or only selected package unit stages are selected.

Condition-Based Filtering in SAP TM 9.6

The additional selection attributes include one tab for condition-based filtering in SAP TM 9.6, which is run after all other selection criteria. All other criteria are evaluated first, resulting in an intermediate selection. Then the hits in the intermediate selection are processed according to the specified condition, which may be much more time-consuming than explicit selection criteria that operate directly on efficient database queries.

Therefore, use as many explicit criteria as possible, and avoid condition-based filtering. Only use condition-based filtering after intensive performance testing and if the performance is satisfactory. See also SAP Note 1765952 for hints on improving performance for planning and, in particular, for the use of condition-based filtering. Note that condition-based filtering won't be offered by SAP TM in SAP S/4HANA.

Planning Profiles and Settings

The planning profile defines numerous parameters that control how planning is to be performed. Besides the parameters defined in the planning profile itself, it contains eight building blocks: the capacity selection settings, the optimizer settings, the load planning settings, the planning cost settings, the carrier selection settings, the incompatibility settings, the manual planning settings, and the scheduling settings. As with the selection profile's building blocks, all these settings can be maintained independently of each other and the planning profile and can therefore be reused in different planning profiles. An additional block covers administrative data to show the dates for creation and last change. You can create a planning profile and additional settings by following the menu path **Profiles and Settings • Create Planning Profile** (in SAP TM 9.6, the menu path is **Application Administration • Planning • Planning Profiles • Create Planning Profile**) and **Profiles and Settings** (in SAP TM 9.6, the menu path is **Application Administration • Planning • Planning Profile Settings**).

The planning profile itself contains many parameters grouped into different sections, as shown in Figure 6.38. The **Planning Horizon** area is identical to the horizon definitions already explained in the context of time-related selection attributes. However, the planning horizon defines the horizon in which new capacity documents can be created by planning.

The **Default Business Document Type** area defines the types of objects that are created by planning. You can use the default types per category, which are all marked as default in the corresponding type Customizing; use a condition for document type determination; or explicitly maintain the document types per category. You can maintain the document types for road freight orders, rail freight orders, ocean freight bookings, air freight bookings, trailer units, railcar units, container units, and package units. If no explicit document type is specified, the corresponding default type is chosen. If the condition doesn't specify the document type, then the explicit type definition is used as the fallback.

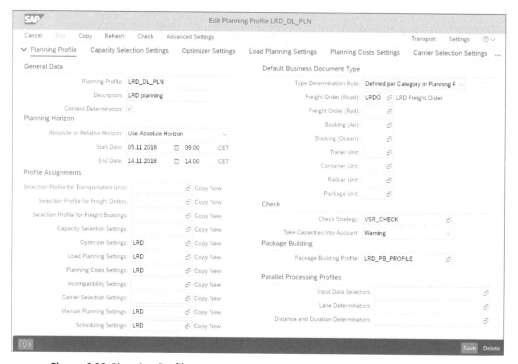

Figure 6.38 Planning Profile

In the **Profile Assignments** area, you can reference these eight planning-relevant settings and include selection profiles to select freight orders, freight bookings, and TUs, which is useful for scenarios in which you want to explicitly include certain freight documents and TUs in planning. With the **Copy** and **New** links, you can copy the assigned profiles and settings or create new ones, respectively.

The **Context Determination** flag in the **General Data** section enables automatic selection of the following objects into a transportation cockpit session based on explicitly selected objects:

- The truck, trailer, locomotive, railcar, and container resources assigned to explicitly selected freight orders and TUs. Drivers of explicitly selected road freight orders are selected, too.
- The freight documents and TUs (in the planning horizon) for the resources selected explicitly or in the previous step. In the same way, it selects road freight orders for the drivers selected explicitly or in the previous step.
- The freight documents and TUs (in the planning horizon) assigned to explicitly selected TUs.
- The TUs assigned to explicitly selected or automatically determined freight documents.

The main purpose of this functionality is to ensure a complete view for the resources at hand, which is particularly important when you deal with your own fleet and need visibility on the usage of your resources (e.g., in the Gantt chart). If you run a fleet operating in Europe and want to select all trucks that have been planned to make a stop in France during the planning horizon, you can do so by explicitly selecting freight documents with France as a source or destination zone and using context determination to select the assigned trucks.

The **Check** section defines the check strategy and the handling of capacity violations. The system issues either a warning (in which case, you can continue planning and save the affected document) or an error (in which case, the planning operation can't be executed), or it simply ignores the capacities.

Package Building in SAP TM 9.6

A **Package Building** section is available in SAP TM 9.6, which allows defining the package building profile to be used in the planning session. Note that this isn't supported by SAP TM in SAP S/4HANA 1809.

The **Parallel Processing Profiles** section allows you to define profiles to control parallel processing for the optimizer input data selection, transportation lane determination, and distance and duration determination. Via the menu path **Logistics • Transportation Management • Current Settings • Define Parallel Processing Profile** (in SAP TM 9.6, the menu path is **Application Administration • General Settings • Define Parallel Processing Profile**), you can specify the server group used for parallel processing, maximum number of parallel processes, package size that determines the number of relevant objects to be grouped together in a package for parallel processing, and queue time that defines how long the system has to wait for resources to become available for further processing. Parallelization can reduce the runtime for large optimization scenarios.

In the **Capacity Selection Settings** area shown in Figure 6.39, you can select the vehicle resources, drivers, container resources, and schedules for the planning scenario at hand. You can define multiple criteria based on attributes of the vehicle resource. The mode of transport can be maintained explicitly, allowing selection of different road and rail resources within one selection. You can use the **Means of Transport** attribute to select active or passive vehicle resources. The definition of criteria for drivers, container resources and schedules is analogous to vehicle resources.

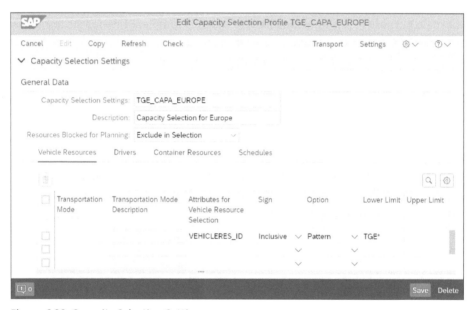

Figure 6.39 Capacity Selection Settings

For the remaining settings, refer to the sections that describe them in detail: The optimizer settings are described in Section 6.7.2, except for the transportation proposal parameters, which are explained in Section 6.6.9. The planning cost settings cover costs and constraints, which are discussed in Section 6.7.3 and Section 6.7.4, respectively. The incompatibility settings are covered by Section 6.7.4, too. The load planning settings are relevant for load consolidation and load planning, which are described in Section 6.7.7 and Section 6.7.8, respectively. The manual planning settings are explained in Section 6.6.8, and the scheduling settings are described in Section 6.7.4. Chapter 7, Section 7.1.4, explains the carrier selection settings.

The menu path **Profiles and Settings** • **Profiles and Settings Worklist** (in SAP TM 9.6, the menu path is **Planning** • **Worklist** • **Overview Settings**) takes you to a POWL containing queries for all profiles and settings. This provides a good overview and allows you to navigate to the individual profiles and settings as well as create new ones.

Transporting Profiles and Settings

Click the **Transport** button for planning profiles and selection profiles to trigger a transport (software) for them from one system into another. This avoids you having to maintain the same profiles in development, quality, and production systems and is less error prone than maintaining the same profiles multiple times—or once per change in each system.

6.6   Manual Planning

Manual planning concerns manually creating or changing the transportation plan. The transportation cockpit is the main UI for displaying the transportation plan and planning manually, but you can trigger automatic planning in it as well.

Section 6.6.1 describes the need to configure the transportation cockpit and provides many examples from different transportation planning scenarios. The page layout concept is key to configuring the transportation cockpit and is explained in Section 6.6.2.

Section 6.6.3 introduces hierarchical views and dual views that provide visibility into the substructures of documents and enable efficient comparisons and replanning of capacity documents.

The main visual components used in the transportation cockpit—the map, Gantt chart, and load plan—are presented in the next sections. Section 6.6.4 presents the map that can be used to display and change the plan from the geographical perspective. The Gantt chart provides an intuitive view on the plan from the time and resource availability perspective and is explained in Section 6.6.5. The load plan view described in Section 6.6.6 is key for package building and load planning, as it shows the packaging hierarchy in detail and offers a 3D view on all relevant aspects.

The entry options for the transportation cockpit are discussed in Section 6.6.7. Section 6.6.8 explains how to use the transportation cockpit by describing all its functionalities (e.g., manual planning, automatic planning, navigation through object lists and hierarchies, changing the optical appearance on the fly, etc.).

Section 6.6.9 presents the transportation proposal, which is a semiautomatic planning approach that combines automatic planning with a UI that enables a manual decision about the determined alternative transportation proposals. We describe how to configure and use the UI, as well as special parameters for automatic determination of transportation proposals.

Section 6.6.10 describes scheduling, which can be triggered out of the transportation cockpit and systematically determines start and end times for selected freight documents.

6.6.1   Transportation Cockpit

The ultimate goal of planning is to define a transportation plan that matches transportation demands with transportation capacities. The *transportation cockpit* is the central UI for performing any planning operation. However, due to the vast structural variety of planning scenarios in practice, it's impossible to define one UI statically that perfectly fits all scenarios of all transportation businesses in the world. Therefore, it's essential to configure the transportation cockpit, adapting it to the planner's needs so that all relevant information is visible and all irrelevant information is hidden.

The configuration of the transportation cockpit is done by *page layouts* that allow you to adapt the appearance of the transportation cockpit to the planning scenario at hand. A page layout defines the number of screen areas, their positions and sizes, the tabs contained in the screen areas, and all buttons that are visible in the cockpit's toolbar, as well as in the individual tabs per screen area. In addition to flat lists, more advanced concepts, such as hierarchical views and dual views, can also be incorporated, as well as graphical components, such as a geographical map, Gantt chart, and 3D visualization of a load plan. Besides the page layout concept, the column sets for all lists and hierarchies can be personalized; that is, the relevant fields can be selected, ordered, sorted, grouped, filtered, and aggregated according to the planner's needs. Moreover, you can use conditional formatting to highlight certain values.

To illustrate the variety of different planning scenarios and the need for flexible page layout definitions, we describe a few examples, each accompanied by a dedicated page layout. Afterwards, in Section 6.6.2, we describe how to configure a page layout and to maintain the underlying Customizing.

Note

It's important that there is an administrative object called page layout that defines the visual page layout of the transportation cockpit in a specific planning session. We don't introduce separate terms to differentiate the administrative and the visual aspect because the meaning becomes clear from the context of the discussion.

Example 1: Local Distribution without Own Fleet

In one local distribution scenario, the company ships goods from a distribution center in Frankfurt to multiple customers. The company doesn't own a truck fleet and therefore only uses external trucks. As the transportation planner is very experienced with geography of the different customers, he or she doesn't need a map. This scenario can be covered by the page layout shown in Figure 6.40. It contains freight unit stages in the top-left area, available truck (types) in the bottom-left corner, a list of road freight orders in the top-right corner, and overview details in the bottom-left area.

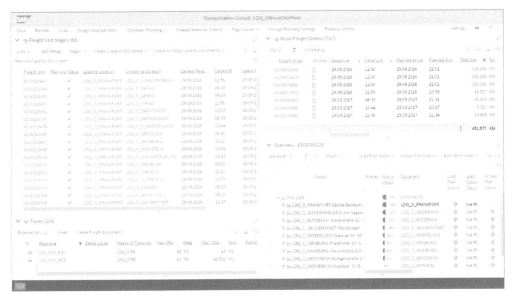

Figure 6.40 Location Distribution without Own Truck Fleet

Example 2: Local Distribution of Palletized Goods with Own Fleet

In another local distribution scenario, the company is using its own truck fleet to ship palletized goods from the distribution center in Frankfurt to multiple customers. The planner may use the page layout shown in Figure 6.41. The top-left area contains a Gantt chart with two views, one for the freight units to be planned and one for the trucks and the assigned road freight orders. The bottom-left area displays a list of road freight orders. The top-right corner shows a map that includes the road freight orders and the current positions of the trucks. The bottom-right area shows the load plan for one of the road freight orders. The screenshot shows the result of automated planning using the VSR optimizer and load planning. The freight units have been palletized using package building.

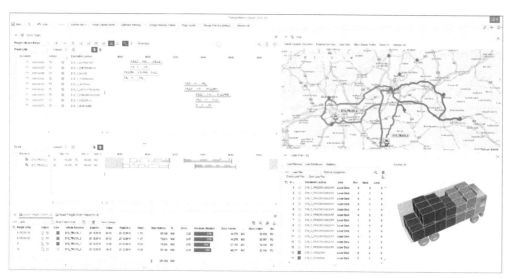

Figure 6.41 Local Distribution of Palletized Goods with Own Truck Fleet

---

Note

See *http://bit.ly/2DjLnCM* for a video showing how you can use manual and automated planning in such a scenario.

Figure 6.41 contains a lot of information. In a realistic scenario, the planner needs to handle many more freight units, trucks, and freight orders than shown here. We recommend running the transportation cockpit on two or three windows and assigning each window to one physical screen. This provides much more space for decision-making, and it's a great usability improvement because this significantly reduces the demand for scrolling (vertically or horizontally) and tab switching. Figure 6.42 shows one window containing the map to focus on the geographical aspect of the plan, Figure 6.43 shows one window consisting of the Gantt chart to focus on the time-related aspect of the plan, and Figure 6.44 displays a window consisting of a road freight order hierarchy (to show the detailed stop information of multiple freight orders) and the 3D load plan view. Using this setup with three screens containing these three page layouts, the planner gets a much better overview and can perform his job much more efficiently.

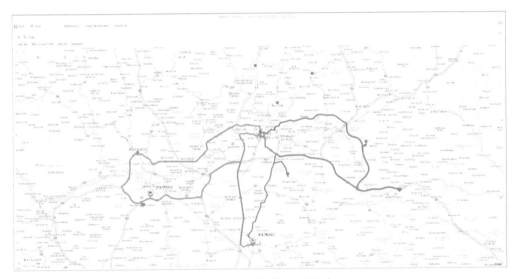

Figure 6.42 Map Window in Planning Session with Three Windows

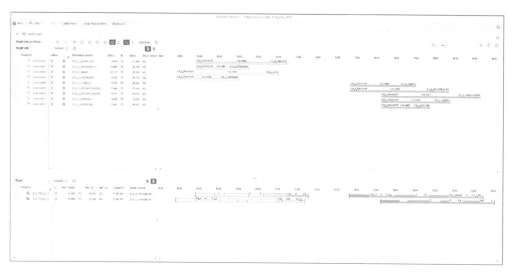

Figure 6.43 Gantt Chart Window in Planning Session with Three Windows

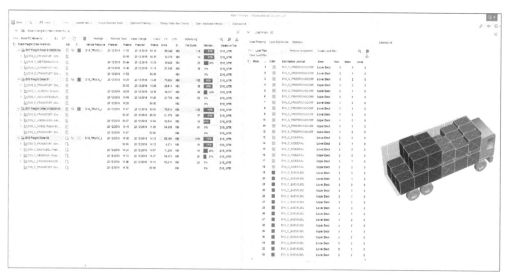

Figure 6.44 Road Freight Order Hierarchy and Load Plan Details in Planning Session with Three Windows

The basic idea of spreading the content of one page layout to three to use three screens for better overview and usability purposes is applicable to all scenarios.

Example 3: Integrated Delivery and Line-Haul Tour Planning without Own Fleet

An integrated delivery and line-haul tour planning scenario as described in Section 6.4.5 can be modeled by two dedicated page layouts.

The delivery planner can use a page layout as shown in Figure 6.45. It contains freight unit stages and package unit stages in the top-left area. Initially, the planner would only focus on the freight unit stages, but after creating package units, he would certainly review the created package unit stages. The bottom-left corner contains the available truck types and additional detailed areas to show the distribution stops of a package unit stage with distribution, and the assignment of a freight unit to multiple package units. The top-right corner lists the created freight orders in a list-based view or in a hierarchical view. Conditional formatting has been used to highlight the progress of the planning process. The bottom-right corner shows the map that initially contains the unplanned freight units and displays a road freight order created by the VSR optimizer. Moreover, the bottom-right area contains the load plan detailed area.

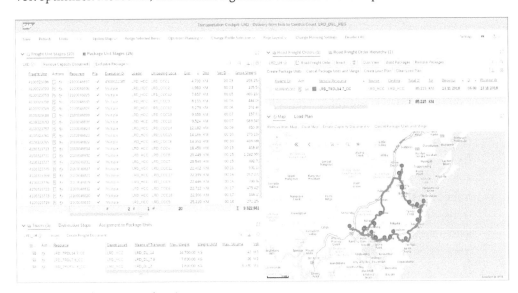

Figure 6.45 Delivery Tour Planning

The line-haul planner can use a page layout depicted in Figure 6.46, which includes two views on package units and their stages in the top-left corner. Available truck and trailer types are displayed in the middle-left and bottom-left areas. The top-right area contains a road freight order list and hierarchy, as well as a trailer unit hierarchy. As in the delivery planning page layout, the bottom-right corner shows the map and the load plan.

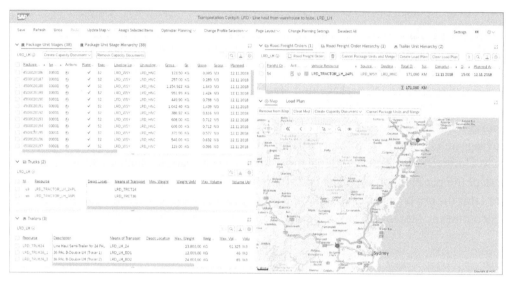

Figure 6.46 Line-Haul Tour Planning

Example 4: Load Planning

A company producing metal products (e.g., rods) is using a two-phase planning process. First, the transportation planner consolidates freight units to multiple road freight orders, minimizing total distance and focusing on weight limits of the available truck types, and then the load planner optimizes the load plans of the determined freight orders with automated and manual load planning. While the transportation planner may use the page layout already shown in Figure 6.40, the load planner can use the page layout depicted in Figure 6.47, which includes a list of road freight orders in the top and the detailed load plan view in the bottom. In the shown example, the load planner manually positioned the rods from the freight units assigned to the freight order at hand in the cargo space of the truck and then manually inserted and positioned wooden blocks between the rods for safety reasons.

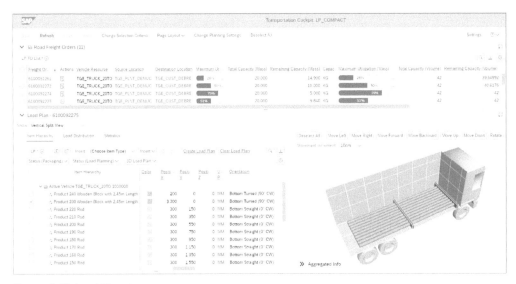

Figure 6.47 Load Planning

Example 5: Road Carrier for Full Truckloads

A road carrier operates a truck fleet and executes full truckloads (FTLs) across the United States. As all freight units fully cover a truck, there are no consolidation decisions to be made. However, the assignments of the freight units to the truck fleet and the sequencing on each truck are crucial to minimize the overall empty mileage of the truck resources. The planner may use a page layout shown in Figure 6.48. It contains a Gantt chart on the left side that includes three views for freight units, truck resources, and road freight orders. The right side shows a map that includes the unplanned freight unit stages as thin arcs, colored by document number to establish the link to the demands in the Gantt chart. Moreover, the map can show the last planned location of each truck resource as pins, and road freight orders are displayed as thick arcs, also colored by document number. This page layout combines the time-related view of the Gantt chart and the geographical view of the map so that the planner can make decisions considering all relevant aspects, for example, the last planned locations of the trucks, their availability times, and the geographical and time aspects of the unplanned freight units.

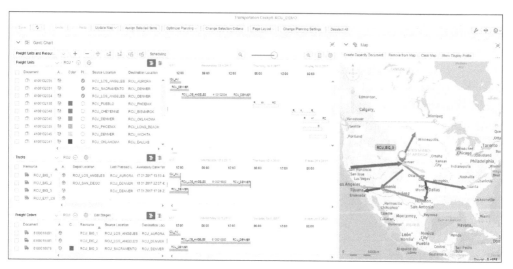

Figure 6.48 Road Carrier Scenario

Example 6: International Container Transportation

In an international container transportation scenario, a company transports pallet-ized goods from a plant in Mannheim (Germany) to a distribution center in Chicago (USA). First, the planner needs to determine the optimal number of 20-foot and 40-foot containers for the transportation orders at hand. Then, the planner needs to determine how to transport the containers through the transportation network.

This planning scenario can be covered by two page layouts that focus on the two main planning steps and are used consecutively. Figure 6.49 shows the first page lay-out, which contains the freight unit stages to be transported from Mannheim to Chicago (top-left corner), the available container types (bottom-left corner), the determined container units that still contain only one stage each (top-right corner), and the load plan consisting of a tabular and 3D view (bottom-right corner). The plan-ner used load consolidation to assign unplanned freight unit stages into the optimal number of container units. The freight units are planned, and the transportation demands are now represented by container units, which get planned in the second step.

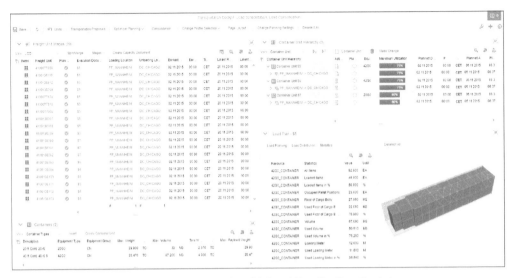

Figure 6.49 International Container Scenario with Load Plan for One Container

Figure 6.50 shows the second page layout, which contains container units and their stages in the top-left corner, schedules and trucks in the bottom-left corner, freight documents in the top-right corner, and the map and overview details in the bottom-right corner. Figure 6.50 shows the result of the VSR optimizer, which determined the two ports, consolidated the main legs of all the container units into one ocean freight booking, and assigned the pre-leg and subsequent leg of the container units into corresponding road freight orders.

Note

See *http://bit.ly/2FJ3MKP* for a video showing this planning process.

Example 7: Freight Forwarding

In a global forwarding company, the ocean freight planner needs freight units, ocean freight bookings, and schedules. Similarly, the air freight planner needs freight units, air freight bookings, and maybe schedules. The planners responsible for the pre-legs and subsequent legs require freight units, road freight orders, and schedules or vehicle resources. Therefore, within the same company, different planners need very different setups.

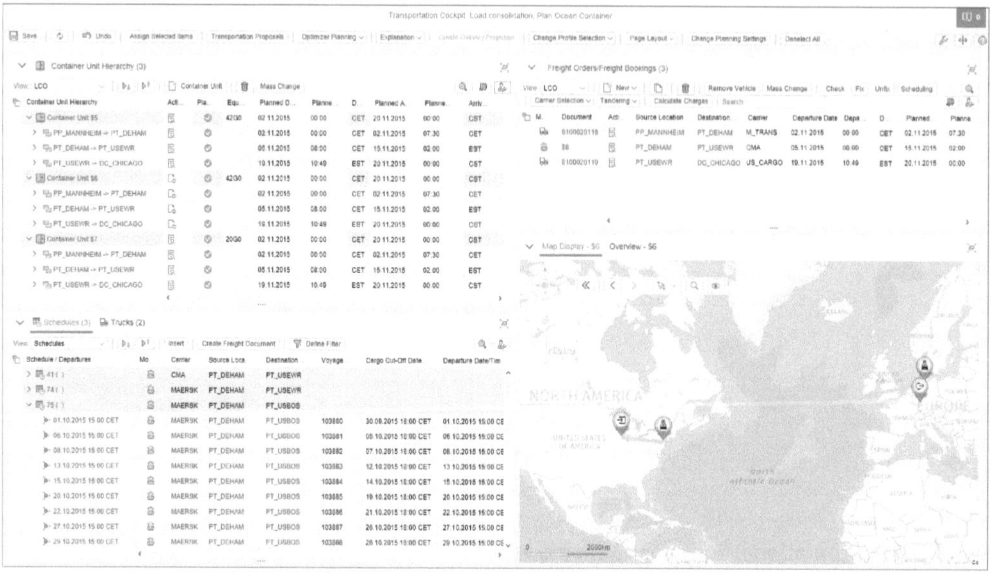

Figure 6.50 International Container Scenario with Planned Container Unit Stages

6.6.2   Page Layouts

The transportation cockpit offers a rich set of building blocks, each tailored to a certain transportation business domain. The planner can compose his or her preferred page layout by choosing the building blocks relevant for his planning scenario and defining their positions and sizes on the screen. Note that certain planners may require multiple page layouts, each dedicated to certain planning phases or decision types, as explained in the previous section for the integrated delivery and line-haul planning and the international container transportation example.

The system already provides a set of more than 20 page layouts tailored to different scenarios and modes of transport whose names all start with "SAP". We recommend you check these first. Ideally, one of them will perfectly meet your needs. Otherwise, you may copy one of them and then adjust it according to your scenario, or you create a new page layout from scratch.

Defining Page Layouts

To define a page layout, go to **Profiles and Settings** (in SAP TM 9.6, the menu path is **Application Administration • Planning • General Settings • Page Layouts**), and choose one of the following contexts for which you want to define a layout:

- **Transportation cockpit**
  This is the central planning UI, as just mentioned. Because it offers the biggest range of configuration possibilities, the rest of this section focuses on the transportation cockpit. Configuration for the next three contexts is much more straightforward and is therefore mentioned only briefly, without discussion of details.

- **Carrier selection**
  This layout focuses on freight documents and their details, which is sufficient for carrier selection purposes. From this perspective, these page layouts are special cases of page layouts for the transportation cockpit. Refer to Chapter 7, Section 7.1, for more details on carrier selection.

- **Delivery creation**
  This layout is required for SAP ERP order integration scenarios in which delivery proposals are created in SAP TM 9.6 for the freight units resembling SAP ERP orders. The layout consists only of freight units and delivery proposals. The delivery proposals can be propagated from SAP TM 9.6 into SAP ERP, where SAP ERP deliveries are then created. See Chapter 4, Section 4.1.3, for more details on delivery proposals.

- **Transportation proposal**
  This is a semiautomatic planning approach in which layouts consist of transportation proposals and may also include screen areas for preferences and a map. Transportation proposals are described in Section 6.6.9.

Next, you reach a page layout worklist, as shown in Figure 6.51. Here, you can create a new page layout, copy and delete a page layout, or transport the layout to another system. It's also possible to declare one page layout as the default, which will be used by the system in case the transportation cockpit is started without defining a page layout.

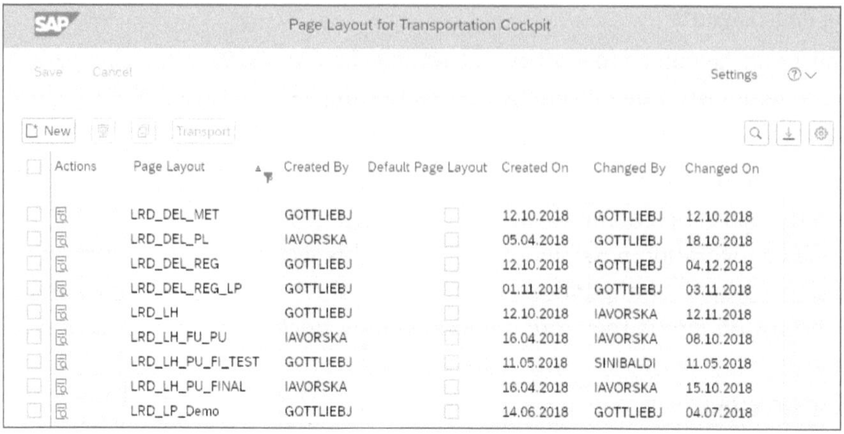

Actions	Page Layout	Created By	Default Page Layout	Created On	Changed By	Changed On
	LRD_DEL_MET	GOTTLIEBJ		12.10.2018	GOTTLIEBJ	12.10.2018
	LRD_DEL_PL	IAVORSKA		05.04.2018	GOTTLIEBJ	18.10.2018
	LRD_DEL_REG	GOTTLIEBJ		12.10.2018	GOTTLIEBJ	04.12.2018
	LRD_DEL_REG_LP	GOTTLIEBJ		01.11.2018	GOTTLIEBJ	03.11.2018
	LRD_LH	GOTTLIEBJ		12.10.2018	IAVORSKA	12.11.2018
	LRD_LH_FU_PU	IAVORSKA		16.04.2018	IAVORSKA	08.10.2018
	LRD_LH_PU_FI_TEST	GOTTLIEBJ		11.05.2018	SINIBALDI	11.05.2018
	LRD_LH_PU_FINAL	IAVORSKA		16.04.2018	IAVORSKA	15.10.2018
	LRD_LP_Demo	GOTTLIEBJ		14.06.2018	GOTTLIEBJ	04.07.2018

Figure 6.51 Page Layout Worklist

You can maintain a page layout by clicking on the icon in the **Actions** column. Figure 6.52 shows the generic sections **General Data**, **Users**, **Additional Windows**, and **Push-buttons for Application Toolbar** of the page layout, which allow you to define the following properties:

- **General Data**
  You can define the name of the page layout and choose a page layout for the transportation proposal, which is used if you determine transportation proposals out of the transportation cockpit, as described in Section 6.6.9. You also can activate command-line planning, which is explained in Section 6.6.8.
- **Users**
  The **Users** section allows you to explicitly assign specific users or roles to the page layout at hand or to declare it available for all users (as shown in Figure 6.52).
- **Additional Windows**
  The **Additional Windows** section allows you to assign one or two additional windows. For each additional window, you can specify its page layout and whether it will be opened by default. The main concept behind planning on multiple windows is a master window to which you can assign one or two additional windows. When planning in such a setup, you can close additional windows and reopen them, but closing the master window terminates the planning session. In the example depicted in Figure 6.42, Figure 6.43, and Figure 6.44, the (master) page layout is shown in Figure 6.44, and it's assigned to two additional windows containing the map and the Gantt chart, respectively.

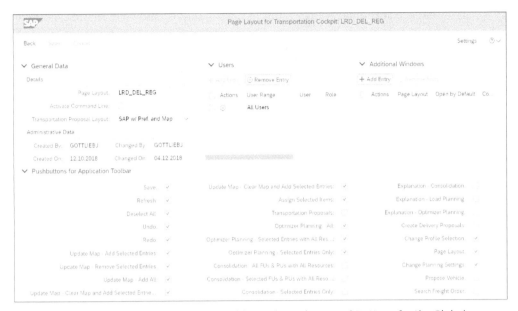

Figure 6.52 Defining General Data, Users, Additional Windows, and Buttons for the Global Toolbar in a Page Layout

- **Pushbuttons for Application Toolbar**
  You can select buttons in the **Pushbuttons for Application Toolbar** section to make them available in the global toolbar of the transportation cockpit. Section 6.6.8 describes the available functionalities.

Figure 6.53 shows the configuration of the content areas, which are placed in the page layout maintenance as they will appear in the transportation cockpit.

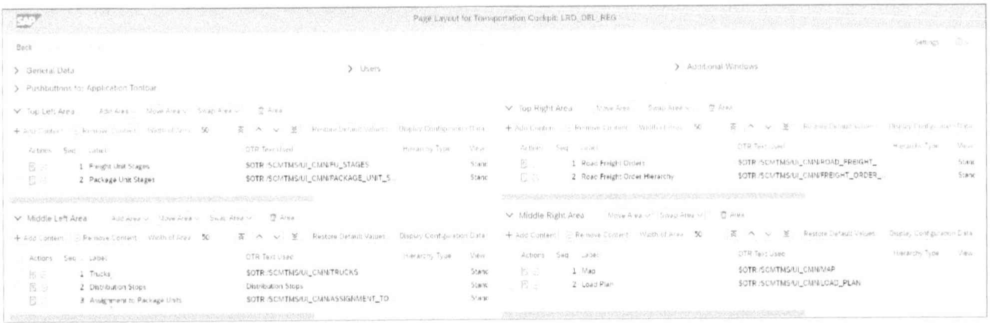

Figure 6.53 Defining Content Areas in a Page Layout

In the depicted example, which results in the page layout shown in Figure 6.45, there are four content areas:

- The top left area contains freight unit stages and package unit stages.
- The bottom left area contains trucks and the detailed areas for distribution stops and assignment to package units.
- The top right area contains the road freight order list and the road freight order hierarchy.
- The bottom right area consists of the map and the load plan.

You can maintain the content areas as follows:

- Add new content areas until you've reached a virtual grid with two columns and three rows.
- Delete a content area.
- Move complete areas to a new position in the virtual grid or swap the positions of two content areas.
- Adjust the relative width of two content areas beside each other. If you maintain the left area as 60, the right one will automatically be adjusted to 40 so that the total is 100.

Within each content area, you can add and remove content and change the relative ordering of the content in the area. This ordering defines the sequence of the tabs shown in the transportation cockpit.

For each content area, you can click on the details icon in the **Action** column and select the buttons to appear in the local toolbar and define additional parameters, as shown in Figure 6.54. For example, you can define that the content will be collapsed initially and specify the configuration and the association to retrieve data. For the graphical components, such as the map, Gantt chart, and load plan, you can stretch them and specify their layout, which will be described in Section 6.6.4, Section 6.6.5, and Section 6.6.6, respectively. You can define dual views and the hierarchy type for hierarchies, which are both explained in Section 6.6.3. The dual view can only be defined if the corresponding button has been activated.

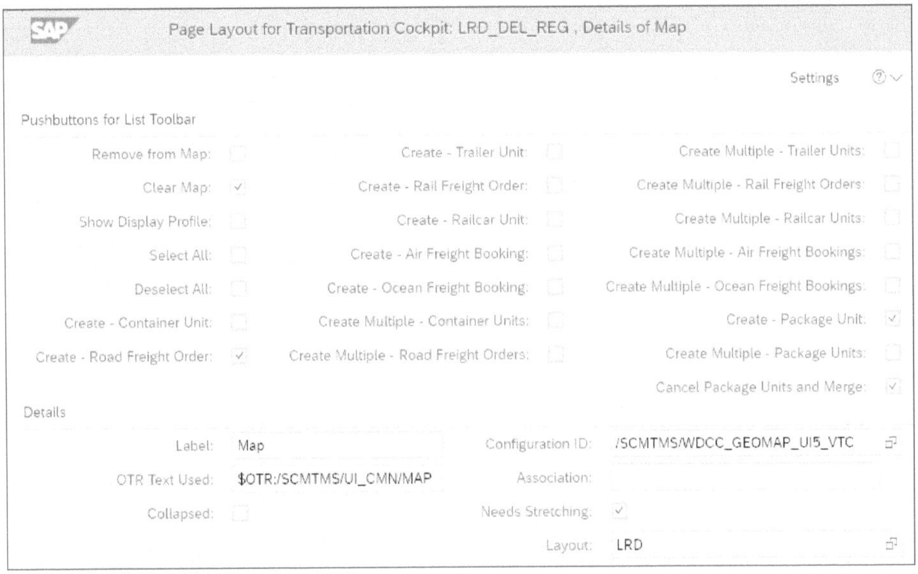

Figure 6.54 Defining Buttons and Additional Parameters for the Map Content Area in the Page Layout

You can place every available content object in any content area. While many content objects can display many objects at the same time, the detailed content objects focus on detailed information for one object at hand. It's possible to put multiple lists, hierarchies, and detailed views into the same content area. When adding content, the system issues a popup to choose the content object (see Figure 6.55) among a list of more than 80 options, including more than 40 detailed views.

Several content objects can even be placed in two content areas. For example, in a combined inbound and outbound planning scenario, you may want to have two freight unit stage lists, one for inbound and one for outbound. You can model these by using the freight unit list twice in the page layout and by defining appropriate filters to ensure that each of the two lists only contains inbound and outbound freight unit stages, respectively.

Figure 6.55 Adding Content for One Area in the Page Layout

The content objects can be structured as follows:

- Freight unit stage lists and freight unit hierarchies represent pure demand documents, which need to be assigned to capacity documents. Different configurations are offered for freight unit stages, with a focus on shipper scenarios as well as forwarder scenarios for ocean freight and air freight.

- Freight document lists and hierarchies for road freight orders, rail freight orders, ocean freight bookings, and air freight bookings can be used to consolidate demands. One list includes freight orders and freight bookings, which is useful for intermodal scenarios. The hierarchies are useful to replan stops in freight orders or to reassign demand documents between freight documents, as described in Section 6.6.3.

- TU lists, TU stage lists, and TU hierarchies for package units, container units, trailer units, and railcar units can be used for multiple purposes. While the stage lists primarily focus on the demand aspect, similar to a freight unit stage, the document list can be used for consolidation purposes. As previously mentioned, hierarchies are useful for replanning and reassigning purposes.

- The combined list for freight unit stages and package unit stages and the corresponding hierarchy are useful for scenarios in which freight unit stages and package unit stages serve as demands at the same time.

- Trucks, trailers, locomotives, railcars, containers, and drivers are contained in the respective resource lists.

- The schedule hierarchy contains the available departures per schedule.

- The map can display all documents and resources at the same time. It offers interactive planning and rich configuration capabilities described in Section 6.6.4.

- In the same way, the Gantt chart can display all documents and resources, enables manual planning, and is highly configurable, as explained in Section 6.6.5.

Detailed views can be triggered in the transportation cockpit by the corresponding buttons in the **Actions** column of any list, of any hierarchy, or of the Gantt chart. The following detailed views are offered:

- The single document hierarchies for road freight order, rail freight order, ocean freight booking, air freight booking, trailer unit, railcar unit, container unit, and package unit provide detailed information and enable replanning by drag and drop, both within the document at hand and from here to another document in a cockpit list or hierarchy. The package unit hierarchy and package unit stage hierarchy get triggered from the corresponding document and stage to provide details for the complete document or the stage at hand, respectively.

- The **Allocation** and **Carrier Ranking** views provide additional information on the affected allocation and the carrier ranking of the freight document at hand.

- The **Assignment to Package Units** view helps to identify how a freight unit's quantities are distributed to package units, which is relevant for the multi-assignment case described in Section 6.4.5.

- Four **Cargo Management** views provide cargo details from the viewpoint of road, rail, air, and ocean modes of transport, respectively.

- The **Cargo per Stage** view shows the assigned requirement documents for a capacity document at hand.

- The **Charges** view offers details on the calculated charges of the freight document at hand.

- The **Distribution Stops** view displays the stops of a package unit stage with distribution, as introduced in Section 6.4.5.

- The **Driver Assignment** view provides details on the driver assignment for the road freight order at hand.

- The **Execution Information** view provides details on planned and actual events for the freight document at hand.

- The **Freight Unit Hierarchy** provides hierarchical information on a freight unit at hand, which may, for example, include its items or original demand document, such as a forwarding order.

- The **Load Plan** and **Load Plan per Stage** views show the load plan for a road freight order, trailer unit, container unit, or package unit at hand. They can be triggered for a document or a TU stage at hand, respectively. Refer to Section 6.6.6 for more details.

- The **Map Display** view displays the document at hand on a geographical map. See Section 6.6.4 for more details on configuring the visual appearance.

- The **Overview** presents the quick overview for the document at hand, including its stop sequence and the assigned demand documents per stop. It includes an overview on utilization and certain status values.

- The **Predecessor Documents** view shows freight documents that must be executed before the capacity document at hand because they are assigned to a predecessor stage of a demand document stage assigned to the freight document at hand. Similarly, the **Successor Documents** view lists freight documents that must be executed after the capacity document at hand.

- Four **Stages** views represent the stages for the road freight order, rail freight order, ocean freight booking, and air freight booking at hand, respectively. Each view provides the stop sequence with detailed address, distance, and execution information, as well as planned and actual arrival and departure date and time, which can be edited.

- The **Status Management** view provides details on the various status values of the capacity document at hand.

- The **Utilization** and **Utilization Overview** views display a graphical and hierarchical view for the capacity document at hand, as shown in Figure 6.56 and Figure 6.57, respectively. The hierarchical view is very helpful for analyzing the capacity calculation, in particular when multiple object levels are involved, such as in the depicted example with a tractor carrying two trailers. The hierarchy isn't available with SAP TM in SAP S/4HANA 1809.

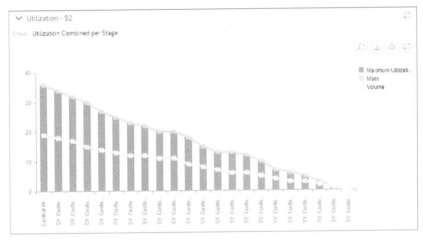

Figure 6.56 Utilization Graph

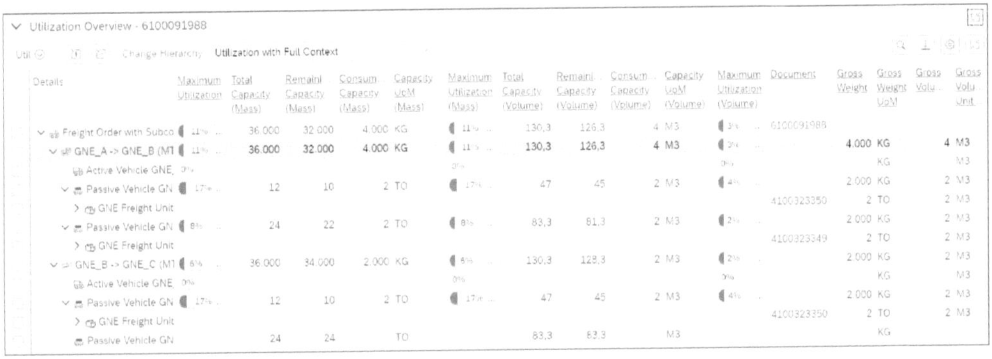

Figure 6.57 Utilization Overview

The number of rows used by the **Maximize** button (see Section 6.6.8) can be specified for any list and hierarchy. If you've created a personalized view for the tab, which defines the number of rows, column set, ordering, and so on, you can set it as the initial view for the tab. Otherwise, the standard view is used. By clicking the **Display Configuration Data** button, you can show the association used and change the UI configuration to use your own configuration.

Defining Settings for Page Layouts

The content offered to be chosen in a page layout can itself be configured in Customizing by following the path **Transportation Management • Planning • General Settings • Define Settings for Page Layouts**. Buttons and content objects represent the main building blocks, and you can configure which of these are offered in a page layout for the four applications mentioned previously (transportation cockpit, carrier selection, delivery creation, and transportation proposal).

You can define the following properties of buttons:

- The **Row Action** parameter defines whether the button is available as a row action or in the toolbar. For example, you can enable the row action for pushing objects to the map or removing them from the map. This is useful because it saves one click when pushing an object to the map. Without row action, the user must select the row first and then use a button in the toolbar, which results in two clicks.
- **Event** defines the action triggered by the button.
- You can also define **Button Text**, **Tooltip**, and **Icon** parameters as well as **Hotkey** to enable a keyboard shortcut to trigger the button.

Content objects allow configuring the following properties:

- You can define content object's **Title** and **Description**.
- The parameters **Detail Area Display** and **Req. Details Area Display** define whether the content object at hand represents a detailed area for a capacity document or a requirement document.
- The **Multiple Display** parameter specifies that the object can be used twice within the same page layout.
- You can assign multiple Web Dynpro configurations to the content object and assign local toolbar buttons to each configuration. For each button, you can define whether it's available for the page layout, whether it's initially selected in a new page layout, and its **Button Text** and **Tooltip**. Moreover, the ordering of the buttons in the local toolbar can be specified.

- For each configuration, you can define it as **Available** for the page layout definition. Moreover, you can define whether the content object needs **Stretching**. For example, for a Gantt chart or map, this is useful to utilize the available vertical space in the transportation cockpit. If two objects above each other use stretching, both will consume the same vertical size.

These configuration capabilities are very powerful because they even allow you to configure what can be configured in a page layout. This enables including your own objects developed in a customer project into the standard page layout maintenance and streamlining page layout maintenance by not offering objects or buttons that aren't relevant at all. However, if you change the preceding configuration, this may have an impact on already-defined page layouts that were based on the previous configuration. Therefore, we recommend synchronizing the page layout with the underlying Customizing after you change the Customizing. You can do so using the menu path **Profiles and Settings** · **Synchronize Page Layouts with Customizing** (in SAP TM 9.6, the menu path is **Application Administration** · **Planning** · **General Settings** · **Page Layouts** · **Synchronize Page Layouts with Customizing**). This tool allows you to choose a layout context and check all existing page layouts regarding new buttons, changed buttons, deleted buttons, deleted content objects, and deleted configurations. You can run the tool in simulation mode to report the affected page layouts or to clean up the page layouts immediately.

6.6.3   Hierarchical View and Dual View

Whereas in many planning scenarios, the information shown in flat lists for requirement documents and capacity documents is sufficient, several planning scenarios require visibility of the substructures of the business objects to make the right planning decisions. For example, if you want to assign an unplanned freight unit stage to one of the existing freight orders, you need to know the stop sequences of the freight orders to choose the best fit. Another example is improving the ratio of volume and weight for your air freight bookings, for which it's necessary to see the reassignment potentials of the freight units already assigned to the air freight bookings.

In this section, we'll dive into two views that achieve this effect: hierarchical view and dual view.

Hierarchical View

Hierarchical views can be used for all demand and capacity documents. The substructure of a hierarchical view is defined by a hierarchy type, which can be configured a priori. Hierarchical views allow planners to dynamically drill down into the substructures of the relevant objects in their transportation cockpit sessions. Figure 6.58 shows an example of a road freight order hierarchy with three hierarchy levels: freight order, location, and freight unit. You can expand all nodes or selected nodes in the hierarchy and collapse them afterward. Using the **Change Hierarchy** dropdown menu in the toolbar, you switch between alternative hierarchical views for the same document type, for example, between a stop-based and a stage-based hierarchy.

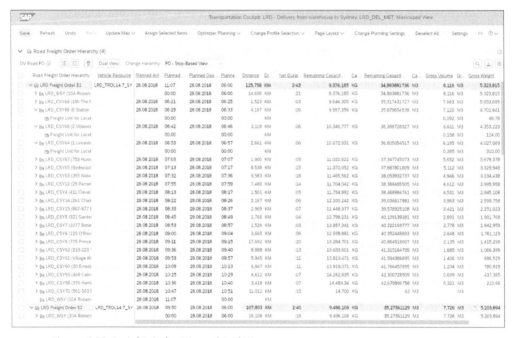

Figure 6.58 Freight Order Hierarchical View

To define a hierarchical view, select the Customizing menu path **Transportation Management • Planning • General Settings • Define Hierarchical Views for Business Documents**. You can edit an existing hierarchy type or create a new one. First, you have to choose its **Consumer** from the following alternatives (see Figure 6.59):

- **Transportation Cockpit: Requirement Document Stages**
- **Transportation Cockpit: Transportation Units**

- Transportation Cockpit: Freight Orders/Freight Bookings
- Freight Document: Overview
- Freight Document: Utilization
- Freight Document: Load Plan
- Freight Document: Cargo
- Freight Document: Equipment
- Freight Document: Simplified Item View
- House Bill of Lading

The consumer ensures that only reasonable hierarchy levels can be defined. Then you choose the **TrM Category** (mode of transport category), which also restricts the possible entries for the hierarchy levels. Filtering preserves parents of the filtered hierarchy level, and you can use the **Filter Type** to specify whether all sublevels of the parents are shown.

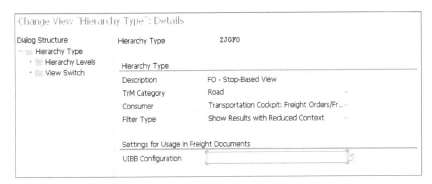

Figure 6.59 Hierarchy Type Header

The next step is to define the hierarchy levels, as shown in Figure 6.60. You choose among the available levels via the **Show Level** column. For each selected hierarchy level, you define whether the hierarchy is initially expanded. The example shows a freight order hierarchy with the freight order on the first level (which is expanded by default), locations on the second level, and assigned requirement documents on the third level.

471

Change View "Hierarchy Levels": Overview

Dialog Structure	Hierarchy Type	ZJGFO							
∨ Hierarchy Type									
• Hierarchy Levels	Hierarchy Levels								
• View Switch									

Object	Level	Show Level	Expanded	Text	Icon	Filter Lvl	Grp. Level
A Document Header	∨ 0	✓	✓			☐	☐
b Documents from LE, SD, and MM	∨ 0	☐	☐			☐	☐
B Forwarding Orders, OTRs, and DTRs	∨ 0	☐	☐			☐	☐
C Requirement Documents	∨ 0	✓	☐			☐	☐
H Packages	∨ 0	☐	☐			☐	☐
I Products	∨ 0	☐	☐			☐	☐
K Shipments	∨ 0	☐	☐			☐	☐
L Locations	∨ 0	✓	☐			✓	☐
M Stages	∨ 0	☐	☐			☐	☐
O Drivers	∨ 0	☐	☐			☐	☐

Figure 6.60 Hierarchy Levels

It's also possible to define the text and icon displayed in the hierarchical view. By activating the filtering option, you can suppress displaying locations at which no loading, unloading, coupling, or uncoupling takes place. For example, if a freight order delivers 50 freight units from one source to 10 different locations, you may want to see for each stop only those freight units that are loaded or unloaded at that stop, as shown in Figure 6.58. Alternatively, you can configure the hierarchy so that all freight units still on the truck are displayed for each stop. Thus, the freight units going to the last destination would be shown at all previous stops.

With the grouping functionality, you can aggregate multiple objects into your own hierarchy level based on a grouping rule, which can be based on a standard grouping attribute, grouping class (implemented by you), or data access definition. For example, if you want to group freight unit stages by their destination location, you can choose the stage object type, activate **Grouping Level**, define grouping rule **Standard Grouping Attribute**, and choose attribute **Destination Location**.

Note that it's even possible to define multiple grouping levels, which is useful if you want to structure your freight units according to source location and destination location. You can define that by adding a second entry for the stage object type, choosing the attribute **Source Location**, and assigning it a higher level. If you have hundreds of freight units to be planned manually, this kind of grouping structures the freight units according to your needs, enabling you to get a quick overview of the different freight unit groups by collapsing all hierarchy levels except for the groups.

You can introduce grouping levels in lower hierarchy levels also (e.g., to structure the freight units assigned to a stop of a freight order by product). Note that you can drag and drop freight unit groups to a freight order, which allows many similar freight units to be handled by one manual planning operation, without worrying about the individual freight units in the group.

The **Empty Grps** parameter defines whether groups without any children are shown. You can use the **Sorting** parameter to specify the sorting behavior for the hierarchy level at hand. By default, sorting is allowed for all hierarchy levels except for locations and stages because these represent the stop sequence of a capacity document at hand and are protected against sorting. For each hierarchy level, you can specify whether it will be sorted or not sorted, or the default will be used.

If you want to switch dynamically between alternative hierarchical views, you can define multiple hierarchy types and list the alternatives in the **View Switch** list of one hierarchy type. In the example shown in Figure 6.61, you can switch from the hierarchy type **ZJGF0** to the alternative hierarchy type **ZJGF1**, which enables dynamic switching between a stop-based and a stage-based hierarchy type.

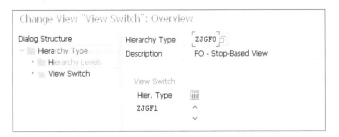

Figure 6.61 Hierarchy Type View Switch

Performance of Hierarchical Views

A hierarchical view contains much more information than a flat list and therefore may be slower than a flat list with the same set of objects. Consider a road freight order hierarchy with locations and freight units on the second and third hierarchy level, respectively. Imagine a scenario with 100 road freight orders, each having, on average, five stops and each stop containing five freight units in the hierarchy. The fully expanded hierarchical view then contains 2,500 rows, instead of 100 rows in the flat road freight order list.

The greater level of detail doesn't come for free. Therefore, if you're defining a hierarchical view, avoid defining too many hierarchy levels, and include only hierarchy levels that are very important for your business. We recommend that you do rough estimations of the average number of nodes per hierarchy level first to get an estimate of the expected number of rows for your hierarchical view if all nodes are expanded. If this number is much too big—for example, if it contains 10,000 rows—check whether you can cut your scenario into pieces by appropriate selection profiles or omit hierarchy levels in your definition.

We recommend displaying only items with action at the current location because displaying all items would yield even more rows in the hierarchical view.

The grouping functionality helps aggregate the objects, but it also creates more rows, so keep this in mind when introducing one or multiple grouping levels.

Although it's nice to see the full substructure of an object, usually not all columns in the hierarchical view can be meaningfully filled for all rows. While the source and destination location, as well as certain times, can be meaningfully defined for the freight order level and stage level, several fields (e.g., carrier or vehicle resource) are only meaningful on the freight order level. Therefore, we recommend checking whether all intended columns are needed and focusing on the most important pieces of information.

In a nutshell, be aware of the number of columns and rows created by your hierarchy type and chosen columns.

Dual View

If you've already created a plan, either manually or automatically, you may want to check it in detail for local improvements, such as reassigning a freight unit from one freight booking to another or moving a whole freight order stop with all its freight units to another freight order. Hierarchical views allow you to browse through the freight documents and their substructures. However, when you've found one freight order that you want to optimize manually by adding or removing freight units, you need to search for another freight order to perform the reassignment. Usually, you want to keep the first freight order and its substructure visible while identifying the second freight order. Because both freight orders are in the same hierarchical view, scrolling within one hierarchy may hide your first freight order. The *dual view* overcomes this issue by offering two hierarchies at the same time, which allows scrolling and searching within one hierarchical view while keeping the other hierarchical view constantly visible. The two views show the same information, but from a different angle, so if you change something in one hierarchy, you immediately see the effect in both hierarchies.

Depending on your scenario, you may want to see as many rows as possible or as many columns as possible. The dual view allows you to switch between the vertical view and the horizontal view, as shown in Figure 6.62 and Figure 6.63.

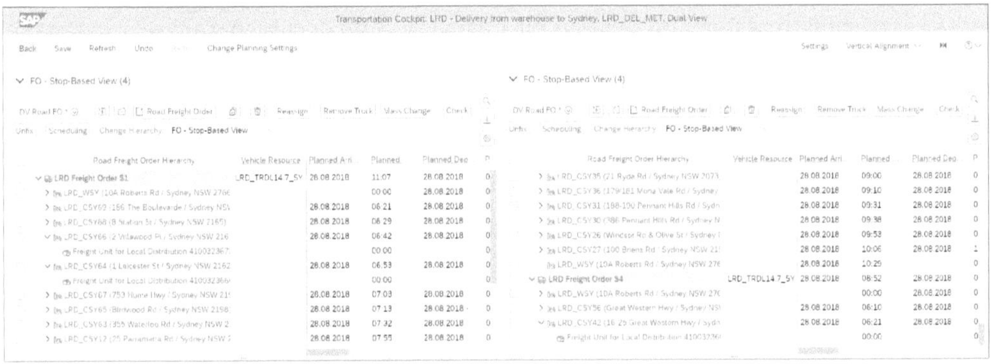

Figure 6.62 Vertical Dual View for Road Freight Orders

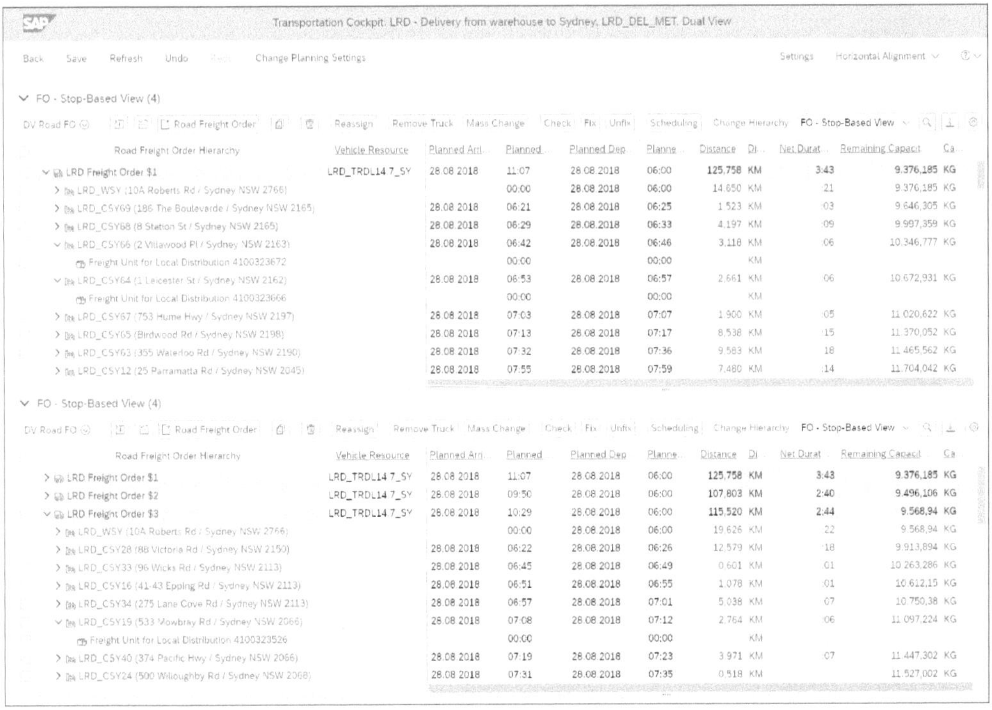

Figure 6.63 Horizontal Dual View for Road Freight Orders

Within the transportation cockpit, the dual view is triggered by the **Dual View** button from a list or hierarchy of capacity documents. If some of the documents in the list or hierarchy are selected, the dual view will only contain the selected documents. Thus, if you want to replan just 3 out of 50 freight documents, you can select the 3 relevant documents and focus on these in the dual view. If no documents are selected in the list or hierarchy, the dual view will contain all documents.

The **Dual View** button can be activated in the page layout definition for the list or hierarchy at hand. Figure 6.64 shows the definition of a dual view for a road freight order hierarchy. In the **Dual View** area below the **Details** area, you can specify the initial alignment of the dual view (either vertical or horizontal) and the hierarchy types for the two hierarchical views in the dual view. If you define only one hierarchical view, it's used for the second hierarchical view, too. If your layout is user specific, you can also define the view for the column sets. It's also possible to define the number of rows and columns; the initial value 0 uses the full space available for the page layout.

The dual view shows only two hierarchical views and can't be combined on one screen with other screen areas, such as resources or freight units. However, you can define a layout with two hierarchical views and other screen areas. If you want to enable an easy switch between the horizontal and vertical views, as is built into the dual view, you can define two layouts: one resembling the horizontal variant and one for the vertical variant.

Figure 6.64 Defining Buttons and Dual Views for Road Freight Order Hierarchy

6.6.4   Map

The map allows the planner to focus on the geographical aspect of the planning scenario, which is particularly important for consolidation decisions and searching demands or capacities nearby. Instead of working with names of objects in lists or hierarchies, the planner can see the objects directly on a geographical map. This enables the planner to judge distances between locations much more intuitively than in a text-based list and therefore supports the planner in making good decisions from a geographical perspective.

Similar to the transportation cockpit in general, the map provides rich configuration capabilities, so that it can perfectly be adapted to the transportation planning scenario at hand.

First, we'll motivate the need for configuration on two planning scenarios, and then we'll describe how to work with and configure the map.

Visualization for Local Distribution Scenario

In a local distribution scenario, for example, the planner needs to see the distribution center and the customers on the map. Figure 6.65 displays a map in which the distribution center is visualized as a square, and the customers are shown as triangles. If customers have the same address, which may be the case if multiple customers are located in the same business complex, they are displayed as a big triangle.

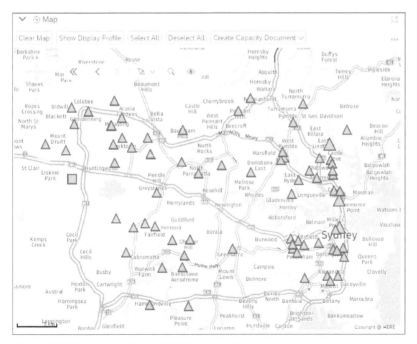

Figure 6.65 Unplanned Freight Unit Stages Displayed on a Map

477

Using the toolbar in the map scene, you can use a lasso to select certain freight unit stages on the map, as depicted in Figure 6.66. The selected freight unit stages are displayed in a different color than the unselected freight unit stages, as shown in Figure 6.67.

Now, the planner can use automated or manual planning to create a road freight order for the selected freight unit stages. The resulting freight order is immediately displayed on the map as well, as shown in Figure 6.68. The stops of a freight order are displayed as circles to differentiate them from unplanned demands.

This visual representation is very intuitive as all demands have the same source, which the planner can easily identify by its special shape on the map. The demands are mainly differentiated visually by the geographical position of the destination locations.

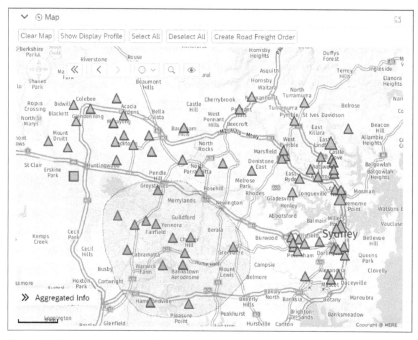

Figure 6.66 Lasso Selection of Unplanned Freight Units

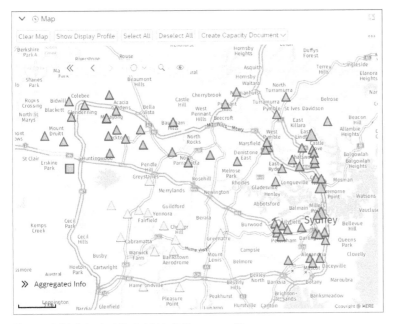

Figure 6.67 Selected Freight Unit Stages on Map

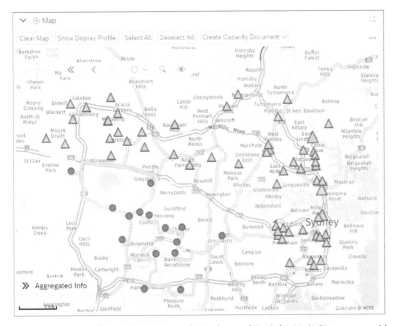

Figure 6.68 Road Freight Order and Unplanned Freight Unit Stages on a Map

Visualization for Road Carrier and Full Truckloads

For a road carrier transporting FTLs, it's more natural to visualize unplanned freight unit stages as arcs connecting source and destination per demand, as shown in Figure 6.48. This gives the perfect overview of the flow of transportation demands across the whole country.

In this scenario, you also need to see the last planned location of each truck, that is, the location in which the last freight order scheduled for the truck ends. You can show this and selected freight orders together with the unplanned freight unit stages on the map, as already depicted in Figure 6.48.

Working with the Map

Using the mouse wheel, you can zoom in or out; pressing the mouse button, you can move the displayed region into any direction with the mouse. Alternatively, the navigation and zoom controls in the top-left corner allow zooming in and out and moving the visible area.

The toolbar in the map allows you to go back and forth between recently used zoom levels. You can use three selection modes: single object, rectangle, and lasso. The two rightmost buttons in the toolbar offer rectangular zooming and optimizing the zoom level so that all objects are visible on the map.

You can push objects to the map by corresponding buttons in the global toolbar of the cockpit or buttons in the **Actions** column in a list, a hierarchy, or the Gantt chart. Individual objects can be removed from the map by the context menu, and the whole map can be cleared by a button in the toolbar above the map.

The **Aggregated Info** window (refer to the bottom-left corner in Figure 6.68) can be expanded and collapsed. It shows the total weight and volume as well as the number of sources and destinations for the requirement documents on the map, and the same information about the selected requirement documents.

In the page layout, you can define the buttons to appear in the toolbar above the map. Basically, you can create any capacity document for the selected documents on the map, and you can assign and create documents by dragging and dropping demand documents to a capacity document or a resource.

The context menu offers the following features:

- **Insert a stop**
  Insert a new stop into the document at hand.

- **Remove a stop**
  Remove a stop from the document at hand.

- **Editing the stages**
  Edit the stages of a capacity document.

- **Find transportation demands nearby**
  Define a distance threshold and then display all demands within this distance from a given resource on the map. This allows the planner to find efficient potential assignments of demands to the given resource.

- **Find resources nearby**
  Find efficient potential assignments of a resource for a given transportation demand.

- **Assigning objects to one object**
  Select unplanned demand document stages and start planning via the context menu. The system then offers possible assignments to the resources from which you can choose.

- **Demand document stage split**
  Split a demand document stage into two new stages by dragging and dropping the stage onto a location. For a freight unit, the location serves as a new intermediate transshipment location.

- **Multi-object planning**
  If multiple objects correspond to the same arc shown on the map, perform the manual planning operation either on one of those objects or on all objects associated with the arc. The latter is a very powerful functionality because you can plan a bundle of demand document stages with one step on the map.

- **Report a resource position**
  Report the current position of a resource and define the time stamp.

- **Color documents by attribute**
  Color-code documents according to their attributes. This is helpful if many freight orders are displayed at the same time. For example, you can color them by their document number, as shown previously in Figure 6.41, or you can color them by assigned resource, which allows you to identify all freight orders assigned to one specific truck resource.

- **Show details**
  For any object on the map, navigate to its detailed UI.

- **Find documents**
  For resources on the map, show the assigned documents on the map.

- **Show transshipment locations**
  In the context menu, trigger the display of the relevant transshipment locations for your scenario.

- **Remove**
  Remove all objects of one kind from the map.

- **Detailed routes**
  Switch between displaying the objects on the map as straight lines and detailed (street-level) routes.

- **Show display profile**
  Show the display profile that includes a legend for the visualized objects and some capabilities to adjust the visual appearance on the fly. For example, the display profile in Figure 6.69 has been used for the visualization of freight units and freight orders in Figure 6.68.

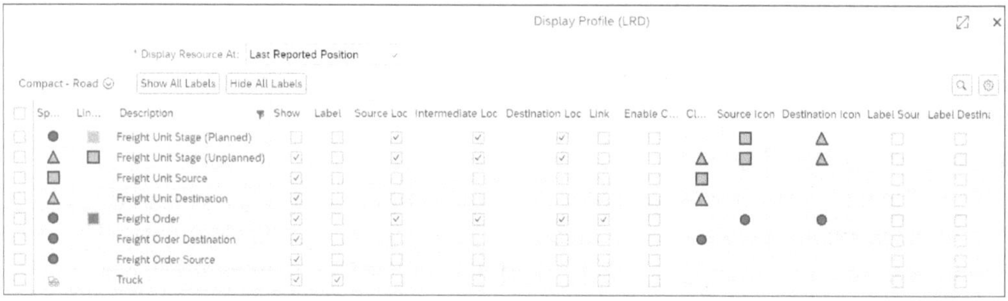

Figure 6.69 Display Profile

You can see that planned freight unit stages aren't displayed; unplanned freight unit stages are shown by a square and triangle for source and destination, respectively, but without arc; and freight orders are shown as circles for their stops and arcs between the stops. Labels aren't shown at all. The display profile allows you to show resources at the depot location, the last reported position, or the last planned location. You can also activate clustering to get a quick overview of the unplanned demands, as shown in Figure 6.70.

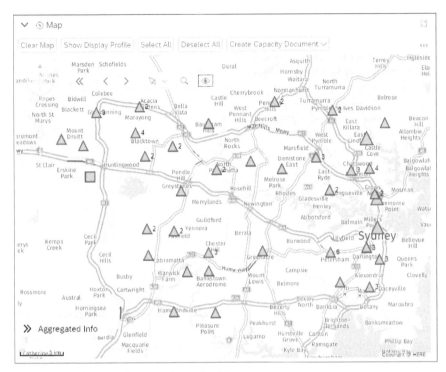

Figure 6.70 Clusters of Demands on the Map

- **Personalize**
  Define the initial map section, for example, the map of Italy if you plan that region most of the time, and choose among available map types configured.

- **Address search**
  Enter an address and show its geographical position on the map. Search results can be cleared afterward.

Configuration

Map layouts can be defined in Customizing using the menu path **Transportation Management • Basic Functions • Geographical Map • Define Layouts for Geographical Map**. You can assign map layouts for one of the following three components:

- **Map Display Component**
  Used to display one single document on the map.

- **Transportation Network Cockpit**
  Shows the network as already described in Chapter 3, Section 3.2.8.

- **Visual Transportation Cockpit**

  Represents the map in the cockpit that allows displaying many objects at the same time and manual planning. In this section, we'll focus on this application because it's the most powerful one.

For each application, you can define one map layout as the default. The definition of a map layout is based on the following abstract concepts:

- **Icons**

  Icons can represent circles, squares, and triangles of predefined size, fill color, border color, and border width. An icon can also be a real icon defined by an image, for example, a truck or driver.

- **Spot**

  A spot is a logical object that combines icons for different states, such as single, multi-object, highlighted, and selected spots. In the previously described local distribution example, a destination spot has been defined as a green triangle for the single state, a big green triangle for the multi-spot state, an orange triangle for the selected state, and so on. An icon can also specify properties for a cluster, such as its visual appearance, distance used for clustering, font color, and size, to indicate the number of objects in the cluster.

- **Link**

  A link is a logical object defining the visual appearance for an arc on the map. You can specify the fill and border color for the normal, highlighted, selected, and multi-link states; determine whether source, destination, and intermediate stops get displayed; and decide whether detailed street-level routing can be used.

- **Object**

  An object is composed of a spot, a link, and a set of description fields.

- **Object scheme**

  An object scheme defines the object for each required document or resource on the map, its label background color and position, and whether it's shown by default. For simplification purposes, the object scheme also defines a default background color and position of labels and refers to a default link configuration and a default spot configuration.

A map layout combines an object scheme and a context menu and defines several global properties, such as the usage of the aggregation window or the quick add function, which automatically pushes all selected objects to the map. You can also define that objects shown on the map will remain displayed when refreshing the planning session and whether resources get displayed at the depot location, last reported location, or last planned location. The map can automatically focus on objects added to the map. You can define the selection behavior for multi-objects, that is, several objects appear on the same position. Selection of a multi-object either triggers selection of all contained objects or triggers a popup in which you can choose among the contained objects. The context menu contains the menu structure, including submenus, ordering of menu entries, and usage of separators in a menu.

For the configuration of the map itself (e.g., geographical information system [GIS] vendor, etc.), refer to Chapter 3, Section 3.2.9.

6.6.5   Gantt Chart

The Gantt chart allows the planner to focus on the time aspect of the planning scenario at hand. Showing the plan from the time perspective in an intuitive graphical fashion, it creates visibility on the usage of your resources. The planner can easily identify which resource becomes available at which time and check the usage of the resources (i.e., when it's used for which activity), as well as the load utilization (i.e., the free capacity per time period).

The status of documents, activities, and delays causing overlaps with subsequently planned activities are visualized, too, allowing monitoring of the execution of the current plan. Moreover, the Gantt chart provides visual warnings for missing stages and incorrect driver assignment. With all these capabilities, the Gantt chart is key to enabling real-time planning, such as adapting the current plan based on progress reported from executing the plan.

The Gantt chart can visualize all planning-relevant documents and resources as well as drivers, and it offers all buttons available in lists and hierarchies in the cockpit.

Overview

The Gantt chart is a very powerful and flexible interactive graphical UI. Figure 6.71 shows its basic structure and main capabilities.

Before describing the functionalities in more detail, we first describe the overall structure of this UI. The global toolbar ❶ contains several buttons. The example contains two views. The view in the top consists of a local toolbar ❷, the selection panel ❸, and the chart ❹. The view in the bottom has the same structure ❺/❻/❼ and offers the same functionalities ⓝ–ⓠ, so we focus our explanation on the view in the top.

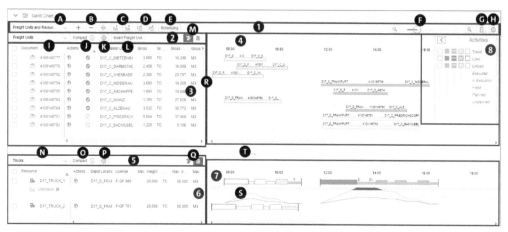

Figure 6.71 Building Blocks and Features of the Gantt chart

The selection panel displays multiple columns per row and allows you to select and sort rows, which you can scroll horizontally (via the scroll bar in the bottom of the selection panel). Using the button ⓚ, you can add or remove columns for the selection panel and reorder them. The button ⓙ allows you to store the column personalization including sorting as a new variant, switching between variants, and managing them, that is, defining one as default or deleting variants.

The selection panel and the chart can be scrolled vertically via scroll bar to the right of the chart (not shown in Figure 6.71 because all objects can be visualized in the available rows), and, of course, they scroll synchronously. The chart area consists of the time axis on top and the rows corresponding to the selection panel. The legend ⓼ can be shown or hidden using the button ⓖ, which contains multiple sections that explain colors and patterns and allows you to show or hide certain aspects of the plan, which we'll describe later.

While the vertical splitters ⓡ/ⓢ allow the ratio between the selection panels and the charts to be adjusted, the horizontal splitter ⓣ enables changing the relative sizes of the top view and the bottom view.

You can use zoom in and zoom out ⓕ by using the plus and minus buttons or dragging the zoom level to the left or right. You can also use bird's-eye view zooming (not shown in the screenshot), which can determine the best zoom rate for the visible rows or all rows at hand.

You can dynamically switch between the document and activity view using the button ⓜ. The document view shows a complete document, such as road freight order or freight unit, as one rectangle. This is particularly helpful if the planner wants to quickly assign a complete document to one resource or reassign it from one resource to another. If the planner needs more details about the documents at hand, he or she can use the activity view to visualize all individual activities of a document (i.e., travel, load, unload, prepare, finalize, couple, and uncouple) as rectangles. In Figure 6.71, the views in the top and bottom show documents and activities, respectively.

The activity types are distinguished by colors, and the corresponding statuses are differentiated by patterns, as shown in the legend for the activities. The activities' statuses are propagated to the corresponding documents:

- If all activities are planned, but execution hasn't started yet, the corresponding document also has the status *planned*.
- If at least one activity is already executed or in execution, and at least one activity isn't yet executed, the document is *in execution*.
- If all activities are executed, the corresponding document also has the status *Executed*.

Moreover, documents can have the status *fixed* or *unplanned*.

The combination of color and pattern allows the planner to quickly understand the progress of execution of the current plan. Of course, colors and patterns can be configured, as described later in this section.

For resources, downtimes and nonworking times are displayed. A downtime may represent a planned maintenance period or breakdown and indicates that the resource can't be used during this time period. In the case of a planned maintenance period, the location is shown as text in the downtime rectangle so that the planner can consider moving the truck to the maintenance location and plan its next trip after the downtime from there. Nonworking times can model weekends or public holidays during which a truck isn't supposed to drive. Note that travel activities can be interrupted by such nonworking time to model, for example, weekend breaks during which the truck rests at some parking place along the highway.

You can display the load utilization of a resource by selecting the corresponding row and using the left load utilization button 🄲. In Figure 6.71, you see the time-dependent load utilization for the truck resource **D17_TRUCK_1**. In the truck row running in activity view, you see two freight orders. The corresponding load utilization is shown in the row below the truck resource and displays two curves, one for volume utilization and one for weight utilization. The over-capacity zone has a back-slashed pattern, and any utilization across the capacity is displayed red. In this example, the planner notices that the second freight order contains one loading activity followed by two unloading activities and that the truck capacity is exceeded. In addition, the over-capacity notification bar appears in the top of the corresponding document/activity rectangle. The planner can solve this problem by assigning one of the unloading activities to another truck or a new freight order on the same truck. The planner can hide the load utilization row by either clicking the cross in the selection panel part of the load utilization row or using the right load utilization button **C**.

Hierarchies and Multiple Views

The user can switch between predefined hierarchies via the local dropdown menus (refer to **I** and **N** in Figure 6.71). This dynamic switch allows the user to view the plan from a different angle, such as from the freight unit perspective, freight order perspective, or truck resource perspective. A real hierarchy (with more than one hierarchy level) visualizes the structural relation between different objects (e.g., trucks and their assigned drivers). Using the dropdown menu **A** in the global toolbar, you can switch between predefined views.

The view control buttons **B** allow you to add a new view until the limit of three views is reached (refer to Figure 6.48 for an example), to remove a view, and to switch between horizontal and vertical display. In the horizontal version, the views appear on top of each other; in the vertical version, the views appear side by side. As already discussed in the dual view concept for lists (refer to Section 6.6.3), the horizontal version provides more horizontal space for the chart and selection panel, and the vertical version provides more rows for the charts.

The concepts of multiple views and dynamic hierarchy switching allow the planner to quickly adapt the Gantt chart to the decisions he wants to make next. For example, if the planner wants to assign unplanned road freight orders to truck resources, he or she can use two views with freight orders in the top and truck resources in the bottom. With this setup, he or she can now assign the freight orders to trucks via drag and drop.

In general, the multiple view concept is perfect for assignment decisions to be made, such as assigning freight units to trucks. You simply define a dual view with freight units in the top view and trucks in the bottom view, and then you can drag and drop freight units to the trucks, thereby creating new road freight orders, as shown in the dual view in Figure 6.71. Other dual view use cases are assignments of drivers to freight orders, freight units to trailer units, trailer units to trailer resources, trailer units to freight orders, trailer units to truck resources, and so on. Using three views at the same time can be useful if you deal with two-level consolidation decisions, such as assigning container units to trailer units, and assigning trailer units to road freight orders.

The dual view also allows you to compare certain aspects of a plan or replan documents from one truck resource to another, as depicted in Figure 6.72. Here, truck resources are shown in the top and bottom, so the planner can bring some resource into focus of the upper view and others in the lower view; compare them; and make reassignment decisions, which he can execute by dragging and dropping the relevant documents or activities.

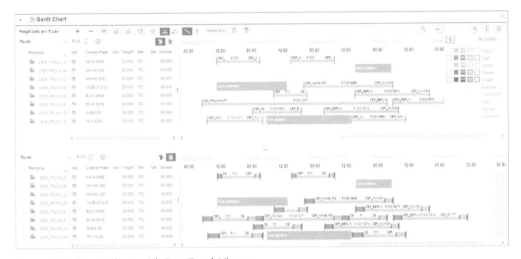

Figure 6.72 Gantt Chart with Two Truck Views

The utilization of handling resources can also be visualized, for example, in a dual view with trucks and handling resources, as shown in Figure 6.73.

The visualization of handling resources is useful when there are bottlenecks or the planner wants to balance the utilization or reduce over-capacity situations on a handling resource. He or she can analyze the handling resource utilization, capacity, non-working times, and downtimes in the upper view and replan the corresponding freight orders and loading or unloading activities in the bottom view. For each handling resource, you can display the detailed activities in the row below the utilization curve by selecting the corresponding handling resource and using the **Show Detail** button (refer to **D** in Figure 6.71).

Figure 6.73 Dual View with Handling Resources and Coloring by Attributes

If certain views (single, dual, or triple) are used frequently, they can be preconfigured, allowing the user to switch between them easily, as described previously for the drop-down menu in the global toolbar (refer to **A** in Figure 6.71).

Attribute-Based Planning

In certain industries, such as retail, the planner doesn't want to plan at the individual freight unit level but at the assortment level, for example, ambient, chilled, and frozen. You can define one attribute and colors for different attribute values in the Gantt chart Customizing. Loading and unloading activities then get colored accordingly, as shown in Figure 6.73, in which the document label was used as the attribute. For usability reasons, all attribute groups at a stop get the same visual duration (as it otherwise would be difficult to see and drag a small group). Now, the planner can drag and drop attribute groups, which may represent many freight units associated with the same attribute value. In this retail example, you can drag the ambient group from one freight order to another, which is much more efficient than selecting all individual ambient freight units. This general principle to work on the group level can also be used by freight unit hierarchies grouped by an attribute, as described in Section 6.6.3.

490

Notifications

Notifications are used to visualize certain critical aspects of the current plan, as shown in Figure 6.74. They are shown as lines on the top or in the bottom of rectangles representing documents or activities. A notification bar on the top visualizes important aspects of load utilization:

- **Empty run**

  The truck or trailer doesn't have any load; in other words, it travels empty. Planners for company fleets usually want to avoid or at least minimize empty runs.

- **Low load utilization**

  The planner can specify a certain threshold, such as 70%, and the system then notifies the planner about loads below this percentage. Many companies work with such thresholds and execute freight orders only if they have a utilization above the threshold.

- **Over-capacity**

  The current load in a capacity document exceeds the capacity of the corresponding resource, as shown for truck **DER_TRUCK_C** in Figure 6.74. The planner may temporarily create such a situation, such as when consolidating multiple freight units into one freight order. Of course, the planner should later reduce the load so that the resource capacity isn't violated.

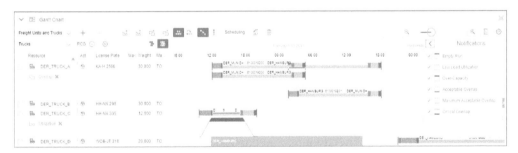

Figure 6.74 Notifications in the Gantt Chart

While a single resource represents an individual truck instance (i.e., a real physical truck with a license plate), multiresources, which are commonly used to represent truck types instead of truck instances, allow scheduling several documents in parallel with the maximum number of allowed documents. A notification bar in the bottom of a rectangle indicates an overlap situation, such as when more than one freight document or activity is scheduled at the same time. Selecting the corresponding row and using the left overlap button (refer to ❹ in Figure 6.71), the planner can show the details of the overlap below the selected row. The system differentiates between three kinds of overlap situations:

- **Acceptable overlap**
  There are at least two overlapping documents, but the number of overlapping documents is below the allowed number of instances.

- **Maximum acceptable overlap**
  The number of overlapping documents equals the allowed number of instances. Although this assignment is still feasible, it's more critical because any new assignment of a document to the resource at hand would lead to exceeding the number of instances.

- **Critical overlap**
  The number of overlapping documents exceeds the allowed number of instances. Thus, the planner has to get additional resources or replan some of the involved documents to meet the original constraint. In the example, truck **DER_TRUCK_A** contains two parallel freight orders, which led to a critical overlap as the truck is a single resource.

The colors for the different overlap situations help to notify the planner in a visual fashion about the criticality of the overlap situation. You can dynamically show and hide each notification by the checkboxes in the legend.

Warnings

While notifications are used to indicate overlap situations or load utilization issues, warnings are provided for other critical situations. Warnings are visualized with icons and can be switched off via a checkbox in the legend, as depicted in Figure 6.75. In this example, two freight orders are assigned consecutively to the truck resource **DER_TRUCK_D**. The first freight order goes from Hamburg to Munich, and the second goes from Frankfurt to Hamburg. Obviously, the truck needs an empty travel from Munich to Frankfurt, which hasn't yet been planned. This fact is visualized by two icons, one at the end of the first freight order and one at the beginning of the second freight order. Hovering over an icon, the planner gets information about the distance and duration of the missing travel activity. Thus, the planner can decide to insert the empty stage or replan one of the freight orders to another truck, if he wants to avoid the empty mileage. By right-clicking for the context menu for the previous or subsequent freight order and choosing **Solve Warnings**, the planner can add the missing stage to the corresponding freight order.

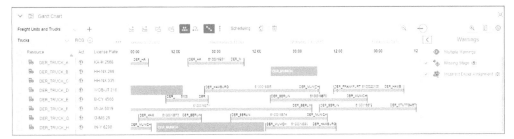

Figure 6.75 Warnings in the Gantt Chart

The second offered warning type displays an incorrect driver assignment. If you configured driver planning to be relevant for the road freight order type at hand, the system issues a warning if the current driver assignment isn't correct. This might occur, for example, if the freight order requires a single driver, but you haven't assigned one, or if the freight order requires a driver team (of two drivers), and you've assigned only one or no driver. The warnings are shown on the document and travel activity level, as you may have configured that different drivers can be assigned on each stage of a road freight order.

Document Separators and Time Windows

Using the **More** part of the legend, you can display acceptable and requested time windows for loading and unloading demand documents, as shown in Figure 6.76. This is helpful to verify the current plan from a service level viewpoint, that is, whether the desired and acceptable time windows are met. The legend also allows you to show and hide the document separators, which you can see in Figure 6.72 and Figure 6.75. They help to identify idle times on a resource between consecutive capacity documents, in particular when using the activity view.

Figure 6.76 Requested and Acceptable Pickup and Delivery Time Windows

Additional Settings

The settings dialog can be triggered by the **Settings** button ⊕ (refer to Figure 6.71) to allow activation of the following:

- **Indicate current time**
  The current time is shown as a vertical line in the charts.

- **Show cursor time**
  When the planner moves the mouse inside the charts, a vertical line is shown in the charts and following the mouse cursor movements. The line contains a time stamp shown in the time axis area. It allows comparison of the times of documents or activities in different rows or charts, or just getting the time stamp for the current mouse cursor position.

- **Show divider lines**
  You can switch off vertical divider lines in the chart area, as shown previously in Figure 6.75.

- **Synchronize scrollbars**
  When using multiple views, all charts have the same time axis by default; in other words, they visualize the same time period and are scrolled (horizontally) synchronously. In some scenarios, the planner may not want to scroll synchronously, such as when replanning a freight document from truck 1 (this week) to truck 2 (next week). He or she may want to do this by keeping truck 1 and this week visible in the view in the top and scrolling in the bottom view to the next week (and keeping the visible area of the other view stable).

- **Display related documents/activities only**
  When showing hierarchies, you can define whether you want the lower hierarchy levels to show only documents and activities that are directly linked to the parent hierarchy level. The trailer swap example depicted in Figure 6.28 shows two views: in the top, you see trailers below trucks, and in the bottom, it's vice versa. Here, the lower levels only show the activities that are linked to the parent level. For example, in the view in the top for trailer **AT_TRAILER1**, only the couple, travel, and uncouple activities are shown because these are performed together with the truck **AT_TRACTOR1** on hierarchy level 1. Therefore, that trailer's activities performed together with **AT_TRACTOR2** aren't shown below **AT_TRACTOR1**. If you want to see the full context—that is, all other activities on the lower hierarchy levels as well—you can activate such visualization as depicted in Figure 6.77.

- **Automatically determine drag and drop target**
  If you drag and drop a demand document to a time period on a resource where

another capacity document has already been scheduled before, the system will automatically assign the demand document to the capacity document. However, in particular when planning with multiresources, you may want to create a new capacity document on the resource at hand, although this would result in an overlap. You can switch off the automatic assignment, and when performing a drag and drop that would offer multiple assignment options for the drop target, the system raises a popup window that allows you to choose one of the identified options. For example, if there are already two freight orders in the drop target time period, you can choose between these two freight orders and the third option to create a new freight order.

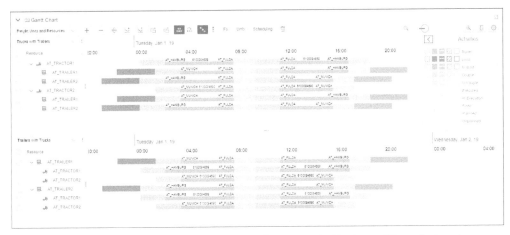

Figure 6.77 Trailer Swap in Gantt Chart Showing All Activities in the Lower Hierarchy Levels

Drag and Drop Modes

The Gantt chart offers different modes for performing drag and drop:

- **Toggle between the rescheduling and the resequencing mode**
  The two buttons to the right of the overlap button in Figure 6.77 are called **Rescheduling** and **Resequencing**. Basically, rescheduling means that a drag and drop triggers a rescheduling, but the location sequence is kept, while resequencing allows changing the location sequence. Rescheduling is the default mode and behaves as follows. When dragging an activity, this activity serves as an anchor scheduled at the drop position's time, and other activities are scheduled accordingly, starting from the anchor. When dragging a document, its first activity serves as an anchor. Independent of which mode is active, drag and drop of an object from one resource to another resource causes a reassignment and, consequently,

495

rescheduling on the new resource. If an activity is dragged, only the corresponding demands are reassigned, and in the case of a dragged document, the whole document is reassigned. With resequencing mode active, drag and drop of a loading or unloading activity removes the corresponding demands (freight units) from their current position and inserts them into the new position on the same resource. This could be a new position in the same document, a new position in another document, or a new position on a free space that would result in creating a new document.

- **Drag and drop with scheduling or assigning**
  The two buttons to the right of the **Rescheduling** and **Resequencing** buttons in Figure 6.77 are the **Drag and Drop Scheduling** and **Drag and Drop Assigning** buttons. If you reassign a document or activity from one row to another, usually you want to specify the desired anchor time for scheduling by the drop position in the target row. However, in some businesses, you may want to preserve the previous times of the document at hand. For example, suppose that you've created road freight orders with the VSR optimizer, considering opening hours and time windows of customers and transportation demands. You may want to preserve this scheduling of the freight order but just assign a driver. Switching to the assigning only option, you can ensure that you drag and drop the freight order to a driver row in the Gantt chart and preserve the freight order's scheduling.

Context Menu

The context menu offers additional manual planning features, such as assigning or unassigning resources or drivers, inserting locations, and fixing or canceling the document at hand. Moreover, you can use the context menu to solve warnings. You can also scroll to the first or last activity in a row or to the current time, select all objects in the row at hand, or open the single document UI. By double-clicking on a document in the chart, you can trigger a quick view that lists some extra information. It also provides a hyperlink to the single document or resource UI, which you can also reach by hyperlinks in the selection panel.

Smart Add

While some customers use the Gantt chart as the primary tool to visualize all resources and documents and perform manual planning, other customers want to work in lists and hierarchies and use the Gantt chart as a kind of detailed area in which only selected resources and documents get displayed. The second usage is offered by the *smart add* mode, which can be activated in the Customizing as described in the next subsection. Basically, this mode makes the Gantt chart only display objects selected in lists and hierarchies outside the Gantt chart. If the user didn't select anything, the Gantt chart is empty. If the user selects a resource or a document, the Gantt chart will show it, including its context. Therefore, if the user selects a road freight order, the Gantt chart will show it as well as its assigned resource (if any) and other documents assigned to that resource.

Configuration

Because the Gantt chart is a very visual tool, it's impossible to provide a color and pattern configuration that all planners like or can work with. Some people have difficulties distinguishing red and green, so they need different colors that they can differentiate. Some companies are used to certain colors in their software and may want to use them in the Gantt chart, too.

While one planner is mainly interested in the start and end times of a freight order, another planner prefers to see the start and end location as text in the Gantt chart. One company is mainly interested in the number of pallets, while another company needs to see volume and weight information. For all these reasons, the Gantt chart provides sophisticated configuration capabilities so that every company and user can adapt it to their needs.

To configure the Gantt chart, select the IMG menu path **Transportation Management · Basic Functions · Gantt Chart**. Note that a lot of Customizing content has been delivered, usually starting with the prefix "SAP." We recommend using that as a starting point and then copying and adjusting it according to your business needs.

Following the activity **Define Color Schemes and Patterns for Gantt Chart**, you can do the following:

- Color schemes for activities define colors and height (full or half row) of activity types and patterns of activity statuses. For example, you can give full height to location-based activities, such as loading, unloading, preparing, finalizing, coupling, and uncoupling, and half height to travel activities to differentiate traveling from other activities in an easy, visual way. You can also define the level that defines which objects are shown in the foreground in case of overlaps. The color scheme also defines an attribute that is used to color loading and unloading activities, and the assigned attribute scheme defines the sequence of attributes and their colors.

- Similarly, color schemes for documents define colors, heights, and levels for document types and patterns for document statuses.

- Set colors for visualizing overlaps on resources.

- The color schemes for resources configure colors for downtimes and nonworking times of resources.

- The color schemes for utilization define the load utilization curves for weight, volume, and quantity. You can also switch off certain loading dimensions, such as if only weight were critical for your business, for example.

- Notification schemes allow you to set thresholds, heights, and colors for notifications about load utilization. For example, a utilization below 70% could be marked yellow, a utilization above 100% marked red, and an empty run marked blue. This helps users quickly identify underutilized and overutilized capacity documents as well as empty runs. You can also define heights and colors for notifications about overlaps and enable visualization of document separators and time windows. For all these graphical components, you can define whether they are active when starting the transportation cockpit.

- Warning schemes enable the usage of warnings for missing stages and incorrect driver assignments and whether they are active initially.

- You can define the colors and patterns that are the basis for all the preceding definitions.

If you choose the activity **Define Field Lists and Label Schemes for Gantt Chart**, the systems allows you to do the following:

- Define the fields that can be displayed in the selection panel and used in labels for the chart. For each field, you can specify its content per object type. Using this principle, you could use one column differently per object type. This may be helpful for hierarchies because you would otherwise consume two different columns, and half of the cells would be unused because the field applies to only one object type.

- Specify field lists that are used for the selection panel. A field list is an ordered set of fields. Per field, you can define whether a quick view is offered.

- Define labels that can combine multiple fields and static texts. For example, you can specify a label that combines source location and destination location, resulting in texts such as "Hamburg → Munich".

- Set label schemes for activity types, to define which label is visualized as text in the chart area and which labels are used as tooltips. Using this concept, the source location could always be shown on the left of a travel activity, the destination location shown on the right, and both the start time and end time shown in the tooltip.

- Define label schemes for document types similar to the label schemes for activities.

Choosing the activity **Define Layouts for Gantt Chart**, you can define the hierarchies, views, and layouts for the Gantt chart as follows:

- A hierarchy refers to a field list and consists of multiple hierarchy levels. For example, the hierarchy **SAP_TRK_WITH_DRV** contains trucks on level 1 and drivers on level 2; therefore, the assigned drivers are shown below the truck resource. All flat lists are modeled as hierarchies with just one hierarchy level, such as the hierarchy **SAP_FO**, which contains only road freight orders (on hierarchy level 1). For all levels in a hierarchy, you can specify whether the level will be expanded and its utilization will be shown initially.

- A view can be a single view, a dual view, or a triple view, meaning that it contains one, two or three Gantt charts. If it's a dual or triple view, you can specify whether it's initially displayed in its horizontal (charts above each other) or vertical version (charts beside each other). For the view, you can specify the initial ratio of the selection panel versus the chart part, and if it's a dual or triple view, you can specify the sequence of the views and ratio between the views. Moreover, you can define for each hierarchy in a view whether it's initially shown in the document or activity view.

- The layout contains an initial view and a set of additional views that may be used in the planning session (using the dropdown menu in the global toolbar). It also contains a list of additional hierarchies that can be used by the dropdown menu in the local toolbar. The layout refers to color schemes for activities, documents, resources, and utilization; to label schemes for activities and documents; and to schemes for warnings and notifications.

- In the layout, you can also define whether the following are true:
  - The current time is shown as a vertical line.
  - The cursor time is displayed.
  - The horizontal scrollbars are synchronized when using multiple views.
  - Lower levels in hierarchies only show activities and documents related to the parent level.
  - Load utilization can be displayed.

- Automatic zoom level detection is active; the zoom level is determined so that all documents are visible in the Gantt chart. Alternatively, you can explicitly choose among predefined zoom levels, ranging from 15 minutes to 2 months.
- Quick views are shown in the selection panel and after which time period they are shown during hovering.
- Rescheduling or resequencing is taken as default mode for drag and drop in a row.
- Scheduling or pure assigning is the default mode for dragging and dropping between rows.
- Bird's-eye view zooming is available and which options are offered (visible or all rows). This function requires SAPUI5 1.54, which isn't part of the current SAP TM 9.6 stack.
- Automatic target detection during drag and drop is active.
- The smart add function is activated.

When choosing the Gantt chart screen area in the page layout (of the transportation cockpit), you can refer to a Gantt chart layout as defined in the previous bullet list.

6.6.6   Load Plan

The load plan view serves many purposes. It enables manual and automatic load planning (Section 6.7.8) and displays the corresponding result, that is, the positions and orientations of packages and products loaded into the cargo space represented by a road freight order, trailer unit, or container unit. The load plan view also allows manual and automatic package building (Section 6.3) for road freight orders, trailer units, container units, and package units, and it shows the result, that is, the packaging hierarchy, including the positions and orientations of products and cartons positioned in a pallet. You can also manage the status from the load planning and package building perspective and create package units based on the packaging hierarchy of a road freight order, as described for the integrated delivery and line-haul tour planning scenario introduced in Section 6.4.5.

In this section, we'll walk through the load plan view types and configuration.

Three-Dimensional View

The load plan view is composed of a hierarchy and a 3D view, showing the current plan from a tabular and visual viewpoint. In the 3D scene, you can show or hide the assigned resource of the capacity document at hand, and you can show the packaging details or omit them; that is, each package is displayed as one big box without the objects positioned in it.

Figure 6.78 shows the package details in the 3D scene without the assigned truck of the road freight order at hand.

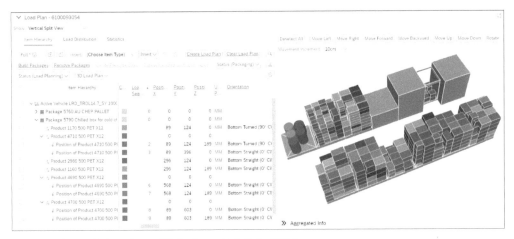

Figure 6.78 Load Plan View with Package Details in 3D View

This view allows you to analyze the result of package building, which includes some kegs on one pallet, some pure product pallets shown as big boxes, many open pallets containing cartons of varying sizes, and a closed package, which resembles a cool pack with some goods in it that require a cooled package. Closed packages represent pallet cages or cool packs and only their skeleton is displayed so that you can see the positioning of products in it. In this example, the products are colored by the destination location, so most pallets represent mixed pallets for many customers and with many different products.

The package details can be switched off, as depicted in Figure 6.79. The pallets with an X symbol indicate that they aren't stackable. This view indicates the pallets' outer volumes very precisely and therefore shows the package information that is considered as input for load planning.

In the previous examples, load planning hasn't yet been performed. The result of load planning is shown in Figure 6.80, again without package details. To verify the result, the truck resource is shown—in the previous two screenshots the truck was hidden. This view is helpful to quickly review the load plan result.

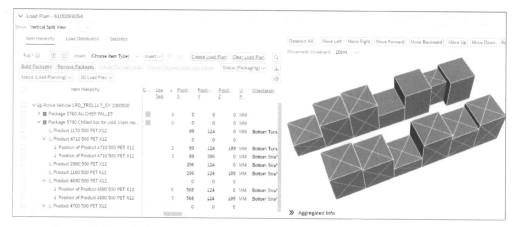

Figure 6.79 Load Plan View without Package Details in 3D View

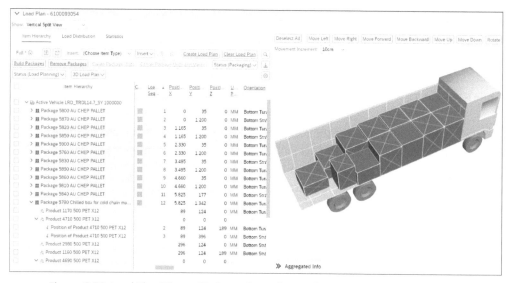

Figure 6.80 Load Plan View with Cargo Space but without Package Details

Of course, you can also show the load plan result by including all packaging details, as depicted in Figure 6.81. This represents the full level of detail determined by package building and load planning.

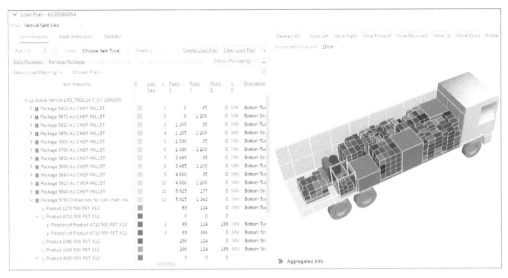

Figure 6.81 Load Plan View with Cargo Space and Package Details

The graphical view allows the planner to rotate the view and zoom in and out using the mouse to verify the plan from any angle. The context menu offers the following features:

- Switch between predefined views (e.g., from back, left, right, or top).
- Color-code the loaded packages and products by freight unit, package unit, destination location, weight, stackability, product, reference product, and orientation. While coloring by destination is very helpful to verify the last-in-first-out principle in case of pallets that serve just one customer, coloring by reference product allows verifying how products of the same reference product are distributed among the mixed pallets. You can use coloring by freight unit to see how goods of one freight unit are spread over multiple pallets.
- To analyze the structure of the load plan, hide selected items, stacks, rows, levels, or the upper deck from the visualization.
- Switch off the grid on the cargo area that is used to show the dimensions if not necessary.
- Display a legend that shows the colors used in the 3D scene.
- Display the package details.
- Show the complete load plan or only the selected packages.

- Use the load chart to display the center of gravity and the constraints imposed by the axle weight constraints. This is helpful to identify the degree of freedom for further objects loaded into the cargo space.

You can perform manual planning using the buttons in the toolbar, keyboard short-cuts, or the editable fields for positions and orientations in the hierarchy. The movement increment used for manual planning in the graphical view can be chosen in the dropdown menu of the toolbar. The aggregated view displays the axle weights, as well as the volume, weight, and quantity of the objects (planned and all) in the scene. You can easily expand and collapse the aggregated view and its sections and move the aggregated view by dragging and dropping to a different position in the 3D view.

Quick views for objects in the 3D scene can be triggered by double-clicking. Tooltips are provided for all visual elements, so you can check the weight on the axle groups or get additional information about the loaded items or the resource. The axles are colored based on their utilization, so you could use green, yellow, and red to differentiate utilizations close to the limit from two other utilization intervals.

Hierarchical View

The **Item Hierarchy** tab provides the item hierarchy from the load planning and packaging viewpoint, as shown in Figure 6.82.

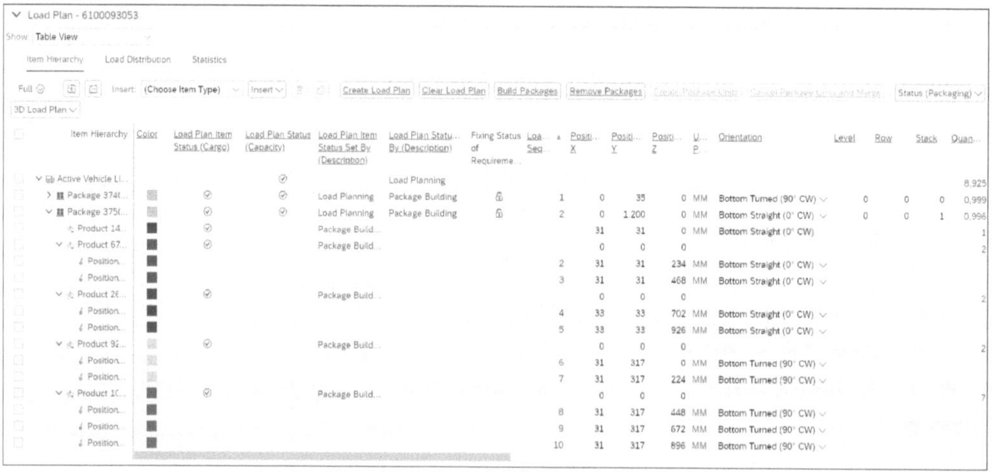

Figure 6.82 Load Plan Hierarchy

This hierarchy provides many useful fields that can be personalized, but we recommend only using the most important fields for your business, as many columns and a huge number of items may become performance-critical, as already discussed in Section 6.6.3. Now, let's review the available fields and their usage:

- **Color** indicates how the item is colored in the graphical scene.

- **Load Plan Item Status (Cargo)** indicates whether the item at hand has been planned into its parent item. **Load Plan Status (Capacity)** informs whether all children of the item have been planned into the item. In the shown example, the first status for the top-level packages yields the status from the load planning perspective, while the second status indicates whether all children have been packaged into the top-level package. For both status values, separate fields indicate how the status got set, for example, by load planning, package building, or manually. Using the buttons in the local toolbar, the status values can be changed. For example, you can finalize packages to protect them again further changes; in this case, the **Fixing Status of Requirement Assignment** is set to **Fixed**, too. In general, these fields are very useful to identify the progress in the planning process that consists of package building, load planning, and finalizing top-level packages, for example, when required to create package units, as described in Section 6.4.5.

- **Loading Sequence** specifies the sequence in which the items need to be loaded. This applies to the top-level items being loaded into the cargo space as well as to top-level items loaded into top-level packages (e.g., cartons into mixed pallets).

- **Position X**, **Position Y**, and **Position Z** define the physical position of the item. Top-level items are positioned in the cargo space of the truck, trailer, or container, while the direct children are positioned in the top-level packages.

- **Row Stack**, and **Level** are useful to identify the position when all pallets in the cargo space have the same footprints.

- **Deck** indicates whether the package is loaded into the lower or upper deck. See Figure 6.83 for an example of a truck with a flexible upper deck.

- **Orientation** specifies whether the item is turned, tilted, and so on.

- **Gross Weight**, **Gross Volume**, **Outer Volume**, **Quantity**, **Length**, **Width**, and **Height** define the dimensions of an item. The utilization, total capacity, remaining capacity, and consumed capacity are provided for both volume and weight.

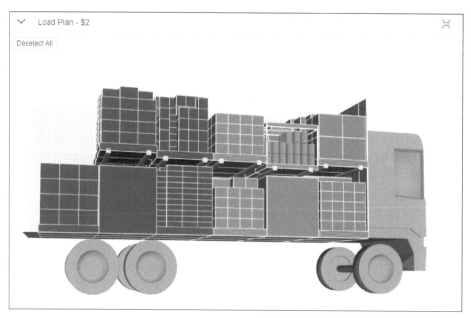

Figure 6.83 Load Plan for Truck with Flexible Upper Deck Based on Beams

- **Product** specifies the loaded product and the packaging material for product items and package items, respectively. For product items, you can also see the **Reference Product for Package Building**. For packaging materials, **Closed Packgng Mat.** indicates whether it's an open or closed package.

- **Loading Location** and **Unloading Location** are presented, together with the **Parent Location (Hard)** and the **Parent Location (Soft)**, which are useful if you use the location hierarchy-based constraints described in Section 6.3.3.

- **Mixed Package** and **Non-Stackable Packages** indicate whether the package item at hand is mixed, that is, contains multiple products, and nonstackable, respectively. **Maximum Top Load** lists how much weight can be stacked on the package at hand.

- You can identify the origin of the item, that is, whether it stems from a freight unit or a TU, and the original requirement document, for example, its forwarding order.

- **Contained In PU** informs you whether the package at hand has already been extracted into a package unit.

- If you want to remove certain items from the next load planning run, you can exclude them via a checkbox in the list and trigger load optimization again.

Load Distribution and Statistics

The **Load Distribution** tab displays the utilizations regarding all weight constraints on the axle groups, split deck, trailing load, and total weight, and the **Statistics** tab provides additional information, such as the number of pallet positions, used floor space on the lower and upper decks, used loading meters, used volume, and percentage of items that could be loaded, as shown in Figure 6.49.

Configuration

Configuration options are offered in the IMG menu path **Transportation Management • Basic Functions • Load Planning • Define Layouts for 3D Load Plan**. Here, you have the following options:

- Specify the units of measure to be used for the statistics.
- Define whether the grid, the load distribution, not loaded items, package details, and the information window will be shown.
- Set the initial coloring scheme, the thresholds for coloring axles, and the colors for loaded items, not loaded items, low loading, medium loading, and high loading.
- Define weight groups and classes that are used for coloring packages by weight.
- Define the content for quick views, tooltips, and context menus.
- Activate manual planning, and define the movement increments in the scene.

After you've defined such a load plan layout, you can refer to it in the page layout. You can choose among different configurations, including the hierarchy view, the 3D view, both together arranged horizontally or vertically, or a combination that includes all previous options and the ability to to dynamically switch between them.

Earlier releases included a flat table instead of a hierarchy. While the hierarchy provides many more features and is therefore the new default, in some simple scenarios, a flat table of packages may be sufficient. The load plan views including flat tables are represented by the following configurations:

- /SCMTMS/WDCC_LSO_LOAD_PLAN_CO displays table and 3D view beside each other.
- /SCMTMS/WDCC_LSO_LOAD_PLAN_CO_2 shows the table above the 3D view.
- /SCMTMS/WDCC_LSO_LOAD_PLAN_TAB includes only the table.
- /SCMTMS/WDCC_LSO_LOAD_PLAN_TAB_C contains all three of the preceding variants and enables dynamic switching between them.

6.6.7   Selection Criteria and Profile and Layout Sets

The previous sections mentioned the need for configuring the cockpit's appearance and introduced page layouts, hierarchical views, dual views, the map, the Gantt chart, and the load plan. Let's turn our attention to how to get started in the transportation cockpit.

The menu path **Planning · Transportation Cockpit** (in SAP TM 9.6, the menu path is **Planning · Planning · Transportation Cockpit**) takes you to the entry screen for the transportation cockpit. You can choose from two entry possibilities in the **Switch Start Screen** choice: one based on selection criteria and one based on profile and layout sets.

In addition to these entry options, the transportation cockpit can be triggered from various POWL queries, such as OTRs, DTRs, road freight orders, and rail freight orders. It's also possible to trigger the transportation cockpit directly out of a business object, such as the forwarding order.

Let's now focus on the most commonly used cockpit entry options, the selection criteria and profile and layout sets.

Selection Criteria

The entry by selection criteria allows you to define ad hoc selection criteria for the various objects or choose from previously defined selection criteria (saved searches), as shown in Figure 6.84. In the **Freight Unit Stages**, **Transportation Units**, **Freight Orders**, **Freight Bookings**, **Resources**, **Drivers**, **Container Resources**, and **Schedules** sections, you can define multiple criteria for the desired object types, each criterion referring to one attribute and one matching criterion. For example, the two criteria for freight unit stages refer to the source and destination location, respectively. Both use the matching criterion **Is** and together result in selection of freight unit stages that meet both criteria. You can add or remove criteria by clicking the plus and minus buttons. The planning profile, transportation cockpit layout, and page layout for the planning result screen can be selected in the **Settings** section. Note that you can suppress display of the planning result screen via the **Skip Planning Result Screen** checkbox in the optimizer settings described in Section 6.7.2. After you've made your choice, click **Continue** to start the cockpit.

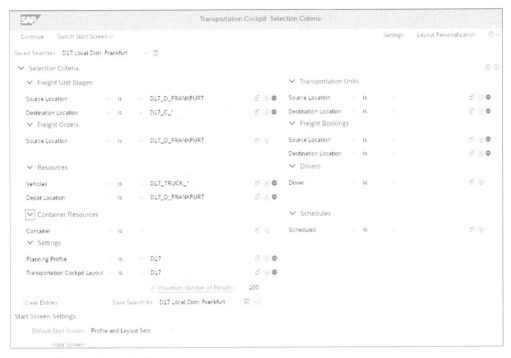

Figure 6.84 Selection Criteria

You can store alternative search criteria, and using the **Settings** button in the **Selection Criteria** row, you're able to do the following:

- Define one of the selection criteria as the default.
- Run the default when opening the selection criteria.
- Collapse the search criteria panel.
- Run the selected search automatically.

Profile and Layout Sets

Figure 6.85 shows the entry by profile and layout sets method. A profile and layout set is defined via a selection profile for freight units, a selection profile for TUs, a selection profile for freight orders, a selection profile for freight bookings, capacity selection settings, incompatibility settings, a planning profile, a page layout for the transportation cockpit, a layout for the planning result screen, and a description.

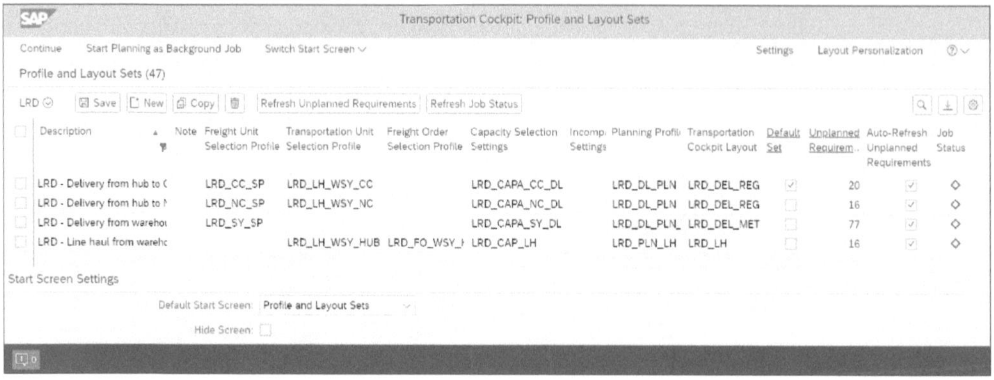

Figure 6.85 User Worklist for Profile and Layout Sets

You can define your own sets but also use predefined sets administrated centrally (see the next section). Working with multiple sets allows you to use the transportation cockpit for different scenarios. You can organize all your sets by maintaining a personal note per set and using the personalization capabilities, including sorting, grouping, filtering, and conditional formatting. If you mainly work with your own sets but occasionally substitute your colleagues on their sets, you can use the **SubstituteSet** field to identify the sets for which you act as substitute.

By selecting one set and clicking **Continue**, you can start the transportation cockpit as defined by the set. If you've defined multiple sets but usually use only one set, you can define it as the default set, which frees you from having to select it every time you start the cockpit. You can trigger a background job for the selected set and check its status in the corresponding column.

The system provides some administrative and statistical information, for example, when the set was created and changed, by whom, the last time it was used, and how many times it was used. Additionally, the system indicates the number of unplanned requirements—that is, freight units, trailer units, railcar units, container units, and package units—which is helpful for comparing the workload for a planner using several sets per day. You can refresh the number of unplanned requirements using the **Refresh Unplanned Requirements** button in the toolbar, or you can activate automatic refreshing when entering this UI. If you deal with several big scenarios, be careful when using the automatic refresh options, as this may be time-consuming.

Comparing entry via profile and layout sets versus selection criteria, the selection criteria are simpler to maintain and very intuitive, allowing a quick start of the transportation cockpit without having to define several selection profiles. However, the entry with profile and layout sets is much more powerful because the selection pro-files provide more sophisticated selections, and the individual selection profiles for the different objects can be combined and reused by multiple users. Moreover, the central administration of profile and layout sets, which will be explained soon, mini-mizes the overall administration efforts significantly. Especially for big companies with many users and planning scenarios, the profile and layout set approach enables structuring the users' scenarios and roles on a very systematic and fine-grained level.

Using the **Default View** choice, you can define whether selection criteria or profile and layout sets are used as the default. If you always start the cockpit with the same profile and layout set, you can set it as the default profile and layout set. Then choose the **Hide Screen** option, which suppresses the whole entry screen when you start the transportation cockpit. If you want to see the entry screen again, just start the trans-portation cockpit, and click the **Change Profile Selection** button. If your layout doesn't permit this, change the layout to activate this button.

Administrating Profile and Layout Sets

The administration of profile and layout sets can be started using the menu path **Pro-files and Settings • PLS Management for Transportation Cockpit** (in SAP TM 9.6, the menu path is **Administration • Planning • General Settings • Profile and Layout Sets • Profile and Layout Set Management for Transportation Cockpit**). Figure 6.86 shows the administration worklist for profile and layout sets, which is similar to the user worklist depicted in Figure 6.85 but offers many useful additional features to simplify maintenance:

- Create, edit, delete, or copy a set, either with or without assigned users.
- Transport selected set to another system.
- Using the user symbol in the **Actions** column, assign explicit users or roles or define them as available for all users. Moreover, you can define individual users as substitutes for the set at hand.
- Use the **Users** button in the toolbar to perform a mass update of users. You can assign all users, remove all users, assign individuals, and remove individuals for the selected sets.
- Show sets assigned to a specific user. Together with the previous mass update function, this is helpful, for example, if you want to remove a user from all its assigned sets.

- View similar sets in the **Similar Sets** column, which detects similar profile and layout sets. Two sets are considered similar if they have identical entries for selection profiles, capacity selection settings, incompatibility settings, and planning profile.

If you upgraded from SAP TM 9.4 or an earlier release that didn't offer administration of profile and layout sets and where each user had to create his or her sets completely manually, this field helps to identify equivalent sets after the upgrade. Using grouping or filtering on this column allows you to merge selected similar sets, which may significantly reduce the number of required sets—in particular if many users have been working with similar sets. Alternatively, you can use **Auto-Merge Similar Sets**, but be careful as this performs many changes automatically.

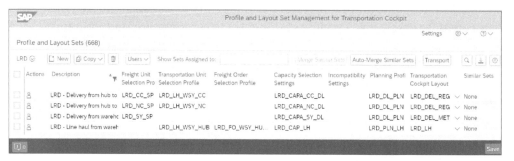

Figure 6.86 Managing Profile and Layout Sets for the Transportation Cockpit

Similarly, you can manage profile and layout sets for carrier selection and delivery creation.

The administration capabilities significantly simplify the usage of profile and layout sets, as the sets can be defined and assigned to users and roles centrally. In addition, this is much less error-prone than the previous approach, in which the sets had to be created individually for each user.

6.6.8   Working in the Transportation Cockpit

All building blocks of the transportation cockpit and entry options have been described in the previous sections. This section presents its functionalities for navigating through the objects, changing the appearance on the fly, manual planning, triggering automatic planning, and performing subcontracting and execution-related tasks.

The transportation cockpit offers a rich set of functionalities that can be triggered by selecting objects in lists, hierarchies, maps, or Gantt charts via buttons or drag and drop.

You can save the results of planning by clicking the **Save** button, and you can refresh the documents in the transportation cockpit session with the the **Refresh** button. This may be useful if, for example, execution information from freight documents has been updated outside the transportation cockpit session.

Using the **Undo** and **Redo** buttons in the global toolbar, you can go back to previous planning states or go forward again. This is helpful if you want to compare certain plans or if you're not satisfied with your planning decision. After saving, you can't go back anymore. You can define the maximum number of steps for undo and redo in Customizing by following the path **Transportation Management • Basic Functions • General Settings • Define Maximum Number of Consecutive Undo and Redo Actions**.

The main decisions made during manual planning refer to assignments of requirement documents (stages) to capacity documents, which can be done explicitly or implicitly by creating a new capacity document for a resource or a driver. Such decisions have an impact on the affected stop sequences, and you can decide on the insertion position explicitly by using, for example, drag and drop into a location-based hierarchy, or implicitly, for example, letting the system determine the position.

Let's walk through the main settings and features you'll encounter while working in the transportation cockpit.

Manual Planning Settings

As different users, businesses, or companies expect a different behavior during manual planning, the *manual planning settings* shown in Figure 6.87 allow you to define the detailed behavior:

- **Manual Planning Strategy**
  Choose from the available strategies (Section 6.5.1). For example, you can choose **VSRI_SCH** and **VSRI_1STEP** to trigger scheduling and carrier selection, respectively, after each manual planning step, or **VSRI_DEF** for the default manual planning operation without any subsequent step. When you use the strategy **VSRI_ALP**, load planning is automatically triggered after each manual planning operation, such as drag and drop.

Figure 6.87 Manual Planning Settings

- **Consider Fixing Status**
  Define the reaction of the system to your attempt to change a fixed document in the cockpit. The system either issues a warning (in which case, you can continue planning and save the document) or reports an error (in which case, the planning operation can't be executed).

- **Document Assignment Strategy**
  Specify how to handle the assignment of a requirement document to a capacity document if the relevant locations aren't yet included in both documents. You can insert new locations only into the capacity document or only into the requirement document. Alternatively, the system can first try to insert new locations into the capacity document and then into the requirement document. You can also

copy the missing locations from the capacity document to the requirement document, or neither change the capacity document nor the requirement document.

- **Loc. Extn. Strategy of Capacity Doc.**
  Define where to insert a new location into a capacity document. You can insert it to minimize the total distance, as the start or end of the sequence, or based on the date and time of the inserted requirement document.

- **Location Movement Strategy**
  Define the result of a drag and drop. The to-be-inserted location can be inserted before or after the target location.

- **Remove Locations Without Activities**
  Define whether stops without any activity get removed after the manual planning operation.

- **Rule for Creating Capacity Documents**
  Consolidate all selected requirement documents into one capacity document. Alternatively, you can create one capacity document for each selected requirement document stage or for all consecutive selected requirement document stages.

- **Depot Location Handling**
  Define whether the depot location is used as first, last, or first and last location in a new capacity document, or whether it's ignored.

- **Default Driver Handling**
  Define how the default driver of a truck resource is considered when assigning a truck to a road freight order. You can ignore it, always assign the default driver to the freight order at hand, or assign the default driver only if the freight order doesn't yet have an assigned driver.

- **Default Truck Handling**
  Similarly, this defines how the default truck of a driver is considered when assigning a driver to a road freight order. You can ignore the default truck or use the default truck if no other truck is assigned to the freight order. Note that a truck is considered as default for a driver if the driver is the default driver for the truck.

Assignment Decisions and Capacity Documents

You can make assignment decisions and create new capacity documents as follows:

- **Create new capacity documents from scratch**
  You can create a new document in a document list or hierarchy, map, or Gantt

chart. Alternatively, you can create it for a resource, driver, or schedule (departure)—in this case, the resource, driver, or schedule departure is directly assigned to the new document. You have the option to specify the number of desired documents, which allows you to quickly create many capacity documents by just one click.

- **Drag and drop**
  You can make any assignment decision by drag and drop, be it a demand document to a capacity document or vice versa, or any document to resources, drivers, schedules, and schedule departures. It's even possible to drag a freight order and drop it to another freight order—in this case, all requirements of the source freight order get reassigned to the target freight order. Drag and drop is supported from any list and hierarchy to any list and hierarchy, within the Gantt chart, and within the map.

- **Assign selected items**
  You can assign the selected objects—in any list, hierarchy, map, or Gantt chart—by clicking the **Assign Selected Items** or **Reassign** button (within a hierarchy).

- **Assign resource, driver, or carrier by editable fields**
  You can edit the resource, driver, and carrier fields in the capacity document lists.

- **Create new capacity document based on demand document (stage)**
  For any set of selected requirement documents or requirement document stages, you can explicitly create one or multiple capacity documents of the same kind. For example, for a freight unit stage, you can explicitly create a package unit, container unit, railcar unit, trailer unit, road freight order, rail freight order, ocean freight booking, or air freight booking.

- **Copy capacity documents**
  You can copy capacity documents, but the document assignments won't be copied. The **Multiple Copies** button allows copying the document at hand many times by just one click.

- **Unassign from capacity document**
  By clicking the **Remove from Capacity Document** button, you can revert the assignments to documents.

- **Unassign from resource or driver**
  You can remove the resource assignment for capacity documents or the driver assignment from road freight orders.

- **Cancel**

  You can cancel capacity documents, which results in unassigning the assigned demand documents.

Document Stages

You can change the stages of a document as follows:

- **Split and merge freight units**

  You can split and merge by stages and quantities.

- **Apply default route**

  For freight unit stages, trailer units, railcar units, container units, or TUs, the system determines a matching default route and creates stages accordingly. See Chapter 3, Section 3.2.6, for more details on default routes.

- **Insert and remove locations**

  You can insert new stops and remove stops from a TU and a freight order.

- **Edit stages popup**

  Using the **Edit Stages** button, you get a popup in which you can maintain the stage sequence and additional information, such as dates and times.

Additional Manual Functions

The following additional useful functions are offered:

- **Fix and unfix**

  Freight documents and TUs can be fixed—that is, they can't be changed by automatic and manual planning unless they are explicitly unfixed.

- **Mass change**

  Using the **Mass Change** button, you can change certain properties, such as dates and times, for many capacity documents at the same time.

- **Editable fields**

  Beyond the assignment decisions mentioned previously, you can also change dates and times, which may trigger rescheduling if configured by the manual planning strategy, and the means of transport.

- **Command-line planning**

  You can also use command-line planning, which allows you to enter an assignment command in a text field. For example, the command 5 6 7 – 2 assigns the freight unit stages with indexes 5, 6, and 7 to the vehicle resource with index 2.

- **Interaction with map**
  Using the **Update Map** button, you can add or remove selected objects, add all objects to the map, or clear the map and add selected objects (with all resources, if desired). Using the **Actions** column in lists, hierarchies, and the Gantt chart, you can add or remove the object at hand; the icon indicates whether the object is already on the map.

- **Last planned location and availability time**
  For manual planning of your own resources and drivers, it's key to know where they are supposed to be according to the current plan and when they are available for new transports after the current plan. The system provides the two fields **Last Planned Location** and **Availability Time**, which can be displayed as columns in any list for resources—of course, including the Gantt chart—as described in SAP Notes 2051868 and 2187025. While the Gantt chart itself creates visibility on the availability time in a graphical fashion and can display the location as text in the chart, these two columns allow sorting and filtering, which is particularly important if you deal with lots of resources that can't be displayed at the same time in the corresponding screen area. If you create a new freight order for a truck resource after its current availability time, the two fields are updated automatically according to the last location and the end time of the last activity in the new freight order.

  As described in Section 6.6.4, you can also display a resource on the map at its last planned location.

Automatic and Semiautomatic Planning

In addition to manual planning, you can also trigger automatic and semiautomatic planning from the transportation cockpit:

- **Scheduling**
  The start and end times for all activities represented by selected freight documents and TUs are scheduled automatically. As defined in the scheduling settings, the scheduling direction can be forward or backward. Refer to Section 6.6.10 for more details on scheduling.

- **Optimization**
  You can run the VSR optimizer on all the data in the cockpit, only the selected objects, or the selected objects together with all resources in the session. See Section 6.7 for more details on the VSR optimizer.

- **Load planning**
  This triggers load planning for the selected road freight orders, trailer units, or container units. The results are shown in the **Load Plan** detailed view as described in Section 6.6.6. Refer to Section 6.7.8 for more details on load planning.

- **Load consolidation**
  Load consolidation is run for all data in the cockpit, only the selected objects, or the selected demands with all resources. This process can create road freight orders, trailer units, and container units based on freight unit and package units as input. If its consolidation mode is based on load planning, you can review the results in the **Load Plan** detailed view, too. See Section 6.7.7 for details on load consolidation.

- **Transportation proposal**
  The system can determine a set of transportation proposals for the selected freight unit stage, from which you can choose one proposal. See Section 6.6.9 for more details.

- **Optimizer explanation tool**
  This tool helps you understand the input and output data for automatic planning—that is, for VSR optimization, transportation proposals, load planning, and load consolidation. See Section 6.7.6 for more details on the explanation tool.

User Interface Adaption

You can adapt the UI in the same cockpit session as follows:

- **Maximize**
  Using the **Maximize** button in the top-right corner of each screen area, you can focus on that screen area shown in full window size and then go back to the original layout.

- **Page layout**
  You can switch between alternative page layouts.

- **Resizing columns of the page layout**
  Using the **Enable Column Resizing** button in the top-right corner of the transportation cockpit and a divider between the left and right column, you can adjust the relative width to any other percentage, such as 40% for the left column and 60% for the right column.

- **Skip result screens**
  If you always accept the result of carrier selection or the VSR optimizer, you can skip the result screen by default, which will always save you one click for accepting it. The result screens can be skipped by a parameter in the optimizer settings and carrier selection settings.

- **Dual view**
  You can trigger the dual view (Section 6.6.3), switch between its horizontal and vertical versions, and then go back to the original page layout. If you've selected objects in the tab from which you trigger the dual view, only these objects are shown in the dual view.

- **Change hierarchy**
  You can switch between alternative hierarchical views.

- **Change (column) view**
  For each list and hierarchy, you can choose which columns are contained, define the ordering of the columns, and define the width (in pixels) for each column. Additionally, you can freeze a selected number of columns so that they remain visible and are protected against horizontal scrolling. You can also define sorting, filtering, and conditional formatting. All this is captured in a personalized view, and you can switch between alternative views that you've defined. The lists also provide a grouping and aggregation functionality, which can be personalized; group objects by predefined criteria; and aggregate columns by determining the maximum, minimum, average, sum value, or distinct count for all entities in a group.

See Figure 6.88 for an example of freight unit stages shown in maximized view and grouped by unloading location. The bottom row provides the total aggregation, and the row above shows the aggregation of selected rows (triggered by the sum icon, highlighted in the top-right corner). Volume and weight are aggregated by sum, while the other aggregations represent the distinct count.

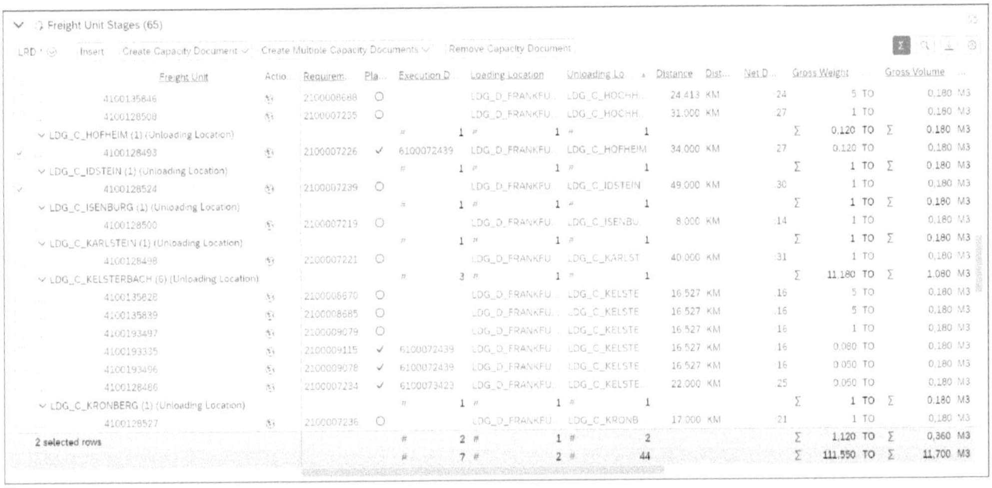

Figure 6.88 Grouped Freight Unit Stage List with Aggregation Rows

Navigation

Navigation through the objects in the various lists and hierarchies is possible as follows:

- **Sorting**
  Sort according to a sequence of columns, and store this information in the personalized view.

- **Filtering**
  Define filters for multiple attributes, and store this in the personalized view.

- **Searching**
  Search by free text field, and iterate through the search results, which get highlighted in the corresponding lists and hierarchies.

- **Expanding and collapsing hierarchies**
  Expand or collapse all nodes or all selected nodes.

- **Hyperlinks**
  Use hyperlinks that are provided for all documents and master data to easily jump to the detailed UI for the object at hand.

- **Quick views**
  Hover over a cell in a list or hierarchy to open a quick view popup, which displays additional information for the object at hand, as shown in Figure 6.89. See SAP Note 2262509 for how to change or enhance the content according to your needs.

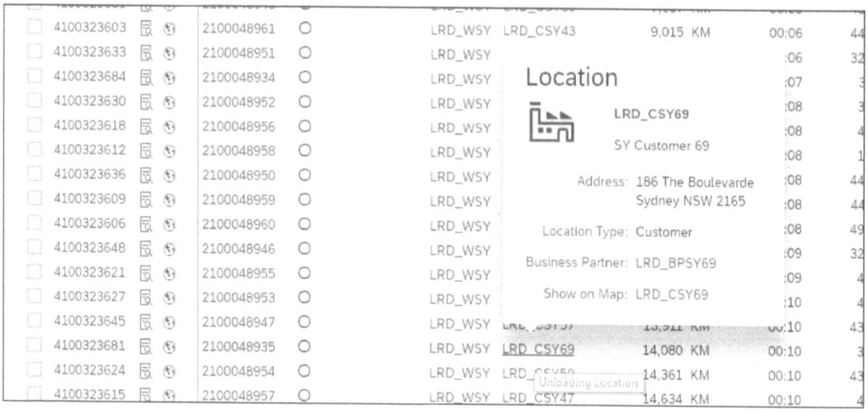

Figure 6.89 Quick View for Location

Usage of Quick Views

We recommend reducing the visible columns in a list or hierarchy to those required for sorting, filtering, grouping, aggregating, conditional formatting, and comparing. Put any extra information into quick views (e.g., street name for a location's address) because you probably won't sort rows by this field. As a consequence, fewer columns are needed in lists, hierarchies, and Gantt charts, leading to performance improvements and less scrolling and searching efforts.

Planning Session Environment

You can adjust the environment for your planning session as follows:

- **Change planning settings**
  Adjust several parameters in the planning session, as shown in Figure 6.90. The initial values stem from the planning profile.
- **Change profile selection**
  Go back to the selection screen to adjust the selection and restart the cockpit.
- **Insert**
  Insert new resources, drivers, and documents into the cockpit session.
- **Context determination**
  Determine the context of the selected resources; in other words, additional freight documents or TUs inside the planning horizon are fetched into the planning session, as explained in Section 6.5.2.

- **Change display settings**
  Using this function in the top-right corner of the transportation cockpit, choose between user or individual time zone, use location-specific time zones, use a short time format, define the format for durations (e.g., hours and minutes, or full days and fraction of days), use the default unit of measure for distances (kilometer), or use an individual one.

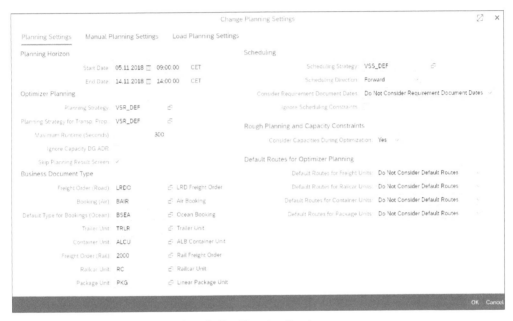

Figure 6.90 Change Planning Settings in the Planning Session

Subcontracting, Execution, and Additional Features

In addition to all its planning capabilities, the cockpit can be used as a work center for subcontracting and execution tasks. You can execute the following subcontracting activities from the cockpit:

- **Carrier selection**
  Start manual or automatic carrier selection, determine the available carriers and store them in the carrier ranking list, remove the carrier assignment, and clear the carrier ranking list.

- **Tendering**
  Start and stop the tendering process, and create requests for quotation.

- **Subcontracting**
  Send a freight document to the carrier.

You can also trigger execution activities for the freight documents at hand:

- **Calculate charges**
  Trigger charge calculation for the selected freight documents.

- **Printing**
  Print freight orders or review the print preview first.

- **Set status**
  For freight orders, update their status (e.g., **In Process**, **In Execution**, or **Completed**), and set the organization interaction status for freight units, as described in Section 6.2.2. You can also update the status regarding load planning and package building (note that this isn't available in SAP TM in SAP S/4HANA 1809).

- **Create and update the SAP ERP shipment**
  Send the freight order information to the SAP ERP shipment. Refer to Chapter 7, Section 7.2.3, for more details on this process.

- **Create delivery proposals**
  The system can create delivery proposals as explained in Chapter 4, Section 4.1.3.

- **Create export declaration**
  Refer to Chapter 9, Section 9.1.4, for more details.

The system provides the following additional features:

- **Check**
  The system performs a check of the selected TUs and freight documents.

- **Export to spreadsheet**
  The content of a list or hierarchy can be exported into a spreadsheet file.

Flexibility

The various planning activities don't have to be performed in a predefined sequence. Therefore, you have full flexibility to use the most efficient and effective sequence of planning steps for your scenario.

For example, you can use the VSR optimizer to create freight documents and then manually adjust the plan. Alternatively, you can create freight documents before the cockpit session via a nightly VSR optimizer background run that assigns freight units to the freight documents or by systematically creating schedule-based freight documents for a certain time period, as described in Chapter 5, Section 5.1.2, and then manually assigning freight units to them. You can also create new schedule-based freight documents in the cockpit by choosing an appropriate schedule and departure.

Resources can be chosen manually or by the optimizer. You can first create road freight orders, then assign freight units, and select a vehicle resource. Alternatively, you can assign freight units directly to a resource to create a a freight document.

In truck and trailer scenarios, you may first determine the stages of the trailer units and then assign appropriate vehicle resources, but you could also first define the stages of the vehicle resources and then assign matching trailer units or let the VSR optimizer determine the whole plan.

6.6.9   Transportation Proposal

The transportation proposal engine automatically determines a set of alternative proposals for a given freight unit stage, thereby considering the complete transportation network definition and all the other constraints for automatic planning, as described in Section 6.7. The alternatives are presented to you for making your choice, as shown in Figure 6.91.

Figure 6.91 Proposal Layout: Only Results

Alternatively, you can refine your preferences or change some parameters and let the system again determine new transportation proposals according to your preferences and parameters. Because the transportation proposal combines automatic planning—for determining the alternatives—and manual interaction choosing from those alternatives, this planning process can be called semiautomatic.

Similar to the transportation cockpit, there are multiple entry options for the transportation proposal UI. You can trigger it directly from a forwarding order by defining the actual route, as described in Chapter 4, Section 4.2.1, or from the forwarding order POWL query by defining the route for a selected forwarding order via the follow-up button. The forwarding order type Customizing allows you to declare the planning profile and page layout for the transportation proposal. There, you can also define how the selected proposal is copied into the forwarding order, considering either only its route or its whole plan, including start and end times.

In the transportation cockpit, you can select a freight unit stage, container unit stage, package unit stage or railcar unit stage, and click the corresponding button to trigger the transportation proposal UI. The manually chosen result is directly applied to the selected demand document stage in the cockpit. If multiple consecutive stages of the same document have been selected, the corresponding transshipment locations are preserved; however, additional transshipment locations could be inserted. Only one alternative is provided for the distribution stage of a package unit of the linear with distribution type.

The transportation proposal UI employs the page layout concept, as already mentioned in Section 6.6. The page layout for transportation proposals offers the following screen areas:

- **Transportation Proposals**
  This screen area contains a hierarchical display of the transportation proposals, structured with proposals on the first level, demand documents on the second level (omitted if you call the proposal for one document only), and stages on the third level. This screen area allows you to choose from the proposals, so it should be activated in the page layout. You can sort the transportation proposals via the available columns or use the filter in the toolbar. Collapsing and expanding the hierarchy allows you to compare the proposals on an aggregated level and analyze the stages of the proposals in greater detail, respectively. Personalization of the hierarchy's columns is supported, too, as in the transportation cockpit.

- **Map Display**
  This area shows a geographical map, enabling comparison of the proposals on the map. You can add and remove proposals from the map using the button in the **Actions** column or add all proposals by using the **Show All on Map** button.

- **Transportation Proposal Preferences**
  This area allows you to define preferences that are considered by the automatic transportation proposal determination.

Like the page layout for the transportation cockpit, one to three of these alternative screen areas can be placed on a grid with three rows and two columns, with each screen area covering either two columns or only one column. See Figure 6.92 for an example that shows the results area on top and the map on the bottom.

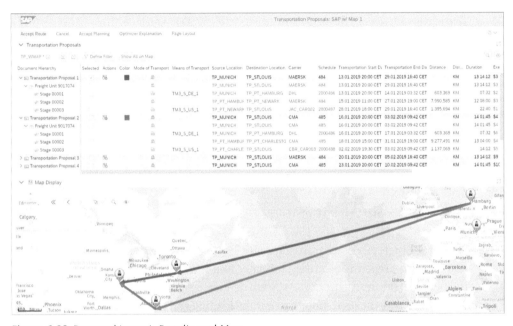

Figure 6.92 Proposal Layout: Results and Map

The preferences can be entered before triggering a new transportation proposal determination. (See Figure 6.93 for a layout that has preferences on the top and results and map on the bottom.) Suppose that you transport goods from Germany to the United States, and you want them to go via ocean and the port in Hamburg. You can use the **Stages** area in the **Preferences** screen area to define that the transport must contain a stage from the port in Hamburg to the destination location and that ocean is used as the mode of transport for this stage. Note that the system would still be allowed to split this stage into one main stage and a subsequent stage, which would then result in an ocean main stage and a subsequent stage that could be handled by road or rail, but not the air mode of transport. You can also predefine a sequence of transshipment locations (e.g., to force the system to determine only transportation proposals going via the ports in Hamburg and Newark).

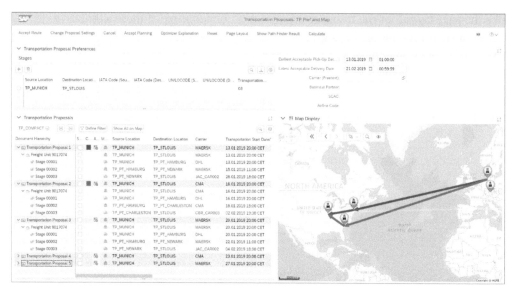

Figure 6.93 Proposal Layout: Preferences Results Map

Besides the preferences for transshipment locations and mode of transport per stage, you can also predefine a carrier and dates and times for loading at the source and unloading at the destination. The system determines proposals that have at least one stage covered by the predefined carrier, and loading and unloading doesn't take place earlier or later than the corresponding preferences.

The **Pushbuttons for Application Toolbar** section in the page layout for transportation proposals offers the following buttons:

- **Accept Route**
  This allows acceptance of only the route of the result; that is, only the stages for the forwarding order or demand document at hand are stored according to the proposal.

- **Accept Planning**
  This stores the complete plan of the proposal, including start and end times.

- **Calculate**
  This triggers a new transportation proposal determination.

- **Change Proposal Settings**
  You get a popup with parameters, which you can change for this transportation proposal session. Initially, these parameters are defined as in the planning profile. Overruling these may be useful, for example, if you're used to considering air

freight bookings' capacities, but no satisfactory proposal is found. Then you can relax the booking capacity check to find better proposals, knowing that you can increase the corresponding capacity as necessary later.

- **Reset**
  This resets the preferences and allows restarting the transportation proposal determination, which may be required if you tried several preferences but didn't find a satisfactory transportation proposal.

- **Page Layout**
  This allows you to switch among alternative page layouts.

- **Show Path Finder Result**
  This allows you to search for connections and display them on the map, which is helpful for analyzing your network definition. This functionality is also available in the transportation network cockpit and is described in detail in Chapter 3, Section 3.2.8.

- **Optimizer Explanation**
  This tool helps in understanding the input and output data of the transportation proposal determination. It's described in more detail in Section 6.7.6.

The optimizer settings contain two groups of parameters dedicated to the transportation proposal. The **Transportation Proposal Settings** section offers the following parameters:

- **Accept Transportation Proposal**
  You can predefine whether only the route of the selected proposal result is stored or the corresponding freight documents are considered, too. Alternatively, you can keep this parameter undefined, letting the user choose between these two options in the transportation proposal UI.

- **Planning Strategy for Transportation Proposal**
  This allows you to define whether only the transportation proposals are determined (strategy **VSR_DEF**) or carrier selection is performed for each transportation proposal (**VSR_1STEP**), as already mentioned in Section 6.5.1.

- **Maximum Number of Transportation Proposals**
  This parameter defines how many alternative proposals are shown in the UI. Note that automatic planning may yield fewer proposals (e.g., if the network or capacity situation doesn't allow offering the defined number of proposals).

- **Do Not Create Transportation Proposals Immediately**
  You can control whether the proposals are determined before you enter the proposal UI. If you want to maintain preferences first, you can activate this parameter so that proposals are calculated only after you click the **Calculate** button.

The **Transportation Proposal Preferences** section contains parameters to control the diversity of the determined transportation proposals. For each diversity criterion, you can define the relevance to be high, medium, or low; set it as not relevant; or rely on the default behavior in the transportation proposal algorithm. The following parameters are offered:

- **Route Variation**
  This determines the relevance of how the demand document is routed through the network. If this aspect is relevant, the system searches for transportation proposals differing in their used transshipment locations, modes of transport, and means of transport.

- **Carrier Variation**
  This parameter controls whether the system searches for proposals differing in their carriers. For example, if this parameter is relevant, but the previous parameter isn't, the system would determine the best routing through the network and search for alternative proposals along this routing that use different carriers.

- **Departure Date Variation**
  Defining this parameter as relevant, the system searches for proposals with alternative departure and arrival dates and times. For example, if the previous two parameters are irrelevant, the system would determine the best routing and carrier and search for alternative departure and arrival dates and times.

- **Time Relevance**
  In the trade-off of timely delivery versus transportation costs, this parameter defines the relevance of timely delivery. If time relevance is high, but cost relevance isn't relevant, the system focuses on transportation proposals that meet the demand document's time windows as closely as possible; if no time windows have been specified, it delivers the goods as early as possible.

- **Cost Relevance**
  In the trade-off of timely delivery versus costs, this parameter defines the relevance of transportation costs. If cost relevance is high but time relevance isn't relevant, the system searches for minimum cost proposals, and compromises on timely delivery are allowed (within the hard time windows of the freight units).

Note that the transportation proposal determination is performed by a special operating mode of the VSR optimizer, for which technical details are described in Section 6.7.2.

6.6.10 Scheduling

Scheduling determines the start and end times for a set of activities, considering multiple constraints, such as a predefined relative ordering among the activities and time windows for the activities. Scheduling can be triggered for one or more selected freight documents. The Gantt chart is the best tool to visualize and explain scheduling. Let's review the example shown in Figure 6.94.

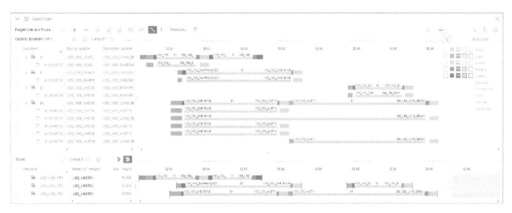

Figure 6.94 Gantt Chart with Freight Order–Freight Unit Hierarchy and Trucks

A freight order represents a sequence of activities. While a travel activity is a movement between two locations, all other activities take place at a location. A loading activity can represent one or multiple freight units being loaded, and the start and end time of the loading activity at the freight order stop is propagated to the assigned freight units, in this example, for freight order $3. Unloading activities are handled analogously. Preparing and finalizing are activities independent of the transported cargo and may represent check-in or check-out activities. Coupling and uncoupling activities (not shown in Figure 6.94) refer to a truck and trailer and are used in scenarios with dynamic recoupling, such as trailer swaps, as described in Section 6.4.2 and shown in Figure 6.28.

The durations for loading, unloading, preparing, finalizing, coupling, and uncoupling can be defined in the scheduling settings, which are explained in Section 6.7.4, and the duration for traveling is determined based on the distance, as explained in Chapter 3, Section 3.2.3.

There is a natural ordering of the different activity types during one stop:

1. Prepare
2. Uncouple
3. Unload
4. Load
5. Couple
6. Finalize

As you would expect, prepare and finalize are the first and last activity types. Uncoupling takes place as early as possible, and coupling takes place as late as possible to maximize the flexibility of handling trailers and not restricting them by the bottleneck—the truck. Unloading takes place before loading because loading could not be possible otherwise, due to the capacity constraint of the resource at hand.

The freight order **$3** represents the stop sequence Cheyenne, Austin, and Long Beach. The stop sequence can be defined by manual or automated planning. Scheduling respects the given stop sequence and doesn't change it—the only purpose of scheduling is to assign start and end times to the activities of the capacity document at hand. If you prefer the stop sequence Cheyenne, Long Beach, and Austin, you can do so by manually changing it and then scheduling it again.

The scheduling algorithm can be run forward or backward, which can be set in the scheduling settings described in Section 6.7.4. Forward scheduling uses the first activity to be scheduled as the anchor, defines its start and end times, and then iterates through the whole activity sequence until the last activity is reached, assigning start and end times for each activity. Backward scheduling uses the last activity to be scheduled as the anchor, defines its start and end times, and then iterates through the activity sequence until the first activity is reached, assigning start and end times for each activity. For both directions, the algorithm tries to schedule the activities as compactly as possible to avoid idle times between the activities. However, time windows and other constraints may make it impossible to avoid idle times entirely.

Forward scheduling is useful if you want to push the goods out of a depot to minimize your inventory. Backward scheduling aims at meeting the delivery time window as closely as possible, and your transportation happens "just in time" before the delivery.

Scheduling can be triggered for freight orders but also for unplanned demand documents, such as freight units, trailer units, railcar units, container units, and package units. The latter requires activating the distance and duration determination in the corresponding requirement document type, and it can be triggered during FUB or by applying a default route. Scheduling unplanned demand documents is useful because it already indicates the expected transportation duration before planning the document at hand.

Scheduling considers the following constraints:

- Time windows for loading and unloading activities, as specified for the corresponding freight units and described in Section 6.2.2
- Durations for loading, unloading, coupling, uncoupling, preparing, and finalizing, as specified in the scheduling settings described in Section 6.7.4
- Calendars of the involved vehicle resources for loading, unloading, transportation, coupling, and uncoupling activities
- Calendar resources and handling resources' calendars and capacities for loading and unloading activities, as described in Chapter 3, Section 3.2.1
- Minimum and maximum goods wait times defined for transshipment locations, as described in Chapter 3, Section 3.2.1
- Scheduling constraints to reflect driving time regulations, as described in Section 6.7.4

The scheduling settings define how scheduling will consider the time windows of freight units: either both hard and soft time windows are considered, only soft time windows are considered, or time windows are ignored. Considering all time windows is the most restrictive version and may cause the scheduler to fail if your time windows make it too hard to find a feasible scheduling for the activities at hand. However, not considering the time windows at all may lead to extreme solutions that fully exploit the boundaries of the planning horizon. Therefore, you should carefully specify these parameters and consider the interplay with the planning horizon to ensure that scheduling can produce the desired results. Refer to SAP Note 1908165 for handling time windows in the scheduling algorithm and the VSR optimizer.

Note that scheduling is performed by a special operating mode of the VSR optimizer, for which Section 6.7.2 provides technical details.

6.7   Automated Planning

In contrast to the previous section, our focus now is on planning processes that don't require user interaction. One way of limiting user interaction is to omit it completely, as in the zero-click process described in Section 6.2.3. Freight orders are created automatically instead of freight units upon the creation of their predecessor business documents, and subsequent planning steps such as carrier selection and tendering are triggered by background jobs. Thus, planning in the background is the first topic here.

In the zero-click process, freight orders are actually rule based (i.e., created using FUBRs). This way, the planning process of creating freight orders (i.e., choosing the right vehicle resource, choosing the shortest path for the vehicle resource, and choosing the best possible time schedule for loading and unloading) is omitted. These tasks can be done manually or interactively, as described in the previous section, by using the VSR optimizer (as standard functionality) or defining custom planning strategies. How the VSR optimizer creates transportation plans in a structured way is the main topic of this section.

Finally, automated planning is also supported in other transactions outside the planning domain. The route functionality to create stages based on default routes directly in the forwarding order (as described in Chapter 4, Section 4.2) or the transportation proposal functionality (as described in Section 6.6.9) are examples of automated planning that requires some user interaction. The direct shipment option (Section 6.2) is a means of using "real" costs in the automated planning step.

When we elaborate on planning in the remainder of this chapter, only the first planning step that creates the freight order is addressed. Subsequent planning steps, such as carrier selection and tendering, are discussed in detail in Chapter 7.

6.7.1   Background Planning and Vehicle Scheduling and Routing

You can initiate background planning in the backend by starting Transaction /SCMTMS/BACKGRD_PLAN from the menu path **Logistics • Transportation Management • Administration • Background Processing • Run Planning** (in SAP TM 9.6, the menu path is **Application Administration • Background Processing**), scheduling the report /SCMTMS/PLN_OPT, or clicking the **Start Planning in Background** button in the transportation cockpit. Figure 6.95 shows the configuration options of this report. The **Freight Unit Selection Profile** field determines the *scope*, that is, which freight units (stages) are selected for planning in the background, whereas the **Planning Profile** field determines the *method*, that is, the planning strategy (e.g., whether carrier selection should be included with planning strategy VSR_1STEP), available capacities, planning costs, and constraints.

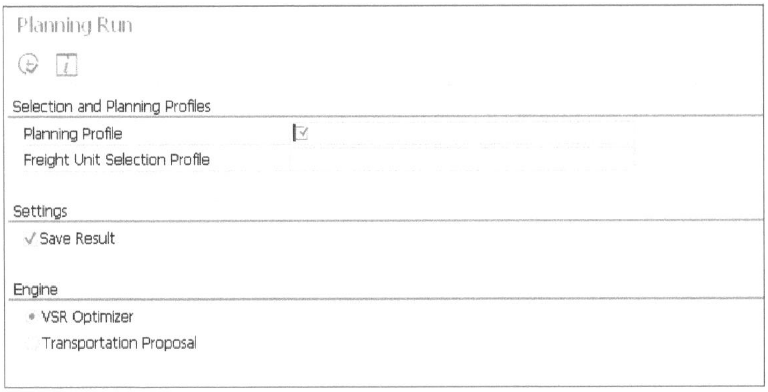

Figure 6.95 Background Planning

Background planning is used when limited or no user expertise is required or even desired for creating a reasonable transportation plan. Thus, it can be used in simple planning scenarios (e.g., to group freight units by temperature requirements and assign them to a suitable resource). Both grouping of freight units with similar temperature requirements and their resource assignment can be expressed by the definition of incompatibilities, which then implies that freight units are sorted and assigned properly. In this type of scenario, automated planning takes the burden of manual assignments from the transportation planner, and a high volume of freight units and freight orders can be processed in a short amount of time.

However, background planning can also be used in rather complex scenarios (e.g., if the consolidation of freight units into freight orders involves complex routing and scheduling decisions) because many freight units with different delivery windows based on fixed appointments have to be delivered to many destination locations with a limited number of vehicle resources. In this case, the decision situation is rather complex because of the combinatorial nature of the planning problem; the VSR optimizer can explore many more alternatives to find the best possible solution than a human planner can in the same amount of time. For this kind of scenario, background planning can be scheduled overnight, and the transportation planner can check and adapt the results in the morning upon arriving to work.

To enable the automatic creation of a systematic transportation plan, a suitable framework needs to be defined that allows the maintenance of the objectives, rules, and constraints to which the planning result should adhere. The VSR optimizer engine provides this framework. For this purpose, the VSR optimizer requires all relevant data for this task:

- **Freight units**
  Freight units (precisely, freight unit stages, because the different stages of a freight unit can be planned independently of each other in a transportation chain) are selected directly via the selection profile.

- **Transportation capacities**
  Transportation capacities are selected via the planning profile and can be vehicle resources, container resources or schedules (selected via capacity selection settings), existing freight orders (selected via the selection profile for freight orders), TUs (selected via the selection profile for TUs), or freight bookings (selected via the selection profile for freight bookings).

- **Master data**
  Finally, the relevant master data (i.e., the transportation network consisting of information about locations, transportation zones, transportation lanes, and transshipment hierarchies) is retrieved based on the selected freight units and transportation capacities.

During automated planning, the system has to consider dependent objects to be able to keep all objects consistent and at the same time consider the effects of parallel processing (e.g., if other users or reports try to change the same objects in parallel).

The selection of dependent objects is called *context determination*. It's relevant, for example, in a scenario in which new freight units are assigned to existing freight orders. In this case, the existing freight orders (created either manually or automatically) already have freight units assigned. These freight units are also relevant because their constraints (i.e., pickup and delivery windows) or properties (i.e., required temperature conditions in transportation) need to be respected if the freight order is adapted. The same is valid in the opposite case. If a freight unit needs to be transported via several stages, some of these stages may already have been planned, so existing freight orders for some stages can apply relevant context information for the current planning scope. Finally, the context information for vehicle resources is determined to limit the timely and geographical availability of a fleet based on already-scheduled freight orders.

Objects that haven't been explicitly selected but have been retrieved via context determination are only for information purposes; that is, they aren't changed by the VSR optimizer but only impose additional (side) constraints.

To keep planning data consistent while several users work in parallel, a locking concept is imposed to allow parallel planning. If different users or processes of the same user try to access the same object (e.g., a vehicle resource) in manual planning or in VSR optimization, a message that the object is locked is issued. Only the user or process that locked the object is allowed to change it. Subsequent processes can't change the locked object until the lock is released. Freight bookings are exempt from this locking concept. The VSR optimizer or a transportation proposal can both access the freight booking in parallel, with both processes being able to use the remaining capacity of the freight booking. Because saving is done in an asynchronous mode, this can result in overbooking the freight booking.

Locking of Multiresources

Recall from Chapter 3, Section 3.3, that multiresources are often used to represent external vehicle resources in subcontracting scenarios. If these are available only in a limited number for certain means of transport, you can specify in Customizing (via **Transportation Management • Master Data • Resources • Define Means of Transport**) whether these multiresources are locked. However, the lock applies to all copies of the multiresources at once.

6.7.2 Configuring Optimizer Settings

The configuration of the VSR optimizer is primarily done in the **Optimizer Settings** view of the planning profile (see Figure 6.96).

Defining a **Planning Strategy** is mandatory because the system needs to know whether only the VSR optimizer should be used (**VSR_DEF**) or another process step should be triggered subsequently, such as carrier selection (**VSR_1STEP**) or load planning (**VSR_ALP**). The freight order building rule (**FO Building Rule**) decides how freight orders are structured. If the same vehicle resource is scheduled to pick up freight units from several locations and deliver to several locations, different freight orders can be created either based on the load of the vehicle (**New Freight Order when Resource is Empty**) or whenever it returns to its depot location (**New FO when Resource is Empty and Depot Location Reached**).

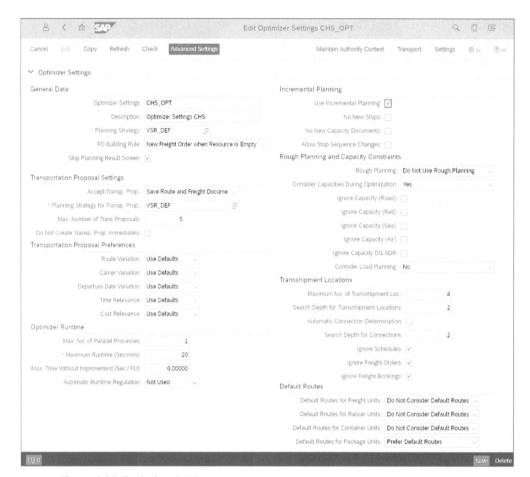

Figure 6.96 Optimizer Settings

Use Incremental Planning is an option to keep parts of an existing transportation plan and only add new freight units to it. While the standard behavior of the VSR optimizer is to delete existing freight orders and create new freight orders, incremental planning allows certain information to be retained from an existing plan. Use cases include adding freight units to freight orders that are already in execution or changing freight orders that have already been published to carriers. In these cases, you can't delete the existing freight orders and replace them with new ones, but you need to retain certain attributes of the freight order (e.g., freight order number, location sequence, and existing assignment of freight units). If incremental planning is selected, the VSR optimizer will keep the existing assignment of freight units to freight orders. In addition, you can choose between three additional options or a combination thereof:

- **No New Stops**
  The VSR optimizer can only add additional freight units to existing freight orders if there is remaining capacity, and corresponding stops exist. The stop sequence of existing freight orders is fixed, but new freight orders can be created.

- **No New Capacity Documents**
  The VSR optimizer can add new freight units to existing freight orders but isn't allowed to create new freight orders. This option may be used if you've defined (empty) default tours that may be changed by the VSR optimizer, but no additional tours should be created.

- **Allow Stop Sequence Changes**
  The VSR optimizer can change the stop sequence of existing freight orders, except for the first and last location. A use case for this option is a scenario in which a planner has manually created freight orders, but you want the system to optimize their routing.

Note

Using a BAdI implementation, more sophisticated limitations can be specified for incremental planning, for example, that new stops in a freight order can only be created for a predefined subset of locations or that a tour may be extended but shouldn't exceed a certain duration. SAP Note 1866364 explains how this is achieved.

You have to define a **Maximum Runtime (Seconds)** to specify the amount of time the algorithm uses to calculate the best possible result. The required runtime depends on many factors (e.g., number of freight units to be planned, number of available vehicle resources, and complexity of the transportation network) and has to be determined during testing. It's possible to define a second termination criterion for the VSR optimizer: **Max. Time Without Improvement (Sec./ FU)**. If the VSR optimizer doesn't improve the best solution found for the defined amount of time per freight unit, then it's automatically terminated prior to the defined maximum runtime. A third option is to leave the decision when to stop with the VSR optimizer by using **Automatic Runtime Regulation**. You can choose from **Not Used, Fastest, Fast, Balanced, Good Quality, High Quality**, and **Highest Quality** options depending on whether you want to fully use the maximum runtime to compute the highest quality solution or whether you want to sacrifice speed versus quality.

Modern hardware can parallelize processes. The **Max. No. of Parallel Processes** field allows you to define how many parallel processes the VSR optimizer is allowed to start. Each process requires one CPU core, so this setting needs to take into account the available hardware as well as the number of parallel users that can run the VSR optimizer at the same time.

The transportation proposal settings and transportation proposal preferences refer to the use of the VSR optimizer for creating transportation proposals, as explained in Section 6.6.9.

Rough Planning and Capacity Constraints deal with exact or rough duration determination in planning (**Rough Planning**) and whether vehicle capacities should impose a constraint for planning with the VSR optimizer. For many business processes, it isn't important to plan complete, end-to-end transportation in detail. For example, it may be important to find the right flights, but it's known that the airport can be reached within a predefined time interval (e.g., eight hours), and planning for this stage of the journey doesn't require the same degree of precision. The assignment of a transshipment location to a transportation zone (i.e., an entry or exit point into a transportation network) can be used to allow planners to specify a duration that can be used for *rough planning* instead of the exact distance and duration determined based on transportation lanes. This means that a detailed transportation network (transportation lanes) isn't required for the pre-carriage/on-carriage in this kind of scenario. Furthermore, capacities of certain transportation modes may be ignored as well as the calculation of ADR points for the transportation of dangerous goods.

While load planning will be a separate topic and covered in detail in Section 6.7.8, in some scenarios, aspects of load planning should be considered already during VSR optimization because, otherwise, freight orders will be created that can't be executed. For this purpose, the VSR optimizer essentially generates additional internal dimensions for floor space and upper deck capacity to respect packages' footprints, stackability (e.g., some packages may not be stacked on each other), and positions (e.g., some packages may be loaded to the lower deck only). Because the consideration of load planning constraints has a performance impact on the VSR optimizer, the **Consider Load Planning** option can be switched on (**Partially**) or off (**No**).

The parameters for **Transshipment Locations** influence the complexity of the transportation network and therefore have a significant impact on the amount of time required to calculate a reasonable planning result. The **Maximum No. of Transshipment Loc.** field defines the number of transshipment locations any freight unit is allowed to be routed through between its source and destination. It should be as small as possible to limit the number of paths in the transportation network that the VSR optimizer has to consider as possible alternatives.

To ease maintenance of the transportation network, you don't need to define transshipment locations that are part of a schedule explicitly as transshipment locations, but **Automatic Connection Determination** can be activated in the optimizer settings. This implies that all possible connection points (stops of flight or carrier schedules) are implicitly considered transshipment locations (see Chapter 3, Section 3.2).

Default Routes (see Chapter 3, Section 3.2.6) can be considered for freight units, container units, railcar units, and package units in the VSR optimizer. You have four options for whether default routes will influence the planning result:

- **Only Consider Default Routes**
  The VSR optimizer considers only default routes as possible routing alternatives.

- **Prefer Default Routes**
  The VSR optimizer chooses a default route if it represents a feasible routing alternative but searches for alternatives if no feasible default route exists.

- **Also Consider Default Routes**
  The VSR optimizer returns the lowest cost routing, independently of whether it has been defined as a default route.

- **Do Not Consider Default Routes**
  The VSR optimizer doesn't consider any default routes.

Technical Configuration of the VSR Optimizer

The VSR optimizer is a separate piece of software that has been developed for performance reasons in C++ and not in ABAP. Technically, the optimizer is called via the *remote control and communication framework* (RCCF) using a remote function call (RFC). You'll find relevant transactions for the technical configuration in the backend system at **Cross-Application-Components • Processes and Tools for Enterprise Applications • Remote Control and Communication Framework** (in SAP TM 9.6, the menu path is **Application Administration • General Settings • Remote Control and Communication Framework**).

In the Edit Destinations transaction (see Figure 6.97), you can define which hardware you have available for the VSR optimizer and the other external engines and how these can be reached. The following applications are other external engines that use the same framework:

- TSPS: Carrier selection
- TVRG: Transportation proposal
- TVSR: VSR optimizer
- TVSS: Manual scheduling
- TVSO: Load optimization
- TSFM: Strategic freight management

The **Communication Connection** column defines the RFC connection and is defined in Transaction SM59 (TCP/IP Connections). The **Max. Slots** column refers to the number of CPU cores available at the destination server. If these are already in use, and an additional optimization run is started, it's canceled immediately because no hardware is available to process the request. If several destinations (**Dest. ID**) are defined for the same application (**Appl.**), the **Priority** column determines the sequence that the VSR optimizer tries to use for these servers.

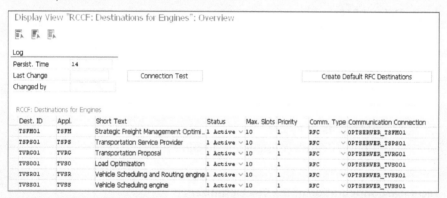

Figure 6.97 Remote Control and Communication Framework: Edit Destinations

The **Persist. Time** field specifies how many days the planning logs are kept in the system before they are deleted. The logs can help you analyze the planning result and are explained in Section 6.7.6 in more detail. The logs are also required for SAP Support to reproduce VSR optimizer behavior in the case of an error in any of these engines. For this purpose, set **Optimizer Trace Level** to **Info** and **Optimizer Dump Level** to **1** in Transaction /SCMTMS/OPT10 (Engine Debug Configuration) shown in Figure 6.98.

The correct installation and technical setup of all destinations can be checked in the Version Display transaction. If a version is displayed as **Version Information,** then everything is fine. Note that the engines are downward-compatible and therefore have to be of the same or a newer version and support pack than the application.

The Display Active Sessions transaction provides a monitoring tool for currently running sessions of all engines using the RCCF. This transaction can also be used to terminate background runs.

Finally, the optimization data can be manipulated prior to the engine run, when the relevant data is sent to the optimizer (e.g., to add additional constraints on the fly) and after the engine run (to adapt the results). This is done in BAdI /SCMTMS/PLN_PRE_PROC to preprocess the optimization data and in BAdI /SCMTMS/PLN_POST_PROC to postprocess the planning result.

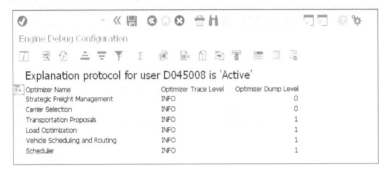

Figure 6.98 Remote Control and Communication Framework: Engine Debug Configuration

6.7.3 Vehicle Scheduling and Routing: Planning Objectives

For the VSR optimizer engine to create a reasonable transportation plan, you need to define an objective. Individual objectives may be different in different implementation projects or even for different planning situations in the same implementation. This can be illustrated by a simple example.

Assume a simple planning situation with only one source location (plant) and only one delivery location (customer). The customer orders the equivalent of half a truck of goods every day. In this situation, there are two possible solutions from a transportation planning point of view:

- Every day, a truck delivers the goods from the plant to the customer. However, this truck is only half full (or half empty). Although this solution isn't very efficient because of the low truck utilization, it provides a high service level because the customer is served exactly as needed.

- The customer is served every other day with a full truckload. This solution is very efficient from a transportation perspective (100% truck utilization), but the customer service level is poor because the customer is provided 50% of his or her orders either one day early or one day late based on the delivery pattern.

Which solution is better and will be created from the VSR engine? The answer depends on the individual situation; either one may be preferred. The first solution may be preferred if there are inventory/warehousing constraints at the customer location or if the shelf-life of goods doesn't allow their storage but forces daily deliveries. The second solution is preferred in competitive situations if cost is the driving decision criterion. The VSR engine can create both solutions, and which one is returned depends on the defined objective. Thus, the relation between different cost elements must reflect the user's business objectives to make it possible to calculate the right solution.

The VSR optimizer is governed by a cost minimization objective. The cost elements depend on the freight units as well as on the transportation capacities. Freight unit–dependent cost elements influence the service level (timely pickup and delivery), whereas transportation capacity–related cost elements influence their efficient usage. In the previous example, the first solution is returned if the freight unit–dependent costs for earliness and lateness are high compared to the transportation capacity-related cost because, in that case, it would be expensive to violate the delivery window for half of the goods. The second solution is returned if the transportation capacity–related costs are higher.

Let's look at which cost elements are considered. Most of them are defined in the Planning Costs Settings app (see Figure 6.99 and Figure 6.100).

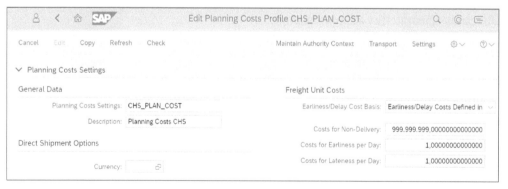

Figure 6.99 Planning Cost Settings Freight Unit Costs

Figure 6.100 Planning Costs Means of Transport Settings

Freight unit costs can be defined either directly in the Planning Costs Settings app or via a condition (type **/SCMTMS/FU_PNLT_COST**) that is assigned in that screen. If a condition is used, different costs can be defined based on the characteristics of each freight unit (e.g., different lateness penalties depending on customer priority) or based on whether pickup or delivery windows are violated:

- Costs for nondelivery are incurred in the cost objective if a freight unit isn't transported. By default, they are set very high to force the VSR optimizer to find a solution because nondelivery isn't usually a valid option.

- Costs for earliness per day apply to both early pickup and early delivery of a freight unit. The duration of the earliness is calculated as the interval between the scheduled time of the pickup/delivery and the requested date to start (Section 6.2.2).

- Costs for lateness per day also apply to both late pickup and late delivery of a freight unit. The duration of the lateness is calculated as the interval between the scheduled time of the pickup/delivery and the requested date to end (Section 6.2.2).

Means of transport costs define the transportation capacity costs and can be maintained directly in the **Planning Costs Settings** app (see Figure 6.100) and, to some extent, in transportation lane master data (see Chapter 3, Section 3.2).

Means of transport costs can be defined differently for all means of transport or even for particular vehicle resources in the scope of the planning scenario:

- **Fixed costs**
  These costs are incurred in the objective function either per freight order or per vehicle resource. Therefore, fixed costs can be used to minimize the number of vehicle resources used or to select between different available vehicle resources.

- **Penalty costs**
  These costs are factors that apply to freight unit–dependent earliness and lateness costs. These factors can be used to distinguish earliness and lateness based on the means of transport. For example, violating a pickup window for an ocean transport is much more expensive than for a truck transport.

- **Distance-dependent costs**
  These costs per means of transport can be maintained in the Planning Costs Settings app or in the transportation lane (**Mns of Trsp. Costs** field). The actual distance of the freight order is multiplied by the costs per distance unit (see Chapter 3, Section 3.2.3, for the determination of transportation distances). In North America and other parts of the world, different concepts for calculating distance-dependent costs exist. In North America, these are known as *destination-based distance costs*; in Europe, they are *route-based distance costs*.

Figure 6.101 provides an example that illustrates the different calculation concepts, which can even result in different optimal solutions. Destination-based distance costs are calculated by multiplying the actual distance of the complete freight order with the distance cost from the transportation lane between the source and the destination. Route-based distance costs are calculated by multiplying the actual distance of each stage with the cost of the transportation lane for this stage and summing up the costs for the individual stages.

Finally, a *minimum cost* can be defined that applies to distance costs calculated for a freight order. A typical example is a scenario in which freight costs are usually variable based on the distance (e.g., $2/mi), but a minimum of $300 applies because short trips less than 150 miles aren't economical with only variable rates. The minimum cost can be defined in the transportation lane master data (**Min. MTr Costs** field).

Distance costs are usually minimized to lower fuel consumption or reduce operating times of the vehicle resources.

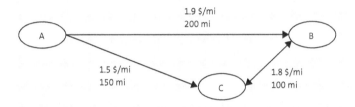

Destination-based cost:
Freight order (A→B→C) = Distance (A→B→C) * Cost (A→C) = 300 * 1.5 = 450 $
Freight order (A→C→B) = Distance (A→C→B) * Cost (A→B) = 250 * 1.9 = 475 $

Route-based cost:
Freight order (A→B→C) = Distance (A→B) * Cost (A→B) + Distance (B→C) * Cost (B→C) = 200 * 1.9 + 100 * 1.8 = 560 $
Freight order (A→C→B) = Distance (A→C) * Cost (A→C) + Distance (C→B) * Cost (C→B) = 150 * 1.5 + 100 * 1.8 = 405 $

Figure 6.101 Destination-Based Cost versus Route-Based Cost Calculation

- **Duration costs**
  These costs refer to the actual use of vehicle resources. They are incurred from its first use (loading) until its last use (unloading). The duration is multiplied with the cost per duration unit. Duration costs can be used to minimize operating times, perhaps to create a compact transportation plan with limited idle time.

- **Quantity costs**
  These costs based on a unit of measure (e.g., kilogram or cubic meter) can be incurred into the objective function or not (**No Costs** selected in the **Basis for Quantity Costs** dropdown box). If quantity costs are considered, they can be distance independent or distance dependent. For distance-dependent quantity costs, the freight order quantity is multiplied by the actual distance. This calculation is done stage by stage. Additionally, you can define quantity costs universally in the Planning Costs Settings app or based on the geography in the transportation lane.

  Transported quantities can have an impact on fuel consumption and may therefore be considered distance-dependent cost elements in the objective.

- **Additional stop costs**

  These costs can be used to minimize the number of stops in a freight order. The costs per additional intermediary stop are incurred for each stop that isn't the source or destination of the freight order. For example, in a freight order from A via B to C, the costs per additional intermediary stop would be incurred once for the intermediary stop at B.

Cost Functions in SAP TM 9.6

In addition, you can define *cost functions* using a BAdI implementation in /SCMTMS/ PLN_PRE_PROC. In SAP TM 9.6, you can define cost functions by following the menu path **Application Administration • Planning • Cost Function Settings • Create Cost Function Settings** and assigning them to the means of transport in the Planning Costs Settings app. A cost function is a stepwise linear function that is referenced to a unit of measure when assigned to a means of transport (see Figure 6.102). The cost function is intended to load vehicles in a more efficient way by associating a cost with the vehicle resource that is dependent on the load of the resource in the referenced unit of measure.

In the example in Figure 6.102, a load cost of 10,000 is defined if the vehicle is loaded with less than 15,000 kg. From 15,000 kg, the load cost is 500 and decreasing linearly to 0 at the vehicle capacity of 20,000 kg. With this cost pattern, the VSR optimizer would try to load a vehicle resource with at least 15,000 kg.

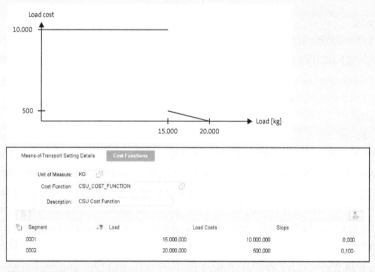

Figure 6.102 Cost Function

Cost functions are sometimes used to achieve a minimum utilization of freight orders. However, keep in mind that sacrificing a good routing for a better utilization is rarely a reasonable choice. More options to deal with a minimum utilization objective are dealt with in the next section.

6.7.4   Vehicle Scheduling and Routing: Planning Constraints

The VSR optimizer tries to minimize all different cost elements introduced in Section 6.7.3. The creation of a minimal cost transportation plan also has to adhere to certain constraints. These planning constraints model the physical or execution-related restrictions of the real world in the planning system. For example, because of physical or legal restrictions, trucks can transport only a certain load, which is expressed as a maximum mass, maximum volume, and/or maximum number of pallets that needs to be considered as a capacity constraint in the freight order. Many constraints are available in the VSR optimizer, which we'll discuss. However, it's important to note that good modeling practice isn't to constrain a planning problem too much; instead, use only those constraints that influence the planning decision.

Capacity Constraints

Capacity constraints are important in transportation planning and are considered hard constraints; that is, the VSR optimizer doesn't create any solution that violates capacity constraints. The VSR optimizer would rather decide not to transport a freight unit (and incur a high nondelivery cost) than violate a capacity constraint. Capacity constraints can be expressed in vehicle resource master data (see Chapter 3, Section 3.3). For each vehicle resource, the VSR optimizer can consider up to eight different capacity dimensions. The prevailing dimensions are mass, volume, and floor space (number of pallets). Only those dimensions that have also been defined as capacity requirements in the freight unit (i.e., those that have been defined as planning quantities in the FUBR; Section 6.2.3) are considered in planning. In addition to capacity constraints, the temporal availability defined in the resource master data is considered a hard constraint by the VSR optimizer.

Capacity constraints are observed on several levels, as illustrated in Figure 6.103. The lowest level is the compartment level. In Figure 6.103, both the vehicle resource and the trailer are physically structured into four compartments (e.g., tanks, C1 to C8).

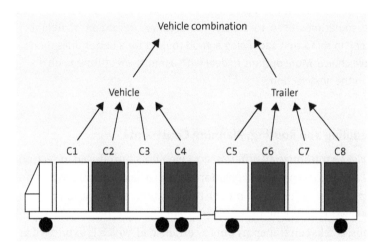

Figure 6.103 Capacity Constraints: Compartment, Vehicle Resource, and Vehicle Combination

You may need to take this property of the vehicle into consideration, for example, if different liquids that can't be mixed have to be transported. Each compartment provides a capacity constraint. In addition, each vehicle resource (the vehicle and the trailer) provides a capacity constraint, and finally the vehicle combination can also have a capacity constraint. Capacity constraints on different levels can be defined independently from each other and are considered independently from each other during planning. They aren't derived from the other levels.

Compartments are defined in Customizing via the menu path **Transportation Management • Master Data • Resources • Means of Transport and Compartment • Define Compartment Types** in the following way:

1. A compartment type is defined by its capacity (in several dimensions) and attributes. Attributes can be used in conjunction with incompatibilities to control whether only liquids or goods that require special temperature conditions can be loaded into the compartment. In Figure 6.103, different colors indicate that the vehicle consists of four compartments with two different compartment types.

2. In the same Customizing transaction, compartment profiles are defined to combine the compartment types with a vehicle configuration. In Figure 6.103, the compartment profile indicates that the vehicle has two compartments of compartment type 1 and two compartments of compartment type 2.

3. Finally, the compartment profile is assigned to the means of transport (in the same Customizing transaction). In the example in Figure 6.103, the same compartment profile can be assigned to the means of transport representing the vehicle resource and to the means of transport representing the trailer.

Compartments are frequently used in planning scenarios that involve liquids or, in retail distribution, to meet the temperature conditions of transported goods.

Vehicle combinations are defined in Customizing via the menu path **Transportation Management • Master Data • Resources • Means of Transport and Compartment • Define Means-of-Transport Combination** in the following way:

1. Means of transport combinations consist of exactly one means of transport that is *not* defined as passive (**Transportation Management • Master Data • Resources • Means of Transport and Compartment • Define Means of Transport**) and any number of means of transport that have been defined as passive. Any means of transport that is used in a means of transport combination can't be defined as multiresource because planning requires tracking individual resources in these scenarios.

2. Like compartments, a means of transport combination is assigned capacities (in different dimensions) and attributes.

As a result of planning with the VSR optimizer, each vehicle resource with a means of transport used in a means of transport combination can be used in a vehicle combination and be coupled to and uncoupled from other vehicle resources based on any defined means of transport combination. Coupling and uncoupling durations are defined in the **Scheduling Settings**.

In the location master data (**Master Data • Transportation Network • Locations • Define Location • TM**), you can define how coupling and uncoupling of trailers is to be handled at a location. A few options are available: to allow coupling/uncoupling activities at the location, *not* to allow these activities, to allow them only if freight units are picked up from or delivered to the location at the same time, or to allow only trailer swaps at this location (Section 6.4.2). The VSR optimizer supports these scenarios and the creation of trailer documents as part of the automated planning process.

Planning with vehicle combinations is used if trailers are frequently exchanged between tractors or the number of tractors and trailers deviates because loading and unloading takes a significant amount of time compared to driving, and a tractor can pull other trailers while one is being loaded or unloaded. However, the use of means of transport combinations introduces a lot of complexity into the planning scenario because tractors and trailers have to be planned independently from each other. Therefore, modeling this constraint should be avoided if possible. Note that this feature is limited to truck and trailer scenarios (e.g., one tractor and one or a few passive resources) and isn't intended for building trains in a railway scenario.

Capacity constraints aren't limited to compartments, vehicle resources, and vehicle combinations. Schedules and freight bookings can also provide capacity in planning.

Decreasing capacities are a capacity constraint that sometimes exists in retail scenarios. If a truck delivers goods to several stores, the goods in the truck are loaded sequentially per store and a separator (thin wall) is used to separate the goods for each store from each other. However, because of the separator, some loading space can't be used and is lost. How much space is lost depends on the number of separators—that is, on the number of stores planned to be delivered to with the vehicle. Thus, the available vehicle capacity isn't a fixed value but depends dynamically on the transportation plan. Decreasing capacities are a planning constraint that addresses this situation and defines how much the vehicle capacity is decreased based on the number of stops on the freight order. Decreasing capacities are defined per means of transport via the menu path **Profiles and Settings** • **Create Decreasing Capacity Settings** (in SAP TM 9.6, the menu path is **Application Administration** • **Planning** • **General Settings** • **Decreasing Capacity Settings**).

In the previous Section 6.7.3, you learned about the load cost function as a means of introducing a utilization objective into the objective function of the VSR optimization algorithm. This can be counterproductive because it may force the VSR optimizer to send a truck on a large detour by adding a freight unit that needs to be delivered in the opposite direction than everything else to fill the truck. To avoid the creation of such tours, you can define a **Minimum Target Utilization in Percent** in the Planning Cost Settings app (see Figure 6.100) instead of defining a cost function. That way, the optimization algorithm isn't misguided by an ambiguous objective, but you can still control what should happen if a utilization objective isn't met for a freight order. If the minimum target utilization has been maintained, the VSR optimizer will try to reach this target utilization in at least one capacity dimension. Based on whether you **Accept Freight Orders Below Target Utilization**, the VSR optimizer will either leave some freight units unplanned or issue a warning for freight orders below target utilization.

Time Constraints

To represent time constraints, you can define a calendar resource in master data (**Master Data • Define Resource**) and assign it to the location in location master data (**Master Data • Define Location • Resources**). You can assign different calendar resources as operating times for inbound (unloading) and outbound (loading) activities. In addition, you can assign operating times that are specific to a means of transport. If the number of parallel loading and unloading activities is restricted, you define handling resources in master data (**Master Data • Define Resource**) and assign them to the location in the location master data (**Master Data • Define Location • Resources**). Similarly to opening times, you can distinguish between inbound and outbound and define these constraints as being specific to a means of transport (see Chapter 3, Section 3.2.1 and Section 3.3, for the definition of master data).

We introduced pickup and delivery time windows in Section 6.2.2. The acceptable start and end dates of both the pickup and delivery time window are hard constraints for the VSR optimizer and are never violated. The requested dates express preferences (soft constraints) and are considered in the objective of the VSR optimizer to incur earliness and lateness costs for freight units (Section 6.7.3).

Pickup and delivery imply that the freight units have to be loaded onto and unloaded from transportation capacities. These activities imply additional constraints for planning. Loading and unloading are activities that require not only the vehicle resource but may also require availability at the location. Some locations may be open only at certain times (e.g., weekdays from 9 a.m. to 5 p.m.). Other locations may limit the number of parallel loading/unloading activities because of limited ramps or personnel available to load and/or unload vehicles. Furthermore, additional activities, such as "gating in" at large locations, some time to do paperwork for the driver, and so on, may require explicit scheduling to obtain a reasonable freight order schedule. While up to SAP S/4HANA 1709 (and SAP TM 9.4), the scheduling was based on the five activity types of loading, unloading, traveling, coupling, and uncoupling, the scheduling concept has changed from SAP S/4HANA 1809 (SAP TM 9.5) to do the following:

- Include additional activities, such as preparation and finalization
- Combine freight unit–specific activities (loading and unloading) into freight order–specific activities (loading and unloading).

In Figure 6.104, the new scheduling concept is explained, and Figure 6.105 shows its configuration.

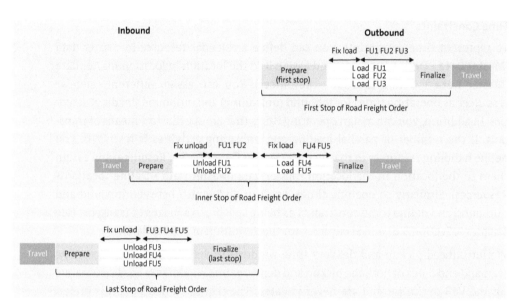

Figure 6.104 Scheduling Concept for Road Freight Orders

A freight order can have pure outbound stops (first stop and first line in Figure 6.104), combined inbound and outbound stops (second stop and second line in Figure 6.104), and pure inbound stops (third stop and third line in Figure 6.104). Each stop consists of one to four activities:

1. Prepare
2. Unload
3. Load
4. Finalize

Their duration can be independently defined based on locations, means of transport, a document attribute, and the loading/unloading quantity. Let's take a closer look at each:

- **Preparation activity**
  Preparation activities are always the first activities in a stop. They are defined on the **Outbound** tab (if it's the first stop of the freight order; in Figure 6.105, it's defined as 30 minutes in the **Prepare First Stop and Finalize Stop** area of the screen) or on the **Inbound** tab for all other stops. Preparation activities can represent "gating in" activities in a location, and a calendar resource can be assigned to allow these activities only during the availability time of this calendar resource.

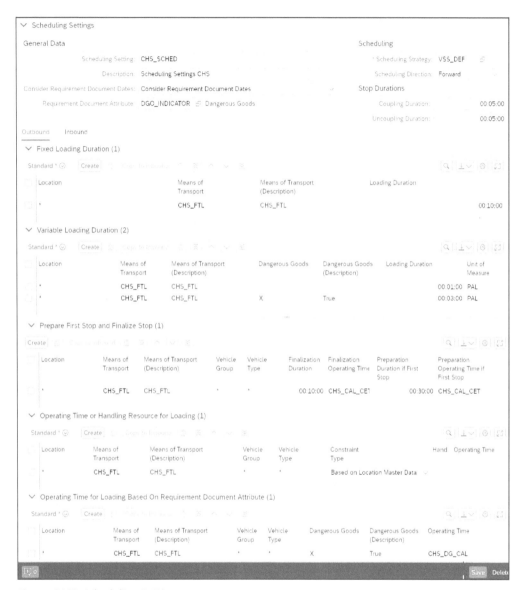

Figure 6.105 Scheduling Settings

- **Loading activity**

  The loading activity is also defined on the **Outbound** tab. One common duration is calculated for all freight units that are loaded at the location. This common duration is used for scheduling in contrast to the individual loading durations of each freight unit according to the previous logic. As shown in in Figure 6.105, the calculation of the common loading duration consists of a fixed part (**Fixed Loading Duration**) plus a variable part (**Variable Loading Duration**), where the variable part may be dependent on an attribute of the requirement document.

In Figure 6.105, the **Dangerous Goods** indicator has been used to define a loading time of 3 minutes per pallet with dangerous goods and 1 minute per pallet without dangerous goods. In addition to the duration, **Scheduling Settings** allow you to define whether these durations have to consider an operating time (calendar resource), handling resource, or none, as well as whether these resources are **Based on Location Master Data** or defined in the **Scheduling Settings**.

- **Unloading activity**
  The unloading activity is similarly defined as the loading activity on the **Inbound** tab. One common duration is calculated for all freight units that are unloaded at the location. This common duration is used for scheduling. Similarly, the calculation of the common unloading duration consists of a fixed part plus a variable part, where the variable part may be dependent on the same attribute of the requirement document as the loading activity. In addition to the duration, **Scheduling Settings** allow you to define whether these durations have to consider an operating time (calendar resource), handling resource, or none, as well as where these resources are defined.

- **Finalization activity**
  The finalization activities are always the last activities in a stop. They are defined on the **Outbound** tab (for all stops other than the last in a freight order; in Figure 6.105, it's defined as 10 minutes in the **Prepare First Stop and Finalize Stop** area of the screen) or on the **Inbound** tab for the last stop. Finalization activities can represent "gating out" activities or paperwork in a location, and a calendar resource can be assigned to allow these activities only during the availability time of this calendar resource.

Note that for the calculation of durations, the first matching row in each area of the screen will be used. Furthermore, because freight units aren't scheduled individually anymore, for the determination of the pickup and delivery time window, the system will use the intersection of all freight units' individual time windows. As a consequence, a prerequisite for successful scheduling is that the acceptable time windows of the individual freight units overlap, which also means that there can't be gaps between individual loading/unloading activities.

Routing Constraints

Section 6.7.2 introduced the maximum number of transshipment locations in a transportation chain as a constraint that drives complexity. Transshipment locations are defined in the Transshipment Assignment Definition app via **Master Data • Assign Transshipment Location** (see also Chapter 3, Section 3.2.5) (in SAP TM 9.6, the menu path is **Master Data • Transportation Network • Locations • Assign Transshipment Location**). This constraint helps the VSR optimizer limit the number of possible alternatives to transport a freight unit from its source to its destination. However, if the constraint maintained is too low, no feasible alternative may be found. Using transshipment locations (e.g., ports or airports) often implies a second constraint that is the cutoff time at the transshipment location. If a flight takes off at 2:15 p.m., it's usually too late to deliver freight to the airport at 2:10 p.m. Thus, a minimum cutoff time should be respected. On the other hand, delivering freight to the airport one week in advance also isn't an option because this may incur additional costs or not be accepted at all. Therefore, minimum and maximum cutoff times can be defined in either the location master data via **Master Data • Define Location • TM** (in SAP TM 9.6, the menu path is **Master Data • Transportation Network • Locations • Define Location • TM**) or schedules via **Master Data • Create Schedule** (in SAP TM 9.6, the menu path is **Master Data • Transportation Network • Schedule • Create Schedule**).

If a fleet is in the scope of transportation planning, then depot or home locations of vehicle resources may be in the scope. If trucks are parked in depot D overnight and need to transport a freight unit from A to B the next day, then the freight order has to include the empty runs from D to A and from B back to D because these stages also require time and incur cost.

Depot locations are maintained in the resource master data (**Master Data • Define Resource**) for each vehicle resource. They are considered as a constraint only for means of transport that are flagged as **Your Own MTr** and aren't flagged as **Multiresource** in Customizing (**Transportation Management • Master Data • Resource • Means of Transport and Compartment • Define Means of Transport**).

If planning local delivery tours from a depot is in the scope of the planning scenario, there may be an additional constraint in place that each tour should last, at most, eight hours, reflecting the working times of drivers. This type of constraint can also be considered by the VSR optimizer. Essentially, the optimizer is allowed to impose limits on one or all of the following:

- Total duration of a freight order
- Total distance of a freight order

- Maximum number of intermediate stops of a freight order
- Maximum number of pickup stops of a freight order
- Maximum number of delivery stops of a freight order

These limits are separate constraints and can be used independently from defining depot locations. For each means of transport, these limits can be maintained in the means of transport settings of the Planning Costs Settings app (refer to Figure 6.100).

Scheduling Constraints

Chapter 3, Section 3.2, explained how transportation duration is calculated based on the transportation distance. However, this isn't a very precise calculation and can't be used universally, which is obvious from even a simple example.

To calculate the transport duration for a container ship from Rotterdam to Boston, you can take the distance (3,200 nautical miles) and divide it by the speed (20 knots/hour) to calculate the expected duration to be 160 hours (approximately one week). The same calculation logic fails for a truck going from Boston to Los Angeles. The distance (3,000 miles) divided by the truck speed (50 miles/hour) would indicate that the truck would arrive after 60 hours (2.5 days) at its destination.

However, in contrast to the ship, which sails day and night, the truck (driver) has to take some breaks that prolong the transportation duration. If the driver were allowed to drive 10 hours per day, the trip from Boston to Los Angeles would take 6 days instead of 2.5 days. Scheduling constraints can be defined to take those breaks into account. As shown in Figure 6.106, scheduling constraints are defined in Customizing (**Transportation Management • Planning • General Settings • Define Scheduling Constraints**) in the following way:

❶ Define an activity group.

❷ Assign activity types to the activity group. The available activity types include **Travel**, **Pickup** (loading), **Delivery** (unloading), **Couple** (vehicle combination), **Uncouple** (vehicle combination), **Prepare**, and **Finalize**. Depending on the origin or purpose of this planning constraint in a specific scenario, either all activity types or just a subset may be relevant for the scheduling constraint. This step maintains the relevant activity types.

❸ Several **Time Constraints** can be maintained in the third step. In the example shown in Figure 6.106, two time constraints are defined. **Constraint ID DAY** represents a constraint in which the maximum duration of activities of activity group **WORKTIME**, defined in step ❷, is 10 hours in any 24-hour time interval (constraint length). The constraint type is defined as a rolling constraint; that is, it doesn't apply per workday but applies to any 24-hour period. If it were defined as a fixed constraint, it would be possible to schedule activities during the last 10 hours of day 1 and during the first 10 hours of day 2, which would allow 20 hours of uninterrupted driving. The second **Constraint ID**, **WEEK**, allows 50 hours of activities within one calendar week.

❹ Because both constraint IDs should be considered together, a constraint set is defined in this step.

❺ Both constraints are assigned to the constraint set in this step.

❻ Finally, the constraint set is assigned to a means of transport.

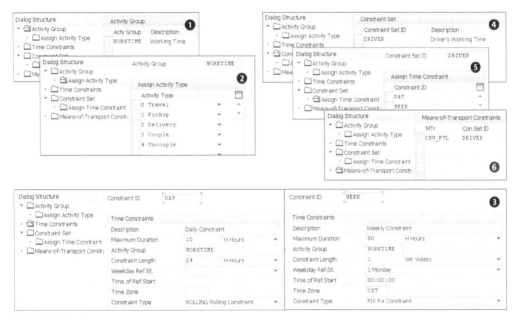

Figure 6.106 Scheduling Constraints

Incompatibilities

We've already mentioned incompatibilities as constraints because they are used in several areas of the application (Section 6.2.3; Chapter 4, Section 4.1.3; and Chapter 6, Section 6.1):

- FUB
- VSR planning (manual, transportation proposal, optimizer)

- Carrier selection
- Delivery proposal

Incompatibilities define which two objects aren't compatible with each other. In VSR planning, the following incompatibility types exist:

- **Freight unit—freight unit (vehicle level)**
  Two freight units aren't allowed on the same vehicle (e.g., they may be explosive if mixed in an accident).

- **Freight unit—freight unit (compartment level)**
  Two freight units aren't allowed in the same compartment (e.g., chemicals shouldn't be mixed with milk in a tank).

- **Freight unit—freight unit (means of transport combination)**
  Two freight units aren't allowed on the same vehicle combination (e.g., they may be explosive if mixed in an accident).

- **Freight unit—vehicle resource**
  A freight unit isn't allowed on a vehicle (e.g., chemicals aren't allowed in a truck intended for food transport).

- **Freight unit—transshipment location**
  A freight unit isn't allowed to be routed via a transshipment location (e.g., a heavy turbine can't be routed through ports that don't have cranes to lift it).

- **Freight unit—vehicle compartment**
  A freight unit isn't allowed on a vehicle compartment (e.g., chemicals aren't allowed in a milk tank).

- **Vehicle resource—vehicle resource**
  Two vehicle resources can't be coupled, although in general it would be allowed by the means of transport combination definition.

- **Vehicle resource—location (stay level)**
  A long vehicle resource can't visit certain locations (e.g., because of maneuvering limitations) on its route.

- **Vehicle resource—location (loading/unloading level)**
  Locations that don't have loading and unloading equipment must not be visited by vehicles that don't carry their unloading equipment (e.g., crane, forklift) themselves.

- **Vehicle MTR combination—location**
  A long vehicle combination must not visit certain locations (e.g., because of maneuvering limitations) on its route.
- **Freight unit—booking**
  A freight unit containing hazardous goods can't be booked on some freight bookings.
- **Freight unit—schedule**
  A freight unit containing hazardous goods can't be booked on some schedules.
- **Freight unit—TU resource**
  A freight unit containing hazardous goods can't be loaded into a food grade container.
- **Container unit—container unit (vehicle level)**
  Two container units aren't allowed on the same vehicle.
- **Container unit—vehicle resource**
  A container unit isn't allowed on a vehicle (e.g., an equipment type isn't allowed on a certain truck type).
- **Container unit—transshipment location**
  A container unit isn't allowed to be routed via a transshipment location (e.g., because of storage constraints).
- **Container unit—freight booking**
  A container unit containing hazardous goods can't be booked on some freight bookings.
- **Container unit—schedule**
  A container unit containing hazardous goods can't be booked on some schedules.

As shown in Figure 6.107, incompatibilities are defined in the Incompatibility app (**Profiles and Settings** • **Create Incompatibility**; in SAP TM 9.6, the menu path is **Application Administration** • **Planning** • **General Settings** • **Incompatibility Definitions**). The incompatibility definition determines the incompatibility area and incompatibility type. It also defines whether violations of the incompatibility are allowed, will result in a warning, or are forbidden. This decision can be made separately for manual planning and automated planning—perhaps to forbid violations in automated planning but to allow a manual override of the decision, resulting in a warning only. The comparison of the evaluation result of two conditions that are evaluated for the two objects defined in the incompatibility type determines whether these two objects are compatible with each other.

In Figure 6.107, an incompatibility between a freight unit and a vehicle resource is defined. Those freight units for which the first condition **CHS_TEMP_FU** returns the result **FROZEN** are incompatible to those vehicle resources, for which the second condition **CHS_TEMP_VEHRES** returns the result **AMBIENT**.

Figure 6.107 Incompatibility Definition

Incompatibility settings (**Profiles and Settings • Create Incompatibility Settings**) are a list of incompatibility definitions that are grouped together because all of them should be considered in a specific planning scenario. The incompatibility settings are assigned to the planning profile.

An overview of all defined incompatibility definitions and incompatibility settings is available in a worklist via one of the queries for profiles and settings (**Profiles and Settings • Profiles and Settings Worklist**).

6.7.5   Vehicle Scheduling and Routing: Optimization Algorithm

The VSR optimizer combines the ideas of several metaheuristics in a population-based optimization algorithm that tries to determine reasonable transportation plans within an acceptable runtime. The algorithm is based on the basic principle of evolutionary local search, so a population of candidate solutions is subject to an evolutionary search process by iterative selection and variation. The initial population is created by several insertion heuristics that iteratively assign all freight units to transportation capacities. In the improvement phase, different variation operators reassign freight units to other transportation capacities, change the routes of freight orders, or adapt the scheduling of activities. In this process, the VSR optimizer tries to minimize total costs defined as the objective (Section 6.7.3) while respecting all active constraints (Section 6.7.4). The best solution found within the maximum runtime (Section 6.7.2) is returned. Figure 6.108 shows how the solution evolves over time.

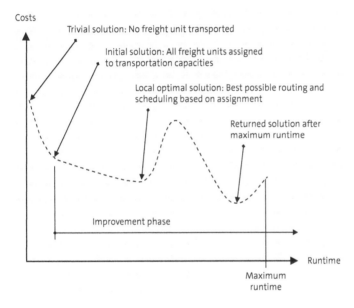

Figure 6.108 VSR Optimizer Runtime Behavior

Complexity of Vehicle Scheduling and Routing Problems

The VSR optimizer is based on an optimization algorithm for the *vehicle scheduling and routing problem* (VSRP). The VSRP is a combinatorial optimization problem that is NP complete—meaning that, based on current research, no polynomial time algorithm is known that solves the problem exactly.

In practical terms, NP completeness means that an exact procedure for large problem instances would require computing time that would be too high to determine the global optimum. That is why the VSR optimizer relies on approximation procedures that achieve an acceptable solution quality in an acceptable computing time.

In the process of generating solutions, the algorithm has to make the following decisions:

- For each freight unit, it decides whether it's transported.
- If the decision is made to transport the freight unit, the path (direct or via which transshipment locations) in the transportation network needs to be chosen.
- Each stage of the freight unit has to be assigned to a transportation capacity (e.g., vehicle resource, schedule, freight booking).
- For each vehicle assignment, the compartment assignment (if defined) needs to be made.
- For each transportation capacity, the sequence of activities (e.g., loading, traveling, unloading, coupling, uncoupling) needs to be determined.
- A date and time need to be determined for each activity according to its sequence.

6.7.6   Explanation Tool

Based on the previous section, you can see that the VSR optimizer is based on a very powerful algorithm; however, to some extent, it isn't transparent to the user how the VSR optimizer created a specific result and why. Therefore, an explanation tool is provided to help the user understand and analyze the optimization results. To activate logging of the optimizer data for optimization runs, a prerequisite is that the user parameter /SCMTMS/EXP is set to X for the specific user. You can access the explanation tool interactively by clicking the **Optimizer Explanation** button either while working in the transportation cockpit or directly after any interactive optimizer run prior to accepting or canceling the result. Both actions take you to the explanation of your last optimizer run.

Another way of accessing the explanation tool, which is also applicable for background runs, is the Log Display transaction in the backend system (**Cross-Application Components • Processes and Tools for Enterprise Applications • Remote Control and Communication Framework • Log Display**; in SAP TM 9.6, the menu path is **Application Administration • General Settings • Remote Control and Communication Framework • Log • Log Display**). This transaction lists and identifies the logs of all engine calls (optimizer, transportation proposal, and scheduling; see also Section 6.7.2) via the user that triggered the engine run, planning profile used, and date and time of this activity. You can access the explanation tool from here for each engine call by clicking the **Explanation Tool** button for the specific run (row of the table).

Explanation Tool: Cleanup

Note that the persistence time for engine logs mentioned in Section 6.7.2 doesn't relate to the explanation tool. For performance reasons, old explanation data should be deleted regularly with report /SCMTMS/PLN_EXP_DELETE.

The explanation tool displays all data that is sent to or retrieved from the engine. Let's walk through Figure 6.109, which shows the input data for the optimizer.

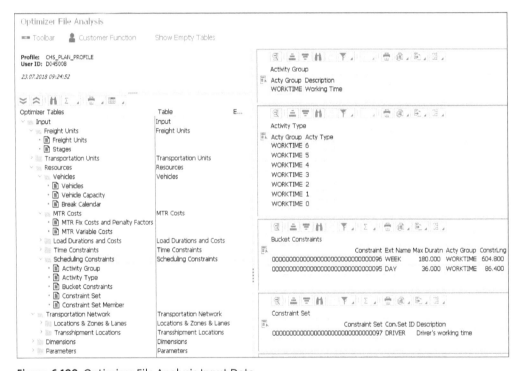

Figure 6.109 Optimizer File Analysis Input Data

On the left side of the screen, it's possible to browse in a folder structure through all the tables, which are organized based on the data origin (e.g., freight unit data, transportation network data, etc.). The right side of the screen displays the content of the tables selected on the left. Often, not all tables contain entries because not all planning constraints mentioned in Section 6.7.4 are present in each optimization problem. You can click the **Show/Hide Empty Tables** button to toggle between the display of all tables or only tables that have at least one entry. Figure 6.109 shows how the scheduling constraints created previously in Figure 6.106 are transferred to the VSR optimizer. Note that for entries in dimension time (**Max. Duratn** and **ConstraintLng** columns in the **Bucket Constraints** table), no unit of measure is transferred, but the unit of measure seconds is always used (10 hours corresponds to 36,000 seconds).

Figure 6.110 shows how the planning result is displayed in the explanation tool. Again, the available tables are displayed in a folder structure on the left, with the table contents displayed on the right. If freight units couldn't be planned as shown in this example (freight unit 300006907, **Planning Status Not Planned**), an explanation would be displayed as **Messages for Freight Units**. In this case, the explanation **No valid connection to destination location** for location 185 indicates that transportation lane information was missing for the optimizer. This is only a hint to the user because the system can't know the real root cause. Other possible root causes for this scenario include the following:

- The resources that have been selected for this planning run are defined for a means of transport that isn't assigned to the (existing) transportation lane.

- A freight booking or schedule should have been used but wasn't selected, so the missing transportation lane wasn't relevant.

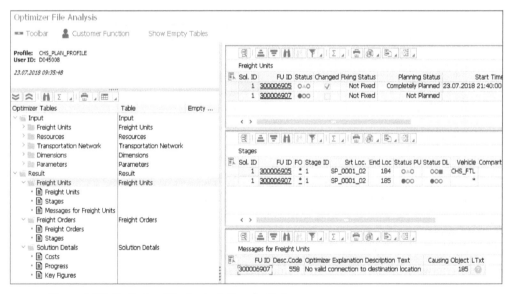

Figure 6.110 Optimizer File Analysis Results Data

6.7.7 Load Consolidation

The load consolidation process supports the planner in the decision to order the correct amount of equipment in case large quantities have to be transported between two locations. In contrast to VSR, no route determination is required in this case, but it has to be done subsequently. Figure 6.111 shows how load consolidation is embedded into a planning process. In this example, freight has to be transported from Mannheim to Chicago. In the package building step, the decision is made regarding which products should be grouped into packages and how many packages and which types are required (Section 6.3 for details on the package building process). The decision regarding how many containers are required as well as which types are needed is made in load consolidation. Furthermore, load consolidation determines the assignment of packages to containers. Finally, VSR determines the routing and scheduling of the individual containers.

The load consolidation isn't limited to containers but can also be used with trucks and trailers as capacity. The result of load consolidation is the assignment of freight units to resources types, while the assignment to actual resources is done subsequently in the vehicle scheduling and routing step.

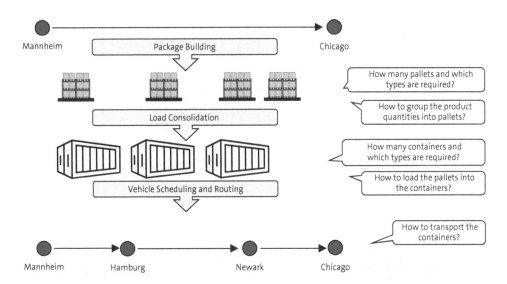

Figure 6.111 Load Consolidation Process

The load consolidation process can be initiated from the transportation cockpit interactively or in the background using report /SCMTMS/PLN_LOAD_CONS_BGD, as shown in Figure 6.112. It's an optimization process that minimizes the fixed costs of the equipment chosen in the process. The fixed cost per equipment type is defined in the Planning Cost Settings app (**Profiles and Settings** • **Create Planning Cost Settings**; refer to Figure 6.100). The number of available equipment items per equipment type can be limited for multiresources in a popup window, if the **Change No. of Individual Resources** checkbox is checked in the Load Planning Settings app (**Profiles and Settings** • **Create Load Planning Settings**; see Figure 6.114 later in this chapter). The load planning settings (**Profiles and Settings** • **Create Load Planning Settings**) control the behavior of the load consolidation process. Load planning settings are assigned to the planning profile but can also be changed interactively in the transportation cockpit via the **Change Planning Settings** button (see Section 6.6.8).

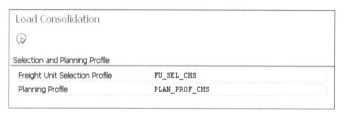

Figure 6.112 Background Report for Load Consolidation

The load consolidation optimizer will select among the available equipment the cheapest set considering capacity constraints and incompatibilities between freight units (e.g., certain dangerous goods must not be in the same container) as well as freight units and capacity types (e.g., reefer cargo requires a reefer container). The capacity check can be defined as **Capacity-Based** or **Load Planning-Based** based on the choice in the Load Planning Settings app (**Profiles and Settings** • **Create Load Planning Settings**; see Figure 6.114 later in this chapter). If the capacity check is based on load planning, the load consolidation process will provide an exact load plan as in load planning, which is described in the next section.

6.7.8 Load Planning

Load planning deals with the creation of a load plan, primarily for loading trucks with pallets. For that reason, master data for vehicle resources and dimensions of freight units needs to be available in more detail (refer to Section 6.2.3 and Figure 6.82). Load planning can be triggered in three ways:

- Manually from the transportation cockpit (refer to Section 6.6.6) or freight order
- Interactively as part of a planning strategy (e.g., manual planning strategy VSRI_ALP or optimizer planning strategy VSR_ALP)
- By scheduling the report /SCMTMS/PLN_LOAD_PLANNING_BGD in the background or from the menu path **Logistics · Transportation Management · Administration · Background Processing · Run Load Planning** in the backend system (in SAP TM 9.6, the menu path is **Application Administration · Background Processing · Run Load Planning**)

Load planning is done by a rule-based optimization engine. The optimization engine is provided with information from the freight order, package information from the items of the freight order, and resource information (number of axles and their specification; interior dimensions, e.g., length, width, and height; etc.). The result of load planning is the exact position of each item of the freight order on the resource. The optimization engine is based on metaheuristics. It runs for a maximum runtime defined in the load planning settings and returns the best found solution within this runtime.

Load planning is limited to box-shaped items (e.g., pallets and cartons) to be loaded onto box-shaped resources (e.g., trucks, trailers, and containers). Other geometries (e.g., barrels or odd-shaped objects) to be loaded on planes or ships aren't within the scope of the solution because either specific equipment exists for their load planning (e.g., unit load devices [ULDs] in air freight) or special trim software exists (for balancing the load on large container ships).

In addition to determining the exact position of each package in the resource, the load planning algorithm also supports determining the best configuration (height position) of a split deck, if this has been defined as flexible for a specific resource. Prerequisites for this case are that the details of the split deck (size and range of movement) have been defined in the resource viewer and that all packages have the same footprint (length and width). Figure 6.113 shows an example with packages that can't be stacked. Without a split deck, the resource can carry only half of the packages (left picture). With a fixed split deck, most of the packages fit onto the truck (middle), and when the beams of the split deck can be adjusted, everything is successfully loaded (right picture).

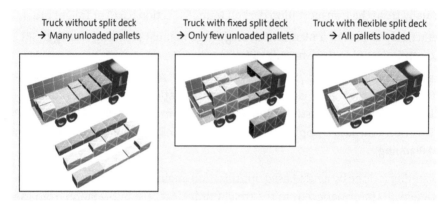

Truck without split deck
→ Many unloaded pallets

Truck with fixed split deck
→ Only few unloaded pallets

Truck with flexible split deck
→ All pallets loaded

Figure 6.113 Load Planning with Split Decks

Depending on the goods to be transported, load planning can become important because legal restrictions and safety considerations may require that the load be distributed inside the vehicle resource based on certain rules. For example, in the United States, the US federal bridge formula establishes the maximum weight any set of axles on a vehicle resource may carry on the interstate highway system. These rules have to be observed when loading a vehicle.

The load optimizer is based on an objective function that is to be minimized and some hard constraints that need to be met. Hard constraints relate to the physical attributes of the resource (maximum gross weight, maximum weight on a split deck, maximum weight on an axle group, etc.) and the physical attributes of the load (pallet dimensions, pallet gross weight, stackability, etc.). The objective is to find a suitable assignment of freight order items to the positions in the resource that meets all hard constraints and minimizes the other objective criteria:

- All freight order items should be loaded onto the resource. Not loading an item results in a penalty cost, which is considered very high because this situation needs to be avoided first.

- All load planning rules must be met according to their priority.

The load planning settings (**Profiles and Settings** · **Create Load Planning Settings**; in SAP TM 9.6, the menu path is **Application Administration** · **Planning** · **Planning Profile Settings** · **Load Planning Settings**) control the behavior of the load optimizer. Load planning settings are assigned to the planning profile but can also be changed interactively in the transportation cockpit via the **Change Planning Settings** button. Load planning settings allow you to define which load planning rules you want to consider and how these different rules will be prioritized (from 1 = highest to 10 = lowest). In addition to priorities, the applicability of load planning rules can be limited to certain equipment groups and types. For some load planning rules, additional parameters can be defined (e.g., maximum height difference of adjacent stacks; see Figure 6.114).

More than 40 different load planning rules are available. Available load planning rules can be grouped into the following areas:

- **Stability of load**
  Motivation for this set of rules is to minimize movement of goods during transport to reduce damages. Examples are ascending or descending stack heights in driving direction or weight balancing regarding load on left/right wheels.

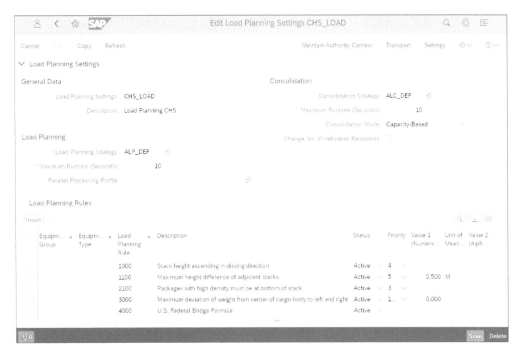

Figure 6.114 Load Planning Settings

- **Positioning of packages**
  Motivation for this set of rules is related to ease of handling (keeping items for the same unloading location together) or the stability of stacks. Examples are maximum weight per stack, density-based sorting from bottom to top of each stack, and consideration of the last-in-first-out (LIFO) principle for trucks/containers that can be loaded from only one end.

- **Double deck-specific rules**
  These rules aim to respect the physical limitations of double-deck equipment and reduce the risk of damages during transportation. Examples are maximum weights per stack or row of the upper deck.

- **Unplanned packages**
  Because not all items assigned to the freight order may physically (based on geometry or maximum [axle] weight considerations) fit onto the assigned resource, these rules allow you to specify preferences for which items will be loaded and which won't. Criteria used to calculate a penalty for any item not loaded can be chosen among weight, volume, or weight × volume.

- **Legal regulations**
  A load planning rule representing the US federal bridge formula allows you to consider legal limitations on axle weights for trucks.

- **Loading patterns**
  Motivations for this set of rules are better weight distribution, load stability, and floor space utilization for customized trucks. More than 20 different rules allow you to define the position and orientation of items. These load planning rules can be defined as vehicle specific or deck specific. Examples are specific loading patterns, such as straight loading, turned loading, or pinwheel loading.

The result of load planning is a list of all loaded items, the sequence of loading, the orientation for each item (straight or turned), and the exact position with stack and row number defining the position on the floor and level in the stacking sequence. The result can be displayed both in list format and as 3D visualization.

6.8   Summary

This chapter explored the depths of planning in SAP TM. We started by reviewing the different documents involved in this process and exploring the decisions to be made in this process. The definition and creation of freight units transformed the various transportation requirements into plannable objects. Package units have been defined to create a package hierarchy from pure products and quantities.

Multiple manual planning options from textual command line planning to visually supported planning in the map or Gantt chart have been explained. However, we focused not only on interactive planning but also on automatic planning options that can be executed in the background.

No matter which planning method is used, all of them produce freight orders, freight bookings, or TU documents. The next chapter focuses on freight orders and how they are subcontracted, tendered, or both.

6

Chapter 7

Carrier Selection and Subcontracting

Transportation execution can be outsourced easily to specialized companies such as logistics service providers or carriers. Therefore, subcontracting is an important component of a transportation management solution because it leaves the supervision of the transportation process in the control of the company while outsourcing its physical execution.

In the previous chapter, we discussed transportation planning as a planning task that deals with the assignment of freight units to available transportation capacities. However, we haven't yet discussed the topic of who will provide these transportation capacities: whether they represent an organization's own fleet of vehicle resources or whether the objective is to subcontract the execution of freight orders.

The focus of this chapter is twofold. One focus is freight order management, and the other focus is choosing the best possible carrier through carrier selection and/or tendering processes.

The objective of carrier selection is to provide a ranking list of carriers that are available to execute a planned freight order. A broad list of options and constraints is available to streamline the selection of the best possible carrier. These options include expected freight order costs, priorities, incompatibilities, transportation allocations, and business shares representing various contractual obligations.

You can perform carrier selection manually, by using an optimization algorithm, or by using an auctioning mechanism as part of the tendering process. The tendering process can itself be used as part of the carrier selection process or as a separate process. In the tendering process, individual freight orders can be tendered to one carrier (peer-to-peer tendering) or to several carriers (broadcast tendering) in parallel. The tendering process involves communication with the carrier in which the carrier can quote prices for the tendered freight order (broadcast tendering) or inform about acceptance or rejection of the freight order (peer-to-peer tendering).

This chapter is structured in the following way: Section 7.1 explains the carrier selection process, objectives, and constraints, as well as the available configuration options. Section 7.2 deals with freight order management, freight order configuration, freight order types, and usage, mainly in land transportation. This section also talks about special processes using freight orders, such as pickup and delivery freight orders in sea and air transportation, customer self-delivery and pickup, and service orders. Finally, Section 7.3 focuses on freight tendering and tendering process configuration options.

7.1   Carrier Selection

The primary objective of carrier selection is to assign a reliable and cost-efficient carrier to a freight order. This can be done in the background, interactively using manual steps, or by using an automated optimization procedure. The various options are described in the next section.

7.1.1   Process

The carrier selection process can be initiated using various methods interactively and in the background. Figure 7.1 shows the carrier selection process when initiated interactively. Carrier selection can be started directly from the freight order user interface (UI) or from any worklist that displays freight orders. It can also be started for freight orders inside the transportation cockpit (**Planning · Transportation Cockpit**) or using an app dedicated to carrier selection (**Planning · Carrier Selection**). Finally, carrier selection can be executed as part of a planning strategy (e.g., by including method VSR_TSPS as in planning strategy VSR_1STEP, which is delivered as a standard planning strategy that combines vehicle scheduling and routing (VSR) optimization and carrier selection; see Chapter 6, Section 6.7) or as part of a creation strategy upon freight order creation.

The input data for carrier selection is one or more freight orders (selected interactively in a worklist) or a selection profile by which the freight orders that need to have a carrier assigned are determined. In addition, carrier selection settings are required to specify exactly how carrier selection should be carried out. The carrier selection settings (Section 7.1.4) are specified explicitly as part of the definition of a background job (/SCMTMS/TSPS_OPT_BGD) (see Figure 7.4); retrieved indirectly, perhaps because they have been assigned to the planning profile that was used to enter the transportation cockpit; or can be determined from freight order type Customizing either via a condition or by direct assignment.

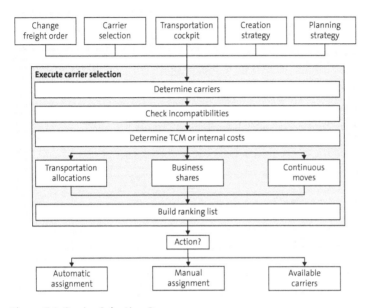

Figure 7.1 Carrier Selection Process

After carrier selection has been initiated, the system determines the available carriers for each selected freight order. A carrier is considered available if it has been defined as a valid carrier for the means of transport used in the freight order for a transportation lane from the source location to the destination location of the freight order. The list of available carriers is reduced by those carriers that are incompatible with the freight order. Incompatibilities arise in a number of ways, such as when a customer doesn't want to be served by a specific carrier or the freight units assigned to the freight order contain hazardous goods that the carrier isn't allowed to handle (e.g., because his or her drivers lack experience, haven't been trained for it, or don't possess a legally required permit).

Available Carriers

To determine which carriers are available, the system proceeds as follows:

1. For each stage of the freight order, the carriers defined for the means of transport used in the freight order in the most specific transportation lane that represents each stage are determined (see top half of Figure 7.2).

2. The carriers defined for the means of transport used in the freight order in the most specific transportation lanes from the source to the destination of the freight order are determined (see bottom half of Figure 7.2).

3. Depending on whether the **Overall Carrier Availability** checkbox has been set, either the carriers are considered available that have been identified for each stage in step 1 and in step 2 (checkbox is set), or only those identified in step 2 (checkbox isn't set) are considered available.

Figure 7.2 illustrates this procedure. If the **Overall Carrier Availability** checkbox is set, only carriers 1 and 2 are considered available, whereas carriers 1, 2, and 5 are considered available if the checkbox hasn't been checked.

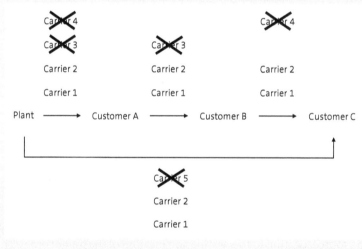

Figure 7.2 Available Carriers

After eliminating incompatible carriers, it's time to decide how to choose one from among the remaining carriers. Decision criteria can include priorities, internal costs, or Transportation Charge Management costs based on the defined strategy.

The next step is an optimization procedure that takes into account the decision criteria calculated in the previous step, as well as all constraints that have been defined. (We outline objectives and constraints in Section 7.1.2 and Section 7.1.3, respectively.) The result of this process is a ranking list of all available carriers from the reduced lists based on the decision criteria. Figure 7.3 gives an example of a ranking list of the relevant information—such as the carrier name, Standard Carrier Alpha Code (SCAC), expected transportation cost, and priority—that a user requires to make a reasonable assignment. Note that the first-ranked carrier isn't necessarily the cheapest because its ranking may have been forced by constraints such as transportation allocations or business shares. All carriers beyond the first position are sorted in descending order of the decision criteria (e.g., cost or priority).

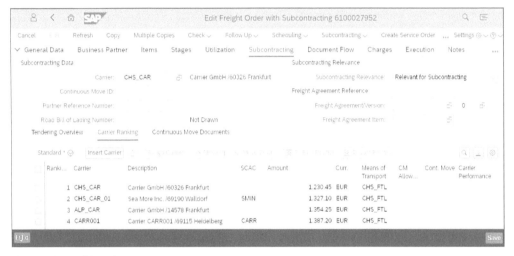

Figure 7.3 Ranking List

Finally, the carrier that is ranked first can be assigned to the freight order as part of the automatic carrier selection process, or the assignment can be delegated to a user in a manual process. If carrier selection hasn't been executed to *determine* a carrier but only to identify the *available* carriers, the ranking list can be used in a subsequent tendering process (Section 7.3). If carrier selection is done to initiate a broadcast tendering process, the optimization step can be skipped because the decision criterion (cost) is determined only then.

In addition to starting manual and automatic carrier selection and determining a list of available carriers, the transportation cockpit also interactively offers the functionality to delete existing carrier assignments, as well as existing carrier rankings for a freight order.

In the background, the carrier selection process can be initiated in the following ways:

- As part of the transportation planning process with background report /SCMTMS/ PLN_OPT and using a planning strategy that includes carrier selection (e.g., VSR_ 1STEP)

579

- By scheduling report /SCMTMS/TSPS_OPT_BGD (see Figure 7.4)
- By assigning strategy **Carr_Sel** as a creation strategy in the freight order type Customizing

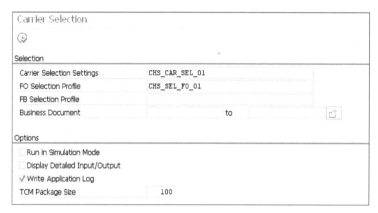

Figure 7.4 Background Report for Carrier Selection

The carrier selection process is predominantly used in land transportation. However, the carrier selection process can also be triggered for freight bookings using the background report or from the freight booking UI. In contrast to carrier selection for freight orders, carrier selection for freight bookings will only consider transportation allocations—no business shares or continuous moves.

7.1.2   Objective of the Carrier Selection Optimizer

The objective of carrier selection is to assign the most suitable carrier to a freight order, which usually means assigning the cheapest one. However, there may be criteria other than cost involved, such as whether another carrier needs to be assigned to a defined minimum transportation quantity based on contractual obligations (minimum transportation allocation), which can force an assignment even if that carrier is more expensive for a specific freight order.

Carrier Selection Optimizer

The carrier selection optimizer converts the assignment problem into a *mixed-integer linear problem* (MILP). Based on the number of freight orders, the complexity of the constraints, and whether the runtime specified in the carrier selection settings is carefully chosen, the carrier selection optimizer usually returns the optimal solution.

If the runtime isn't sufficient to determine the optimal solution, the best solution found within the specified runtime is returned.

Automatic carrier selection is based on an optimization algorithm that minimizes costs. The algorithm considers the following cost components:

- **Transportation charges for the freight orders of the assigned carrier**
  The transportation charges of the assigned carrier are often the only relevant cost component. For each freight order, the transportation charges are evaluated for all available carriers. The transportation charges can have two different origins. The transportation charges are calculated either via Transportation Charge Management (which we cover in Chapter 10) and thus represent the expected real freight cost for a freight order or via internal costs. Internal costs can be defined in the transportation lane master data or, if they don't depend on the geography, in the carrier profile. You can also use a combination of both, if required.

- **Nonassignment charges for freight orders to which no carrier could be assigned**
  While the objective of carrier selection is to find an assignment of a carrier to each freight order, it's not always possible, and the result is nonassignment. For example, finding a carrier may not be feasible because it would violate the maximum transportation allocation of all possible carriers. Because this situation should be avoided, the system defines a penalty cost for not assigning any carrier to a freight order. This penalty can't be influenced by the user and is calculated to be prohibitively high to outweigh the other cost components and avoid nonassignment charges.

- **Penalty charges for violating minimum transportation allocations**
  If minimum transportation allocations refer to a monthly quantity, these may often not be fulfilled in the beginning of the month. Thus, minimum transportation allocations can't be considered a hard constraint because if there aren't enough freight orders waiting for assignment, it's impossible to fulfill all minimum transportation allocations. Therefore, this constraint is considered a soft constraint, and violation of minimum transportation allocations is penalized by costs. Similar to nonassignment charges, this penalty cost is calculated automatically by the system and set higher than the other cost components to avoid violation, if possible.

- **Penalty charges for noncompliance to business shares (outside negative and positive tolerance)**
  Business shares can be defined to yield a predefined distribution of freight orders

among several carriers. This constraint can be used due to contractual obligations or simply to avoid assigning all freight orders to one carrier and therefore becoming too reliant on this carrier. To allow the assignment of carriers that have higher transportation charges, noncompliance with defined business shares is penalized, as outlined in Figure 7.5.

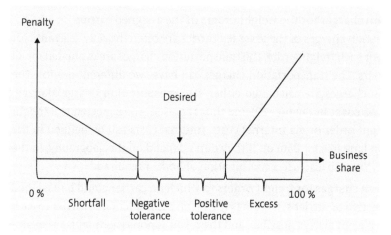

Figure 7.5 Business Shares

A negative and positive tolerance can be defined based on a desired business share for a carrier; actual business shares within these tolerances are cost free. A shortfall of the desired business share minus the negative tolerance or an excess assignment beyond the desired business share plus the positive tolerance is penalized with different penalty costs. Because the user is allowed to specify these penalty costs, he can influence to what extent the consideration of business shares overrules the assignment of carriers based on transportation charges.

- **Discounts granted by the creation of continuous moves**
  In certain situations, carriers grant discounts to transportation charges. These discounts are also taken into account by the carrier selection optimizer.

Continuous Moves

Sometimes carriers grant discounts if they are assigned several freight orders for the same vehicle resource because the incentive reduces effort on their end to look for additional freight after having completed a single freight order. This situation is addressed in carrier selection by defining *continuous move* options. When carrier selection allows it, continuous moves are a way to save money on transportation costs.

Continuous moves may be offered for transports between regions that have economic disparities, such as mainland Europe and the United Kingdom. Because many more goods are transported from mainland Europe to the United Kingdom, many trucks have to return empty from the United Kingdom. A carrier may therefore be inclined to offer a discount on the transportation charges if it's also offered to transport freight on the return trip.

Figure 7.6 shows two continuous move types:

- **Simple continuous move**
  There is no relation between the destination of the second freight order **D** and the source of the first freight order **A**. Only the destination of the first freight order **B** and the source of the second freight order **C** have to be close.

- **Round-trip**
  The destination of the second freight order and the source of the first freight order have to match **A**. In addition, the destination of the first freight order **B** and the source of the second freight order have to be close **C**.

A round-trip is limited to two freight orders, whereas an unlimited number of freight orders can be combined by simple continuous moves. Closeness, or proximity, has the following two dimensions and is defined in the transportation lane:

- **Distance**
  A continuous move provides commercial benefit to the carrier only if the source of the second freight order isn't too far away from the destination of the first freight order. A maximum distance can be defined in the transportation lane master data.

- **Time**
  The departure time of the second freight order has to be reasonably close to the arrival time of the first freight order. It doesn't help the carrier if his vehicle has to wait for a week. Therefore, time constraints for these windows are also defined in transportation lane master data.

The continuous move types allowed for a carrier are also defined in the transportation lane and therefore can deviate by geography. In addition, the carrier needs to be marked as eligible for offering discounts on continuous moves in the carrier profile (**Continuous Move** checkbox).

If certain freight orders shouldn't be combined in a continuous move—even if these definitions would allow it—this can be specified via an incompatibility of type 82.

Before the carrier selection optimizer is started, an evaluation is carried out regarding whether two or more freight orders and carrier assignments qualify for continuous moves. These continuous move opportunities and their associated discounts are then provided as additional information to the optimizer, which takes these discounts together with the other cost components (freight charges, penalties) into account when calculating the optimal (cost minimal) solution.

If two or more freight orders build a continuous move, this is identified by a continuous move ID that is visible in the freight order (see the **Continuous Move Documents** tab in the **Subcontracting Data** section of Figure 7.3).

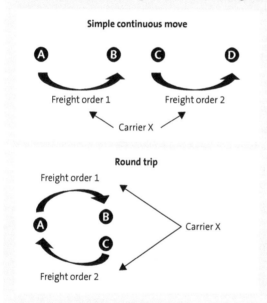

Figure 7.6 Continuous Move Types

While cost is the most obvious objective, carrier selection can also be based on priorities or a combination of priorities and costs as an alternative. Using priorities may be an option if the focus of the implementation project is planning, and it's deemed to be too much effort to actually set up Transportation Charge Management or internal transportation costs. If the contractual setup with carriers allows you to express preferences based on geographical information (transportation lane master data), priorities can be used as a selection criteria for carrier selection.

One way of combining priorities and costs is to use the multiplication of both numbers as a decision criterion (*priorities* × *costs*). In this case, priorities can be interpreted as a key performance indicator (KPI) for carrier reliability. A value smaller than 1 indicates a bonus in the selection because of good customer service, whereas a value larger than 1 corresponds to a disadvantage, which increases the perceived costs of this carrier. Similarly, you can argue for using the sum of both decision criteria (*priorities + costs*).

7.1.3   Constraints

We recommend considering the following constraints during carrier selection:

- Transportation allocations
- Business shares
- Incompatibilities

In the carrier selection settings, each constraint can be switched on or off individually by geography (transportation lane level) or globally for one carrier selection optimizer run (Section 7.1.4). Transportation zone hierarchies and means of transport hierarchies are considered with these constraints.

Chapter 5, Section 5.2, introduced transportation allocations in detail. A *transportation allocation* allows you to define minimum and/or maximum allocations (capacities) that *need to be* assigned to a carrier (minimum) or that *can be* assigned to a carrier (maximum).

The transportation allocation type customization defines whether a transportation allocation is valid for carrier selection (**Transportation Management • Planning • General Settings • Define Transportation Allocation Types**) and the unit of measure that is relevant for carrier selection. A transportation allocation can be created via the menu path **Master Data • Create Transportation Allocation** (in SAP TM 9.6, the menu path is **Planning • Allocation**) and is defined by the following characteristics, which are shown in Figure 7.7:

- Trade lane
- Source location or transportation zone
- Destination location or transportation zone
- Orientation (see Chapter 3, Section 3.2.7, for details)
- Transportation mode and/or means of transport
- Carrier
- Validity period

585

- Planning period
- Relevant unit of measure defined via the allocation type

Trade lanes and orientation define the geographical validity of the transportation allocation. Transportation mode, means of transport, and carrier identify exactly for whom and for what the transportation allocation is defined. The validity period defines the temporal validity of the transportation allocation. This time period is divided into buckets according to the setting of the planning period (e.g., daily, weekly, monthly, quarterly, or yearly).

Customizing the transportation allocation type also specifies the unit of measure for which the transportation allocation is defined. In the example used in Figure 7.7, gross weight has been defined as the relevant dimension. Therefore, in the transportation allocation, you can maintain a minimum and maximum weight for each bucket, as well as display what has already been allocated to the carrier for this transportation allocation (current gross weight).

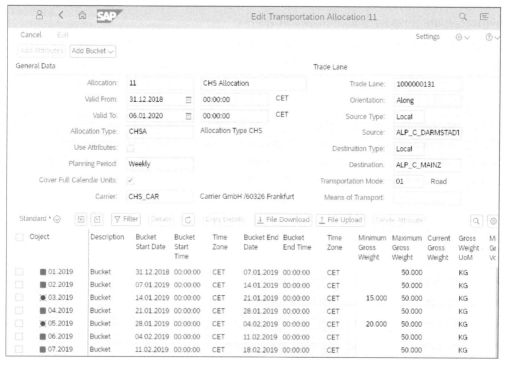

Figure 7.7 Creation of Transportation Allocations for Carrier Selection

Furthermore, in the transportation allocation type, you've specified how to account for transportation allocations. The **Bucket Overlapping** checkbox specifies whether only the first date (the requested start date) or the complete period of the freight order allocates capacity. If a freight order covers a period of three days (e.g., a truck driving from Spain to northern Germany), and the planning period for the transportation allocation is daily, this checkbox determines whether the transportation allocation takes this freight order into account on all three days or only once on the first day.

A freight order is considered relevant for a transportation allocation if all of the following characteristics are met:

- The means of transport in the allocation is the same or superior to the means of transport used in the freight order.
- The requested start date of the freight order falls into the validity period of the transportation allocation.
- The geographical criteria (trade lane and orientation) are met for the source and destination location of the freight order, considering also the transportation zone hierarchy.
- The check for transportation allocations has been set in the transportation lane corresponding to the freight order or in the carrier selection settings.

One Freight Order Can Consume Several Transportation Allocations

Note that one freight order may consume several transportation allocations because means of transport hierarchies, transportation zones, and transportation zone hierarchies are taken into account when determining the relevant transportation allocations for a freight order. You can't automatically assign a carrier if even one transportation allocation is violated, but you can force the assignment manually.

For example, let's say that a carrier leaving plant P is allowed to take a maximum of 10 freight orders per week. A maximum of 3 freight orders per week is allowed for the same carrier from plant P to warehouse W. If 3 freight orders from P to W have been assigned to this carrier in a particular week, no additional freight order from P to W can be assigned to this carrier, even though there is an open allocation of 7 freight orders outbound from plant P. This assignment would violate the second transportation allocation (P to W).

If a freight order is created or changed, this updates all relevant transportation alloca-tions, meaning that potential violations are checked. However, an update of the transportation allocation doesn't have an impact on existing carrier *assignments* to freight orders.

Business shares have a lot of similarities with transportation allocations. They can be created by selecting **Master Data · Create Business Share** and are defined by the fol-lowing characteristics, as shown in Figure 7.8:

- Trade lanes
- Source location or transportation zone
- Destination location or transportation zone
- Orientation
- Means of transport and/or transportation mode
- Validity period
- Business share period
- Positive and negative tolerances
- Penalty costs
- Target business shares per carrier
- Unit of measure

Figure 7.8 Business Shares

Similarly to transportation allocations, defining and using business shares takes into account means of transport hierarchies, transportation zones, and transportation zone hierarchies. When you're calculating the actual business share, you consider not only the orders that are part of the selection for carrier selection but also those that already have a carrier assigned and that fall into the business share period (historical business share).

The major difference between transportation allocations and business shares is that business shares express preferences of carrier assignments in relative numbers (percentages), while transportation allocations represent capacity restrictions and are defined in absolute numbers. In addition, business shares are represented as soft constraints that are considered based on penalty costs, whereas transportation allocations are hard constraints.

For carrier selection, two incompatibility types are relevant:

- **Freight order—carrier (type 81)**
  Incompatibilities between freight orders and carriers are used if a carrier won't be assigned to a freight order for any reason. Possible reasons are typically driven by the business, such as if a carrier is blacklisted by a customer and should therefore not be used in freight orders for this customer, or if a carrier won't process certain goods because it isn't certified for those goods.

- **Freight order—freight order (type 82)**
  Incompatibilities between freight orders are relevant for the determination of continuous move options only. For example, a truck's cleaning requirement prevents it from being used for backhaul activities.

Individual incompatibilities are defined as *incompatibility definitions* (**Profiles and Settings • Create Incompatibility**), which are grouped into *incompatibility settings* (**Profiles and Settings • Create Incompatibility Settings**) to finally be assigned in the *carrier selection settings* (**Profiles and Settings • Create Carrier Selection Settings**). This has been described in detail for planning-related incompatibilities in Chapter 6, Section 6.7.4 .

Figure 7.9 illustrates an example in which information is considered for automatic carrier selection. Although the example doesn't consider alternative carriers or several means of transport, it shows that a lot of information needs to be processed to adhere to all constraints relevant for carrier selection. In real-world situations, several available carriers or means of transport organized in a hierarchy with transportation allocations or business shares defined on several levels may add complexity to the decision.

The example consists of four locations (**A**, **B**, **C**, and **D**), which are assigned to transportation zones **Z1** (**B** and **C**), **Z2** (**C** and **D**), and **Z3** (**A**, **B**, and **C** via **Z1**).

Freight orders are for the following:

- Freight order 1 (FO1) from source **A** to destination **B**
- Freight order 2 (FO2) from source **A** to destination **C**
- Freight order 3 (FO3) from source **D** to destination **C**
- Freight order 4 (FO4) from source **D** to destination **A**

Three transportation allocations are in the scope of this scenario: one from **A** to **Z1** (orientation: along), one from **D** to **Z2** (orientation: along), and one for **D** (orientation: from). In addition, business shares have been defined from **A** to **Z1** (orientation: along) and from **D** to **Z3** (orientation: along).

In this example, FO3 has to respect two transportation allocations and one business share, whereas one transportation allocation and one business share are relevant for the other three freight orders each.

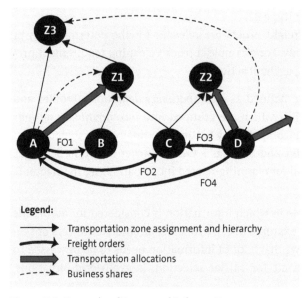

Legend:

→ Transportation zone assignment and hierarchy
→ Freight orders
⇒ Transportation allocations
--→ Business shares

Figure 7.9 Example of Processed Information

7.1.4   Configuration

The configuration of carrier selection with all of its constraints is controlled by many objects. These objects have been explained in earlier chapters:

- Carrier profiles (see Chapter 3, Section 3.1.2)
- Transportation lanes (see Chapter 3, Section 3.2.3)
- Transportation zones and transportation zone hierarchies (see Chapter 3, Section 3.2.2)
- Transportation allocations (see Chapter 5, Section 5.2, and Section 7.1.3)
- Business shares (Section 7.1.3)
- Means of transport hierarchies (see Chapter 3, Section 3.3)

One central configuration step is the carrier selection settings (**Profiles and Settings • Create Carrier Selection Settings**), which are shown in Figure 7.10.

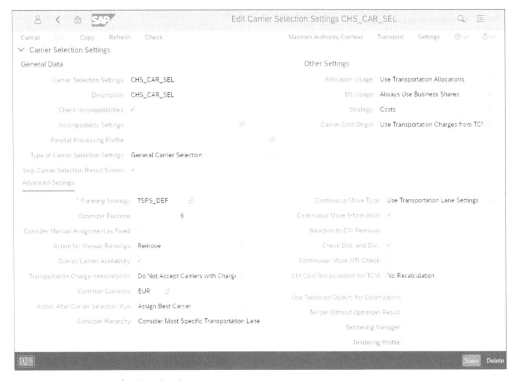

Figure 7.10 Carrier Selection Settings

These settings control the carrier selection process and determine which constraints are used and how. Therefore, configuring carrier selection settings for automatic carrier selection is mandatory.

The following fields are the most important to influence the carrier selection process:

- **Check Incompatibilities**
  Incompatibilities (Section 7.1.3) are checked only if this checkbox has been selected.

- **Incompatibility Settings**
  If the **Check Incompatibilities** checkbox is selected, incompatibility settings define which incompatibility definitions need to be adhered to.

- **Type of Carrier Selection Settings**
  This parameter defines the purpose of carrier selection. Available options are **General Carrier Selection**, **Carrier Selection for Tendering**, and **Carrier Selection for Direct Shipment**.

- **Allocation Usage**
  This parameter determines the consideration of transportation allocations. Available options are to use transportation allocations, not to use them, or to decide on the transportation lane level.

- **BS Usage**
  This business share usage parameter determines the consideration of business shares. Available options are to use business shares, not to use them, or to decide on the transportation lane level.

- **Strategy**
  The strategy determines how the objective of carrier selection is calculated in optimization. The objective can be based on cost, priority, the sum of cost plus priority, or the product of cost times priority. In addition, the **Use Transportation Lane Settings** option can delegate this decision by geography to the individual transportation lanes, so that in different geographical areas, different objectives can be pursued (e.g., priority in one transportation lane and costs in another transportation lane).

- **Carrier Cost Origin**
  Carrier cost origin defines how costs are calculated. Transportation charges from Transportation Charge Management or internal costs can be used (Section 7.1.2).

The **No Cost Determination** strategy may be used if carrier selection for tendering searches for the available carriers in a broadcast tendering process (Section 7.3). Like the settings for strategy with the **Use Transportation Lane Settings**, you can delegate this decision by geography to the individual transportation lanes.

- **Planning Strategy**
  The left column of Figure 7.11 shows the default planning strategy for carrier selection **TSPS_DEF**. The assigned methods illustrate the carrier selection process with all relevant steps from gathering relevant data (carriers, step 20; incompatibilities, step 30; continuous move opportunities, step 40; other constraints, steps 50 to 70) to optimization (step 80).

Method assignment to Strategy			
Strategy	Method	Sequence	Description
TSPS_DEF	TSPS_PRE	10	CS: Preprocessing
TSPS_DEF	TSPS_CARR	20	CS: Get carriers
TSPS_DEF	TSPS_INC	30	CS: Check incompatibilities
TSPS_DEF	TSPS_CM	40	CS: Build continuous moves
TSPS_DEF	TSPS_FILT1	50	CS: Optimizer restrictions
TSPS_DEF	TSPS_TAL	60	CS: Load relevant TAL/BS
TSPS_DEF	TSPS_FILT2	70	CS: Process TAL Bucket Restrictions
TSPS_DEF	TSPS_EXEC	80	CS: Execute Process
TSPS_DEF	TSPS_POST	90	CS: Postprocessing

Figure 7.11 Planning Strategy TSPS_DEF

- **Optimizer Runtime**
  This parameter specifies the maximum runtime for the optimizer (in seconds). The optimizer returns the optimal solution prior to this runtime or the best solution found at this runtime.

- **Consider Manual Assignments as Fixed**
  Dealing with manual assignments in automatic carrier selection is an important topic because there is likely a reason for manual assignments, and they shouldn't simply be overridden. Therefore, manual assignments can be considered as fixed when this checkbox is selected.

- **Action for Manual Rankings**
  A similar question is how to deal with manual rankings. Available options for manual rankings are to keep them, remove them, or keep the carrier only when it's considered available (Section 7.1.1).

- **Transportation Charge Interpretation**
  If, for any reason, the transportation charges for a carrier for a freight order are evaluated as zero, this parameter determines how to deal with it. Available options are to either ignore the carrier availability for this freight order or accept the carrier for this freight order as either the cheapest available carrier or the most expensive one.

- **Action after Carrier Selection Run**
  Available actions after the carrier selection run are the automatic assignment of the highest ranking carrier to the freight order or doing nothing (i.e., leaving this decision to a manual process/user, based on the created carrier ranking). In addition, automatic or manual tendering based on the parameters for tendering (tendering profile, tendering manager) can be initiated. The tendering process is explained in detail in Section 7.3.

- **Consider Hierarchy**
  This parameter chooses the available carriers. Options include considering only those carriers defined on the most specific transportation lane or considering all transportation lanes to retrieve available carriers. The sequence that hierarchies (based on source location, destination location, and means of transport) are evaluated to determine the most specific transportation lane are defined in Customizing activity **Transportation Management · Master Data · Transportation Network · General Settings for Transportation Network Determination**.

- **Continuous Move Type**
  With this parameter, you decide whether only simple continuous moves are allowed, only round-trips are allowed, continuous moves aren't considered at all, or this decision is made on the transportation lane level (Section 7.1.2).

7.2   Freight Order Management

For the most part, freight orders are created as the result of planning, especially in land transportation, whereas freight bookings are used in air or sea transportation. In a subcontracting scenario, the freight order is the document that is sent to the carrier after the carrier is assigned via either carrier selection or tendering (Section 7.3). In this section, we focus on the role of the freight order and its automatic or manual creation from a planning perspective; the next chapter covers the view from the execution perspective, including the printing of freight documents.

7.2.1   Configuration and User Interface

You can create a freight order either manually or automatically. Choose the manual process if you already know what to order because you regularly create similar freight orders for a carrier. In this case, you manually enter the relevant information (logistical data, e.g., source and destination locations, as well as dates/times and items to be transported) in the freight order UI, or you copy an existing freight order and change the required fields in your version. You can also create a freight order based on a freight agreement.

On the other hand, there are different options for automatic creation of freight orders:

- **Result of planning**
  Freight orders can be created as a result of two kinds of planning: manual planning in the transportation cockpit and automatic planning using either the VSR optimizer or transportation proposal functionality.

- **Direct creation via a background process**
  Freight orders can be created directly from the freight unit building rule (FUBR) (shortcut planning process; see Chapter 6, Section 6.2.3) or as a result of a direct shipment option (see Chapter 6, Section 6.2.2).

Freight Orders Based on SAP ERP Shipment Integration

In a deployment scenario in which SAP TM 9.6 is connected to an SAP ERP system with Logistics Execution (LE-TRA) still in use, freight orders can be created based on integration of a shipment document from SAP ERP.

The most important settings for the freight order are defined in the Customizing activity of the freight order type, which you can access by following the menu path **Transportation Management · Freight Order Management · Freight Order · Define Freight Order Types**. Figure 7.12 shows the freight order type Customizing with all of its options.

Freight Order Type	CHS1 Freight Order with Subcontracting		
☐ Default Type			
☐ Default Type for ERP Shipment Integration			
Number Range Settings		**Integration Settings**	
Time for Drawing	I Draw Number Immediately ⌄	Dangerous Goods Profile	
Number Range Interval	F0	Customs Profile	
		Document Creation Relevance	N No External Document Creation ⌄
Basic Settings		Delivery Profile	
Transportation Mode	01 Traffic Direction ⌄	EWM Integration Profile	
Freight Order Can Be Subcontracted	01 Relevant for Subcontracting ⌄	Application Object Type	ODT20_TO
Sequence Type of Stages	01 Defined and Linear ⌄	☑ BW Relevance	
Self-Delivery/Customer Pick-Up	⌄		
Shipper/Ship-to Party Determ.	P Determination Based on Predeces... ⌄	**Checks and Blocks**	
☐ Fix Document When Saving		☐ Enable Compliance Check	☐ Enable Additional Execution Checks
☐ Freight Order Can Be Deleted	☐ Track Changes	☐ Enable Air Cargo Security Check	
		Block Profile	
Planning Settings			
Planning Profile		**Service Definition**	
Distance/Duration Determination	Use Default for Document Category ⌄	Default Service Level	⌄
Def. MTr for DocType		Service Level Condition	
Condition for Def. MTr			
Enable Pkg Building	Do Not Enable ⌄	**Default Units of Measure**	
		Default Weight UoM	KG Kilogram ⌄
Execution Settings		Default Volume UoM	M3 Cubic meter ⌄
Execution Tracking Relevance	2 Execution Tracking ⌄	Default Quantity UoM	⌄
Check Condition "Ready for Exec"			
Display Mode for Execution Tab	Actual Events from TM and EM, Ex.. ⌄	**Default Types**	
Last Exp. Event	ARRIV_DEST	Default Service Order Type	
☐ Immediate Processing		Import Freight Order Type	
Execution Propagation Mode	Standard Propagation ⌄		
Discrepancy Profile		**Driver Settings**	
		☐ Settings Can Be Changed in Freight Order	
Output Options		Number of Required Drivers	0 Not Relevant for Driver Plann... ⌄
Output Profile	/SCMTMS/TOR	Driver Assignment Type	Per Freight Order ⌄
Add. Output Profile	/SCMTMS/TOR_PRINT_ROAD		
Text Schema		**Tendering Settings**	
Default Text Type		◉ Use Default Settings	
☐ Dynamic Determination of Output		○ Use Condition for Sett. Determ.	
		Tendering Condition Definition	
Organizational Unit Determination		○ Use Type-Specific Settings	
☐ Default Org Unit		Process Settings	
Execution Organisation		Communication Settings	
Purchasing Organization	50010476		
Execution Group		**Change Controller Settings**	
Purchasing Group		Default Change Strategy	NO_ACTION
		Change Strategy Det. Cond.	
Determination Rules		Quantity Tolerance Cond.	
1. Condition		Date Tolerance Condition	
2. ☐ Consider Organization Unit of User			
		Additional Strategies	
		Creation Strategy	
Charge Calculation and Settlement Document Settings		Save Strategy	
☑ Enable Charge Calculation	☑ Automatic Charge Calculation	Deletion Strategy	
☐ Enable Internal Charge Calculation			
Default Charges View	2 Grouped View ⌄	**Partner-Related Settings**	
Event Profile		Partner Determination Profile	0001
☐ Enable Settlement	☐ Enable Cost Dist.	Default Carrier Selection Settings	
Default FSD Type	001 Freight Settlement ⌄	Carrier Selection Condition	
☐ Enable Internal Settlement	☐ Enable Int Cost Dist		
Default ISD Type	⌄	**Additional Settings**	
		HBL or HAWB Strategy	
Residence Periods		Draw BoL Number	Draw Manually ⌄
Completeness Criteria	Execution and Settlement Compl.. ⌄		
Residence Period	100	**Application Configuration Settings**	
Res. Time (Compl.)	Res. Time (Canc.)	Web Dynpro Application Configuration	/SCMTMS/FRE_ORDER

Figure 7.12 Freight Order Type Customizing

Let's walk through the most important settings:

- **Freight Order Type**
  The freight order type has to be unique with respect to freight unit types, freight booking types, transportation unit types, and service order types because all of these objects technically originate from the same business object: /SCMTMS/TOR.

- **Default Type/Default Type for ERP Shipment Integration**
  Depending on how a freight order is created, the freight order type is manually entered, determined by a condition, or determined from the planning profile.

  Two freight order types can be marked as default types. One default type is used if the freight order is created based on a predecessor document in SAP TM, and no other freight order type is being determined; the other default type is used if the predecessor document was an SAP ERP shipment.

- **Number Range Settings**
  The number range settings specify a number range interval and whether a number is drawn immediately or only when the business document is saved.

- **Basic Settings**
  The basic settings define whether the freight order is relevant for subcontracting. They also define how the shipper and consignee are determined. Furthermore, you define whether changes are tracked, whether freight orders are fixed when saving, and whether freight orders of this type can be deleted.

  Sequence Type of Stops determines the structural design of the stages of the freight order. Freight orders created via planning have a **Defined and Linear** stop sequence because the stages of the freight order represent the route that the assigned vehicle resource is expected to drive (e.g., from A to B, from B to C). However, other stop sequences can be defined, such as **Nonlinear Star-Shaped** (from A to B, from A to C) or **Disconnected** (from A to B, from C to D). These stop sequences, which physically can't be executed as such, may be used in freight orders that are relevant only for charge calculation and can be created only using customer-specific functions or from SAP ERP shipments. No planning activities are allowed for these freight orders. Freight orders created from the parcel process using direct shipment options may be created with the **Star-shaped based on FU stages** option because all freight units would have the same origin but different destinations.

- **Planning Settings**
  The means of transport of a freight order is usually determined from the vehicle resource assigned to the freight order. However, if the freight order isn't created from planning (e.g., in the shortcut process), the means of transport can be determined

from the default value defined here or using the specified condition. Similar, the planning profile can be defaulted here, which may be required for, for example, scheduling activities, if these are triggered from the freight order directly and not from the transportation cockpit.

- **Execution Settings**
  The execution settings deal with the execution tracking relevance of the freight order type. Tracking and tracing is done with SAP Event Management, which is described in Chapter 8. The discrepancy profile defines the settings for handling discrepancies (general and quantity discrepancies). A discrepancy profile can contain several discrepancy types.

- **Output Options**
  Two output profiles can be assigned to the freight order type. The output options are explained in detail in Chapter 8.

- **Organizational Unit Determination**
  For a freight order, the purchasing organization is relevant in subcontracting scenarios because, in this case, transportation services are purchased from an external vendor or carrier. Alternatively, the execution organization may be relevant if the freight order isn't subcontracted. The relevant organizational unit for a freight order is first determined from the condition maintained here, second based on the assignment of the user that creates the freight order to an organizational unit, and third from the default values.

- **Charge Calculation and Settlement Document Settings**
  You can enable or disable whether freight orders of this type are relevant for charge calculation, settlement, internal charge calculation, internal settlement, and/or cost distribution, as well as default views and default settlement document types for these options.

- **Residence Periods**
  The residence period defines the minimum time between completion of a document and archiving. Completeness of a freight document is based on the completion of execution, settlement, and, optionally, discrepancies.

- **Integration Settings**
  You can define a delivery profile to control creation of delivery proposals based on freight orders. Furthermore, the document creation relevance and SAP EWM integration profile control the integration to SAP Extended Warehouse Management (SAP EWM). The dangerous goods profile relates to processing of dangerous goods content, and the customs profile relates to global trade integration.

- **Checks and Blocks**
  Compliance checks, air cargo security checks, and additional execution checks can be enabled or disabled. Additional execution checks limit the execution of activities related to cargo management in the freight order based on the handling execution status of the items.

- **Service Definition**
  The service level for the freight order is determined based on the default setting or retrieved via a condition.

- **Default Units of Measure**
  You can specify a default unit of measure for weight, volume, and quantity.

- **Default Types**
  You can specify the default service order type for service orders created from the freight document and default the import freight order type.

- **Driver Settings**
  The driver settings define whether freight orders of this type are relevant for driver determination, the relevant number of drivers (one or two), and the driver assignment type (per stage or per freight order).

- **Tendering Settings**
  Settings related to the tendering process are defined here. These settings are explained alongside the freight tendering process in Section 7.3.

- **Change Controller Settings**
  The change controller settings specify which change controller strategy is used for freight orders of this type or which conditions are used to determine the change controller strategy.

- **Additional Strategies**
  Similar to the change controller strategy executed for document changes, additional strategies can be defined to be executed at document creation, save, and deletion.

- **Partner-Related Settings**
  In the partner determination profile, you can define which business partner roles are relevant to the document and how corresponding business partners are retrieved. The carrier selection condition can be used to derive the carrier selection settings, for example, in a shortcut process when carrier selection is initiated by creation strategy CARR_SEL. If the condition doesn't return a result or hasn't been defined, default carrier selection settings as defined here are used.

- **Additional Settings**

  The additional settings deal with house bill of lading (HBL) or house air waybill (HAWB) creation.

- **Application Configuration Settings**

  Finally, the Web Dynpro application assigned to this document type can be specified.

Freight orders can be accessed for editing or displaying via worklists (**Order Management • Freight Orders (Worklist)**; in SAP TM 9.6, the menu path is **Freight Order Management • Road/Rail • Overview Road/Rail Freight Orders**), from the document flow of predecessor or successor documents, from the transportation cockpit (**Planning • Transportation Cockpit**), or directly via **Order Management • Edit Road Freight Order**. Figure 7.13 shows the UI for the freight order.

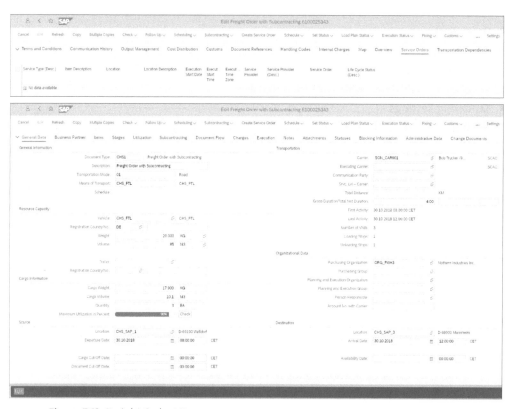

Figure 7.13 Freight Order UI

Accessing Freight Orders in SAP TM 9.6

In SAP TM 9.6, the initial menu path you use to access freight orders is **Freight Order Management • Road/Rail • Overview Road/Rail Freight Orders**.

The information stored in the freight order is organized into the following tabs:

- **General Data**
  The content of the **General Data** tab is depicted in Figure 7.13. It gives an overview of the freight order, including logistical information (source and destination location, dates and times, cumulative quantities for the cargo assigned to the freight order), assigned capacities (vehicle resources), and carrier and organizational assignments (responsible purchasing organization or planning and execution organization).

- **Business Partner**
  The business partners for the relevant business partner roles are displayed here. The most important business partner roles for the freight order are carrier, shipper, consignee, executing carrier, and communication party.

- **Items**
  All items assigned to any stage of the freight order are displayed on the **Items** tab. All information related to cargo is consolidated here: product details, quantities, dangerous goods information, content identification information, customs information, and notes. From this tab, discrepancies can be reported, documented via attachments, and resolved. You can also show and create the load plan for the freight order. The load plan is displayed in tabular format and as a 3D visualization (see also Chapter 6, Section 6.7).

- **Stages**
  The **Stages** tab displays the logistical information about the freight order. For each stage, distance, duration, planned dates and times, and assigned requirements (freight units) are shown. Stage-dependent block statuses—one for planning and one for execution of the stage—can be checked on this tab.

- **Utilization**
  The utilization of the freight order is visualized on this tab.

- **Subcontracting**
  The **Subcontracting** tab shows all information related to the subcontracting process. This includes the carrier ranking, continuous move information (Section 7.1), and tendering process documentation (Section 7.3).

- **Document Flow**

  The document flow lists all business documents that have a direct or indirect relationship to the freight order. Predecessor documents of freight orders that are linked here include the following:

  - Freight units
  - Order-based transportation requirements (OTRs)
  - Delivery-based transportation requirements (DTRs)
  - Forwarding orders
  - Deliveries
  - Sales orders (SOs), purchase orders (POs), or stock transfer orders (STOs)

  A successor document would be the freight settlement document. Both predecessor and successor documents are displayed in a hierarchical structure.

- **Charges**

  This tab shows the calculation result and all individual charges for external (carrier) settlement. How the charges are determined is the focus of Chapter 10.

- **Execution**

  On the **Execution** tab, you can compare expected and actual dates and times of the events for this freight order, as well as report events. SAP Event Management integration is explained in Chapter 8, Section 8.2.

- **Notes**

  This tab allows the display of freight order texts in different languages.

- **Attachments**

  This tab allows you to link files and URLs to the freight order.

- **Statuses**

  The freight order can be monitored using various statuses:

  - The lifecycle status shows whether the business document is new, in process, completed, or canceled.
  - The fixing status prevents changing existing planning results (e.g., you're not allowed to add additional freight units to a fixed freight order). The reason can be that the freight order has been subcontracted and the carrier has confirmed the requested quantities. Adding freight units at this point could lead to situations in which the carrier can't transport the additional (unconfirmed) freight units. For manual planning activities, you can specify to ignore the fixing status in the manual planning settings of the planning profile.

- The subcontracting status deals with the current status of the subcontracting process (e.g., whether a carrier has already been assigned), and the corresponding confirmation status shows whether the carrier has confirmed this assignment. Additionally, the invoicing status shows whether an invoice has been received for the freight order, and the dispute case status shows whether a dispute has been created.

- The execution status is adapted based on the execution information.

- The manifest status shows whether documents have been created for the freight order.

- The customs status is set based on information from SAP Global Trade Services (SAP GTS) (see Chapter 9, Section 9.1).

- Consistency check statuses (for the document and cross-document) report the integrity of the business document data.

- **Blocking Information**
  A freight order can be blocked for planning, execution, and invoicing. This is controlled with three separate blocking statuses available on the **Blocking Information** tab. Blocks can be set and removed manually and automatically. Manual blocks can be defined for an entire business document or only for individual document items or stages.

  You can set multiple planning or execution blocks and choose from different block reasons. If blocks were set in a predecessor document, blocks are set by the system automatically. In this case, the information displayed includes which predecessor document caused the block, the type and reason for the block, the date on which the block was created, and the person responsible. When removing a block, a comment can be entered that is stored along with the information regarding which user has removed the block and when.

  The invoicing block is set automatically or manually but can't be propagated from a predecessor document.

- **Administrative Data**
  The administrative data shows information about the creation and latest change date/time and user.

- **Change Documents**
  If change tracking has been activated in the corresponding freight order type, the change documents allow you to keep track of who changed what in the freight order.

- **Internal Charges**
  The **Internal Charges** tab shows the calculation result and all individual charges for internal settlement. Internal settlement is covered in Chapter 12, Section 12.3.5.

- **Terms and Conditions**
  Terms and conditions include information about the incoterms for the freight order and about the value of goods (for customs and insurance).

- **Cost Distribution**
  The **Cost Distribution** tab shows how the charges (from the **Charges** tab) are distributed among the cargo transported by the freight order. If goods for two customers (and therefore originating from two SOs) are transported together, the transportation cost has to be borne by these two accounting objects. How the costs are split is shown here (see also Chapter 11, Section 11.2).

- **Output Management**
  Print documents or electronic messages can be the result of the output process and are listed here based on their action status (**Unprocessed Actions**, **Successfully Processed Actions**, and **Errors**). Output actions can be generated and triggered from here. More details about this topic are provided in Chapter 8.

- **Customs**
  The **Customs** tab displays customs-relevant information (see Chapter 9, Section 9.1, for details).

- **Overview**
  The **Overview** tab displays the logistical information about the freight order in a hierarchical view similar to the freight order details in the transportation cockpit (see also Chapter 6, Section 6.3). The displayed hierarchy consists of the following levels: vehicle resource, location, freight unit, and freight unit item. You can define appointment times for each stop in the **Overview** tab and the **Stages** tab.

- **Map**
  On this tab, the exact route of the freight order is shown on a map.

- **Drivers**
  If the driver settings can be changed in the freight order (based on Customizing **Transportation Management** • **Freight Order Management** • **Freight Order** • **Define Freight Order Types**), you change the number of required drivers (single driver, driver team, not relevant) and driver assignment type (per stage, per freight order) here. Correspondingly, drivers can be displayed and assigned/removed.

- **Service Orders**
  Service orders related to the freight order are displayed on this tab. Service orders

are listed here and on the item level in the **Items** tab depending on whether they relate to the complete document or only to individual items.

- **Document References**
  The **Document References** tab shows additional external references.

- **Handling Codes**
  This tab is invisible if not personalized and available only for freight orders and air freight bookings. Handling codes are used to model certain properties of the freight (e.g., whether a unit load device [ULD] can be loaded only on the lower deck).

- **Transportation Dependencies**
  The **Transportation Dependencies** tab shows logistical information from dependent freight order management documents (e.g., freight booking for the main carriage of a freight unit assigned to the freight order, if the freight order represents the pre-carriage).

- **Communication History**
  The communication with carriers is listed here. This includes inbound and outbound messages, carrier's document number, and stage information from the XML messages.

Rail Freight Orders

Compared to road freight orders, which has been the focus of this chapter, freight orders for rail have some specifics. They can represent a train with one or more locomotives and one or more railcars. If several locomotives need to be assigned, they have to be modeled as multi-items. Only one locomotive can be assigned on the header level, which is relevant for scheduling and incompatibilities. The other locomotives can be assigned as subitems of the multi-item. Railcar items can come from railcar units that are assigned to the rail freight orders (similar to trailer units assigned to road freight orders) or can be created directly in the rail freight order. Cargo items are then assigned to railcars. Multi-items can also be used to assign railcars of the same category instead of assigning each individual railcar.

For the most part, the rail freight order UI (**Order Management** • **Edit Rail Freight Order**) is similar to the one for road freight orders. For rail freight orders, the **General Data** tab shows the source and destination rail location, the number of railcars, and whether there are multiple executing carriers.

On the **Stages** tab, you can specify the invoicing carrier, which invoices the shipper for the corresponding stages. This is commonly referred to as "rule 11" in rail scenarios in North America. In these rail scenarios, the electronic bill of lading is sent to just one carrier. This carrier then forwards the routing instructions to all of the invoicing and executing carriers involved. This carrier is usually the carrier responsible for the first or last main stage. In rule 11 scenarios, one carrier accepts the actual rail freight order, but the invoices for the individual stages are submitted by all involved carriers assigned to the different stages.

The **Items** tab indicates the position of the railcar in the train, equipment groups and types, and railcar details, such as whether the railcar is owned by the shipper or carrier. On this tab, you can change the handling execution status of your cargo and the cargo execution status of your railcars. Any change of one status adjusts the other. For example, if you set the cargo item to **Loaded**, the system also changes the cargo execution status of the corresponding railcar to **Loaded**.

The **Routing** button in the rail freight order UI initiates the following steps to determine possible routing options from the source to the destination rail location:

1. Determine all default routes for which the first and last location (or transportation zone) matches the source and destination rail location.

2. For each default route, determine freight agreement items for each executing carrier in the default route filtering by trade lane and commodity code.

3. For each default route, determine rates from the freight agreement item for all location combinations within the default route.

4. Show a list of routing options and rating alternatives. A rating alternative includes any combination of rates from different executing carriers from the source to the destination rail location.

5. Based on the selection of a routing option from the list, the system generates the stages of the rail freight order.

For further details on rail freight orders specific to planning, see Chapter 6, Section 6.4.

Many actions can be triggered from the freight order UI. The user can change statuses on the document header level and on the item level for the cargo included in the freight order. In addition, planning activities (scheduling the freight order, starting the transportation cockpit, and creating a load plan) and actions related to subcontracting (e.g., carrier selection, tendering, and document transfer to the carrier) can be initiated here. Charge calculation and the creation of a freight settlement document, creation and printing of freight documents, and actions related to the logistical integration (creating deliveries, sending and cancellation of loading/unloading instructions) can be triggered via buttons on the freight order UI.

From the freight order worklist (**Order Management • Freight Order (Worklist)**), it's also possible to mass change many freight orders at the same time. Data to be changed in mass include transportation data (e.g., means of transport, resource), carrier data (e.g., SCAC, executing carrier), and source and destination data (e.g., locations, dates, and times).

Planning Profile

The planning profile includes some important information for the freight order, such as whether capacity violations result in an error or warning and which incompatibility settings need to be watched. Therefore, a planning profile needs to be associated with the freight order even when the freight order needs to be changed in transactions that aren't planning related, such as the freight order UI.

For that purpose, a planning profile is stored in the **Plan_Prof_Key** field of the root node of business object /SCMTMS/TOR. This field is populated with the planning profile that has been used to create the freight order (e.g., in the transportation cockpit or via a background planning run) or via evaluation of a condition with condition type /SCMTMS/TOR_PLN_PROF. If no planning profile can be determined, then the defaults are applied (e.g., no incompatibility check).

7.2.2   Freight Order Items

Items in freight order management documents can represent either capacity or demand (with the exception being containers, which can represent both). Freight order management items that haven't been transferred from predecessor documents can be changed in the freight order or freight booking.

The following items represent capacity:

- Vehicle resources (active)
- Passive vehicle resources (e.g., trailers and railcars)
- Containers

The following items represent demand:

- Containers
- Packages (e.g., pallets or cartons)
- Products

In addition, nonphysical items (services) can be assigned to items of the freight document. Capacity items are displayed on the **General Data** tab, while demand items are displayed on the **Items** tab of the freight order UI.

Except for railcar units, each freight order management business document can have only one main item and any number of subitems. Railcar units can have several main items. The item hierarchy defines which items can be loaded into which other items; for example, a product is loaded onto a pallet, which is loaded into a container, which is loaded onto a trailer. You can define item types in Customizing by following the menu path **Transportation Management · Freight Order Management · Define Item Types for Freight Order Management** and defining which item types are valid for a document type by assigning the item type to the freight document type (e.g., for freight orders, **Transportation Management · Freight Order Management · Freight Order · Define Freight Order Type**).

7.2.3   Special Processes with Freight Orders

This section summarizes some special scenarios that can be represented by freight orders. First, freight orders for pickup and delivery are focused on allowing you to model the transfer between, for example, a gateway and a port, in an ocean freight booking. Then we discuss customer self-delivery and pickup, which are two non-transport-relevant stages in the transportation chain. Finally, we examine the parcel process and the integration of SAP ERP shipments into freight orders.

Freight Order for Pickup and Freight Order for Delivery

Freight orders for pickup and freight orders for delivery can be used in an ocean freight process or an air freight process. In an ocean freight process, they are created out of the freight booking for the transfer of containers from the export gateway to the port of loading (freight order for pickup) and for the transfer from the port of destination to the import gateway (freight order for delivery), as shown in Figure 7.14. In an air freight process, these orders are created similarly between the gateways and the airline's delivery/pickup address to transport either ULDs or loose cargo.

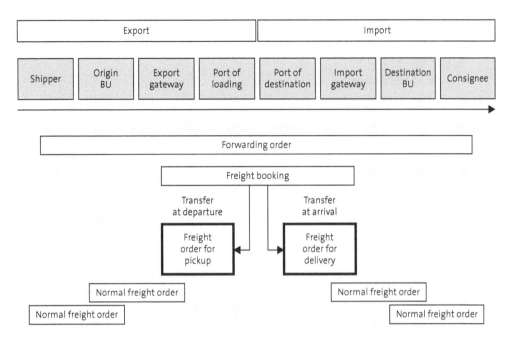

Figure 7.14 Freight Order for Pickup and Freight Order for Delivery

A prerequisite for this process is that the freight booking (ocean or air) has been created from the export gateway to the import gateway. In this situation, the freight orders for pickup and delivery can be created from the freight booking UI (**Items** tab) or from a freight booking worklist (**Order Management · Freight Bookings (Worklist)**; in SAP TM 9.6, the menu path is **Freight Order Management · Air/Ocean · Overview Air/Ocean Freight Bookings**). The freight order type used for the creation of these freight orders is defined in the Customizing of the freight booking type (**Transportation Management · Freight Order Management · Freight Booking · Define Freight Booking Types**). You can create one or several freight orders for pickup and delivery from each freight booking, but you can also consolidate freight from several freight bookings into one freight order for pickup and delivery.

The advantage of tight integration between the freight booking and its freight orders for pickup and delivery is that changes in one document automatically update the other document. The following information is copied from the freight booking to the freight orders for pickup and delivery:

- Seal information and changes to seals
- Item changes
- Location changes
- Date/time changes
- Adjustment of handling execution status

The following information is copied from the freight orders for pickup and delivery to the corresponding freight booking:

- Change of cargo receipt status
- Reporting/resolution of discrepancies

Customer Self-Delivery or Pickup

Freight orders for customer self-delivery and pickup are only used for documentation purposes. They offer limited functionality and aren't relevant for planning or charge calculation and settlement. This is indicated in the Customizing of the freight order type (**Transportation Management • Freight Order Management • Freight Order • Define Freight Order Types**), which is marked as a freight order for customer self-delivery or pickup (see Figure 7.12), and the use of a "light version" of the freight order UI by defining Web Dynpro application configuration /SCMTMS/FRE_ORDER_SDCP in the freight order type Customizing.

Freight orders for customer self-delivery and pickup can be created directly from the forwarding order UI (**Actual Route** tab) or a forwarding order worklist (**Order Management • Forwarding Orders (Worklist)**) in an air or ocean process. If these freight orders are created based on the forwarding order, it's a prerequisite that the corresponding stages are defined based on a stage type with either category **Customer Self-Delivery** or **Customer Pick-up** (in Customizing: **Transportation Management • Forwarding Order Management • Define Stage Types**). In addition, these stages need to be set to **Never Relevant for Planning** in the stage type sequence of the movement type used in the forwarding order (in Customizing: **Transportation Management • Forwarding Order Management • Define Stage Type Sequence for Movement Types**) or in the corresponding stage profile (in Customizing: **Transportation Management • Forwarding Order Management • Define Stage Profiles**).

Parcel Process

A parcel process is represented in SAP TM by freight orders from one shipping point to several consignees based on deliveries (or DTRs) and includes the following steps:

1. **Creation of parcel shipments**
   A parcel shipment is a freight unit. For each delivery, exactly one freight unit must be created.

2. **Determination of direct shipment options**
   Determination of direct shipment options can be triggered manually from the freight unit UI or automatically upon the creation of the freight unit by configuring **Automatic Determination of Direct Shipment Options** in the Customizing of the freight unit type (**Transportation Management • Planning • Define Freight Unit Type**; see Figure 7.15).

3. **Assignment of parcel shipment to a parcel freight order**
   The assignment of the parcel shipment to a parcel freight order is governed by the **Direct Shipment Strategy** (see Figure 7.15). Strategy **Dso_Result** assigns the freight units automatically to an existing freight order or creates a new freight order and assigns the freight unit. Strategy **Dso_Def** only creates the direct shipment options and leaves the assignment to a freight order to a user or background report /SCMTMS/ DIRECT_SHIPMENT_BATCH.

   Suitable freight orders must have matching source location, pickup date, and carrier.

4. **Editing the parcel freight order**
   Parcel freight orders require specific Customizing settings in the freight order type (**Transportation Management • Freight Order Management • Freight Order • Define Freight Order Types**). The default setting for the sequence type of stops in the parcel process is **Star-Shaped Based on FU-Stages**. To allow for printing of parcel manifests and labels, you can use /SCMTMS/TOR_PRINT_PARCEL_ROOT as an additional output profile, and to adapt the UI for parcel requirements, you can use /SCMTMS/FRE_ORDER_MANIFEST as Web Dynpro application configuration.

5. **Sending and confirmation from carrier**
   The freight order is sent to the carrier and confirmed or rejected by the carrier.

6. **Document printing and execution**
   The parcel manifest and labels can be printed from the **Output Management** tab of the freight order UI. After the **Cargo Ready for Loading** status has been set to start execution and tracking, no automatic assignment of additional freight units to the

freight order is allowed, and the parcel freight order is processed like any other freight order.

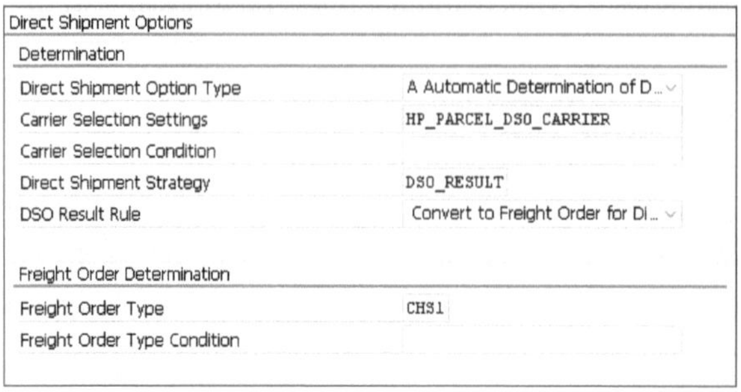

Direct Shipment Options	
Determination	
Direct Shipment Option Type	A Automatic Determination of D... ∨
Carrier Selection Settings	HP_PARCEL_DSO_CARRIER
Carrier Selection Condition	
Direct Shipment Strategy	DSO_RESULT
DSO Result Rule	Convert to Freight Order for Di... ∨
Freight Order Determination	
Freight Order Type	CHS1
Freight Order Type Condition	

Figure 7.15 Direct Shipment Options

SAP ERP Shipments

In SAP TM 9.6 for the time being, freight orders can also be created based on SAP ERP shipments (Section 7.2.1). Shippers that want to continue to use their already established processes in SAP ERP (LE-TRA) and want to use functionality in SAP TM that isn't available there can take advantage of this option. Use cases include processes involving carrier selection, tendering, or Transportation Charge Management and settlement. When a freight order is being created based on an SAP ERP shipment, the system first determines the freight order type. You can define the freight order type in three ways (sidecar only):

- In Customizing using a mapping table between SAP ERP shipment types and freight order types (**SAP Transportation Management • Transportation Management • Integration • ERP Logistics Integration • Shipment Integration • Assign Freight Order Types to ERP Shipment Types**)

- Using a condition with condition type /SCMTMS/FRO_TYPE_SHP

- Using the default type defined in freight order type Customizing (**SAP Transportation Management • Transportation Management • Freight Order Management • Freight Order • Define Freight Order Types**)

Note that SAP TM can't create freight orders based on any type of SAP ERP shipment because only certain stop sequence types (Section 7.2.1) are allowed in SAP TM. Thus, any SAP ERP shipment that creates a freight order needs to respect this limitation. Once created, the freight order can be used for subcontracting purposes (e.g., carrier selection and tendering) and for updating the SAP ERP shipment with the results of this process.

7.2.4   Service Orders

Cleaning containers, fumigating, and performing security services or documentation are typical examples of services that can occur for items of a freight order or freight booking. The *service order* is used to account for and track services, calculate charges, and enable settlement of the charges for services that have been provided for individual items in a freight order/booking or for the entire freight order/booking.

Service orders are created from the freight order/booking UI (refer to Chapter 5, Section 5.4). The **Service Order** tab in the freight order/booking UI displays an overview of the service orders created for the freight order/booking, while similar information for items is provided on the **Items** tab of the freight order/booking UI. The service order UI (see Figure 7.16) provides the following information:

- **General Data**
  The **General Data** tab shows the involved parties (purchasing organization and service provider), as well as the service order type and status information. The service order type is defined in Customizing (**Transportation Management · Freight Order Management · Service Order · Define Service Order Types**). In the service order type Customizing, you define options similar to those in the freight order type Customizing. That is, you can enable charge calculation and settlement, define number range settings, define output options, define how organizational units are determined for service orders of this type, and define change controller and execution tracking settings.

- **Services**
  Under **Services**, the link to the freight order/booking or freight order/booking items is displayed, as well as the service types that have been or will be provided for the freight order/booking or freight order/booking items, their location, and the execution time per service type. Service types are defined in Customizing (**Transportation Management · Basic Functions · General Settings · Define Service Types**). Service types can be assigned to item types (**Transportation Management · Freight Order Management · Define Item Types for Freight Order Management**), which are then linked to service order types (**Transportation Management · Freight Order Management · Service Order · Define Service Order Types**).

The **Charges, Document Flow, Notes, Attachments, Change Documents, Output Management**, and **Administrative Data** tabs of the service order UI provide similar information as the corresponding tabs on the freight order UI covered in Section 7.2.1.

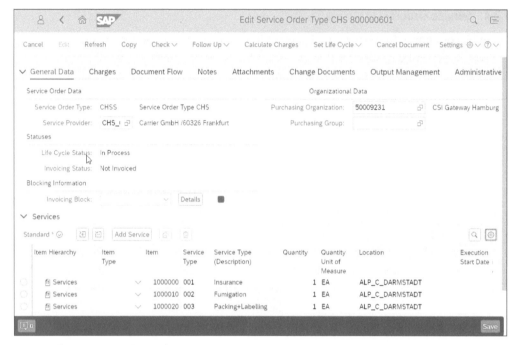

Figure 7.16 Service Order UI

You can edit or display the service order by following the menu path **Order Management • Edit Service Order**, by selecting the service order from a worklist (**Order Management • Service Order (Worklist)**), or via the document flow of a related document (e.g., freight booking).

Edit or Display Service Orders in SAP TM 9.6

To edit or display the service order in SAP TM 9.6, the menu paths change. Follow the menu path **Freight Order Management • Service Order • Edit Service Order**, or select the service order from a worklist (**Freight Order Management • Service Order • Overview Service Orders**).

7.3   Freight Tendering

After you've created a freight order and potentially identified a suitable carrier, the final step prior to executing the freight order is tendering. The freight tendering process can be used to tender freight orders to one or more carriers. Numerous process variants exist for this process, as shown in one variant in Figure 7.17.

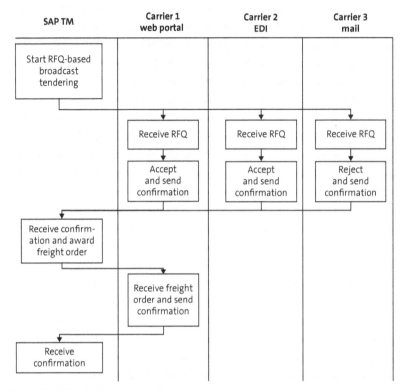

Figure 7.17 Tendering Process Example

In this example, you initiate the tendering process in SAP TM by sending a freight request for quotation (RFQ) for a freight order to several carriers. These carriers receive and review the RFQ via different communication channels (web portal, electronic data interchange [EDI], etc.). The carriers can accept or reject the tendered freight orders and quote prices in a freight quotation. SAP TM evaluates the carriers' responses and awards the freight order to one carrier (carrier 1, in the example). This carrier receives the freight order and acknowledges receipt of the freight order with a confirmation message.

In this section, we'll walk through the configuration for freight tendering, the tendering process, and your communication options focusing on the SAP Logistics Business Network.

7.3.1   Configuration

The tendering process can be configured in various ways using a tendering profile (**Profiles and Settings · Create Tendering Profile**), as displayed in Figure 7.18.

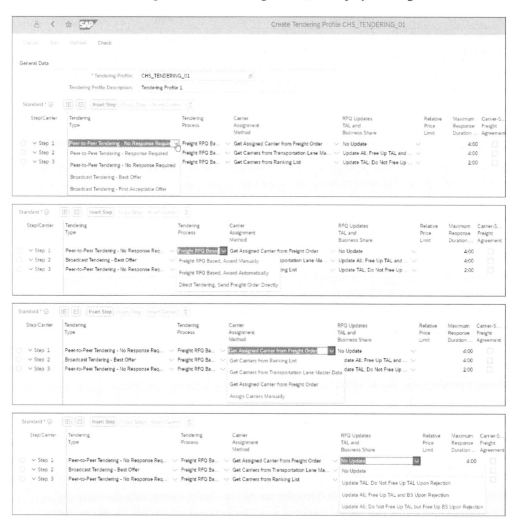

Figure 7.18 Tendering Profile

Tendering processes can consist of several steps, for example, because you want to limit the number of carriers to those you prefer in a separate step before you publish an RFQ to a larger group after none of the preferred carriers has responded in the previous step. In the tendering profile, you can combine different steps. The first step can be a peer-to-peer tendering process with the preferred carrier selected based on carrier selection (Section 7.1). A broadcast tendering to all available carriers defined in the transportation lane is a second step to quickly make an assignment if the preferred option (step one) failed. You can define the individual steps of a tendering process in the tendering profile. For each step, you define the following criteria:

- **Tendering Type**
  The tendering type specifies the auctioning mechanism that is used in the tendering process. Four available tendering types are offered:
  - **Peer-to-Peer Tendering - Response Required** initiates the tendering process with one or more carriers sequentially. This means that the system waits for a negative response from the first carrier before contacting the second (or third, etc.) carrier. **Response Required** indicates that the lack of a response is considered a rejection.
  - **Peer-to-Peer Tendering - No Response Required** also initiates the tendering process with one or more carriers sequentially, but, in this case, the system treats no response within the specified duration as acceptance of the tendered freight order. This tendering type can be used if carrier acceptance is the usual and expected behavior and thus reduces the number of messages exchanged between the involved parties.
  - **Broadcast Tendering - Best Offer** is an auctioning mechanism in which several carriers are contacted simultaneously. The evaluation of the different offers is based on the quoted price of the carrier.
  - **Broadcast Tendering - First Acceptable Offer** is also an auctioning mechanism in which several carriers are contacted simultaneously, but here the focus is on a fast response rather than the best price. With this tendering type, the first carrier to quote a price below the specified price limit is chosen.

- **Tendering Process**
  The tendering process can be specified as **Freight RFQ Based** or **Direct** tendering. The difference is that in the first method, a freight RFQ is sent to the carrier, whereas in the second method, the freight order is sent directly. The freight RFQ process always requires an award step (manual or automatic) after the freight quotation has been received from the carrier. The award step determines which carrier receives the freight order, and the freight order itself is only sent at this stage of the process as a separate message. In the direct tendering process, the freight order

is automatically awarded to the carrier if the carrier hasn't rejected it explicitly within the maximum duration.

■ **Carrier Assignment Method**
An important decision in each step of the tendering process is the selection of the carriers that are included in each step. Four different options are available:

– The carriers can be taken from the carrier ranking list, which has been created by the carrier selection process (Section 7.1) or selected manually.

– Carriers can be retrieved from the transportation lane.

– The carrier that is currently assigned to the freight order can be used.

– Carriers are manually assigned to a process step.

■ **RFQ Updates TAL and Business Share**
Section 7.1 introduced transportation allocations and business shares as a means of influencing the carrier selection decision based on, for example, contractual obligations. How are transportation allocations and business shares considered in a tendering process? If a minimum allocation of three freight orders per week has been agreed upon with a carrier, how is a rejection of a freight RFQ accounted for? Does this freight RFQ count against the minimum allocation? The answers to these questions can be influenced by this setting. The following options are available:

– No update

– Update of transportation allocations, but no update (free up) upon rejection

– Update of transportation allocations and business shares, and update (free up) of both upon rejection

– Update of transportation allocations and business shares and update (free up) of transportation allocation, but no update (free up) of business share upon rejection

■ **Relative Price Limit**
The relative price limit is important for the automatic award mechanism of freight orders to a carrier. It's used as a threshold to avoid awarding a freight order based on too high a price quotation. The relative price limit is therefore relevant for all four tendering types.

■ **Maximum Response Duration**
The maximum response duration specifies the time limit within which SAP TM waits for carriers' responses. With tendering type **Broadcast Tendering - Best Offer**, it specifies the time after which the best available offer is selected.

- **Carrier-Specific Freight Agreement**
  If this checkbox is selected, the price limit is calculated per carrier with the carrier's specific freight agreement.

- **Price Details**
  The price details define whether the calculated price limit is visible to the carrier as a lump sum (**Price Limit Only**) or whether the full hierarchy of charges calculated in Transportation Charge Management is shown (**Charge Hierarchy**). Depending on the visibility settings, the carrier can change either the total amount or the total value of the individual elements in the charge hierarchy.

- **Visibility Settings**
  The visibility settings are defined in Customizing (**Transportation Management** · **Freight Order Management** · **Tendering** · **Define General Settings for Tendering**) and determine the following:

  - Whether the price limit is disclosed to the carrier (read-only) or not (hidden)
  - Whether the submitted price can be edited, is read-only, or is hidden
  - Whether the stop dates can be edited, are read-only, or are hidden

  This allows you to specify whether the carrier is allowed to change stop dates of stages of the freight order to better accommodate the freight order into its vehicles' schedules. Any changes made by the carrier need to be reviewed to determine whether they fit into your plans before the freight order is awarded.

Which tendering profile is chosen can be decided manually or is specified in the tendering settings of the freight order type (see Figure 7.19). The process settings and communication settings can be defined per freight order type, based on a condition (with condition type /SCMTMS/TEND), or per using default settings. The tendering profile is part of the process settings defined in Customizing (**Transportation Management** · **Freight Order Management** · **Tendering** · **Define General Settings for Tendering**).

Figure 7.19 Tendering Settings

In addition to the visibility settings, process settings, and communication settings, you can define the following in the tendering Customizing:

- Rejection reason codes
- Email and short message service (SMS) content, if these communication methods will be used
- Carrier-specific communication settings
- Default settings for the tendering process

7.3.2   Tendering Process

The tendering process can be initiated interactively from the freight order UI or from the transportation cockpit. Additionally, you can initiate the tendering process in the background via report /SCMTMS/TOR_TENDERING_BATCH (see Figure 7.20) or by defining strategy **Tend_Start** as a creation strategy of the freight order. To be run automatically in the background, report /SCMTMS/TEND_CONT_PROCESS must be regularly scheduled. This report evaluates the responses received from the carriers.

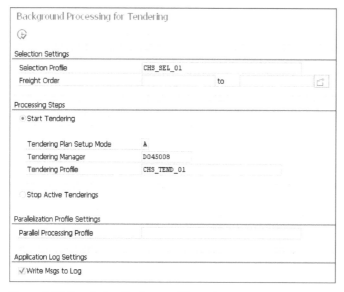

Figure 7.20 Tendering Background Report

Freight RFQs and freight quotations can be monitored by the responsible user via worklists (**Order Management • Tendering (Worklist)**); in SAP TM 9.6, the menu path is

Freight Order Management • Road • Overview Tendering). Here, alerts are visible in separate queries (**Freight Quotations to be Reviewed**, **Unsuccessful Tenderings**, and **Tenderings Stopped Due to FO Changes**).

You can monitor the tendering process for a freight order with its individual steps in the **Subcontracting** tab of the freight order UI. Figure 7.21 shows an example. In the first step, the carrier **CHS_CAR** accepted **RFQ 4600004607** and was therefore awarded with the freight order. Because the first step of this tendering process is peer-to-peer tendering, no RFQ has been created for the second carrier CHS_CAR_01. The second step in the tendering profile, which is a broadcast tendering to a group of three carriers, has been omitted completely because of the successful completion of the first step. If a carrier submits more than one freight quotation, the system considers only the last freight quotation of each carrier that is submitted within the maximum duration.

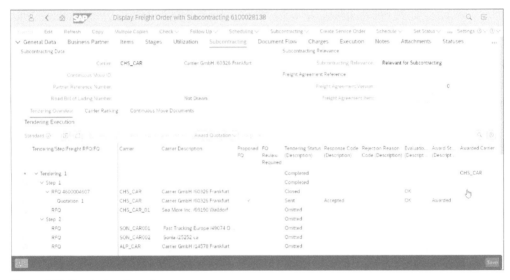

Figure 7.21 Tendering Overview

7.3.3   Freight Tendering with SAP Logistics Business Network

From a communication perspective, the interaction between shippers or LSPs and carriers can be via EDI, email, SMS, or web portal. From SAP S/4HANA 1709 and SAP TM 9.3, integration with SAP Logistics Business Network is supported. SAP Logistics Business Network is a cloud solution for logistics collaboration. The infrastructure, onboarding, support, and operations are provided by SAP, while applications and content can be provided from SAP and partners. A general overview of SAP Logistics Business Network is provided in Chapter 13.

Collaboration Portal

The Collaboration Portal is a web portal hosted by the owner of the SAP TM system (only available in SAP TM 9.6). The Collaboration Portal offers similar functionality as SAP Logistics Business Network in the area of freight order management:

- Freight RFQ
- Freight quotation
- Freight orders for confirmation
- Event handling

Related to tendering, there are two relevant processes that are supported by SAP TM and SAP Logistics Business Network. The first one is the administrative onboarding process, which is illustrated in Figure 7.22. The second process is the processing of freight RFQs and freight quotations illustrated in Figure 7.23.

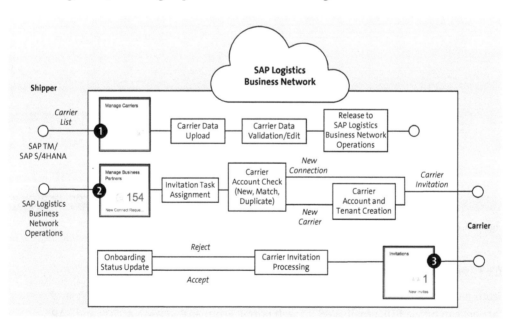

Figure 7.22 Onboarding Process with SAP Logistics Business Network

Figure 7.22 shows the three steps of the onboarding procedure. A prerequisite to initiate the process is that the shipper has purchased an account on SAP Cloud Platform and created users for this account with relevant roles. In addition, the purchasing organization used in a subcontracting/tendering process needs to be assigned a unique network ID created from the SAP Logistics Business Network. This unique network ID is assigned on the **Identification** tab of the business partner linked to the purchasing organization (**Master Data · Define Business Partner**).

The first step in the onboarding process is the creation of a list of carriers that the shipper wants to collaborate with on SAP Logistics Business Network. This list can be created using report /SCMTMS/LBN_CARRLIST. In the Manage Carriers app, this list is uploaded to SAP Logistics Business Network. It can be edited and validated and finally needs to be submitted.

Once submitted to SAP Logistics Business Network, the SAP Logistics Business Network backend operations team manages the carrier invitations. This is the second step of the process. Depending on whether the carrier already has an account and/or connection, the invitation is linked to an existing account and connection, or a new one needs to be created. The carrier can respond to invitations in the Invitation app by accepting or rejecting. When a carrier accepts an invitation to connect with the shipper/LSP, the unique network ID of the carrier must be updated. The unique carrier network IDs can be updated in SAP TM by downloading them from the Manage Carriers app in SAP Logistics Business Network and uploading to SAP TM via report /SCMTMS/LBN_BPID_UPD.

Figure 7.23 shows the processing of freight RFQs and freight quotations in SAP Logistics Business Network. A freight RFQ is sent from SAP TM to SAP Logistics Business Network, where it can be accessed from the carrier using an Internet connection. The freight RFQs are displayed in a list view or detailed view, showing relevant data (source location, destination, location, intermediate stops, dates and times, items to be transported). The carrier can filter, sort, and search within the freight RFQs and accept or reject one or more freight RFQs at the same time. Reason codes for rejection can be defined and are sent from SAP Logistics Business Network to the SAP TM system. The carrier can also accept freight RFQs with changes (price and dates) and add a text message. After the carriers' responses have been processed (in SAP TM as described before), the status of their quotations (**Pending**, **Award**, or **Reject**) can be checked by the carrier in the Freight Quotations app.

SAP Logistics Business Network can also be used by carriers to confirm freight orders to the ordering party (shipper or LSP), as shown in Figure 7.23. In this process, freight orders are sent for confirmation from SAP TM to SAP Logistics Business Network. In the Freight Orders for Confirmation app, the carrier can confirm or reject freight orders. The carrier is also allowed to propose changes or add a text, which becomes available on the freight order UI as a note.

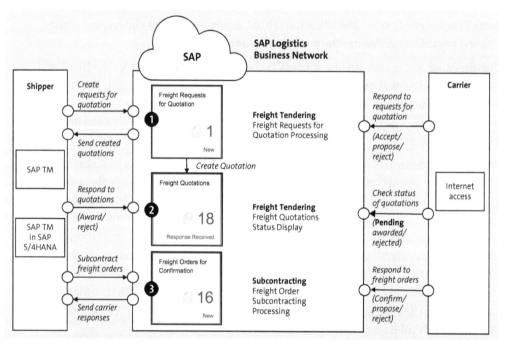

Figure 7.23 Processes in Freight Order Management (SAP Logistics Business Network)

The last process in the area of freight order management that is supported using SAP Logistics Business Network is event reporting. Carriers can report expected and unexpected events for the freight order on SAP Logistics Business Network. Comments, reason codes, and attachments can be added for the event. Supported events include the following:

- Departure
- Arrival
- Proof of delivery
- Delay

Connecting to External Marketplaces

Frequently, marketplaces are used to bring together companies that want to ship goods with carriers that offer these services. With small enhancements, the standard freight tendering process can be used to take advantage of freight marketplaces. In this process, the marketplace is specified as the carrier to which the freight RFQ is sent. The marketplace assigns the real carrier, and its response includes the real carrier and price information. Thus, based on the marketplace's response, only the real carrier and its price need to be assigned to the freight order.

7.4   Summary

This chapter has dealt with freight orders that are created primarily as a result of planning, especially in land transportation. These can get subcontracted with a carrier selected via the carrier selection process, the tendering process, or a combination of both. The carrier selection process is typically based on cost and can consider several constraints, such as business shares or transportation allocations. The tendering process can deal with a group of carriers sequentially or simultaneously and combine several tendering steps into one process.

Now that the planning process is complete, the next chapter covers the view on freight orders from the execution perspective, including the printing of freight documents.

Chapter 8

Transportation Execution and Monitoring

SAP Transportation Management, SAP Event Management, and SAP Global Track and Trace provide documentation and status management as well as track and trace capabilities for end-to-end cargo movements.

Transportation execution and monitoring includes a set of process steps and corresponding functionalities in SAP Transportation Management (SAP TM), SAP Event Management, and the new SAP Global Track and Trace that allow you to organize and document activities involving the physical movement and handling of cargo along the supply chain. The SAP system supports employees working in documentation and freight-handling departments of logistics service providers (LSPs) and shippers' logistics departments to fulfill their responsibilities in a compliant manner and create an audit trail for the actual cargo movement.

Freight movement processes are executed and monitored using one or more of the following components:

- **SAP TM Freight Order Management**
  Before and during execution, the Freight Order Management component allows you to create documents related to the cargo movement and its compliance to document actual quantities and details of the cargo. You can record discrepancies that occur between order capture and planning on the one hand and physical checking and handling on the other. Moving cargo also results in updates of order and cargo status, such as documenting a loading status either manually out of the SAP TM system or automatically in conjunction with SAP Event Management. The organizational aspect of the cargo movement is supported by export/import handling, which provides you with the handover capability between multiple organizational units along the path of a cargo move.

- **SAP Event Management**

  SAP Event Management is an extremely flexible, efficient, and generic software tool for management and visualization of track and trace processes, status management processes, and key performance indicators (KPIs) based on these process types. You can use SAP Event Management in logistics and beyond to automatically record activity information related to cargo movements, order processes, resource lifecycles, and financial management aspects related to shipments (e.g., cargo prepayment).

- **SAP Global Track and Trace**

  Fueled by the innovation of the SAP logistics technology, SAP Global Track and Trace was first released in 2018 as a new tool for collaborative process tracking. From technology and use cases, this tool was designed for parties engaging in a joint process in the public cloud. The first releases are limited, however, to scenarios driven out of SAP S/4HANA.

In this chapter, we explain the features and background of transportation execution and tracking.

8.1   Transportation Execution

Transportation execution comprises all activities involved with handling and documenting shipments in transit. It's more than just tracking a vehicle on the road: it includes recording any changes to the planned transport and handovers to other business partners or entities.

In previous chapters, we mainly talked about how to use the SAP TM functionality to record, plan, and subcontract transportation requirements. Actual pallets, containers, and wagons hadn't yet been loaded, let alone put into motion.

The Freight Order Management component within the SAP TM functionality not only supports transportation management during the planning phase but is also used after the vehicle has left the loading location.

Before the vehicle actually leaves for the transit, the loading process gathers new information that might be relevant for the shipper or carrier. So far, we've been dealing with planned quantities, but now the carrier has to deal with actual quantities, which could differ from the freight quantities ordered. These discrepancies between ordered and actual quantities can be recorded and, depending on the agreement between the ordering party and the carrier, taken into consideration for charge calculation.

In international, multimodal transports, more than one LSP unit is often involved in the overall transportation. Sometimes importing in the destination country can be very specialized, and a local LSP unit or organization can support the import leg much better than a foreign LSP unit. Therefore, we can observe a handover between the exporting LSP unit (which is also the single point of contact for the customer) and the local importing LSP unit.

In addition, transportation isn't only about moving goods from point A to point B. Sometimes it seems like it's more about moving paper or information from point A to point B. Waybills, customs declarations, bills of lading, and other documents need to be generated, printed, and transported with the goods or transmitted in advance. Often legal requirements also need to be respected.

More than moving goods from one place to another, transportation execution involves significant administrative effort, legal requirements, transparency, and organizational interactions. The Freight Order Management component supports all these areas, so we now delve deeper into each of them to show you how you can leverage these requirements with the SAP TM functionality.

8.1.1 Document Creation

Regardless of which transportation mode is involved, creating, printing, and carrying documents is very important in the transportation process. Depending on the perspective from which we look at the transportation process, several documents are involved. In this section, we concentrate on the creation of bills of lading and waybills.

The difference between these two documents is their legal and practical purposes. The *bill of lading* (B/L) serves as proof that a contract or order has been issued between a shipper and a carrier stating that certain goods need to be transported. A *waybill* is the more logistical document, listing the goods that need to be transported.

However, in a process involving a freight forwarder as an agent between an actual carrier and shipper, the B/L and waybill can mean the same thing. The LSP now issues its own B/L, called the *house bill of lading* (HBL), which is at the same time also called a house waybill. Because waybills are usually seen in the context of the transportation mode, the terminology for waybills is usually used together with the mode of transport (e.g., sea waybill for ocean transports or air waybill for air transports).

If we look at it from a shipper's perspective, for some modes of transport (e.g., ocean), we're obliged to hand over a B/L to the consignee that lists all goods to be transported. The B/L is a legal and negotiable document enabling the receiver—who is usually the consignee—to claim the goods at the port of discharge. On the other hand, the consignee may also sell the goods during ocean transit and hand over the B/L to the buyer.

The LSP or carrier who manages the order for the shipper issues the B/L. For consolidated transportation for different shippers, the LSP issues itself a B/L or receives one from the carrier for the consolidation and issues multiple HBLs, which the LSP provides to the involved shippers.

Making It Simple

Recall that the terminology of waybills is often used in combination with its mode of transport. To make this chapter easier, we use air transportation as an ongoing example from now on; therefore, we refer to *house air waybills* (HAWBs) and *master air waybills* (MAWBs).

HAWBs can be created from the forwarding order as well as from the freight units, freight orders, or freight bookings. By customizing the forwarding order, you can define how the number of the HBL or HAWB should be put together. We talked about this already in Chapter 4, Section 4.2.1. Nevertheless, you can also define in Customizing how the HBL should be composed by defining a process controller strategy that takes over the job of creating HBLs.

Several possibilities are offered with the standard strategies. In general, the HBL is built out of the *items* of a document, not the header data:

- **By shipper and ship-to party**
  All items containing the same shipper and ship-to party combination are consolidated into one HBL. There are also additional, more specific strategies available that group the items on a HBL by container or transportation group of the material in addition to the shipper and ship-to party information.

- **By destination location**
  In some cases, the goods are transported to the same location, but different consignees will later receive the goods. This is the case if an importing business unit will take over the goods at the port of discharge.

- **By forwarding order**
  If the HBL or HAWB is created by an LSP, all items belonging to the same forwarding order can be put together in one document.

- **By freight documents**
  Again, this scenario is built for LSPs. All items planned on the same document on the main carriage are consolidated into one HBL.

Which strategy you use and from which document you would like to create the HBL depends on your business case and industry.

The waybill, on the other hand, is the logistical document passed between two parties cooperating in a transportation business. The waybill document comprises the information about the cargo, transportation route, and terms.

The consumer of a transportation service and the provider of that transportation service share a common number range from which the consumer can draw a number to give to the provider. This number is then a unique referral for both parties of the transportation business. In the SAP TM functionality, the number ranges are stored in *waybill stock IDs* that define agreed-upon number ranges.

Waybills in SAP TM can be separated into house waybills and master waybills. The house waybills represent the transportation documents between the sales side of the company using SAP TM and a sold-to party. The master waybills represent the purchasing document between the company using SAP TM and a carrier. You can compare this differentiation with freight settlement documents and forwarding settlement documents—they are similar-looking documents but are built for different parts of the transportation process.

Waybills Aren't Separate Entities

Other than with freight settlement documents and forwarding settlement documents, waybills aren't represented with their own separate entities in the SAP TM system. Waybills serve as print documents only on the forwarding order and freight orders, freight bookings, and freight units. These documents provide the functionality of drawing the right number. However, there is no separate business object designed for the waybills.

To create waybill stock IDs, you need to carry out some Customizing activities. Remember that the number ranges in SAP TM are stored as waybill stock IDs. To create these waybill stock IDs, you need to define *waybill stock types,* which you can do in Customizing via the IMG menu path **Transportation Management • Master Data • Waybill Stock • Define Waybill Number Stock Types**.

As shown in Figure 8.1, you can customize several details about the waybill number stock before you define the waybill number stock itself. Waybill number stocks are always dependent on the transportation mode, so the assignment of a transportation mode is mandatory in this Customizing activity. With the stock category, you specify whether the number stock is used as a waybill number or as a tracking number.

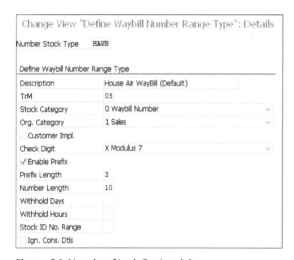

Figure 8.1 Number Stock Customizing

Waybill Numbers and Tracking Numbers

Technically, there is no difference between a waybill number and a *tracking number*. Both numbers are used to identify a transport uniquely in communication between the transportation service consumer and the provider.

However, the different terms are used in different transportation scenarios. Air, sea, road, and rail transportation use the waybill number; we refer to tracking numbers in parcel scenarios.

Later in this chapter, you'll see that tracking numbers are maintained the same way waybill numbers are.

The organization category defines whether the waybill number stock we're creating is supposed to be used for master waybills or house waybills. Recall that house waybills are used between the sales side and a sold-to party, while master waybills are used between the purchasing side and a carrier. Therefore, the house waybill usually represents the entire transportation ordered, and the master waybill represents only a certain transportation leg.

The lower part of the Customizing activity illustrated in Figure 8.1 addresses how the number should be composed. First, you can define that a carrier-specific prefix should be added by selecting the **Enable Prefix** checkbox.

Carrier Prefix

The prefix for the carriers is also defined in Customizing. In the Customizing activity found via the IMG menu path **Transportation Management • Master Data • Business Partner • Define IATA Airline Codes**, you can assign a waybill prefix to the carriers.

In addition, waybill numbers may have a check digit. SAP TM offers two possibilities for automatically adding a check digit to the waybill number. The waybill number is calculated with either Modulus 7 or Modulus 10. If none of the provided calculation rules fit the specific waybill number stock requirements, you can implement custom implementation using a business add-in (BAdI).

Calculation with Modulus

Calculation with modulus is often used in IT. When you use the calculation operation MOD, the base number is first divided by the divisor. But it's the remainder after the division that's important, not the result of the division.

For example: 11 MOD 3 = 2.

As you would expect, the waybill number stock type also defines the general length of the waybill number. The waybill number is always extended with leading zeros to match the waybill number length defined in the waybill stock type.

In certain processes, master waybill numbers can be returned, such as the cancellation of a freight booking for which a waybill number was already assigned. Although the returned number can't be directly reused by other documents, it needs to be withheld for a certain time because the cancellation might be replicated into other systems, as well. Therefore, a withholding time in days and hours can be maintained in the waybill stock type.

After defining a waybill stock type, we can create the actual waybill number ranges. In the SAP Fiori launchpad, you can find the corresponding **Waybill Number Stocks** tile in the **Master Data** tab. Here you can see a personal object worklist (POWL) that differentiates among house waybills, master waybills, and tracking numbers.

Waybill Stocks in SAP TM 9.6

In SAP TM 9.6, you'll find the POWL for waybill stock mentioned in the preceding with menu path **Master Data • General • Overview Waybill Stock**.

When creating a new waybill stock with the **New** button on the top of the POWL list, you'll see that you need to select a waybill stock type first. After you've chosen a waybill stock type, the definitions from Customizing are automatically propagated into the waybill stock.

Terminology

In this chapter, we use the terms *waybill stock, waybill stock IDs*, and *waybill number ranges*. All these terms describe the same entity in SAP TM: the waybill stock.

With the waybill stock, you now define the actual number range for the waybill document in the **From Number** and **To Number** fields. For air waybills, the waybill stock needs to be assigned a specific airline's prefix, as you can see in the top-right corner of Figure 8.2.

However, as you can see in the lower part of the figure, the waybill stock can be defined among several organizational units (sales organizations for a house waybill and purchasing organizations for a master waybill) and several external parties (sold-to parties in house waybills and carriers in master waybills).

Waybill numbers can automatically be drawn on all SAP TM documents that are related to waybills. In air freight bookings, you can do this with a follow-up activity called **Draw MAWB Number** (in ocean freight bookings the action is called **Build House Bill of Lading**); in forwarding orders, you have a separate button in the global toolbar called **HBL**, where you find the **Draw HBL Number** action.

Numbers are drawn for waybills based on the waybill stocks that we defined earlier. For house waybills, the system looks for waybill stocks that has the sales organization and sold-to party of the corresponding forwarding order assigned. If several waybill stocks are found, a popup appears, where you can choose between the different relevant waybill stocks. During searches for waybills stocks, the validity dates of the waybill stock are also considered; only waybills stocks that are currently valid are taken into consideration.

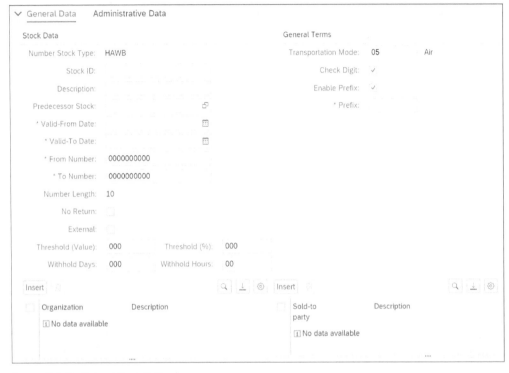

Figure 8.2 Defining Waybill Stock

Predecessor Stocks

If several valid waybill stocks represent the required organizational unit/ordering party combination, you need to choose the waybill stock manually from a popup.

However, you can use the predecessor stock functionality to define a priority among waybill stocks that are valid at the same time. You can see in Figure 8.2 that you can insert an ID of another waybill stock as the predecessor stock. If a predecessor stock is maintained, numbers from this predecessor stock are drawn first.

Only when the predecessor stock is exhausted will the next waybill stock be considered.

If there is no valid house waybill stock that represents the combination of sales organization and sold-to party, the system next looks at waybill stocks that have only a sold-to party assigned. If no waybill stocks are found in this case, either, waybill stocks that have only sales organizations assigned are then considered.

This logic doesn't exist for master waybills because these should always represent a certain combination of carriers and purchasing organizations.

If the waybill stock is running out of numbers, you can define a threshold value (either an absolute value or a relative value) for your waybill stock. When the use of the waybill stock exceeds the threshold value, the user sees a warning message when drawing another number from the almost-exhausted waybill stock.

When a waybill stock that represents a number range agreed upon between an organizational unit and an external party is eventually exhausted, the organizational unit has to approach the external party to agree on a new number stock. However, if the organizational unit foresees that only one more number is needed, this number can be drawn from another waybill stock that wasn't designed for the relationship between this organizational unit and the external party. This process is called *delegation* of a waybill number. When you access your waybill stock in the lower part of the SAP Fiori screen, you can see which waybill numbers have already been used and on which documents they were used.

You could access the freight document directly from this list. If a number was returned, but the withholding time hasn't yet expired, the number is still displayed together with the freight document it was previously used on, but the status of the number is **Returned**.

If you want to delegate a number to another organizational unit as just explained, you can also do this in the waybill stock. If you click the **Delegate** button, the next available number from the waybill stock is drawn and added to the list of numbers in the **Details** area of the waybill stock. The status is set to **Delegated**, and you can now enter the organizational unit to which you would like to delegate the number.

Restrictions on Delegation

Note that delegating waybill numbers is possible only for master waybills, not for house waybills. Furthermore, the number will only be delegated to another purchasing organization; the carrier has to remain the same.

After the delegation is entered in the waybill stock, the next automatic drawing of a waybill number takes the delegated number into consideration.

As you know from Chapter 3, organizational units can be created hierarchically, representing the responsibilities of some organizational units to other units. The organizational hierarchy is considered in the number drawing of waybill numbers as well. In waybill stocks, you can enter not only purchasing organizations as organizational units but also other functional roles such as forwarding houses and companies.

If different waybill stocks are defined for purchasing organizations and forwarding houses, the automatic number drawing only considers the more specific organizational unit; in this example, this is the purchasing organization. Only if the waybill stock of the most specific organizational unit is exhausted is the next higher level considered as a fallback solution. With this functionality, you can make sure you have some fallback numbers maintained if a waybill stock unexpectedly runs out of numbers.

Now that we've discussed the process of drawing waybill numbers, let's look at the waybill itself. In Customizing of the freight order or freight booking type, you define which documents can be printed out of the corresponding document. Via the IMG menu path **Transportation Management • Freight Order Management • Freight Booking • Define Freight Booking Types** (or the definition of freight order types), you can assign two output profiles to the document type, as shown in Figure 8.3.

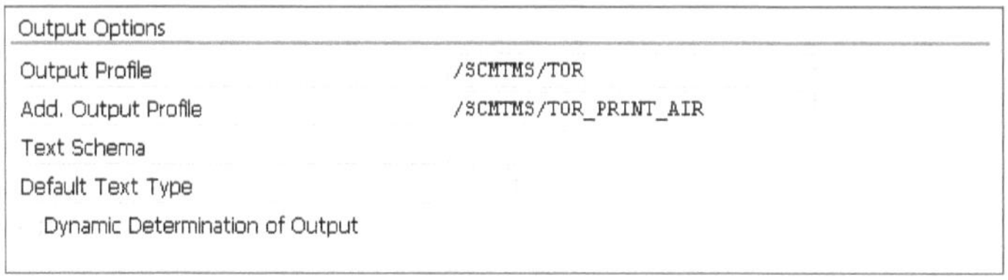

Output Options	
Output Profile	/SCMTMS/TOR
Add. Output Profile	/SCMTMS/TOR_PRINT_AIR
Text Schema	
Default Text Type	
Dynamic Determination of Output	

Figure 8.3 Assignment of Output Profiles to a Document Type

The output profile defines which documents may be printed for the document. Therefore, you can find output profiles for each supported transportation mode in Customizing. If you want to define your own output profiles, you can do this in the Post Processing Framework that was discussed in Chapter 2, Section 2.3.3.

SAP TM provides a standard format for MAWBs. You can change the layout of this document in Transaction SFP with Adobe Document Server, as we described in Chapter 2, Section 2.3.4.

When you want to print a waybill from a freight document, such as a freight order or freight booking, define the printing options in the configuration of the corresponding action of the PPF. In the freight booking or freight order itself, you can navigate to the **Output Management** tab, where you'll be able to preview the waybill documents when selecting a corresponding action.

House waybills on forwarding orders can be printed and viewed on the **Output Management** tab. If the output profile was assigned to the forwarding order type, the document automatically appears on this tab.

8.1.2   Discrepancies

So far we've discussed only transportation process steps that deal with requested and planned quantities. However, in some cases, the actual quantity can't be estimated precisely beforehand, for example, when transporting bulk freight. When the transportation execution starts, the actual quantity needs to be recorded as well. This process in the SAP TM functionality is called *discrepancy handling*.

Discrepancies are a hassle for transportation execution because they might affect the choice of vehicle resource being used for the transportation or lead to a different charge calculation. Therefore, discrepancies need to be discussed with the shipper before transportation can continue.

The transportation process starts as usual, requested quantities are entered into a forwarding order, and freight units are created out of this document. After the freight units are planned, the execution of the transportation may begin. The carrier now physically receives the cargo and checks the actual quantities against the requested quantities.

This checking and reporting is performed by the carrier and communicated to us as the freight forwarder. We'll then enter the actual quantities in the freight order's items.

Carrier Collaboration Portal for SAP TM 9.6

In SAP TM 9.6, this can also be done in the Collaboration Portal by the carrier. The carrier employee logs on to the Collaboration Portal and is able to view all freight orders that are assigned to him or her. On the **Freight Order Management** area of the Collaboration Portal, the carrier can then report execution information, such as actual quantities for a particular freight order.

Note that the carrier Collaboration Portal is only available in the standalone SAP TM 9.6 variant. In the SAP TM in SAP S/4HANA functionality, this portal isn't available.

As you can see in Figure 8.4, the freight order contains planned quantities, but the carrier reported deviating actual quantities.

Figure 8.4 Reporting Actual Quantities in the Collaboration Portal

If the carrier doesn't receive the cargo as planned, you need to report the discrepancy. In general, you can differentiate between two types of discrepancies:

- **Quantity discrepancies**
  The actual quantities are different from the requested quantities because of a change in the quantity, gross weight, or volume.

- **Other discrepancies**
  Discrepancies that aren't caused by a change in quantities are called *other discrepancies*. If the cargo is damaged, or documents are missing for the cargo, these events can be recorded as other discrepancies.

When the carrier discovers a quantity discrepancy, the carrier can report it using SAP TM or enter the actual quantities in the corresponding fields of the Collaboration Portal if using SAP TM 9.6, as shown on Figure 8.4. The system automatically checks the actual quantities against the requested quantities. If a discrepancy exists, it's automatically reported.

You can define different types of discrepancies in Customizing by following the IMG menu path **Transportation Management** · **Freight Order Management** · **Define Discrepancy Profile**.

For the discrepancy type, you can define a tolerance range, meaning that if the actual quantities are within the defined tolerance range, no discrepancy is recorded. The tolerance range is defined as a percentage.

Discrepancy types are clustered in a *discrepancy profile* in the same Customizing activity. The discrepancy profile is assigned to a freight order or freight booking type so that different freight documents can react to discrepancies differently.

After a discrepancy is recorded, the actual quantities of the subsequent transportation stages and the actual quantity of the freight units are updated. The carrier now has to discuss the discrepancy with his customer before the execution of the transport may continue. Therefore, after a discrepancy is reported, all transportation stages carrying a freight unit with unresolved discrepancies get a planning and execution block. In discrepancy type Customizing, however, you can specify that the reported discrepancy of a special discrepancy type doesn't lead to a planning and execution block. If you remove the freight unit with unresolved discrepancies from the freight document, the planning and execution block is also removed.

In the freight order on the **Items** tab, you can select the item for which you've entered discrepant quantities. In the **Details** area below the table of items, the reporting of discrepancies is protocolled on the **Discrepancies** tab, and a corresponding event (assigned to the discrepancy type in Customizing) is triggered.

If the carrier discusses the discrepancy directly with the shipper, you can report the resolution of the discrepancy directly on the **Items** tab. From the toolbar above the list of discrepancies, select **Resolve • Resolve Discrepancy**, as shown in Figure 8.5.

Figure 8.5 Resolving Discrepancies in the Freight Order

After the discrepancy is set to **Resolved**, the planning and execution block is removed.

In other cases, the carrier notifies only the freight forwarder of the discrepancy, and that freight forwarder has to discuss the discrepancy with the shipper. Therefore, the discrepancy is also propagated to the forwarding order. If you select the item of the forwarding order, you'll see the **Discrepancies** tab in the **Details** area of the forwarding order items.

As you can see in Figure 8.6, the freight forwarder can now also set the discrepancy to **Resolved** by selecting **Resolve** • **Resolve Discrepancy**, which leads to the removal of the planning and execution block of the stages in the assigned freight documents.

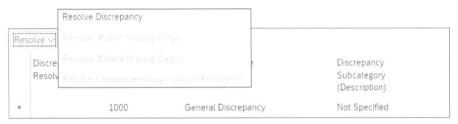

Figure 8.6 Resolving Discrepancies in the Forwarding Order

If the cargo was already damaged when handed over to the carrier, the carrier can report discrepancies, as well. In Figure 8.5, shown earlier, you can also insert discrepancies on the **Discrepancies** tab without entering actual quantities in the cargo information of the freight order or freight booking. The processing of other discrepancies is exactly the same as the processing of quantity discrepancies.

If you've reported a wrong discrepancy, or the discrepancy was resolved by changing the quantity, you can click the **Delete** button to reset the discrepancies so that the actual quantities no longer differ from the requested quantities.

8.1.3   Export/Import Processing

In international, multimodal transports, several organizational units or even business partners are often involved in the planning and execution of the transport.

It's not uncommon for an export organization to organize the pre-carriage and main leg of the transportation while an import organization deals with the on-carriage of the same transport. Due to customs regulations and special circumstances in the importing country, this makes sense because organizations with local knowledge can participate in the transportation planning, making the transport more efficient and, in most cases, cheaper.

Let's take a deeper look at how the interaction between export and import organizations is established in SAP TM. As an example of the process, we concentrate on an ocean transport ordered at the export organization. The export organization deals with the pre-carriage and main carriage, while the import organization is responsible for the organization and execution of the import transportation leg. Figure 8.7 illustrates this division of labor.

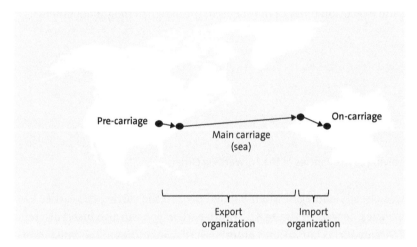

Figure 8.7 Responsibilities in an Export/Import Process

In general, we can differentiate among different scenarios in the export/import process:

- **Full container load (FCL)**
  Because a full container is shipped completely from the shipper to the carrier, there is exactly one transportation request on the export side and one transportation request on the import side. The number of freight documents is also exactly one on each side.

- **Less than container load (LCL)**
  The number of transportation requests on either side still matches. However, because several transportation requests are now consolidated into one container, more than one transportation request is created on each side, but there is still only one freight document on each side.

- **Buyer's consolidation**
  In this scenario, the export side needs to deal with several pickup transports from many shippers and consolidate them at the port. The import side, however, receives only one container that can be delivered as a whole to the ship-to party.

Therefore, the export side creates several transportation requests and one freight document (for the main leg), but for the import side, it's sufficient to create only one transportation request.

- **Shipper's consolidation**
  As in the buyer's consolidation scenario, consolidation effects should be exploited. In this scenario, the shipper creates only one transportation request (because the pre-carriage and on-carriage are transported in one container) and one freight document, but the import side now needs to create one transportation request and one freight document per ship-to party (also because one waybill needs to be created per consignee).

As you've seen while browsing through the different scenarios, two documents in the SAP TM functionality are crucial to using the export and import process: the transportation request (in our case, a forwarding order) and the freight document (in our case, freight booking).

If you know the forwarding order quite well, you'll be wondering how the information about the export and import organizations is stored on the forwarding order. In the forwarding order, you can define whether the forwarding order should be for export or import purposes with the **Traffic Direction** field. If it's an export forwarding order, the sales organization of this transportation request is the export organization of the entire transport. If you're viewing an import forwarding order, the sales organization of this forwarding order acts as the import organization for the transport.

Forwarding Houses

Recall from Chapter 3 that an organizational unit can be a sales unit, purchasing unit, or forwarding house.

In the export/import process, the organizational units used as sales organizations of the forwarding order and purchasing organization of the freight documents should be created as forwarding houses so that the same organizational units can be used for purchasing and selling.

On an export forwarding order, the import organization is assigned on the **Business Partner** tab shown in Figure 8.8. With the partner function **Import Organization**, you can assign the business partner created for the organizational unit to the export forwarding order as the import organization. This also applies to import forwarding orders, where you can assign an export organization in the same way.

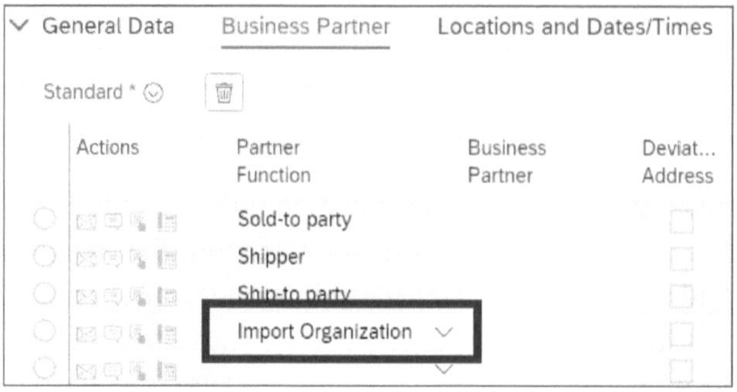

✓ General Data	Business Partner	Locations and Dates/Times	
Standard * ⊙ 🗑			
Actions	Partner Function	Business Partner	Deviat... Address
⊙	Sold-to party		☐
⊙	Shipper		☐
⊙	Ship-to party		☐
⊙	Import Organization ⌄		☐
⊙			☐

Figure 8.8 Import Organization on an Export Forwarding Order

Business Partners for Organizational Units

To assign the import organization to the export forwarding order as shown in the preceding figure, the import and export organizational units have to be created as business partners as well. They also need to be assigned to the organizational units.

There are several ways to create organizational units and business partners and to link these two entities. The easiest way is to ensure that a business partner is automatically created upon creation of the organizational unit. Maintain the following entry in database table T77S0:

GRPID = HRALX
SEMID = HRAC
GSVAL = X

If you've already created organizational units and business partners separately, you can also assign the business partner to the organizational unit in Transaction PPOME. Manually assign the business partner in the **Org. Data** tab.

The report /SCMB/ORG_CREATE_BP_ASSIGNMENT automatically links organizational units to business partners if both entities have already been created. To establish the link between organizational unit and business partner, the business partner's search term 1 needs to be the name of the organizational unit, and search term 2 needs to be the description of the organizational unit.

Let's look at how the export and import organizations interact and which documents need to be created in SAP TM. In general, we can differentiate between an internal communication of two organizational units and an external communication. In the internal communication, both organizational units use an SAP TM system and even access the same client; this means that no web service-based information flow needs to be established. In the external communication, the two parties use different transportation management systems (TMSs), but at least one of them uses SAP TM (otherwise, we wouldn't describe this case in this book!).

Let's first look at the ideal case of both organizational units working in the same SAP TM system.

The general transportation process starts as usual with the creation of a forwarding order. In our case, we create an export forwarding order. The traffic direction (which defines whether we're dealing with an export or import forwarding order) can be entered manually in the document or predefined in the forwarding order document type via Customizing in the IMG menu path **Transportation Management · Forwarding Order Management · Forwarding Order · Define Forwarding Order Type**. It makes sense to define one dedicated forwarding order type for export forwarding orders and another for import forwarding orders.

As we've already discussed, the export organization acts as the forwarding order's sales organization, while the import organization is an additional partner function on the **Business Partner** tab. For the shipper's consolidation scenario, you might not want to define one import organization for the entire forwarding order but, instead, define several import organizations for each item of the forwarding order in the **Details** area of the forwarding order items (discussed in Chapter 4, Section 4.2.1).

After the forwarding order is defined, the export organization can start planning the pre-carriage and main carriage. The method of planning the two stages is completely up to the planner. We've taken a look at the different planning methods in Chapter 6.

Because the export and import processes usually take place in ocean or air scenarios, SAP TM supports these processes only when you're using freight bookings for the main carriage, which can be either an ocean booking or an air booking. For you to realize the interaction between the export and import organizations, the main leg has to be planned on a freight booking.

The traffic direction of the freight booking must now also be **Export** because it was created by the export organization. In addition, we again enter the import organization on the **Business Partner** tab of the freight booking. Alternatively, this is done automatically due to the setting in the freight booking's document type Customizing that business partners should be taken over from the predecessor document, which, in our case, is the forwarding order. The export organization now has to deal with all the necessary process steps regarding the customs declaration for exporting the goods. The freight booking in this case is therefore used as the supporting document for the export declarations but also in general for the capacity reservation at the carrier.

After the freight booking is **Set to Shipped on Board** (in air freight booking, the status is **Uplift Confirmed**), as shown on Figure 8.9, the SAP TM system automatically starts generating the import documents. From a process perspective, this means the import organization is notified by the upcoming transportation request only after the cargo is loaded onto the vessel or aircraft.

Figure 8.9 Setting the Ocean Freight Booking to Shipped on Board Status

After the **Execution Status** of the freight booking is **Set to Shipped on Board**, the automatic generation of import documents is triggered by the PPF.

To enable the internal communication—that is, create the import documents within SAP TM—the corresponding output profile has to be activated and assigned to the document type of the export freight booking in Customizing, as shown in Figure 8.10.

Output Options	
Output Profile	/SCMTMS/TOR_PRINT_SEA
Add. Output Profile	/SCMTMS/EXP_IMP_PROC
Text Schema	
Default Text Type	
☐ Dynamic Determination of Output	

Figure 8.10 Assigning the Output Profile for Export/Import Processing to the Freight Booking Type

The import documents are created by a PPF action. For this to occur, import document types for the import freight booking, import forwarding order, and import freight units need to be defined up front. The correct document types can be determined during the automatic creation of import documents in two ways:

- **Assignment of import document type based on export document type**
  In Customizing of the forwarding order type and of the freight booking type, you can directly assign a corresponding document type for the import document. During the creation of the import document from the export document, the corresponding document type is taken into consideration.

- **Condition-based document type determination**
  SAP TM offers two condition types for the condition-based determination of the import forwarding order type and the import freight booking type:
  - The condition type /SCMTMS/FWO_TYPE can be used to determine the forwarding order type for the import document.
  - The condition type /SCMTMS/FRB_TYPE_IMP can be used to determine the import freight booking type.

Both condition types are singleton conditions, meaning they can't be assigned anywhere in Customizing, and you need to define one global condition for all use cases.

The SAP TM functionality first creates an import freight booking out of the export freight booking. The import organization can use this import document to carry out the import declarations for customs, and it's also the basis on which to plan the on-carriage.

After the import freight booking is created, the import forwarding order and freight units are also created from the booking. The freight units are now created by the freight unit building rule (FUBR) assigned to the import forwarding order type, so the automatic import document creation actually has nothing to do with the creation of import freight units. This is done independently by the forwarding order functionality.

Relation of Forwarding Orders and Freight Bookings

Remember the beginning of this chapter when we discussed buyer's and shipper's consolidation? For a shipper's consolidation, one import booking is created, but because the items will eventually be delivered to different ship-to parties, several import forwarding orders are created—one for each ship-to party.

With the import documents created, the import organization can now start with the import declarations and plan the on-carriage based on the freight units created out of the import forwarding order.

On the import freight booking, the purchasing organization is now automatically the import organization, and the export organization is entered as the additional partner function in the **Business Partner** tab. The same applies to the import forwarding order that was automatically created. The import organization now acts as the sales organization of the forwarding order, and the export organization is shown on the **Business Partner** tab in the corresponding partner function.

The import forwarding order and import freight booking were created in the **Draft** status. In a document with this status, data can't be changed, except for the purchasing organization in the freight booking or the sales organization in the forwarding order. The import organization now has to check the forwarding order and the freight booking for completeness; then it can set the status manually to **In Process** when starting the on-carriage planning.

Import Documents and Service Items

In SAP TM, the standard process is to copy only cargo items from the export documents to the import document. Service items aren't transferred. However, you can influence the system's copy logic by implementing a BAdI via the IMG menu path **Transportation Management · Business Add-Ins (BAdIs) for Transportation Management · Basic Functions · Export/Import Processing · BAdI: Service Item Processing for Import Forwarding Orders**. With this BAdI, you can make changes to the copy logic so that service items are copied to the import document.

The external communication scenario isn't especially different from the internal communication scenario because the physical and legal process doesn't differ from the internal communication. Only the use of TMSs is different here.

With the external communication, we need to differentiate between two cases:

- **Only the export organization uses SAP TM**
  In this case, we can start the process just like in the internal communication scenario because we're going to create an export forwarding order and export freight booking. After that, the information concerning the import is sent out to the import organization's TMS.

- **Only the import organization uses SAP TM**
  If the import organization uses SAP TM, the transportation request communicated by the customer is recorded in an external TMS. Only after the cargo is loaded into the vehicle executing the main transportation leg is a message sent to SAP TM to create import documents.

We'll now look at both cases, starting with the export organization using SAP TM.

As already mentioned, the export organization—just like in the internal communication scenario—starts creating an export forwarding order and plans the freight units created out of this forwarding order on an export freight booking. Now when **Execution Status** is **Set to Shipped on Board**, as shown earlier in Figure 8.9, the system needs to react differently.

Import Organization in SAP TM 9.6

To determine whether the import documents should be created in the same SAP TM 9.6 system of web services and should be sent to the import organization, you need to activate the corresponding PPF action in the business partner's master data record on the **Output Management** tab (as shown in Figure 8.11). To enable the creation of import documents in the same SAP TM 9.6 system, activate PPF **Action /SCMTMS/ COPY_EXP_BOK_IMP_BOK** and deactivate PPF action **/SCMTMS/TOR_BKWBIL_NTF_ EXT**.

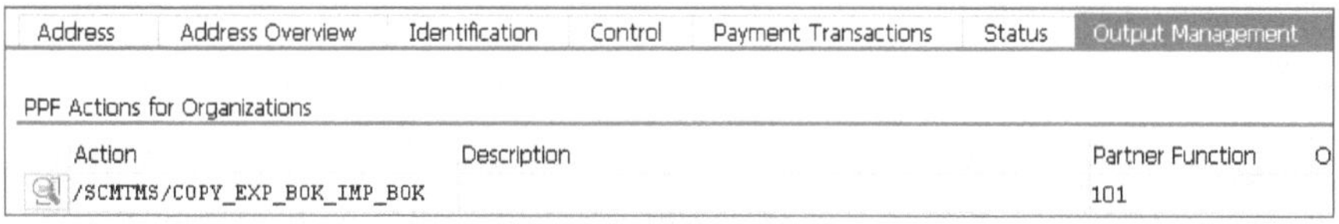

Address	Address Overview	Identification	Control	Payment Transactions	Status	Output Management

PPF Actions for Organizations

Action	Description	Partner Function	O
/SCMTMS/COPY_EXP_BOK_IMP_BOK		101	

Figure 8.11 Assignment of PPF Action to Business Partner

If you want to send web service messages to the import organization, activate and deactivate the two PPF actions just mentioned the other way around.

SAP S/4HANA no longer provides the **Output Management** tab for the business partner, which is why the differentiation isn't available in SAP S/4HANA. Thus, while both internal document creation and web service messages are triggered, only one of the two activities will be successful due to subsequent configuration. However, this can be prevented with the deactivation of the corresponding PPF action in Customizing by following the IMG path **Cross-Application Components • Processes and Tools for Enterprise Applications • Reusable Objects and Functions for BOPF Environment • PPF Adapter for Output Management • Maintain Output Management Adapter Settings**.

For external communication, a web service is called that sends out all the necessary information to the import organization's connected external TMS. The service interface TransportationOrderBookingWaybillNotification_Out is sent to SAP Process Integration, where the routing of the message is processed.

System Landscape Setup

To use external communication between the export and import organizations, the external TMS needs to be connected to the system landscape on which the SAP S/4HANA system is located that is running the SAP TM functionality. We recommend that you connect the external TMS with the SAP S/4HANA system using SAP Process Integration or any other middleware.

When the import organization uses the SAP TM system, another service interface can be used. The service interface `TransportationOrderBookingWaybillNotification_In` integrates the information from an external TMS into SAP S/4HANA and triggers the creation of an import freight booking, as well as the creation of an import forwarding order, based on the information provided by the service interface.

Let's compare internal and external communication. First, the SAP TM functionality within SAP S/4HANA—as well as the standalone deployment of SAP TM 9.6—supports both scenarios. However, internal communication offers some advantages because export document updates are received seamlessly on the importing side. In addition, internal communication provides more transparency because the import organization, using the same system, can be notified by upcoming imports earlier. They can proactively look for export documents with shipments to the region the import organization is responsible for. Furthermore, internal charging between export and import organizations can be performed, which we'll look at in Chapter 12.

In rare cases, manual creation of freight bookings is necessary. Import freight booking can therefore be created manually in the system. As always with the manual creation of freight bookings, you need to ensure that the necessary information from the export freight booking is correctly copied into the import freight booking. For manually created import freight bookings, you can't use all the functionalities that you usually use on an export freight booking, such as the following:

- **Subcontracting the freight booking**
  Because the export organization handles the planning and execution, the import organization doesn't have to do anything about subcontracting the freight booking.

- **Assignment of schedules**
  As with subcontracting of the freight booking, planning (and therefore also schedule assignment) is done by the export organization.

- **Automatic drawing of master waybill number**

  The waybill number has been negotiated by the export organization and the carrier. Therefore, the import organization isn't aware of the number ranges available for the freight booking. However, if the waybill number is already known from the export document, the user can manually enter the waybill number in the import freight booking.

After the import freight booking is manually created, the user can also manually create the import forwarding order as a follow-up action, as shown in Figure 8.12.

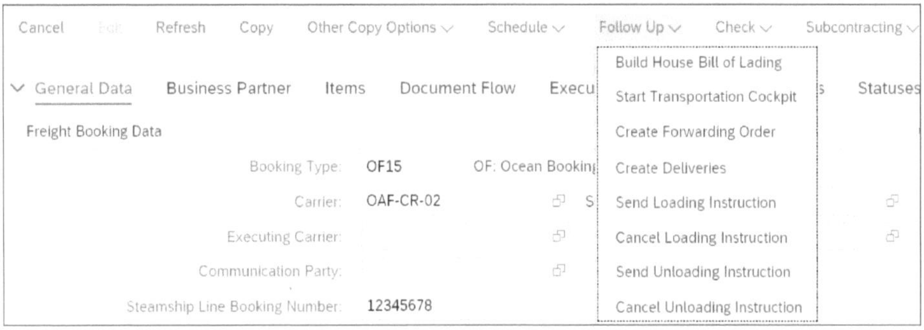

Cancel	Edit	Refresh	Copy	Other Copy Options ∨	Schedule ∨	Follow Up ∨	Check ∨	Subcontracting ∨

						Build House Bill of Lading		
∨ General Data	Business Partner	Items	Document Flow	Execu		Start Transportation Cockpit	s	Statuses
Freight Booking Data						Create Forwarding Order		
	Booking Type:	OF15		OF: Ocean Booking		Create Deliveries		
	Carrier:	OAF-CR-02		S		Send Loading Instruction		
	Executing Carrier:					Cancel Loading Instruction		
	Communication Party:					Send Unloading Instruction		
	Steamship Line Booking Number:	12345678				Cancel Unloading Instruction		

Figure 8.12 Creating a Forwarding Order from the Import Freight Booking

8.1.4   Statuses of Execution Documents

On execution documents, such as the freight order or freight booking, a **Statuses** tab shows the statuses of the document (see Figure 8.13). This tab shows not only statuses of the execution of the freight booking, but also process steps that are handled before the actual execution. They include **Subcontracting**, as well as statuses that are of a more technical nature, such as the **Fixing Status**. However, this section is only concerned with statuses of the execution of the transport.

Among the execution statuses, we can differentiate among three types: the **Handling Execution Status**, the **Cargo Execution Status**, and the **Load Plan Status**.

To understand the difference between these three statuses, let's look at an example. We have a freight booking that is supposed to consolidate different freight units into one container to transport these freight units together on the main leg. The **Cargo Execution Status** tracks the progress of loading these freight units (meaning package items) into the container. The **Handling Execution Status**, on the other hand, tracks

the progress of the container being loaded onto the vessel. The **Load Plan Status** identifies whether the execution data collected in the document is fit to be transmitted to
the next stop, advising what freight will arrive and how it's loaded.

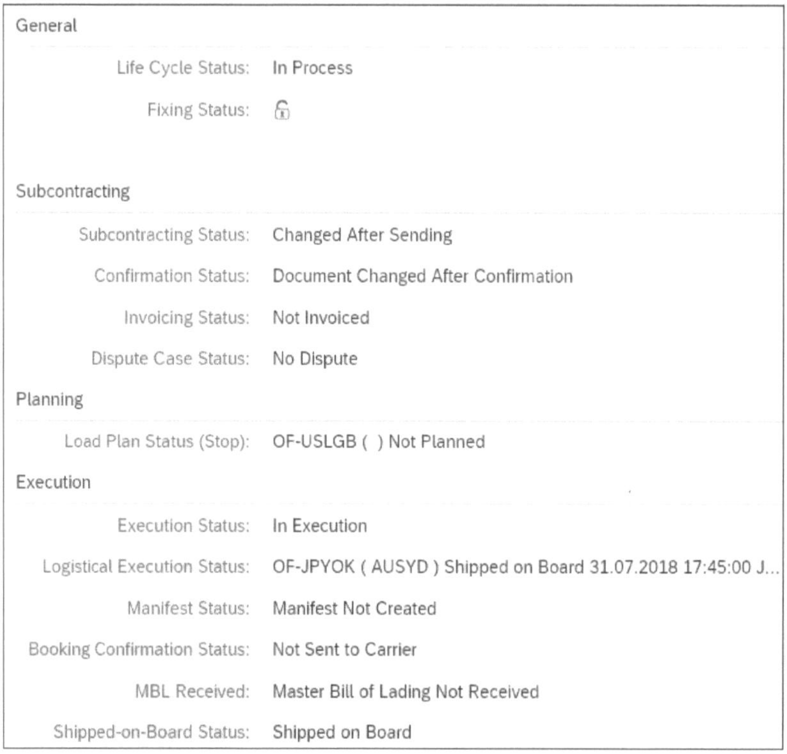

General	
Life Cycle Status:	In Process
Fixing Status:	🔓
Subcontracting	
Subcontracting Status:	Changed After Sending
Confirmation Status:	Document Changed After Confirmation
Invoicing Status:	Not Invoiced
Dispute Case Status:	No Dispute
Planning	
Load Plan Status (Stop):	OF-USLGB ( ) Not Planned
Execution	
Execution Status:	In Execution
Logistical Execution Status:	OF-JPYOK (AUSYD) Shipped on Board 31.07.2018 17:45:00 J...
Manifest Status:	Manifest Not Created
Booking Confirmation Status:	Not Sent to Carrier
MBL Received:	Master Bill of Lading Not Received
Shipped-on-Board Status:	Shipped on Board

Figure 8.13 Freight Booking Statuses

Load Plan Status and Unload Plan Status

As you'll see in Figure 8.14, there both a **Load Plan Status** and an **Unload Plan Status**.
Both statuses relate to the fact that a plan on what needs to be loaded or unloaded is
finalized and can be communicated to the location where loading or unloading will
take place. To simplify the flow of this chapter, we'll only mention the **Load Plan Status** in the course of this section. Keep in mind, however, that the functionality
described for the **Load Plan Status** also holds true for the **Unload Plan Status**.

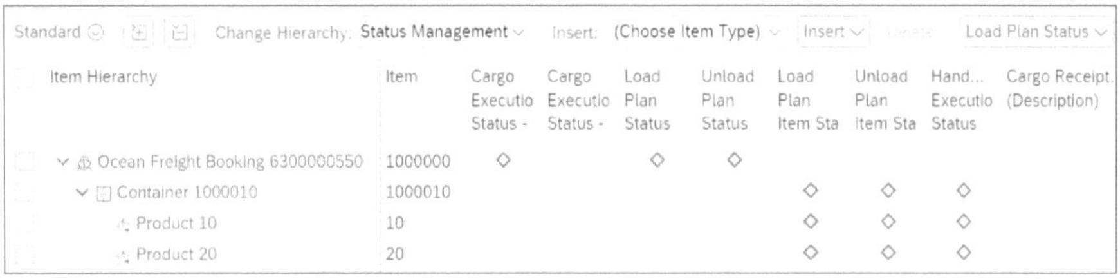

Item Hierarchy	Item	Cargo Executio Status -	Cargo Executio Status -	Load Plan Status	Unload Plan Status	Load Plan Item Sta	Unload Plan Item Sta	Hand... Executio Status	Cargo Receipt. (Description)
⌄ 🚢 Ocean Freight Booking 6300000550	1000000	◇		◇	◇				
⌄ ☐ Container 1000010	1000010					◇	◇	◇	
⚓ Product 10	10					◇	◇	◇	
⚓ Product 20	20					◇	◇	◇	

Toolbar: Standard ⊙ | 🔼 🔽 | Change Hierarchy | Status Management ⌄ | Insert (Choose Item Type) ⌄ | Insert ⌄ | Load Plan Status ⌄

Figure 8.14 Execution Statuses for the Items of the Freight Booking

Because freight bookings can have multiple stops (e.g., in the case of connecting schedules), the **Handling Execution Status** needs to be tracked on every stop and for every item of the freight booking. If the **Handling Execution Status** is updated for an item, the same status is propagated to the subordinate items. The **Cargo Execution Status**, on the other hand, is defined only on the container item level because it's assumed that the container will only be loaded and unloaded once during the transportation part covered by the freight booking.

Both the **Handling Execution Status** and the **Load Plan Status** can be seen on the **Items** tab in the freight booking or freight order. (In air freight bookings, this tab is called **Operations**.)

Keep It Simple

In this chapter, we refer only to a very simple example to show the course of the execution statuses. In addition, we refer to the freight document as a freight booking, meaning an ocean freight booking.

Bear in mind that the execution statuses for the freight documents also apply to more complex scenarios and are used (and work in the same way) on freight orders or freight bookings for other modes of transport.

For the **Handling Execution Status** on the item level, SAP TM provides the following statuses:

- **Not Determined**
  This is the initial status after the freight document is created. After the freight document is ready for execution (covered later in this chapter), the initial status changes to the first status in the process.

- **Not Loaded**

  After the freight document is ready for execution, the **Handling Execution Status** for the items changes to this status because the system now awaits the loading of the container onto the vehicle or vessel.

- **Loaded**

  The packed container is confirmed to be loaded to the transporting vehicle.

- **Not Unloaded**

  At its destination, the container is still sitting on the transport vehicle waiting for unloading.

- **Unloaded**

  The container was unloaded from the vehicle.

Because the last three statuses are probably self-explanatory, we need to add here that the **Handling Execution Status** on the item level always adapts to the current location. This means that in a multistop freight booking, the item status changes from **Not Loaded** to **Loaded**, and at the destination location of the first transportation stage, it changes to **Not Unloaded** and **Unloaded**. However, if the first transportation stage is finished, the status of the item changes to **Not Loaded** again.

The **Handling Execution Status** on the stop level represents the statuses on the item level and offers the additional events **Departed** and **Arrived**. Usually, these two events are reported by SAP Event Management, as we explain later in this chapter. In addition, the **Handling Execution Status** on the stop level also represents all the statuses in the **Cargo Execution Status**. If the current stop is the first stop of the freight booking, meaning this is where the cargo is loaded into a container, then the **Handling Execution Status** on the stop level also shows the current progress of the loading of the cargo into the container. If the current stop is an intermediate stop, these statuses aren't shown.

Now let's look at what statuses in **Cargo Execution Status** the system offers. As already mentioned, the **Cargo Execution Status** is only *defined* on the item level but is also *shown* on the stop level using the **Handling Execution Status** if the current stop is a stop where cargo is loaded or unloaded.

SAP TM offers the following statuses in **Cargo Execution Status**:

- **Not Determined**

  As with the **Handling Execution Status**, the **Cargo Execution Status** is first set to this initial status before the execution process is started.

- **Cargo Ready for Loading**
  Before the cargo can actually be loaded, it needs to arrive at the loading location. In an ocean scenario, we can imagine that the cargo is brought to the port with trucks, and the container waits for the cargo at the port. Therefore, the container and subordinate items are ready for loading only when the cargo items have arrived, meaning that the prerequisite freight order has arrived at its destination location.

- **Cargo Not Loaded**
  None of the cargo items have been loaded yet. Because the previous status **Cargo Ready for Loading** is optional, this status can also show that cargo loading hasn't started yet.

- **Cargo Partially Loaded**
  In an example as shown in Figure 8.14, each subordinate item needs to be loaded into the container separately. If some package items have already been loaded into the container and others haven't yet, the container's **Cargo Execution Status** would be **Cargo Partially Loaded**.

- **Cargo Loaded**
  After all the cargo items have been loaded, the **Cargo Execution Status** of the freight booking or freight order is changed to this status.

- **Cargo Ready for Unloading**
  As already mentioned, when the freight booking has arrived at its final destination, the cargo needs to be unloaded from the container again. Note that this applies only to the last location of the container item; the **Cargo Execution Status** isn't changed on intermediate stops. All statuses regarding the unloading process correspond to the loading statuses, so we'll only list the unloading statuses without going into details.

- **Cargo Not Unloaded**
  Similar to the **Cargo Not Loaded** status, this status indicates that the system expects unloading to happen next. This can mean that the truck is still traveling to the loading location, or it's already there but waiting for an available door. The difference from **Cargo Ready for Unloading** is that the status **Cargo Not Loaded** can also mean the truck is hasn't yet arrived.

- **Cargo Partially Unloaded**
  This status indicates that unloading has started, and some of the cargo items that are supposed to be unloaded at this location have already been unloaded. However, more cargo items are still due to be unloaded.

- **Cargo Unloaded**

  When the **Cargo Execution Status** shows this status, it means that all cargo was unloaded at this location. If this was the final location of the freight order, this would also mean that the overall **Execution Status** of the freight order is changed to **Executed**. If there are more unloading stops after the current one, the overall **Execution Status** remains in status **In Execution**.

The **Load Plan Status** is used to define when information on the cargo can be passed to the next locations where loading and/or unloading takes place. This is connected to the transit warehousing scenario, which we'll describe in further detail in Chapter 13, Section 13.2. After the **Load Plan Status** is set to **Finalized**, the application will send a message to the SAP Extended Warehouse Management (SAP EWM) functionality to create the corresponding documents to prepare unloading and loading. The **Load Plan Status** can be set to the following statuses:

- **Not Planned**

  There isn't yet a load plan defined for this stop.

- **Planned**

  The load plan is created, however, it may be preliminary. No message is sent to the SAP EWM functionality in this status.

- **Finalized**

  The plan is finalized. After this status is set, a message with the information about the cargo to be unloaded/loaded at the next stop is sent to the SAP EWM functionality.

- **Invalidated**

  The plan is invalidated. A message is sent to the SAP EWM functionality to cancel any documents that were already created on the SAP EWM side. The plan therefore needs to be put back to **Finalized** to create new documents in the SAP EWM functionality.

The **Items** tab on the freight booking is used not only to monitor the current statuses of the cargo items but also to manually set these statuses. Recall that the **Handling Execution Status** and **Cargo Execution Status** can be linked to SAP Event Management events. Because we cover this in Section 8.2, for now, we just focus on setting these statuses manually. This is applicable in many use cases because the loading and cargo loading is often done not by the shipper or LSPs (which created the freight booking in the SAP TM functionality), but by the carrier, who doesn't have access to the SAP S/4HANA system and therefore can't set the **Execution Status**. Because of this, the carrier calls the LSP to report the current status of the cargo and container.

If the freight booking is ready for execution, you can start setting the execution statuses in the freight booking.

Readiness for Execution

A freight booking's readiness for execution depends on various factors and information in the freight booking. For example, if a freight booking type is defined in Customizing as relevant for subcontracting, then the freight booking needs to have a carrier assigned to it before the freight booking is ready for execution.

You can check the readiness for execution by selecting **Check • Ready for Transportation Execution** in the global toolbar of the freight booking.

If you want to set the **Cargo Execution Status** or **Load Plan Status** manually in the freight booking, click the **Execution Status • Set to Loaded** button above the item hierarchy displayed in the **Items** tab, which should be set to the **Status Management** hierarchy.

As you can see in Figure 8.15, the choice of statuses combines the different statuses of the **Cargo Execution Status** and the **Handling Execution Status**. Note also that not all of the statuses are selectable. Which statuses are selectable depends on the current status of the items. For example, if the freight booking has already left the port of loading, you can no longer select any statuses that are concerned with loading cargo into the container.

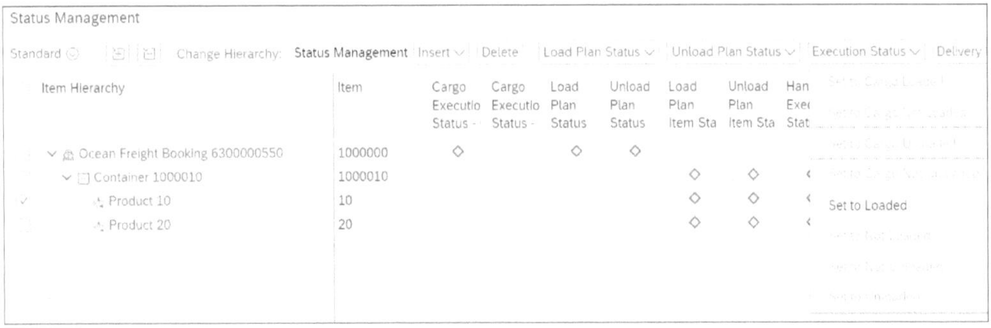

Figure 8.15 Setting Execution Statuses Manually

In addition, you can set the **Handling Execution Status**, **Cargo Execution Status**, and the **Load Plan Status** by clicking on the corresponding buttons shown in Figure 8.15.

The Statuses Need to Be in Order

The statuses have a defined sequential order in which they can appear. Therefore, the cargo must be loaded into the container before the container can be loaded onto the vessel. The same applies at the port of discharge; the container needs to be unloaded from the vessel before the cargo can be unloaded from the container.

This reflects the common use case at ports and airports, where the containers are usually unloaded outside the vessel or aircraft.

You can see in Figure 8.16 that the execution statuses of the items change depending on the overall execution progress of the freight booking.

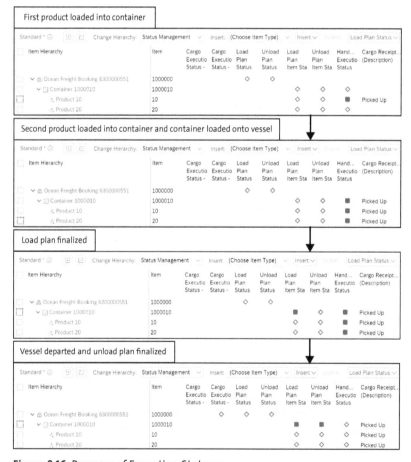

Figure 8.16 Progress of Execution Statuses

The vessel leaves the port after the cargo is loaded into the container and the container is loaded onto the vessel. After the vessel has left the port, the **Handling Execution Status** is reset to a status awaiting the next execution at the next port.

Recall from Figure 8.13 the overall status, called the **Execution Status**, which we haven't yet discussed. The following are some of the most important execution statuses:

- **Not Started**
  This is the initial status of a newly created freight booking.

- **Ready for Transportation Execution**
  All preparations for the shipment have been successfully finalized, and the shipment is ready to go.

- **In Execution**
  The resource used in the freight booking has left the source location but hasn't yet reached the destination where the container and cargo can be unloaded. Think of this as en route.

- **Executed**
  The resource has reached its final destination, and the cargo has been unloaded from the container. In Customizing of the freight order type, as described in Chapter 7, Section 7.2, you can specify which event from SAP Event Management is supposed to set the overall **Execution Status** to this status.

- **Not Relevant**
  If you've defined in the Customizing of the freight booking type that the freight booking isn't relevant for execution tracking, the execution status will always be **Not Relevant**.

The overall **Execution Status** is influenced by the handling execution level on the stop level. If the **Handling Execution Status** on the first stop changes to **Loaded** or **Partially Loaded**, the overall **Execution Status** changes to **Loading in Process**.

The same applies to the actual transportation of the goods. If the **Handling Execution Status** has been set to **Departed** (which, as we said, is usually done by an event in SAP Event Management), the overall **Execution Status** changes to **In Execution**.

Now that we've discussed some execution statuses, it's time to delve deeper into the area of execution tracking. Recall from this section that many of the statuses described are tied to SAP Event Management that will automatically set these statuses.

8.2   SAP Event Management

SAP Event Management is a versatile and adaptable on-premise tool that manages processes for object and status tracking and tracing, performing collection, and analysis of KPI data. SAP Event Management can be integrated into an SAP and legacy system landscape that communicates with partner systems in a worldwide network.

AMR Research breaks SAP Event Management's functions into five core areas:

- **Monitoring**
  Monitoring of processes and objects is based on their statuses and events that are expected to happen within the process or with the object. Usually, monitoring has certain real-time requirements; there sometimes need to be immediate reactions to occurring or missing events. An example of monitoring is the tracking and tracing of a shipment.

- **Notification**
  Decision makers need to be notified if a process deviates from a planned progression. First, the deviation needs to be detected (which is an outcome of the monitoring function). Then a notification via an appropriate channel is raised, giving information about and access to the critical situation (e.g., sending an email that alerts the recipient of a delay in the delivery of a shipment).

- **Simulation**
  In the case of process deviations or delays, it can be sensible to simulate different options for recovery or alternative progression. Simulation is a tool for decision-making that allows evaluation of the impact of actions in terms of complying with definitions at the customer or internal service level.

- **Control**
  Any situation within a process that is monitored through events or status values can lead to reactions that allow you to control the process itself or dependent activities within a business system. The decision on the type of control required for a situation is based on a rule set. An example of control is posting a goods receipt in a distribution system if a customer reports the complete arrival of the goods at his or her premises.

- **Measure and analyze**
  The planned and actual process data, status, and event information can be used in a variety of ways to identify weak points in processes or determine KPIs of the

capabilities of an organization. This data can be collected by SAP Event Management and evaluated in a business warehouse. An example is the average delay time of deliveries made by a certain carrier.

SAP Product Roadmap for SAP Event Management

As an extremely versatile tool, SAP Event Management has a very widespread and flexible use and footprint in many customer implementations. However, it's an on-premise tool, which soon reaches a maturity of 20 successful years. Despite being extremely useful, the SAP strategy moves toward providing track and trace functionality as a software service in the public cloud. Therefore, SAP Event Management will still be available and used by customers, but no new releases will follow the current SAP Event Management 9.2 version, which also implies that no version inside SAP S/4HANA is planned. Maintenance for SAP Event Management is guaranteed until 2025. SAP Event Management can also be used in integrated scenarios with SAP S/4HANA, but as of the time of writing (winter 2018), such a case requires a separate installation, as it's not deployable on the SAP S/4HANA stack.

SAP Event Management will be accompanied by SAP Global Track and Trace, which is accessible in its first cloud releases and under further development. It will slowly catch up with the familiar SAP Event Management capabilities.

SAP Global Track and Trace starts with providing integration to SAP ERP and SAP S/4HANA delivery processes before offering track and trace integration for SAP TM in a future version.

Real-world business processes usually entail a variety of process requirements that need to be reflected in an implementation of an event management process. Because SAP Event Management isn't bound to any predefined designated business objects (e.g., a sales order [SO]), you have flexibility in deciding which object type, process steps, and reactions you want to model and implement in a tailor-made event management process. Yet, because SAP Event Management is the standard tracking and tracing system within SAP logistics applications, many of the processes it covers are connected to a corresponding preconfigured scenario (in SAP TM, enabling plug-and-play integration to process visibility).

Event Management Processes

An event management process is an implementation of a real-world process in an event management system (EMS), where major milestones and characteristics of the process are reflected in the system. The event management process can have different flavors depending on the main emphasis:

- Control processes keep control over a business process.
- Track and trace processes show the current status of a process.
- Visibility processes provide an end-to-end overview of a process.

Let's dive into SAP Event Management, including event handling, the event management process, configuration, processing, and integration.

8.2.1   Event Handlers and Event Messages

The key business object of SAP Event Management is the event handler. All event management processes are based on at least one event handler, which allows you to define main characteristics, statuses, and steps that need to be tracked and controlled. Event handlers can represent a material object, process, or virtual operation. The following are examples of material objects that need to be tracked:

- A pallet that is used as the package for a shipment that needs to be tracked (you're interested in the shipment, but the pallet carrying it is the object that is identifiable from outside)
- A container asset that needs to be tracked during its complete ownership lifecycle
- A production device whose correct operation needs to be monitored and logged
- A shipment such as an express parcel that needs to be tracked from pickup to delivery

Examples of more process-specific visibility scenarios include the following:

- A customer order handled in various order processing statuses
- A payment process that should result in the balance of an invoice
- A purchase order (PO) that needs to be tracked from ordering time to delivery and quality inspection of goods

Event Handlers for a Multiview Example (Car)

Let's consider an example of a process with multiple views, which can be set up in SAP Event Management: In the automotive industry, a car can be tracked from two different viewpoints:

- As a to-be-produced material object that will be sold in the future
- As an order from a customer who wants a made-to-order car

In such a process, either form may occur first (i.e., an order for a specific car that isn't produced yet or the production of a specific car that hasn't yet been ordered by a customer). Because the sequence isn't known up front, all of the related objects (customer order or car production order) need to be modeled in SAP Event Management and be instantiated independently of each other. For this purpose, you can create two linked event handlers:

- One event handler will represent the order.
- A second event handler will represent the production order.

Both can be created independently from the other and linked as the process requires it.

Each event handler has a lifecycle that corresponds to the lifecycle of the object or process it represents. An event handler is instantiated by an incident in a business process, which could be related to a certain status (e.g., order accepted) or to the creation of a business object (master data object for a container created). During its lifetime, the event handler processes a variety of events and reacts to them according to a defined rule set. It can be put to sleep and woken up again before being deactivated and finally archived. Table 8.1 lists some examples of typical event handler lifecycles and event counts.

Characteristics	Event Handler Type (Business Usage)		
	Tendering Process	Shipment Tracking	Container Resource Tracking
Lifecycle	2 hours	4 weeks	5 years
Number of processed events	3–5	approx. 20	>10,000

Table 8.1 Examples of Event Handler Lifecycles

To underline the flexibility and comprehensive applicability of SAP Event Management, let's consider a few examples of how it's used throughout various SAP industry segments:

- Order management, including production monitoring, delivery, and invoice settlement (mill industry)
- Tendering and visibility for logistics execution (high tech industry)
- Distribution processes in a complex environment (industrial machines and components)
- International ocean freight, including customs management (retail industry)
- PO management process for LSPs managing the supply chain of their customers
- Returns management (automotive industry)
- Tracking of handling units in logistics outbound processes (LSPs)
- Spare parts and equipment management (aerospace and defense industry)
- Tracking of parcels, including hierarchical loading (postal services)
- Railcar management (chemical and mill industry)
- Integration with vehicle management systems (automotive industry)
- Integration with the Trader's and Scheduler's Workbench (TSW) (belongs to oil and gas industry)

High-Performance Tool

SAP Event Management is designed to process scenarios with large amounts of data. Many large postal companies use SAP Event Management for parcel tracking, where several billion events need to be processed every year. Big data isn't new to SAP Event Management.

Starting with SAP Event Management 9.1, it runs on the SAP HANA database, which enables in-memory use of event handler and event message data. Data access has been adapted to SAP HANA, resulting in the capability of processing more than 1,000 events per second.

Event messages are announcements related to real-world processes or objects represented in an event management context. These messages are communicated in a standardized form to SAP Event Management; they carry information to identify the related process, incident, time and location, and further contextual details. Event messages can be created and communicated in various ways:

- Interactive creation by humans (e.g., with a mobile device, scanner, Internet application, or business system)
- Automatic creation by machines (e.g., a technical system, production system, or RFID scanner)
- Forwarded by business systems (e.g., EDI or XML messages with business content)

We can define events by some essential characteristics:

- **Event type**
  The event type is a definition of the incident that should be reported by the event message (e.g., acceptance of an order, departure of a shipment at a location, or proof of delivery of a shipment).
- **Repeatability**
  The repeatability defines whether the event type occurs only once in the context of the current process, or the same event type can reoccur at the same or another location (e.g., an *arrival event* may happen multiple times during a truck tour as several customers are visited).
- **Expected event date/time**
  Expected dates/times define a point in time or time frame when an event should happen; an earliest and latest point in time may be assigned to the expected event.
- **Expected message date/time**
  Even if an event is expected to happen within a certain time frame, it may be reported via an event message at a different time. The expected message date/time or time frame is a characteristic that can be defined as a benchmark for reporting compliance.
- **Actual event date/time**
  If an event is reported, the actual date and time of event occurrence are defined. At this point, they can be measured against the expected date and time.

An event management process usually has initialization and termination events. The various other events happening during the process can be assigned to four event categories. Event categories are determined as part of the monitoring function of SAP Event Management and lead to different behavior in terms of notification, simulation, control, and analysis. Figure 8.17 shows an overview of the event categories in the context of an event handler lifecycle, which moves from left to right.

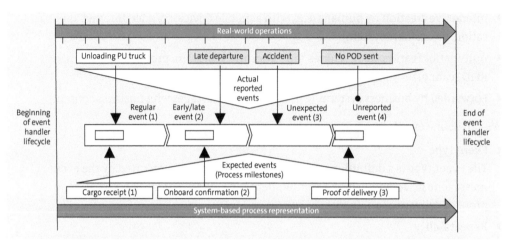

Figure 8.17 Event Types and Event Handler Lifecycle

We can divide the example events in Figure 8.17 into four event categories:

- **Regular events**
  A *regular event* is defined by a milestone in a business process that is reflected in the definition of the expected event and its expected time frame. The actual event occurs within the expected time frame and is reported within the expected message time frame.

  Say, for example, a container should arrive at a terminal between 9:00 a.m. and 10:00 a.m. The confirmation is expected until 1:00 p.m. The container arrives at 9:43 a.m., and the confirmation (event message) is sent at 10:35 a.m.

  In some cases, a regular event can occur without a defined expected time frame (e.g., it can happen anytime, but it needs to happen at least once).

- **Early or late events**
  Like a regular event, the *early or late event* is a milestone that is expected to happen within a defined time frame. The actual event occurs either earlier or later than the expected time frame, or it's reported earlier or later than the expected messaging time frame.

  Say, for example, a container should arrive at a terminal between 9:00 a.m. and 10:00 a.m.; the confirmation is expected until 1:00 p.m. Instead, the container arrives at 10:33 a.m., and the confirmation (event message) is sent at 3:27 p.m.

  A specific real-time reaction to the early or late event isn't planned. Instead, the fact that the process isn't executed according to the expected milestones is registered and used for analytical and process improvement steps (perhaps to evaluate the quality of service of a business partner).

- **Unexpected events**
  Unexpected events don't have a corresponding milestone in the business process, and there is no expectation that the event is reported. We need to differentiate between two situations:
  - The event simply happens and is registered (e.g., location is reported by a GPS device in a truck).
  - The event indicates a serious problem, and some corrective measures must be taken (e.g., accident report of a delivery truck).

  In some cases, the situation needs to be evaluated based on further event characteristics (e.g., if a railcar is reported to be in a switchyard in Chicago when it should be routed from Denver to Los Angeles).

- **Unreported events**
  Unreported events are also based on an expected and time-defined milestone, but either the actual event doesn't happen, or an event message isn't received within the required time frame. The nonoccurrence of the event is rated as noncompliance and immediately leads to exception handling. This allows at least the raising of a notification to a person who can assess the situation and take further actions. For a well-defined escalation process, an automatic control process can be initiated as the reaction.

8.2.2   Event Management Process

An event management process is usually triggered by one of the following sources:

- A transactional object in a business system is created or set to a status (e.g., an order that reaches the status **Accepted**).
- A master data object is created in a business system (e.g., truck resource).
- A process in a business system reaches a state (e.g., a delivery process reaches the state of goods issued).
- A message from external sources indicates that an event management-relevant process has been kicked off, and event messages are expected in the future.
- A process implemented in SAP Event Management starts with manual creation of an event handler for pure event management-based handling. This kind of process

is special because SAP Event Management is creatively used to run a business process on the implemented event handlers without a backend business system (e.g., returns management process on SAP Event Management).

Business Objects and Application Objects

In a business system, manifold business objects represent substantial entities of the business processes (e.g. SO, shipment, or invoice), which are configured by Customizing to represent the real entities (e.g., a domestic truck shipment or the ocean leg of an international shipment). In the context of event management, *application objects* define even a more granular and semantic classification of objects, which depends on the individual characteristics of a business object. This is necessary because an event management process may differ considerably depending on what a business object represents. In the context of event management, the business systems are generally also referred to as *application systems*.

Per the previously mentioned example, a shipment business object can, for example, represent a domestic less than truckload (LTL) truck tour or an ocean FCL container shipment. You can determine the nature of the business object only by looking up characteristics (e.g., mode of transport, stage type, or type of cargo) or an indicator (e.g., shipment type).

Depending on these characteristics, SAP Event Management needs to initiate a different event management process and use an individual type of event handler. Therefore, based on the business object characteristics, the *application object type* and the related data are determined to control the event management process.

Figure 8.18 illustrates the elements of SAP Event Management that are involved in an event management process. Usually, the process starts in a business system such as SAP TM, where the originating object or process is created. In the course of running the event management process, the following stages or steps are executed:

1. A business process is started in the backend business system. At a certain step, the process reaches a status when an event management process needs to be triggered (e.g., shipment is planned). When the business object is saved, the business object data is handed over to a BAdI layer (SAP TM) or the PPF for post-save action handling. In both cases, the business object data is handed over to the SAP Event Management application interface, which is a configurable integration component that manages the communication with SAP Event Management.

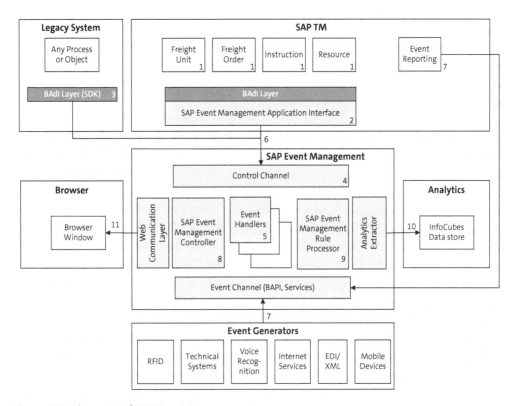

Figure 8.18 Elements of SAP Event Management

2. The application interface determines the tracking relevance of the business object by checking the relevance of an application object type and analyzing the related business object status (e.g., ocean shipment status is switched from **Not Planned** to **Planned**). If an application object type is relevant for tracking, and the object status requires communication with SAP Event Management, the relevant context data is extracted from the business object, and several data packages containing object data in a standardized way are created (e.g., expected events, tracking IDs, and general parameters). In addition, the SAP Event Management instance to be used is determined (it's possible to use multiple SAP Event Management instances for different purposes). Finally, the data packages are sent asynchronously to the SAP Event Management instance. The same procedure applies in the case of updates or deletions of business objects, where change or delete requests are sent to SAP Event Management.

3. Legacy systems don't have an application interface (unless they are built on an SAP NetWeaver ABAP stack). Therefore, a legacy system needs to determine the tracking relevance on its own, build the application data packages, and send them over to SAP Event Management using a business application programming interfaces (BAPI) or web service call. This integration isn't uncommon; one of the largest customer installations of SAP Event Management uses this integration technique.

4. The control channel in SAP Event Management receives the request from the application interface of the business systems or from the legacy systems. The received data is forwarded to the event controller, which determines if an event handler exists or, if not, which type of event handler needs to be created.

5. If an event handler is created, SAP Event Management checks to see if messages have already been received. If so, the buffered messages are processed in sequential order. If an event handler already exists, it's first changed according to the new data (e.g., it may contain changed or new expected events). Then the already-received messages can be reprocessed to check whether the altered event handler is still compliant with the previously received event messages.

6. SAP Event Management finally sends back a status protocol of applied change steps to the application systems, where this information is logged in the application log (Transaction SLG1, object **SAPTRX**, subobject **APPSYS**).

7. Event messages can be received from various sources as single messages or a batch of messages. The messages are sequenced and related to event handlers before being forwarded to event processing by an event controller and rule processor.

8. The event controller retrieves the event handlers for the event messages to be processed and hands over the individual batches of messages to each event handler.

9. Each event handler processes its batch of event messages sequentially using the rule processor. The rule processor analyzes the received event message and applies the rules of the rule set to the event and event handler context. Based on current and previous data of the event handler, a decision on reactions to reported events can be made.

10. Extraction of event management data for analytics is one sort of reaction. The extracted data on process performance is sent to the analytics system and stored in InfoCubes or DataStores.

11. The web communication layer allows data to be retrieved from one or multiple event handlers and to be presented in a role-based web interface. Due to its configurability, the web communication layer can be used to present visibility data to customers and provide access for partners or internal employees.

8.2.3   SAP Event Management Setup and Configuration

SAP Event Management configuration requires changing settings on the SAP application side (e.g., in SAP S/4HANA, SAP ERP, or SAP TM), as well as the SAP Event Management side, which need to match in some places. In this section, we describe how to set up SAP Event Management system instances, data extraction, and communication in the application interface, and how the directly related Customizing is done in SAP Event Management. Visibility process configuration components are also explained.

SAP Event Management Installation

Up to now, SAP Event Management installation could be done together with an instance of SAP TM or SAP ERP, or as a standalone version. With the release of SAP TM in SAP S/4HANA, this changes slightly.

Because SAP Event Management 9.2 has no installation as part of SAP S/4HANA, an implementation on the same instance together with SAP TM on SAP S/4HANA isn't possible. If SAP Event Management needs to run together with an SAP TM operated on SAP S/4HANA, the SAP Event Management should reside on its own instance. Figure 8.19 shows this situation. In addition, it also depicts the installation together with SAP TM 9.6 (SAP HANA or any other database (AnyDB)) and on a separate instance respectively, together with SAP ERP integrated with a standalone SAP TM.

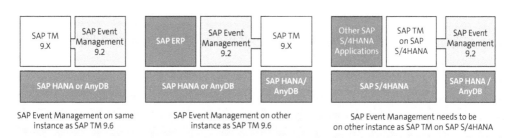

Figure 8.19 Installation Options for SAP Event Management Running Integrated with SAP TM

The previously mentioned requirements may impact some installations done with SAP Event Management and SAP TM on the same instance, as an upgrade of SAP TM to SAP S/4HANA would require a cross move of the SAP Event Management onto a separate instance. However, as the upgrade of SAP TM will usually require a move onto a new instance (SAP S/4HANA), there is a good chance to have SAP Event Management reside in its current place and connect it to the new SAP TM instance remotely. In a properly decoupled implementation, this would not cause much overhead.

Configuration in SAP Application Systems

The SAP Event Management-related configuration capabilities of SAP application systems are provided by the application interface and are part of the application basis software layer of SAP NetWeaver. Therefore, you can use it in all systems of the SAP Business Suite or SAP S/4HANA.

The technical integration between the business processes and the application interface is delivered out of the box for various business objects. Table 8.2 provides an overview of the logistics-related SAP Event Management integration objects.

Object	Component	Event Management Usage
Freight unit	SAP TM	Cargo item/container tracking
Freight order/ freight booking	SAP TM	Shipment tracking, master bill tracking
Resource	SAP TM	Equipment tracking
Standard operating procedures (SOP) instruction	SAP TM	Tracking of standard operating procedures

Table 8.2 Logistics-Related SAP TM Objects with SAP Event Management Integration

The application interface provides a standardized way of configuring the integration between business processes and the corresponding event handling. Depending on the semantic context of a business object, configuration can control which process in SAP Event Management is fed with data and expected milestones. The configuration is controlled mainly by definition of business object type and application object type.

The business process type is directly related to the business objects as they are defined in the business object repository of the application system (e.g., a transportation order object). It relates to a technical integration of the business object with the application interface and a list of data tables with object content that can be used for extracting data and events to be sent to SAP Event Management.

You can customize the business process type by following the IMG menu path **Integration with Other SAP Components • Event Management Interface • Define Application Interface • Define Business Process Types**. For each business process type, settings for technical data posting (dialog task, V1 update task) and queuing are defined. In addition, a list of data structures is provided that allows you to characterize the Data Dictionary (DDIC) structure used and gives an indication of how to evaluate business object changes. The indicator allows you to define, for example, which value in a structure field indicates a newly created object that needs to be communicated to SAP Event Management.

Figure 8.20 shows the business process types of an SAP TM system and some details of the application table definition of the business process type of the transportation order object.

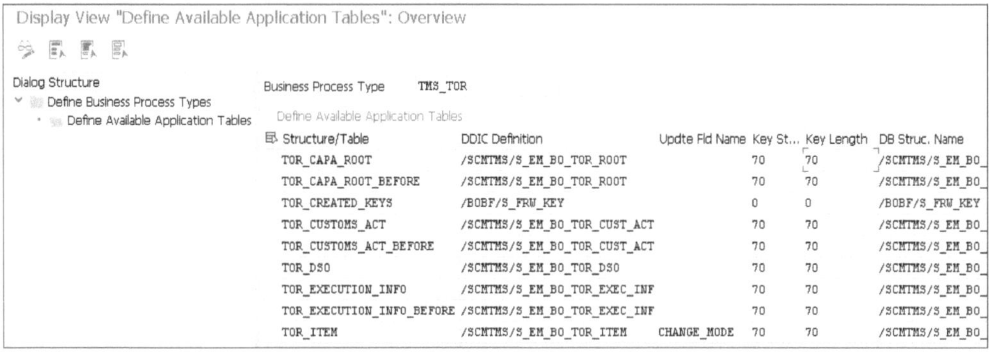

Structure/Table	DDIC Definition	Updte Fld Name	Key St...	Key Length	DB Struc. Name
TOR_CAPA_ROOT	/SCMTMS/S_EM_BO_TOR_ROOT		70	70	/SCMTMS/S_EM_BO_
TOR_CAPA_ROOT_BEFORE	/SCMTMS/S_EM_BO_TOR_ROOT		70	70	/SCMTMS/S_EM_BO_
TOR_CREATED_KEYS	/BOBF/S_FRW_KEY		0	0	/BOBF/S_FRW_KEY
TOR_CUSTOMS_ACT	/SCMTMS/S_EM_BO_TOR_CUST_ACT		70	70	/SCMTMS/S_EM_BO_
TOR_CUSTOMS_ACT_BEFORE	/SCMTMS/S_EM_BO_TOR_CUST_ACT		70	70	/SCMTMS/S_EM_BO_
TOR_DSO	/SCMTMS/S_EM_BO_TOR_DSO		70	70	/SCMTMS/S_EM_BO_
TOR_EXECUTION_INFO	/SCMTMS/S_EM_BO_TOR_EXEC_INF		70	70	/SCMTMS/S_EM_BO_
TOR_EXECUTION_INFO_BEFORE	/SCMTMS/S_EM_BO_TOR_EXEC_INF		70	70	/SCMTMS/S_EM_BO_
TOR_ITEM	/SCMTMS/S_EM_BO_TOR_ITEM	CHANGE_MODE	70	70	/SCMTMS/S_EM_BO_

Figure 8.20 Business Process Types of SAP TM and Application Tables of the TOR Object

You can define the settings for application object types via the IMG menu path **Integration with Other SAP Components • Event Management Interface • Define Application Interface • Define Used Bus. Proc. Types, Appl. Obj. Types, and Evt Types**. Each application object type is directly related to a business process type.

In the **General Data** settings of the application object type, you must define the EMS where the visibility process is started. In addition, you can set the behavior of the application object creation (e.g., whether the application object is relevant to trigger an SAP Event Management communication; you can use this to deactivate an application object type).

The **Control Table** settings define which of the business object data tables represent the main object. An application object may, for example, be created for a shipment (header level) or each shipment item (item level). In the first case, the main table would be the object's header table; in the second case, the main table would be the item table, and the header table should be assigned as a master table. For some objects, deleted records are kept in separate tables. In this case, the table for deleted objects could deviate from the main object table.

On the **Object Identification** tab, you can configure how the application object ID is compiled. You can extract it from one or two fields of the business object data tables or use a function module for extraction.

The **Event Management Relevance** settings determine when an application object is communicated to the EMS. The determination can be done by either a Boolean function or an ABAP function module. Alternatively, the application object can be set to be always relevant, which triggers a communication to SAP Event Management as soon as a business object is created or changed.

copies of existing modules. If you assign such a function module in Customizing, you first need to create an entry for it in Customizing because the function module name isn't directly entered, but a logical name is assigned to it. You can find the assignment via the IMG menu path **Integration with Other SAP Components • Event Management Interface • Define Application Interface • Define SAP EM Extraction Functions**.

In the **Parameter Setup** tab, you can define which data of the business object is handed over to SAP Event Management to create or update an event handler. There are multiple categories of data to be extracted, as follows (Figure 8.21 shows the Customizing screen):

- Tracking identifications (IDs) and code sets are used to identify the event handler when event messages are received. Tracking IDs are usually numbers such as shipment numbers, B/L numbers, pallet numbers, or order numbers. The code set associated with the number helps you find the correct event handler (there might be a shipment with number 12345 identified by SHP 12345, and an order with number ORD 12345, where SHP and ORD represent the tracking code set, and 12345 represents the tracking ID). Tracking IDs can be extracted via a table field reference or an ABAP function module.

- Control and information data extraction provides containers to hand over any kind of data in the format name-index-value to SAP Event Management. This data is related to the object or process and gives additional information. The control data container holds information that can directly influence the SAP Event Management logic (e.g., an indicator that a shipment contains dangerous goods or that the cargo type is bulk). The information data container holds additional object characteristics (e.g., the name of the truck driver), which usually aren't used to control the process. The index is used to relate several entries belonging to the same group (PRODUCT[1] = "Television", QUANTITY[1] = "200", TYPE[1] = "Yamamoto DXTV-230").

- Query IDs provide the option to assign additional code set/ID pairs to an event handler that can be used for data retrieval from SAP Event Management but not for message processing.

- Expected event extraction allows the retrieval of milestones from the application object that are later used to create the expected events in the event handler. Because the extraction is done in an ABAP function module, you have the option to enhance the expected event list by calculating or enriching the milestones given in the business object context. If, for example, a shipment object contains only a departure date, you can additionally create a gate check-out date 30 minutes later, which allows you to track your internal operation schedule compliance.

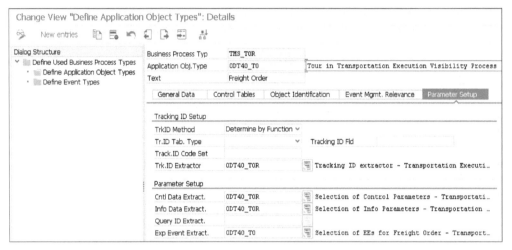

Figure 8.21 Parameter Setup of an Application Object Type

For each business object type, you can configure one or multiple event types in the application system. Event types allow you to set up event messages to be sent from the application to a connected EMS in the context of the backend process. An example is the confirmation of goods issue in an SAP S/4HANA delivery, which needs to be registered in the shipping process tracking in SAP Event Management or via a load status on a freight order in SAP TM.

Data extraction from the application is done in an assigned ABAP function module that allows you to build the event message context in a very flexible way. Figure 8.22 shows the event types defined for the SAP TM transportation order objects (freight order and freight booking).

The standard application log, which you can start via Transaction SLG1, provides detailed information on the success or failure reasons for the activities happening within the application interface. You can access details about the event management relevance of application objects, data extraction and application data, or event transmission to the EMS. The response of SAP Event Management to the application system requests is transmitted back to the application system and stored in the log (e.g., no suitable event handler type could be determined in SAP Event Management). You can see the complete process by accessing the log via Transaction SLG1 for object **SAP-TRX** and subobject **APPSYS**.

Figure 8.22 Definition of Event Types for the Transportation Order Object of SAP TM

Configuration of SAP Event Management

The configuration of SAP Event Management allows you to define the behavior and characteristics of the visibility processes. The main activities in SAP Event Management configuration are to define the following:

- Event handler types, expected event messages, and status settings
- Event handler type determination and data mapping from the application system data
- Event messages and event codes to be processed
- Rules about how to react to received or missing event messages
- Setup of personalized web transactions for accessing event management data

To allow process synchronization between application systems and SAP Event Management, you need to make a few essential settings to connect application system processes with SAP Event Management configuration. You can find these settings in the SAP Event Management IMG by selecting **Event Management • General Settings in SAP Event Management**:

- Define remote function call (RFC) connections to enable technical communication.
- Define logical systems to identify application systems and EMSs.
- Define application systems to give a name to the systems for which you set up processes in SAP Event Management.
- Define business process types because you need them to synchronize the application system extraction process to the event handler creation process.

Definition of different event handler types allows you to control the creation, composition, and behavior of individual visibility processes on the event management side. Event handler types are directly related to a business process type, which you need to define in the event handler type settings. Figure 8.23 shows the setup of an event handler type that you can find in SAP Event Management Customizing by selecting **Event Management • Event Handlers And Event Handler Data • Event Handlers • Define Event Handler Types**.

The main fields of the event handler type are as follows:

- **Bus. Proc. Type**
  You must assign the event handler type to a *business process type*.

- **Priority** and **Condition**
  You can set a *priority* to allow a ranking within event handler type determination. You define a *condition* that specifies the applicability of the event handler type (e.g., only to be used for a specific application object type).

- **Rule Set**
  The rule set defines how the created event handler reacts to incoming or overdue event messages.

- **Stat.Attr.Prof**
  Using the status attribute profile, you can detail the creation of status fields and set an initial value to it during event handler creation.

- **EE Profile**
  The expected event profile summarizes the expected events that are created with the event handler based on application system milestones or other expected events.

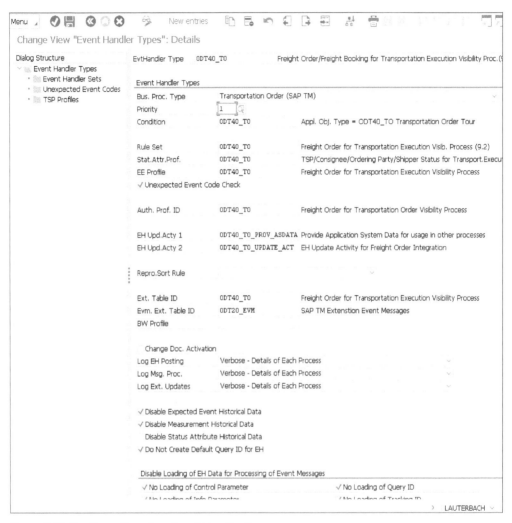

Figure 8.23 Configuration of an Event Handler Type

- **Auth. Prof. ID**
  Using the authorization profile, you can define who has access to which part of the event handler data.

- **EH Upd.Acty 1** and **EH Upd.Acty 2**
  The event handler update activities allow you to specify ABAP function modules to update data of the application system before creating the event handler or

update the event handler after running through the standard event handler creation process. They can be used like traditional user exits.

- **Ext. Table ID**
  The extension table IDs for event handlers and event messages allow you to add fields on the header level of event handlers and messages.

- **BW Profile**
  The **BW Profile** defines which data is extracted from the event handler to be sent to a connected data warehouse system (SAP Business Warehouse [SAP BW] or SAP HANA).

- **Change Doc. Activation**
  Changing document activation and logs allows you to capture additional data for auditing purposes.

Event Handler Header Extension Tables and Use of Logs

You can use an extension table to extend the event handler header for various purposes. Most important is the ability to create fields specifically to a particular event handler type that are part of a database index and allow a fast search (e.g., a field for location of last sighting) without modifying the header table for all event handler types. Each event handler type can have its own extension table and therefore may have specific indexing and access characteristics.

Event handler logs—especially in the verbose mode—should be used very carefully or mainly for testing when running SAP Event Management in high-performance scenarios or with high data volumes. They may create multiples of the data load of the pure tracking process and slow down the process.

Figure 8.24 gives example data of an event handler. The event handler header keeps the references between the application system and SAP Event Management and provides identification and control characteristics for the process. Milestones, tracking IDs, and other attributes are stored in related tables. The header extension table contains important context data for the process. Control and information parameters store more detailed information that can be used in rules or presented upon request.

An event handler that needs to work with milestones must be assigned an expected event profile. You can define expected event profiles in the IMG by selecting **Event Management · Event Handlers and Event Handler Data · Expected Events · Define Profiles for Expected Events**.

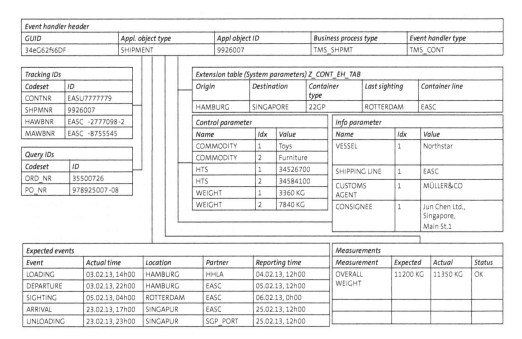

Figure 8.24 Example Data of an Event Handler (Incomplete)

When an event handler is created, SAP Event Management uses the information in the expected events profile to generate a list of expected events to serve as milestones for processing actual received event messages and as a basis for detecting overdue events. The right side of Figure 8.25 shows an example of an expected event list for an air freight tracking scenario that has been set up to support Cargo 2000-like event processing.

The expected events of a profile can be bundled into groups to allow alternative processing of events. One example is a group of events where either an approval or rejection event is expected. Either of these two events fulfills the requirement to receive an answer for a request and therefore satisfies the necessity to receive an answer within a defined time frame.

The detailed setting for expected event generation (see the left side of Figure 8.25) allows you to define how an expected event is created. You can relate the event to an expected event communicated from the application system. Dates and times can be directly moved or manipulated as required. You can also create an expected event by referencing a previously generated expected event (e.g., loading end is always

30 minutes after loading start). If the event scheduling follows a more complex rule or needs to reference other data, you can use an ABAP function module to determine the correct date and time.

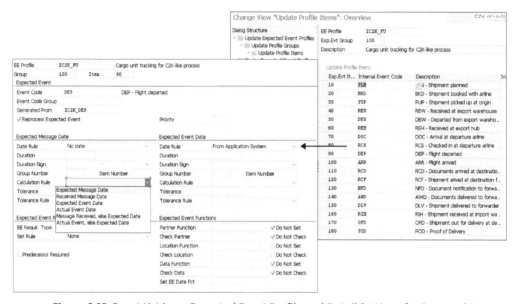

Figure 8.25 Event List in an Expected Event Profile and Detail Settings for Expected Event Generation

Each expected event can have event and message dates with a defined earliest/latest time frame. If an event code occurs multiple times in a process, the individual event instances can be enriched by event locations or sending partners (e.g., if a departure event occurs multiple times on a distribution tour).

Keeping Track of Original Plans

Within the expected event structure, an event handler keeps track of the expected and actual event date and time. In addition, an original expected event date and time is kept. Even if a plan changes multiple times, the first (original) plan is retained in the expected event structure.

Because business processes often require quite specific status settings, SAP Event Management provides a tool to define the status of each event handler type individually. You can configure the Customizing for status attribute profiles by selecting

Event Management • Event Handlers and Event Handler Data • Statuses • Define Status Attribute Profiles. The profiles, which are assigned to one or multiple event handler types, consolidate a list of status attributes, each offering a status definition, possible status values, and an initial value that is set when the event handler is instantiated. Transition of the status values from one setting to another is accomplished by rules processing with specific status modification activities. Figure 8.26 shows an example of a status attribute profile (SAP TM transportation order event handler) with status attributes for block, delivery, and transportation status.

Change View "Status Attribute Profiles": Overview

Dialog Structure	Stat.Attr.Prof.	ODT20_TOR			
∨ Status Attribute Profiles	Description	TSP/Consignee/Ordering Party/Shipper Status for Transport.Execution.Visib.Proc.			
* Status Attribute Profile Items					
	Status Attribute Profile Items				
	StatusAtt. Name	Description		St. Attr. Value	Description
	ODT20_BLOCK_STATUS	Transportation Execution Block Status	NOT_BLOCKED		Not Blocked
	ODT20_DELIVERY	Delivery Status		ON_TIME	On Time
	ODT20_TRANSPORT	Transportation Status		NEW	New

Figure 8.26 Status Attributes of an Event Handler for Transport Order Tracking

When an event handler is created by request from an application system, the extracted and transmitted data is used to determine the appropriate type of the event handler. The first step is to compare the business process type assigned to the application object against the business process type assigned to event handler types. The two should match. Optionally, the alternative business process type assigned to the application object is compared. Event handler types matching the business process type are now ranked by their priority. Subsequently, the conditions of the event handler types are checked until the first applicable one is found. This event handler type is then used to instantiate the event handler.

Because not all application systems are structured the same way, you can harmonize individually created parameters in a common process using the parameter mapping functionality. Even in the SAP world, orders of different kinds exist (SAP Customer Relationship Management [SAP CRM] orders, sales and distribution [SD] orders, etc.). To avoid a cross-system harmonization of transmitted parameters, SAP Event Management offers a parameter mapping tool to assign parameter entities to a joint EMS-specific naming definition. For example, an ORD_NUM parameter from SAP CRM and an ORDERNUM parameter from SAP S/4HANA can be mapped to an ORDERNUMBER parameter in the event handler. The setup of a corresponding mapping profile in the

IMG under **Event Management** · **Event Handlers and Event Handler Data** · **Parameters** · **Define Parameter Mapping** is mandatory; otherwise, the event handler can't be created, and you'll find a mapping error in the application log. In a simple case, the mapping profile just defines that all parameters are routed through the way they are received from the application system.

8.2.4   Event Messages and Event Processing

An event message is a structured set of data that conveys information about the what, when, where, who, and why of a real-world incident to SAP Event Management. SAP Event Management uses this information to identify potential event handlers as receivers by comparing the tracking ID of the message with the tracking IDs of the event handlers. All active event handlers with matching tracking IDs and code sets get a feed of the event message.

Technical Processing of Event Messages

Event message processing is mass enabled for support of high volumes of event messages to be passed to SAP Event Management with a single transmission. All received raw event messages are first saved in the database before being forwarded to message processing, which can be done either synchronously or asynchronously.

Message processing then packages all received messages by tracking ID, sorts the packages by actual event time stamp, and pushes each package into the event handler update process. In the end, the processing status and logs are saved with the messages. The event handler update process assigns the internal event code, checks the feasibility of message processing, and finally executes the rule processing for each message.

Synchronous processing of event messages should be used when you expect an immediate response on the success or outcome of an event message (e.g., if a truck departure is posted on a mobile device and the status update is immediately shown on the open mobile user interface [UI] after refresh).

An event code characterizes the purpose of an event message. They are divided into an external and internal view. Because there are many standards that define how to report a specific incident (e.g., EDIFACT, ANSI X.12, and Rosetta Net), the external view needs to be flexible. Therefore, you can define external event codes and a mapping rule to harmonize and transform them into an internal view defined by internal event codes.

You configure the event codes in Customizing under **Event Management • Event Handlers and Event Handler Data • Codes**. There are multiple settings to define external and internal views and the possibility to group them. Figure 8.27 shows the definition and grouping of internal event codes.

Change View "Allocate Int. ECs to Group": Overview

Dialog Structure	Int. EvCd Group	ZC2K
⌄ Internal Event Codes	Description	C2K-like events group
• Assign Reason Codes		
⌄ Internal Event Code Groups		
• Allocate Int. ECs to Group	Allocate Int. ECs to Group	

Int. EvtCd	Description
ARR	ARR - Flight arrived
AWD	AWD - Documents delivered to forwarder
BKD	BKD - Shipment booked with airline
DEP	DEP - Flight departed
DEW	DEW - Departed from export warehouse
DLV	DLV - Shipment delivered to forwarder
DOC	DOC - Arrival at departure airline
NFD	NFD - Document notification to forwarder

Figure 8.27 Internal Event Code Definition and Grouping

Event message processing is organized through the definition and use of rule sets. A rule set is a sequence of activities conditionally applied upon receipt of an event message or, alternatively, if an expected event is overdue with respect to either an expected event or message data.

A rule set is directly associated with an event handler. It can be a comprehensive list of rules, where each rule contains a condition under which it's executed, and a definition of which activity should happen if the condition is true or false. The activity may be an ABAP function module, method, or procedure containing multiple other activities (see Figure 8.28). You can also define a next rule that should be executed based on the result of a called activity, which could be true, false, or an error.

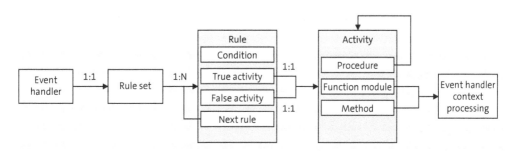

Figure 8.28 Associations among Event Handler, Rule Sets, Rules, and Activities

Using Rules to Build an Event Handler Hierarchy

If you need hierarchical relations of event handlers (e.g., a tracked box in a tracked container), inheritance of tracking IDs allows you to easily indicate this reference. As soon as the box is packed into the container, the container event handler passes its tracking ID to the box event handler so that each message for the container event handler is now also processed by the box event handler (same tracking ID). This can be easily managed by rules and activities in the SAP Event Management activity repository (see the IMG under **Event Management • General Settings in SAP Event Management • Functions, Conditions, and Activities in SAP Event Management**). After the box is de-containerized, the box event handler deactivates its relation to the container event handler, and it can then be tracked on its own.

You define rule sets in Customizing under **Event Management • Reaction to Event Messages • Define Rule Sets**. Here you can manage rule sets and define the single activities and logic in them. You also have access to activity definitions, multitasking activities (procedures), and rule conditions.

To provide a better overview of complex rule sets, you can also display rule set details, which takes you to a screen where the complete rule set with all its rules, conditions, and activities are displayed.

Figure 8.29 shows the rule set maintenance and the rule set details display. In the details display, you can identify the procedural structure of the rule set, for example, in the **LOADING_BEGIN** section.

To ease and support the development and distribution of SAP Event Management settings, you can use solutions and scenario definitions to package all settings done for a scenario implementation on the SAP Event Management or application system side. In the IMG, the setup can be found under **Event Management • Solutions and Scenarios**. Here you can assign event handler types, rule sets, extension tables, parameters and conditions, functions, activities, web interface transactions, users, and document flow to a scenario. Each scenario can then be exported from SAP Event Management as a business configuration (BC) set, which allows you to import it into another EMS.

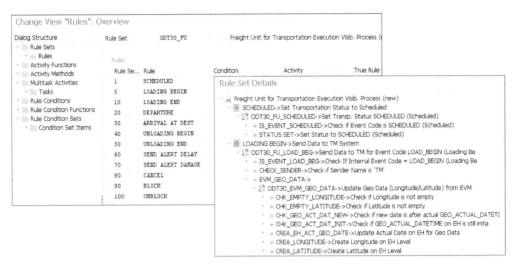

Figure 8.29 Rule Set Maintenance and Details Display

8.2.5 End-User Interaction, Lists, and Background Processing

SAP Event Management offers different methods of user interaction:

- Role-based web end-user interaction to retrieve data from SAP Event Management or interaction based on event messages
- List processing for power users to execute maintenance, retrieval, and inspection tasks
- Transactions for simple event message input

The role-based web interface allows you to define web transactions for event handler data retrieval and posting of event messages. It can be used to provide tracking information to end users and customers or partners and offers them the possibility to take part in the event reporting. An example is a transaction for parcel tracking, where a customer can follow the status of its parcel, and the receiver can send a proof of delivery event if it receives the package in the correct condition.

Because the web transactions are role based, you can assign different authorizations to each role and define the kind of event handlers and event messages, as well as the details a user can see. In addition, the event reporting feature can be authorized or restricted. You can find the setup of the web interface in the IMG under **Event Management • Event Messages, Status Queries, and Web Interface • Web Interface**, where you can define the web interface transactions, configure the visibility of data

8

and authorization, and assign users or roles to the web interface transactions. Figure 8.30 shows an example of a web interface transaction where drilldown capabilities have been configured to do complex intermodal container tracking for an LSP.

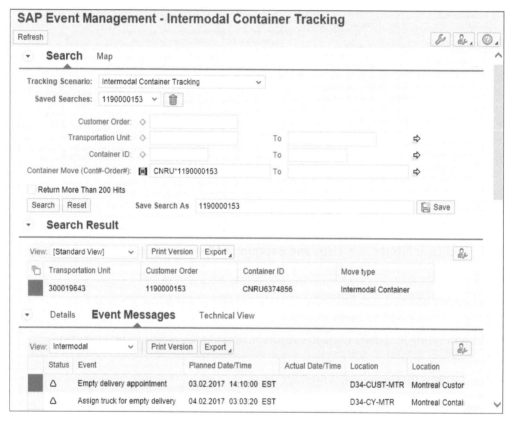

Figure 8.30 Web Interface of SAP Event Management

With the lists in SAP Event Management, you can either retrieve information as a professional user or control the processing of data. Control processing can be done interactively, when a user starts the corresponding transaction, or as a background process started by a batch job to regularly do data processing. The following list processes are provided in SAP Event Management:

- **Event handler list (interactive)**
  Using the event handler list, you can find and retrieve event handlers from SAP Event Management. You can drill down into the event handler overview and the detail display, which offers an in-depth overview of all event handler data.

From the event handler details, you can also update event handler data, which is a functionality that should be used only for maintenance purposes because it may corrupt data consistency.

- **Unprocessed message list (background or interactive)**
  The unprocessed message list allows you to process received messages that could not be processed (e.g., due to a locking situation). If an event handler receives two independent messages within a millisecond time frame, the second message may find the event handler locked while processing the first message. In this case, the unprocessed message processor can be scheduled and run regularly to resolve this situation.

- **Expected event overdue processing (preferably background)**
  The expected event overdue processing should be done regularly, best triggered by a batch job in less than an hour time frame (usually 5–10 minutes, depending on the on-time criticality). The processing checks whether any expected event was overdue and raises an exception processing of the corresponding event handlers that can be handled in the rule set.

- **Event message reprocessing (interactive)**
  In situations where event handler rules need to be tested, reprocessing can support the process so that not every test requires new event messages.

- **Status list for event message processing**
  This status list shows the processing status of the event messages that have been received for the selected event handlers.

8.2.6   Integrating SAP Event Management with Other Components

In Section 8.2.2, we described the integration of application systems (which includes SAP TM) with SAP Event Management for creating event handlers or posting event messages. On top of this very fundamental integration, SAP Event Management offers a variety of predefined content and additional integration points with SAP TM and other components and legacy systems, which we'll discuss in this section.

Predefined SAP Transportation Management Content

For SAP TM application objects, there is a corresponding preconfigured process, which you can use out of the box just by enabling it in Customizing, as follows:

1. Activate the SAP Event Management integration in the corresponding settings of the SAP TM object type (e.g., in the freight order type).
2. Enable and set up the application interface for the corresponding process (Section 8.2.3).
3. Enable and set up the SAP Event Management process (Section 8.2.3).

The following visibility processes are ready to use, as shown in Table 8.3.

Visibility Process	Application Object	Event Handler Type
SOP instruction tracking	ODT30_INS	ODT30_INS
Freight unit tracking	ODT30_FU	ODT30_FU
Freight order tracking	ODT30_TO	ODT30_TO
Resource tracking	RES30_RESOURCE	RES30_RESOURCE

Table 8.3 Visibility Processes and Their Implementations

Integration between SAP TM and SAP Event Management

There are two additional integration points between SAP TM and SAP Event Management:

1. The first is the posting and update of SAP TM-relevant data from SAP Event Management to SAP TM as result of rule processing. In many scenarios, receipt of an event needs to update corresponding data in SAP TM. If, for example, an event handler has an expected event for arrival at a destination that is derived from an SAP TM freight unit arrival date, then the rule processing can call an activity, which updates the SAP TM freight unit actual date upon receipt of the arrival event message (see Figure 8.31).
2. SAP TM and other systems can retrieve event handler data for displaying inside the application context. With this integration, a user can see the event handler status without calling a web transaction. The data is displayed as part of the current transaction (e.g., in the SAP TM **Execution** tabs). SAP TM also offers the sending of event messages to SAP Event Management upon manual setting of the actual dates, for example, in the freight unit maintenance. Figure 8.31 shows an example of displayed event message data in an SAP TM railcar unit context.

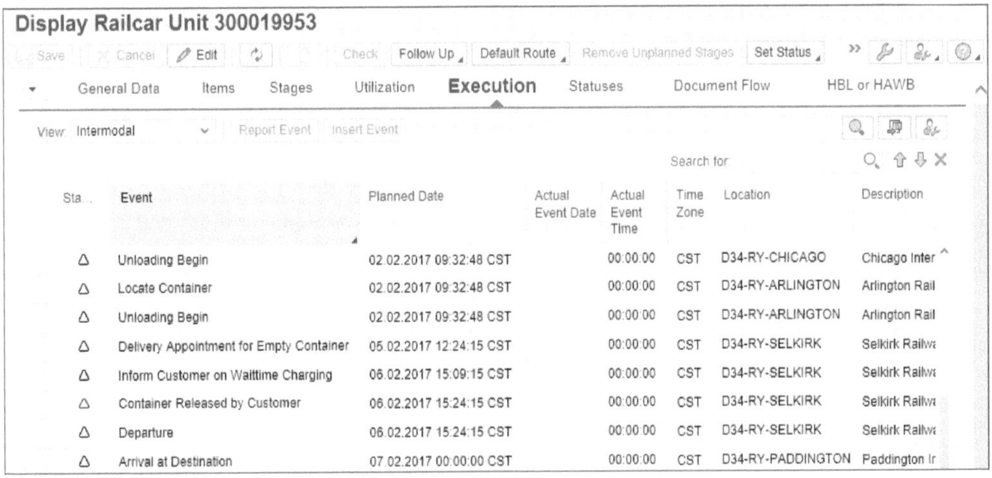

Figure 8.31 Event Message Data Displayed in SAP TM Railcar Unit Context

Integrating SAP Event Management with Other Systems

SAP Event Management offers three important interfaces for communication, which can be used as BAPIs, enterprise web services, or intermediate documents (IDocs). The interfaces can also be used to integrate with non-SAP systems such as legacy systems running in a customer's landscape.

Due to its flexibility and universality, SAP Event Management can also be connected and integrated with many other SAP components. The following integration cases have been done within SAP environments as prototypes, as part of standard products, or as custom development projects:

- Integration of SAP Event Management with SAP Global Trade Services (SAP GTS) for tracking customs approval status
- Integration of SAP Event Management with SAP EWM to track the detailed movements of items in a warehouse or yard
- Integration of SAP Event Management with SAP CRM incident management as a custom development add-on to create incidents to be handled by customer service in the event of critical situations in the supply chain that effect service-level agreements for handling of customer cargo

8.3   SAP Global Track and Trace

SAP Global Track and Trace is a public cloud-based service, which allows joint access and scenario usage. The event processing, visualization, and process handling capabilities are provided for all related and registered parties. The implemented scenarios don't represent the view of one company anymore (i.e., the process owner) but a common view on a scenario where all relevant companies can view and contribute. As tracking processes in SAP Global Track and Trace can be jointly used due to the cloud access capability, implementation of complex product provenance proofs can be implemented more easily. A trust chain from raw material to point of consumption with a complete electronic record and forward as well as backward traceability of the material can be expected to be implemented in future.

The availability of new Internet of Things (IoT) and sensor integration technologies coming with SAP Leonardo opens a large field of integration possibilities to enrich the data and event reporting in logistic chains. The SAP platforms also allow embedding of the relevant tracking information into workspaces and platforms.

Industry-Related Utilization of SAP Global Track and Trace

SAP Global Track and Trace is a quite new tool, which is reflected in its capabilities and ongoing development progress as well as in its industry-related utilization. Due to the necessary efforts, usage in all industries currently isn't possible. Therefore, typical use cases that match capabilities and integration paths are provided for the shipper industries. An integration with SAP TM, as it's required for LSPs, will be developed in a future release. Specific process industries (e.g., consumer products or chemicals) also use a specific tool named SAP Global Batch Traceability (SAP GBT), which can be integrated with SAP Global Track and Trace.

In Figure 8.32, you can see an example process, which explains the different characteristics of the SAP tracking systems. The main process deals with tracking over multiple company instances and goods consistencies. A raw material (e.g., for sanitary products) is produced and shipped via an exporter and a trader to a semifinished goods manufacturer. The semifinished goods are purchased by a consumer products manufacturer to make sanitary articles, which subsequently are sold to retailers, from there to smaller shops and finally to an end customer. In all these subprocesses and business relations, transportation may be used, which is done by an LSP. For many parties in the supply chain, the origin and quality of the different product consistencies is important. Faulty raw products may cause issues anywhere in the following chain. Each party in the supply chain may report and query its event data to and from SAP Global Track and Trace, which connects all participants from the raw material producer to the end customer. However, because the LSPs usually have a very strong interest in tracking and controlling their own logistics operations and due to release availability, they would usually run SAP Event Management, which on the other side could also feed selected data into SAP Global Track and Trace to complete the supply chain information. In the same way, the finished goods producer may use an instance of GBT, which also can be connected to SAP Global Track and Trace. Doing so, SAP Global Track and Trace provides the end-to-end status of the supply chain and material or product provenance to all authorized participants.

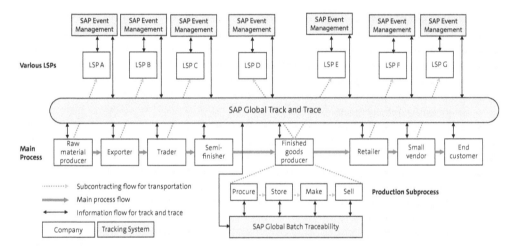

Figure 8.32 Utilization of Available SAP Global Track and Trace Solutions in a Long Supply Chain

SAP Global Track and Trace offers quite a range of new features and technologies when it comes to collaborative tracking and data evaluations. This allows for a certain strength compared to SAP Event Management, which is based on the innovative architecture and foundation. Table 8.4 shows you a comparison of the features of SAP Global Track and Trace and SAP Event Management.

Feature	SAP Global Track and Trace	SAP Event Management
Onboarding support	X	
Master data consolidation	X	
Integration to SAP S/4HANA	X	X
Integration to SAP TM		X
Role-based access	X	X
Role-specific view and filtering		X
Standard tracking	X	X
Tracking of parts/items	X	
Alerting, rules engine, process control		X
Attachments to events		X
High configurability/Customizing in model setup		X
Event handler sets		X
Serialization support, Electronic Product Code Information Services (EPCIS)		X
Analytics		X
On-premise installation		X
Cloud service	X	
Cloud scalability on demand (performance)	X	
Multitier visibility	X	
Archiving		X
SAP Leonardo stack	X	

Table 8.4 Comparison of SAP Global Track and Trace and SAP Event Management Features

Feature	SAP Global Track and Trace	SAP Event Management
Strong business network support	X	
Machine learning and blockchain integration	X	
Shipper processes	X	X
LSP processes		X

Table 8.4 Comparison of SAP Global Track and Trace and SAP Event Management Features (Cont.)

As SAP Global Track and Trace is a public cloud-based solution, the deployment cycles for new functionalities and features are much shorter compared with an on-premise version. Therefore, existing, updated, and new features that users need to be made aware of are directly accessible through the UI of the SAP Global Track and Trace launchpad start page. In Figure 8.33, you can see the help function for a selected topic displayed for each main menu entry.

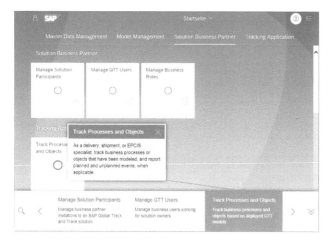

Figure 8.33 SAP Global Track and Trace Launchpad Start Page with Menu Content and Tile Explanation

As part of the help functionality, the news for the current cloud release of SAP Global Track and Trace is accessible. Figure 8.34 shows you the release news of SAP Global Track and Trace version 2018.08a, which allows you to get an overview on the impact of the newly available scope.

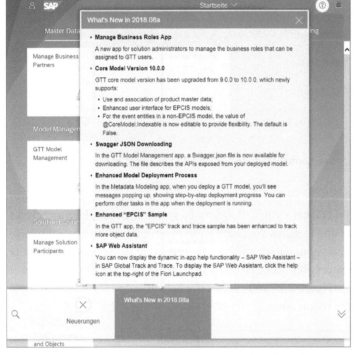

Figure 8.34 Release News View in the SAP Global Track and Trace Launchpad Start Page

In the implementation as of Q3/2018, SAP Global Track and Trace has some major scenarios embedded, which are directly integrated with logistics functionality of SAP S/4HANA:

- **SO fulfillment**
  Ensure on-time, in-full delivery to customers by surveying all relevant milestones to increase customer satisfaction.

- **Procurement**
  Get granular, real-time PO status information from your business partner ecosystem to avoid costly firefighting.

- **Goods and assets in transit**
  Track goods that are in transit and keep track of assets/returnables as they move along the entire supply chain to reduce operational costs.

- **Product lifecycle**
  Set up a repository for your finished products, and track downstream distribution or even after-sales events for advanced customer service.

Figure 8.35 shows the details of an event message view for a PO item in a procurement process of SAP Global Track and Trace. Data accessible in the detailed views corresponds to some extent with what SAP Event Management provides. However, the UI provides the innovative features of the SAP Fiori technology.

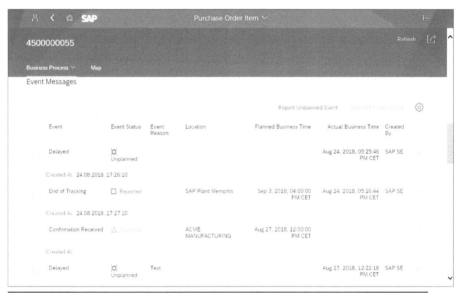

Figure 8.35 Event Message View on a PO Item in SAP Global Track and Trace with Geographic Overview

Concerning flexibility of models, there is still a much higher configurability and customizing capability in SAP Event Management. In SAP Global Track and Trace, models are also very flexible, but must be created using a metadata modeling app with a language called CDS definition language (CDL), which runs as a part of the SAP Global Track and Trace Plug-in for SAP Web IDE Full-Stack. There you can define, design, and deploy SAP Global Track and Trace projects, which allow you to activate it in the cloud. For maintenance purposes, an SAP Global Track and Trace Model Management app is available. In Figure 8.36, you can see the metamodels and their status, which are deployed into SAP Global Track and Trace (left screen) and an example of event handling within the model for **Purchase Order Item Tracking** for the events **Transportation Planned** and **Supplier Goods Issue**.

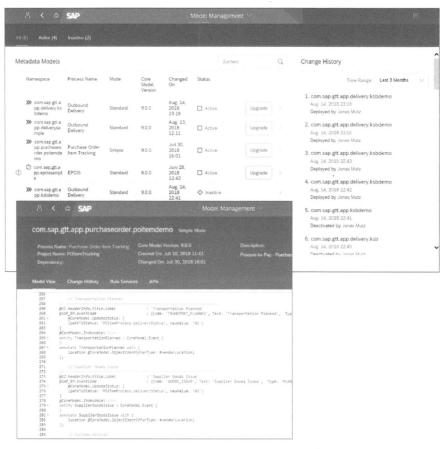

Figure 8.36 SAP Global Track and Trace Metadata Models (Left) and View into the CDL Representing the Model

SAP Global Track and Trace will see a lot of developments and features in the future and is already prepared to support the processes coming with the new digital age of logistics.

8.4 Summary

This chapter gave an overview of how to execute and monitor transportation processes. Regarding transportation execution, we explained how you can work with the result of planning and execute freight orders and bookings, introducing the concept of print documents and discrepancies in Sections Section 8.1.1 and Section 8.1.2.

In Section 8.1.3, we introduced the concept of interaction between an export and import organization and how this can be handled with different sets of documents on either side.

In the SAP Event Management and SAP Global Track and Trace sections, you learned which visibility options you have with the traditional SAP Event Management or what the new SAP Global Track and Trace will bring.

In the next chapter, we offer insight into transportation compliance handling in terms of legal and trade compliance and dangerous goods regulations. In addition, we'll look into processes of SAP TM that are supported by connecting to third-party providers in terms of compliance and security.

Chapter 9

Transportation Compliance

Functional capabilities in the SAP portfolio can support your daily processes around transportation-related legal, environmental, and trade compliance. In this chapter, we focus on two SAP applications: SAP Global Trade Services and SAP S/4HANA for product compliance. In addition, we introduce you to the option to interface with compliance services of external providers, such as Descartes.

Highly globalized markets and integrated supply chains offer many opportunities to companies acting in international economies. International business can involve risks for supply chains and the environment, as well as numerous underlying national and international regulations. Dealing with such hurdles in an effective manner without neglecting a company's core business is a challenge for many businesses. SAP applications for transportation compliance support you in overcoming these obstacles.

Transportation compliance describes the expectation of abiding by local and international laws and regulations in transportation and logistics. The following list categorizes the different areas of transportation compliance, in line with SAP software applications:

- **Import and export management**
  Every country checks incoming and outgoing cargo regarding customs obligations and ensures conformance with national and international trade laws. This requires the creation of export/import declarations to authorities, embargo checks, and sanctioned party screenings for each foreign shipment. In addition, trade finance services can fall under this category to ensure payment of goods via a letter of credit. Import/export systems that require a data exchange between companies and customs authorities include the following:
  - U.S. Automated Export System and Automated Broker Interface
  - Brazil Nota Fiscal Electronica

- European New Computerized Transit System (NCTS)
- German ATLAS System

■ **Special customs procedures**
The usage, categorization, and further processing of goods can entail various exceptions to regular import/export customs requirements, which are called special customs procedures. Goods that remain in bond, for example—that is, remain in a warehouse before being exported again—aren't subject to customs duty. Inward/outward processing prevents custom obligations if goods are being exported, processed abroad, and reimported. Only the value added is subject to customs duty. The same applies for raw materials that are imported and exported again after processing or assembly.

■ **Trade preference management**
Countries have preferences about importing goods from certain countries and prohibitions against others. Trade preference management is the process of managing the eligibility of products for reduced import duty rates.

■ **Security filing**
Security filing is a legal requirement demanded by more and more countries to collect and check information on any kind of shipment and cargo entering the borders or sovereign territory of a country. The process of filing mainly concerns air and ocean cargo. It's defined by countries such as the United States, China, Canada, Japan, or countries within the European Union and implemented in individual IT-based services, such as the Advanced Manifest System (AMS) in the United States, Importer Security Filing (ISF) in the United States, or Advance Commercial Information (ACI) in Canada. Security filing requires the carrier or forwarder to send detailed information on the shipped cargo and its related business partners at least 24 hours before the corresponding transport leaves the exporting country to receive clearance. The cargo may not be shipped with uncleared security status.

■ **Dangerous and hazardous goods**
Dealing with dangerous and hazardous goods exposes companies to additional risks and therefore responsibilities. Multiple legal regulations must be followed depending on a categorization of products according to both national and international law. This includes specific requirements for documentation and operational limitations, such as mixed loading prohibitions and averting the use of wrong container types, trucks, or even aircrafts with certain goods. Entire import bans or quantity restrictions can be applied to certain dangerous and hazardous goods classes.

The two core applications in the SAP portfolio that support your business in dealing with challenges regarding transportation compliance are SAP Global Trade Services (SAP GTS) and SAP S/4HANA for product compliance. Both applications are integrated into SAP Transportation Management (SAP TM) and contain individual functional components:

- SAP GTS is part of SAP's Global Risk and Compliance portfolio. It's integrated into SAP S/4HANA, SAP ERP, SAP Customer Relationship Management (SAP CRM), SAP Extended Warehouse Management (SAP EWM), SAP Event Management, and SAP TM. We look at SAP GTS in Section 9.1.

- SAP S/4HANA for product compliance offers extensive functionality, such as employee health and safety management, Product Safety and Stewardship (PS&S), and environmental and product compliance, as well as registration, evaluation, and authorization of chemicals (REACH) and dangerous and hazardous goods management. We look at SAP S/4HANA for product compliance in Section 9.2.

Furthermore, SAP TM offers a variety of integration scenarios with compliance and booking service providers via web services. These services are open to be utilized with any provider via SAP Process Integration if the integration and data mapping is provided on the service provider side. We explain these services in Section 9.3.

9.1   SAP Global Trade Services

SAP GTS is the most extensive application in the SAP portfolio for trade compliance management. It's highly integrated into the SAP landscape, especially into SAP S/4HANA and SAP TM, where it's now part of SAP S/4HANA for international trade. In this area, SAP GTS has the following five functional components to support your business:

- **Export management**
  SAP GTS helps you to streamline complex export processes to ensure faster delivery to your customers. SAP GTS automates your interactions with authorities due to its numerous interfaces with customs applications.

- **Import management**
  Like the export process, you can expedite customs clearance for import shipments and reduce costly buffer stocks, aiming for just-in-time inventory management. SAP GTS allows you to easily classify products, calculate duties, streamline electronic communication with customs authorities, ensure import compliance, and manage letters of credit.

- **Trade preference management**
  You can determine the eligibility of your products for preferential customs treatment and issue certificates of origin to your customers.

- **Special customs procedures**
  This functional component supports you in managing your in-bond customs warehouses. You can drive process efficiency for duty reliefs regarding inward and outward processing and decrease costs by referring duty obligations.

- **Special regional procedures**
  Businesses operating in the European Union (EU) can use SAP GTS to manage and calculate the restitution for the export of common agricultural products (CAP) out of the EU with capabilities to assign securities, manage export licenses, maintain recipes, and calculate and apply for refunds.

9.1.1   Functional Overview

Let's take a closer look at specific SAP GTS functionality related to logistics and transportation to explain how you can use it in a standard implementation.

SAP S/4HANA versus SAP ERP

SAP GTS functionality is integrated with both SAP S/4HANA and SAP ERP. Keeping in line with our pattern, our discussion will use SAP S/4HANA as the base system, with key differences for SAP ERP and SAP TM 9.6 noted where needed.

Import and Export Management

The first key functionality in import and export management is the import/export classification. Companies are required to ensure that they have licenses for certain goods and declare their license codes when filing customs declarations with authorities. SAP GTS allows you to assign import/export control classification number codes to your existing materials from your SAP S/4HANA system (products in SAP GTS). This functionality is mainly used for shippers because most LSPs don't maintain product masters for goods they ship for their customers.

The second core functional component, import and export compliance, is supported by three capabilities: sanctioned party list screenings, embargo checks, and license management. You can use complex checks to screen your business partners for denied parties. This functionality is used with integrated sales orders (SOs) and purchase orders (POs), financial accounting (to prohibit financial interactions), SAP TM order management, and transport execution. Embargo checks follow the same concept. For both embargo checks and sanctioned party lists, you can use SAP GTS to manage all blocked documents centrally.

Third, SAP GTS has a strong functional component that supports you in generating and processing customs declarations, as well as interacting and communicating with customs authorities. If you work as a shipper, you'll benefit from the goods classification of your materials and product master data. If you work as a freight forwarder, you'll collect most customs-relevant information directly from the shipper/consignee; however, due to missing product master, the functionality may be limited. SAP GTS offers numerous interfaces to local authorities with standardized e-filing formats.

Special Customs Procedures

Besides numerous obligations and regulations in international trade, authorities still support your international business with certain customs exceptions. SAP GTS supports three key processes to benefit from such duty exemptions.

First, SAP GTS supports you in your customs warehouse activities to store duty-unpaid goods. This is permitted in two situations. If you keep cargo in transit before it's shipped to another (possibly yet unknown) country, no duties apply. Alternatively, you can keep a stock of duty-unpaid goods if they are being processed for free circulation with a prescribed end use for industrial assembly. For both cases, SAP GTS is tightly integrated into SAP S/4HANA and SAP EWM for warehouse processes. When you're receiving inbound deliveries based on POs, SAP GTS can automatically detect whether they are to be treated as in-bond goods. SAP GTS helps you in its integration with SAP EWM to manage stocks of in-transit and duty-unpaid products.

Second, you can manage your processes of free circulation with prescribed end use and processing under customs control. The goods you've imported have a higher duty obligation than the finished product they might be used for in an assembly or industrial process. SAP GTS supports identification of goods that qualify for such treatment, monitoring stocks, warehouse movements, and interactions with authorities to calculate duty deductions. It's integrated with both SAP S/4HANA and SAP EWM.

Third, you can declare goods for outward and inward processing. This process aims at you as a manufacturer, exporting products into another country for processing and reimporting them for assembly/disposition (outward processing). You must pay customs duties only for the newly added product components/value. The import process works the other way around. You must declare products for inbound processing if you intend to reexport them after processing. Again, SAP GTS is the core application that supports this process, integrated into billing documents and orders.

9.1.2   Integration of SAP GTS and SAP TM

The previous section explained how logistics-relevant functional components of SAP GTS are integrated into systems, such as SAP S/4HANA, SAP TM, SAP EWM, and SAP Event Management. Table 9.1 summarizes the SAP applications that are linked to different functional components of SAP GTS.

Functional Components of International Trade (SAP GTS)	SAP ERP	SAP EWM	SAP TM	SAP Event Management
Import and Export Management				
Import/export classification	X			
Customs services export	X		X	X
Customs services import	X			
Custom services transit	X			
Letter of credit	X			
Embargo checks	X		X	
Sanctioned party list screening	X		X	
Trade preference management	X			
Special customs procedures	X	X		
Special regional procedures	X	X		

Table 9.1 Functional Components Using SAP GTS

Let's shift our focus to the functionality that is used in the integration between SAP TM and SAP GTS only. From a transportation perspective, the transactional process is enabled for two major technical objects in SAP TM: the transportation request (TRQ) representing the customer order side, and the transportation order (TOR) for the subcontracting side.

Integration of Master Data

With SAP TM in SAP S/4HANA, master data no longer needs special integration. You only need to synchronize the master data from your backend SAP S/4HANA or SAP ERP system to SAP GTS if SAP TM is running standalone. After a successful integration of master data, you need to enrich records with additional SAP GTS-specific information, such as product classifications (to identify goods based on customs authority definitions) or product groupings (which allow logical grouping of goods with equal customs requirements). Additional master data needs to be maintained directly in SAP GTS because it's used solely in SAP GTS, for example, country groupings (assignment of country of departure and country of destination to country groups), customs list (import/export classification numbers), licenses for import/ export, and sanctioned party lists.

Integration of Transactional Data

The transactional integration between SAP GTS and SAP TM is based on web services using SAP Process Integration. Alternatively, it's possible to define point-to-point (P2P) connections without going via SAP Process Integration but still facilitating the Enterprise Service Repository (ESR) in SAP Process Integration. Freight orders and forwarding orders are the main transactional documents, which are interfaced with SAP GTS for specific functionality. Figure 9.1 shows which objects can be used for which functionalities in the integration with SAP GTS.

The forwarding order, for example, can be validated against a sanctioned party list because this is where you maintain your shipper, consignee, and other business partners. In the upcoming sections, we'll introduce the details of the functionalities in the transactional context. It's important to highlight that the integration between SAP TM and SAP GTS for customs services is currently available only in the standard for export customs services, export compliance, and import services and compliance.

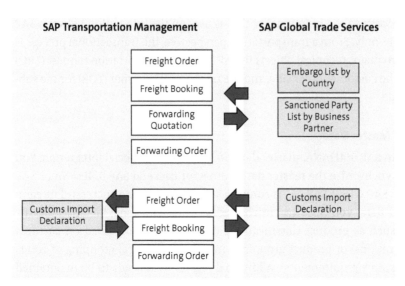

SAP Transportation Management

Freight Order

Freight Booking

Forwarding Quotation

Forwarding Order

SAP Global Trade Services

Embargo List by Country

Sanctioned Party List by Business Partner

Customs Import Declaration

Freight Order

Freight Booking

Forwarding Order

Customs Import Declaration

Figure 9.1 Integration of SAP TM and SAP GTS

9.1.3   Export Compliance for Sanctioned Party Screening and Embargo Checks

Various historical events, especially the terrorist attacks of September 11, 2001, led to stricter legal regulations to monitor and blacklist companies if they violate local law. Different countries and legal authorities have issued blacklists that name all businesses and individuals with whom it's prohibited to have a business relationship, including importing and exporting goods. Companies are now legally obliged to check their business partners against government blacklists of sanctioned parties. The challenges in this process are that companies can have thousands or even millions of records of business partners with various spellings and addresses. Blacklists frequently change and require updates, which makes manual maintenance very difficult, if not impossible.

It's similarly relevant for both shippers and freight forwarders to validate business partners and check destination or transit countries against sanctioned parties and embargo lists that appear in your orders and freight documents. Figure 9.2 gives an overview of the entire process for both a shipper and an LSP.

In the right white boxes, you can see the LSP-specific objects, such as the forwarding order/quotation. The left white boxes illustrate the shipper scenario. Some objects are relevant for both an LSP and a shipper, such as the freight units. As a shipper, you can start the process for compliance checks by creating orders and deliveries in SAP S/4HANA. Alternatively, as a freight forwarder or carrier, you would start the process by creating a forwarding order directly in SAP TM.

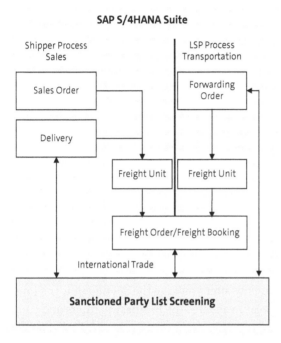

Figure 9.2 Sanctioned Party Checks with SAP TM and SAP GTS (International Trade)

Figure 9.3 shows that an LSP performs the compliance checks directly when capturing a forwarding order or providing a quotation to a customer. This allows you to prevent the creation and execution of an order very early in the process. After a forwarding order is created, it's automatically blocked for execution with the category **Compliance**.

After the document is saved, the business partners and country information are handed to sanctioned party list screening for the validation. SAP GTS returns the compliance status as either **Not Compliant** or **Compliant**. If a business partner or country is detected as blacklisted or under an embargo, you can cancel the forwarding order or manually release the business partner or document as compliant in SAP GTS to release the execution block in the forwarding order.

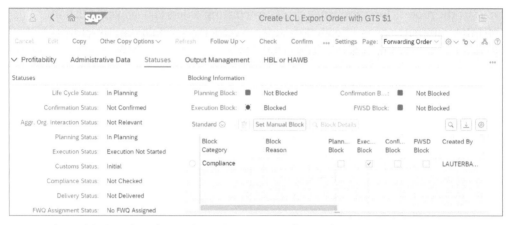

Figure 9.3 Sanctioned Party Screening in Forwarding Order

If you work as a shipper, you don't use the forwarding order. Instead, you can perform the compliance checks either from the sales documents or after transportation planning from either the freight order or the freight booking. As an LSP, you can use the same functionality to validate freight orders and bookings. After you've successfully created a freight order or booking, the compliance status is set to **Not Checked**, and the execution block is activated. Only after you save the document is the interface to SAP GTS triggered. SAP GTS again validates the business partners and countries against blacklists and embargos. The document is released or blocked, depending on the screening result. You can now handle the exceptions of blocked freight orders or bookings in SAP GTS. You can monitor all blocked documents and business partners and manually release them with the appropriate reason code (e.g., a mistaken identity).

In SAP TM, very few Customizing settings are required to enable embargo checks and sanctioned party screenings. You must select the **Enable Compliance Check** checkbox for the following document types: forwarding order type, forwarding quotation type, freight order type, and freight booking type.

To enable the sanctioned party screening and embargo checks in SAP GTS, you have to configure activities in international trade Customizing:

- Maintain the Customizing table to enable the sanctioned party checks for different business partner functions.

- Define the check rules for the sanctioned party screening (e.g., using address information and keywords).

- Assign the defined check rules to a legal regulation, such as the German Foreign Trade Regulations. You can specify which types of sanctioned party lists should be considered, as well as audit trails and notification workflows.

- Enable embargo checks, and implement active legal regulations (e.g., the UN embargo regulation). For each legal regulation, you can select settings to assign business partner groups that are relevant for checks.

9.1.4   Export Customs Services

To process your international shipments successfully, as both a freight forwarder and a shipper, SAP TM offers integration with international trade for export customs services. You can check whether your outgoing shipments are customs relevant, depending on the origin and destination country of the shipment. You can't process a shipment without appropriate legal documentation, so the application blocks orders and shipments until appropriate documentation has been issued. SAP GTS supports the generation of the customs declaration and the electronic communication with authorities via electronic data interchange (EDI). SAP GTS supports the creation and printing of export documentation based on customs (e.g., legally required documentation), compliance (legally required certificates), and customer-specific requirements (individual documents).

Figure 9.4 shows the process overview for both a freight forwarder (top row) and a shipper (bottom row). As the central application, SAP GTS is used the same way for shippers and freight forwarders. The major difference is that a freight forwarder triggers the generation of a customs declaration directly from the order, whereas a shipper starts the generation of a customs declaration from a freight order or booking.

The first activity in export customs processing is to check whether the forwarding order or freight order/booking requires customs documentation at all. For shipments within the European Union, for example, no export customs declaration except Intrastat reporting (standard with SAP GTS) is required. When you save your document, the customs relevance check is automatically performed directly in SAP TM. If the result is customs relevant, you see that the order/booking is automatically blocked from execution for the reason **Customs Declaration Check Required**.

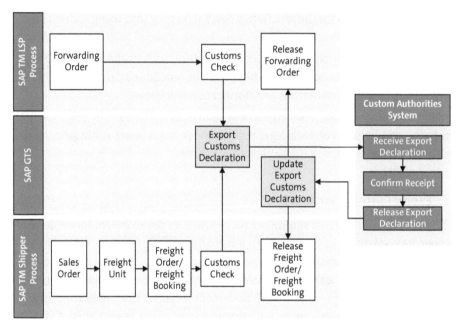

Figure 9.4 Process Overview for Export Customs Services

Export Customs Declaration Management

After a freight order/freight booking or a forwarding order has been identified as customs relevant, you need *customs groups* because each freight order/booking or forwarding order can contain multiple consignees or goods sellers, and you might need to generate a separate customs declaration for each one. The freight unit items are grouped together in a customs group. Each customs group created in SAP TM generates one export customs declaration in SAP GTS. You'll see that the generation of customs groups happens automatically and is flexibly configurable. At least one customs group is required to generate an export declaration in SAP GTS. Each SAP TM object—the forwarding order, freight order, and booking—has a **Customs** tab on the items to manage customs details and show the latest statuses.

You can create the export customs declaration by choosing **Customs · Create Export Declaration**. SAP GTS offers you the ability to monitor all incoming and generated declarations. You can perform the setup for customs checks in the IMG under **Transportation Management · Basic Functions · Global Trade**. Here you can define and assign customs-relevant checks, activities, and profiles.

After the communication has been sent, and a successful answer is received from the authorities, a reference number (e.g., the movement reference number [MRN]) is returned to both the export declaration in SAP GTS and the related forwarding order or freight order/booking in SAP TM. The customs status in SAP TM changes to **Approved**. Only now is the SAP TM document released from the execution block. For a rejection or hold, the corresponding documents in SAP TM stay blocked with an appropriate status.

Configuration for Export Customs Management and Services

To enable the process of export customs integration between SAP TM and SAP GTS, you need to perform settings in both components. You can define multiple ways to split the items of a freight order or freight booking. There are two standard methods provided to group the items: per consignee and per LSP. This is defined in a method that you can access by following the menu path **Transportation Management • SCM Basis • Process Controller • Define Method**.

The last step is to assign the method to a strategy. As a result, the strategy combines the service and method for splitting and grouping items. We use the strategy later and assign it to a customs profile.

The customs relevance check defines whether an order or booking in SAP TM requires customs clearance. This differentiates all national shipments from international transports. The customs relevance check can be defined via the menu path **Transportation Management • Basic Functions • Global Trade • Define Customs Relevance Check**. You must maintain the status values that you want to be displayed depending on the processing status of a customs procedure (e.g., **Requested**, **Approved**, etc.). Follow the menu path **Transportation Management • Basic Functions • Global Trade • Define Cumulation of Customs Statuses**.

A customs activity combines some of the settings we described, such as the customs relevance check and the process controller grouping strategy. These settings determine what status an object (e.g., freight order) needs to have for SAP TM to trigger the check of customs requirements. Last, the customs activity contains the list of all status values related to the customs process that will be displayed in your documents.

9.1.5   Import Customs Services

To ensure end-to-end transportation across countries, more than an export declaration is required from a customs service perspective. You also need an appropriate import declaration to declare goods and determine customs duty. Alternatively, you can issue a transit procedure if goods aren't declared at the border and will be transported duty-unpaid or under bond. The importing country can have very specific requirements for the content and procedure for import declarations and transit procedures.

We must emphasize that this functionality in standard SAP TM doesn't have an integration with SAP GTS. The process is executed standalone and manually in SAP TM. A business add-in (BAdI) is provided to implement a custom integration, which we cover shortly. The functionality of the import customs declaration is aimed solely at LSPs and freight forwarders acting as the customs broker for a shipper. Consequently, the functionality is enabled only for the freight unit object in combination with the import forwarding order. The transit procedure also involves your freight documents.

When generating an import forwarding order in SAP TM for a customer, you first need to select the **Import Declaration by LSP** checkbox in the **General Data** tab. If a customer always requires import customs clearance, you can maintain this checkbox on the business partner as well, which defaults it to the forwarding order. Per forwarding order item (e.g., products and containers), you can find the **Customs** tab. In this tab, it's necessary to specify what customs activity needs to be performed for the forwarding order item. You can choose between a transit procedure and, in our case, the import declaration. You also need to specify in which location the cargo is imported to a country. Select **Customs • Create Import Declaration** in the top panel of the forwarding order to generate the customs groups, for example, based on the customs location. The forwarding order is blocked for execution because processing and approval of the import declaration is required. You need to set the status to **Customs Declaration Approved** as you receive the actual approval from the customs authorities. As mentioned earlier, the entire generation of the customs declaration—as well as its submission to and handling by customs authorities—currently isn't supported. After the status for all freight unit custom groups is set to **Customs Declaration Approved**, the forwarding order is released from the execution block.

As an alternative to the import customs declaration, you can generate a transit procedure. Navigate to the **Customs** tab in the forwarding order items, and set the inbound customs activity as **Transit Procedure**. You can enter relevant data, such as commodity codes. In the **Stages** tab, you can mark each transportation leg (each stage) that requires a transit procedure for each freight unit in the forwarding order. After you've planned your forwarding order and assigned the freight units to freight orders and bookings, SAP TM automatically marks the same stages in the freight documents as **Transit Procedure Relevant**. The freight documents that are affected can be blocked for execution. You can open and close transit procedures to indicate whether the goods are currently in transit (e.g., between the border to a trade union and the transit end location). To open a transit procedure, navigate to the freight document, and select **Customs • Open Transit**. You can manually interact with the authorities, and, as soon as the transit is approved, change the status to **Open Transit Approved**. You can also store the customs document number and MRN manually; these are provided by the authorities. The freight document is released from an execution block.

A similar process can be followed to close the transit procedure: choose **Customs • Request Unload**. SAP TM generates a new customs activity and customs group, which can be processed manually to reflect the offline interaction with authorities. Each customs group's status can be changed to **Transit Unload Approved**. In addition to the capability of opening a transit procedure from a freight document, you can trigger it directly from a freight unit. The closure still happens from the freight document.

To enable import customs management in SAP TM, you must perform configuration in Customizing. First, you need a forwarding order type with a traffic direction of import. Set **Customs Handling** to **Automatic**. Only forwarding orders that have been set to automatic customs handling are considered for import customs. All other required settings are very similar to the export declaration.

Another requirement is to set up the process controller by using an import declaration strategy (IMP_FU) and a method (GT_B_IM_FU). The transit procedure must be set up the same way (e.g., strategy TRA_OPEN, TRA_CLOSE, and TRA_OPENFU). To do this, follow the menu path **Transportation Management • Basic Functions • Process Controller**. In SAP TM 9.6, you can find the configuration under **SAP Transportation Management • SCM Basis • Process Controller**. You must also implement the customs relevance check, a customs activity, and a profile—just like the export process. A key difference from the export process is that you need to assign the customs profile to a freight unit type. To enable both the transit procedure and import customs declaration, you need to generate two separate customs activities and assign them to a customs profile.

To enable automated communication with customs authorities via a customs management application, such as SAP GTS, you can implement a BAdI provided in standard SAP TM. You can find the BAdI in SAP TM Customizing via the menu path **Transportation Management • Business Add-Ins (BAdIs) for Transportation Management • Basic Functions • Global Trade • Declarations**.

9.2   SAP S/4HANA for Product Compliance

Cargo moved in shipments needs to comply with product compliance regulations. Product compliance—also known as dangerous goods handling, hazardous materials, hazmat, or dangerous and hazardous (DnH)—refers to dealing with material solids, liquids, and gases that can harm people, other organisms, or the environment. Shipments moving these dangerous goods can therefore have a direct influence on the environment, the health of people that are in contact with them, and the safety of all surrounding material objects. The risk of moving dangerous goods is based on multiple factors and characteristics:

- The characteristics of the material itself and its impact on the environment, including whether it's flammable, explosive, corrosive, radioactive, oxidizing, toxic or asphyxiating, pathogenic or allergenic, or biohazardous in nature
- The risk of inappropriate transportation or handling, which includes improper or damaged means of transport; unsuitable transportation routes; and unqualified, unreliable, or overworked personnel
- Risk factors due to external influences, such as terrorism

In SAP S/4HANA, you can perform checks to ensure safe and compliant transportation of dangerous goods. These checks reflect the international and national regulations regarding dangerous goods transport and depend on transportation mode, transit countries, and other factors. SAP S/4HANA for product compliance provides a framework for delivering certain checks. It's used in combination with SAP TM and consists of several components:

- Basic data and tools
- Product safety
- Occupational health
- Industrial hygiene and safety
- Waste management
- Dangerous goods

From this set of components, basic data, tools, and dangerous goods are integrated with SAP TM.

9.2.1   Dangerous Goods Regulations

Dangerous Goods Regulations (DGR) differ by mode of transport, issuing country or region, and activity category or material status. For example, warehouse handling rules for flammable materials in the United States may differ from regulations that determine flammable materials transportation rules in Swiss tunnels.

Several globally valid dangerous goods agreements and regulations are relevant for transportation. The following are the most important ones:

- **International Maritime Dangerous Goods (IMDG) Code**
  The IMDG has been defined by the International Maritime Organization (IMO) to standardize terminology, packaging, labeling, and markings of dangerous goods and advice on stowage, segregation, handling, and emergency reactions for dangerous goods transport on vessels.

- **IATA Dangerous Goods Regulations**
  The International Air Transport Association (IATA) is the governing body of airlines and published the 54th edition of the *Dangerous Goods Regulations* in 2013. *Dangerous Goods Regulations* is a guide to safely shipping cargo or passenger luggage by air.

- **ICAO Safe Transport of Dangerous Goods by Air**
  The International Civil Aviation Organization (ICAO), which is an association of countries, has defined joint rules for safe air cargo transportation in annex 18 of their international standards and recommended practice (SARP).

- **Hazardous Materials Regulations (HMR) of the Code of Federal Regulations (CFR)**
  The HMR is regulated by the US Department of Transportation (DOT) in Title 49 CFR Parts 171-180. The HMR applies to transportation of hazardous materials in interstate, intrastate, and foreign commerce by aircraft, railcar, vessel, and motor vehicle.

Some European regulations are also commonly used:

- **Regulations concerning the International Carriage of Dangerous Goods by Rail (RID)**
  The RID, issued by the Intergovernmental Organization for International Carriage by Rail (OTIF), regulates dangerous goods processes on rail cargo for European, Middle Eastern, and some North African countries.

- **European Agreement concerning the International Carriage of Dangerous Goods by Road (ADR)**
  ADR regulations are targeted at transnational transport of dangerous goods in Europe and were launched by the UN Economic Commission for Europe (UNECE).
- **European Agreement concerning the International Carriage of Dangerous Goods by Inland Waterways (ADN)**
  Like ADR, ADN regulates the transport of dangerous goods on inland waterways in Europe.

9.2.2 Dangerous Goods Classification

Dangerous goods classification is to some extent harmonized through the UN Recommendations on the Transport of Dangerous Goods with the goal of making it easy to understand what kind of cargo is transported and what hazards are entailed without having in-depth knowledge of chemistry or physics. Dangerous goods are divided into the following classes:

- Class 1: Explosive substances and articles:
  - 1.1: Substances and articles that have a mass explosion hazard
  - 1.2: Substances and articles that have a projection hazard but not a mass explosion hazard
  - 1.3: Substances and articles that have a fire hazard and a minor blast hazard, minor projection hazard, or both, but not a mass explosion hazard
  - 1.4: Substances and articles that present no significant hazard
  - 1.5: Very sensitive substances that have a mass explosion hazard
  - 1.6: Extremely insensitive articles that don't have a mass explosion hazard
- Class 2: Gases, including gases and vapors compressed, liquefied, and dissolved under pressure:
  - 2.1: Flammable gases (e.g., butane and propane acetylene)
  - 2.2: Nonflammable and nontoxic, likely to cause asphyxiation (e.g., nitrogen and $CO2$), or oxidizers (e.g., oxygen and fluorine)
  - 2.3: Toxic (e.g., chlorine and phosgene)
- Class 3: Flammable liquids:
- Class 4.1: Flammable solids, self-reactive substances, and solid desensitized explosives

- Class 4.2: Substances liable to spontaneously combust
- Class 4.3: Substances that, in contact with water, emit flammable gases
- Class 5.1: Oxidizing substances
- Class 5.2: Organic peroxides
- Class 6.1: Toxic substances and poison
- Class 6.2: Infectious substances and biohazardous materials
- Class 7: Radioactive material (e.g., uranium and plutonium)
- Class 8: Corrosive substances (e.g., acids and alkalis)
- Class 9: Miscellaneous dangerous substances and articles (e.g., asbestos, airbag inflators, self-inflating life rafts, and dry ice)

Detailed material classification is given by the four-digit UN number (currently, the number range is from 0001 to 3600). We recommend referencing UN resources for a detailed list of UN numbers.

9.2.3   Requirements for Dangerous Goods Checks in Transportation

DGR cover various aspects of dangerous goods handling, movements, accident avoidance, and legal documentation. In transportation, a subset of these requirements is applicable, and they differ slightly from a shipper's and an LSP's perspective.

Shippers involved in transportation usually have very detailed master data on the products and materials they manufacture or trade. The corresponding master data records are home to the related dangerous goods characteristic that controls the processing and documentation behavior in transportation. For shippers, the dangerous goods master data is maintained in SAP S/4HANA material master definition. The applicability of a dangerous goods check for a shipper depends on whether the shipper is executing and planning transportation versus subcontracting it to an LSP.

In the first case, the shipper is obligated to thoroughly execute all checks required and provide its personnel with appropriate training and transportation documentation, such as a shipper's declaration for dangerous goods or dangerous goods sheets. If the shipper subcontracts complete dangerous goods transportation, the shipper needs to simply provide accurate dangerous goods data for the forwarding orders to the LSP.

An LSP that actively handles dangerous goods transportation usually doesn't have detailed master data records for the materials shipped (unless it's a contract logistic business, where the LSP manages the supply chain for the shipper). In this case, the forwarding order needs to bring the correct and detailed classification for the forwarding order items that allow running the transportation of dangerous goods check process.

Checking for dangerous goods in transportation encompasses the following auditing steps (see also Figure 9.5):

1. Check the forwarding order to determine whether transportation of the ordered items can be done at all. It may not be feasible for the following reasons:
   - There are no appropriate vehicles or trained personnel.
   - Certain materials (e.g., ammunition) aren't accepted.
   - Origin, destination, or transit countries don't allow the materials to be shipped.

2. Check a single forwarding order to determine whether quantities, packaging, and shipment properties comply with the regulations:
   - Certain quantities can't be exceeded.
   - Certain material combinations can't be shipped together at all or together in one transportation or packaging unit (on a pallet, in less than x yard distance, in the same container, on the same truck, etc.).
   - The evaluation of all cargo items must not exceed a certain limit in an evaluation scale (e.g., "1,000-point rule").
   - Certain materials aren't allowed to be shipped on certain routes (e.g., flammable liquids in Swiss road tunnels).

3. Check a consolidation of cargo or transportation plan details during or after transportation planning. All rules for the single forwarding order are applicable here, too:
   - Respect quantity limits, prohibited combinations, overall evaluation of hazard potential, allowed vehicles, and allowed shipping routes for the consolidated cargo.
   - In multistop shipments, loading limits for each stop need to be checked individually. For example, for a container line business, there are certain limits on the number of containers that can be loaded or unloaded in a port.

SAP TM can perform many of these checks, but for some (e.g., the load restrictions per port), the use of custom extensions is required.

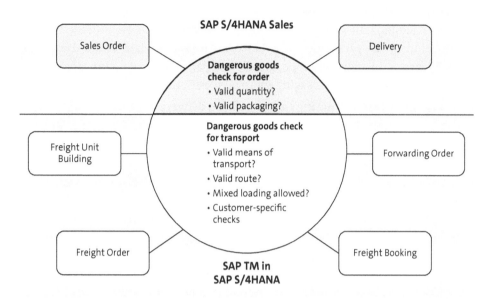

Figure 9.5 Dangerous Goods Checks for SAP TM in SAP S/4HANA

9.2.4 Configuration of Dangerous Goods Checks for SAP TM

Companies handling dangerous goods in transportation need to prepare their SAP S/4HANA system for use of the product compliance functionality in the following areas:

- Product master–related product compliance settings
- Sales and distribution–related product compliance settings
- Transportation-related product compliance settings

We'll discuss each in the following sections.

Product Master–Related Settings

Manufacturers and shippers need to maintain their product master data for raw, semifinished, and finished goods to be procured, used in production, or sold in materials management (MM) or sales and distribution (SD). For each maintained product (as described in Chapter 3, Section 3.1.4), you can define additional dangerous goods data. SAP S/4HANA offers a variety of processes for dangerous goods compliance for shippers and manufacturers in terms of handling their distribution requirements:

- **Packaging proposals in deliveries**
  In the handling unit (HU) functions of delivery, the system can propose allowed dangerous goods packaging codes based on packaging data in the dangerous goods master. In addition, proposing allowed packaging materials is done based on packaging codes and packaging approval specification.

- **Packaging and mixed packing checks within a delivery**
  If incompatible or noncompliant dangerous goods are packed together but have UN numbers that aren't allowed to be packed together, the system sends an error message and blocks further processing.

- **Mixed loading checks and transit country checks for SAP S/4HANA basic shipping**
  Shippers using transportation functionality may use the dangerous goods checks embedded in the SAP S/4HANA basic shipping scope. The HU-based mixed packing checks work the same way here as in the delivery. In addition, the checks are implemented across all deliveries assigned to the shipment. If the route and stages of the shipment have been defined, dangerous goods checks can also be done for the transit countries passed.

Dangerous Goods–Related Integration for SAP TM 9.6

In scenarios and systems where the SAP S/4HANA is the main operational system for production and delivery processes, data integration for dangerous goods is already embedded in the system. If you're using SAP ERP and SAP TM on a SAP Business Suite, master data integration between the instances is still required. In this case, the following data transmission procedures are used to synchronize SAP ERP with SAP TM 9.6:

- Transfer of dangerous goods master data from SAP ERP to SAP TM 9.6:
  - Dangerous goods master data and text phrases are distributed via Application Link Enabling (ALE) integration.
  - Material master of SAP ERP is transferred via the Core Interface (CIF).

- Transactional data transmission is embedded in the integration processes between SAP ERP SD SOs and order-based transportation requirements (OTRs) and between SAP ERP Logistics Execution (LE) deliveries and delivery-based transportation requirements (DTRs). The required dangerous goods data and master data records are provided by SAP ERP via web services to SAP TM 9.6 business objects, where they are available as references to the SAP Supply Chain Management (SAP SCM) dangerous goods master.

After material and dangerous goods master data have been transmitted from SAP ERP to SAP TM 9.6, transactional processing of forwarding orders and transportation orders (freight orders and freight bookings) can start. The integration of the checks is technically done in the same way, independently of the ordering or subcontracting side.

Configuration of Dangerous Goods Checks for SAP TM

Many settings can be found under the PS&S services topic of transportation basic functions in the Customizing IMG of the SAP S/4HANA system. Before you can use the dangerous goods checks of SAP S/4HANA for product compliance, you must enable the checks in Customizing. If you follow the IMG menu path **Transportation Management · Basic Functions · Dangerous Goods · PS&S Services · Basic Services · Specify Environment Parameters** (in SAP TM 9.6, it's **SAP Transportation Management · SCM Basis · EH&S Services · Basic Services · Specify Environment Parameters**), you need to set the environment parameter DG_SERVICES_ACTIVE to value X.

The SAP S/4HANA for product compliance component has a variety of settings where you can configure the behavior of dangerous goods management and phrase management:

- Phrase management settings allow you to define phrase libraries and language definitions for the phrases.
- Dangerous goods management provides setup for the different DG codes, categories, regulations, and classes that build the legal framework.
- Dangerous goods checks provide the configuration for the check rules and the reaction of the system on success or failure of a check.
- Dangerous goods documents allow you to set up the output conditions, formatting rules, and languages for dangerous goods paperwork.

You can find these Customizing settings in SAP TM via the IMG menu path **Transportation Management · Basic Functions · Dangerous Goods**. Here you can define, for example, the error behavior of the SAP TM–related dangerous goods checks or quantity definition for the 1,000-point rule according to ADR 1.1.3.6.

Because many dangerous good checks within SAP S/4HANA for product compliance are based on check rules, which must be embedded in a rules framework, you need to maintain individual rules. Alternatively, you have the option to load dangerous goods content via a loader so that not everything needs to be set up from scratch. Figure 9.6 shows the maintenance of check methods and the level of granularity for operations (e.g., header level and item level).

You can maintain the check methods in Customizing via the menu path **Transportation Management · Basic Functions · Dangerous Goods Management · Dangerous Goods Checks and Dangerous Goods Documents · Dangerous Goods Checks · Specify Dangerous Goods Check Methods** (in SAP TM 9.6, the menu path is **Transportation Management · SCM Basis · EH&S Services · Dangerous Goods Management · Dangerous Goods Checks and Dangerous Goods Documents · Dangerous Goods Checks · Specify Dangerous Goods Check Methods**).

Change View "EHS: Specify Dangerous Goods Check Methods": Overview

New Entries

EHS: Specify Dangerous Goods Check Methods

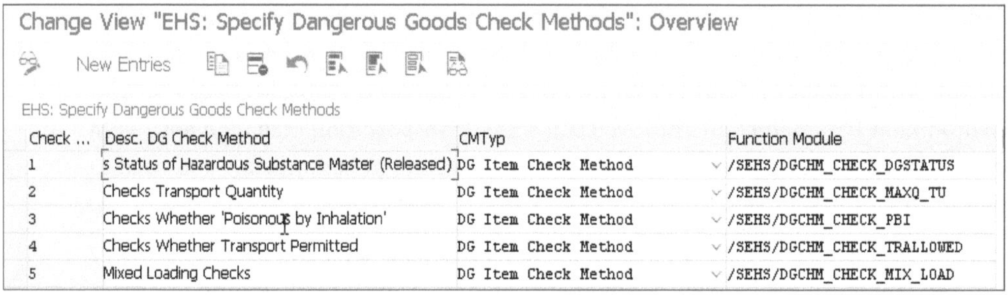

Check ...	Desc. DG Check Method	CMTyp	Function Module
1	s Status of Hazardous Substance Master (Released)	DG Item Check Method	/SEHS/DGCHM_CHECK_DGSTATUS
2	Checks Transport Quantity	DG Item Check Method	/SEHS/DGCHM_CHECK_MAXQ_TU
3	Checks Whether 'Poisonous by Inhalation'	DG Item Check Method	/SEHS/DGCHM_CHECK_PBI
4	Checks Whether Transport Permitted	DG Item Check Method	/SEHS/DGCHM_CHECK_TRALLOWED
5	Mixed Loading Checks	DG Item Check Method	/SEHS/DGCHM_CHECK_MIX_LOAD

Figure 9.6 Dangerous Goods Check Methods Maintenance in SAP TM

Segregation keys are used to define criteria to keep materials apart from each other in stowage, loading, and consolidation. Segregation key definition is done as part of dangerous goods master data maintenance. Segregation keys are maintained on the **Mixed Loading** tab. In PS&S Customizing, you can set up the segregation rules for mixed loading and define the system response if you plan to load two cargo items with segregation keys together. The result of rules also depends on the individual dangerous goods regulation and can be either a warning or an error.

9.2.5   Dangerous Goods Content Loader

The dangerous goods content loader allows you to import dangerous good regulatory content into the dangerous goods master data tables. The content can be found in the software download center of the SAP Service Marketplace (*https://support.sap.com/swdc*) via the menu path **Installations and Upgrades · A–Z Index · E · EHS RegCont DG · EHS RegCont DG 1805**. The provided content files contain DGR, regulation texts such as substance names and phrases, and Customizing data to implement the regulations and its check rules. Figure 9.7 shows the content load UI, which you can call in the SAP TM application under **Application Administration • Dangerous Goods Content Loader.**

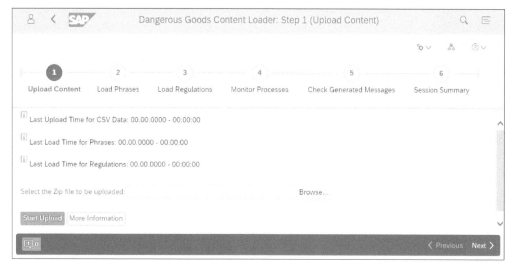

Figure 9.7 Dangerous Goods Content Loader

The content loader can be very useful for LSPs to get the system quickly set up with the data and regulations that concern the shippers. The imported content can be used to perform consistency checks on the forwarding order data provided by shippers. In addition, it provides template data for document-based dangerous goods records.

9.2.6   SAP TM Application-Level Setup for Dangerous Goods Support

You can create individual user interfaces (UIs) for document-based dangerous goods data that reflect the specific data and phrase requirements of the DGR.

The UIs specified in a UI profile can hold tabular and field data with individual field labels (see Figure 9.8). Fields can be assigned to UI groups. You can define check functions for a UI profile and use them by invoking them on the forwarding order.

You can find the tool for defining dangerous goods UI profiles in the SAP TM application menu via **Application Administration • Edit UI Profile for Dangerous Good** (in SAP

TM 9.6, the menu path is **Application Administration • General Settings • Edit UI-Profile for Document-Based Dangerous Goods Data**). The assignment of the UI profile to the forwarding order happens on the forwarding order item level. You can set the dangerous goods UI profile in the Customizing of the item types for forwarding order management.

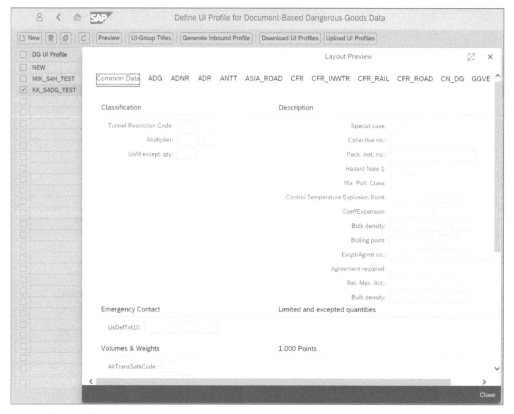

Figure 9.8 Configuration for a Dangerous Goods UI Profile

9.2.7   Dangerous Goods Data and Checks in SAP TM

As described in Section 9.2.3, dangerous goods data definition and dangerous goods checks happen mainly on the forwarding order and transportation order level (freight order and freight booking). Additionally, dangerous goods are considered in freight unit building and transportation planning.

Figure 9.9 shows a forwarding order item with a UI profile that has only an **ADR** tab. To execute the check, you can click the **Check Record** button on the forwarding order's **Dangerous Goods** tab.

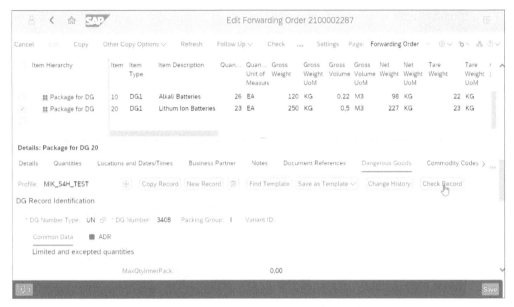

Figure 9.9 Dangerous Goods Item Details Screen in a Forwarding Order

In the forwarding order, most of the dangerous goods data is made available on the item level. The header contains only status and summary information, such as the dangerous goods indicator, ADR points, or an ADR exemption indicator. Recall from the previous section that you can assign individual, regulation-dependent UI profiles to the item types of the forwarding order. If multiple regulations are assigned, you'll see as many subtabs under the forwarding order item as you have regulations defined.

If you invoke the check functionality in the forwarding order, the configured dangerous goods checks are also executed, and the result of the checks is displayed in the message log of the forwarding order. When you start planning in the transportation cockpit (see Chapter 6), the mixed loading checks are applied to the consolidated items of the freight units that you plan to be moved together in one vehicle. Material compatibilities are inspected in any mode of transport. Additionally, the system summarizes the ADR points of all cargo items that should go on a truck in road transportation.

9.3   External Compliance Service Providers

SAP TM already has a comprehensive coverage of export and import functionality in conjunction with SAP GTS. However, as customers—especially LSPs—often need a broader scope in terms of supported countries or functional depth, SAP has introduced enterprise services to connect to external compliance service providers and booking service.

These interfaces have been developed with the Descartes Systems Group, which offers a wide range of shipment- and connectivity-related services for the logistics industry as part of their Global Logistics Network (GLN).

The SAP side of the interfaces is designed generically as a web service. There isn't a direct integration with a security filing service such as Automated Manifest System (AMS) available, but the SAP interface is mapped by the provider into the relevant format and the actual data exchange, and detailed process handling is done through the provider. This means that the scope of possible compliance scenarios is defined mainly by the service provider enabling the various country- and regulation-specific procedures, which, in many cases, also need to be certified by the government agencies behind them.

The compliance interfaces are initiated in SAP TM via the Post Processing Framework (PPF). A decision on when to trigger communication via the interfaces is controlled through settings in Customizing via the menu path **Transportation Management • Basic Functions • Global Trade**, where you find settings to define customs activities, profiles, customs relevance checks (including security filing related settings), and so on. Figure 9.10 shows Customizing settings for the definition of customs activities, where you can, for example, set up the status handling and relevance checks for US security filing for import processes.

After the relevance checks for customs activities have been successfully completed, and the activity is triggered either manually or automatically, the communication is initiated via PPF. The security filing information is transmitted using the same physical message format as the customs filing/declaration. The type of filing required is defined in the message content. The system also uses the same message types for triggering and handling the filing processes from the transportation request/forwarding order and transportation order objects.

Figure 9.10 Customizing Settings for Security Filing (Example)

During the filing process, the SAP TM order isn't updated but stays blocked for execution. An intermediate filing status can be reviewed in the integrated compliance partner system, such as the Descartes GLN. After the government agencies respond with a release or rejection, the corresponding information is converted back by the compliance service provider into the SAP TM web service message and then transmitted back to update the SAP TM order. For a release, the execution block is reset, and the processing can continue. For a rejection, the execution block stays. You may view the detailed reasons for the rejection in the compliance partners portal. You can see the available integration scenarios in Figure 9.11.

Export and import declaration handling, as well as trigger of a transit procedure, can be achieved in a similar way as the security filing. Relevance determination starts the configured relevance rules for customs filing.

The air freight booking process with partner systems, such as Descartes Global Freight Exchange (GF-X), uses the standard mechanisms supplied with SAP TM in the scope of the freight booking. Sending a booking request message is triggered by invocation of the **Send Booking** action in the air freight booking object. The same functionality can, of course, also be used for ocean freight bookings; however, the necessary adaptation and mapping of messages hasn't been provided so far with respect to partner booking systems.

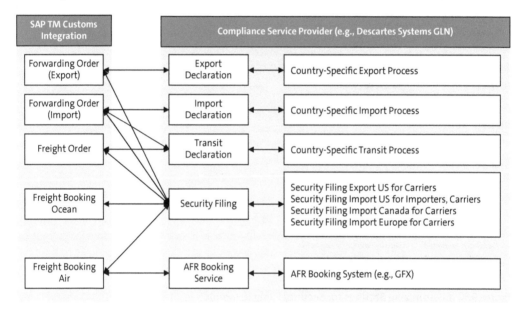

Figure 9.11 Integration Scenarios between SAP TM and External Compliance Service Providers

The action to send the booking sets the corresponding communication status in the freight booking, which is subsequently updated by receiving a booking confirmation or booking rejection from the carrier or partner booking system.

9.4   Summary

This chapter showed how for customs and trade compliance, dangerous goods compliance, security compliance, and air freight booking processes can be run with SAP TM and SAP GTS, PS&S, or compliance partner systems.

In the next chapter, we'll give you an overview of transportation agreements (contracts) and the mechanisms of charge calculation.

Chapter 10
Transportation Charge Management

Understanding the flexible contract management and charge calculation capabilities in SAP Transportation Management will benefit your supply chain processes. In this chapter, you'll learn how to maintain freight contracts with carriers and logistics service providers, store complex rate agreements, and calculate charges in your shipping documents.

Managing transportation charges is a core process requirement for shippers and logistics service providers (LSPs). From a shipper's perspective, it's necessary to maintain contracts with carriers or freight forwarders and to ensure full visibility of transportation costs. As a freight forwarder, you equally need transparency of your carrier contracts and costs. In addition, it's a key requirement for your commercial processes to maintain and manage customer contracts and have visibility of your profitability.

The Transportation Charge Management component of SAP Transportation Management (SAP TM) is a very powerful and flexible engine; it allows you to maintain transportation contracts and fully integrate them into your operational processes. This means that contracts are centrally maintained and will be cardinally used for the automated charge determination in your freight documents: forwarding orders and quotations, freight orders, freight bookings, service orders, freight units (for parcel rate calculation) and settlement documents. Consequently, charge calculation processes across all modes of transport for shippers, freight forwarders, and carriers are supported.

In this chapter, we introduce to you the basics and some details of SAP TM Transportation Charge Management. We start by setting up the master data objects in Section 10.1. We explain each master data element and its core Customizing settings. With this foundation, we dive into Section 10.2 and focus on how these master data objects are derived to calculate charges in freight documents. In Section 10.3, we clarify the actual charge calculation logic using various scenarios as an illustration. Mode specifics for road and rail are covered, and the concept of event-based charge calculation is explained. Finally, in Section 10.4, strategic vendor contract management is addressed. This includes freight procurement planning and analytics as well as the process to establish a freight agreement request for quotation (RFQ).

Let's start by introducing the architecture in Figure 10.1. In the center of the figure, you can see the core master data objects: agreements, calculation sheets, rate tables, and scales. These allow you to store contracts with all their details, such as validity periods, currencies, payment terms, prices, and calculation rules.

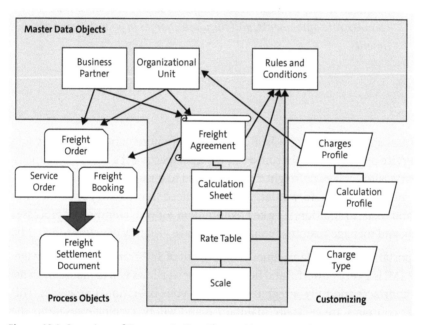

Figure 10.1 Overview of Transportation Charge Management

The relevant freight agreement is determined from freight orders, freight bookings, service orders, and freight units (for direct parcel shipments) to calculate the transportation cost. When any of these business documents needs to be settled, the calculation is redone in the freight settlement document. The determination of the relevant freight agreement, which will be explained in more detail in Section 10.2, is usually based on the business partner and organizational unit (purchasing organization), which must match in the order/booking and the agreement.

Rules and conditions can control the determination of agreements, calculation sheets, and rate tables. These are referenced in the agreement header, agreement items, calculation sheet, and calculation profile. The charges profile, which is assigned to the organizational unit, provides the link to other profiles, such as the calculation profile or settlement profile in Customizing.

The introduction of master data objects is the starting point of the journey into the depths of Transportation Charge Management.

10.1   Charge Calculation Master Data and Customizing

The following elements constitute master data and are the basis for the configuration of Transportation Charge Management:

- **Freight agreements**
  Freight agreements serve as contracts with companies providing transportation services, such as carriers and LSPs, as well as service providers for transportation-related services, such as warehousing or port operations. They contain charges and rate information, as well as capacity commitments.

- **Calculation sheets**
  Calculation sheets have an n:m cardinality to agreements. Each agreement has at least one calculation sheet that lists all charge types (e.g., basic freight charges and surcharges) of an agreement. It also controls the behavior of the actual charge calculation for each charge element.

- **Charge type**
  Each line in a calculation sheet uses a specific charge type. Any number of charges types can be used in a calculation sheet.

- **Rate tables**
  Rate tables are the central place where all the actual values of your rates and charges are maintained. Rate tables have an n:m cardinality to charge types and calculation sheets. Each calculation sheet can contain multiple rate tables, but the same rate table can also be used in multiple calculation sheets.

- **Scales**
  Several scales can define the dimensions of a rate table.

The left side of Figure 10.2 depicts the hierarchical relationships among agreements, agreement items, calculation sheets, charge types, rate tables, and scales. On the right, we apply these concepts to a business example to show how you can use this flexible structure in an ocean freight scenario. Here, the freight agreement is a contract with an ocean carrier and can have the scope of multiple trade lanes as items of the agreement, for example, based on geography.

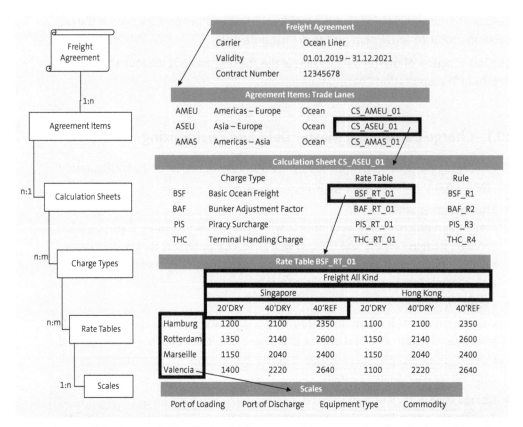

Figure 10.2 Transportation Contract Management Component with a Business Example

Each trade lane has its own calculation sheet with different global and country-specific charges (basic ocean freight, bunker adjustment factor, terminal handling charge, etc.). For each charge, an applicability rule or condition can be maintained. In addition, a rate table that contains all the actual rates is assigned to each charge. Rate tables are constructed based on multiple scales, such as origin, destination, equipment, and commodity.

You maintain all freight agreements in a central repository. Select **Charge Management • Charge Management Worklist • Master Data Cockpit for Freight Agreements** to get an overview, query all charge-relevant master data objects, and search through different agreements, rate tables, calculation sheets, and much more. The *master data cockpit* is extremely useful when you want to update charge types and rates of multiple agreements. Numerous search attributes help you find an agreement (e.g., based on the organizational unit or an involved business partner). From the cockpit, you can also trigger currency conversions and Microsoft Excel downloads. One benefit of this functionality is that you can search for agreements based on the most granular components, such as a single rate table entry or source destination, and the results are all agreements that contain this specific rate table line.

Central Repository in SAP TM 9.6

In SAP TM 9.6, the overview page is accessed by following **Master Data · Charge Management and Service Product Catalogs · Overview Charge Management and Service Product Catalogs**.

Let's turn our attention to the individual elements in more detail.

10.1.1   Freight Agreements

The freight agreement is of great relevance for both shippers and LSPs because both parties use freight agreements to store contracts with trucking companies, airlines, ocean carriers, railways, and freight forwarders. Freight agreements are created using **Contract Management · Create Freight Agreement**. Each freight agreement requires the choice of a freight agreement type, which controls the user interface (UI), number range assignment, whether multiple parties can use it, and whether a duplicate check is performed during save or check. You define the freight agreement type in Customizing via **Transportation Management · Master Data · Agreements and Service Products · Define Freight Agreement Types**. Freight agreements can be created manually from scratch, can be based on freight agreement templates, either as master data (**Contract Management · Define Freight Agreement Template**) or as Customizing (**Transportation Management · Basic Functions · Charge Calculation · Basic Settings · Templates · Define Freight Agreement Templates**), or can result from a strategic freight procurement process as described in Section 10.4.

Figure 10.3 shows the header section of a freight agreement. The **Basic Data** area lists the internal and external reference as well as the agreement status. Only released agreements can be used for freight charge calculation. The **Involved Parties** are the purchasing organization on one side and the carrier on the other side. If the agreement type allows, multiple parties can be maintained here. The **Details** area contains the validity dates of the contract and the document currency. It can also contain a dimensional weight profile and an exclusion rule in case you want to exclude an agreement for specific charge calculations (see Section 10.2.2 for more details on rules and conditions).

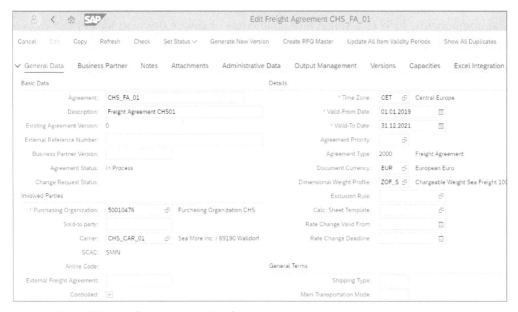

Figure 10.3 Freight Agreement Header

On the **Business Partner** tab, the relevant business partners can be maintained based on their function. The confirmed capacities are stored on the **Capacities** tab. Freight agreements support versioning, and other versions of the freight agreement can be accessed via the **Versions** tab. You can add notes and store attachments on the **Notes** and **Attachments** tabs, respectively. The entire capabilities of the output management to print a document or trigger a workflow, email, or alert are available on the **Output Management** tab. Downloading into an Excel format and uploading from Excel are also supported from the **Excel Integration** tab.

From the freight agreement header, you can change the agreement status; check for duplicates, that is, search for freight agreements that cover the same scope; generate new versions of the agreement; or generate an RFQ master to start a strategic freight procurement process. Furthermore, you have the option to trigger a rate change request and initiate the update of the items' validity periods. A freight agreement can have one or more items, as shown in Figure 10.4. Each item has one calculation sheet (or determination rule) assigned and has its own validity. Preconditions are used to define which item is selected for charge calculation in a freight order, freight booking, or service order, if you want to distinguish in the same agreement between different calculation logic, for example, for ocean and inland transport.

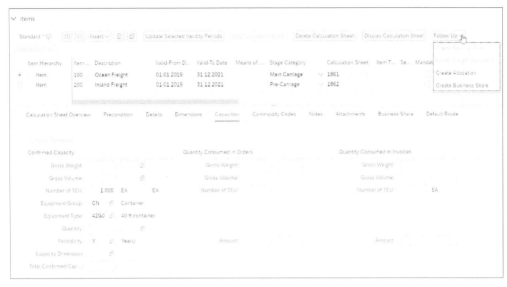

Figure 10.4 Freight Agreement Items

While the main elements of each item are its calculation sheet and preconditions, additional information can be maintained at this level. One of these is the maintenance of **Capacities**, as you can see in Figure 10.4. When you negotiate a contract with an LSP, it's a common business practice to not only agree on rates but also capacities to be shipped under a contract. This allows you as a consumer of space to better forecast and manage capacities. Higher capacities can be associated with discounts on the rates for you as a shipper or LSP. Besides the **Confirmed Capacity** in the contract, you can actively monitor the consumption of capacities. Consumption in both freight orders and invoices is tracked in the agreement. Various reports are available based on an embedded dashboard to display the year-to-date or periodical consumption of confirmed capacities. Different dimensions, such as containers (20-foot equivalent units [TEUs]), gross weight, or gross volume, are available.

From the **Capacities** tab shown in Figure 10.4, you can trigger the creation of allocations as a follow-up action. This will generate an agreement allocation based on the maintained capacities of the agreement item. To enable this capability, you need to assign an allocation type to your freight agreement type in Customizing. The navigation from the agreement item to the allocation document is then possible via the

Allocation Details button. Besides generating allocations from a freight agreement, it's also possible to generate business shares. This capability allows you to distribute your total demand in capacity among different suppliers. Business shares are considered during carrier selection for freight orders. (Refer to Chapter 5, Section 5.2, for more on allocations, and refer to Section 5.3, for more details on business shares. Chapter 7, Section 7.1, describes carrier selection.)

The functionalities to add notes and attachments are available on the item level as they are on the header level.

Each item can have an item type, which is defined in Customizing (**Transportation Management · Master Data · Agreements and Service Products · Define Freight Agreement Item Types**). Item types can default the freight order or freight booking types, if these are created directly from the freight agreement item. Furthermore, preconditions can be linked to the item types. A freight agreement type can be linked with none or any number of item types and none or any number of preconditions.

10.1.2   Calculation Sheet

As mentioned in the previous section, the calculation sheet is the main element of each freight agreement item. The calculation sheet will store the charge types and assigned rate tables for each charge line. This setup is mandatory to do charge calculation for freight orders, freight bookings, service orders, and settlement documents.

The calculation sheet contains all charges you need to pay to your carrier or LSP as part of an agreement. Calculation sheets control the behavior of the charge calculation logic, which we describe in Section 10.3. It's tremendously important because in the calculation sheet, you map rate tables to each charge. Calculation sheets contain the logic for how to apply charges and the sequence in which they need to be calculated. In addition, any advanced or mode of transport-specific charge logic is defined and set up in the calculation sheet.

Let's dive into calculation sheet structure, setup, and Customizing.

Calculation Sheet Structure

To generate a calculation sheet, you generally have two alternatives:

- **Embedded calculation sheet**
  You can create the calculation sheet directly from an agreement. Notice the buttons at the top of the screen to add, display, or delete calculation sheets in the

freight agreement item shown earlier in Figure 10.4. Clicking the **Add Calculation Sheet** button will automatically generate a calculation sheet in the background and assign it to the agreement item. By clicking the **Display Calculation Sheet** button, you navigate directly to the calculation sheet for maintenance or display based on whether you had opened the freight agreement for maintenance or display.

- **Standalone calculation sheet**
  You can also create a calculation sheet separately and assign it to agreement items later. For this purpose, you can use the **Create Calculation Sheet** tile, which you can find in **Charge Management · Create Calculation Sheet**.

The calculation sheet contains very little header information, as you can see in Figure 10.5. Most important here is the **Charge Usage** field, which you can use to limit potential assignments to agreements because, unlike an agreement, calculation sheets can be generically used in forwarding, freight, or internal agreements.

The main element of the calculation sheet is the item table. Each item represents a charge line. Each line is calculated individually starting at the lowest hierarchy level and sequentially based on the line number ascending on each hierarchy level. In the example in Figure 10.5, the calculation will start with the line numbers 20 to 70, which represent the lowest hierarchy level, and then the sum (line number 10) will be calculated. The example shows a business scenario for ocean freight charges with a base freight, bunker adjustment factor, currency adjustment factor, terminal handling charges, and a piracy risk surcharge. Each line has assigned a charge type, which is defined in Customizing and will be explained in Section 10.1.3. This flexible structure can also be used for any other mode of transport or business context, and you can define your own charge types.

Each charge line needs to be assigned either a fixed rate amount or, most commonly, a rate table. Charges can be absolute values maintained in a currency or relative values defined as percentages either in rate tables or directly in the calculation sheet. If they are defined as relative values, they need to reference another charge line or a range of charge lines (reference from and reference to), which is used as a basis for their calculation. Each line item in the calculation sheet has a **Details** section with multiple tabs, such as **Basic Data**, **Rate**, and **Classification**, which you can use to maintain important settings to control the charge calculation logic. These item details are covered in detail in the next section of this chapter.

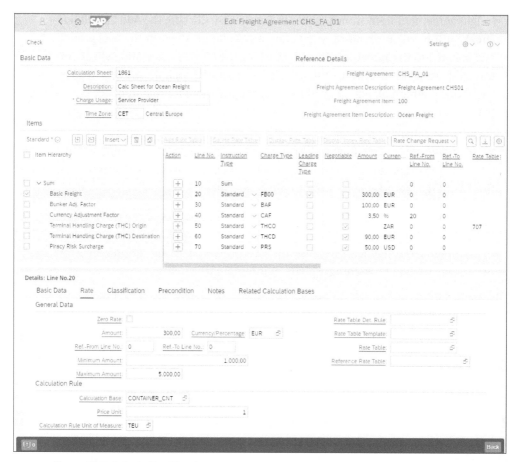

Figure 10.5 Calculation Sheet

Calculation sheets don't need to be created from scratch every time. Calculation sheet templates can be defined as master data using the **Create Calculation Sheet Template** tile from **Charge Management • Create Calculation Sheet Template** or as Customizing via **Transportation Management • Basic Functions • Charge Calculation • Basic Settings • Templates • Define Calculation Sheet Templates**. The calculation sheet template contains the most important elements of a regular calculation sheet. When you generate a new calculation sheet, you can pick a template as a source, which will automatically populate all specified charge types and other settings defined in the template. Furthermore, a calculation sheet template can be assigned to an agreement type in Customizing. As a result, that calculation sheet template is defaulted when you generate a calculation sheet from the agreement.

Calculation Sheet Setup and Customizing

The details of each calculation sheet line item can contain many settings that are evaluated by the system during charge calculation. While we describe many of the available settings here, more detail about the impact of some of these settings will become obvious only when the charge calculation logic itself is explained in Section 10.3. Keep in mind that most of these settings are optional and are only required if you want to model specific use cases, such as handling codes for air freight or provisioning and return of empty containers in ocean freight.

On the **Basic Data** tab in Figure 10.6 you specify the charge type of each item.

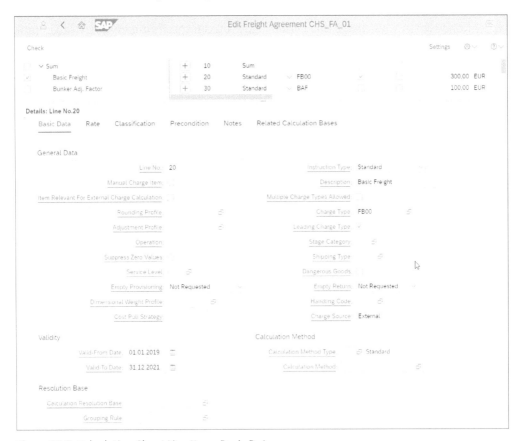

Figure 10.6 Calculation Sheet Line Item: Basic Data

You can mark a charge type as the leading charge type. If the system identifies more than one charge calculation sheet as valid during charge calculation, it checks the leading charge of each calculation sheet to determine which one to use. If you don't require this logic, you can disable this feature in the charges profile.

You can assign a rounding profile—which you must define in Customizing via **Transportation Management • Basic Functions • Charge Calculation • Rounding • Define Rounding Rules**—to round calculated charges up or down. A commonly used feature is the manual charge calculation where a user can specify an amount for the charge item in the transactional document (freight order, freight booking, or service order). The **Manual Charge Item** checkbox must be enabled in the calculation sheet in this case.

As a shipper or freight forwarder, you'll find that the chargeable weight is very important in your charge calculation logic. You can specify dimensional weight profiles in Customizing (**Transportation Management • Basic Functions • Charge Calculation • Data Source Binding • Define Dimensional Weight Profile**) to calculate the correct chargeable amounts (e.g., 1000 kilogram to 1 cubic meter for the metric system or 1 pound to 166 cubic inches in the imperial system). Besides maintaining the dimensional weight profile per charge in the calculation sheet line item details, you can also maintain it on the agreement line item, on the agreement header, or in the calculation profile. The calculation logic will check in the same sequence to determine the relevant dimensional weight profile on the lowest defined level.

A very powerful option is the definition of a **Calculation Method**. Whenever you expect the system to simply read a rate from a rate table, no specific calculation method is required. However, if a more complex computation is needed, such as clipping or for break weights in air freight, a set of standard calculation methods is available. You can also develop your own calculation methods as an enhancement and assign them in Customizing (**Transportation Management • Basic Functions • Charge Calculation • Enhancements to Charge Calculation Engine • Define Calculation Methods**) to use them in the calculation sheet.

Furthermore, the **Calculation Resolution Base** and **Grouping Rule** are of great importance for charge calculation. The calculation resolution base defines on which level you apply a charge in your transactional document (e.g., per container, per package, or once per document [root]). On the other hand, the grouping rule allows the system to calculate one combined charge for multiple items. Let's assume you want to calculate charges for a freight order that transports five packages from your warehouse to customer A and three packages from your warehouse to customer B. While the calculation resolution base "package" would calculate eight charges (one for each package), the grouping rule "by destination" would allow you to calculate two charges only (one for the five packages to customer A and another one for the three packages to customer B). If weight breaks are defined in a rate table, it obviously will make a big difference if you check for the applicable rate eight times (once for each package) or only twice (once for the combined weight for each customer). Your choice of calculation resolution base and grouping rule will lead to a different calculation result.

How to determine the relevant rate for each charge line in the calculation sheet is defined on the **Rate** tab in Figure 10.5. The simplest way of defining a rate is to enter a fixed amount and currency here. The most common scenario is to store a rate table because it offers much more flexibility. You can either associate exactly one rate table to the charge line or reference a rate table determination rule (e.g., per origin country). As the name indicates, this option allows you to define a rule that is evaluated during charge calculation to determine the relevant rate table for the transactional document. A use case may be the definition of country-specific surcharges with different organizations being responsible for their maintenance. More details on the implementation of rules related to charge calculation and conditions can be found in Section 10.3.1.

The **Calculation Rule** determines how to calculate a charge based on a fixed amount or inside the rate table. For example, if you maintain a charge per distance (kilometers), you must multiply this rate by the actual distance a vehicle has traveled, which is retrieved from your transactional document. The actual rule needs to specify a calculation base, which specifies the data access to the transactional document (in our example, this is **CONTAINER_CNT** for the number of containers). The calculation logic in Figure 10.5 is as follows:

1. The rate amount is 300 EUR.
2. This rate will be multiplied by the number of TEUs.
3. A minimum of 1000 EUR or a maximum of 5000 EUR will be applied.

If you maintain a rate table for the charge line item, the calculation rule will be defined in the rate table itself. Refer to Section 10.1.4 and Section 10.1.5 for more details on the calculation base and scales, respectively.

Next, in the **Classification** tab, you indicate whether a charge is a statistical charge, a tax, or a mandatory charge. Statistical charges are used in the charge calculation like any other charge, but they aren't settled in the invoicing process. Using the tax indicator, you can classify a charge as a tax. If you specify a charge line as being mandatory by activating the appropriate checkbox, and this charge fails to calculate a value in a transactional document, an error message is displayed to the user, and the transactional document is blocked for subsequent processing steps (settlement).

The **Preconditions** tab provides an important functionality for the charge calculation logic. This setting allows you to maintain flexible rules and conditions as well as to define trade lanes to control whether this charge line is evaluated or not. A precondition can be maintained in three ways:

- Use trade lanes to maintain geographical limitations.
- Specify that a charge line is applicable only to specific business partners.
- Assign a precondition rule to the calculation sheet item.

Business Examples for Conditional Charges

In the air, rail, and, especially, ocean freight business, you can find numerous rules and conditions for various charges. Some regional examples are as follows:

- All ocean freight transports with the destination Spain must pay a mandatory banking charge that is a percentage value of the amount to be paid in Spain.
- In India, a mandatory service and education tax must be paid for every inbound and outbound shipment.
- For all shipments going to the United States, a mandatory surcharge must be paid for legal filings.
- Surcharges apply if a ship crosses the Panama Canal or Suez Canal.

Similar examples in air freight apply, such as specific terminal handling charges, screening charges to x-ray cargo, and other security surcharges that are based on origins and destinations.

Because each charge line has a charge type assigned to it, let's turn our attention to the configuration of charge types.

10.1.3   Charge Type

The initial configuration already includes a basic set of charge types, which can be extended based on project needs. Charge types are defined in Customizing (**Transportation Management • Basic Functions • Charge Calculation • Basic Settings • Define Charge Types**). Figure 10.7 shows the definition of charge type **CAF** as an example. A charge type can be linked to a charge category and charge subcategory, which may be defined based on global standards such as UN/EDIFACT code list 5237. Charge categories and charge subcategories can be defined in Customizing themselves (**Transportation Management • Basic Functions • Charge Calculation • Basic Settings • Define Charge Categories** and **Define Charge Subcategories**). Charge type descriptions can be maintained in multiple languages.

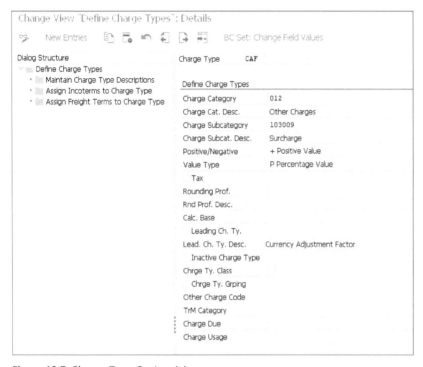

Figure 10.7 Charge Type Customizing

You can define whether a charge type can result only in a positive or negative value (e.g., for discounts) or whether it can be an absolute or percentage value. For either setting, you can specify that both options are valid and enter the details in the calculation sheet line item details. The rounding profile is optional and either defaulted to the calculation sheet charge line or directly defined there. To limit the usage of a charge type to specific use cases, you can specify a transportation mode category (e.g., to limit the usage to air transports) or charge usage (e.g., to limit the usage to freight opposed to forwarding charges).

Charge types can be used in a calculation sheet and can be assigned to rate tables, which are covered next.

10.1.4   Rate Table

Rate tables contain all prices that are required for the charge calculation. A rate table can never be used standalone. It must be assigned to a calculation sheet, which itself needs to be assigned to an agreement. You can maintain rate tables manually, by using the upload and download function for single rate tables, or by using mass update functions.

In this section, we'll discuss the creation, structure, and maintenance of rate tables.

Creation and Structure

You have two options for creating a rate table: from a calculation sheet or standalone.

First, you can generate it from a calculation sheet. You select one charge line in the calculation sheet and choose **Add Rate Table** to generate a new rate table in the background. If you've maintained a rate table template in the calculation sheet item details, this will prepopulate the new rate table. Rate table templates can be defined as master data in **Charge Management • Create Rate Table Template** or as Customizing via menu path **Transportation Management • Basic Functions • Charge Calculation • Basic Settings • Templates • Define Rate Table Templates**.

Second, you can generate and maintain a standalone rate table by navigating to **Charge Management • Create Rate Table Definition**. You can specify a rate table type or a rate table template to prefill certain elements of the rate table and define attributes of the rate table.

The rate table type is defined in Customizing via **Transportation Management • Master Data • Rate Tables • Define Rate Table Type**. In Figure 10.8, you can see which attributes of the rate table are defined in the rate table type. You can enable a rate table for workflow approval. In this case, a user with the relevant authorization is required to approve changes made to validity periods in a rate table. Furthermore, you can specify whether the rate table or its values should be editable or not. If rate validity split (**Rate Val. Split**) is enabled in a rate table, you can change rates without needing to update all the rates of the parent validity period in the rate table.

The rate table has a **General Data** section, as you can see in Figure 10.9. A rate table can be used to store selling, buying, or internal rates. As a result, you need to maintain the **Charge Usage** as a mandatory field. It's possible to set the **Charge Usage** for one or more purposes.

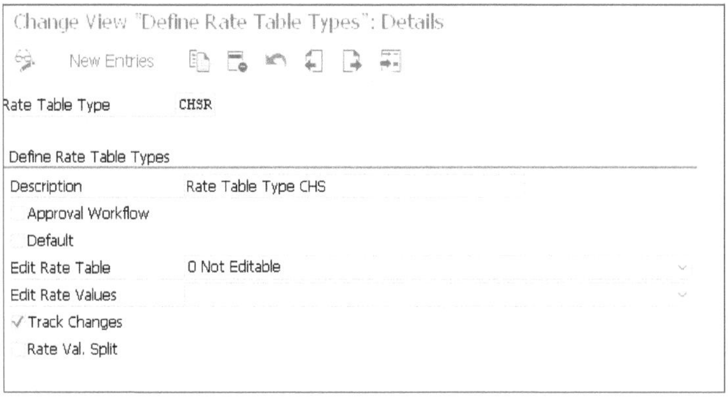

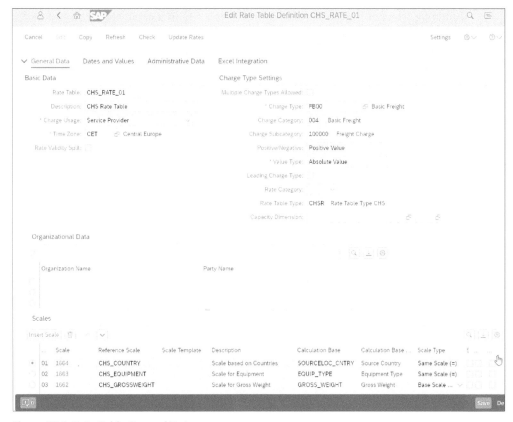

Figure 10.8 Rate Table Type

Figure 10.9 Rate Table General Data

Another important section is the **Charge Type Settings** area. The dimensions for storing the rate values can be very different for each charge type. As a result, you maintain a rate table for each charge in most scenarios. Consequently, you need to maintain the charge type in the rate table. If you generated the table from the calculation sheet, the charge type is automatically pulled from the calculation sheet item. The **Multiple Charge Types Allowed** checkbox enables the use of one rate table for multiple charge types. In this case, you can maintain the charge type as its own dimension (scale).

The most important section in the **General Data** tab is the **Scales** area where you design the layout (rows and columns) of the rate table. The scales can best be described as the dimensions of a rate table. In the example, three scales are maintained, meaning the rate value will be determined based on three different criteria. The first scale is based on countries. The **Calculation Base** defines which country should be relevant for the determination of the rate in a cross-border transport. In Figure 10.9, the source country is defined as the relevant country. The second scale is based on the equipment type, and the third scale is based on weight. Because different types of weight also can be relevant for pricing (gross weight, net weight, dimensional weight, etc.), the calculation base is used to define which one should be used to determine the correct rate value. For each scale, several attributes can be defined, such as whether a match is required in the scale items of a scale (**Item with No Value Allowed**) or whether a **Minimum Value** or **Maximum Value** should be defined. The maximum number of scales that you can define in a rate table is 14, but to manage and maintain rate tables efficiently, you should use more rate tables with fewer dimensions instead of one with too many dimensions.

The **Dates and Values** tab shown in Figure 10.10 contains the actual rate values for one or more different validity periods. You need to create an entry in the header item table with a valid-from date, valid-to date, and currency before you can maintain rate values. Afterward, the specified dimensions in the form of the rate table scales will become visible in the lower part of the screen. Each validity period has a **Life Cycle Status**. Initially, the **Life Cycle Status** is **In Process** and needs to be changed to **Released** before the rate values of the validity period can be used for charge calculation. To prevent fraud, the authorization to release a rate table validity period can be assigned to a user, and an approval workflow can be triggered to this user after a second user has maintained the rate values.

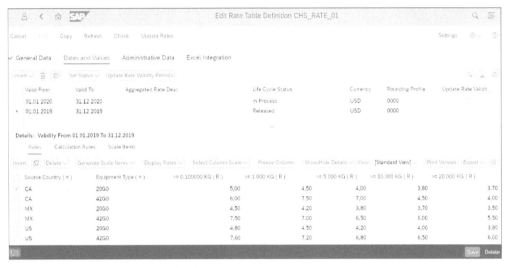

Figure 10.10   Rate Table Dates and Values

In the lower part of Figure 10.10, the rate values for the selected validity period are shown along the three dimensions that have defined the rate table structure on the **General Data** tab. Here you can maintain rate values, which are then used in charge calculation. You have the option to toggle between different layouts of the rate table and to display or hide descriptions and notes. You can easily imagine how rate tables can grow, so you can use the filter functionality to display only a specific set of rows.

The **Scale Items** tab defines the actual characteristic values of each scale. The example rate table in Figure 10.10 will be used for transports originating in North America because the scale items for the source country have been maintained as **CA** (Canada), **MX** (Mexico), and **US** (USA). Scale items can be entered directly row by row in the **Rates** tab of the rate table using the **Insert** button, or you can maintain the entire list of scale items in the **Scale Items** tab. The scale items for source country and equipment type will be compared for exact matches, indicated by the **(=)** next to the scale description. This is reasonable for alphanumeric fields such as countries, cities, or equipment. For numerical values, a smaller or equal **(<=)** comparison or a larger or equal **(>=)** comparison should be used. In the example, different weight breaks have been defined for gross weight, so that different rate values can be specified depending on the gross weight of the transported container.

Section 10.1.2 explained that you can maintain a calculation rule in the calculation sheet or directly in the rate table. Recall that a calculation rule is used in the charge calculation logic to multiply a retrieved rate value from the rate table with a certain data field. The calculation rule in Figure 10.11 specifies that the rate values from Figure 10.10 are the amounts in USD for each 100 kg of gross weight.

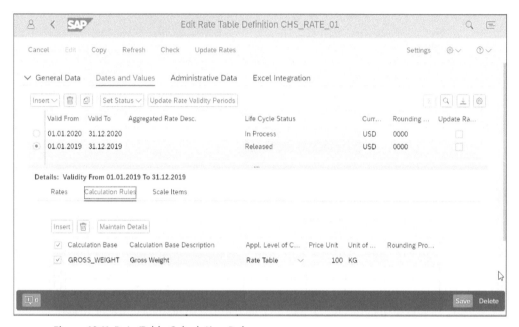

Figure 10.11 Rate Table Calculation Rule

Maintenance Tools

The manual creation and maintenance of large rate tables can be a very tedious process. Especially in the environment of large LSP or carrier contracts, a rate table can contain tens of thousands of entries. Two options to ease this maintenance process are offered in the system, but a certain level of manual effort may still be required.

The first option is the **Update Rates** function, which is available via a button in the Edit Rate Table Definition app. In Figure 10.12, you can see that it allows you to increase or decrease rate values by an absolute amount or a percentage. Rate value changes can be applied to a certain validity period, limited to a combination of scale items, or both. Additionally, it's possible to create new validity periods with this function. The same functionality is also offered using report /SCMTMS/RATE_MASS_ UPDATE or from the master data cockpit.

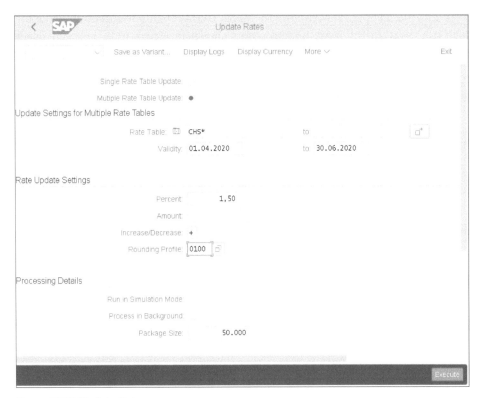

Figure 10.12 Update Rates

Second, **Excel Integration** is offered for entire rate tables on a separate tab (refer to Figure 10.11). You can download one, multiple, or all validity periods into an Excel file where a separate sheet is created for each validity period. Then you can maintain the rate values and even change the scale items in the spreadsheet to take advantage of all the capabilities of an Excel spreadsheet that aren't available in SAP TM. The spreadsheet will be protected in such a way that you're not able to change its structure because, otherwise, it couldn't be uploaded again. When you upload the file, the system validates the newly added or changed scale items against the master data. You can also use report /SCMTMS/TCC_RATE_MASS_CREATE to download rate table templates for later maintenance in Excel or upload Excel files in the background.

In the freight industry, it's a common business practice to regularly (e.g., quarterly) adjust freight charges and surcharges with batch updates. In ocean freight, these are called *general rate adjustments* (GRA). Such mass updates of rates usually impact multiple rate tables across numerous agreements. Other industries have similar requirements. Report /SCMTMS/RATE_MASS_UPDATE supports mass updates for such use cases. In the mass update report shown in Figure 10.13, you can select numerous rate tables and apply a markup or deduction.

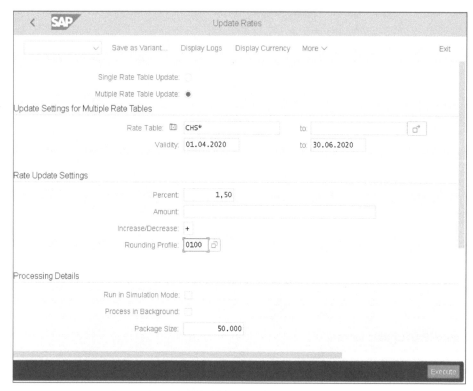

Figure 10.13 Report /SCMTMS/RATE_MASS_UPDATE

Unfortunately, it's not possible to specify the scope for a mass update by limiting the updates to specific scale items. If this is required, the update must be done for a single rate table at a time with the **Update Rates** function described earlier.

Release Your Agreements and Rate Tables

It's easy to forget this small step when setting up Transportation Charge Management, which leads to there being no results in the rating. Therefore, remember that both agreements and rate table validity periods must be released before they can be used. This contingency prevents you from using rates while they are still in negotiation or setup. Always change the **Life Cycle Status** of the rate table validity periods and the agreement header to **Released** after the maintenance is completed. You can also release both the agreement and all its rate tables directly from the agreement header.

10.1.5   Scale

Scales are a prerequisite for maintaining a rate table. They are the lowest layer of master data for Transportation Charge Management. A scale itself is always generic, and you have to associate a calculation base to it to refer to the correct data element for charge calculation. The configuration of scales and their assignment to a rate table must follow the steps shown in Figure 10.14:

1. **Define the scale base in Customizing**
   The scale base is the scale's technical foundation where you define its description and the technical field assignment a scale value is stored in. Furthermore, you define whether a scale is a numerical value, whether a currency is required, whether a unit of measure is required, and which dimension needs to be maintained for the unit of measure (mass, volume, density, etc.). You can customize the scale base via menu path **Transportation Management · Basic Functions · Charge Calculation · Data Source Binding · Define Scale Bases**.

2. **Specify the calculation base in Customizing**
   While a scale base only defines the basic data element, the calculation base defines its context. For scale base WEIGHT, the calculation bases CHRG_WEIGHT for chargeable weight, DIM_WEIGHT for dimensional weight, and GROSS_WEIGHT for gross weight exist, among others. You've learned already that calculation bases are used within calculation rules. Calculation bases are also used in the scale definition of rate tables to specify in which context the rate value should be determined.

   Calculation bases are defined in Customizing via menu path **Transportation Management · Basic Functions · Charge Calculation · Data Source Binding · Define Calculation Bases**. Note that you need to assign a scale base to any calculation base. Additionally, you can specify whether the calculation type is absolute or relative. Relative can only be chosen if the underlying scale base is numeric. It defines whether the obtained rate value is used as maintained in the rate table (absolute) or whether it needs to be calculated from the referenced relative scale (relative). Other attributes of the calculation base are technical settings, such as those that specify database fields.

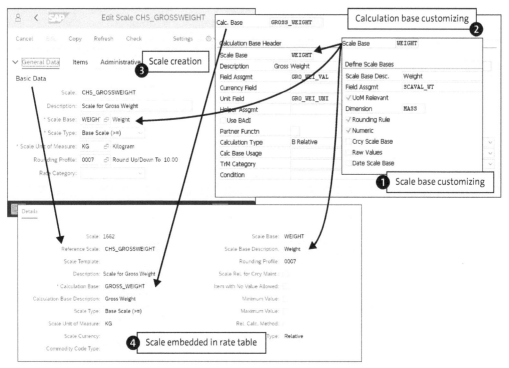

Figure 10.14 Configuration of Scales and Their Assignment

3. **Define the reference scale (optional)**

You can create a standalone scale with the **Create Scale** tile that you find in the **Charge Management** folder and assign it later as a reference scale in a rate table. Scales can be created from scratch or based on a scale template. When you define a scale, you must specify its scale base, scale type, unit of measure, and rounding profile. Three different scale types exist: **Same Scales** are used for alphanumeric values, whereas **Base Scales** or **To scales** are used for numeric values depending on whether you want to define rate values *from* a certain scale value or *up to* a certain scale value, respectively. On the **Items** tab, you can define the individual scale items. Scale templates can be defined as master data in **Charge Management • Create Scale Template** or as Customizing via menu path **Transportation Management • Basic Functions • Charge Calculation • Basic Settings • Templates • Define Scale Templates**.

4. **Embed the scale in the rate table**

   Finally, a scale is embedded as a dimension into a rate table. As shown in Figure 10.14, the association to a calculation base is mandatory. All settings specified in the calculation base are populated into the dimension of the rate table, especially the **Scale Base** and **Calculation Type**. Optionally, you can assign a reference scale to prefill certain fields from the reference scale, such as a scale unit of measure, scale type, or even the scale items. Obviously, the scale base of the calculation base and the scale base of the reference scale must match.

Because there are limits on how many scales/calculation bases can be embedded in a rate table, it's possible to embed a condition into a scale to increase the flexibility of rate tables. When such a scale/calculation base is determined in a rate table to look up a specific rate, it's possible to run through an entire Business Rules Framework plus (BRF+) condition table as part of the rate value determination. For this process, you can use calculation base CONDITION with scale base CONDTN, and assign it to a scale. The actual condition can then be entered in the **Rates** section of the rate table for each entry.

After establishing all relevant master data elements for charge calculation, let's focus now on how these get determined in a transactional document.

10.2   Contract Determination

The creation of master data allows you to store and manage your carrier and LSP contracts. The real added value is raised when you use the integration of this master data into your transactional documents to automatically calculate the charges of freight orders, freight bookings, and service orders based on the contract determination logic. This functionality is the key to automatically finding and determining an appropriate contract with your business partners. There are numerous ways to set up this determination logic because it's tremendously flexible and can serve all industries and modes of transport.

Contract Determination versus Charge Calculation Logic

It's important to highlight the key difference between the contract determination in this section and the charge calculation logic in Section 10.3: contract determination finds a correct agreement, agreement item, calculation sheet, and charge type. As soon as this level is reached, the charge calculation logic determines the actual value from a rate table of a charge type and how to use this value in charge calculation.

10.2.1   Contract Determination Logic

The contract determination logic is triggered with the charge calculation for a trans-actional document (e.g., a freight order) either explicitly by clicking the **Calculate Charges** button in a freight order or worklist, or implicitly by executing save strategy CALC_CHARGE when a freight document is saved. It follows this process:

1. Determine an appropriate freight agreement.
2. Determine the relevant items of the appropriate agreements.
3. Check all qualifying calculation sheets.

Let's walk through header and item determination.

Agreement Header Determination

First, the appropriate freight agreement header is determined based on the involved parties (purchasing organization and business partner). Both parties must match in the freight agreement with the corresponding parties in the transactional document by considering hierarchies. In addition, the calculation date in the freight document must be within the validity period of the freight agreement, and the freight agreement must have agreement status **Released**.

If multiple agreements qualify based on a similarity in the described attributes, there are several ways to identify the appropriate agreement:

- The simplest approach is to specify a freight agreement or freight agreement item manually for a freight order stage. In this case, the charges are calculated based on the specified freight agreement or freight agreement item, and no other agreement gets determined.

- Another approach requiring manual interaction is to enable the manual selection by choosing **Display All Agreements** in the **Agreement Det. Type** dropdown list of the corresponding calculation profile. In this case, the system calculates the charges based on all appropriate agreement items and displays the results in a popup window for the user to decide. This option is valid only for manual and interactive charge calculation. If charge calculation is triggered in the background or from a worklist, charge calculation will fail, and the calculation status will be set to **Automatic Charge Calculation Failed**.

- If the **Agreement Det. Type** in the calculation profile is set to **Minimum Charges** or **Maximum Charges**, the system calculates the total for all appropriate agreement items and selects the one with the lowest or highest charges. The calculation profile and its impact are explained in Section 10.2.2.

- The appropriate agreement can be selected via an agreement determination rule, if one is maintained in the calculation profile.

- The appropriate agreement and relevant agreement items can also be selected via the leading charge type. Only those agreement items that include at least one leading charge type are used in the evaluation, and only those agreement items in which all included leading charge types can determine a valid rate are considered. The leading charge type is only considered in the selection of the appropriate agreement if the **Evaluate All Agreements** checkbox is selected in the charges profile, which is explained in Section 10.2.2.

- An agreement can only be selected for charge calculation if its **Exclusion Rule** doesn't prevent its usage. The exclusion rule is assigned on the **General Data** tab of the freight agreement.

- If after all these checks, there are still several potential agreements available for charge calculation, the agreement priority, which is defined on the **General Data** tab of the freight agreement, can be used as a tiebreaker. The freight agreement with the highest priority (lowest number) will be selected.

- Finally, if none of the previous criteria helped to identify one freight agreement and its relevant items, the choice will be random, which you should avoid.

Agreement Item Determination

The determined agreement can contain multiple agreement items. Before checking the assigned calculation sheet in detail, the system needs to find out how many agreement items it's looking for. This depends on the calculation level and there are three options:

- **Calculation at header level**
  The contract determination logic runs only once on the header of the transactional document and identifies exactly one agreement with one matching agreement item (calculation sheet).

- **Calculation at item level**
  The determination logic runs once per each main cargo item in the freight document. One agreement item is determined for each cargo item and charges are calculated separately for each cargo item of the transactional document.

- **Calculation at stage level**
  The determination logic runs once for each stage in a freight order or freight book-ing. One agreement item is determined for each stage, and charges are calculated accordingly.

A frequent use case is the combination of charge calculation both at the stage and at header level. These two calculation levels can coexist. To configure this use case, you must select **Calculation at Stage Level** as the relevant calculation level in the calcula-tion profile to calculate charges for each stage. In addition, you need to flag one agree-ment item in your freight agreement as a **Header-Level Charge**. This agreement item will then be used for the calculation of the header-level charges.

It's important to note that charge lines from different calculation sheets can't be combined within one transactional document other than using this concept of calcu-lation levels.

Furthermore, to check the relevance of an agreement item, the attributes of the agreement item must match the same of the transactional document for which the determination logic has been triggered. The following attributes can be used:

- Shipping type (e.g., less than container load [LCL], full truckload [FTL], or unit load device [ULD])
- Transportation mode (e.g., sea, air, rail, or truck)
- Stage category (e.g., pre-carriage, main carriage, or on-carriage)
- Stage type (e.g., pickup or delivery)
- Service level, such as those of a carrier (e.g., express, standard, cold chain, or fumi-gation)

After one or multiple agreement items have been determined, an appropriate calcu-lation sheet needs to be identified and validated. This can be influenced by the lead-ing charge types contained in the calculation sheet and by preconditions.

An agreement item with an assigned calculation sheet that contains a leading charge type can only be selected if a valid rate can be determined for this leading charge type. As a rule of thumb, you should always try to use just one leading charge type per calculation sheet (e.g., the basic ocean freight charge, the main air freight charge, or the basic freight charge, depending on your mode of transport).

Preconditions can be based on BRF+ (see Chapter 2, Section 2.3) for more complex condition expressions. In the next section, we elaborate more on the use of these preconditions for contract determination. Additionally, there are also standard preconditions available. These are either assigned in Customizing to freight agreement types (**Transportation Management · Master Data · Agreements and Service Products · Define Freight Agreement Types**) or freight agreement item types (**Transportation Management · Master Data · Agreements and Service Products · Define Freight Agreement Item Types**). These standard preconditions relate to attributes such as transportation mode, shipping type, or stage category. Furthermore, trade lanes or business partner roles can be used as preconditions and assigned to the agreement items.

If you want to deviate from the standard logic to determine the agreement items, you have the option to define a calculation sheet determination rule in the calculation profile.

10.2.2   Configuration of Contract Determination

There are essentially two pillars in the configuration of the contract determination logic. The first one consists of the calculation profile and charges profile defined in Customizing, and the second one is the charge calculation rules. We'll discuss both in the following sections.

Calculation Profile and Charges Profile

The calculation profile is defined in Customizing via **Transportation Management · Basic Functions · Charge Calculation · Basic Settings · Define Calculation Profile**. One of the most important settings of the calculation profile in Figure 10.15 is the calculation level explained in the previous section. An agreement determination rule (**Agr. Det. Rule**), a calculation sheet determination rule (**Calc Sheet Det. Rule**), and the agreement determination type (**Agreement Det. Type**) are also defined here.

Furthermore, the calculation profile contains the calculation date type (**Calc. Date Ty.**), which specifies the date to use to check the validity of an agreement and calculate the charges. Possible calculation date types include the system date, the order (creation) date, the order start date, or order end date. If charges need to be calculated in multiple currencies, it's also important to define how the exchange rate date is determined. The exchange rate date type (**Exch. Rate Date Type**) can be the same as the calculation date or defined differently.

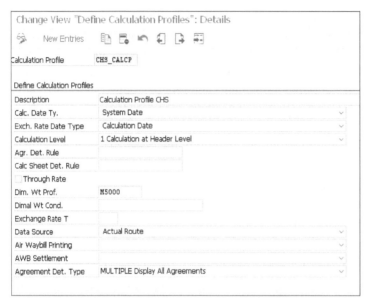

Figure 10.15 Calculation Profile

The calculation profile is assigned either to a carrier in the business partner master data or to the charges profile. The charges profile itself can be assigned to an organizational unit. Thereby, you default a calculation profile via the charges profile for a purchasing organization except for cases in which a calculation profile is defined for a carrier business partner explicitly.

Besides the calculation profile, the charges profile in Figure 10.16 contains the links to the settlement profile and the cost distribution profile, which we'll introduce in Chapter 11. The charges profile is defined in Customizing via **Transportation Management · Basic Functions · Charge Calculation · Basic Settings · Define Charges Profile**.

In the charges profile, you can select the **Evaluate All Agreements** checkbox to allow the system to evaluate all agreements that have an appropriate business partner and organization for valid rates based on the leading charge types and priorities as it has been explained in the previous section. Finally, you define whether item-based charges should be displayed in a grouped or ungrouped view in the **Default Charges View** dropdown.

Let's conclude with the second pillar of the contract determination logic: charge calculation rules.

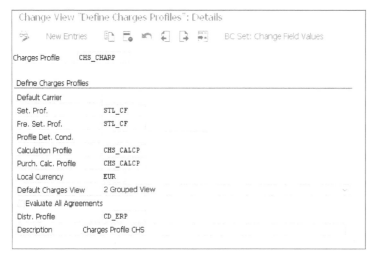

Figure 10.16 Charges Profile

Charge Calculation Rules

To enhance the flexibility of both the contract determination logic and the charge calculation logic itself, you can specify charge calculation rules and conditions based on BRF+.

The basic principle is identical for all BRF+ based conditions: all attributes in a transactional document—such as the freight order or freight booking—can be used to design a condition and for validation against a BRF+ decision table. If an attribute is stored on a line-item level (e.g., a rate table line item), it must be available as a calculation base. Attribute values are retrieved via data access definitions. They are then used as columns in a decision table and for the validation between transactional data and the table structure. Figure 10.17 shows a calculation sheet determination rule as an example for a BRF+ based condition using a decision table.

In this example, the determination is based on three criteria: mode of transport, dangerous goods, and the bill-to-party. The decision table is evaluated sequentially row by row until the first row matches the attributes of the transactional document. Typically, the last row can be used to default a result (here: calculation sheet **CHS_ Default**) by not specifying any attribute value to match, as shown in Figure 10.17.

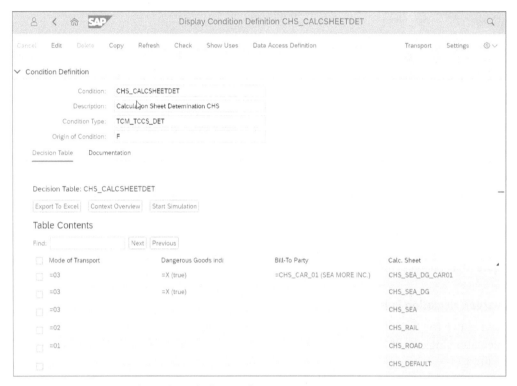

Figure 10.17 Condition for Calculation Sheet Determination

Business Add-Ins versus Charge Calculation Rules

There are various enhancement spots in charge management where a business add-in (BAdI) can be implemented. You can find the available BAdIs in Customizing via the menu path **Transportation Management • Business Add-Ins (BAdIs) for Transportation Management • Master Data • Agreements/Rate Table/Calculation Sheets** and **Transportation Management • Business Add-Ins (BAdIs) for Transportation Management • Basic Functions • Charge Calculation**.

The actual logic developed in a BAdI has a slight performance advantage compared to charge calculation rules using BRF+. On the other hand, a condition is much easier to implement because it's configured purely in decision tables and can be flexibly maintained without hard-coding values. Whether to enhance Transportation Charge Management via a BAdI or a charge calculation rule is an individual decision based on the complexity and required flexibility of the enhancement.

Charge calculation rules can be based on conditions or based on custom code (BAdIs). Wherever charge calculation rules can be assigned, a condition can also be assigned directly. Charge calculation rules are defined only on the classic GUI via path **Logistics • Transportation Management • Master Data • Maintain Charge Calculation Conditions**. In this transaction, charge calculation rules can be defined for the following use cases:

- Agreement Determination Rules–Standalone
- Agreement Determination Rules–Exclusion
- Calc. Sheet Determination Rules–Standalone
- Calc. Sheet and Calc. Sheet Item Precondition Rule
- Grouping Rules for Resolution Base
- Rules for Rate Table Determination
- Rules for Charge Calculation by Formula

For the area of contract determination, only the first four use cases are relevant:

- **Agreement determination rule–standalone/exclusion**
  The entire logic of how to perform the contract determination can be bypassed using an agreement determination rule–standalone. That way, you can define your own custom logic. Alternatively, you can still use the standard contract determination logic but apply an additional filter that takes the form of an exclusion rule.

- **Calculation sheet determination rule–standalone**
  A calculation sheet determination rule defined as a condition in Figure 10.17 can be used to determine a calculation sheet.

- **Calculation sheet (item) precondition rule**
  Precondition rules can be assigned on the level of agreement items to help select the right calculation sheet or on the calculation sheet item level to check the applicability of a specific charge line item as described in Section 10.1.2.

The remaining charge calculation rules are relevant for the actual rate retrieval and calculation. They are explained as part of the calculation logic in the next section.

10.3   Charge Calculation Logic

In the previous section, you learned how one or multiple agreements are automatically determined for charge calculation. In this section, we focus on the pure logic of how charges are calculated per charge type in a calculation sheet. The charge calculation process can vary wildly in different industries, for different types of charges, and for different modes of transport. In ocean freight, for example, there can be hundreds of surcharges that are all calculated differently, such as bunker adjustment factors based on a formula, a charge for out-of-gauge cargo, or country-specific surcharges. Similarly, in air freight, there are complex requirements for charge calculation, such as a charge calculation for ULD ratings with pivot rates. In trucking, there can be charges such as fuel adjustment factors based on index values.

The general principles of how charges are calculated are explained in Section 10.3.1. In Section 10.3.2, we describe some special capabilities in truck and rail transportation. Finally, Section 10.3.3 deals with event-based charge calculation. SAP TM's strong capabilities to manage air freight charges, sea freight charges, and LSP-specific scenarios will be covered in Chapter 12 and Chapter 13.

10.3.1   Basics

Charges can be calculated for any freight or service order, freight booking, forwarding order, quotation, settlement document, or freight unit. You need to ensure that charge calculation is enabled in the relevant transactional business document type in Customizing. You can calculate the charges manually by selecting **Charges · Calculate Charges** in the top panel of any transactional document, from a worklist, or in the transportation cockpit. In addition, you can enable automated charge calculation in the document type Customizing. Furthermore, a background report allows you to mass-calculate charges (/SCMTMS/TOR_CALC_BATCH). Finally, charges are also automatically calculated when you generate a settlement document (depending on the strategy for settlement documents in Customizing; refer to Chapter 11) or recalculated in credit memos.

In this section, we'll discuss calculation processing logic, rules, and methods.

General Processing Logic

Let's rewind for a moment. The result of the contract determination logic is one agreement item per calculation level (e.g., per stage or item) and a corresponding calculation sheet. Now each charge line item of the calculation sheet is evaluated, as follows:

1. Each charge line is checked regarding whether it's required for the calculation. You can maintain preconditions for this purpose. Standard preconditions include trade lane, service and business partner, and complex preconditions rules based on BRF+ as explained in the context of the contract determination logic (calculation sheet item precondition rules).

2. The instruction type of the charge line gets evaluated. Instruction type **Standard** points to a normal calculation of a rate amount, whereas other instruction types initiate some special logic. **Sum** will calculate an intermediate sum of all charge lines that are defined hierarchically below this charge line. **Line Item Selection** will evaluate the subordinate charge lines and choose its highest or lowest value based on its defined operator (**Highest Value**, **Lowest Value**, **Check in Sequence**) or the first charge line to return a value.

3. The rate amount is determined for charge lines with instruction type **Standard**. The rate amount can be a fixed amount, or it can be determined from a rate table. The rate table is either assigned to the charge line or determined via a rate table determination rule. In a scenario where charges are maintained on a regional or country level, you can assign each country its own rate table and determine the appropriate one via a charge calculation rule for rate table determination. After the rate table is found, the correct rate amount is retrieved from the relevant validity period of the rate table. To retrieve the rate amount, the calculation bases for each dimension (scale) of the rate table are evaluated.

The three most important settings that influence the retrieval and calculation of the rate amount are the resolution base, the calculation method, and the calculation rule. These have been introduced briefly in Section 10.1.2 and will be explained in more detail here.

The resolution base can optionally be maintained for each charge line in a calculation sheet. The calculation resolution base determines on which level a rate needs to be applied. Therefore, it defines how often the charge line of the calculation sheet will occur in the result of charge calculation in the **Charges** tab of the transactional document. If a freight booking includes three containers, and a charge line of the relevant calculation sheet has calculation resolution based defined as **Container**, then three rates need to be determined, one for each container. The following are the most important resolution bases:

- **Root**

  This is the default. Only one charge line will be the result with this resolution base. It can be used for charges that are calculated once on the document header level only, such as a documentation fee, bill of lading charges, or air waybill charges.

- **Container**

  The resolution base **Container** generates one row in the **Charges** tab for each container in a freight order or freight booking. It's the most common resolution base for air freight and ocean freight charges. In air freight, it can be used for ULDs. Because multiple containers with different attributes—such as weight, volume, commodity, equipment type, and so on—can be contained in a freight document, the determined rates can vary per container.

- **Package**

  A charge line is generated, and the rate is calculated for each package in a transactional document. This resolution base can be used for charge types, such as commodity handling, loading and unloading, and less than truckload (LTL) charges.

- **Product**

  You can generate a charge line for each product to differentiate product-dependent transportation charges.

- **Service**

  When you work with service items, you can apply the calculation resolution base **Service** for charge types that are mapped against service types. One charge line per service will be created.

- **Stage**

  One charge line per stage will be created, and a corresponding rate will be calculated.

- **Active and passive resource**

  Especially in trucking and for railways, the calculation based on resources is a common business practice. For example, you can maintain the resolution base **Passive Resource** to calculate a charge for each trailer or rail wagon individually.

The calculation level introduced in Section 10.2.1 has a strong impact on the resolution base. If the calculation level is chosen as an item level, but the resolution base of a charge type in the calculation sheet is selected as root (header), then the charge is still applied for the item (e.g., a container) and not the header (freight order). This means that the calculation level takes precedence over the resolution base; that is, the resolution base is applied based on the selected calculation level. Resolution bases can't be customized but are provided as part of the standard functionality.

Grouping rules are charge calculation rules that allow you to cluster different elements with the same resolution base to calculate a consolidated rate. Let's assume you want to calculate charges for a train that consists of 10 rail wagons of type A and another 10 rail wagons of type B. Calculation resolution base **Passive Resource** allows you to retrieve 20 rates, one for each wagon. However, you can't calculate the cost advantage from using several wagons with identical types. This is possible by using the wagon type in a grouping rule to only retrieve two rates, one for each wagon type. In a collective freight settlement, document grouping can be done across transactional documents by selecting the **Group Across Orders** flag in the grouping rule.

Because the resolution base can be defined differently for each charge line, it's also possible to combine them in one calculation. Let's assume you calculate charges for a road freight order that delivers packages from your warehouse to several customers:

- A waybill fee is charged with the resolution base root.
- A destination-based fee is charged with the resolution base stage for each destination.
- A handling fee is charged with the resolution base package for each pallet.
- An equipment-based charge is calculated for the truck and trailer based on the active resource and passive resource resolution bases.

Calculation Rules and Methods

In the charge calculation logic, the calculation rule greatly influences how a rate is calculated. To construct a calculation rule, you need to define three components: the calculation base, price unit, and unit of measure.

From Section 10.1.4 and Section 10.1.5, you learned that many calculation bases are available, such as source location, equipment type, and gross weight. When constructing a calculation rule, you can use only calculation bases with a numerical value (e.g., gross weight) because its value needs to be multiplied with the price and divided by the price unit. For example, to maintain a charge line with the calculation base actual distance and a price of 0.45 EUR per kilometer, you can enter the amount 45 with currency EUR, the price unit would be 100, the calculation rule unit of measure KM, and the calculation base actual distance. For a freight order that travels 2,000 kilometers, the calculation logic would divide this value by 100 and multiply with 45 to determine 900 EUR as a final rate.

In a rate table, you can maintain multiple calculation rules to model more complex business scenarios. For each calculation rule in a rate table, you must define its application level. This can be either maintained as **Rate Table**, if you expect to apply the rule for the full rate table, or you can define calculation rules with different price units per scale item. In this case, the application level for the calculation rule is **Scale Item**, and you must maintain the corresponding price unit for each scale item in the **Scale Items** tab.

Calculation methods are relevant for the correct interpretation of the values retrieved from a rate table. Several calculation methods are available, but you can also develop your own calculation methods and assign them in Customizing (**Transportation Management • Basic Functions • Charge Calculation • Enhancements to Charge Calculation Engine • Define Calculation Methods**) to become available in the calculation sheet. The most common calculation methods are the following:

- **Standard**
  This is the simplest calculation method. The standard calculation method multiplies the rate retrieved from the rate table (e.g., 0.45 USD per mile) with the corresponding value from the calculation base (e.g., 100 miles) to compute the final amount (here: 45 USD). If you don't maintain a calculation method in the charge line, this calculation method is used by default.

- **Clipping**
  A calculation method that is also frequently applied is clipping. When you're working with tiered rates in a rate table, the clipping method takes a value that is relevant for the charge calculation (e.g., weight) and applies each tier until the total is reached or exceeded. At the same time, the clipping method is accumulating the calculated charge.

Let's compare calculation methods standard and clipping by an example: The calculated charge will be based on gross weight, and the total gross weight to be charged for is 11 tons.

Based on the rate table in Table 10.1, the standard calculation method would identify the relevant rate as 14 USD per ton and therefore return 11 × 14 = 154 USD as a final amount. In contrast, the clipping calculation method would return 209 USD because it would have calculated different amounts for the first ton, second to fifth ton, and so on, as outlined in Table 10.1. Thus, the same rate table can yield different results based on the applied calculation method.

Scale	Rate	Calculated Amount	Value
Up to 1 ton	35 USD absolute	35 USD	1
Up to 5 tons	20 USD per ton	80 USD	4
Up to 10 tons	16 USD per ton	80 USD	5
Up to 15 tons	14 USD per ton	14 USD	1
Sum		209 USD	11

Table 10.1 Rate Table and Clipping Results

- **Break-weight**

  The break-weight calculation method deals with an undesired anomaly of the standard calculation method. Based on the rate table in Table 10.1, the standard calculation method calculates 90 USD for a gross weight of 4.5 tons (4.5 × 20 = 90 USD) but calculates only 80 USD for a gross weight of 5 tons (5 × 16 = 80 USD). Thus, a higher weight would result in a lower charge. To avoid this anomaly, the break-weight calculation method calculates two values: (1) the same as the standard calculation method and (2) the entry price of the subsequent scale item. Then it compares these two values and returns the lower one. For a gross weight of 4.5 tons, the break-weight method will first calculate 90 USD (per the standard calculation method), then calculate 80 USD (lowest price in the subsequent scale item), and finally return 80 USD (the lower value).

- **Deficit weight rating**

  Deficit weight rating is a calculation method used especially in US land transportation. If you have a tiered rate table, and the weight of a cargo item isn't high enough to reach the tier with cheaper rates, the system sums up the weight of similar cargo from different freight classes and rounds up the weight to reach the next available tier. The charges for all cargo items are calculated based on this cheaper tier. The deficit that was added is rated with the cheapest freight class rate in the appropriate tier and added to the total rate.

  Table 10.2 and Table 10.3 show an example of the deficit weight rating. The weight of freight class A is 350 kilograms, and the weight of freight class B is 600 kilograms. As depicted in the rate tables, the total rate with the standard calculation method is 20,200 USD (7,000 + 13,200). With the deficit weight calculation method rating, the total rate is 18,000 USD (5,250 + 750 + 12,000) USD because the total weight is rounded up by 50 kilograms to 1,000 kilograms to achieve the next-cheapest tier. Each freight class is rated in its individual tier (350 × 15 = 5,250 and 600 × 20 = 12,000). In addition, the deficit weight of 50 kilograms (1,000 − 950) is rated with the cheapest rate in all tiers across the two freight classes (50 × 15 = 750).

In the transactional document, a new charge line called *deficit charge* concatenated with the charge type description is automatically created. This additional charge line will show the deficit weight and deficit rate-related information corresponding to the charge type.

Tier	Rate	Standard	Deficit Weight Rating
Up to 500 kilograms	20 USD per kilogram	7,000 USD	
Up to 750 kilograms	19 USD per kilogram		
Up to 1,000 kilograms	15 USD per kilogram		5,250 USD
			750 USD
			(50 × 15)

Table 10.2 Rate 1 with Freight Class A: 350 Kilograms

Tier	Rate	Standard	Deficit Weight Rating
Up to 500 kilograms	25 USD per kilogram		
Up to 750 kilograms	22 USD per kilogram	13,200 USD	
Up to 1,000 kilograms	20 USD per kilogram		12,000 USD

Table 10.3 Rate 2 with Freight Class B: 600 Kilograms

- **External system**
  The external system calculation method allows you to call an external rating engine, such as SMC3. In this case, the rates are retrieved from the external system without being calculated in SAP TM.

10.3.2 Mode-Specific Calculation for Road and Rail Freight

Each transportation mode has its peculiarities when calculating charges. While specifics for sea, air, and forwarder businesses are discussed in Chapter 12, road and rail freight are addressed here.

Parcel Freight Charges

The transportation of freight with courier, express, and parcel services (CEP) requires specific functionality to calculate charges accordingly. A key difference from all other charge calculation scenarios is that in this scenario, charges are retrieved already in the freight unit that represents a parcel or package. This process is called direct shipment, which must be enabled in the freight unit type Customizing (**Transportation Management • Planning • Freight Unit • Define Freight Unit Type**) by selecting either **Automatic Determination of Direct Shipment Options** or **Manual Selection of Direct Shipment Options Enabled** as the direct shipment option type. In this case, each applicable freight agreement is determined for the freight unit as well as the available services each carrier offers. A user can choose the best direct shipment option in the freight unit based on the charges for various service levels. For the setup of these kinds of charges in agreements, it's crucial to maintain the service levels of each carrier for CEP services as agreement items. This allows you to differentiate charges for an overnight versus a three-day delivery service, for example. Each such agreement item can use additional dimensions as a precondition, such as weight, height, or length of a parcel. The retrieved charges per service are displayed on the **Direct Shipment Options** tab of the freight unit.

Charge Calculation for Road Freight

In most economies, much of the freight volume is still transported via road. Compared to rail transport, truck transports are typically faster but also more expensive. The following situations are typical in road freight:

- To enable a charge that is dependent on the number of stops in the freight order, you can use calculation base NUMBER_OF_STOPS that counts all stops of a freight order or calculation base NO_OF_INT_STOPS that only counts the number of intermediate stops without the initial start and the destination stop. You can multiply this figure with a fixed stop charge or use it in a rate table.

- To model fuel surcharges you can use index-based rate tables. This is very typical for many truck carriers to apply flexible surcharges depending on a fluctuating fuel index. A special calculation method type (**Fuel Surcharge Calculation**) and calculation method (FUEL_SURCHARGE) is available for this scenario. Two flavors of this calculation are offered: either the system retrieves the latest fuel index to look up the relevant rate in a regular rate table based on the order date, or the system compares the fuel index on the order date against a fuel index for a base date and multiplies it with a percentage or the actual fuel surcharge value.

To configure the first variant of index-based charges, you must maintain a corresponding charge line in your calculation sheet and use calculation base FSC (fuel surcharge) in a regular rate table assigned to this charge line. This (regular) rate table holds the rate amounts depending on the index value. A second rate table, from which the index value is retrieved needs to be maintained in the same charge line in the **Index Rate Table** field.

In the second variant, two charge lines are required. The first charge line holds the regular rate table. The second charge line holds the index rate table, the index base date, and the reference line number to the first charge line. The index rate table is defined like the first variant, but instead of using the actual rate amount, the system determines the value for the scale item that is valid on the date specified in the **Index Base Date** field. An index value is calculated and used in conjunction with the amount or percent specified in the relevant (first) line item in the calculation sheet to determine the fuel surcharge amount.

- Another useful functionality for road freight is to base charges on the vehicle resources used. This allows you to apply different charges, depending on whether a truck, trailer, or specific combination thereof has been used. The calculation resolution bases ACTIVE_RESOURCE and PASSIVE_RESOURCE are available to influence whether a charge such as a fuel surcharge is only applied for the truck or for both truck and trailer.

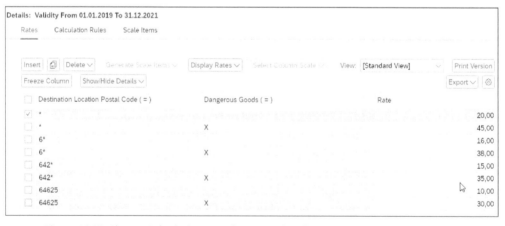

Figure 10.18 Charge Calculation Based on Postal Codes

- Frequently, charges in road transportation are based on transportation zones or postal codes. Because using individual postal codes for the definition of freight charges can lead to rather large rate tables, wildcard operator * can be used in place of numerals of the postal code. The most specific rate value will be retrieved with this setup. In the rate table in Figure 10.18, the value 30 would be retrieved for transporting a dangerous good to postal code 64625, whereas 35 would be retrieved if the same item were sent to postal code 64626.

Charge Calculation for Rail Freight

Like road transports, rail transports also have their transportation mode-specific calculation logic:

- **Interline shipments with rule 11**
  The railway network in different countries or even within large countries such as the United States is divided among several rail carriers. If a shipper wants to transport goods across a railway network, it's very likely that multiple rail carriers will be involved in executing this transport. Rule 11 is the rail industry regulation governing interline shipments with one tender and multiple service provider invoices. A rail freight order will typically have one stage for each of the different rail carriers involved in the transport. However, to simplify the contractual relationship, a shipper might have a freight agreement with only one (or a subset) of all rail carriers involved in the transport. In this kind of scenario, the system will retrieve the relevant freight agreement based on the *invoicing carrier* that will be maintained in the corresponding rail freight order against each stage. The invoicing carrier can therefore be different from the executing carrier of a stage and is determined based on rail routing.

- **Railcar charge calculation with day-of-week pricing**
  It's possible to maintain rates in absolute numbers or markups in percentages depending on the delivery date. Especially in rail transportation, the charges often deviate depending on the weekday. Calculation base WEEKDAY may be appropriate to use in these cases.

  This can also be relevant for the determination of rail fuel surcharges. If the order date isn't used to look up the fuel index, but the in-gate date (e.g., the end date of main carriage) is used instead, then you should specify the calculation date type in the calculation profile accordingly.

- **Railcar specific charges**
  Like road freight, the calculation resolution bases ACTIVE_RESOURCE and PASSIVE_
  RESOURCE are frequently used to differentiate charges applied to either the locomotive or individual rail wagons. Calculation base NO_OF_AXLES can be used to determine axle-based charges for rail wagons of different sizes and types.

10.3.3   Event-Based Charges

Any company managing freight in containers will have experienced detention and
demurrage charges. These fees are charged if containers are released or returned to
the provider of the container, mostly freight forwarders or ocean carriers, later than
agreed. Demurrage charges usually apply if a shipper or consignee (e.g., a manufacturing company) picks up the container from the port of discharge too late. These
charges are meant to cover the cost that occurs for the service provider when storing
the container in a port or terminal. Detention fees follow the exact same principle.
They apply for extra days the empty container isn't returned after it has been delivered to the consignee. The rationale is that the provider of the container has an
opportunity cost if the provider can't use this container for another customer. Detention and demurrage charges can even apply for entirely chartered ocean vessels.
Especially for bulk transportation, it's common to charter an entire vessel for a transport (e.g., of oil or iron ore). The carrier charges detention and demurrage fees for the
late release of the vessel from its service.

Detention and demurrage fees are the most prominent but certainly not the only
example of where a charge is applied upon the occurrence of a certain event. Other
examples include accessorial charges in the railway business (e.g., storage services or
diversions), service charges in the ocean carrier industry (e.g., reissuance of documentation, detention in transit, or container cleaning charges), or any other conditional charges that aren't known prior to the execution.

Event-based charge calculation allows you to use event information in the charge calculation process. That way, charges can be retrieved depending on whether certain
events happen and the deviation of time between the planned and actual event time
or between the actual time and a reference event. Depending on the individual contractual agreement, a service provider usually grants some number of free days prior
to starting to charge. If we apply this capability to detention and demurrage fees, this
means that during the tracking of the delivery of the container and its empty return
to the container depot in SAP Event Management, this information can be provided
to the charge calculation logic. During charge calculation, the system retrieves the

total days between full container delivery and empty container return and subtracts the free days to derive the chargeable delay days. This number is then multiplied with the detention/demurrage fee per the charge line/rate table.

Limitations of Event-Based Charge Calculation

Managing detention and demurrage charges can be increasingly complex. Depending on the exact contractual commitment, LSPs might have stringent clauses when the count of delay days goes up. Some contracts exclude, for example, force majeure or other incidents from counting toward detention/demurrage days. If there is, for example, a labor strike in a port of discharge that prevents the consignee from picking up its container, the corresponding days might not count as demurrage-relevant days. In addition, the free day commitments can be very granular and different per each port-pair and equipment type.

Another important aspect of basing charge calculation on actual event dates is the accuracy of how this event information is captured. If reported event dates and times aren't accurate, charge calculation based on this inaccurate information will be wrong from the beginning.

To enable event-based charge calculation, you need to create an event profile and map charge types to events in Customizing via menu path **Transportation Management • Basic Functions • Charge Calculation • Basic Settings • Define Event Profiles**. Figure 10.19 illustrates the creation of an event profile. In this example, three charge types are maintained, which are based on different events. When these events are reported in SAP Event Management (see Chapter 8, Section 8.2) the corresponding charge type is added to the execution document (e.g., a freight order or freight booking), and charges are calculated.

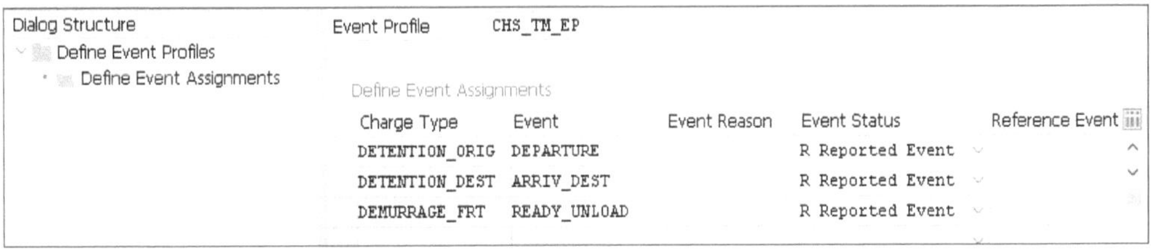

Dialog Structure	Event Profile	CHS_TM_EP			
∨ Define Event Profiles					
• Define Event Assignments	Define Event Assignments				
	Charge Type	Event	Event Reason	Event Status	Reference Event
	DETENTION_ORIG	DEPARTURE		R Reported Event	
	DETENTION_DEST	ARRIV_DEST		R Reported Event	
	DEMURRAGE_FRT	READY_UNLOAD		R Reported Event	

Figure 10.19 Event Profile for Event-Based Charge Calculation

Notice that the event profile is influencing only whether and when a charge type is applied in a transactional document. The charge calculation logic still resides in the calculation sheet. For the detention/demurrage calculation, you still need to maintain the appropriate charge types in the calculation sheet. To model the logic to apply a threshold of free days into the calculation, you can use calculation base Delay_Tot (delay days) and unit of measure as Day in the calculation rule of the appropriate charge line and assign in Customizing the calculation base Grace_Days as a related calculation base to calculation base Delay_Tot. This allows you to maintain the number of free days directly in the calculation sheet.

So far, we've put a lot of emphasis on the options for how to configure the contract determination and charge calculation logic. Finally, let's look at the result and the options for analyzing it.

10.3.4   Charge Calculation Analysis and Charge Estimation

After a successful calculation of the charges, you can find the results in the **Charges** tab of your transactional document. How you can read and understand this information, especially if the result doesn't match your expectation, is the focus of the remainder of this section.

Figure 10.20 shows an example of calculated charges for a road freight order. The freight order consists of two stages (from **CHS_SAP_1** via **CHS_SAP_2** to **CHS_SAP_3**) and includes three items (**MATERIAL 1, MATERIAL 2,** and **MATERIAL 3**). From the **Logistical Reference**, you can see that the basic freight of the first charge line has been calculated on the header/root level, whereas the stop off charge has been calculated on the stage level, and the handling charges have been calculated on the product level. This has been achieved by using the different calculation resolution bases ROOT, STAGE, and PRODUCT) for the corresponding charge lines in the calculation sheet. On this overview, you can also see the following for each charge result line:

- The rate amount that has been determined from the rate table or calculation sheet
- The price unit and unit of measure
- The logistical quantity
- The calculation base

This information is used to compute the calculated amount for each charge line as well as the final amount.

Figure 10.20 Charge Calculation Result in a Freight Order

To increase the transparency of the calculation, you can display details for each charge line. You can toggle between the display of this information or hide it using the **Show/Hide Details** button. Figure 10.21 and Figure 10.22 show some of the details that are displayed when this function is turned on. The details show systematically how the charges have been determined. They are always displayed for the charge line that is currently selected.

More specifically, Figure 10.21 and Figure 10.22 show the details for the stop off charge for the second stage from **CHS_SAP_2** to **CHS_SAP_3**. In Figure 10.21, you can see that freight agreement **CHS_FA_02** with **Calculation Sheet 1913** and **Rate Table 752** have been used to retrieve a rate amount of **16 EUR**. Figure 10.22 shows the logistical data that has been used to retrieve this value from the rate table. The **Data Source Value** for dangerous goods was empty, such that also the empty value has been retrieved as **Scale Value**. For the postal code, the value retrieved from the freight order was **68900** (**Data Source Value**). Because no such value exists among the scale items in the rate table shown earlier in Figure 10.18, the postal code that comes closest, that is, **6***, is used as a **Scale Value** to retrieve the rate amount.

Details: Line Number 000030, Charge Type STOP_OFF, Stop Off

Overview   Basic Data   Charge Calculation Log   Calculated Amounts and Exchange Rates   Calculation Rules   Notes

Calculation Parameters

Rate Amount:	16,00
Manually-Changed Rate Amount:	☐
Rate Currency/Percentage:	EUR
Zero Rate:	☐
Calculated Amount:	16,00
Calculated Currency:	EUR
Logistical Reference:	CHS_SAP_2 - CHS_SAP_3
Group Type:	
Group Type Description:	
Class Rate:	
Reference Rate Class:	
Percent:	0,000000
Class Rate Amount:	
Rate Table Notes:	

Charge Management Master Data

Agreement:	CHS_FA_02
Calculation Sheet:	1913
Rate Table:	752
Index Rate Table:	
Rate Table Determination Rule:	

Printing

Additional Notes:

Figure 10.21 Charge Calculation Analysis: Overview

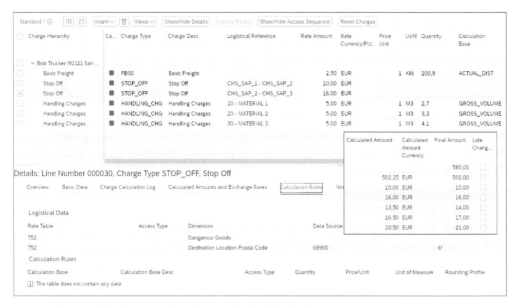

Figure 10.22 Charge Calculation Analysis: Calculation Rules

If manual changes or additions are required, you have the option to add charge lines by choosing **Insert • Charge Line**. For manually entered charges, you need to specify the charge type and rate amount.

If no freight order or freight booking exists, but an estimate of freight charges is required, this can be done with the Estimate Freight Charges app available in order management. This app can support you in estimating the transportation cost without generating a transactional document. Technically, the object used in this process is like a freight order, but the results can't be persisted and saved. Furthermore, it's possible to skip entering certain information that may be unknown at the time. The UI of this app is a simplified freight order screen as shown in Figure 10.23.

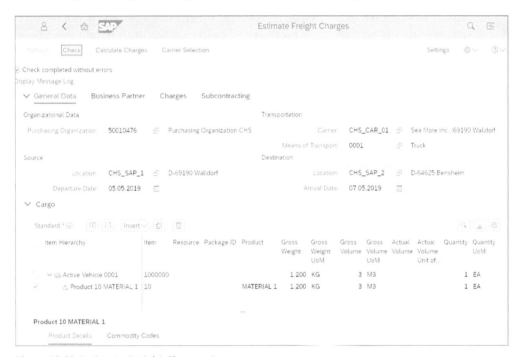

Figure 10.23 Estimate Freight Charges App

Let's change our focus now from an operational view to a more strategic perspective. In the next section, we introduce the available capabilities around strategic freight procurement. While we started this chapter with manually creating freight contracts, the next topic is to show their automatic creation via a streamlined quotation process.

10.4   Strategic Vendor Contract Management

SAP TM offers capabilities for long-term procurement and selling decisions and an integration into carrier portals, SAP Logistics Business Network, or SAP Customer Relationship Management (SAP CRM) for contract management (see Chapter 13, Section 13.7, for detailed information). Earlier releases of SAP TM offered limited functionalities for selling and procuring transportation services, mainly to support operational and ad hoc scenarios, but this has been widely improved in SAP TM in SAP S/4HANA and SAP TM releases starting with SAP TM 9.2. In this chapter, we summarize these new capabilities under the umbrella of strategic freight management, which can be broken down into strategic freight procurement and strategic freight selling (see Chapter 12, Section 12.5). Strategic freight management is relevant for shippers and LSP businesses, as most parties need to subcontract freight services to external vendors.

Figure 10.24 shows the high-level architecture of strategic freight management. In terms of freight service contracting, the architecture shows a clear distinction between strategic customer and vendor contract management, symbolized by the sections on the left and the right.

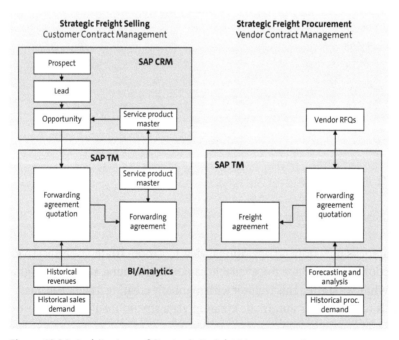

Figure 10.24 Architecture of Strategic Freight Management

On the right side of Figure 10.24, you can see the capabilities for a strategic freight procurement (also known as vendor contract management), which we focus on in this section. This includes integration with SAP analytics solutions to analyze historical demands and even forecasting based on different strategies and what-if scenarios. You can generate a freight agreement quotation, which serves as an RFQ to one or many vendors, shown in the center-right.

It's possible to perform a carrier ranking and carrier analysis directly from the freight agreement quotation. You can generate multiple vendor RFQs for publishing and collect various responses. In addition, you can compare answers from your vendors, both manually and via an optimizer engine, to award carriers. Finally, you can generate a freight agreement as a new contract from a freight agreement quotation.

Use of Analytics Functions in Strategic Freight Management

Concerning analytics usage in strategic freight management, there is a difference in availability of analytics functions and analytics integration between SAP TM in SAP S/4HANA and SAP TM 9.6. Functionality based on SAP BusinessObjects Business Intelligence (SAP BusinessObjects BI) is no longer included in the standard scope of SAP TM in SAP S/4HANA, as this release has its own analytics technologies and views. Many analytical reports that are available based on SAP BusinessObjects BI therefore can't be used in SAP S/4HANA 1809, unless it connects with SAP BusinessObjects BI. Based on the SAP Fiori technology, Business Context Viewer (BCV) functionalities also can't be used anymore. Instead, the user must rely on available analytics content in SAP S/4HANA, which unfortunately doesn't include analytics of contracts and what-if simulation results as of release 1809.

10.4.1   Strategic Freight Procurement

Strategic freight procurement supports the streamlined management of RFQs from the perspective of a shipper or LSP, requesting capacities and rates from a carrier or freight forwarder. The SAP TM functionality for strategic freight procurement focuses on mid-term and long-term planning and procurement decisions. The intention is to support and enable a quotation and contract management process to establish freight agreements.

The strategic freight procurement process begins by analyzing and planning future demand based on historical data. A forecast is the foundation for procurement decisions about freight capacities. After capacities are forecasted and planned, the actual vendor selection and quotation process can be executed.

The freight order and freight booking tendering functionality is limited to single shipments only, as discussed in Chapter 7. The innovative aspect of strategic freight procurement is that it supports an entire RFQ process from analyzing historical demands, to generating forecasts, to managing an RFQ until the vendor is awarded and a contract is created.

In SAP TM, we differentiate between two supported functional processes, as shown in Figure 10.25:

- **Planning and analytics**
  This process is either executed using the analytics of SAP S/4HANA or outside SAP TM 9.6 in SAP BusinessObjects BI. The bases for procurement planning are historical shipments from SAP TM: freight orders and freight bookings and their analytical data stored in SAP Business Warehouse (SAP BW). These historical demands are the foundation for generating forecasts by using strategies such as trending and smoothing. After you've successfully generated a volume forecast, you can use this information for the freight agreement quotation process.

- **Freight agreement quotation process**
  You can generate freight agreement RFQs to subcontract freight capacities and agree on rates. You can use the forecasted volumes as an input to define capacities you want to request from your vendors. The freight agreement RFQ allows you to define scope, requested capacities, charge structures, and service products that will be contracted. A carrier ranking tool allows you to short-list potential carriers and forwarders. You can generate vendor RFQ documents and publish them individually to providers. To award a carrier or service provider, you can use a comparison optimization tool and then generate freight agreements.

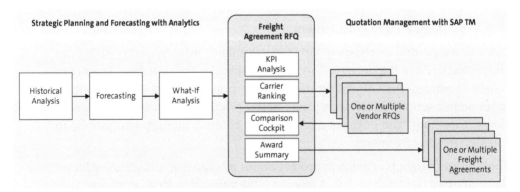

Figure 10.25 Overview of Strategic Freight Procurement

10.4.2   Freight Procurement Planning and Analytics in SAP TM 9.6

The procurement planning and analytics functionality has three components that support you in your sourcing decisions: you can analyze historical demands, generate forecasts, and consider alternative scenarios with what-if analyses. All three functionalities are part of the SAP transportation procurement cockpit, which runs completely in SAP BusinessObjects BI. You can access the transportation procurement cockpit from SAP Business Client by navigating to **Analytics · Strategic Freight Management**. The analytical cockpit currently isn't available in SAP S/4HANA 1809.

Historical Demand

After you've started SAP BusinessObjects BI, you see a table that shows historical shipments and breaks down your shipped containers, weights, volumes, and planned and actual costs. Furthermore, you have a list of filter parameters in the top panel that you can apply to drill deeper into the report. For example, you can specify the scope for the report from a total of container types to a breakdown per specific container type carrier and trade lane. In addition, the time horizons can be flexibly adjusted. A clear advantage of the SAP BusinessObjects BI analytics solution is that you can flexibly adjust a report to your needs by setting filters and dragging and dropping additional dimensions in the table. This allows very intuitive navigation and capabilities for drilling down. Figure 10.26 shows one example of a specified scope for a historical demand report.

Source Location	Destination Location	Carrier	Equipment Type	Calendar Year	Number of Documents	Container Count (TEU)	Gross Weight in KG (KG)	Gross Volume in m3 (M3)	Planned Costs (EUR)	Actual Costs (EUR)
Port Newark	Port of Rotterdam	AV_CAR_002	22G0	2012	23	8,664.000	222,900.000	111,450.000	445,291.00	453,971.00
			22H0	2012	27	9,080.000	228,798.000	114,399.000	541,917.00	553,537,00
			42G0	2012	20	8,048.000	202,394.000	101,197.000	368,780.00	376,155,00
			42G1	2012	17	5,968.000	150,458.000	75,229.000	341,740.00	349,042,00
			Result		87	31,960.000	804,550.000	402,275.000	1,697,728.00	1,732,705,00
		AV_CAR_004	22G0	2012	37	5,632.000	143,196.000	71,596.000	569,592.00	590,470,00
			22H0	2012	37	6,496.000	164,356.000	82,176.000	578,529.00	598,353,00
			42G0	2012	40	6,288.000	159,810.000	79,905.000	643,693.00	666,413,00
			42G1	2012	43	8,160.000	205,808.000	102,904.000	651,620.00	674,104,00
			Result		157	26,576.000	673,170.000	336,585.000	2,443,434.00	2,529,340,00
Overall Result					244	58,536.000	1,477,720.000	738,860.000	4,141,162.00	4,262,045,00

Figure 10.26 Historical Demand per Carrier and Equipment Type

Capacity Forecast and What-If Analysis

In the second tab of the transportation procurement cockpit for planning, you can generate capacity forecasts. First, you need to define a planning version and describe the scope for the historical data. You can specify the historical basis with start and end dates and whichever trade lanes, origins, and destinations you want to include.

As a result, you see the historical demand based on your selection. If you select the forecast, you're prompted to specify the forecast period you want to generate.

After you confirm the scope, the actual demand projections are computed, including the number of TEUs and the projected cost. You can generate various forecast planning versions using different strategies to calculate the projections. To compare the different forecast planning versions that you've created, you can use the forecast version analysis. Select the versions you want to compare via the filter capabilities, and you'll see the overview of projections for each version. It's possible to export generated forecasts into an Excel spreadsheet.

Figure 10.27 shows a forecast for a specific origin and destination pair in a given calendar year. Two forecast versions are shown.

				No of Documents	Container Count	Gross Weight in KG	Gross Volume in m3	Projected Cost	Actual Costs
Source Location	Destination Location	Forecast Version	Calendar Year/Month		TEU	KG	M3		
Port Newark	Port At Honk kong	SAP02	AUG 2013	0	0	2.975.504.000	0	0,00	0,00
			SEP 2013	0	0	2.879.520.000	0	0,00	0,00
			OCT 2013	0	0	2.975.504.000	0	0,00	0,00
			NOV 2013	0	0	2.879.520.000	0	0,00	0,00
			DEC 2013	0	0	2.975.504.000	0	0,00	0,00
			Result	0	0	14.665.551.999	0	0,00	0,00
		SAP01	AUG 2013	0	0	116.553.605	0	0,00	0,00
			SEP 2013	0	0	116.553.605	0	0,00	0,00
			OCT 2013	0	0	128.208.966	0	0,00	0,00
			NOV 2013	0	0	116.553.605	0	0,00	0,00
			DEC 2013	0	0	116.553.605	0	0,00	0,00
			Result	0	0	594.423.386	0	0,00	0,00
	Result		Result	0	0	15.279.975.385	0	0,00	0,00
Overall Result				0	0	15.279.975.385	0	0,00	0,00

Figure 10.27 Forecast with Version Comparison

One essential task is to define the logic of the actual strategy being used to generate the forecast. In SAP BusinessObjects BI, you can specify your own planning functions, each with a different forecasting strategy. You can define planning functions in your SAP BusinessObjects BI system using Transaction NRSPLAN. Several standard strategies are available and can be used in a new function, such as simple exponential smoothing, linear regression, seasonal exponential smoothing, and trend-seasonal exponential smoothing. After you've defined and copied a new planning function and assigned a strategy, you need to establish a planning sequence as part of the same transaction. After a new planning function and sequence are defined, they can be used for forecasting runs.

To get comparable results in SAP TM in SAP S/4HANA 1809, you can, for example, utilize analytical pages such as the freight order quantity analysis, as shown in Figure 10.28.

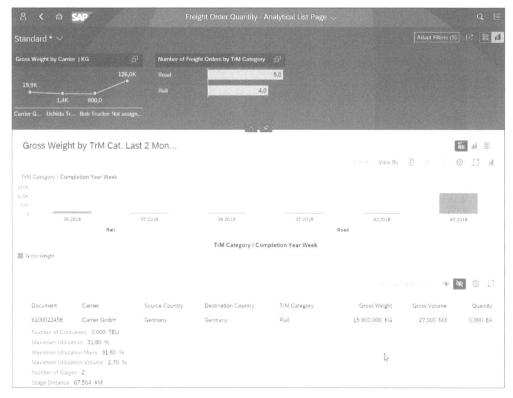

Figure 10.28 Freight Order Quantity Analysis: Analytics List Page

After a successful forecast, you can manually alter the projected results. Click the **Enable Change** button (refer to Figure 10.27) to enter deviating container amounts or weights and volumes. If you select **Simulate**, the system automatically calculates impacts on other parameters, such as the projected cost. You can save the simulated versions.

10.4.3   Freight Agreement Request for Quotation Process

In the previous section, you analyzed historical demands and generated or calculated a capacity forecast. Knowing your future demand is a key input for making strategic procurement decisions. In this section, we use both capacity information and past shipment data to issue an RFQ to short-listed vendors. The goal is to sign a long-term freight agreement with the highest-ranked and cheapest service providers. This process is driven mainly by the freight agreement quotation, which is needed to start a new RFQ process.

Create Freight Agreement Request for Quotation

You can find agreement quotations by following **Contract Management • Freight Agreements** or **Create Freight Management RFQ Master**. You're prompted to enter an RFQ type. The RFQ type is a new Customizing setting that you can find in SAP TM Customizing via the menu path **Transportation Management • Master Data • Agreement RFQs and Quotations • Define Freight Agreement RFQ Types**. The RFQ type specifies number ranges, activates approval workflows, and contains important settings for carrier ranking and the comparison cockpit, as we describe in the following sections. After you've generated the freight agreement RFQ, you can specify basic header information, such as the purchasing organizations responsible for the RFQ, validity dates, deadline for the quotation, and desired contract duration, as shown in Figure 10.29.

The **Carriers** section is used to define the list of vendors you want to consider for the quotation. It doesn't represent the short list to which you're submitting the RFQ, but instead shows the long list of possible vendors. To specify the scope for your RFQ, you need to generate RFQ items. An RFQ item can, for example, resemble different geographical trade lanes, a different set of commodities, or different service products you want to request. You can also maintain a budget against each agreement quotation line to limit your maximum expenditure.

SAP TM offers a ranking functionality for your vendors based on a configurable carrier key performance indicator (KPI) profile. You can set up a profile in SAP TM Customizing and assign it as the default profile to the freight agreement RFQ type. Alternatively, you can select it in the RFQ header or line item directly.

Figure 10.29 Freight Agreement RFQ Master

After you've successfully short-listed your vendors based on the KPI analysis and carrier ranking, you can proceed to the quotation preparation. An important step in the preparation is to define the surcharge structure with which you want your vendors to comply. As with a regular freight agreement, you can assign a charge sheet to each line item and add charge types. The list of charges you select is used for submission to the vendors and dictates the charge structure the carrier is expected to reply to. To define the scope of your RFQ with detailed request line items, generate a rate table for each charge type in SAP TM. For charges where you expect a fixed lump sum across all line items, you don't need to assign a rate table (e.g., a currency adjustment factor). Usually, you generate a rate table for at least the basic freight charge and key surcharges, depending on your mode of transport. You can enter the scope for the RFQ by adding lines in the rate table (e.g., per origin, destination, equipment type, and commodity). The rate table structure is flexible; you can use various scales and calculation bases to model the rate table for the scope of your RFQ. This rate table for the basic freight charge is the central input tool for your vendors to reply with a rate for each request line item. Each rate table you assign to a surcharge generates output that your vendors need to fill in.

Capacities in SAP TM 9.6

In addition to rates and surcharges, another vital piece of the freight agreement RFQ is the capacities. In the previous section, we covered how to generate a demand forecast; now we bridge the gap and walk through how to include the requested capacity information in your RFQ. By selecting **Business Context Viewer** in the top panel of your RFQ, you can directly access the demand and forecast reports, as shown in Figure 10.30. This is only available in SAP TM installations on SAP Business Suite (e.g., SAP TM 9.6).

You can select the **Historical Demand and Forecast** content in the side panel of the BCV. This allows you to view the historical demands you've shipped with your carriers directly in the RFQ. It's possible to personalize the chart and change the parameters, shown in this example by different trade lanes, origin–destination pairs, modes of transport, or time buckets.

You can also view the forecast you generated as part of the procurement planning and forecasting process. You can display your own forecasted capacity demands with the specific carriers in the BCV by selecting the content of **Forecasted Version Analysis.** You can filter the demands (e.g., by the geographical scope). It's even possible to switch between different forecast versions that you created prior to the freight agreement RFQ by entering a different forecast version in the RFQ line item table.

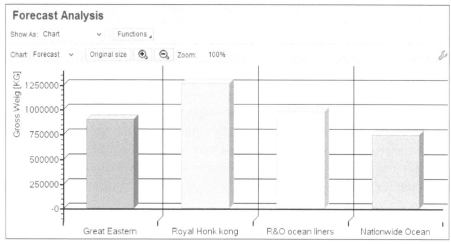

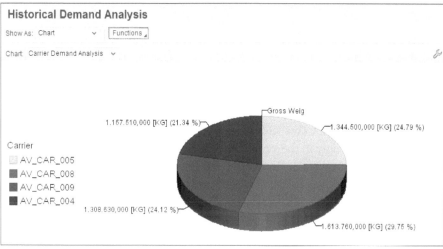

Figure 10.30 Historical Demand and Forecast (SAP TM 9.x Only)

After you've decided which capacities to request, you need to enter your decision in the freight agreement RFQ. You can request capacities both by RFQ line item and in the more granular rate table lines. In the RFQ line items, you can specify your requested capacities in various types, perhaps per weight, volume, or TEU per defined time bucket (e.g., per month or per year). A vendor can respond with promised capacities and, after a negotiation, with a confirmed capacity that can be agreed upon. In addition, you can enter requested capacities for each origin–destination pair in the more detailed rate table items. The rate table lines were enhanced in SAP TM to store requested, promised, and confirmed capacities.

In addition to the capacities you want to transport, you can also specify a range of target rates. This is a very common business practice for freight RFQs across various modalities. In ocean freight, for example, a shipper is likely to publish its requested target rates. This puts the carrier under pressure to match the expectations of the potential customer and be competitive. Consequently, shippers use this functionality to achieve cost savings. Target rates in an RFQ in SAP TM can be added in both the calculation sheet for each charge type and, more importantly, the rate table lines. You can also specify tolerances (e.g., 4%), which may be quoted by the carrier or LSP. Enable this functionality in the freight agreement RFQ type by choosing the **Publish Target Rates** checkbox.

Communication of RFQs and Collaboration Portal in SAP TM 9.6

After you've successfully prepared the RFQ but before you publish it to your vendors, SAP TM supports a standard approval workflow that you can enable in the freight agreement RFQ type; it generates a vendor RFQ document for each carrier that you included in your short list. Each vendor RFQ has a similar layout and UI as the master RFQ. It inherits all RFQ line items, the charge sheet for each line item, and the rate tables. Only one carrier is stored in the header of the vendor RFQ because it's unique for each vendor. The vendor RFQ document is used mainly to either upload it or input the carrier responses. The fields for promised capacities and offered rate values are editable for input only in the vendor RFQ. You can use the standard SAP TM output management functionality that is enabled for RFQs to generate output files. In addition, you can use the rate table Excel integration to generate RFQ spreadsheets and submit to your vendors. It's also possible to download the entire freight agreement RFQ into an Excel spreadsheet for publishing with a carrier or LSP.

SAP Collaboration Functionality for Contract Creation

In SAP Business Suite releases of SAP TM (i.e., SAP TM 9.x), the collaboration with carriers and LSPs was supported by the Collaboration Portal. This functionality isn't available any longer in SAP TM in SAP S/4HANA 1809. It will be replaced in multiple steps by the SAP Logistics Business Network. However, a complete feature parity hasn't been reached with the release of SAP TM in SAP S/4HANA 1809.

A support functionality for the interaction with carriers and LSPs is the Collaboration Portal, which, as of the time of writing (winter 2018), is limited to SAP TM 9.x releases. Let's briefly look at its capabilities for strategic freight procurement. Managing RFQs and agreements only via email or offline communication can be a very inefficient process. You can consequently use the Collaboration Portal to publish your freight agreement RFQs to LSPs and carriers. Your business partners will be equipped with user access to the portal. They can view RFQs with their corresponding status (**Submitted** or **Closed**) in a comprehensive worklist.

In the details of a selected RFQ, you can see any attachments to the freight agreement RFQ. This can be, for example, the terms and conditions of the RFQ. The actual details for the freight agreement RFQ are attached to the entry in the Collaboration Portal as an Excel spreadsheet called *Bid_Structure*. The carrier can download this spreadsheet to enter the reply of rates and capacities. A specific Customizing setting allows you to define which fields in the spreadsheet are editable and can be changed by the carrier: **SAP Transportation Management** • **Transportation Management** • **Master Data** • **Agreement RFQs and Quotations** • **Define Editable Fields in TM-Formatted Excels.** This works very similarly to the forwarding order quotation process.

After the carrier has uploaded the reply, you can retrieve the information directly into your master freight agreement RFQ in SAP TM to proceed with the RFQ evaluation. It's even possible to upload delta changes; therefore, if a carrier provides additional rates after a first submission, the delta of the rates can be pulled into SAP TM. You can use report /SCMTMS/UPLOAD_RFQ_RESPONSE in Transaction SE38. Besides the pure bid structure, it's also possible to attach any legal requirements, such as terms and conditions or a boilerplate that the carrier must comply with.

A very useful functionality is the list of all the existing agreements in the menu path **Freight Agreements**. This can further support the communication with the carrier. The actual SAP TM freight agreement is available for download and viewing as an Excel spreadsheet.

If you don't use the Collaboration Portal, you can use the Excel integration to upload all results into your vendor RFQ documents manually. After a successful upload or manual entry, mark each agreement RFQ line item as **Responded**. Clicking the **Submit** button in each vendor RFQ makes the rates and capacities available in the initial master RFQ so you can analyze and compare the results. In the master freight agreement RFQ, you can see the status of each vendor RFQ in the document flow.

Request for Quotation Evaluation and Awarding

A key functionality in the RFQ process is the comparison of the results of the vendors to help you decide on the capacities you're going to source for each vendor. In the master RFQ, you can select a single line item and click the **Open Comparison Cockpit** button.

The comparison cockpit is divided into four sections, which are shown in Figure 10.31. There are two ways to compare the vendor offers:

- **Manual comparison**
  With manual comparison, you use the **Response Comparison** section and **Response Comparison Graph** to select the vendors that have replied and submitted their responses. You can see the breakdown of their charges with amounts. Alternatively, you see rate tables assigned to each charge type if those are maintained. You click the **Selection Options** button to select multiple charges of the same type for each carrier to compare them. When you select **Compare**, the graph in the right section is compiled, and you can switch among multiple chart types to help you make your decision. You can also add RFQ line items for comparison. SAP TM doesn't support the analysis of amounts stored in rate tables or the their display in the graphs for comparison. If any charge type has a rate table assigned to it, the charge type doesn't appear in the graph. You can use the rate table comparison functionality to automatically generate one consolidated rate table in Microsoft Excel and list the offered rates for each carrier against each line item in the table. Select **Compare • Rate Tables in Microsoft Excel** to compare the rate tables.

- **Automated comparison**
  SAP offers the functionality to automatically suggest a cheapest option via an RFQ optimizer based on defined conditions that must be met (e.g., a minimum of two carriers must be awarded). You can add these conditions before running the optimizer. Alternatively, define a target share strategy in Customizing and assign it to the agreement type via the menu path **Transportation Management • Master Data • Agreement RFQs and Quotations • Define Target Share Strategies**. The outcome of the optimizer run is a suggestion of a target share as a percentage of the required capacity for each vendor. When you select **Simulate Estimate Spend**, the expected cost is calculated based on the provided rates and given capacities. You can compare multiple strategy versions displayed in the graph in the right section.

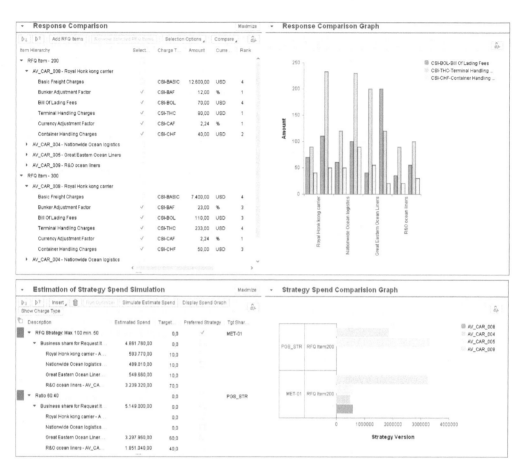

Figure 10.31 Comparison Cockpit (SAP TM 9.x Version)

The automated comparison contains multiple useful functionalities to steer a decision for strategic procurement and influence the target share. A crucial part of the automated comparison is to project the future estimated spend. This will eventually allow you to choose the best carrier. The automated RFQ optimizer has different possibilities for how to influence the estimated expenditure to derive the suggested capacity allocation to the tendered carriers:

- The basic concept of the RFQ optimizer is to simulate the estimated future expenditure by multiplying the capacities tendered in the RFQ with the responded rates from the carrier. The settings as part of the target share strategies can then influence the capacity split across carriers—for example, by defining minimum/maximum quantities a certain carrier must be allocated.

- As part of the RFQ optimization, it's crucial to consider not just quantitative factors, such as the quoted rates. You should also consider the performance of carriers. With every shipment you execute with carriers and LSPs in the past, you collect data concerning their performance (e.g., the historical on-time delivery). With the bonus–malus functionality, SAP TM applies penalties or rewards on the quoted rates of the LSPs. This results in cheaper or more expensive rates and impacts the target share SAP TM suggests. Activate the **Enable Bonus-Malus** checkbox in your target share strategy. After you've applied the bonus-malus, you can change the calculated values, which influence the carrier ranking in the **Carriers** tab.

- Another very important factor to consider is the historical expenditure with carriers. When you specify an RFQ, there is only limited knowledge of how many freight orders you're going to have on each trade lane or per origin–destination pair. As a consequence, it's possible to estimate the future expenditure by using the quoted freight charges and historical freight orders. This improves the accuracy of the RFQ optimizer. This functionality is called the historical spend analysis.

- The last influencing factor on the RFQ optimizer is transit times. It can be an imperative part of your freight agreement RFQ to get a commitment of the carrier/LSP concerning the transit times for your shipments. Regardless of whether it's for air or ocean, or even trucking or rail freight, the transit time is a crucial KPI for shippers.

  It's therefore possible to specify your expected transit time (e.g., in hours) both on a charge item and per individual rate table line item. The carrier/LSP is obliged to reply. You can use the deviation of the carrier committed transit time to mark up or reduce the offered rates of the carrier. For example, you expect a carrier to transport your shipment from Singapore to Hong Kong in 168 hours via ocean freight. You expect an indirect service where the cargo might be co-loaded onto another vessel. The carrier offers you a direct service that takes only 120 hours. You can apply a discount of, say, 1% for each 10 hours of reduced transit time. This consequently benefits carriers that have attractive transit durations and penalizes carriers that don't comply with your requested transit times. You need to implement the following BAdI to define the penalty/reward rule based on transit times: **Transportation Management • Business Add-Ins (BAdIs) for Transportation Management • Master Data • Agreement RFQs and Quotations • BAdI: Specification of Transit Time for Optimizer.**

RFQ Evaluation with Multiuser Assignment

It's very common in the transportation and logistics industry for RFQs to be of enormous size. A manufacturing company might request thousands of different rates from a carrier/LSP for a multitude of origin and destination pairs, equipment types, and shipping commodities. This results in freight agreement RFQs that can have many RFQ items and very large rate tables.

As a consequence, it's impossible for just one user to evaluate the results. You can split a master RFQ into several workable packages and allocate them to different users. This functionality is called concurrent user work.

It's possible in SAP TM to choose a master RFQ line item after having received the carrier responses and assign it to a certain user, such as the manager for the trade lane. Choose the RFQ line item, and select **Create/Update RFQ Assignment**. If you work as a rating expert, you can now evaluate the subportion of the overall RFQ you're responsible for. Other users, for example, trade lane managers, perform similar work on the same RFQ in parallel. Alternatively, you can create a new RFQ assignment from scratch and then pull line items into the assignment. After the evaluation is concluded, and each analyst has chosen preferred carriers, you can choose the **Merge to RFQ Master** action on the RFQ item. This merges the subscope of the RFQ back into the master RFQ.

The final step in the freight agreement RFQ process is the awarding and creation of the contracts. You can choose one strategy as your preferred option and choose **Accept Preferred Strategy** in the RFQ line item table. The **Award Summary** tab is available to compare the business share between the vendors and your budget against the actual cost. Last, you can create new agreements for the awarded carriers or amend existing agreements with the new rates and capacities.

With the successful generation of a new freight agreement based on a carrier RFQ, you've concluded an entire walkthrough of strategic freight management.

10.5 Summary

This chapter shifted the focus from a pure operational view to a strategic view of procuring freight space and freight-associated services. The process supports you as shipper or LSP in requesting RFQs from other third-party vendors. We highlighted the surrounding procurement planning, forecasting, and sales demand analysis capabilities and provided a comprehensive overview of procurement management functionalities for both customers and vendors.

After looking into the details of rating and vendor contract, we'll continue with details on freight settlement for shippers, carriers, and LSPs with external vendors in Chapter 11. We'll explain how to generate and process carrier invoice verifications.

Chapter 11

Charge Settlement

This chapter introduces the basics of charge settlement for vendors, integration with SAP S/4HANA billing and invoicing, as well as cost distribution. Learn how to monitor, settle your third-party freight charges, and manage disputes.

The previous chapter introduced to you the capabilities of SAP Transportation (SAP TM) charge calculation and strategic vendor contract management. This gives you the background to dive into the process of charge settlement with vendors of freight services, such as forwarders or carriers. We'll focus on charge settlement with logistics service providers (LSPs) in Chapter 12.

Settling of charges comes with three different concepts that we need to differentiate:

- **Settlement of supplier freight services**
  Regardless of whether you work as a shipper or freight forwarder, you always procure transportation capacities with incurring costs. Both shippers and LSPs procure transportation capacities from airlines, ocean liners, railways, and trucking companies. Even for carriers, it's common to procure complementary transportation services (e.g., trucking or railway services). Similarly, costs can occur when you work with agents or alliance partners from a carrier perspective and with freight forwarders as shippers.

- **Settlement of customer charges**
  The settlement of customer charges is an important factor for all companies selling professional logistic services because billing customers for transportation services is part of the core business model. You'll read about this process and its implementation in Chapter 12.

- **Internal settlement**
  An LSP's or shipper's logistics department might bill other internal departments to settle costs that need to be reimbursed internally for activities that contributed to the overall services. This common business practice will also be explained in more detail in Chapter 12.

Before we describe the different sections, let's clarify the overarching principle and commonality across the three ways of settling charges. If you want to use this capability of SAP TM, you can use either SAP S/4HANA or an SAP ERP system as the backend system, regardless of whether you're working as a shipper with order integration or as an LSP or carrier. The standard SAP TM solution uses the existing capabilities of SAP S/4HANA (or SAP ERP, although SAP S/4HANA will continue to be our base system) sales and distribution (SD) billing application and materials management (MM) for invoice verification and payment. In either case, it's always required to calculate freight charges based on SAP TM's charge calculation functionality before triggering a settlement.

In the following sections, we'll introduce you to the charge settlement for vendor charges and the cost distribution.

11.1   Charge Settlement and Billing

We've highlighted how the settlement process for billing resembles invoice settlement. For both billing and invoicing, a standard integration with a backend system is required. You can find more commonalities when you look at the architecture. Figure 11.1 illustrates the standard integration and flow of documents between SAP TM, SD, and MM as part of SAP S/4HANA.

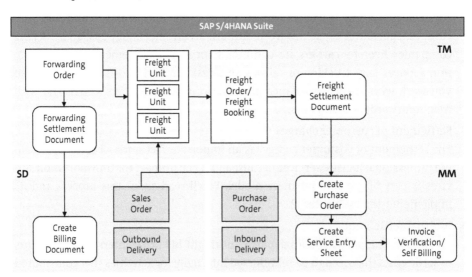

Figure 11.1 Integration of SAP TM to SD and MM for Charge Settlement in SAP S/4HANA

The diagram is applicable for both shippers and LSPs or carriers. The dark boxes are the documents you use as a shipper and that resemble your transportation requirements created based on SAP S/4HANA orders. The white boxes show the forwarding order document that is relevant for you as a freight forwarder or carrier. (Recall both options from Chapter 4.) The gray boxes are the common documents relevant for both freight forwarders and shippers that are required for the settlement process. For both the billing of freight charges to your customers and the settlement of procured services, you generate an SAP TM *settlement document*. The settlement document contains all billing- and invoicing-relevant information, such as the invoicing parties, calculated charges, and currencies. It can be considered as a draft invoice/bill.

Two different business objects differentiate between the customer settlement and the invoicing to service providers: the forwarding settlement document and the freight settlement document. For the billing side, the forwarding settlement document directly generates a billing invoice in SAP S/4HANA SD. The freight settlement document triggers the creation of a purchase order (PO) in MM in SAP S/4HANA, and a *service entry sheet* (SES) is created. Both documents are generated in the background to eventually enable posting of accruals, invoice verification, or self-billing.

SAP S/4HANA versus SAP ERP

The process works similar when an SAP ERP system is used as backend instead. The main difference is that the settlement information must be transmitted via an XML interface from SAP TM 9.6 to SAP ERP.

From Section 11.1.1 to Section 11.1.3, we explain freight settlement and invoicing via the MM functionality. In Section 11.1.4, you'll learn about the latest functionality in SAP TM to allow a self-billing process for LSPs as well as an embedded dispute handling capability. Finally, in Section 11.1.5, we introduce SAP TM credit memos for corrections of settled amounts.

11.1.1 Creating Freight Settlement Documents

The functionality of freight settlement is used by any company procuring freight-related services, regardless of whether you work as a shipper, forwarder, or carrier. The invoicing of supplier/service provider bills always originates from your freight documents, that is, a freight order, freight booking, or service order in SAP TM. The freight settlement document can be described as the draft invoice that is generated in SAP TM. It's used to store all invoicing-relevant information from your freight orders, freight bookings, and service orders. The freight settlement document is the document that triggers the interface to the backend system for verifying the actual invoice. You'll see many similarities in the process of the forwarding settlement document.

Functional Process Flow

To create a freight settlement document, start by navigating to your freight documents (e.g., a freight order), and select **Charges/Settlement • Create Settlement Document**. Next, you can create the settlement document from a personal object worklist (POWL). Finally, you can use the standard batch job for mass creation: /SCMTMS/SFIR_CREATE_BATCH.

We start by answering the question of how many settlement documents are created when you trigger the settlement document generation. In a standard scenario, the system creates one freight settlement document for the entire freight order, service order, or freight booking. The reason for this is that each order or booking can have exactly one supplier who performs the services. Hence, it's expected that you receive one invoice per freight order, service order, or booking from this supplier. After the successful generation of a freight settlement document, the invoicing status of the originated freight document is updated.

Alternatively, perhaps you have more than just one service provider as part of a freight order or freight booking. Besides the pure transportation service from a carrier, additional services might be performed by a customs broker or a provider of container cleaning or fumigation. You can capture such additional parties in the **Business Partner** tab in your freight order or freight booking. When you trigger the settlement document creation, you can select one or multiple parties in a popup window. You can create the freight settlement document for the carrier, one or more additional parties, or both. The charge calculation determines freight agreement and a charge calculation sheet per party. If you store the charges for the different services in two separate charge calculation sheets, the system can automatically calculate the charges and uses one charge calculation sheet per party. The only restriction applies if a business partner plays a hybrid role with two freight agreements (one for main carrier rates, one containing rates for specific services). If a service provider plays a role as the main carrier in a first freight booking but interacts as an additional agreement party in a second freight booking, there is no determination rule available to decide which of the two freight agreements to use.

You can collectively create freight settlement documents from the POWL. SAP TM combines all selected freight orders or freight bookings based on splitting criteria into one or multiple freight settlement documents. The key criteria that need to be equal among the different freight orders or bookings include the carrier, invoicing party, payee, payment term, and document currency.

Basic Customizing

The essential Customizing in SAP TM includes the following steps to enable the freight settlement process:

1. **Freight settlement document type**
   You can define the freight settlement document type in SAP TM via the Customizing menu path **Transportation Management · Settlement · Freight Settlement · Define Freight Settlement Document Type**. The type contains the number range that is being assigned to newly created freight settlement documents as well as enablement of cost distribution. You must assign the freight settlement document types to your freight order and freight booking types.

2. **Settlement profile**
   You can use one settlement profile for both the forwarding and freight settlement side. You need to assign the settlement profile to a business partner or, alternatively, to a charges profile.

3. **Process controller**
   As an optional step, you can implement an alternative way to create and group or split freight settlement documents in the creation process. SAP provides a standard method, but you can also develop your own methods and strategies, which you can assign to your settlement profile.

11.1.2   Structure of Freight Settlement Documents

The freight settlement document has a very similar structure to the forwarding settlement document. It stores the invoice-relevant information inherited from the freight order, service order, or freight booking.

The **General Data** tab shows the sum of the invoicing amount, the payment terms, and the organizational data, such as the purchasing organization that was responsible for procuring the services. You can also see the expected invoicing date, which you can change manually. After invoice creation and verification, the settlement document shows the verified invoice amount in the freight settlement document.

In the **Charges** tab, you see the list of all charge items inherited from the corresponding freight order. If you collectively created a freight settlement document for multiple freight orders or freight bookings, you'll see the sum of the charges per freight order. The view depends on your settings in the calculation profile in Transportation Charge Management. If you calculated the charges with calculation-level stages, you'll see the details of cost per order and cost per stage. You can see an example of the freight settlement document **Charges** tab in Figure 11.2.

Figure 11.2 Charges Tab in Freight Settlement Document

The settlement document shown lists the charges per cargo item from an associated freight order. Figure 11.3 shows a different example.

Charge Items	Exchange Rates	Charge Calculation Log	Charge Analysis Log									

Quotation BL * ⊙   ⊞ ⊟   Insert ∨   Views ∨   Show/Hide Details   Multiple Rates   Show/Hide Access Sequence

Charge Hierarchy	Ac...	Ca...	Charg...	Charge Desc.	Rate...	Rate Curre	Calc...	Ca... Amou Curre	Final Amount	Doc. Currency	Price Unit
∨ Q1: FO05 6100027318 , stage from Shipper 01 to Q1 HUB Guan				Q1: FO05 6100027318					250,00 USD		
Basic Freight	⊕	■	FB00	Basic Freight	250,00 USD		250,00 USD		250,00 USD		
∨ Q1: FO05 6100027318 , stage from Q1 HUB Guangzhou to Q1 C				Q1: FO05 6100027318					250,00 USD		
Basic Freight	⊕	■	FB00	Basic Freight	250,00 USD		250,00 USD		250,00 USD		

Figure 11.3 Details of Charges per Stage in a Freight Settlement Document

Here, the charges are grouped per transportation leg (stage) of, for example, a freight booking for ocean freight. Two stages are visible and expanded to show the details of the applicable charges and surcharges per leg.

The **Business Partner** tab lists all relevant parties for the invoicing. For the settlement process, you require at least the invoicing party and payee. You can include other parties in the settlement document, such as the carrier, which is automatically inherited from the freight order. You can assign a business partner determination profile to your freight settlement document type to steer the correct assignment of involved parties to the freight settlement document.

Depending on how the freight settlement document was created, it might contain multiple freight orders or freight bookings that are grouped into one settlement document. All such orders are listed in the **Orders** tab. If you created a settlement document for each stage based on a freight order with nonlinear stages and then activate the **Stage Split** checkbox in the settlement profile, you'll see the freight order and the stage details of the invoiced stages. This is determined by the calculation level of your calculation profile.

The **Document Flow** tab in the freight settlement document always gives you an overview of the related predecessor and successor business documents of the settlement document, such as the freight order or freight booking for which it was created. This is especially valuable in the integration scenario, where SAP TM is operated with a financial SAP backend, which can be either SAP S/4HANA or SAP ERP. The document flow shows the generation of the succeeding documents, such as the SES and the PO, as it also captures cross-system document relations. Other tabs in the freight settlement document are the **Notes** tab, where you can enter information as free text, the **Administrative Data** tab; the **Change Information** tab; the **Attachments** tab; and the **Output Management** tab. In the **Statuses** tab, you can see the latest lifecycle and confirmation statuses, which again, support the cross-system integration. Finally, the **Cost Distribution** tab supports a scenario for shippers with integration for order management. We describe the details of this functionality in Section 11.2.

11.1.3   Integrating Freight Settlement Documents with Materials Management

The freight settlement process is integrated into the MM functionality in SAP S/4HANA. SAP decided to integrate with an existing application for invoice verification and the actual posting of accruals and cost. In the following sections, we highlight the required Customizing settings for the integration, the functional process flow, and some technical basics. In SAP S/4HANA, it's essential to create both an SES and a PO.

Basic Customizing for Service Entry Sheet and Purchase Order Creation

To set up your integration between SAP TM and the MM functionality, there are a few essential Customizing steps to generate an SES and a PO. A PO is created to provide an order reference in your SAP system. The SES comprises all the individual services provided by your service provider. It also contains additional information, such as descriptions of your services. An SES is generated with reference to the PO.

We focus on the essentials to enable vendor invoicing by integrating SAP TM with MM. A service master for the transportation services needs to be created. The service master in SAP is a standardized list containing all items that a company might procure in MM. You must maintain the service master as master data and map your SAP TM charge types to the service master in Customizing. The valuation class on the service master can optionally be used in General Ledger (G/L) account determination.

You can find the Customizing activity for charge type mapping by selecting **Integration with Other SAP Components • Transportation Management • Invoice Integration • Invoicing • Definition for Transportation Charge Types • Define Charge Types**. You can also define category and subcategory codes and assign them to the mapped charge types. Next, you must assign your charge types to service master records and account assignment categories in SAP. You must make sure that you've maintained entries in your service master record, as described previously. Navigate to the Customizing menu path **Integration with Other SAP Components • Transportation Management • Invoice Integration • Invoicing • Assignment of Transportation Charge Types • Assign Service Master Record and Account Assignment Category**. Based on this setting, the system can relate your SAP TM-specific charges to actual procurement service master records. The account assignment category also plays an important role in the determination of accounts, cost objects, and, eventually, SAP financial postings.

Another required setting is the assignment of your SAP TM freight settlement document types to the purchasing characteristics in MM. You can find the settings by following Customizing menu path **Integration with Other SAP Components • Transportation Management • Invoice Integration • Invoicing • Mapping of Organization Units • Assign Purchasing Information for Posting**. The purchasing information on the MM side impacts account determination and invoice verification in SAP S/4HANA. In addition to the mapping of organizational units, you can map the SAP

TM purchasing organization against internal orders or cost centers. This setting is very important for posting freight costs to the correct internal cost centers.

Basic Customizing for Invoice Verification and Automated Postings

The previously mentioned settings allow you to generate the SES and PO in an existing SAP S/4HANA system. You can also allow automated posting of accruals and invoice verification with message integration with the SAP TM freight settlement document. To enable these functional components in the MM and controlling (CO) functionality in SAP S/4HANA, additional Customizing settings are required. Here, we'll provide you with a quick overview of the key Customizing settings.

To enable the automated account assignment, you need to first define a mapping for your impacted company code, cost elements, and cost centers. Navigate to Customizing, and follow the menu path **Controlling · Cost Center Accounting · Actual Postings · Manual Actual Postings · Edit Automatic Account Assignment**. The next important step is to configure the automatic postings so that your SAP system is capable of automatically posting to the correct G/L accounts. This must be maintained per impacted *chart of accounts* in the SAP S/4HANA system of each company code. Navigate to SAP Customizing via the menu path **Materials Management · Valuation and Account Assignment · Account Determination · Account Determination Without Wizard · Configure Automatic Postings** to enable inventory postings (Transaction GBB) for your impacted chart of accounts.

If using a standalone SAP TM system with a separate financial backend (SAP S/4HANA or SAP ERP), the systems are technically integrated via SAP Process Integration. SAP provides a standard integration scenario that needs to be enabled in the SAP Process Integration system (`TM_ERPInvoiceIntegration`). Four messages are supported in a standard system for the integration between SAP TM and the backend:

- `TransportationOrderSUITEInvoicingPreparationRequest` sends a request to create or change a freight settlement from SAP TM and receive it in the backend system.
- `TransportationOrderSUITEInvoicingPreparationConfirmation` sends the confirmation of received supplier invoices from the backend and receives them in SAP TM.
- `TransportationOrderSUITEInvoicingPreparationCancellationRequest` sends a request to cancel a freight settlement document from SAP TM and receive it in the backend system.
- `InvoiceNotification` sends the invoice notification from your backend system and receives it in SAP TM.

Functional Process Flow

After you've configured your SAP S/4HANA system and—if used—the integration for the freight settlement process, you're almost ready to transfer a generated document from SAP TM to the MM functionality in SAP S/4HANA. In Figure 11.4, you can see the different statuses of a freight settlement document.

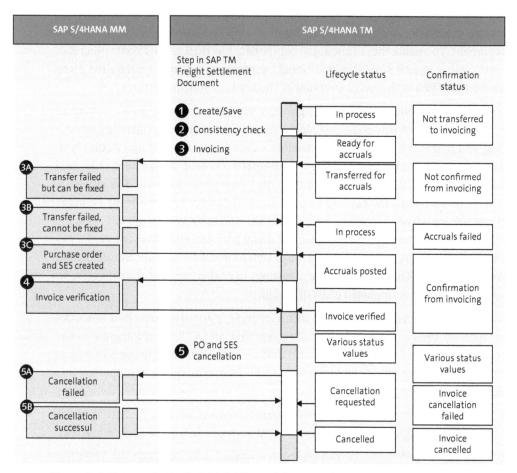

Figure 11.4 Statuses in the Freight Settlement Document

After you've created a settlement document, the lifecycle status is set to **In Process** ❶. Before transferring it now to invoicing in MM, you can perform an automated consistency validation by clicking the **Check** button on the top panel in the freight settlement document ❷. If no inconsistencies are detected, the lifecycle status is automatically changed to **Ready for Accruals**. It's always required to have charge items in the settlement document; otherwise, you can't transfer the freight settlement document to MM.

If you generated your freight settlement documents collectively with a batch job, the system automatically performs the consistency check. In the batch program, you can also generate and transfer the freight settlement document in one step. In a more manual approach, you can click the **Save and Transfer** button in the freight settlement document or from a POWL and trigger the interface to MM. The corresponding lifecycle status is **Transferred for Accruals**, and the confirmation status isn't **Confirmed from Invoicing** ❸. If all settings are correct, the system automatically performs three actions in MM:

- Generate a PO in MM.
- Create an SES based on the PO.
- Post the accruals based on the PO and SES.

The PO is required for purely technical reasons. The SES enables the posting of accruals and invoice verification in MM. Figure 11.5 shows a freight settlement document and the related PO in MM.

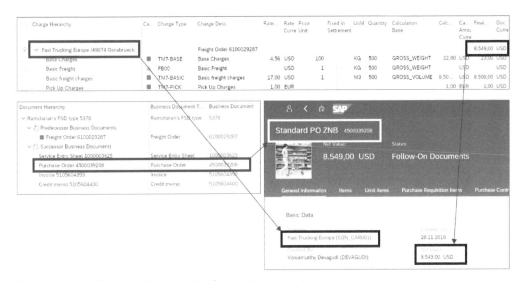

Figure 11.5 Creation of a PO from a Settlement Document

The document flow in the freight settlement document shows the generated PO, SES, and invoice after the document has been verified. The PO contains all the charge types as service line items based on the mapping introduced in Customizing: the carrier, statuses, and other references from the freight settlement document.

If the accruals haven't been posted, the lifecycle and confirmation status in the freight settlement document stay unchanged unless an error can be corrected in the MM side. While the lifecycle status is **Transferred for Accruals**, it's no longer possible to manipulate any data in the freight settlement document in SAP TM (refer to Figure 11.4 **③A**). If the failed accruals posting can't be fixed, the lifecycle status is automatically updated to **In Process**. The confirmation status indicates **Accruals Failed ③B**. If no discrepancies are detected, the lifecycle status is changed to **Accruals Posted**, and the confirmation status to **Invoice Verified ③C**.

After you've successfully transferred your freight settlement document to MM, and the lifecycle status shows **Accruals Posted**, it's possible again to manipulate the data in the freight settlement document in SAP TM. Any changes require a retransmission of the freight settlement document to MM, which triggers a few additional steps. First, the SES posted earlier is reversed. Second, items of the SES and PO are deleted. Last, the regular process flow is similarly followed as described earlier; a new PO and SES are created, and the accruals are posted again. After the actual invoice from the supplier is received, you can perform the invoice verification in MM via Transaction MIRO, usage of the new SAP Fiori invoice management apps, or customer self-billing (refer to Figure 11.4 **④**). After the invoice verification has been performed, the SAP TM freight settlement document is updated with a corresponding lifecycle status of **Invoice Verified.** The PO and SES in MM are locked for any manual changes or manipulation. You can issue a credit memo to correct the charges in case of any discrepancies.

You can cancel a PO and SES from SAP TM only by canceling the freight settlement document itself. Keep in mind that even this doesn't work in all statuses of the freight settlement document: **Transferred for Accruals** or **Invoice Verified**. The cancellation action triggers another status change in the SAP TM freight settlement document (refer to Figure 11.4 **⑤A**). If the cancellation request isn't successful, the freight settlement document is updated with confirmation status **Invoice Cancellation Failed in SAP ERP ⑤B**. For a successful cancellation, the status changes to **Invoice Canceled.**

Settlement Scenarios for Air Freight

In the air freight business, cargo is often handled through a freight forwarder or booking agent. To standardize the billing process, most airlines outsource their billing services to the International Air Transport Authority (IATA). The IATA has introduced the Cargo Accounts Settlement System (CASS) as the clearinghouse for this purpose. Airlines send their air waybills together with other settlement-relevant data to CASS. Based on the air waybill data, such as weights, volumes, charges, and cargo details, CASS generates a monthly or bimonthly billing cycle and lists all charges and credits per air waybill for each freight forwarder. This billing document is called the *cargo sales report* (CSR). A freight forwarder can download the report or introduce an interface via electronic data interchange (EDI) (message `CARGO-IMP FCI`). The CSR is used by the forwarder for invoice verification, which can be done manually or electronically.

When an error is detected by either side (i.e., the freight forwarder or the airline), and a billed amount is too high or too low, corrections are required. Because the IATA billing cycle happens monthly or bimonthly, corrections can be made only for an already-paid invoice in the subsequent billing cycle. In this case, the IATA supports airlines with two documents:

- Cargo charges correction advice document (CCAD)
- Debit credit memo (DCM)

CCAD

The CCAD is a different category of freight settlement document, but technically it's the same object. You can't create a CCAD if you haven't yet generated the freight settlement document or if it hasn't yet been set as status **Accruals Posted**. The reason is that before the freight settlement document has been generated or the accruals posted, you can still include all corrections in the first settlement document.

Let's consider an example. A freight forwarder has been invoiced for the weight of its cargo. The airline detects that the actual cargo weight is higher than originally stated. As a result, the airline issues the deviation to the IATA and submits a cargo CCAD. The CASS includes the correction amount as part of the new billing cycle in the CSR to the freight forwarder. The old amount paid is reversed (comparable to a credit memo process), and the corrected amount is added.

The Cargo Accounts Settlement System

Since IATA introduced CASS in 1999, more than 200 airlines and ground handling companies have joined the CASS billing system. Today, the total billing value handled through CASS exceeds $32 billion every year.

SAP TM offers some support for this billing process for freight forwarders. You can generate one collective freight settlement document for the same airline for all freight bookings in one month and thereby simulate the CSR in your system. The integration with your invoicing system follows the standard settlement process. A PO and an SES are created that contain the appropriate charges. After the receipt of the CSR from IATA, in your SAP S/4HANA system (specifically, the MM functionality), you can perform the invoice verification of the accrued charges versus the received invoice amounts and pay the settled amount.

In case of a discrepancy after the forwarder has made the payment, the airline triggers the CCAD to the IATA. As a result, the forwarder receives the corrected settlement amount with the next cargo settlement report. To reflect this discrepancy in your system as the freight forwarder, you should follow these steps:

1. Navigate to your originally created and already-completed freight booking that generated the troublemaking air waybill.

2. It's possible to correct the freight booking despite its status. You might change the weight of the cargo to the correct weight per your agreement with the airline.

3. Because the freight settlement document has already been generated for the freight booking, you can't correct or change the existing freight settlement document. You can generate your own cargo correction advice document instead. The CCAD serves as a simulation of the actual CCAD and contains the originally posted amount from your old freight settlement document, the delta amount that needs to be corrected, and the final billing amount.

4. The CCAD needs to be transferred to the MM functionality in SAP S/4HANA, where a new PO is generated. The PO stores both the old settlement amount with a reverse indicator and the corrected amounts.

5. Based on the new PO, two SESs are generated:

   - The first SES posts the initial erroneous settlement amount with a reverse indicator.

   - The second SES posts the accruals for the fully corrected settlement amount.

You're now ready to perform a new invoice verification based on the actual cargo settlement report from the IATA.

11.1.4   Carrier Self-Billing and Dispute Management

We've already introduced how to create freight settlement documents and how to verify and pay invoices in the MM functionality in SAP S/4HANA (or SAP ERP). This process assumes a classic communication with a carrier or freight forwarder, where you receive hard copies of invoices and pay them after verification. The disadvantage of this process is that the responsibility to detect any errors as well as the workload lies with you as the customer.

In SAP TM 9.6, you may use the Collaboration Portal to manage this process more efficiently and to push the responsibility to the LSP's side. In addition, you can now manage dispute cases with LSPs. We'll walk through both processes in the following sections.

SAP S/4HANA versus SAP ERP

For SAP S/4HANA systems, the corresponding process will be provided via SAP Logistics Business Network in the future.

Carrier Self-Invoicing via Collaboration Portal

Using the Collaboration Portal in SAP TM 9.5 or 9.6, you can manage the interaction with the carrier via self-invoicing. Instead of waiting for the carrier's invoice and having to verify the charges, the carrier can instead log in to the Collaboration Portal and submit an invoice online. Figure 11.6 shows the process flow of this new functionality.

The process starts with the carrier logging on to the Collaboration Portal. If a carrier selects the **Freight Orders for Invoice Submission** button, all freight orders that are ready for invoice creation are shown in a worklist. Clicking the **Create Invoice** button begins the invoice posting workflow. Technically the invoice document is a freight settlement document that gets created in SAP TM and is visible in a corresponding POWL.

As a shipper, you can enable a workflow to inform you about any invoice deviations between your own calculated charges and the carrier's submission. You can define tolerances that will be applied to automatically approve deviations below a certain threshold. From this point on, you can use the new dispute management functionality to deal with any deviations in invoices. After the deviations are resolved and invoice approved, you can post any changes to the actual freight settlement documents, which will respectively update the PO and SES in SAP ERP's MM component.

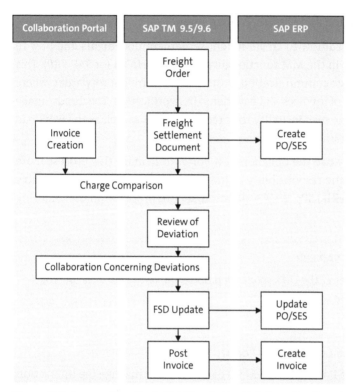

Figure 11.6 Process Flow for Self-Billing in the Collaboration Portal

Dispute Management

Whenever a carrier invoice deviates from your freight settlement document, SAP TM can automatically create a dispute case, which can then be processed by a user in SAP TM. You can enable an approval workflow to inform relevant users of the dispute. The dispute document is also published in the Collaboration Portal for the carrier to review it. After you process the dispute case, it's immediately updated in the Collaboration Portal for the carrier to review the requested changes. This process can have multiple iterations until a consensus is achieved. After any changes have been agreed upon, you can directly update your freight settlement document and the MM documents. Most of the settings for dispute management can be found in a new section in the SAP TM Customizing: **Transportation Management • Settlement • Freight Settlement • Freight Settlement Dispute Management**. The following are the key settings required in Customizing:

- Define the tolerance rules for disputes, which steer the behavior when SAP TM automatically creates a dispute case and escalates charge deviations to a user. You can maintain tolerance groups and even assign them to individual charge types. Tolerances can be maintained as absolute values or percentages. The tolerance rules are assigned to the settlement profile.

- Maintain reason codes for the communication of dispute cases.

- A new freight settlement category is available that is used for the dispute document. Maintain the dispute type to influence text types, number ranges, and more.

- Use the approval workflow to define approval levels and user roles, that is, who will be informed via email about the disputes.

11.1.5 Credit Memos for Freight Orders

Billing customers and settling supplier invoices may not always be straightforward. Sometimes bills to your customers have errors, and invoices from your suppliers can be too high or too low, perhaps because the cargo measures, weights, or volumes deviated between an order and the actual amounts. In addition, any delays in the transportation chain can cause errors and require you to decrease your bills or receive deductions from your suppliers.

The *credit memo* is a document in SAP TM that you use to post corrections of incorrect settlement amounts. A credit memo can be generated for the forwarding settlement document to give a credit to a bill-to party for incorrect billings. You can also generate a credit memo for a freight order or freight booking to trigger a deduction of an invoiced amount from your supplier. As settlement documents can't be changed after they reach a certain lifecycle status, you can still use the credit memo for any corrections, especially from a document process flow and audit visibility point of view. The same behavior is relevant for the freight settlement document. The following describes credit memos for freight orders. Concerning forwarding orders, you'll find the details in Chapter 12.

With a credit memo for freight settlement documents, you can correct payments to your service provider, freight forwarder, or carrier, in case they charged you too much for transportation services. The credit memo can come from your original freight order, booking, or service order, and it can include any changes in the document. If your freight forwarder charged you based on weight, but the cargo items weren't as heavy as listed in the freight booking, you can correct the weight directly in the freight booking. The credit memo automatically posts the delta amount. To create the credit memo, select **Follow Up • Create Credit Memo** in the top panel of the document. SAP TM generates the credit memo automatically. Like the CCAD, every credit memo generates a new PO in MM. In contrast to the CCAD process, the PO has only one line as the returns item with the correction amount. Based on the POs, an SES is created that posts the corrected amount.

In the Customizing for credit memos on the freight settlement side, you need to create a credit memo type and reason codes. The credit memo type for freight settlement can be created via the Customizing menu path **Transportation Management • Settlement • Freight Settlement • Define Credit Memo Reason Codes and Types for Freight SDs**. In the credit memo type, you can define how changes in the invoicing status of the freight order, freight booking, and service order should be handled. The invoicing status of the documents changes automatically to **Completely Invoiced** as soon as you've successfully generated a freight settlement document with the full amount, as calculated for the charges. You can activate the **Influence Invoicing Status** checkbox in the credit memo type. When you generate a new credit memo, the invoicing status of a freight order, booking, or service order is reset to **Not Invoiced**. If you deselect the **Influence Invoicing Status** checkbox, the creation of a credit memo doesn't have an impact on the invoicing status. In the same Customizing path, you can maintain reason codes and assign them to the credit memo.

11.2   Cost Distribution

Working as a shipper or LSP, you might encounter challenges in apportioning transportation costs to the correct organizational units, accounts, or sales orders (SOs). SAP TM offers two capabilities to support automated distribution of transportation charges and the settlement of these between different organizations. In this chapter, we'll explain cost distribution. The second way of apportioning is the internal settlement for LSPs, which is described in Chapter 12.

The SAP TM cost distribution functionality supports both shippers and LSPs. It gives you the capability to distribute incurred costs from freight orders and freight bookings in SAP TM to the individual originating forwarding order items. You might have, for example, a freight order for trucking that contains several pallets as items from multiple forwarding orders. The cost distribution ensures an apportionment of the cost for the entire freight order down to each individual cargo item. You can use different apportionment rules (e.g., based on the weight or volume of each cargo item). Looking at this functionality, we need to differentiate between shippers and LSPs:

- **Cost distribution for shippers**
  First, you can manage your transportation costs for inbound deliveries by assigning charges to the materials valuation component in your SAP S/4HANA system. This enables calculations with actual costs from your SAP TM freight order or freight booking documents. Second, you can gain better visibility of your SO profitability by assigning transportation charges for outbound deliveries to the correct orders and company codes. In Profitability Analysis (CO-PA) in SAP S/4HANA, you have the capability to include any transport-related charges in your SO profitability analysis.

- **Cost distribution for LSPs**
  You can distribute incurred costs from your procured transportation services and capacities (freight orders or freight bookings) to other organizational units. The distribution can be performed completely in SAP TM, and this enables an internal settlement process. Cost distribution outcomes are the input for the **Order-Based Profitability** tab in the forwarding orders, which allow an LSP to judge the margin related to a single customer order.

The concept of apportioning cost is similar in shipper and LSP scenarios, but how we use the cost information is different. In either case, you break down the cost of a freight order or booking to the order document items (e.g., SO items and forwarding order items). A shipper can use the cost distribution for inbound shipments to perform product costing and pricing. The transportation cost is automatically used in MM materials valuation. For all outbound shipments, the distributed cost can be used for Profitability Analysis. This allows improved visibility regarding actual profitability. For an LSP, the distributed cost can be used as the basis for an internal settlement process. The apportioning of cost is always done per delivery or cargo item.

For a shipper, the freight settlement document contains the distributed cost and offers visibility in its own tab, as you can see in Figure 11.7. The transportation cost is split and broken down into each individual item of an order. You can also see the distribution percentage that was assigned to each item. The cost distribution is executed for every charge type. In this example, the distribution rule is the net weight of the items. Other rules are available, which can be set in Customizing.

✓ Cost Distribution

Distribution Category (Description)	Net Amount in Document Currency	Document Currency	Distribution Date	Distribution Level
● External Charges	2.170,00 USD		31.07.2018	Forwarding Order

Details: External Charge Distribution

Standard * ⊙ ⊞ ⊟

Distribution Hierarchy	Charg…	Distribution Percentage	Distribution Amo…	Currency	Logistical Refere…	Requirement	Distributi… Rule	Quantity	Un… Meas	Distributi… Status
∨ Freight Booking 400001355 , Forwarding Order 1100001212		60,6	1.315,15	USD	1100001212	1100001212				
Low Sulphur Surcharge	LSFS	60,6	6,06	USD	10 - CNNGO_20G0		Net Weight	2.000	KG	Allocated
Peak Season Charge	PEAK	60,6	66,67	USD	10 - CNNGO_20G0		Net Weight	2.000	KG	Allocated
Terminal Handling Charge (THC) Destination	THCD	60,6	242,42	USD	10 - CNNGO_20G0		Net Weight	2.000	KG	Allocated
Terminal Handling Charge (THC) Origin	THCO	60,6	121,21	USD	10 - CNNGO_20G0		Net Weight	2.000	KG	Allocated
Bunker Adj. Factor	BAF	60,6	212,12	USD	10 - CNNGO_20G0		Net Weight	2.000	KG	Allocated
Basic Freight	FB00	60,6	666,67	USD	10 - CNNGO_20G0		Net Weight	2.000	KG	Allocated
∨ Freight Booking 400001355 , Forwarding Order 1100001213		39,4	854,85	USD	1100001213	1100001213				
Low Sulphur Surcharge	LSFS	39,4	3,94	USD	10 - CNNGO_20G0		Net Weight	1.300	KG	Allocated
Peak Season Charge	PEAK	39,4	43,33	USD	10 - CNNGO_20G0		Net Weight	1.300	KG	Allocated
Terminal Handling Charge (THC) Destination	THCD	39,4	157,58	USD	10 - CNNGO_20G0		Net Weight	1.300	KG	Allocated
Terminal Handling Charge (THC) Origin	THCO	39,4	78,79	USD	10 - CNNGO_20G0		Net Weight	1.300	KG	Allocated
Bunker Adj. Factor	BAF	39,4	137,88	USD	10 - CNNGO_20G0		Net Weight	1.300	KG	Allocated
Basic Freight	FB00	39,4	433,33	USD	10 - CNNGO_20G0		Net Weight	1.300	KG	Allocated

Figure 11.7 Distributed Cost in Freight Settlement Document

For a freight forwarder, the cost information of a freight settlement document is less relevant, as no material valuation is required, which targets only shippers. Profitability analysis in CO-PA, however, may be of interest to LSPs, as the slicing and dicing of freight charges and forwarding revenues related to logistical parameters such as trade lanes or container types has significance.

A key question at the beginning of the cost distribution process is how cost is distributed to the order items in the freight order or freight booking. You can define different rules for how to distribute the charges. SAP offers four methods of distribution: gross weight, net weight, gross volume, and distance times weight. You can define your own logic via a business add-in (BAdI): /SCMTMS/TCD_DISTRIB_RULE. This BAdI allows a lot of flexibility, so you can implement your own methods for cost distribution.

The distribution rule must be added in a mandatory *distribution profile* in SAP TM. This profile contains both the distribution rule and the level, which must be the order item for shippers or the forwarding order for freight forwarders. You can configure the profile in SAP TM Customizing via the menu path **Transportation Management** •

Basic Functions · Cost Distribution · Define Cost Distribution Profiles. The cost distribution profile needs to be assigned to a charge profile, just like any other profile relevant to the settlement or charge calculation process in SAP TM Customizing. To do so, follow the menu path **Transportation Management · Basic Functions · Charge Calculation · Basis Settings · Define Charges Profile**. In addition, you need to enable cost distribution in your corresponding freight settlement document types. Freight forwarders are required to select the **Cost Distribution** checkbox in the freight order or freight booking types.

11.3   Summary

In this chapter, we provided an overview on charge settlement, integration to invoicing, and cost distribution for vendor settlement. In the next chapter, we'll explain the charge calculation for the buying side, which is interesting for service providers, who are selling freight services and must settle those.

Chapter 12

Charge Calculation and Settlement for Logistics Service Providers

As discussed in previous chapters, SAP Transportation Management differentiates between buying transportation services and selling them. Regarding charge calculation and settlement, we've so far only focused on the functionality from a buying perspective. Now we'll start selling services and charging customers for these services.

In the previous chapters, you've learned how the SAP Transportation Management (SAP TM) functionality calculates accurate transportation charges and settles those against service providers. However, as you know, SAP TM can also be used by logistics service providers (LSPs) that use the SAP TM system to capture customer orders. When capturing customer orders, the goal is to obtain revenue from the transportation services sold to customers. In this chapter, we'll look at how to use the charge calculation and settlement functionality to *sell* transportation services to customers and what other functionalities in this area help LSPs stay profitable in their business.

In a similar fashion as we did for the charge calculation and settlement for shippers, we'll start with examining the specific master data required (Section 12.1), before delving into the charge calculation logic (Section 12.2). We'll then look at the billing and settlement process (Section 12.3) and specifically with SAP Billing and Revenue Innovation Management (SAP BRIM) (Section 12.4). Finally, we'll cover strategic customer contract management in Section 12.5.

Note

This chapter will only delve into the specifics of charge calculation and settlement for the selling side that is different to the functionality on the buying side. It's therefore essential to understand the basics of charge calculation and settlement described in Chapter 10 before going into this chapter.

12.1   Charge Calculation Master Data

As described in Chapter 10, some master data is essential to drive charge calculation. In Chapter 10, we've examined the freight agreement as the contract between the purchasing organization and the carrier that is selling the transportation service to us. Now that we sell transportation services to customers ourselves, we'll use the following sets of master data:

- **Forwarding agreements**
  Forwarding agreements serve as customer contracts and contain charges and rates, as well as capacity commitments, optionally based on service products.

- **Internal agreements**
  Internal agreements represent rate agreements among your own internal organizations for the internal settlements process. You can maintain standard costs for intercompany and intracompany charges.

Agreements can represent both short-term and long-term relationships between your company and business partners.

Furthermore, Transportation Charge Management allows you to maintain a configurable *service product catalog*. You can set up your own service products based on individual service items, which can represent value-added services or customer-specific services. Using service products when you set up agreements and order documents is optional. You can assign standard operating procedures (SOP) to the service products to operationalize them.

12.1.1   Forwarding Agreements

First, let's differentiate a forwarding agreement from a freight agreement, as follows:

- The *forwarding agreement* represents a customer contract, which is highly relevant to all LSPs.

- The *freight agreement* represents a carrier contract with the rates of your vendors, which is relevant for both shippers and LSPs. We already discussed freight agreements in Chapter 10.

You can create a forwarding agreement by navigating to the **Create Forwarding Agreement** tile in the **Contract Management** tab of the SAP Fiori launchpad. You need to specify a forwarding agreement type, which is to be defined in Customizing, and then assign the agreement to one or multiple sales organizations.

In Chapter 3, you learned the essentials of the organizational structure. The sales organization represents a customer-facing organization that issues forwarding orders. If you work as a freight forwarder, your individual freight stations might have autonomous agreements with your customers. Alternatively, it's possible to maintain multiple sales organizations for an agreement. Besides the sales organization, you need to store the business partners who are permitted to use the contract. You have two options:

- Define exactly one business partner (your contracting party).
- Maintain a list of business partners in a table format. All parties are permitted to book forwarding orders under this contract, unless they are excluded from an item of the forwarding agreement.

Last, it's mandatory to maintain the validity dates of a contract.

Another attribute on the header of a forwarding agreement is the version number. This functionality both supports regulatory filings and keeps track of changes in agreements. You can generate new versions of an agreement by clicking the **Generate New Version** button. A deep copy of the entire contract with all rates is generated. A history of the different versions is also available.

Figure 12.1 shows an example of the general header information of a forwarding agreement. This contract is maintained for one business partner only but is valid for three sales organizations. To prevent use while agreements are in maintenance, you must activate each agreement. As a result, you see **In Process** in the **Agreement Status** field.

Items in the agreement line differentiate the scope inside an agreement. Figure 12.2 shows an example of agreement line items. There are a few important requirements to take into consideration here. You must assign one calculation sheet to each agreement item, and each forwarding agreement must have at least one line item. When you execute the charge calculation for forwarding orders, the system picks up the rates from a line item in the determined agreement only if the defined scope between your forwarding order and the agreement line item match. We call this scope for an agreement item a *precondition*.

Figure 12.1 General Data of a Forwarding Agreement

Consider these examples of agreement line items and preconditions:

- Maintain only one line item per transportation stage category (e.g., pre-carriage, main carriage, and on-carriage, as shown in Figure 12.2). As a result, an item would only be used to determine trucking charges for an individual stage (pre-carriage) in the forwarding order.

- Agreement items can also represent service products; we discuss this further in Section 12.1.3.

- Mode of transport, movement type, and service level are examples of preconditions. If you don't want to maintain services as proper master data, note that the service level is a simplified concept of a service product catalog. Service levels are also used to describe services of courier, express, and parcel providers (e.g., an overnight service).

You can enhance agreement item preconditions through Customizing. On the forwarding agreement line items, you can also maintain the **Settlement Basis**. This setting determines how your settlement documents are generated (e.g., if you want to generate an invoice based on all goods loaded on a resource). The standard setting is **Per Forwarding Order**. We already discussed details of the settlement process in Chapter 11.

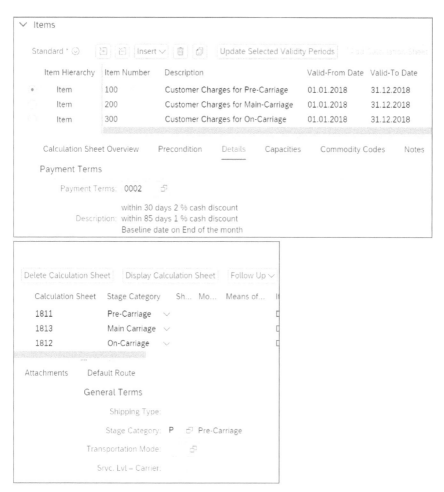

Figure 12.2 Items of a Forwarding Agreement

The tabs in the forwarding agreement item provide more information, such as the **Details** and **Calculation Sheet Overview** tabs. In the **Calculation Sheet Overview** tab, you can see the information from the calculation sheet after it has been assigned to the item. The **Precondition** and **Commodity Codes** tabs allow you to store more conditions for the calculation sheet determination, which we detail in Section 12.2. Last, you can maintain capacities that you've agreed upon with a customer. It follows the same concept as for agreed capacities with carriers maintained in freight agreements that we already discussed. SAP TM can't yet maintain space or capacity allocations from forwarding agreements to customers of, for example, a freight forwarder or ocean carrier. The capacities in the forwarding agreement are used mainly for reference purposes and in the RFQ process for strategic freight selling, as described in Section 12.5, but they aren't used operationally yet.

Both the agreement header and items have other useful tabs, such as **Notes**, where you can maintain free text clauses and other text elements. You can also upload any document to the agreement, such as a signatory page or a legal filing confirmation.

For proper contract management, you need to be able to print agreements and define other output modes, such as email or fax. For this, define the settings for output management as part of the Post Processing Framework (PPF) in Customizing via the IMG path **Cross Application Components · Processes and Tools for Enterprise Applications · Reusable Objects and Functions for BOPF Environment · PPF Adapter for Output Management · Maintain Output Management Adapter Settings**. We covered this in Chapter 2, Section 2.3.3.

After you've configured output management for agreements, you can generate actions in the **Output Management** tab by selecting **Generate · Actions Including Condition Checks**. Figure 12.3 shows some examples of configured actions for agreements.

∨ General Data	Notes	Attachments	Administrative Data	Output Management	Versions	Capacities	Business Partner		Excel Integration
Standard ⊙	Deselect All	Generate ∨	Regenerate	Execute Actions ∨					
☐ Action Status		Processing Type	Document Number		Deactivate		Partner Dependent	Language	Print
☐ ∨ ⚠ Unprocessed									
☐ Freight Agreement		External Communication			☐		☐	EN	☐
☐ /SCMTMS/SPC_PRINT		External Communication			☑		☐	EN	☐

Figure 12.3 Output of a Forwarding Agreement

Let's highlight the key Customizing settings required for using a forwarding agreement. The forwarding agreement has its own type, which you need to configure. You can maintain the type in Customizing via the IMG path **Transportation Management · Master Data · Agreements and Service Products · Define FWA and Service Product Catalog Types**.

The agreement type is a key setting; for example, it controls the user interface (UI) layout. You can select the **Multiple Parties** checkbox to maintain more than one business partner and organizational unit, as shown earlier in Figure 12.1. In the same Customizing section, you can specify preconditions for the agreement items, such as the stage category, movement type, and so on, as just described.

The forwarding agreement items have their own type; you can maintain them by following the menu path **Transportation Management · Master Data · Agreements and Service Products · Define FWA and Service Product Item Types**. The forwarding agreement item types need to be assigned to the forwarding agreement type.

Let's turn our attention to another agreement—the internal agreement—which represents your contracts with the LSP or carrier.

12.1.2   Internal Agreements

The internal agreement is important to the management of internal settlements. For example, a freight forwarder can use internal agreements to maintain the internal rate agreements between freight stations and purchasing organizations. Each purchasing organization could have its own independent standard rates, which would be charged internally to the sales organizations generating the revenue. A manufacturing or retail company might similarly have a separate in-house logistics department that cross-charges other business units (BUs) for managing their transportation.

Alternative Use of Internal Agreements

In implementation projects, the internal agreement has been modeled differently from the internal charge settlement process. Companies decide to maintain internal agreements to store their internal standard cost of shipments. The standard cost contains many more components than just the purchasing charges for the transportation service. Such additional cost components can contain the cost of operations of the company's fleet, container repositioning, or other overhead costs that aren't directly related to a shipment. Because this data flows into the profitability analysis of the forwarding order, it gives an even more precise insight into the margin.

The structure of the internal agreement is almost the same as the forwarding agreements and freight agreements. In the header section, you maintain the purchasing organization that is offering internal services to other organizations.

The unique aspect of the internal agreement is that you also need to maintain the agreement partner. For example, a purchasing organization grants the same internal rates to all sales organizations in the same country but different rates to stations in other countries. As a result, a table is provided to maintain the involved parties for each internal agreement.

The internal agreement items are very similar to forwarding agreement/freight agreement items. Functionalities such as preconditions, commodity codes, notes, and attachments are supported. Capacities can't be stored on the items, assuming that internal organizations wouldn't negotiate on capacities that need to be consumed by internal sales organizations or other lines of business. You need to assign a calculation sheet or determination rule to each agreement item.

You need to define an internal agreement type before you can use this functionality. Maintain internal agreement types by following the menu path **Transportation Management • Master Data • Agreements and Service Products • Define Internal Agreement Types**. You also need to configure the internal agreement item types and assign them to internal agreements: **Transportation Management • Master Data • Agreements and Service Products • Define Internal Agreement Item Types**. The configuration of internal agreement types and internal agreement item types is similar to the configuration of forwarding agreement types and forwarding agreement item types described in the previous section.

12.1.3   Service Products and Standard Operating Procedures

The professional services industry, which includes marketing, consulting, and the business-to-consumer (B2C) service industry, has been kicking around the concept of packaged service products for a long time. For LSPs, especially carriers and freight forwarders, the concept of modular and packaged service products is increasingly prominent. Offering nonfreight-related, complementary services can provide multiple benefits for an LSP, such as increasing revenue potentials, achieving cost savings due to standardization, and establishing a unique selling proposition.

With SAP TM, you can maintain service products and service items as master data. A *service item* is a granular component that can be combined with a basic freight transportation service, such as container fumigation or reduced cutoff hours in a port of loading. A *service product* is a bundle of multiple service items (e.g., expedited air freight or cold-chain services). You can define a service product catalog and use it when setting up agreements and generating orders. SAP TM can also operationalize the production of services with SOP.

Let's look into these options now.

Services in Agreements and Orders

You can maintain service product catalogs to create service products as bundles of multiple service items. You can use these service products as the basis to generate customer contracts representing service agreements. Remember that a service agreement is nothing more than a forwarding agreement or freight agreement that contains service products. In the case of a forwarding agreement, it represents the service offerings to your customers. Freight agreements with service items represent the services you choose from your LSPs. When setting up your agreement with services, you can choose whether a service will be considered as **Mandatory** or **Flow Service**. Both can be retrieved to an order, but the latter can be removed again—not so with the mandatory services.

You can work with service products and service items in your transactions in two ways:

- Generate a forwarding order/freight order directly from a service agreement. The new forwarding order/freight order automatically inherits all service items, which are bundled under the service product in the service agreement.

- Generate a forwarding order /freight order manually and insert service items. You can enter the carrier in the freight order to limit the input help values of service items from that carrier. You can also enter agreement, item, and version, and SAP TM automatically retrieves the services to the order.

It's not mandatory to maintain a service product catalog. A limitation is that you can't insert an entire service product, only service items.

Now let's introduce the creation of a service product catalog. You can generate a service product catalog in SAP Fiori launchpad by choosing the **Create Service Product Catalog** tile on the **Contract Management** tab (in SAP TM 9.6, follow menu path **Master Data • Charge Management and Service Products • Service Product Catalogs**). In the structure, the catalog is like a forwarding agreement, but you don't maintain any agreement parties, validities, or capacities. Most important, you can create service products in the item table. Select **Insert • Service Product**, and assign a service product item type as specified in Customizing.

You can now give the product its own ID and bundle service items under the product by selecting **Insert • Service**. It's possible to directly assign a calculation sheet to each service product. In the calculation sheet, you can include all the charge types that are relevant to calculate the charges for the individual service items. However, you can't assign a charge type directly to a service product (e.g., to offer a price for an entire bundle).

You can maintain more than one service product catalog to distinguish the scope of service products with preconditions in Customizing. In a service agreement, you can insert a service product in the item table. You can search through your repository of service products for each service catalog and select a suitable product. All service items and charge types are pulled into the agreement when selected in a service agreement. Choose **Follow Up • Create Forwarding Order** to generate an order directly from the agreement to default a service product into the order.

When generating a freight order or forwarding order, you can enter service items in the item table. You can assign services either to single containers only or to all containers as a header service. After you execute the charge calculation, the rates for service items are calculated based on the maintained amounts in the service agreement.

Settings for Services in SAP TM

To generate a service product catalog and use services in orders, you need to define a repository of service types in Customizing, together with various other settings, as follows:

- **Service types**
  You need to set up your individual repository of service types, such as fumigation, providing generator sets, customs brokerage, container cleaning, expedited delivery, and GPS cargo tracking. To do this, navigate to the Customizing IMG path **Transportation Management • Basic Functions • General Settings • Define Service Types**. Service types are the most granular items (e.g., value-added services that can be bundled under a service product or that are particularly used in orders).

- **Forwarding and freight order item types**
  Recall from Chapter 4, Section 4.2, that in the forwarding order, you can use item types mainly to enter cargo items, containers, railcars, and trailers. To also enter service items in the forwarding order and freight order item table, you need to maintain a new item type in Customizing by following the IMG path **Transportation Management • Forwarding Order Management • Define Item Types for Forwarding Order Management**. The same is required for freight order item types. Maintain at least one entry with the item category **Service**, and assign this item type to your forwarding order type in Customizing by following the IMG path **Transportation Management • Forwarding Order Management • Forwarding Order • Assign Item Types to Forwarding Order Types**.

- **Service product item types**

  Besides the granular definition of your individual service types, you need to establish a repository of your service products to generate the list of all the service products you want to offer. You can establish the repository by following the IMG path **Transportation Management · Master Data · Agreements and Service Products · Define FWA and Service Product Item Types**. In this setting, you can define the description for your service product, such as guaranteed on-time delivery, expedited services, or temperature control deluxe.

  It's crucial now to assign the list of granular service types to the service product item type, under which it could be bundled. Note that this isn't the actual bundling of services, which happens in the master data.

  Optionally, you can specify preconditions that influence whether a service product can be used with the scope of an order or agreement.

- **Service product catalog type**

  The service product catalog is technically a forwarding agreement object, so you need to generate a service product catalog type that influences the number ranges and UI design and contains templates and defaults. You can create a service product catalog type in Customizing via the IMG path **Transportation Management · Master Data · Agreements and Service Products · Define FWA and Service Product Catalog Types**. To enable the use of service products in the service product catalog, you need to assign the possible service product types to the catalog types in the same Customizing path.

You've now made the basic Customizing settings to enable service products in SAP TM. To allow a charge calculation for services in forwarding orders, you need to map your service types to charge types. You must maintain at least one charge type per service type, but, alternatively, you can map a service type to multiple charge types. Navigate to Customizing to maintain the mapping (**Transportation Management · Basic Functions · Charge Calculation · Basic Settings · Assign Charge Types to Service Types**).

Standard Operating Procedures

Imagine an end-to-end transportation process of an LSP, freight forwarder, or carrier. You'll find that numerous tasks and actions need to be performed to execute a single shipment. Such tasks can include anything from taking and validating an order, planning and executing the transportation, issuing transportation documentation, performing customs clearance, and then finally invoicing a customer. In addition, specific agreements in customer contracts might outweigh the standard handling of a shipment and require additional services.

Standard operating procedures (SOP) support consistent and structured handling of all such tasks by generating instructions to be executed from user-specific worklists, which ensures process standardization, compliance, and clear guidance for staff. Figure 12.4 gives an example of instructions for one forwarding order. The SOP list can be considered as an individual to-do list for a user that needs to be completed daily.

Standard * ☺ ⊞ ⊟	Insert	Set Status ∨	Edit Note	Delete Note	Set Completion Date			
☐ Attribute Description	Sequence	Instruction	Instruction Description			Status	Due Date	Set Due Date
☐ ∨ New Lane Request								
☐	5	Z0001	Request Business Model			Pending		Set Due Date
☐	10	ZNL_SO...	Complete Source Location Data			Pending	31.07.20...	Set Due Date
☐	20	ZNL_DEST	Complete Desination Location Data			Pending	02.08.20...	Set Due Date
☐	30	ZNL_EX...	Complete External Sourcing Data			Pending	09.08.20...	Set Due Date
☐	40	ZNL_IM...	Complete Import Analysis			Pending	28.07.20...	Set Due Date
☐	50	ZNL_TEST	Complete Testing			Pending	31.07.20...	Set Due Date
☐	60	ZNL_SI	Complete Shipping Instructions			Pending	06.08.20...	Set Due Date

Figure 12.4 Instructions on a Forwarding Order

In SAP TM, you can define instructions to represent executable tasks for a user, such as arrange fumigation, generate customer invoice, verify shipping instructions, perform cargo screening, and so on. The example in Figure 12.4 is about the customer's request for a new transportation lane and therefore includes tasks such as completing location master data and the analysis of how the import process can be handled.

For each instruction, you can also define which user role needs to execute this task and provide notes and descriptions. To bring these instructions in the proper sequence and context, you need to group them in *instruction sets*. Instruction sets serve as a framework to define due dates for tasks to appear before or after a specific event. You can define, for example, that a task needs to appear in a user's worklist 12 hours before cargo cutoff. You can also define time-dependent alerts for a user in case a task hasn't been executed in time. After an initial setup, SAP TM automatically generates instructions in a user's worklist after a forwarding order has been generated, depending on the scheduled time. You can generate instructions and instruction sets in Customizing via the IMG path **Transportation Management · Basic Functions · Instructions · Define Instructions and Instruction Sets**.

Instructions are always stored on the forwarding order, where you can find the entire list of relevant instructions in the **Instructions** tab that was depicted on Figure 12.4. You have four options for how to assign an instruction set to ensure it's appropriate for the forwarding order:

- **Forwarding order type**
  The most generic assignment allows you to assign instruction sets to forwarding order types. Whenever you use the specific forwarding order type, the instructions are pulled into the forwarding order.

- **Item type per forwarding order**
  The instruction set is based on the item type in the forwarding order.

- **Stage type**
  An instruction set is pulled into a forwarding order if a specific stage type is used.

- **Service type**
  When you work with the service product catalog, you can assign an instruction set to each service type. This ensures the compliant execution of services you sold to a customer.

The assignment of instruction sets is performed in Customizing via the IMG path **Transportation Management • Basic Functions • Instructions • Assign Instruction Sets**.

12.2   Charge Calculation Logic

In Chapter 10, we introduced the concept of charge calculation and how the SAP TM functionality makes use of the master data defined. Charge calculation for forwarding orders follows the same principles as calculating charges for freight orders or freight bookings. The only difference is that we're now using a forwarding agreement instead of a freight agreement to draw rate tables and calculation sheets. When calculating charges on the forwarding order, the system determines a forwarding agreement that is valid for the combination of sales organization and sold-to party and fulfills all potential preconditions defined for the agreement itself as well as for the item. Because this is the only difference, we won't delve into the basics of charge calculation again. Chapter 10 covers this part, even though it's primarily focused on purchasing transportation services instead of selling.

This section will look at particularities that LSPs will require the charge calculation to cover that go beyond the basic charge calculation features.

12.2.1   Charge Calculation for Air Freight

Transportation Charge Management offers comprehensive capabilities for the calculation of air freight charges for freight forwarders or shippers. There are multiple methods and variants for calculating charges in air freight. Because this book focuses on the bigger transportation management picture, we don't cover the details of the pure air freight charge calculation or attempt to cover all available functions and setup, but instead we aim to convey a general overview of the capabilities in SAP TM. If you're an SAP customer or partner, you can find a comprehensive implementation guide for air freight with SAP TM on the SAP Service Marketplace.

SAP TM supports two ways of calculating air freight charges: rating based on the International Air Transport Association (IATA) or rating based on individual contract rates. The IATA globally standardizes processes in air freight and acts as a service organization for most airlines for charge calculation and settlement processes. One of the services the IATA offers is to calculate and manage cargo rates in its own database, representing more than 100 airlines.

IATA-Based and Contract-Based Charge Calculation

SAP TM can use the same methods and tools that the IATA uses for charge calculation to determine the cost for a freight forwarder. The core principle is that as a freight forwarder, when setting up agreements with your customers, you can configure your own forwarding agreements or base them on the IATA logic. Similarly, when maintaining contracts with airlines, you can be charged based on IATA or individual contract terms. For both IATA and contract rates, three rate categories are supported: unit load device (ULD) rates, special commodity rates (SCRs), and general cargo rates (GCRs).

Upload of TACT Rates

SAP TM has the capability to upload the Air Cargo Tariff (TACT) into SAP TM database tables to enable a charge calculation based on IATA. TACT rates represent a generic tariff available to any customer of an airline.

You can upload TACT rates via a report in SAP TM. Navigate to Transaction SE38 in the SAP GUI, and run report /SCMTMS/TACT_RATE_UPLOAD. You can select a file containing the TACT rates. SAP TM generates the appropriate entries in the database with report /SCMTMS/TACT_RATE_PROCESS.

Air Freight-Specific Calculation Logic

A common way of calculating rates is to have different weight tiers with flat charges per ULD type. This rating logic can be used both by the IATA and if rates are contractually agreed upon. If the chargeable weight exceeds a weight tier, an over-pivot rate is applied and added. SAP TM calculates the chargeable weight of a ULD and applies the flat rate of the next higher weight tier. This rate is compared against the flat rate of the next lower weight tier, plus the delta in chargeable weight, multiplied by the over-pivot.

Let's illustrate this using the simplified example shown in Table 12.1.

ULD Class	Weight Tier for Chargeable Weight	Rate
04	300	$20,000
04	400	$22,000
04	500	$25,000
–	Over-pivot	$40

Table 12.1 ULD Rating Example

Let's say that the ULD in a forwarding order has a chargeable weight of 450. The flat rate would be $25,000. The lower weight tier rate is $22,000 plus the over-pivot rate of 50 × 40 = $2,000, which results in $24,000. The lower rate of $24,000 is rated. IATA provides the weight tiers for each ULD class and the flat rates/over-pivot rates for each carrier. The rates are normally dependent on the source and destination IATA cities. This logic is implemented in SAP TM via the air freight break-weight calculation method.

Pure commodity rates are rarely used in air freight. They can be maintained as rates per chargeable weight and are simply multiplied by the chargeable weight of the cargo with a similar commodity class (see example in Table 12.2). It's possible to also apply tiers for the commodity rates, but no over-pivot or comparison logic is applied. A pallet of chocolate on a flight from Frankfurt to Singapore has a chargeable weight of 350. The rate calculated would be 350 × $5 = $1,750.

Origin	Destination	Weight Tier for Chargeable Weight	Commodity: Chocolate	Commodity: Gold
Frankfurt	Singapore	>100	$6	$30
Frankfurt	Singapore	>300	$5	$25

Table 12.2 Commodity Rating Example

Finally, the GCR is always used if no specifically discounted ULD or SCR is found. Three rate classes are used for the calculation: minimum charge, normal rate, and quantity rate (see example in Table 12.3). The logic is that a normal rate is multiplied by the chargeable weight of the cargo. If it's lower than the minimum, the minimum rate is applied. If the chargeable weight of the cargo is higher than the normal rate weight, the quantity rate of the appropriate tier is used. For example, a piece of cargo on a flight from London to Newark has a chargeable weight of 80. The calculated rate is $80 \times \$8 = \$640$.

Origin	Destination	Class	Weight Tier	Rate
London	Newark	Minimum	–	$124
London	Newark	Normal	<50	$9.50
London	Newark	Quantity	>50	$8.00
London	Newark	Quantity	>100	$7.00

Table 12.3 General Cargo Rating Example

When creating an air freight booking, for example, you can specify which rate category to use. SAP TM can also automatically determine the rate category with a specific sequence.

Nature of Goods

As of SAP TM 9.2, you can enter the *nature of goods* (NOG) against each charge line in the air waybill view. The NOGs are used in air freight to give more detailed cargo information, such as concerning quantities, dimensions, dangerous goods, or live animals. It's often printing relevant in several documents (e.g., manifest and air waybill). The NOG can be entered in any execution document (e.g., forwarding order or freight booking) and is inherited by the predecessor documents.

The charge calculation logic is implemented based on two calculation methods: the air freight break-weight rating and air freight standard rating can be used for all scenarios. It's also possible to combine the ULD and GCR rate categories, which you might do for mixed loose cargo and ULD cargo scenarios:

1. If you're transporting ULDs, the booking needs to contain a ULD with weight and volume information. SAP TM checks for a ULD rate based on chargeable weight.

2. If no rate is found, or the cargo is loose/packages (but not consolidated in an air freight ULD), the SCR is calculated. The commodity code in the booking for the cargo is required.

3. If no specific commodity-based rate is maintained, the generic rate calculation is used as a fallback option.

When you work with contract rates, you can flexibly change this sequence. You can enter specific handling codes in air freight bookings that can indicate, for example, that a cargo screening is required, dangerous goods are being transported, or other services need to be performed. Handling codes can be used to determine additional charge types that need to be included in the calculation.

Additional Capabilities for Air Freight

An option for charge calculation in air freight is to derive the charges of a direct shipment by pulling the cost calculated in the main air freight booking into a forwarding order (use the calculation method AIR_COST). Such an IATA direct shipment means that one order (house air waybill [HAWB]) equals to one air booking (air waybill). No order consolidation happens, for example, in a ULD with other customer orders. This is relevant particularly if LSPs have agreed upon rates based on actual cost plus a markup, or simply the actual cost. By choosing the COST_PULL calculation method in the forwarding agreement, you can choose both the source (e.g., air waybill charges) and the strategy for cost pull. The Active_Copy strategy determines whether charges pulled to the forwarding order are editable. Very important in the behavior of the cost pull functionality are the incoterms in the forwarding order and the *freight terms* in the freight booking. Freight terms specify which of the freight forwarder's organizational units will pay the carrier. Depending on the selection of the freight terms, the cost pull might happen from the export, the import, or both the export and import freight booking.

When you work with an airline as a shipper or freight forwarder, you might deal with a sales agent in particular countries. Instead of having your freight agreement defined directly with the airline, you might have it with the airline's agent. This is common practice especially in small countries or countries with low service offerings of the airline. The possible behavior of SAP TM is to first check for an agreement with the sales agent and, if none is found, to check for an agreement with the airline as a fallback. Remember from Chapter 10 that this is a specific behavior. You can enable this feature by maintaining the airline in the **Vendor Data** tab of the sales agent business partner. Make sure to also establish a business partner relationship between the two business partners with relationship category **Is Agent Of**. Furthermore, it's possible to use a weight-to-volume ratio for charge calculation. This very common way of using a chargeable weight is described in more detail in Chapter 10, Section 10.3. Specifically, in air freight, a volumetric weight factor is often crucial to calculate the actual chargeable weight.

Configuration Highlights

To configure Transportation Charge Management according to air freight charges, you need to apply a few settings. In Customizing, the following configurations are required. Let's highlight the core differences from a regular charge calculation, as described in Chapter 10.

- TACT rates
  - ULD rate types are maintained and mapped against ULD types: **Transportation Management • Basic Functions • Charge Calculation • Air Freight Settings • Define ULD Rate Types** and **Map ULD Types to ULD Rate Types**.
  - TACT rates are uploaded.
- A calculation profile is maintained with the calculation level **Header** and the air waybill printing and air waybill settlement definitions. The calculation profile is assigned to a charges profile of an organization or business partner.
- A dimensional weight profile is assigned to the calculation profile or the agreement/agreement item.
- The charge types you use have the transportation mode category **Air**.

Besides pure Customizing, it's essential to set up your agreements, calculation sheets, and rate tables accordingly. Consider this summary of the possible settings:

1. The agreement contains a dimensional weight profile. Alternatively, it's stored on the calculation profile.
2. The charges in the calculation sheets are set up for air freight:

- The rate categories are maintained as **ULD**, **SCR**, or **GCR**.
- The rate type is selected as either **Contract** or **TACT**.
- Charge type classifications and IATA charge-due definitions are maintained.
3. One of the two air freight calculation methods—air freight break-weight or air freight standard—is assigned to the charge types.
4. Rate tables contain the appropriate rate category for a corresponding charge type.

You can also use other functionalities, such as a multirate hit or minimum/maximum rates, as well as working with preconditions in the air freight charge calculation.

12.2.2   Charge Calculation with Freight Forwarders

In this section, we highlight charge calculation capabilities specific to freight forwarders or when you, as a carrier or shipper, have contracts with a freight forwarder. Crucial to mention at the beginning is that freight forwarders provide air freight services. In this chapter, we now focus on other capabilities freight forwarders can use in the context of air, ocean, trucking, or rail charges.

Charge Calculation Based on Chargeable Weight

In the freight forwarding industry, especially in air freight and less than container load (LCL) ocean cargo, it's a very common business practice to maintain rates not per weight or volume but per chargeable weight. The chargeable weight is a combination of weight and volume based on a specific factor. For the calculation of rates, it's common to use the higher value out of weight versus chargeable weight.

Let's look at an example. In air freight, the space of an aircraft and the weight that a plane can carry are limited. Consequently, the perfect piece of cargo to meet both the total volume and weight limits of the plane weighs 1 kilogram (kg) per 6,000 cubic centimeters (cm^3). In Example 1 in Table 12.4, the chargeable weight used for rating is 83.33 kg. In Example 2, the chargeable weight is 47 kg.

Example	Volume (in cm^3)	Divided By	Dimensional Weight	Actual Weight
1	500,000	6,000	83.33 kg	60 kg
2	240,000	6,000	40 kg	47 kg

Table 12.4 Air Freight Weight Scenarios

You can maintain dimensional weight profiles to store the specific weight-to-volume ratios in the SAP TM Customizing via the IMG path **Transportation Management** · **Basic Functions** · **Charge Calculation** · **Data Source Binding** · **Define Dimensional Weight Profiles**. You can assign the dimensional weight profile to a calculation profile or on the header/line items of an agreement to use it for the charge calculation and even in the charge details.

Through Rates, Cross Rates, and Uncontrolled Shipments

In a regular rating scenario for customers of a freight forwarder, you can calculate charges per transportation leg. SAP TM checks for a rate for each start location and destination location for each leg when using the resolution base **Stage**.

In the ocean freight industry, however, it's a common business practice of carriers to charge a freight forwarder an end-to-end rate from origin to final destination. This is called the *through rate*. Alternatively, any other combination of stage-dependent rating is possible based on *cross rates*, meaning that one rate is maintained for the pre-carriage, another rate for the main carriage, and a third rate for the on-carriage.

To pass this concept on to customers of the freight forwarder, SAP TM supports the through rate/cross rate calculation logic for forwarding orders and forwarding quotations. This calculation logic always tries to find the most direct rate with as few individual stages as possible. If no through rate is found, the logic systematically breaks up the end-to-end route into pieces of mixed stage categories (pre-carriage and main carriage) to find cross rates, including two-stage categories. If no cross rate is found, the logic checks for a rate for each stage category. If a rate isn't maintained for each stage category, then each start–destination pair is analyzed for a rate. Figure 12.5 shows how SAP TM breaks down the legs of the tour.

The trip starts with a charge calculation, which checks the rate table for a rate from **A** to **F**. If no rate is found, a second call to the rate table (Rating 2) is performed to check for a rate from **A** to **D** and from **D** to **F**, and so on. To enable the through rate/cross rate calculation logic, you need to select the **Through Rate** checkbox in the calculation profile in Customizing (refer to Chapter 10, Section 10.2.2). The calculation level needs to be maintained as the stage level. Note that if a rate isn't found for specific legs, SAP TM performs a partial determination, where a rate is determined (e.g., only for main and on-carriage).

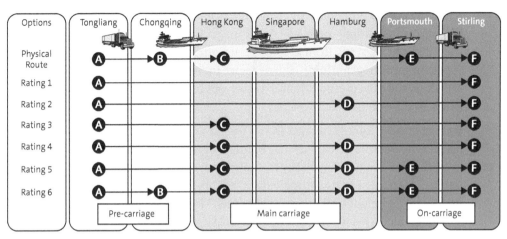

Figure 12.5 Through Rate and Cross Rate Concept

A common business scenario for a freight forwarder is to handle uncontrolled shipments. A customer uses rates for the main carriage that are directly agreed upon with the carrier. A forwarder can be requested to perform invoice verification for the carrier. Consequently, the charge calculation for both the forwarding order and freight booking are still performed by the forwarder to validate an invoice received. You can maintain a forwarding agreement item, deactivate the **Controlled** flag, and enter both the carrier and external agreement ID. In the freight agreement with the carrier, you need to mention the uncontrolled agreement party and the external agreement ID.

Customer Charge Calculation Based on Cost Pull

A very useful functionality in SAP TM is the cost pull capability, through which you can pull the actual transportation cost from a freight order or freight booking into a forwarding order for customer charge calculation. We briefly introduced this in Section 12.2.1 for air freight. For example, you can maintain markups in percentages that are applied on top of the transportation cost when you calculate the customer charges. As you saw in Chapter 11, Section 11.2, you must configure the cost distribution before you can use this functionality.

When setting up your calculation sheets in the forwarding agreement, you need to enter a line item with the new instruction type **Cost**. In the basic data of this line item, assign the calculation method **COST_PULL**, which enables the underlying logic of

retrieving cost information from a freight document and using it for charge calculation on the forwarding order side. You can specify whether all charge types or only
dedicated charge types from a booking are retrieved, as well as whether they are
applied as an aggregated lump sum or shown individually as in the booking. To apply
a markup, you can enter additional charge types under the cost line item in the calculation sheets with percentage values.

You can retrieve internal charges from a freight order to the forwarding order. This is
particularly important if an LSP has multiple organizations that are involved in the
execution of a shipment, typically an export and import organization. In this case, an
internal agreement between the export and import organization applies internal
charges to the freight booking or freight order—for example, from the export side to
the import side. This is very common for an LSP, as we explain in more detail in Section 12.3.5. To enable the internal cost pull, you need to add a specific charge type in
your calculation sheet of the forwarding agreement. Maintain the **Charge Source** field
in the **Basic Data** tab as **Internal**. A similar calculation method and instruction type as
described earlier are needed.

12.2.3   Charge Calculation for Container Management

For an LSP such as a freight forwarder or an ocean carrier, it's common to provide
containers to customers as an additional service to the actual transportation of the
freight. A shipper might provide its own container, and provisioning isn't required. In
other examples, the customer might require only an empty container but no transportation service. In SAP TM, it's possible to manage these different provisioning and
return processes of containers. SAP TM introduces container units, which can optionally be created during freight unit building (FUB). Refer to Chapter 4, Section 4.2.1, for
more details on the order processing of such containers. It's essential for your profitability that you invoice relevant fees for container provisioning and return. For this
purpose, it's possible to maintain a container-specific charge type, maintaining values for the **Empty Provisioning** or **Empty Return** attributes in the **Basic Data** tab of a
charge type in a calculation sheet. For both empty provisioning and empty return,
it's possible to choose any of three options, as depicted on Figure 12.6:

- **Requested**
  An empty container is provided to the shipper/returned from the ship-to party.
  The cargo transportation of the container is managed as the main service.

- **Not Requested**
  The shipper has its own container, and only the cargo transportation is requested from the LSP.

- **Provisioning/Return Only**
  The shipper/ship-to party doesn't need the actual cargo transportation, just the provisioning/return of an empty container.

Figure 12.6 Applying an Empty Container Provisioning or Return Charge Type

If a forwarding order is created, and a container provisioning or empty provisioning only (no cargo movement) is requested for the container items, the relevant charges from the calculation sheet are retrieved. You can use a resolution base container to retrieve the corresponding charge types for each container.

Technical Container Object

When you offer all three container options (cargo movement, container provisioning/return with cargo movement, and only container provisioning/return) to a customer, you must pay attention to the charges setup. If you, for example, maintain separate charge types for the cargo movement, the container provisioning/return, and the empty provisioning/return, SAP TM applies each applicable charge type per container item on the forwarding order. Remember that the resolution base is Container. This might result in an overcharging of the customer because SAP TM creates technical container units in the background. Such a container unit is created for the empty container leg and *additionally* for the leg of the cargo movement. If a forwarding order, for example, has two containers—one requires provisioning and cargo movement and one container is needed only for empty provisioning—SAP TM creates three container units: one for the provisioning of the cargo container, one for the cargo movement, and one for empty provisioning. In reality, only two containers exist. In this case, the charge to provide only empty provisioning is also applied for the technical container created for the empty provisioning of the cargo movement.

12

This section walked through the specific capabilities offered in SAP TM for managing forwarding contracts and charges and demonstrated the different ways of deriving rates for eclectic use cases and transportation modes.

Now, we need to make sure the charges calculated against our customers are also paid. To facilitate this, we need to create customer invoices. The next section will focus on the functionality SAP TM provides to create invoices based on the charges calculated in forwarding orders.

12.3   Billing and Settlement

When talking about settlement in SAP TM, we usually differentiate between settlement toward a transportation service provider and settlement against a customer. Chapter 11 already dealt with freight settlement, which will serve as a basis for this section. This section will now take a closer look at the following types of settlement:

- **Settlement of customer charges**
  The settlement of customer charges is significant for LSPs and carriers (e.g., railways, trucking companies, and ocean liners). Billing customers for the provided transportation services is part of the core business model. This can be a very straightforward process or become increasingly complex. The settlement of charges depends greatly on the incoterms of a shipment. The incoterms define whether freight charges need to be paid by the shipper or the ship-to party. Consequently, different settlement documents and invoices are sent to the involved shippers to pay for prepaid charges, and the involved ship-to party or parties to pay the collect charges, according to the agreed incoterms. Certain customers have preferences about how to split and group invoices, which can become a challenge for logistics companies. The logistics departments of shippers can benefit from the same functionality if they act as an LSP/carrier to external customers. However, as a shipper, your logistics department is probably a cost center and doesn't bill customers.

- **Internal settlement**
  A shipper's logistics department might bill other internal departments—let's call them internal customers—for transportation services. For freight forwarders and trucking companies, this is a very common business practice. LSPs usually organize themselves in such a fashion to increase operational efficiency. They have gateways and hubs that are responsible for the optimization of costs for procurement and generating a profit through consolidation services. In such situations,

LSPs tend to operate as internal service providers for their own BUs. Incurred cost and profit is commonly settled/shared across the organizations. A selling branch/ booking office of an LSP might sell transportation services to a customer, but multiple hubs and gateways are responsible for procuring and providing capacities along the global supply chain.

In the next sections, we'll look at how forwarding settlement—the settlement of customer charges—is performed, meaning how we create settlement documents, what these documents look like and how these are integrated with the billing functionality in SAP S/4HANA. We'll also dive into internal settlement and Profitability Analysis (CO-PA).

12.3.1   Creating Forwarding Settlement Documents

During this section, you'll notice that the high-level process of creating and processing forwarding settlement documents is similar to the way we created and processed freight settlement documents in Chapter 11, Section 11.1. The forwarding settlement process, however, is highly integrated with and dependent on the way we calculate the charges in the forwarding order. You'll quickly see that a multitude of scenarios and requirements have come from LSP customers concerning how their invoices are created and structured. As a result, SAP TM supports a variety of functionalities to serve specific scenarios. We'll introduce the different scenarios step by step, including both the business background and the most important Customizing settings.

Incoterm-Based Forwarding Settlement Documents

Our process starts with creating the forwarding settlement document, if we've already generated and executed a forwarding order. There are generally three ways to generate a forwarding settlement document:

- Navigate to a forwarding order, and select **Charges/Settlement · Create Forwarding Settlement Document** from the top navigation panel.
- Run a batch report, which periodically generates forwarding settlement documents.
- Collectively or individually generate forwarding settlement documents from a personal object worklist (POWL) by selecting **Create Forwarding Settlement Document · Individual, Collective** or **Use Default Settings**.

Mass Creation of Forwarding Settlement Documents

SAP TM offers a standard report that you can run manually or automatically in the background. Navigate to Transaction SE38 in SAP GUI, and run report /SCMTMS/ CFIR_CREATE_BATCH.

The first question to answer is how many forwarding settlement documents are generated when the creation is triggered. For a freight forwarder, customer invoices are generated based on global incoterms. From Chapter 4, you learned how to maintain and use incoterms in a forwarding order, and you've seen that incoterms can significantly influence the way we calculate charges. Now we show you how incoterms influence the generation of forwarding settlement documents. Figure 12.7 shows an example of a settlement process based on incoterms.

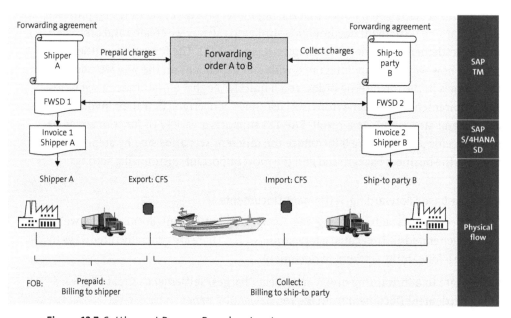

Figure 12.7 Settlement Process Based on Incoterms

Let's assume you have a forwarding order with the incoterm free-on-board. The shipper is responsible for paying all charges until the port of loading, including the export customs declaration. The ship-to party pays all charges from the port of loading to the final destination, including insurance and import customs. We have two forwarding agreements in place, one with the shipper and one with the ship-to party.

The definition of which agreement party is responsible for paying which part of the forwarding order is defined on the **Actual Route** tab of the forwarding order (or the **Ordered Route** tab if the charge calculation is performed based on the ordered route). As you can see in Figure 12.8, the forwarding order in our example is an ocean transport from the Tokyo metropolitan area to Tucson, Arizona. The prepaid agreement party will pay for the stages in Japan, while the collect agreement party will pay for the main carriage and the road stages in the United States. Note that the **Agreement Business Partner** is automatically determined from the **Business Partner** tab of the forwarding order, where a business partner was assigned to an agreement partner function.

Stage Description	Stage Type	Mode of Transport	Source Location	City (Source)	Destination Location	City (Destination)	Agrmt Prtnr Function	Agreement Business Partner
⌄ Route			OAF-CU-02	Ota-ku	OAF-CO-02	Tucson		
Stage 1	01 (Pick-Up)	01	OAF-CU-02	Ota-ku	OAF-STA-JPTYO	Tokyo	Prepaid Agrmt. Party	OAF-CU-02
Stage 2	02 (Pre-Carriage)	01	OAF-STA-JPTYO	Tokyo	OF-CFS-JPYOK	Naka-ku	Prepaid Agrmt. Party	OAF-CU-02
Stage 3	03 (Main Carriage)	03	OF-CFS-JPYOK	Naka-ku	OF-CFS-USLAX	Long Beach	Collect Agrmt. Party	OAF-CO-02
Stage 4	04 (On-Carriage)	01	OF-CFS-USLAX	Long Beach	OAF-STA-USPHX	Tempe	Collect Agrmt. Party	OAF-CO-02
Stage 5	05 (Delivery)	01	OAF-STA-USPHX	Tempe	OAF-CO-02	Tucson	Collect Agrmt. Party	OAF-CO-02

Figure 12.8 Assigning Agreement Parties to Transportation Stages

Assuming we've made all the required settings, you should see the following system behavior after navigating to the forwarding order and selecting **Charges/Settlement • Create Forwarding Settlement Document**. The system prompts you with a user selection to define which forwarding settlement document to create (see Figure 12.9).

Figure 12.9 Selecting the Agreement Party for Forwarding Settlement Document Creation

The system recognizes that two forwarding settlement documents will be created based on our configuration settings. The first business partner represents the prepaid agreement party, as maintained in the **Business Partner** tab in the forwarding order. The second business partner is the collect agreement party that must pay the charges from the port of loading. You now choose whether to create just one settlement document for either business partner or both at once.

Note

If you create a forwarding settlement document for only one business partner in this step, not all charges of the forwarding order will be settled, as the charges against the other business partner will remain pending settlement.

When choosing **Prepaid and Collect Party**, a minimum of two settlement documents are generated in total from the forwarding order because both the ship-to party and the shipper pay a proportion of the overall charges. The first forwarding settlement document contains the charges of the shipper who is responsible for paying the prepaid charges from origin to port of loading. The charges are calculated for each transportation stage.

The second forwarding settlement document contains the collect charges to be paid by the ship-to party. The invoicing status in the forwarding order is updated to **Partially Invoiced** if not all settlement documents have been generated. The status changes to **Invoiced** after all forwarding settlement documents have been generated. After the successful creation of multiple forwarding settlement documents based on incoterms, you see an item table of forwarding settlement documents that contains all the settlement documents that were created. You can now select each document to drill down into the details, which we cover in Section 12.3.2.

Additional Forwarding Settlement Documents

You can create additional forwarding settlement documents manually by selecting **Other Business Partner**. This functionality has been developed for exceptional and unplanned cases only, where a user wants to bill a customer manually for charges that weren't retrieved from the customer's forwarding agreement or services billed to another business partner that is neither the prepaid nor collect agreement party. These additional settlement documents don't impact the invoicing status of a forwarding order, and the charges for these settlement documents need to be calculated on the settlement document directly.

It's important to mention that in an export/import scenario, the settlement of customer charges can be based on two forwarding orders for one shipment: the export and import forwarding orders. As you learned in Chapter 8, Section 8.1.3, SAP TM can generate an export and an import forwarding order for international shipments. As a result, the export organization of a company in the exporting country might be responsible only for settling the prepaid charges to a shipper. The responsible import organization consequently settles the collect charges with the ship-to party. Depending on the incoterm, you generate one forwarding settlement document to the shipper from the export forwarding order and a second forwarding settlement document to the ship-to party from the import forwarding order. In addition, you can cross-charge the incurred transportation cost between the export and import organizations for an equal split. We detail this scenario of internal settlements in Section 12.3.5.

If a customer cancels a forwarding order, it's still possible that costs occurred, and, consequently, the charges need to be applied. You can create a forwarding settlement document for forwarding orders that are in the **Canceled** lifecycle status. You must create the forwarding settlement document manually. It's not yet possible with the standard SAP TM installation to calculate the charges automatically for canceled orders. As a result, you must manually add them in the settlement document, which is created as an empty shell. After you've entered the charge types and actual amounts, you can follow the standard settlement process flow.

Basic Customizing in SAP TM

Let's look at the basic settings required to achieve this system behavior. For the creation of forwarding settlement documents, you need to take a few basic Customizing steps in the forwarding order management and charge calculation areas. You need to have defined the incoterms and maintained the default agreement party roles for stages, where a stage type is assigned a default agreement party role. The forwarding order you created stores the actual incoterm. In addition, you need to have defined the resolution base as **Stage** in your calculation profile (see Chapter 10), as the charge split between prepaid and collect agreement party is usually done on a stage basis.

The following Customizing settings are required in charge settlement:

- **Settlement document type**
  When using SAP TM settlement functionality, you must define at least one forwarding settlement document type in Customizing and assign it to your forwarding order type by first following the IMG path **Transportation Management ·**

Settlement • Forwarding Settlement • Define Forwarding Settlement Document Types. The forwarding settlement document type specifies the number range, output profile, and multiple default settings. The assignment of the forwarding settlement document type to the forwarding order document type is done in the IMG path **Transportation Management • Forwarding Order Management • Forwarding Order • Define Forwarding Order Types**. More details about this Customizing activity are provided in Chapter 4, Section 4.2.

- **Settlement profile**

  Second, you need to maintain a settlement profile via the IMG path **Transportation Management • Settlement • Define Settlement Profile**. Figure 12.10 shows a standard settlement profile in SAP TM. The settlement profile is the key configuration that influences the behavior of a forwarding settlement document. A settlement profile can be directly assigned to a business partner. Alternatively, it can be assigned to a charges profile that is mapped to an organizational unit, in our case, the forwarding house or sales organization.

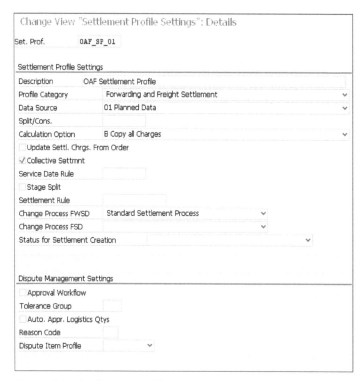

Figure 12.10 Settlement Profile

In the following Customizing path, you need to assign your settlement profile to a charges profile: **Transportation Management** • **Basic Functions** • **Charge Calculation** • **Basic Settings** • **Define Charges Profiles**. If the settlement profile is assigned to both the business partner and the charges profile, the priority lies with the business partner. The settlement profile is used for both freight and forwarding order settlement documents, unless the profile category in Figure 12.10 restricts the usage to only freight settlement or forwarding settlement. An additional capability of the settlement profile is the **Stage Split** checkbox. As an alternative to the described incoterm scenarios, selecting this checkbox causes a forwarding order to generate one settlement document per leg for the entire transportation process, independently of the incoterm and involved parties.

- **Process controller**
  Third, you must set up the process controller for creating settlement documents. SAP TM offers two standard methods for the settlement process: either split the forwarding order based on incoterms to generate multiple forwarding settlement documents or consolidate multiple forwarding orders to generate one settlement document. In addition to the SAP TM standard capabilities, you can develop your own process controller methods and assign them to a strategy that will be used in the charge settlement process and steer the creation process of a forwarding settlement document. Custom logic won't replace the standard methods.

Collective Creation of Forwarding Settlement Documents

In addition to the generation of settlement documents based on incoterms, which allows you to split a forwarding order and generate multiple settlement documents, you can also create one forwarding settlement document across multiple forwarding orders. You can select multiple forwarding orders in a POWL and create a collective forwarding settlement document. One document is created for your selection if the basic settlement data is the same. You can configure your own strategies to determine the attributes that have to be similar across forwarding orders to generate a common forwarding settlement document. Examples of such attributes are bill-to party, payer, sold-to party, payment term, credit segment, and source or destination location. To activate this grouping logic, you don't need to assign a split/consolidation strategy in the settlement profiles. A default logic is available in standard SAP TM. A customer-specific logic can be optionally assigned to the settlement profile, which runs in addition to the default in standard SAP TM (refer to Figure 12.10).

Trailer-Based and Route-Based Settlement

Billing the customer based on the distance traveled between origin and destination is a common business practice in the trucking industry. Recall from Chapter 6, Section 6.4.2, that a trailer can be used to pick up multiple forwarding orders across different origins and drop off the cargo at multiple destinations. In this case, you can invoice one bill to your customer for multiple forwarding orders that are transported on the same trailer. This gives you an alternative way of generating one forwarding settlement document for multiple forwarding orders.

A key aspect of the trailer-based settlement is that the charge calculation logic is different from a regular rating scenario. The charges are calculated for the entire group of forwarding orders in a trailer, not per individual order. They are treated as one virtual forwarding order document, and the consolidated weights, volumes, and so on are used for the charge calculation. Consequently, you can use a trailer-based settlement process to generate one settlement document per trailer document per customer.

In cases where the trailer contains forwarding orders from multiple customers, multiple forwarding settlement documents are created. The settlement document has a slightly different layout of the **Orders** section than regular forwarding settlement documents, as shown in Section 12.3.2. You can see the trailer document used for the settlement creation as a line item. Select the line item to see the forwarding orders that were loaded on the trailer on the line item details. These scenarios are also referred to in a similar fashion as execution-based settlement because the cargo execution information plays a vital role in the settlement process.

For you to enable trailer-based charge calculation and creation of settlement documents, one additional setting is required: the **Trailer-Based Settlement** indicator needs to be selected in the line item details of your forwarding agreement that you want to use to calculate the charges of the corresponding business partner. This automatically serves as the main item for charge calculation; use of a specific resolution base isn't required.

Trailer-Based Settlement

For a trailer-based settlement process, you can only use the calculation levels **Header** and **Stage** as possible settings for the charge determination. From Chapter 10, you know that the calculation level, which is maintained on the calculation profile, defines how many forwarding agreements are used when resolving the charges. The calculation-level item would not make sense in this business context because the system would try to retrieve one forwarding agreement per item (e.g., per package of an order).

In the trailer scenario, the opposite is the case. We want to settle all the packages collectively from one customer that are loaded on the same trailer, based on the distance a trailer has traveled. Consequently, there is no need to use a different forwarding agreement for one package or another because the agreed-upon rate based on the distance would be stored in one forwarding agreement of the business partner only.

Another functionality of SAP TM is to generate forwarding settlement documents based on the freight order they are loaded to (which is called the route-based settlement). It's similarly targeted at trucking companies. SAP TM allows you to generate a forwarding settlement document for all forwarding orders on the same freight order. The distinctive feature we want to highlight here is that you can use your freight document (and the data contained) as the basis for the settlement to your customers. This bypasses the individual settlement of forwarding orders, such as a trailer-based settlement. For example, you could combine the route-based settlement with trailer-based settlement in a scenario where a forwarding order is transported on a first stage in a freight order without trailer assignment and for a second leg in a trailer object. Consequently, two forwarding settlement documents are generated per customer—one for the stage of the freight order and one for the stage of the trailer. You can activate this functionality by selecting the route-based settlement basis in the line item details of your forwarding agreement.

12.3.2   Structure of Forwarding Settlement Documents

The forwarding settlement document contains all billing-relevant information inherited from a forwarding order. Think back to Chapter 4, Section 4.2, about forwarding order management and to Chapter 10 about Transportation Charge Management; a lot of the fields and information will already be familiar to you. Therefore, we now want to highlight the most crucial information with respect to the billing process.

The **General Data** tab contains the type of your settlement document, which determines, among other things, the screen design (Web Dynpro application configuration, as described in Chapter 2, Section 2.2). In addition, this tab contains the sales organization, which is determined based on the sales organization from the forwarding order. The incoterms are available based on the forwarding order, as well. They can have a major impact on the creation of the settlement document, as we discussed in the previous section. There is also a screen area listing the payment terms from the customer's forwarding agreement. Payment terms can be maintained in Customizing via the IMG path **Sales and Distribution · Master Data · Business Partners · Customers · Define Terms of Payment**. In addition, there is the invoice date. You can manually change some information in the forwarding settlement document, such as the invoice date and payment terms.

Defining Terms of Payment in SAP TM 9.6

The IMG path for Customizing terms of payment in SAP TM 9.6 can be found in **SAP Transportation Management · SCM Basis · Master Data · Business Partner · Define Terms of Payment**.

To be able to issue a bill to your customers, maintain at least the bill-to party and the payer. The business partners for these two partner functions are defaulted from the forwarding order. You can use business partner determination rules to automatically determine which parties will be maintained for which partner function. For more details on how to maintain and use business partner determination profiles, refer to Chapter 4, Section 4.2. You can overwrite the address of a bill-to party in the forwarding settlement document if you want to send the invoice to a different address. In this case, the settlement and invoice creation in SAP S/4HANA considers the different address to generate the billing document.

The forwarding settlement document is created based on actual forwarding orders. As a result, you can always see which forwarding orders were settled in a forwarding settlement document. You might see only one forwarding order assigned to the forwarding settlement document, but remember that we described how to settle multiple forwarding orders collectively in one settlement document. Therefore, the **Orders** tab provides you with the list of all forwarding orders you grouped into a settlement document. For a trailer-based or freight order–based settlement, you'll see the freight orders or trailer documents in the **Orders** tab, which contains the forwarding orders as line items. If you resolve the charges based on the calculation level of forwarding order items, you can see the list of forwarding order items in the **Orders** tab.

In the **Orders** tab, you might notice the *service date*; this can be different from order to order. When settling the charges to a customer, you're probably confronted with a legal taxation requirement to activate only your revenues when a service has been rendered. SAP TM supports this requirement with the service date. It allows you to set up flexible rules to define at what time you consider the service of a forwarding order fulfilled. The date is transferred with your settlement document for the actual billing (mapped to the *service rendered date* in sales and distribution [SD] billing). You can define such rules in the SAP TM Customizing by following the IMG path **Transportation Management • Settlement • Define Service Date Rules and Rule Prioritization**.

SAP TM offers you the choice between multiple transportation-related dates that are stored in your forwarding order and even in the freight order (e.g., expected start date of first stage main carriage or actual end date of loading). You can maintain multiple dates that are considered as the service date and assign priorities among them if a date isn't available in a forwarding order. You can assign the service date rule to a settlement profile, and it will be converted to the relevant time zone. For further flexibility, a business add-in (BAdI) is offered to plug in your own service date rule (/SCMTMS/ BADI_FCP_SRV_DATE of enhancement spot /SCMTMS/ES_FCP).

The **Charges** tab contains the core information on the forwarding settlement document, which gives you the comprehensive overview of all charges that need to be billed to a business partner. All charges are retrieved from your forwarding order; however, they can be recalculated in some cases, such as collective order rate lookup where the charge is, for example, determined based on the aggregated weight of multiple forwarding orders that are collectively charged on one forwarding settlement document. Which charge items appear in the **Charges** tab depends on how you've configured the charge calculation and settlement process.

You have the same ability to switch the view of the charges and display them grouped or ungrouped as described in Chapter 10 for the charge calculation of the forwarding order. If you use a collective forwarding settlement document to settle multiple forwarding orders, then the charges appear as a sum for each charge type across all forwarding orders. In a standard settlement scenario based on incoterms, the charges are calculated per stage. As a result, you see a breakdown of the charges per stage in each settlement document (for both the shipper and ship-to party). You can see two forwarding settlement documents that were created to bill the charges to the prepaid and collect party based on incoterms in Figure 12.11.

The first settlement document is for the shipper—the prepaid agreement party. In our example, this is a customer in Tokyo, Japan. The second settlement document (below the first one) is for the ship-to party (the collect agreement party) who is a customer in Tucson, Arizona, in the United States.

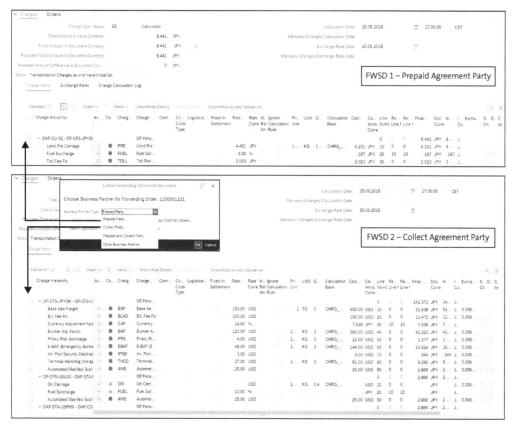

Figure 12.11 Forwarding Settlement Document Charges for Prepaid and Collect Agreement Party

After successful generation of a forwarding settlement document, the actual billing process and posting to SAP S/4HANA SD still must be accomplished. The **Statuses** tab gives a comprehensive overview of the various process steps from creation of a forwarding settlement document until the final billing in SAP S/4HANA SD. Two statuses ensure visibility of the progress of the entire settlement process. We provide you with example values of both statuses as we describe the posting to SAP S/4HANA:

- **Life Cycle Status**

  This status describes what step was performed last, along the entire billing process. After the initial creation of a new forwarding settlement document, the status is set to **In Process**.

- **Confirmation Status**

  Based on the interaction between the SAP TM functionality and SAP S/4HANA SD, multiple activities are performed when transmitting a settlement document to SD. Hence, a separate status is provided that meticulously tracks the interaction between the two modules. The initial status after the creation of the forwarding settlement document would be **Not Yet Posted** in SD.

12.3.3 Integrating Forwarding Settlement Documents with SD in SAP S/4HANA

You've learned throughout this chapter that SAP TM uses the SAP S/4HANA SD billing application to invoice customers. In Section 12.4, we'll highlight an alternative way of invoicing your customers by integrating SAP TM with SAP BRIM.

For now, let's dive into the details of the interaction of SAP TM and the SD functionality for billing.

Basic Customizing in SAP S/4HANA

To enable the SAP TM to SD communication, you must customize your SD billing functionality. Moreover, you're required to set up mapping rules between SAP TM and SD billing. Let's start with the essential settings in SAP S/4HANA SD billing:

1. As a first step in SD billing, you need to maintain *condition types*. Condition types are used to steer the logic of how the charges for a sales document are retrieved and calculated. In the communication with SAP TM, you must define a condition type for each charge type used in the SAP TM documents. In SD Customizing, follow the IMG path **Sales and Distribution • Basic Functions • Pricing • Pricing Control • Define Condition Types • Set Condition Types for Pricing**.

2. You must create a *pricing procedure*. You're required to assign the condition types to the pricing procedure that you've just defined. The pricing procedure is responsible for defining which condition types are used when creating an invoice. You can maintain hundreds of different condition types, but when you generate a billing document, only the ones that were assigned to a pricing procedure are picked up. You can group the condition types in a pricing procedure logically (e.g., by origin port charges, sea freight charges, and destination port charges in an ocean freight scenario). You can maintain multiple pricing procedures because they are assigned for each sales organization or customer. In Customizing, follow the IMG path **Sales and Distribution • Basic Functions • Pricing • Pricing Control • Define And Assign Pricing Procedures • Set Pricing Procedures**.

3. Last, you need to assign your pricing procedure to a sales organization. A sales organization can be assigned multiple pricing sequences. Navigate to Customizing by selecting **Sales and Distribution** · **Basic Functions** · **Pricing** · **Pricing Control** · **Define And Assign Pricing Procedures** · **Set Pricing Procedure Determination**.

Now let's focus on the mapping between SAP TM and SD billing:

1. First, you need to assign the forwarding settlement document type to an SD billing document type and assign a pricing procedure, item category, and sales document type to it. You can do this in the IMG path **Transportation Management** · **Settlement** · **Forwarding Settlement** · **Settings for Posting Forwarding Settlements** · **Assign SD Information for Posting**.

2. Furthermore, navigate to the following Customizing IMG path to perform the mapping of the SAP TM charge types and the SD condition types: **Transportation Management** · **Settlement** · **Forwarding Settlement** · **Settings for Posting Forwarding Settlements** · **Assign Condition Types**.

3. In addition to the mapping of charge types, you need to map your sales organizations as defined in SAP TM to sales organizations in SD. Recall from Chapter 3, Section 3.1.1, that the organizational structure defined in the SAP TM functionality differs from the organizational structure defined for SD and materials management (MM), which is defined in Customizing. Therefore, to post SD billing documents from forwarding settlement documents, you need to map the sales organization defined on the forwarding settlement document to the sales organization that is to be used on the SD billing document. As you can see in Figure 12.12, the ID of the SD sales organization is entered into the **BSG Org. Unit** field in Transaction PPOME.

If the organizational structure in SAP TM was created based on the integration report, this field is already prepopulated.

Integrating SAP TM 9.6 with SAP S/4HANA

If you want to transfer forwarding settlement documents from an SAP TM 9.6 system or a standalone instance of SAP TM functionality in SAP S/4HANA, the assignments mentioned in the preceding are configured in IMG path **Integration with Other SAP Components** · **Transportation Management** · **Billing** · **Settings for Posting Forwarding Settlements**.

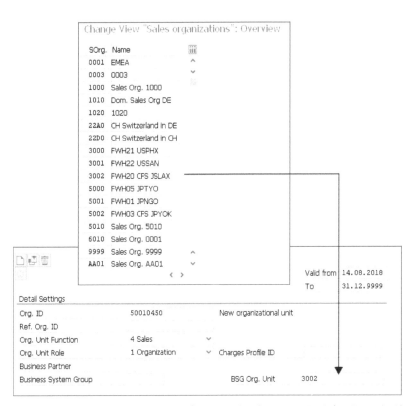

Figure 12.12 Mapping an SAP TM Sales Organization to an SD Sales Organization

Functional Process Flow

After you've successfully created the forwarding settlement document in SAP TM, you can execute a billing simulation in SAP TM before posting it to SAP S/4HANA SD. The charm of this capability is that you combine the logistical information from SAP TM with the tax data available in SAP S/4HANA. Click the **Preview Invoice** button in the top panel of the forwarding settlement document. SAP TM communicates the relevant logistical information to SD. SD, in turn, generates a PDF output file that you can view in SAP TM for each forwarding settlement document. This synchronous processing isn't visible to users. When you select the preview functionality, the actual PDF output file is visible immediately.

To enable this feature, you need to set up the corresponding output types in Customizing via the menu path **Sales and Distribution** • **Basic Functions** • **Output Determination** • **Output Determination** • **Output Determination Using the Condition**

Technique • **Maintain Output Determination for Billing Documents** • **Maintain Output Types**.

Because the logic of billing simulation is active and implemented in standard SAP TM, it doesn't require any particular Customizing. It's possible for you to enhance the logic (e.g., if you have additional SAP TM fields that need to be sent to SD). A provided BAdI on both the SD and SAP TM sides is available for such enhancements. On the SD side, use the enhancement implementation `TM_BIL_IMPL01` for enhancement spot `BADI_SD_BIL_PRINT01`. In SAP TM, the BAdI `/SCMTMS/BADI_FWSD_PRINT_SIM` needs to be implemented for enhancement spot `/SCMTMS/ES_FWSD`. This is the same enhancement spot used for the regular printing of SD invoices.

After the forwarding settlement document is consistent and ready to be posted to SD, you can click the **Post** button in the top panel of the forwarding settlement document. Alternatively, you mark multiple forwarding settlement documents and execute the action from a POWL. You can also use a batch job to post the data to SD.

Mass Posting of Forwarding Settlement Documents

SAP TM includes a standard report to mass-create forwarding settlement documents. You can use the same report to post your created forwarding settlement documents to SAP S/4HANA SD billing en masse. Navigate to Transaction SE38 in your backend system and run report `/SCMTMS/CFIR_CREATE_BATCH`.

A billing document is created directly in SD as depicted in Figure 12.13. Depending on your charge calculation level in SAP TM, the corresponding billing items are generated in SD. If you did a header calculation of charges, the corresponding billing document in SD contains one billing item. If you calculated the charges per transportation stage, one billing item is created per stage.

Integration of SAP TM 9.6 with an External SAP S/4HANA System

As mentioned in other sections of this book, this book concentrates on the SAP TM *in* SAP S/4HANA. Therefore, we've only described the process of posting a forwarding settlement document that is created in SAP S/4HANA.

However, we can still use the forwarding settlement functionality in a separate SAP TM system. In this case, we need to configure the integration with an SAP S/4HANA system to transfer the forwarding settlement documents. The processing of these documents in the SD functionality of SAP S/4HANA is equivalent to the process we described in this section.

Figure 12.13 Posted Forwarding Settlement Document and SD Billing Document

In Figure 12.14, you can see the overview of the most important statuses of a forwarding settlement document. After a forwarding settlement document has been created and saved in SAP TM in step ❶, the **Lifecycle Status** is set to **In Process**. As we've mentioned, it's possible to change certain information in the forwarding settlement document—such as an alternative address for a business partner—without causing inconsistencies. If you change billing-relevant information in the forwarding order, the two documents won't be consistent anymore. This might happen if, for example, the route of a forwarding order needs to be changed due to a missed cutoff, such as a missed aircraft or vessel departure, and it results in a recalculation of charges.

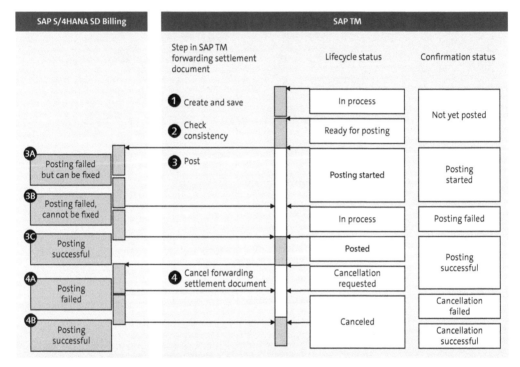

Figure 12.14 Functional Process of SAP TM to SD Billing Integration

Only if the document is consistent is the **Lifecycle Status** updated to **Ready for Posting ❷**. Without consistency, you can't trigger the posting to SD, and the forwarding settlement document is marked with an **Inconsistent** flag in the **Statuses** tab. As soon as you trigger the posting of the forwarding settlement document to SD in step ❸, the **Lifecycle Status** changes. The **Confirmation Status** shows **Posting Started** until you receive a confirmation that the SD billing document is created successfully. In the event of a failed transfer, it depends on the error handling whether a message is returned to the SAP TM functionality.

If it's possible to fix a transfer error directly in SD—say, because of locking issues or a financial period closure—then the posting can be reprocessed in SD. Until the reprocessing, the **Lifecycle Status** and **Confirmation Status** in SAP TM remain as **Posting Started ❸Ⓐ**, respectively. Only if the error can't be fixed ❸Ⓑ or the transfer is successful ❸Ⓒ are both the **Lifecycle Status** and **Confirmation Status** updated on the forwarding settlement document accordingly. Similarly to the inconsistencies that occurred before you posted the forwarding settlement document to SD, you might still have to change invoicing-relevant data in the forwarding order.

Consequently, you can cancel the forwarding settlement document in both SAP TM and SAP S/4HANA SD in step ❹. The **Lifecycle Status** and **Confirmation Status** are updated accordingly in steps ❹Ⓐ and ❹Ⓑ. It's still possible to cancel the forwarding settlement document by creating a credit memo.

Credit Memos for Forwarding Orders

The credit memo on the forwarding order side is used by freight forwarders and carriers to correct originally invoiced amounts on a billing document. You can generate a credit memo by navigating to your forwarding settlement document and selecting **Follow Up • Create Credit Memo**. This is also possible directly from a POWL. Remember that a credit memo can be created only after your forwarding settlement document has been posted to SD, and a billing document has been generated.

With SAP TM, you can generate credit memos for both individual forwarding settlement documents and collective settlement documents that contain multiple forwarding orders. After you've generated a credit memo, you'll see that it has the same structure as the forwarding settlement document. The major difference is that the **Charges** tab contains three columns listing the charges. In Figure 12.15, you can see that in addition to the invoiced amount, a credit amount can be entered.

In the **Credit Amount** column, you can enter all deductions from the settlement amount. It's possible to generate multiple credit memos for one settlement document. As a result, the **Credit Remaining Amount** column shows the remaining billing amount. SAP TM validates and ensures that you can't give a higher credit than the invoiced amount.

Prior to the posting to SD, you can use the **Preview Invoice** functionality if you want to simulate a preview of the credit memo in SD together with the tax information. Like the settlement document, you must ensure consistency in the credit memo before you can transfer it. After you've successfully posted the credit memo to SD, a new document is generated of type credit memo. The **Lifecycle Status** of the credit memo is updated after it has been successfully posted to SD as **Credit Memo Posted**. It's also possible to cancel a credit memo, which changes its status to **Cancellation Requested** and **Canceled** if successful.

Charge Hierarchy	Item Description	Charge Type	Line Number	Invoiced Amount
☑ ⌄ TM9-CU-DLS1 TM9-CU-AHM			0	110,90
Base Charges	Base Charges	TM7-BASE	10	20,00
Basic freight charges	Basic freight charges	TM7-BASIC	20	56,67
Pick Up Charges	Pick Up Charges	TM7-PICK	30	8,00
Fuel Surcharge	Fuel Surcharge	TM9-FUEL	40	4,23
Subtotal	Subtotal		50	
service tax	service tax	TM9-TAX	60	
⌄ Sum	Sum		70	
Documentation Charges	Documentation Charges	TM7-DOCF	80	3,33
Packing/Unpacking Charges	Packing/Unpacking Char	TM7-PACK	90	6,67

Currency - Invoiced Amount	Credit Amount	Currency	Credit Remaining Amount	Currency - Credit Remaining Amount
EUR	64,23	EUR		
EUR	20,00	EUR	20,00	EUR
EUR	10,00	EUR	56,67	EUR
EUR	8,00	EUR	8,00	EUR
EUR	4,23	EUR	4,23	EUR
EUR				
EUR				
EUR				
EUR	3,33	EUR	3,33	EUR
EUR	6,67	EUR	6,67	EUR

Figure 12.15 Charge Details of a Credit Memo

To use the credit memo for the forwarding settlement document, you need to perform a few Customizing steps:

1. A credit memo has its own document type that contains a number range and a reason code for a credit memo. You can define a credit memo type in Customizing in IMG path **Transportation Management · Settlement · Forwarding Settlement · Define Credit Memo Reason Codes and Types for Forwarding SDs**. The credit memo type can be assigned to your forwarding settlement document type.

2. In the same Customizing path, you can maintain reason codes and assign them to the credit memo. A description of a reason code could, for example, be **Delay in Transport** or **Deviating Cargo Measures**. The reason code generally has three characters with a free-text field for a description.

3. All other Customizing settings for the forwarding settlement document on both the SAP TM and SD sides must be in place. In addition, you need to map the reason

codes from the SAP TM credit memo to SD order reason codes. Navigate to Customizing by following the IMG path **Transportation Management · Settlement · Forwarding Settlement · Settings for Posting Forwarding Settlements · Assign SAP TM Credit Memo Reason Code to Order Reason Code**.

Technical Integration

The posting of a forwarding settlement document from SAP TM to SD is processed via direct business logic. However, if you're using a standalone SAP TM instance in SAP S/4HANA that isn't in the same system as the SAP S/4HANA SD functionality, the integration needs to be done via service-oriented architecture (SOA) services. In this case, the terminology changes from *posting a forwarding settlement document* to *transferring a forwarding settlement document*. Alternatively, it's also possible to set up the connection between a SAP TM system and an SAP S/4HANA system via Web Services Reliable Messaging (WSRM).

Standard SOA Services for SAP TM–SAP S/4HANA SD Integration

SAP delivers eight standard SOA services for transactional integration:

- `CustomerFreightInvoiceRequestSUITERequest_Out_V1` (and `_In`)
  Send a request to create or change a forwarding settlement from SAP TM and receive it in SAP S/4HANA.
- `CustomerFreightInvoiceRequestSUITEConfirmation_Out_V1` (and `_In`)
  Send the confirmation and status change for customer invoices from SAP S/4HANA and receive them in SAP TM.
- `CustomerFreightInvoiceRequestSUITECancellationRequest_Out_V1` (and `_In`)
  Send a request to cancel a forwarding settlement from SAP TM and receive it in SAP S/4HANA.
- `CustomerFreightInvoiceRequestSUITESimulate_Out` (and `_In`)
  SAP TM offers to show a preview of an invoice in SAP TM. Send the forwarding settlement from SAP TM to SAP S/4HANA. Receive a PDF of the SAP S/4HANA SD billing document.

12.3.4   Business Scenarios in the Forwarding Settlement Process

You've learned so far about the standard capabilities of the SAP TM forwarding settlement process. However, because different companies can have entirely different billing requirements, we want to highlight specific scenarios in this section that SAP TM supports.

Prepayment Scenario

In the freight-forwarding and ocean liner industries, it's a common business practice to grant customers a certain credit limit. To minimize risks, there are cases where customers aren't conceded any credits. A *cash customer* must pay the invoice for all prepaid charges of the transportation in advance. In such a scenario, you allow creation of a forwarding order for a cash customer but prevent it from being executed until the payment has been received. As a result, for the system to block the forwarding order, you need to indicate that the specific business partner is a cash customer.

When setting up your customer contracts, the forwarding agreements, you can maintain a **Pre-Payment** payment term. Alternatively, you can store this payment term directly in the business partner master data of your customer. In Customizing for payment terms, you can define a block reason (e.g., **Payment not Received**). Whenever you have a contract (i.e., a forwarding agreement) with a cash customer, you can assign a payment term containing the block reason **Payment not Received** to the agreement or business partner record. After a forwarding order is created for the cash customer, you can calculate the charges. Based on the charge calculation from the forwarding agreement, the payment term is retrieved into the forwarding order, and the document is automatically blocked for execution. The same behavior is invoked if you store the payment term on the business partner and as soon as you assign the business partner to the forwarding order. To still allow the settlement of this order, the creation of a forwarding settlement document is possible despite the block status of the forwarding order. As a result, you can follow the forwarding settlement process as described and create an invoice.

Unfortunately, this feature isn't yet fully integrated with the SAP S/4HANA SD billing component. The receipt of the actual payment from the customer in the SD functionality doesn't automatically release a blocked forwarding order. Instead, a user must manually navigate to the **Business Partner** tab in the affected forwarding order and select the checkbox for the corresponding business partner (e.g., select **Payment Received** for the shipper). As you learned in Chapter 4, Section 4.2.1, SAP TM is integrated with the credit limit check application. SAP TM automatically deactivates the credit limit check after the payment term is marked as **Pre-Payment**.

Settlement for Buyer's Consolidation

A buyer's consolidation is a very common service that freight forwarders and carriers offer to their customers. A buyer's consolidation is a scenario where the LSP picks up cargo from multiple origins (e.g., manufacturers in different countries). The cargo is transported to a container freight station (CFS) and consolidated into one container. From the CFS onward, the cargo travels in the same container until the final destination. It's relevant for the settlement process that a customer—in this case, a ship-to party—needs to be invoiced for the consolidated amount and not for each individual forwarding order. As a result, you can generate one forwarding settlement document for all forwarding orders in the same container in a freight booking. Each container in the freight booking (**Cargo Management** tab) can be marked with the value **B** in the **Consolidation Container** field. You can create the forwarding settlement document directly from the freight booking or from one of the consolidated forwarding orders. As a result, the combined charges for all forwarding orders that are consolidated in this container are calculated.

The actual creation of the forwarding settlement documents depends on the incoterms: if the incoterm is maintained as free-on-board, multiple forwarding settlement documents are generated for the pre-carriage legs. One forwarding settlement document per forwarding order is generated because every forwarding order has a different shipper. For both the main carriage and on-carriage, one consolidated forwarding settlement document is generated for the collect agreement party containing all forwarding orders that were consolidated in the same container in the freight booking. The freight booking is shown as a reference in the **Orders** section. In the example of the incoterm, where the ship-to party pays all charges, only one forwarding settlement document is generated on the importing side. This document contains all charges for the pre-carriage based on the individual forwarding orders and the charges for main carriage and on-carriage based on the consolidation in the freight booking.

Export versus Import Forwarding Orders

Keep in mind that you always have two forwarding orders in an international shipment: one export forwarding order and one import forwarding order. You generate all settlement documents for the shippers from the exporting side and the settlement document for the ship-to party from the import forwarding order. Depending on the incoterm, an exporting organization might settle its charges with the importing organization, to be compensated for any incurred cost. This is always required when the shipper doesn't pay for pre-carriage and main carriage.

We provide a deeper insight into the settlement process between exporting and importing organizations in Section 12.3.5 for internal settlements.

The charge calculation follows a specific logic to find the correct forwarding agreement item to retrieve the charges for the forwarding orders:

1. Set the calculation level to Stages so that the consolidated charges are calculated only for distances the cargo traveled together in the container.

2. You can maintain your own forwarding agreement item and select the **Buyers Consolidation** checkbox for it. In the creation of the settlement document, the charges are picked up from this item in the customer's forwarding agreement for all stages that were transported in a consolidated container.

3. If no such item is maintained, SAP TM retrieves the rates from an agreement item with shipping type *full container load* (FCL) or *full truckload* (FTL) but never *less than truckload* (LTL) or *less than container load* (LCL).

You also need to follow a specific process in the sales organization. Each forwarding order that has been consolidated into the buyer's consolidation might have been captured by a different sales organization. If all sales organizations across the forwarding orders are equal, the buyer's consolidation functionality can be used. If the organizations in the forwarding orders deviate, SAP TM uses the purchasing organization of the consolidated freight booking. It's crucial that this organization is maintained as a forwarding house, so it can be used as a sales organization, as well.

One forwarding settlement document is generated for all forwarding orders. The **Orders** tab in the forwarding settlement document lists the freight bookings where the buyer's consolidation has been marked and that contain the corresponding freight units. In the **Details** section, the container item is displayed together with the forwarding orders.

Settlement for Shipper's Consolidation

We can apply the concepts introduced in the buyer's consolidation scenario to a shipper's consolidation scenario as well. In this scenario, a shipper sends consolidated goods in a full container for both pre-carriage and main carriage. In the importing country, the container is deconsolidated, and the cargo items are separately transported to multiple ship-to parties. Depending on the incoterms, SAP TM generates one settlement document to group all pre-carriage and main carriage charges in one forwarding settlement document that is charged to the shipper. The charges for the delivery legs are included in the same forwarding settlement document only in the case of an incoterm, where the shipper pays for all charges. Otherwise, separate invoices are generated for each delivery leg to settle with each ship-to party separately.

Whether multiple forwarding orders are shipped in a consolidated way as a shipper's consolidation is determined by SAP TM. You must select the container in the **Cargo Management** tab of a freight booking to mark the container as a shipper's consolidation. This triggers the **SC** flag to be set in each forwarding order, which can also be done manually. The rest of the settings are like the buyer's consolidation. For example, you must mark at least one agreement line item as a shipper's consolidation item.

Flexible Invoicing

We've introduced to you various ways to generate a forwarding settlement document. Apart from the functionality introduced so far, you have even more flexibility in how to generate the settlement documents. This capability strongly supports LSPs and, in particular, rail carriers. Flexible invoicing allows you to cluster your relevant charge types into *settlement groups*. An example is that a railway company might decide to invoice all charges from the main transportation in one invoice, all accessorial services of an order in a second invoice, and, finally, any peripheral charges in a third invoice. After you create your settlement document, an enhanced popup opens. You can choose for which party and settlement group the forwarding settlement document should be created, as shown in Figure 12.16.

You can trigger the generation of the settlement document for either of the two business partners and any group of charges individually. In addition, the batch report to generate forwarding settlement documents generates forwarding settlement documents only for a specific settlement group. You can still use the collective creation of forwarding settlement documents from a POWL. All selected forwarding orders are combined in one forwarding settlement document for the same settlement group. You can create a settlement group in Customizing via the IMG path **Transportation Management • Settlement • Define Settlement Groups and Settlement Rules**. Note in Figure 12.16 that there is also a default settlement group **Unassigned** that will collect all charge types that aren't assigned to a settlement group in Customizing. This settlement group will be displayed even if all charge types on the forwarding order are assigned to settlement groups.

Figure 12.16 Creation of Forwarding Settlement Documents with Flexible Invoicing

Multiple settlement groups can be clustered in a *settlement rule*. In a settlement rule, you can define more time-relevant parameters for the settlement document generation, such as a billing schedule and the service date rule. To use the settlement rule, which contains the settlement groups, you need to assign it to your settlement profile.

12.3.5   Internal Settlement

In Section 12.1.2, we already introduced the master data object of an internal agreement. In this section, we'll now delve into how the internal settlement process is performed in the SAP TM functionality and how it needs to be set up. We'll also look at different scenarios in which the internal settlement functionality is used.

In general, the internal settlement process is defined like this: a purchasing organization cross-charges the cost for a shipment to a sales organization, which generates the actual revenue with a customer. Let's take a few examples of different business practices:

- In the freight-forwarding industry, it's very common for CFSs/gateways to procure their own capacities with ocean liners or airlines. Capacities are procured and internally provided. A CFS/gateway charges an internal rate to the exporting organization. The incoterms play a major role because an exporting organization might only partially settle the charges with the customer.

- Importing organizations in freight forwarding are generally in charge of any inland transportation via rail or truck in the importing country. This means that an importing organization can settle the charges of the transportation cost to the exporting organization.

- In the trucking industry, it's a common business practice for a service center to own a pool of resources such as trucks and trailers. The service center provides other internal sales or planning organizations with the required capacities. In this case, the sales or planning organization is charged internally by the service center.

SAP TM supports the internal settlement process for both intracompany and intercompany charge settlement. Intracompany charge settlement happens between branches or divisions of the same company code; for example, a gateway in Newark, New Jersey, settles the transportation cost to a freight station in New York City. An intercompany settlement takes place between legal companies with independent company codes (e.g., if a CFS and export station are in separate countries).

Internal Settlement Process for Logistics Service Providers

Let's use an example to illustrate an intracompany settlement process with a cross-company shipment execution. Section 12.3.1 covered the settlement process based on incoterms. Now let's complicate this picture to represent an authentic example of the interaction in the settlement process among internal organizational units. We summarize the lessons learned in this chapter and include both a forwarding and freight settlement document creation.

In Figure 12.17, Shipper 1 in England transports cargo to Ship-To Party 1 in Singapore. Shipper 1 and Ship-To Party 1 have arranged the incoterm free-on-board (FOB). Consequently, Shipper 1 is responsible for paying for the transport to the port of loading, and Ship-To Party 1 pays for the rest of the transportation, including customs duty. Any mode of transport and business scenario can be supported, but our example is based on ocean freight (the equivalent for air freight appears in parentheses).

In step ❶, you receive an export forwarding order in the export station in London. The shipper contacts the local forwarding office to arrange for the transport. Shipper 1 is listed as the prepaid agreement party. Ship-To Party 1 is listed as the ship-to party, but the importing station in Singapore is marked as the collect agreement party.

In step ❷, the export station in London arranges for a pickup service (a local trucker, perhaps) to transport the goods from the customer to the CFS (gateway) in Southampton. A freight order is generated.

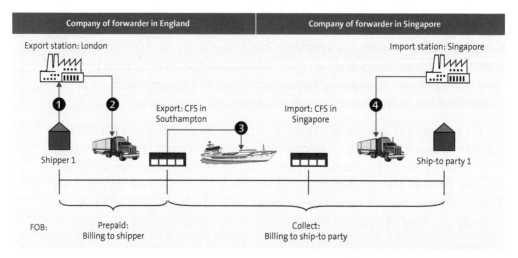

Figure 12.17 Business Scenario for Settlement Process in SAP TM

In step ❸, the CFS (gateway) in Southampton has already procured capacity on a vessel (on a plane), leaving on a voyage (departure) from Southampton to Singapore with an ocean liner (airline), reflected by a freight booking. As you learned in Chapter 4, Section 4.2, the generation of an export freight booking triggers the generation of an import freight booking and consequently an import forwarding order.

In step ❹, after the vessel (plane) arrives in Singapore, the importing station is informed and generates another freight order for the pickup of the freight in the CFS (gateway) and delivery to Ship-to Party 1.

In this example, a total of seven settlement documents are generated. Figure 12.18 shows the creation of the settlement documents.

Let's walk through this figure. Based on the free-on-board incoterm, the exporting station in London creates forwarding settlement document 1 for the prepaid party (Shipper 1) from the export forwarding order ❶. These are the only charges the shipper must cover. The same exporting organization also arranges the pickup and must settle the charges for the trucker. Freight settlement document 1 is generated for the pre-carriage ❷. The CFS (gateway) in Southampton generates a freight settlement document to settle the main leg charges with the ocean liner (airline) ❸.

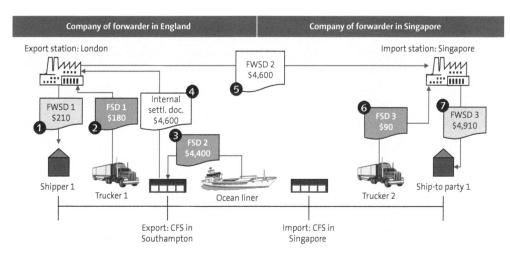

Figure 12.18 Creation of Internal Settlement Documents

An internal settlement document is generated between the CFS (gateway) and the exporting station, again based on the export forwarding order ❹. The intracompany settlement document recovers the cost for the procurement organization—in our example, the CFS (gateway) Southampton of the main leg. To calculate the internal charges, in the top menu of the forwarding order, select **Charges/Settlement** • **Calculate Internal Charges**.

The creation of the intracompany settlement document can be executed manually from a POWL that lists all freight bookings/freight orders that require intracompany settlement. To find this POWL in the SAP Fiori launchpad, navigate to the **Settlement** tab, and open the **Forwarding Orders for Internal Settlement Worklist** tile in which you can open the query **All Forwarding Orders for Internal Settlement**. Notice that not only the forwarding orders are listed in this POWL but also the freight order/ freight booking documents that are associated with the forwarding order for the internal settlement process. You can click the **Create Internal Settlement** button to generate the internal settlement document. Alternatively, you can use a batch job for report /SCMTMS/CFIR_CREATE_BATCH to generate the internal settlement documents.

Internal Settlement Document

The POWL shows relevant freight bookings or freight orders for the generation of an internal settlement document only if you've specified a corresponding settlement rule. A settlement rule is defined in Customizing and determines the behavior for generating internal settlement documents based on the execution status of a freight booking or freight order. In our example, we assume the settlement rule is **Executed**. Consequently, the internal settlement document is ready for generation only after the freight booking of the main leg is fully executed.

In our example, the agreed-upon incoterm is free-on-board. Consequently, the exporting organization transfers the cost to the importing organization in Singapore, which will bill Ship-To Party 1 as the collect payer for the main leg service (**❺** in Figure 12.18). This settlement document FWSD 2 is considered an external settlement document and is generated as a regular forwarding settlement document. In step **❻**, the importing organization generates FSD 3 for the delivery charges. Last, in step **❼**, FWSD 3 is generated based on the import forwarding order to bill the collect charges to Ship-To Party 1.

Now let's highlight the difference between the intracompany settlement process and the flow for intercompany settlements. Let's assume our CFS (gateway) is located in a different country—say, Ireland, instead of England. In this case, the sales organization in London and the CFS (gateway) in Ireland are assigned to different company codes. The internal settlement between the CFS (gateway) and the station are considered an *inter*company settlement. The major change in the process lies in the integration with the SD functionality. You would not see a difference in the actual internal settlement flow in SAP TM.

Table 12.5 summarizes the different cost and revenue components of each organization for our intracompany settlement example.

Export Station London		Export CFS Southampton		Import CFS Singapore		Import Station Singapore	
Cost	Rev.	Cost	Rev.	Cost	Rev.	Cost	Rev.
$180 pickup charges	$210 prepaid charges	$4,400 main leg charges	–	–	–	$90 delivery charges	$4,910 collect charges
$4,600 main leg intracompany settlement	$4,600 main leg charges	–	$4,600 main leg intracompany settlement	–	–	$4,600 main leg intercompany settlement	–
–	$300	–	$200	–	–	–	$220

Table 12.5 Cost and Revenue per Organizational Unit

There are generally two ways to calculate the rates that are to be settled internally. First, you have the choice to set up internal rates in an agreement between the sales and purchasing organizations. These rates represent the standard cost for a purchasing organization. The standard cost is an average price of procuring transportation services and can even include a profit margin. As a result, it's possible to handle purchasing organizations as profit centers that compete to offer the best rates for capacities in the organization. You can maintain such rates in internal agreements, as described in Section 12.1.2.

Recall the introduction to cost distribution in Chapter 11, Section 11.2. Based on the cost distribution functionality, you can determine the actual cost of a freight order or freight booking allocated to the forwarding order items. You have the option to use these actual costs, which need to be paid to the service provider for an internal settlement between the purchasing organization and the sales organization. The core difference from the standard cost scenario is that instead of an average of the cost, the billing-relevant amounts of the actual service provider charges are used. For consolidated shipments, the cost distribution supports the apportionment of the cost to all affected forwarding orders.

Basic Customizing and Master Data in SAP TM

The functionality of internal settlement in SAP TM is well integrated with and dependent upon other master data and several settings. In this section, we highlight the essentials of setting up an internal settlement process.

The basis for every settlement process is the charges and the setup of SAP TM Transportation Charge Management. Refer to Chapter 10 to learn what basic settings are required. You can directly assign a calculation profile to a business partner of type sold-to party or to the regular charges profile. If both are maintained, the profile assigned to the business partner takes precedence.

As with the regular settlement process in SAP TM, you need to define a settlement profile. You can use an existing profile from the regular settlement process that is assigned to a charges profile, as you're used to from Section 12.3.1. Remember that the settlement profile of the purchasing organization will be picked up. Like the calculation profile, you could assign a settlement profile to a business partner in the type sold-to party, which would take precedence.

Since the internal settlement document uses the same object as the forwarding settlement document, there is no separate document type Customizing for internal settlement documents. You need to define an internal settlement document type in Customizing. Navigate to **Transportation Management • Settlement • Forwarding Settlement • Define Forwarding Settlement Type**. The forwarding order type needs to be enabled for internal charge calculation and settlement in Customizing.

You can define a specific time you want an internal settlement document to be ready for generation. This is achieved by an internal settlement rule that you can assign to each stage type of a movement type. Navigate to **Transportation Management • Forwarding Order Management • Define Stage Type Sequence for Movement Types** to determine the point in time when internal settlement should be performed (e.g., only when the stage was executed).

Most important, you must have maintained an internal agreement between the purchasing organization and the sales organization. As introduced in Section 12.1.2, an internal agreement can be valid between one or many purchasing organizations and one or many sales organizations. If you want to base the internal charges on the standard cost, you must maintain charge types with amounts or internal rate tables.

Purchasing Organizations

Be sure to model your purchasing organizations with the organizational unit function *forwarding house*. The reason is that a purchasing organization interacts as a
sales organization internally when settling internal charges to another organizational unit. In our example, this would be the case for the CFS (gateway) in Southampton.

To use the actual transportation cost for internal settlements, you require a slightly
different setup. The way you generate your internal settlement documents and the
integration to the SD functionality are similar. You've performed the setup of the
cost distribution for LSPs, as introduced in Chapter 11, Section 11.2, and all the Customizing steps. The key difference lies in the creation of an internal agreement. You
still need to define an internal agreement but no rates or rate tables. Instead, you set
the **Charge Usage** field of the transportation charge calculation sheet as **Internal**. In
addition, you must maintain one charge type with the calculation method **9—Internal Charge Calculation**. The cost is picked up from the corresponding execution documents, freight order, and/or freight booking.

Integration with the Sales and Distribution Functionality in SAP S/4HANA

After you've successfully generated the various settlement documents, they need to
be posted to the SD functionality. For the internal settlement, we need to distinguish
between the intracompany and intercompany settlement documents. The intracompany settlement document doesn't generate a billing document in SAP S/4HANA SD;
a regular forwarding settlement document does. Instead, reposting would take place
in SAP S/4HANA SD. Remember that the cost of procuring a service is always posted
to the purchasing organization (in our example, the CFS in Southampton). When you
post the intracompany settlement document to the SD functionality, the settled cost
in the forwarding order from the corresponding freight orders or bookings is
reposted from the purchasing organization (the CFS in Southampton) to the sales
organization (the exporting station in London). As a result, it's possible to map the
primary cost to a cost center or an internal order. We already discussed how the intercompany settlement document has a different sort of integration with the SD functionality. It simply generates a regular billing document in SD.

12

> **Integration of SAP TM 9.6 with an External SAP S/4HANA System**
>
> As mentioned in other sections of this book already, this book concentrates on SAP TM *in* SAP S/4HANA. Therefore, we've only described the process of posting an internal settlement document that is created in SAP S/4HANA.
>
> However, we can still use the internal settlement functionality in a separate SAP TM system. In this case, we need to configure the integration with an SAP S/4HANA system to transfer the internal settlement documents. The processing of these documents in the SD functionality of SAP S/4HANA is equivalent to the process we described in this section.

Let's take a high-level look at the Customizing steps required to set up the SD functionality (refer to the SAP S/4HANA configuration guide for more details):

- The standard integration for forwarding settlement needs to be configured to enable the intercompany process, as described in Section 12.3.1 and Section 12.3.3. A mapping of SAP TM sales organizations to SD organizational units is required.

- You need to map your sales organizations and purchasing organizations to the corresponding cost centers or internal orders in SD. This is required for intracompany settlements where the charges are being posted from the original purchasing organization of a freight order or booking to the sales organization of the forwarding order.

  Navigate to Customizing by selecting **Transportation Management · Settlement · Forwarding Settlement · Settings for Posting Intracompany Settlements · Assign Internal Order/Cost Center to Sender Organization** as well as **Assign Internal Order/Cost Center to Receiver Organization**. In this case, the purchasing organization is the sender of the intracompany settlement document, and the sales organization is the receiver organization.

- In addition, you're required to assign your charge types to primary cost elements in SD. Navigate to Customizing by selecting **Transportation Management · Settlement · Forwarding Settlement · Settings for Posting Intracompany Settlements · Assign Transportation Charges to Cost Elements**.

- You have the flexibility to enhance the methods for intracompany scenarios based on available BAdIs. This gives you the flexibility to develop a custom logic for determining cost elements, cost centers, and internal orders. The available BAdI is called `TCM_SE_CFIRSUITE_RQ` with the method `INBOUND_PROCESSING` (parameter `CS_CO_DOC`). Similarly, for intercompany settlement, you can implement a BAdI to influence the assignment of cost objects (e.g., cost centers): BAdI `TCM_SE_CFIR-SUITE_RQ` and method `INBOUND_PROCESSING` (parameter `CT_KOMFKGN`).

Configuring the Integration of Internal Settlement with an SAP TM 9.6 System

When not using SAP TM in the same SAP S/4HANA instance as the SD and MM functionalities, the configuration of the integration will be different. The mapping of charge types and organizational units will then be performed via the IMG path **Integration with Other SAP Components • Transportation Management • Invoice Integration**. In subsequent menu entries, you'll find the same Customizing activities as described earlier, but they are tailored to the scenario of integrating external SAP TM functionality to SAP S/4HANA (e.g., an SAP TM 9.6 system).

Internal Settlement Process for Trucking Businesses

In addition to the process of internal settlements for LSPs based on forwarding orders, as described for the international shipment scenario, you can generate internal settlement documents for resources. This functionality supports trucking companies that own trucks and trailers, for example. A procurement organization arranges a trucking service by using the truck and trailer of another organization that owns the resources. An internal agreement can be maintained between the procurement organization and the organization that owns the resources. These rates are used to generate internal settlement documents between the two organizations. After a successful internal charge calculation, you can generate the internal settlement document directly from the freight order by selecting **Charges/Settlement • Create Internal Settlement Document**.

The settlement integration with SD works similarly as described in the previous section. The resource-owning unit is the sales organization that sends the internal settlement document. The purchasing organization using the truck and trailer is the receiver of the internal charges. Based on the sales organization, the system derives the purchasing organization, the cost centers, or internal orders.

Group Logistics Settlement for Shippers

A very common scenario for large companies with shipping demands is to consolidate all transportation tasks in one BU. This is usually an independent BU within a shipper company that is focused only on organizing and managing transports. Such BUs often act as internal LSPs, which is why we also deal with this process in this chapter. We call such a scenario *group company logistics*. The main advantage is that, as a shipper, you can bundle the transportation demand of your company in one organization, giving it respectively more buying power to negotiate freight rates. In addition, the visibility and process standardization are improved in an organization that solely focuses on transportation.

The key difference in a group logistics scenario is that the BU that manages the transports consolidates orders from multiple other lines of business of the group. A manufacturing company might have different lines of business for the various product segments it produces. The demand for transportation of all these shippers will be consolidated by the logistics company. The transportation services are paid by the logistics branch. Because freight orders will contain goods from multiple orders, it's imperative for the logistics branch to distribute the charges back to the BUs that caused the demand. This process can be managed with internal settlements:

1. You can use cost distribution to allocate the charges from freight orders to the order documents.

2. The internal settlement document is created for each BU that had freight involved in the transportation.

3. The internal settlement document creates an intercompany SD billing document, which in turn creates an entry in financial accounting.

The key settings to support this process are very similar to the internal settlement process we described earlier in this chapter.

12.3.6 Profitability Analysis

CO-PA in SAP TM is used to provide an LSP or carrier with a view on the margin per forwarding order. It's not applicable for shipper solutions. The foundation of CO-PA lies in the Transportation Charge Management and settlement, which was introduced earlier in this chapter and in Chapter 10. It accumulates all revenue components in a forwarding order and calculates the delta against all cost components that were incurred as part of the shipment execution to calculate the profitability of a shipment.

The forwarding order has a **Profitability** tab. You can trigger the calculation of the profitability by selecting **Charges/Settlement** • **Calculate Profitability**.

Figure 12.19 shows an example of the results in a forwarding order with calculated cost, revenue, and profitability. Note that not only the aggregated costs and revenue is shown but the costs and revenue per charge category. Recall from Chapter 10 that charge types are assigned to charge categories to classify their purpose. This configuration is useful also in this context as we usually use different charge types for buying charges than for selling charges. With the use of the charge categories in CO-PA, however, we can analyze the margin per charge category, which could represent, for example, a service product.

Planned Profitability						Expected Profitability					
Profit	45.337 JPY	Profit Percentage		13.72 ■		Profit	48.796 JPY	Profit Percentage		14.77 ■	
Revenue	330.431 JPY					Revenue	330.431 JPY				
Cost	285.094 JPY					Cost	281.635 JPY				

Profitability Status

Profitability Status Calculated
Profitability Details

Standard

Charge Category	Charge Type	Planned Cost	Planned Revenue	Planned Profit Amount	Planned Profit Perc...	Pla...	Expected Cost	Expected Revenue	Expected Profit Amo...	Expected Profit Per...
> Additional charges		142	38.973	38.831	99.64	■	142	38.973	38.831	99.64
> Transport charge & A		2.500	187	2.313-	92.52-	●	2.500	187	2.313-	92.52-
> Basic Freight		159.675	206.550	46.875	22.69	■	156.216	206.550	50.334	24.37
> Destination Port Char		45.898	7.918	37.980-	82.75-	●	45.898	7.918	37.980-	82.75-
> Miscellaneous Charge		13.769		13.769-	100.00-	●	13.769		13.769-	100.00-
> Origin Port Charges		22.949	3.797	19.162-	83.50-	●	22.949	3.797	19.162-	83.50-
> Other Charges		40.161	66.785	26.624	39.87	■	40.161	66.785	26.624	39.87
> Transport Costs (Carr			6.231	6.231	100.00	■		6.231	6.231	100.00

Figure 12.19 Profitability Analysis in a Forwarding Order

To calculate the profitability, you first need to calculate revenue and cost. The revenue is calculated based purely on the charge calculation for forwarding orders, which are based on forwarding agreements. The cost components are derived from three sources: freight orders, freight bookings, and internal rates. Consequently, you first need to set up the Transportation Charge Management component as a prerequisite, as described in Chapter 10. You need to make sure that the charge calculation for forwarding orders, freight orders, and freight bookings has been executed. Both the cost distribution and internal charge calculation need to be set up and executed as described in Chapter 11, Section 11.2 and Section 12.3.5, respectively, to enable CO-PA.

Which cost or revenue components are included in CO-PA isn't configurable. SAP TM generally uses all charge types of revenue and cost for the comparison. SAP TM calculates both a *planned* and *expected profitability*. The major difference between planned and expected profitability is that planned profitability is based on the charge calculation in forwarding orders, freight orders, and freight bookings. The expected profitability is calculated based on the settled amounts in the forwarding, internal, and freight settlement documents.

12.4   Settlement with SAP Billing and Revenue Innovation Management

Customer billing done with the billing and financial components of SAP S/4HANA is quite flexible. It supports full control of integration and many localizations to special billing and taxation standards of a variety of countries worldwide. However, for companies selling logistics services, the billing flexibility of SAP S/4HANA may sometimes not be sufficient. Cargo and logistics customers need end-to-end solutions that allow them to execute invoice services efficiently according to service-level agreements (SLAs) defined in customer contracts. Services need to be invoiced the way customers expect or demand in their SLAs. Additionally, an LSP often needs to deal with bad credit history, short payments and nonpayments, credit and collection issues, freight payments to be prepaid in cash before cargo moves, and disputes raised by customers. All these processes need to be handled efficiently with integration into the customer service workplace. Figure 12.20 shows the process steps and the business focus of an end-to-end process concentrating on financial tasks (dark shaded boxes).

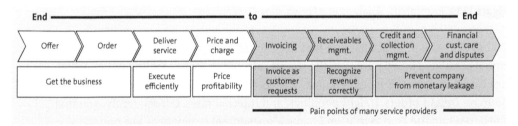

Figure 12.20 End-to-End Process with Billing Focus

A second issue for LSPs is the recognition of revenue in line with legal regulations. If shipments span multiple countries or even continents, or if payments must be made by multiple parties, you need to properly manage revenue recognition.

Usually, the revenue for a service may be recognized only upon progression of the shipment in the supply chain. Depending on local legal regulations, the following situations may occur:

- A customer orders a rail move across the United States. The payment term is prepaid. The invoice is sent to the customer five days before the pull of the railcars, and the customer pays one day before the pull. The carrier is only allowed to recognize the received revenue upon delivery of the railcar at the destination.

- A customer orders a multimodal FCL ocean shipment with truck inland haulage in the country of origin, an ocean leg, and inland haulage in the country of destination. Pre-carriage and the ocean move are prepaid by the shipper; the destination haulage is collected from the ship-to party before delivery of the containers. The carrier can recognize the shipper's revenue in multiple steps. Revenue for origin haulage can be recognized upon delivery of the container at the port of loading. Ocean carriage revenue can be recognized 50% after half of the trip is done; another 50% is recognized after the container arrives in the port of discharge. Ship-to party revenue is recognized after the container has been delivered in the destination country.

The required flexibility in billing and the ability to handle financial customer care and revenue recognition as just described are part of SAP Billing and Revenue Innovation Management (SAP BRIM) (formerly known as SAP Hybris Billing).

SAP Hybris Billing Becomes SAP BRIM Again

In Q3/2018, the re-rebranding of SAP Hybris Billing back to SAP Billing and Revenue Innovation Management was announced. Despite the confusion that may arise, the following name changes apply:

- SAP Hybris Revenue Cloud is changed to SAP Subscription Billing
- SAP Hybris Billing is changed to SAP Billing and Revenue Innovation Management
- SAP S/4HANA for subscription billing is changed to SAP S/4HANA for billing and revenue innovation management

---

SAP TM has the capability to integrate with SAP BRIM via its subcomponent Convergent Invoicing (CI). The technical integration is currently handled by a custom development project component. There are two integration options. In the beginning, SAP TM creates settlement documents from calculated charges as the basis for invoicing. When invoicing needs to be done, the subsequent financial steps can be done either via SAP S/4HANA billing or via SAP BRIM.

Looking at the extended billing and collection requirements of LSPs, CI as part of SAP BRIM is an important building block in their transportation processes. About 80% of LSPs using SAP TM as a core solution for their businesses chose SAP BRIM as their customer billing solution. SAP BRIM offers a rich portfolio of services around customer invoicing and receivables management. Figure 12.21 shows an overview of the major abilities of SAP BRIM.

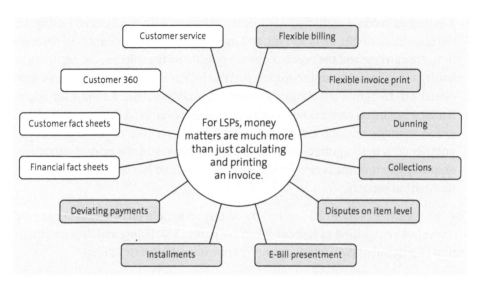

Figure 12.21 Features of SAP BRIM and Its Integration into SAP CRM Customer Service and SAP C/4HANA

Let's walk through each of these supported functions:

- **Invoice convergence**
  SAP TM creates settlement documents with multiple invoice items. If such a settlement document is sent to SD billing, the whole settlement document is used to create an invoice. With CI from the SAP BRIM solution, a billable item is created for each charge item of the settlement document. Subsequently, customer profiles (contract account settings) can be used to control a rules engine that assembles the individual customer invoices from the available charge items. In this case, the content of the invoices isn't controlled by agreement and settlement rules in SAP TM, but by contract accounts in SAP BRIM. You can easily use this, for example, to converge fuel surcharges over a longer time while invoicing freight revenue immediately per shipment.

- **Flexible billing and invoice printing**
  Bill creation and communication (technology and paper forms) are also controlled by contract account settings, enabling you to bill according to customers' service requirements.

  The invoice may contain a large selection of logistics and customer context data. In SAP S/4HANA billing, this context data is very limited. SAP BRIM, however, offers a powerful concept about how any kind of logistical context data can be stored with each billable item. Examples for the logistics context are as follows:

- Bill of lading number
- Container number or pallet ID
- Vehicle identification number
- Railcar or train ID
- Equipment type used
- Buyer's reference number

Therefore, you have all logistics-related data available to sort, filter, and group items for invoicing. In Figure 12.22, you can see an example for logistical context data in a SAP BRIM billable item.

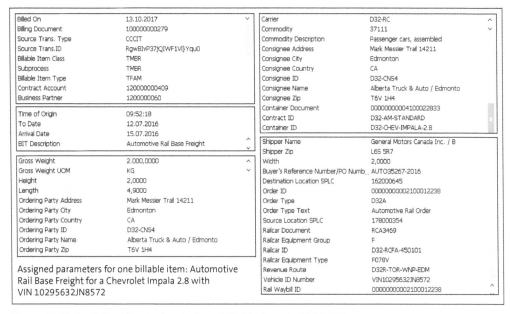

Billed On	13.10.2017		Carrier	D32-RC	
Billing Document	100000000279		Commodity	37111	
Source Trans. Type	CCCIT		Commodity Description	Passenger cars, assembled	
Source Trans.ID	RgwBIvP37jQIWF1Vl}Yqu0		Consignee Address	Mark Messier Trail 14211	
Billable Item Class	TMBR		Consignee City	Edmonton	
Subprocess	TMBR		Consignee Country	CA	
Billable Item Type	TFAM		Consignee ID	D32-CNS4	
Contract Account	120000000409		Consignee Name	Alberta Truck & Auto / Edmonto	
Business Partner	1200000060		Consignee Zip	T6V 1H4	
			Container Document	00000000004100022833	
Time of Origin	09:52:18		Contract ID	D32-AM-STANDARD	
To Date	12.07.2016		Container ID	D32-CHEV-IMPALA-2.8	
Arrival Date	15.07.2016				
BIT Description	Automotive Rail Base Freight		Shipper Name	General Motors Canada Inc. / B	
			Shipper Zip	L6S 5R7	
Gross Weight	2.000,0000		Width	2,0000	
Gross Weight UOM	KG		Buyer's Reference Number/PO Numb...	AUTO35267-2016	
Height	2,0000		Destination Location SPLC	162000645	
Length	4,9000		Order ID	00000000002100012238	
Ordering Party Address	Mark Messier Trail 14211		Order Type	D32A	
Ordering Party City	Edmonton		Order Type Text	Automotive Rail Order	
Ordering Party Country	CA		Source Location SPLC	178000354	
Ordering Party ID	D32-CNS4		Railcar Document	RCA3469	
Ordering Party Name	Alberta Truck & Auto / Edmonto		Railcar Equipment Group	F	
Ordering Party Zip	T6V 1H4		Railcar ID	D32-RCFA-450101	
			Railcar Equipment Type	F078V	
Assigned parameters for one billable item: Automotive Rail Base Freight for a Chevrolet Impala 2.8 with VIN 10295632JN8572			Revenue Route	D32R-TOR-WNP-EDM	
			Vehicle ID Number	VIN10295632JN8572	
			Rail Waybill ID	00000000002100012238	

Figure 12.22 Logistical Context Data for a Billable Item in SAP BRIM

It shows a forwarding settlement item for base freight for an automotive move by rail (finished vehicle), which has been enriched by a variety of context information from SAP TM forwarding order, freight unit, railcar unit, and freight order.

- **Dunning and collections**
  Dunning and collection mechanisms are very flexible in SAP BRIM. Payment clearing rules and clearing worklists support efficient processing of open receivables items.

- **Invoice and dispute management and customer service**
  Invoice correction capabilities and dispute management are highly flexible in SAP BRIM. Integration into the customer service workplace and the interaction center of SAP CRM is provided. A customer service representative can work directly with invoices in SAP BRIM and manage customer disputes on the charge item level. This has the huge advantage that only the disputed part of an invoice needs to stay open, and the rest can be paid. If, for example, only one item in an invoice with 100 items is disputed, the other 99 items can be collected. This is a big relief for days sales outstanding processing.

- **E-bill presentment**
  SAP BRIM uses financial supply chain management functionality for e-bill presentment. A customer can directly access his or her bills in a portal.

- **Deviating payments and installments**
  If a customer pays an amount that deviates from his or her invoices or if he or she pays in installments, these payments can be easily processed against the open receivables.

- **Cash payments**
  In logistics services, especially for ocean cargo or outside of Europe or the United States, cash payments are still a common way of managing receivables. SAP BRIM offers a cashiering functionality for cash desk operation.

- **Customer information**
  To be fully informed about the customer, the customer service workplace offers 360-degree analytics and fact sheet functionality that gives you an overview of customer contracts, orders, payments, disputes, credit history, and other details.

SAP BRIM can do invoicing for SAP TM and, at the same time, also process billing data from other system (even legacy systems) and converge multiple receivables streams into joint invoices. You can bring freight invoice data from SAP TM together with warehouse billing data from a legacy warehouse management system and accessorial data delivered from SAP Event Management, which is used to calculate demurrage. You can even use the SAP BRIM component Convergent Charging (CC) to calculate additional prices before going into the invoicing step.

The process integration between SAP TM and SAP BRIM is triggered from the SAP TM side. Figure 12.23 shows how the process is executed. In SAP TM, customer draft invoices (SAP TM forwarding settlement documents) are created based on the charge information in forwarding orders. For a logistical context, the example shows a container shipment from Shanghai, China, to San Pedro, California. The charge items are sent to SAP BRIM, where billable items (BITs) are created for each charge item. Based on invoicing rules, the available BITs are converged into three invoices: one for freight charges, one for terminal charges, and a third for additional fees such as a security surcharge.

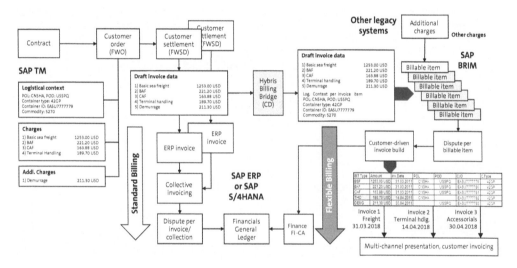

Figure 12.23 Logistics Invoice Creation with SAP BRIM

Accounting is finally done in SAP BRIM contract accounting (FI-CA), which is a subledger accounting system in SAP S/4HANA that integrates into the general ledger.

12.5 Strategic Customer Contract Management

We've seen how strategic vendor contract management (strategic freight procurement) functions in Chapter 10, Section 10.4, and also covered the basics of strategic freight management as a whole. In this section, we'll look at the selling side of the strategic freight management picture: customer contract management (strategic freight selling) with LSPs.

Contracts can have a wide meaning in the world of logistics because an LSP can handle the complete transport business for a manufacturer of goods. Thus, the path from initial customer contact to the contract is often quite lengthy and cumbersome. Strategic customer contract management, which is named strategic freight selling in SAP TM, is a functionality that is usually only used by professional logistics companies, as manufacturers and shippers don't sell freight services.

The process of initiation of contracts often begins in marketing with documenting the first sales calls, resulting in leads and opportunities (related to SAP CRM lead and opportunity management). For more concrete contacts, the customer often requests a quote from the LSP, which is submitted as an electronic- or file-based request for quotation (RFQ). The RFQ is answered by the LSP with a quotation, which corresponds to a contract offer.

Because the quotation reply of the LSP usually doesn't immediately match the customer's expectations in terms of pricing structure, price level, service details, or other conditions, multiple follow-up phases of quote adjustments may be required. Finally, if the customer decides to completely or partially accept the quotation, a contract can be created by the LSP.

12.5.1   Constraints, Expectations, and Activities in Customer RFQ Management

The process of creating a quotation that matches a customer's RFQ and expectation well isn't a simple task because customer RFQs often contain thousands of request items that need to be matched with the LSP's product offering and answered within an often relatively short time frame. A single request item is usually structured to include the following constraints:

- Origin and destination of cargo
- Container types and commodities of cargo
- Quantity details on number of containers or weight of cargo to be shipped within a certain time frame to get high-volume rebates
- Additional wishes for value-added services, shipment routing, or assigned carriers
- Additional wishes for rate structure and included or excluded surcharges

To respond properly to the RFQ, the LSP must do the following activities for each of the request items:

- Understand the requested items.
- Match the items with its services.
- Share the items logically among the LSP's sales teams to jointly or separately work on the items (e.g., according to customer or trade lane responsibility).
- Find appropriate existing tariffs and contracts that are applicable to the request.
- Determine appropriate price structures and prices to be offered.
- Push the processed items through various workflow stages.
- Converge the distributed items into an overall offering to be sent out to the customer.

On top of these activities, there may be a lot of commercial and route analytics required to make a good decision that leaves a good margin for the LSP and doesn't overdraw the customer's allocated budget.

12.5.2   The RFQ Management Process

Looking at SAP TM, the customer RFQ management process can be split into four main sections, each involving several activities that either must be done centrally or are executed in a distributed manner among multiple departments or responsible persons. Figure 12.24 shows the phases and detailed steps of the customer RFQ management process.

Looking at the four phases kicked off by the RFQ, we can highlight the following activities:

- **Customer adaptation**
  Customer adaptation provides you the means of receiving RFQ data from a customer in an electronic format and converting and mapping it into a representation that SAP TM can understand and handle. Because customers in many cases uses their own Excel templates to send the RFQ data, the Excel document must be analyzed, and data must be either extracted and filled into an initial new forwarding agreement quotation or fitted into an existing one, which is then updated and stored as a new version.

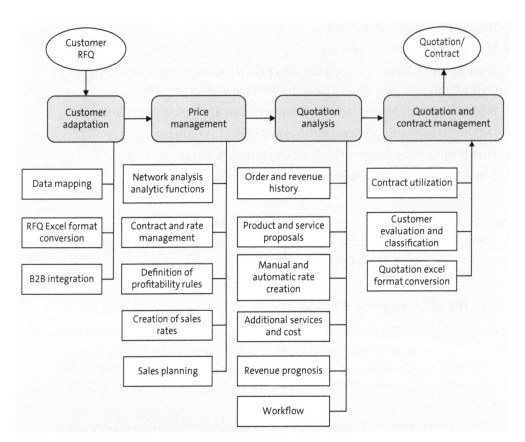

Figure 12.24 RFQ Management Process

- **Price management**
  Price management allows you to relate the RFQ data back to existing rates and tariffs, which are applicable under comparable requirements as stated in the RFQ. New sales rates can be created where required either from scratch or based on existing rates (e.g., with uplift). Analytical functions allow you to do sales planning and network analysis. For an applicability check of rates, profitability rules may be defined that allow a better judgement on appropriate sales prices. The price management phase can already be relevant for a split of the forwarding agreement quotation to several teams. For this purpose, the forwarding agreement quotationforwarding agreement quotation created from the RFQ is split into multiple

forwarding agreement quotation assignments, which are technically again forwarding agreement quotation objects but usually contain only a part of the items of the original forwarding agreement quotation and can be assigned to specific sales teams.

- **Quotation analysis**
  Analysis of the quotation and its postprocessing allows you to evaluate the created offer in the context of an existing contract and sales history with the customer. You can add additional services to the offer and adjust rates as required. Approval workflows and revenue prognosis tools round up the capabilities of this phase. Again, as in price management, the quotation analysis phase can be done in a distributed or overall manner.

- **Quotation and contract management**
  After you finalize the split forwarding agreement quotation assignments in the corresponding teams, the overall quotation can be merged from the single assignments. Again, you have the option to run through an approval workflow and do further analysis and classification. The final quotation can then be converted back into the customer's data or Excel format and be sent out to the customer.

  If the customer accepts the quotation, the LSP can directly create a contract from the last quotation version and activate it for use within SAP TM forwarding order management.

12.5.3   Strategic Freight Selling Functions

In this section, we explain and visualize some of the important steps of strategic freight selling. You can see the Excel upload function to load customer RFQ Excel sheets into forwarding agreement quotations in Figure 12.25.

The upload function can be called via the **FWAQ Excel 07 Integration** tile, which is reachable via **Launchpad · Home · Transportation – Contract Management** in SAP S/4HANA or **Forwarding Agreement Management · Forwarding Agreement Quotations · Forwarding Agreement Quotation Excel 07 Integration** in SAP TM 9.6. The Excel file to be uploaded can be selected, and you can define whether you want to create a new forwarding agreement quotation or a new version of an existing one. The mapping profile determines how SAP TM interprets the data provided by the customer and feeds it into the forwarding agreement quotation. Further parameters allow you to set validity dates or quotation types, for example.

Figure 12.25 Excel Upload Integration for Customer Quotation Requests

The mapping profiles used to convert the Excel document into an appropriate format for the upload are defined in Customizing via the path **SAP Transportation Management • Master Data • Agreement RFQs and Quotations • Define Excel and Flat View Profiles**. This takes you to a Customizing transaction where you can define which column or row of the Excel document contains which type of data (e.g., mode of transport or destination location). Figure 12.26 shows the details of the field assignment for the Excel upload. New Excel layouts always require an individual profile; therefore, the LSP always tries to standardize the RFQ process with its customers.

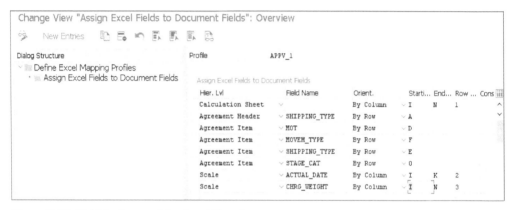

Figure 12.26 Field Assignment for Excel Mapping

After the forwarding agreement quotation is created by upload or created manually, you can manage the quotation similarly to a forwarding agreement. If you want to distribute the work to several subteams, you can either create forwarding agreement quotation assignments with a subset of items directly from the forwarding agreement quotation (push scenario; see Figure 12.27) or create a new forwarding agreement quotation assignment and then insert selected lines of other forwarding agreement quotations into the new assignment (pull scenario). The individual team would then work with the forwarding agreement quotation assignments until they are approved and can be merged back into the original forwarding agreement quotation.

Then, rate building happens in the **Rate Builder Cockpit** screen shown in Figure 12.28, which you can start from the forwarding agreement quotation or forwarding agreement quotation assignment item by invoking the corresponding follow-up function.

Figure 12.27 Splitting a Forwarding Agreement Quotation into Assignments

Figure 12.28 Rate Builder Cockpit

On the left side, you can see the related forwarding agreement items, and for the marked item, the breakdown into charge elements as assigned in the charge calculation sheet. On the right side, you see the list of matching agreements and service products, which are applicable to be used as a foundation or copy source for building rates on the left side. You can either copy or assign complete items from the right side or copy and adjust charge elements and their rates from the bottom-right table to build up the calculation sheet on the left.

The flat view for rates introduces a very comfortable technique to get an overview on rates and rate structures, as well as maintain the rates in that view. You can start the flat view by marking an item in the forwarding agreement quotation and clicking the **Display Flat View** button shown in Figure 12.29.

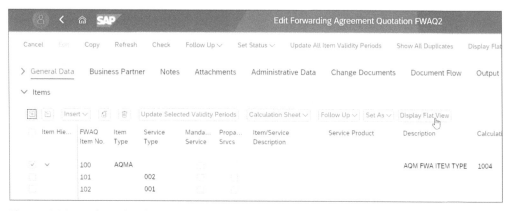

Figure 12.29 Invoking the Flat View for Rate Maintenance

This opens the flat view screen for the rates, where all rates of the calculation sheet of the forwarding agreement quotation item are displayed in a kind of table containing the characteristics columns on the left side and the various charge elements with their rates and currencies on the right side. With this table you can, for example, get an overview on the charge element relevant to a move of cargo between certain locations and the ability to see all applying charges, without explicitly drilling down into each rate table that is related by the charge calculation sheet. Figure 12.30 shows an example of a flat view screen.

The rate flat view screen can be configured and controlled by flat view profiles. These are comparable to the Excel mapping profiles and can also be configured in the Customizing via the path **Sap Transportation Management • Transportation Management • Master Data • Agreement RFQs and Quotations • Define Excel and Flat View Profiles**. When you enter the flat view screen, the flat view profile must be selected. You can instantaneously switch the view by selecting another profile. Figure 12.31 shows the configuration details of the flat view profile.

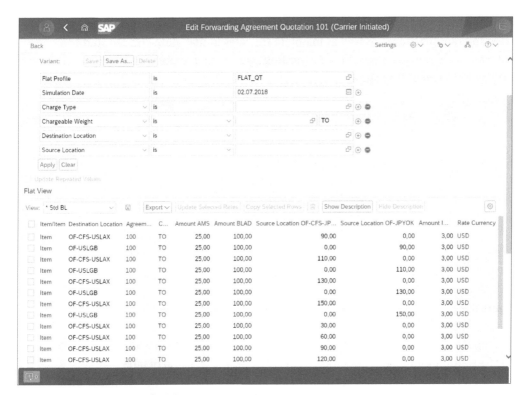

Figure 12.30 Rate Flat View

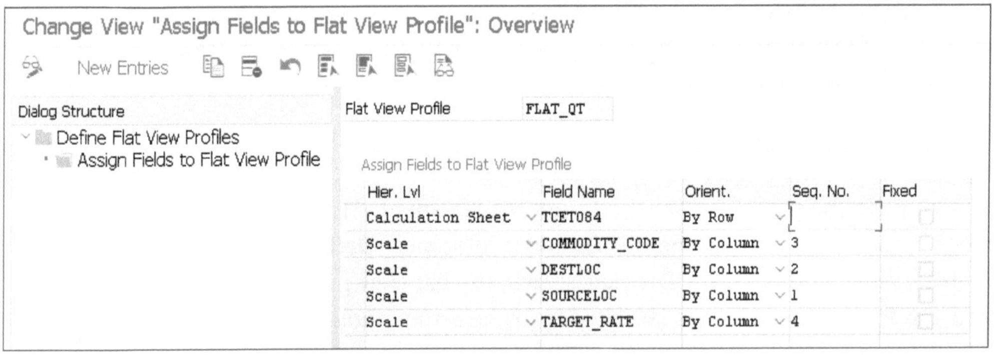

Figure 12.31 Configuration of the Flat View Profile

After all rates are properly built and the quotation is checked and approved, you can export it into an Excel file either in an internal format or with a conversion into a customer-specific format. Figure 12.32 shows a sheet of such an Excel table exported from a forwarding agreement quotation. The Excel file contains a header sheet with all forwarding agreement quotation header details and separate sheets for each item with the corresponding rates.

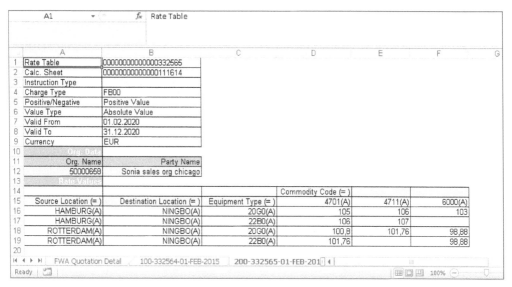

Figure 12.32 Excel Output of a Rate Table of a Forwarding Agreement Quotation

Another comfort function is the duplicate agreement check, which allows you to verify whether duplicate agreements or items exist in the system. Checked characteristics are many and include stage categories, validity dates, trade lane assignment, service level, and so on.

12.6   Summary

This chapter provided an overview of charge settlement, integration to SAP S/4HANA billing and invoicing, integration to SAP BRIM as an alternative way of customer billing for LSPs, and strategic freight selling.

We started by looking at the master data focusing on forwarding and internal agreements, as well as a service product catalog. You learned about the relationship between and integration of these items.

Additionally, we dove deep into the logic for industry-specific charge calculation capabilities and scenarios for air freight, freight forwarder business, and container management. Corresponding charge sheets with assigned rate tables are used for the actual calculation logic.

Only calculating costs wouldn't be sufficient, however, to actually generate revenue. Therefore, we looked into the process of preparing the documents for the customer invoice. The corresponding document in the SAP TM functionality is the forwarding settlement document. Furthermore, this chapter introduced the aspect of cross-charging costs among internal and external organizations of the LSP and calculating profitability.

In the next chapter, we offer insight into SAP TM integration aspects such as analytics, SAP Extended Warehouse Management, SAP Transportation Resource Planning, SAP Yard Logistics, and more.

Chapter 13

Integration with Other Components

A task deemed as too hard or too complex to be solved by one person can in most cases be done by engaging a group of individuals. The same principle applies in software, where integration between individual business systems allows us to address the challenges of the digital age.

Modern supply chains are often dependent on a multitude of participants to reach the goal of a perfect delivery. Such a delivery is achieved only if the goods arrive at the right time, in the ideal quality, and at the desired place. Efficient supply chains orchestrate the participating business partners, while following another principle: efficiency. This last ideal is met when all formerly listed parameters are kept reliably and at the lowest achievable cost.

Efficient supply chains are hence relying on business software to gain the transparency for measuring success, mitigating risks, and optimizing planning processes.

You already know that SAP Transportation Management (SAP TM) can map the complex business processes of *logistics service providers* (LSPs) and shippers. Frequently, such business processes must be represented across system boundaries. Furthermore, a large volume of data is gathered and added to the business process to satisfy the requirements of carriers, authorities, customs, and receiving business partners. Such data is imported electronically and/or automatically ascertained by the system. Today, the volume of data generated during a transportation process is immense, so it's not always easy for an end user or enterprise to draw conclusions from a success or failure at the document or aggregated level.

In this context, SAP TM not only offers strong integration capabilities with analytics solutions from SAP but also uses the potential and opportunities of mobile devices. We cover these in Section 13.1.

When it comes to supply chain operations, SAP TM offers both strong implementation capabilities with third-party solutions and seamless integration with other applications from SAP S/4HANA or SAP Business Suite.

In previous chapters, we've already seen that tight integration with other SAP components is used mainly to facilitate transportation planning and execution in SAP TM. SAP Global Trade Services (SAP GTS) is used to perform compliance checks and customs processing (see Chapter 9). SAP Event Management is used to track and monitor events and statuses for various business objects within the supply chain (integration with SAP Event Management was explained in Chapter 8). Integration with analytics is explained in the next section.

From end to end, however, supply chain management goes far beyond transportation planning and execution. The fulfillment process also uses warehouse operations to source, store, and handle products within the transportation network. Section 13.2 explains the process integration with SAP Extended Warehouse Management (SAP EWM).

In a logistically connected world, the movement of resources, such as containers, is essential to allow a seamless flow of goods. Planning the provisioning and movement of resources at the right place and time is essential for disruption-free transportation. Therefore, we explain the SAP Transportation Resource Planning solution in Section 13.3.

Section 13.4 explains the SAP Yard Logistics solution and elaborates on the resource management within large areas, such as container or railway terminals.

In Section 13.5, we explain the SAP Logistics Business Network, which provides a platform to collaborate with LSPs and sets a technological basis for process integration across company borders.

The applications of blockchain are numerous. Today we can only assume how big the impact on our daily lives and business reality will be. Naturally there are applications that affect supply chain operations and logistics execution as well. Section 13.6 of this book will give a few insights on this topic in relation to SAP TM.

Finally, we explore the SAP Customer Relationship Management (SAP CRM) integration into logistics execution processes in Section 13.7.

13.1 Analytics

Because they make fact-based decisions, enterprises can benefit greatly from detailed analyses on available data. This way, they can identify profitable and less profitable transportation and shipping routes for example. They can use historical data as a basis for learning for the future, structuring their business differently, negotiating with new customers, or plotting shipping routes. A consolidated view of all data from day-to-day activities can give LSPs an important competitive edge. Analyses that connect logistical data with financial data are an important corporate management tool in competition-intensive and low-margin logistics.

In this scenario, analysis-oriented information systems are used to support both planning and strategic processes. They provide enterprises with current and historical data. These systems are frequently based on a data warehouse in which relevant data is collected, formatted, and made available. The core of a data warehouse is a database. The latest business warehouse solutions of SAP are available both in the cloud and on premise, and they use a SAP S/4HANA database.

Due to technical advancements both in business systems and their underlying technology, such as in-memory operations, operational analysis of data in real time is gaining momentum. Based on the SAP S/4HANA system, operational reports are represented across all functional areas as part of the core functionality to track key performance indicators (KPIs).

In this section, we explain how analytics and the integration with SAP TM help decision makers answer business-related and specific questions.

Within this book, we split the analysis section into three parts:

- Business intelligence (BI) content (Section 13.1.1)
- Operational reporting and data provisioning (Section 13.1.2)
- Embedded analytics with SAP TM (Section 13.1.3)

When it comes to analytics, we usually distinguish among the following:

- Role- or user-specific worklists
- Embedded contextual analytics
- Ad hoc reporting and queries
- Graphical dashboards

User-specific worklists have already been explained as part of the user interface (UI) technology in SAP Fiori (refer to Chapter 2, Section 2.2).

Both, the overview pages in SAP TM as well as the content for SAP Business Warehouse (SAP BW) allows for ad hoc, embedded, contextual analysis that is or can be supplemented by graphical dashboards.

The overview pages of SAP TM in SAP S/4HANA provide an overview of the KPIs of data stored in the same system. SAP BW is still the tool of choice when data out of several systems is to be consolidated.

The following sections will explain the methods in further detail.

13.1.1   Business Intelligence Content

With SAP BW, SAP provides a solution that includes all required components for setting up data warehouse architecture for transportation reporting. In addition to the basic technology for data retention, the system provides all the essential components for evaluating the transportation-relevant data stored in SAP BW (i.e., reporting tools, data mining methods, and an option for a portal/SAP Fiori connection). This chapter focuses on analytical reporting, integrating SAP TM with SAP BW, which content is provided, and how the data will be provisioned.

We assume that you're familiar with the main concept of SAP BW, so we provide some further details about how this data is extracted from the source system, as well as how—and in which context—the data can be used for operational reporting.

Where to Find Help

Contrary to other SAP S/4HANA areas, all SAP BW extractors for SAP TM in SAP S/4HANA are still working (refer to SAP Note 2500202 for further details). However, there is no separate content section on this topic in the SAP Help for SAP S/4HANA.

For operational data provisioning, as of SAP TM 9.0, most of the documentation of data sources and BI content has been moved from the BI content documentation to the SAP library for SAP TM 9.X. You'll find the description at *http://help.sap.com* (search for "Transportation Management", and then select product version 9.0 or higher).

In the transportation industry, reporting ranges from structural data analysis in day-to-day activities and complex analyses of individual cost components to determining KPIs for use by corporate management. It demands knowledge and access to data from various operational systems, such as transportation, tracking, financial accounting, and sometimes even purchasing.

In practice, system landscapes are complex, and cross-system enterprise reporting must be possible. Furthermore, both current transaction data and historical data are required to achieve the best possible results. In many enterprises, employees still integrate and prepare data by consolidating Excel tables at the end of the month and generating charts. This process is not only laborious but also prone to errors. Furthermore, it can be performed by data warehouse systems such as SAP BW.

A reporting system must permit both incoming and outgoing access to data, irrespective of the data format. SAP TM uses SAP BW to create analyses and reports. SAP BW can be used to process data from SAP systems, legacy systems, web services, and flat files. The data is then displayed in either tabular form or a meaningful dashboard that consists of traffic lights, meter displays, or charts. SAP BW allows the relevant people within an enterprise to obtain the latest data at the press of a button, thus allowing them to make informed decisions and manage day-to-day activities accordingly.

The latest technologies in BI use encapsulated enterprise services to extract data from very different systems and display it in an easy-to-configure UI. Therefore, reporting is no longer just programming; it also involves business process design, which can be performed by almost all employees because drag-and-drop functionality can be used to configure both the data extraction and display levels.

13

Let's consider a brief example that shows how reporting based on transactional transportation data can be used to monitor indicators in different enterprise areas. This carbon dioxide example is based on data obtained directly from SAP TM, but it can also be based on or enhanced with data obtained from flat data structures or legacy applications.

Figure 13.1 shows a dashboard that provides the user with a great deal of information. The example concerns an analysis of carrier performance and general transportation KPIs. At the click of a button, the user can view the extent to which each carrier contributes to the overall performance. Data can be visualized as a graphic or explored in table format.

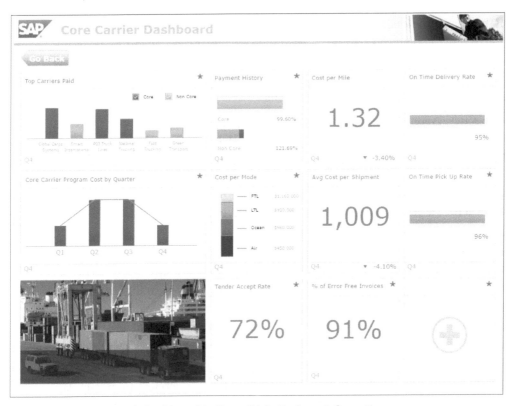

Figure 13.1 Sample Dashboard to Consolidate Business Information

Let's apply this SAP TM example to explain the provided BI content of SAP TM and the integration with SAP BW in much greater detail.

SAP provides delivered content within SAP BW and delivered extractors for transferring data from SAP TM to SAP BW to further analyze transportation-related data.

SAP TM supports you in managing the physical transportation of goods from one location to another. The BI content of SAP TM empowers decision makers and employees with the queries and analytic tools to evaluate, analyze, and interpret transportation-related business data.

In this section, we explain the principles of data extraction from the SAP TM source system and data sources, as well as the content that provides the data basis and analytical foundation to support and answer the following daily questions:

- How much weight or volume is transported per trade lane, business share, or transportation allocation, and how long was the distance or duration of individual transports on average?

- How many containers have been shipped from one location to another, and what is the percentage of dangerous goods shipments compared to the overall number of shipments per trade lane?

- What are the average transport costs per trade lane, carrier, shipper, or consignee, and how reliable was the shipper, carrier, or consignee?

Data Extraction from SAP TM

After examining the application examples and economic background of KPIs and reporting, we now continue with a look at the integration of logistics applications with SAP BW.

In general, SAP logistics applications run either via the UI or through planning or batch reports; a data backup generally takes place before the end of the transaction. After the backup is completed (i.e., when the transaction is obviously finished, and new data has been updated), we need to extract the data relevant to characteristic and key figure determination. Figure 13.2 shows the principles of the integration process.

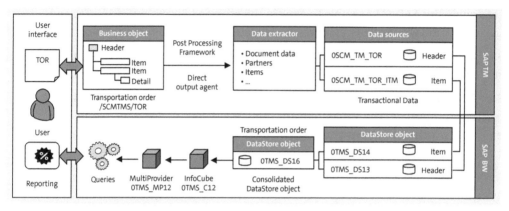

Figure 13.2 Integration with SAP BW

Let's walk through it.

In previous releases of SAP TM for the SAP Business Suite, the action definitions and processing types that refer to data extractors are defined in the *Post Processing Framework* (PPF) action profile for the shipment request, shipment, and shipment order. Here, a method call is referenced in each case. If you want to enhance or change the standard extraction in any way, you can replace this extractor with your own extractor. The data extractor is called only if the PPF condition for the extraction action is identified as being a true condition. You can define this condition in Customizing for the PPF conditions. The standard condition defined here is such that the business objects obtain the status **Completed**, meaning that no further changes are made. It generally makes the most sense to use the **Completed** status if the data of the processes that are currently running doesn't have to be included in the SAP BW analyses.

In SAP TM in SAP S/4HANA (and SAP TM 9.6), however, SAP BW integration is based on outputs that don't involve the PPF. Although the configuration is still part of the PPF adapter configuration, output determination and relevance are based on the direct output agent relevance of the business object.

You can maintain this relevance and direct output configuration in the PPF settings for extracting data for SAP BW in the Customizing of SAP TM. In the IMG for SAP TM, select **Cross-Application Components · Processes and Tools for Enterprise Applications · Reusable Objects and Functions for BOPF Environment · PPF Adapter for Output**

Management · Maintain Output Management Adapter Settings. Figure 13.3 shows the Customizing screen for the delta upload configuration of a transportation order.

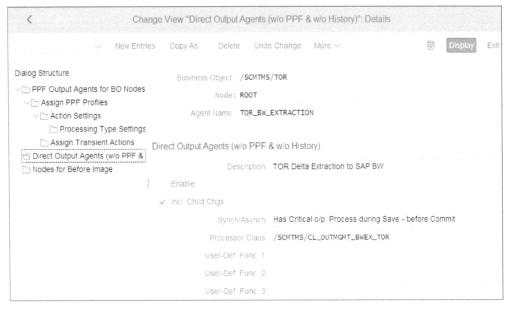

Figure 13.3 Transportation Order: Delta Upload Configuration

General Settings in SAP TM

Before you can use SAP BW for reporting, you must connect SAP TM with the reporting system. You can find the relevant settings in the IMG for SAP TM by following the menu path **Integration with Other SAP Components · Data Transfer to Business Warehouse · General Settings**. Here, you enter the necessary parameters to specify the source system and the maximum size and rows of the data packages that will be transferred into SAP BW. These settings are mainly cross-client.

Before the data extraction and integration can be configured, use Transaction RSA9 to transfer the application component hierarchy. The necessary DataSources are then delivered as part of the business content of SAP TM and can be activated with Transaction RSA5. These DataSources belong to the source system (here, SAP TM) and contain all relevant fields that can be transferred to SAP BW.

Figure 13.4 shows Transaction RSA5 in SAP TM. The relevant DataSources for master data, texts, and transactional data can be found under hierarchy node **OSCM_TM_**

DATASOURCES on the screen. In this context, we must distinguish between an initial or delta upload from SAP TM to SAP BW.

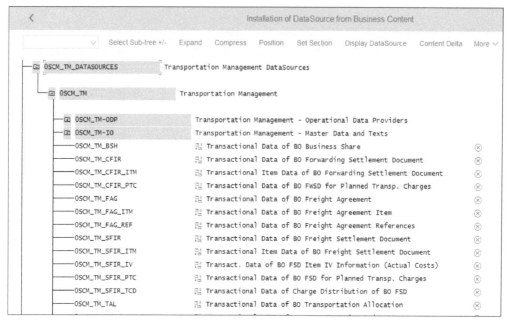

Figure 13.4 Business Content Installation in SAP TM

The initial upload of data to SAP BW can be initialized with or without a physical data transfer. The initial data upload of existing data with data transfer is done using setup tables in SAP TM. After the data in these setup tables has been deleted, they can be filled with data from the relevant SAP BW extractor. You can find the initialization of these setup tables, the relevant transactions to fill them with existing data, and the execution of the data upload into the SAP BW system in the SAP Easy Access menu of SAP TM: **Application Administration • Initial Data Upload to SAP NetWeaver BW** (see Figure 13.5).

Finally, use Transaction RSA6 to perform an extraction test and display the data records of a specific DataSource.

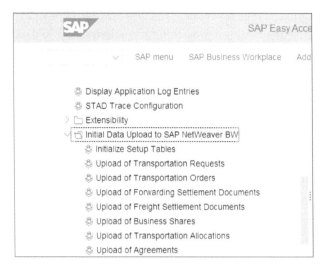

Figure 13.5 Initial Data Upload to SAP BW

Recall that settings in the PPF are used to control the process of extracting data from SAP TM. For the standard delivery, the following business objects have been integrated into SAP BW:

- Transportation order
- Forwarding settlement document
- Freight settlement document
- Transportation request
- Business share
- Trade lane
- Transportation order execution
- Transportation allocation

As part of normal storage of one of these business objects, processing is triggered in the PPF (refer to Figure 13.2). In previous releases of SAP TM, after the PPF condition has been successfully checked, the data is extracted using an extraction method built specifically for the business object. This method then makes the data available in a DataSource so that it can be transferred to SAP BW. In the current release of SAP TM (for SAP S/4HANA and SAP TM 9.6), the extraction relevance is based on the settings made for the direct output agent configuration (see Figure 13.3).

Analytics is based mainly on the extraction, processing, and visualization of business data. In the next section, we describe both the provisioning and extraction of data from SAP TM and how it's ultimately used for reporting.

13.1.2   Data Provisioning and Operational Reporting

The data is loaded from the SAP TM system to SAP BW into the persistent staging area (PSA). In SAP BW, the DataSource information is stored in DataStore objects (DSOs), which then fill InfoCubes with information that is subsequently used by the Multi-Providers from the various sources of data. After the data has been made available in the MultiProvider, you can use different queries to access the information in SAP BW and then combine this information with other available data, specifically for conducting analyses.

Data Provisioning

Before it can be stored in SAP BW, the content is systematically structured based on the technical relevance of the content that is supposed to be mapped. This structure in turn determines and provisions the available options for transportation analytics.

To become familiar with the core elements of analytics, you need to understand the definition of core objects and structures and how these InfoProviders provide a basis for the provisioned queries in SAP BW.

InfoProvider

An *InfoProvider* is an SAP BusinessObjects Business Intelligence (SAP Business-Objects BI) object that can be used as a source of data for a query. SAP divides InfoProviders into two categories: those that physically contain data (in a database table) and those that don't. The data objects that contain InfoProviders are *InfoCubes*, *DSOs*, and *InfoObjects*. Those that don't contain any data themselves refer to other InfoObjects and/or systems for data. Among these are the *VirtualProviders*, *InfoSets*, and *Multi-Providers*.

Four of these objects are an important part of the provided standard content and are the basis for the provisioned queries in SAP BW (see Figure 13.6):

- InfoObject
- DSO
- InfoCubes
- MultiProviders

Let's look at these four in more detail. To understand the integration and relationship among these objects, reconsider the example provided in Figure 13.2. In addition, to learn more about the relationship, characteristics, and how the data is ultimately modeled in SAP BW, look at the *Data Warehousing Workbench* in SAP BW via Transaction RSA1 (Figure 13.6) to start the discussion.

Figure 13.6 Data Warehousing Workbench

An InfoObject is a basic building block in SAP BusinessObjects BI data modeling. It acts as a definition for the data (metadata), describing elements such as the type and length of the data, but it can also contain data itself. InfoObjects are divided into key figures (which contain numerical values, amounts, currencies, etc.) and characteristics (texts and IDs of objects). A characteristic, which contains other InfoObjects (either key figures or other characteristics) as attributes, can be used as an InfoProvider.

A DSO is a store for transactional data that is described by InfoObjects. Some of the InfoObjects are defined as key fields, and the rest contain the "trunk" of the data. Data records with an identical key part can be summed or overwritten.

There are three types of DSOs: standard, write-optimized, and direct-update. In the context of transactional reporting of SAP TM data, the term always refers to the standard DSO. Physically, the standard DSO consists of three database tables: one for new data (has additional, technical key elements), an active data table (only the semantic key), and a change log. DSOs can act as InfoProviders alone but usually are part of an InfoSet or act as an intermediate step in updating the data into an InfoCube (refer to Figure 13.2).

Figure 13.7 shows the DSO OTMS_DS14 for the transportation order line items in SAP BW. It contains all data fields from the corresponding data source OSCM_TM_TOR_ITM in SAP TM. Together with the header data from the business object /SCMTMS/TOR (transportation order), it's consolidated into the DSO OTMS_DS16 (refer to Figure 13.6).

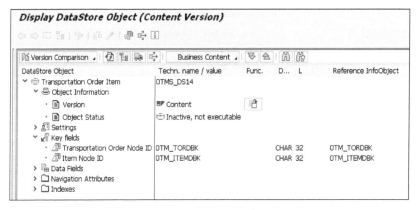

Figure 13.7 DataStore Object: Transportation Order Item

From a reporting perspective, an InfoCube is possibly the most commonly used Info-Provider for reporting purposes. It's built from multiple InfoObjects that are grouped together into dimensions. The transaction data is stored in a fact table to which these dimensions are linked. InfoCubes in SAP BW are either standard or real time. In this chapter, the term always refers to standard InfoCubes.

An InfoCube always has three technical dimensions (unit, time, and package) in addition to the user-definable dimensions. The unit dimension contains the units or currencies of the key figures, the time characteristics are included in the time dimension, and the package dimension contains technical characteristics relevant to each data load.

In SAP BW, these InfoCubes exist for virtually all transactional data of SAP TM business objects. Table 13.1 shows which InfoCubes are provided and used for which data.

InfoCube	Description
0TMS_C11	Transportation request
0TMS_C12	Transportation order
0TMS_C14	Planned costs
0TMS_C15	Actual costs
0TMS_C16	Revenue
0TMS_C18	Transportation order execution
0TMS_C19	Business share
0TMS_C20	Transportation allocation
0TMS_C21	Trade lanes
0TMS_C22	Transportation request stages
0TMS_C23	Transportation order stages

Table 13.1 InfoCubes for SAP TM

Other than the basic InfoCubes, several other InfoProviders are available in SAP BW. As an example, the MultiProvider is a special type of InfoProvider that can combine data from several InfoProviders. They are then available for reporting. Like InfoSets and VirtualProviders, MultiProviders themselves are simply based on a logical definition and don't contain any data. Their data comes exclusively from the InfoProviders on which they are based. MultiProviders can be based on any combination of the following InfoProviders:

- InfoCubes
- DSOs
- InfoObjects
- InfoSets
- Aggregation levels

Therefore, if a MultiProvider allows you to run reports using several InfoProviders, then it's used for creating reports on more than one InfoProvider at a time. Each of the MultiProviders contains information about the data package, time stamps, units, locations, document numbers, partners, and other dimensions, as well as the business object's KPIs. The MultiProviders are defined the same way as the aforementioned InfoCubes.

MultiProviders are often used "on top of" other InfoProviders to simplify the structure for end users and join two InfoProviders of similar structure together (refer to Figure 13.2).

A classic example is joining two InfoCubes that are identical in design, but one contains actual values and the other contains planned values. The MultiProvider allows easy creation of queries, where these two sets of values can be compared. Table 13.2 lists the MultiProvider definitions for SAP TM.

MultiProvider	Description
OTMS_MP11	Transportation request
OTMS_MP12	Transportation order
OTMS_MP13	SAP TM cost analysis
OTMS_MP16	SAP TM revenue analysis
OTMS_MP18	Transportation order execution
OTMS_MP19	Business share
OTMS_MP20	Transportation allocation
OTMS_MP21	Trade lane analysis
OMTS_MP22	Transportation request stages
OMTS_MP23	Transportation order stages

Table 13.2 MultiProviders for SAP TM

Standard Reporting Content

After the data has been placed in a MultiProvider, you can access information in SAP BW with various queries and combine this information with other available data to perform targeted analyses. These analyses can be displayed in spreadsheets, reports, or dashboards.

You can use queries to analyze transportation processes. The queries delivered with SAP TM are typically based on the information extracted from the transportation request, the transportation order business objects, and the MultiProviders described in the previous section.

Figure 13.8 describes the transportation-specific queries available in SAP BW. If you want to enhance any of the existing queries, you can use your own queries, which are based on the MultiProviders in SAP TM and other application areas.

MultiProvider	Query	
Transportation request	0TMS_MP11_Q0001 0TMS_MP11_Q0002	Customer analysis Party/location analysis
Transportation order	0TMS_MP12_Q0001 0TMS_MP12_Q0002	Carrier analysis Transport analysis
Transportation cost analysis	Planned/actual costs per …	
	0TMS_MP13_Q0001 0TMS_MP13_Q0001_1_EXT 0TMS_MP13_Q0001_2_EXT 0TMS_MP13_Q0001_3_EXT 0TMS_MP13_Q0001_4_EXT	Transport Carrier Consignee Shipper Transportation mode
	Costs per …	
	0TMS_MP13_Q0003 0TMS_MP13_Q0004	Number of units shipped per period and mode of transport Carrier
Transportation revenue analysis	0TMS_MP16_Q0001 0TMS_MP16_Q0002	Planned revenue per customer Planned revenue for top 5 customers
Transportation allocation	0SCM_TMS_MP20_Q0001	Carrier by transportation allocations
Business share	0TMS_MP19_Q0001	Business share by carrier
Trade lane analysis	0TMS_MP21_Q0001 0TMS_MP21_Q0002 0SCM_TMS_MP21_Q0002	Transported weight per trade lane Trade lane analysis per transport Carrier analysis by trade lane
Transportation order execution	0TMS_MP18_Q0001) 0TMS_MP18_Q0002 0TMS_MP18_Q0003 0TMS_MP18_Q0004	Delivery reliability Expected events reliability Unexpected events Duration analysis

Figure 13.8 SAP TM Queries and Data Sources

In addition to these InfoProviders and queries, SAP provides standard reporting content. The **Cost Analysis for Transportation Management** dashboard example in Figure 13.9 shows how data can be made available, visualized, and used as a basis for your own reports.

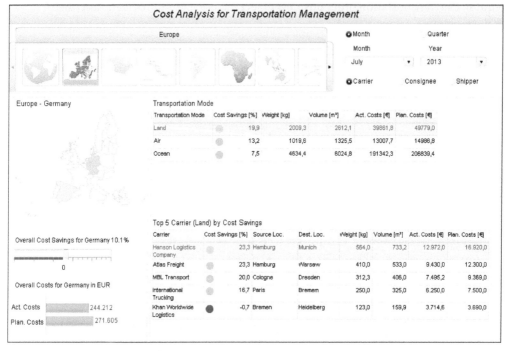

Figure 13.9 Dashboard: Cost Analysis for Transportation Management

You can use this dashboard in SAP TM to do many things:

- Get an overview of costs from the perspective of a carrier, consignee, or shipper.
- Display key figures, such as actual costs, planned costs, or cost savings.
- Access this information for all transportation modes and shipments for any month in the past two years.
- Display additional information about the associated source and destination locations.

The system extracts the key figures from the SAP BW system when you choose a country in a particular region. The dashboard is intended for managers in the transportation and logistics areas.

13.1.3 Embedded Analytics with SAP S/4HANA

Typically, three levels of analytics support decision-making in organizations:

- At the corporate level, analytics mainly supports the strategy concerning the direction, composition, and coordination of various business activities within a large and diversified transportation network.
- At the business level, the strategy relates to the creation of competitive advantage.
- At the operational level, analytics usually supports a combination of resources, processes, and competencies to put a strategy into effect or be competitive.

In previous editions of this book we described the *Business Context Viewer* (BCV) as the intended solution to address these operational analytics processes. With the introduction of SAP TM in SAP S/4HANA, a new option is available and endorsed by SAP: embedded analytics. This technology was designed to combine online transactional processing (OLTP) and online analytical processing (OLAP) on one system based on the SAP HANA database to enable real-time analysis of existing data without the need for separate reporting systems.

In this section, we'll address how this new reporting method can be used to gain valuable business insights for planning and executing transportation processes. In addition, there will be a short introduction and information on the technical background and adaptation possibilities of the embedded analytics functionalities.

Further Information on the BCV Functionality

For further information on the BCV, refer to the SAP TM 9.6 documentation at *https://bit.ly/2SUeqBF*.

As the BCV is currently not delivered with standard content for SAP TM in SAP S/4HANA, we decided to focus on the description of operational reporting on the currently endorsed embedded analytics functionality for SAP S/4HANA. Even though this reporting method doesn't require integration of external systems, we decided to keep it as part of the content in this chapter to provide a holistic view on the analytical capabilities of SAP TM.

Embedded analytics as such has numerous applications in the SAP S/4HANA environment. Within this book, we'll focus on the applications built and delivered as part of the SAP TM in SAP S/4HANA software. All the functionality shown is consumed via the SAP Fiori UI.

Embedded Analytics for SAP TM in SAP S/4HANA

Within SAP TM, several overview pages have been created that reflect contextualized KPIs relevant for freight planning and execution. Those pages are tailored to business roles and hence show KPIs relevant for a certain area in SAP TM. A person who supervises transportation execution would hence start the day by navigating to the **Freight Order Execution Overview** page to understand where his attention is required. As these overview pages are the cornerstone of operational SAP TM reporting, we'll discuss them in more detail. In Figure 13.10, one such page is shown, which allows insight on the current freight order quantity KPIs.

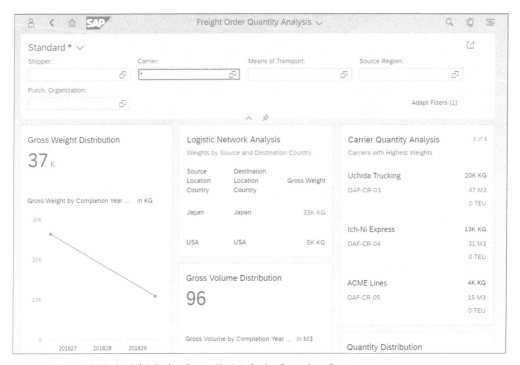

Figure 13.10 Freight Order Quantity Analysis: Overview Page

Multiple KPIs are combined in one screen, and the individual KPI boxes are called *cards*. These cards display graphs, charts, or consolidated figures. The individual cards can be reorganized by dragging and dropping them in a different screen area.

On the upper part of Figure 13.10, the filter bar is shown, where based on criteria such as source region, carrier, purchase organization, and others, the KPIs shown in each section of the screen are being recalculated. The shown numbers and graphs are all determined in real time, allowing for decision-making based on the latest information.

Personalizing Overview Pages

You can decide which KPIs are relevant within your current role and functions, and all other cards can be hidden. This is achieved by clicking on the **User** button on the top-left corner and then selecting **Manage Cards**.

Each of the displayed cards follows the "insight to action" principle; that is, it can be clicked on for further, more detailed information as depicted in Figure 13.11.

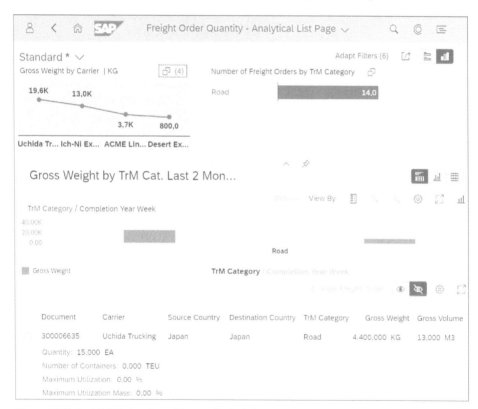

Figure 13.11 Freight Order Quantity: Analytical List Page

These *analytical list pages* show graphs and figures on the selected KPIs. By clicking on the respective area, for example, the quantities of the last week, the list on the lower part of the screen gets filtered further. Only those freight orders are shown that fall into the specific time frame.

As a final step of the analysis, individual freight orders can be opened from this screen by selecting one of the list entries on the lower part of the screen.

This insight to action principle was designed to enable the end user a simple way to execute follow-up actions after getting insight in the past and current transportation situation.

The overview pages shown in Table 13.3 are currently available within SAP TM.

Overview Pages	Description
Allocation Analysis	KPI overview on existing allocations for weight volume and amounts transported
Business Share Analysis	KPI overview on business share fulfillment ratios
Cost Analysis	KPI overview on costs per time frame and distributed by carrier, charge type, purchasing organization, source, and destination country
Freight Booking Execution Monitoring	KPI overview on the freight booking executions status for the current and previous month
Freight Booking Quantity Analysis	KPI overview on quantities transported with freight orders for and with certain business partners and between locations
Freight Order Execution Monitoring	KPI overview on the freight order executions status for the current and previous month
Freight Order Quantity Analysis	KPI overview on quantities transported with freight orders for and with certain business partners and between locations
Tendering Analysis	KPI overview about running and completed tendering processes

Table 13.3 Available Overview Pages in SAP TM

Each of the overview pages has individual cards that lead to further analytical list pages.

Available SAP Documentation

For further information on the available content for overview pages and analytical list pages, refer to the online help at *https://help.sap.com*, search for "SAP S/4HANA", and navigate to the **SAP Transportation Management** · **Analytics** part of the help document.

You've now learned how to navigate the overview pages in SAP TM. All content displayed is delivered out of the box; that is, no further configuration is necessary.

Embedded Analytics Enhancement

The overview pages are just one aspect of the possibilities that SAP S/4HANA offers. Within this subsection, we'll briefly give a glimpse of the background technologies and adaptation options for SAP Fiori tiles, reports, and overview cards.

SAP offers best practice analytics content, that is, analytical tiles that are tailored to the needs of a significant number of end customers. As analytical models need to reflect the specific business realities of a corporate environment, which can deviate from the predelivered content, additional analytical apps can be programmed reusing the SAP *Core Data Services* (CDS) views, which provide access to the data stored on the SAP HANA database.

13

Virtual Data Model

With the emergence of the SAP HANA database, a new concept for providing and consuming analytical data was also devised: Core Data Services (CDS). CDS was developed as a semantically enriched data model defined and consumed directly on the database. Hierarchical consumable CDS views form a *virtual data model* (VDM).

These VDMs can be used to create new consuming applications, and custom views can be created to allow even more flexibility.

The authorization concept for CDS views is in line with the overall profile and role concept of SAP S/4HANA; hence, access on certain views is restricted to certain roles.

We don't do a deep dive into embedded analytics in this book. For a complete picture of SAP S/4HANA embedded analytics, we recommend *SAP S/4HANA Embedded Analytics* by our colleagues, Jürgen Buntsmann, Thomas Fleckenstain, and Anirban Kundu (SAP PRESS, 2018, at *www.sap-press.com/4690*).

Certain functions can be achieved without the need for programming within the SAP TM standard content, however. For this purpose, SAP created several apps to adapt and create reports, cards, and tiles at design time, as shown in Figure 13.12:

- **View Browser**
  This app allows you to see all created CDS views.

- **KPI Workspace**
  This app shows all created KPI tiles and cards and allows you to change certain values, such as currency or criticality ranges.

- **Report Workspace**
  This app allows you to browse newly created (Z_) reports based on the CDS views.

- **Create Tile/Create Reports**
  These apps enable you to create your own tiles that can be published.

Figure 13.12 Analytics Apps

Access to the Analytics Apps

To access the business modeler, role *SAP_BR_ANALYTICS_SPECIALIST* (or an equivalent of this standard role) is required.

With these runtime functions, the possibility for creating new analytical capabilities has undergone a major shift from developers to end users. Self-created reports can be published and transported throughout the system landscape to allow testing in a nonproductive environment.

In this section, we described the analytical capabilities of SAP TM and introduced the capabilities it has when combined with a SAP BW system. In the next section, we'll introduce the options to connect to and execute processes with a SAP EWM system.

13.2   Integration with SAP EWM

Across all phases of process evolution in the delivery of goods, one thing remains certain. The warehouse and transportation functions of a business are its cornerstone for successful supply chain execution.

Orders and deliveries serve as common logistical objects within SAP S/4HANA. They interconnect all logistics functions of the SAP software in the context of supply chain business processes. Within SAP TM in SAP S/4HANA, these objects are used to build freight units, which represent transportation demands.

This tight connection allows SAP TM to continuously react to changes to orders and deliveries and support the optimization of transportation costs and efforts in a flexible and optimized way. From a cargo handling perspective, the results of transportation planning have a direct impact on warehouse logistics and operations.

A warehouse is typically defined as a structural unit with all resources and organizational provisions necessary for the execution of processes connected to inventory management and warehouse management, including the organizational units involved with goods receipt (GR) and shipping. In a nutshell, warehouse logistics involves the storage, maintenance, and handling of goods in warehouses, while warehouse management (or warehousing) is in the realm of materials management, a process where goods are temporarily stored or rerouted to a different channel in the network.

From a transportation logistics perspective, the results of transportation planning influence the warehouse-internal processes, such as the retrieval, staging, and provisioning of goods and cargo. In a connected warehousing and transportation process, efficiency is achieved by optimizing the cost for handling a truck, starting from its arrival at the gate to its final departure after loading and therefore using the data of both systems for planning and execution.

We introduce warehouse operations based on SAP EWM in Section 13.2.1, and delivery-based SAP EWM integration is explained in Section 13.2.2. The integration of these systems enables smooth inbound and outbound processing with an optimized warehouse internal process according to the transportation planning result. Section 13.2.3 explains the integration with SAP EWM from a transit warehouse perspective. Finally, Section 13.2.4 will give a brief overview of the warehouse billing process.

Recall that detailed integration guides with step-by-step introductions and process configuration are available. In addition to these guides, we explain the relevant process flow of these integration scenarios for outbound processing. We use screenshots of a sample process to document and explain the most relevant integration points.

13.2.1   Introduction to SAP EWM

Let's begin by moving our focus from warehouse management in general to SAP EWM. The administration of and transparency regarding existing materials is essential to making precise statements about the availability of a material. Goods movements are usually caused by procurement, distribution, and the associated GRs and goods issues (GIs) or through stock transfer.

SAP has been providing warehouse management functions since the release of SAP R/3 2.0. Thus, it can look back on more than 16 years of experience in warehouse management and countless successful implementations. Ever since the first SAP R/3-based versions and leading right up to the current SAP Supply Chain Management (SAP SCM)-based systems, functionality has been continually expanded and adjusted according to customer demands. In addition to Warehouse Management (WM) as part of SAP ERP, in 2005, SAP introduced the considerably more efficient SAP EWM, which is based on SAP SCM.

Today, SAP EWM is an independent application that can be used in any warehouse environment and integrated with SAP TM. SAP EWM was developed for complex warehouse and distribution centers with several different products and a high document volume. In contrast to WM, it offers many new and expanded functions and business objects. As of SAP S/4HANA 1609, SAP EWM is embedded within the suite— we'll focus on SAP EWM for SAP S/4HANA throughout this section. As in previous chapters, this content also applies to SAP EWM for SAP TM 9.6, unless otherwise noted.

To better understand the SAP TM integration scenarios and how SAP TM documents are mapped and integrated to their corresponding counterparts in SAP EWM, we first briefly explain the most relevant SAP EWM documents and terminology for a standard, outbound scenario. We then use this outbound scenario as the basis for the described integration scenarios.

From an SAP EWM perspective, the process starts with an SAP S/4HANA outbound delivery: the central document in GI. It typically represents a follow-up document to a sales order (SO) but can also be created directly, without reference to a preceding document. The physical shipment, which forms the completion of a GI procedure, thus begins with the generation of an outbound delivery document in SAP S/4HANA. Whether it's necessary to distribute this document to a decentralized SAP EWM system or process it in SAP EWM for SAP S/4HANA depends on the WM warehouse number that is allocated to a delivery item. If an outbound delivery is relevant to processing in SAP EWM, the follow-up activities, such as picking, packing, staging, and so on, are performed in the SAP EWM system.

Outbound Deliveries in SAP EWM

In the context of SAP EWM, the outbound delivery records the goods that are delivered to a goods recipient. From an SAP ERP perspective, it describes the process of picking goods, reducing the storage quantity, and finally shipping the goods to their destination (determined by a ship-to party). The outbound delivery process begins with goods picking and ends when the goods are delivered to the recipient. In the SAP system, this operation is represented by the outbound delivery document that is generated during the following activities:

- Goods shipment based on a SO
- Stock transfer order (STO)
- Goods return to the vendor

Before the introduction of SAP EWM into SAP S/4HANA, SAP ERP inbound deliveries and outbound deliveries were always replicated to a decentralized SAP EWM warehouse system where an *outbound delivery request* (ODR) was created. This document contained basically the same information, had the same structure as an outbound delivery in SAP ERP, and was activated upon successful replication.

With the introduction of SAP EWM for SAP S/4HANA 1609, it was decided that this object was no longer required and that a direct access of SAP EWM on the delivery was the preferred way forward on an SAP S/4HANA system. In the outbound example, that means skipping the creation of an ODR and directly starting the process with an outbound delivery order (ODO) in SAP EWM.

Within the outbound logistical process of SAP EWM for SAP S/4HANA, deliveries form *outbound delivery orders* (ODOs) in SAP EWM. An ODO is a document that contains all the relevant data required for triggering and monitoring the complete outbound delivery process. This process starts with the first planning activities for the outbound delivery and extends to the loading and shipping of the goods.

Goods are typically packed and handled on pallets. In this context, the *handling unit* (HU) represents a physical unit consisting of packaging materials and the products they contain. HUs have a single, scannable identification number.

In the context of SAP EWM, packaging materials are products that are intended to surround or contain products to pack. Products to pack can be packed into or onto the packaging material. The packaging material can be a load carrier. From a warehouse perspective, some examples of the most important packaging materials are crates, boxes, containers, wire baskets, and pallets.

As soon as the materials have been packed, the resulting packages (which are HUs) can be loaded on *transportation units* (TUs), and the GI is then posted. The system can also automatically determine the staging area and door for GI in advance, which is typically based on the route determined when the ODO was generated. The GI can be posted at various times.

Technically, this TU is a special kind of HU used to reflect the truck, trailer, or container that is used for shipping. A TU is assigned to delivery items and therefore contains all relevant information (e.g., carrier, license plate of the truck, and the information regarding which items are supposed to be loaded on the truck). Because loading is an optional step, the GI can be posted without previous loading, depending on system settings. Alternatively, posting can be done after loading or, if the Yard Management functionality is used, at the latest after the TU has left the warehouse grounds. When the GI is booked, SAP EWM informs inventory management in SAP S/4HANA of the change in stock.

13.2.2 SAP EWM for Delivery-Based Execution

SAP EWM was initially designed as a decentralized warehouse management system. Like SAP TM, which was also initially decoupled from SAP ERP, it was designed as an autonomous application of SAP SCM. SAP EWM requires integration with an SAP ERP system for master and transactional data. Like SAP TM, SAP EWM has moved to the SAP S/4HANA core, making the replication of master and transactional data obsolete within this deployment scenario.

SAP EWM was developed for complex warehouse and distribution centers with a variety of products and a high document volume. That is why the design of this warehouse management system has special emphasis on the flexible mapping of warehouse-internal processes. The extent of functions has been expanded considerably in comparison to the existing WM and supplemented by several warehouse structure elements. With this software, SAP enabled the setup and management of highly automated, high-volume operations and complex procedures.

As for SAP TM, the technical link between an external SAP EWM and SAP ERP and such functions as the transfer of inbound deliveries and outbound deliveries between the systems takes place in real time via defined interfaces. These interfaces enable the seamless integration of both systems by distributing, altering, and returning data relevant to deliveries. Inbound and outbound processing is performed asynchronously based on the sequence stored in the inbound and outbound queues. In the event of an error, such as a missing network connection, this queue saves all transfers and allows processing to continue seamlessly as soon as the error has been located and eliminated. The queue enables the real-time and bidirectional exchange and processing of information.

For systems embedded in SAP S/4HANA, many of the existing interfaces were altered or became unnecessary, such as the removed outbound delivery requests and inbound delivery requests. Refer to SAP Note 2668150 for further details.

From a technical standpoint, close integration of SAP EWM and SAP S/4HANA is achieved via interfaces (external SAP EWM) or direct access within the same system (SAP EWM for SAP S/4HANA), while process integration is done primarily via organizational data. As in the case of integration of the WM system, in SAP EWM, organizational allocation of warehouse numbers is initially achieved by their allocation to specific plant/storage location combinations.

From a purely technical standpoint, SAP EWM can also be operated as an autonomous system without direct connection to SAP ERP, SAP S/4HANA, or a non-SAP system. However, when it comes to integrating SAP TM—depending on the project base of the interfaces to be established and the processes to be implemented—standard integration with SAP ERP or embedded in SAP S/4HANA are preferred. In this section, to illustrate the SAP TM integration and processes, we assume the use of SAP EWM for SAP S/4HANA.

Direct Integration with SAP TM and SAP TM in SAP S/4HANA

Since the days of SAP TM 9.0 (and the first edition of this book!), the integration of SAP TM with SAP EWM ran via SAP ERP using SAP ERP shipments as an intermediate step. Data wasn't sent directly between SAP TM and SAP EWM. Since release 9.1, SAP TM supports direct integration between SAP TM and SAP EWM without creating shipments in SAP ERP. The next step in the evolution is the current scenario, where both SAP EWM and SAP TM run as part of the SAP S/4HANA system since release 1709.

The SAP EWM for SAP S/4HANA design was adapted to reflect the *principle of one* design idea, which was the basic guideline for the development of the new system. Thus, the changes were very similar to the ones in SAP TM described in this book. For SAP EWM for SAP S/4HANA, this meant both direct access to master data without the need for replication and also structural changes in its architecture.

As mentioned in Section 13.2.1, as part of its first release in SAP S/4HANA 1610, the inbound delivery notification and the ODR were removed. The purpose of these objects was to reflect the information of the delivery and form the basis for further warehouse execution. With the introduction of SAP EWM for SAP S/4HANA, this intermediate step was no longer necessary to be part of the overall design and thus was removed.

In this section, we explain the current, direct integration in SAP S/4HANA within an SAP EWM for S/4HANA. The integration scenarios are still based on orders and deliveries. Shipments, however, are part of the compatibility scope of solutions in SAP S/4HANA, which have a specific end-of-life date announced. They will no longer be supported after the year 2025.

Standard Integration Scenarios

To optimize transportation costs and efforts in a flexible and optimized way, SAP TM supports transportation planning based on either SO requirements or outbound deliveries. As part of transportation planning, the results influence warehouse-internal processes such as staging. The integration of the SAP TM transportation planning results into SAP EWM warehouse management processes is beneficial because it enables smooth outbound processing with an optimized warehouse-internal process according to the transportation planning result.

From a logistics perspective, GIs serve the controlled reduction of stock. Such stock reduction is executed based on sales and distribution processes. Hence, from the viewpoint of distribution logistics, a GI represents the completion of a shipping procedure to the customer and serves as an interface between internal and external logistics. Like a GR, the information flow in the GI process is based primarily on spatial circumstances, the materials to be picked, and individual process requirements in the warehouse. These requirements can vary from warehouse to warehouse and may even depend on the goods recipient.

For this core process, SAP EWM offers a variety of design options and enables the integration of individual process steps. In the following scenario descriptions, we focus on the main integration points and therefore don't illustrate the basic GI process in SAP EWM. Both SAP TM and SAP EWM support key use cases.

We now explain this direct integration and process flow for the standard integration scenarios shown in Table 13.4.

	Outbound	Inbound
Order based	Sales orders	Purchase orders
Delivery based	Outbound deliveries	Inbound deliveries

Table 13.4 Standard Integration Scenarios

For both inbound and outbound core processes, SAP EWM offers great flexibility to model the necessary warehouse operations and seamlessly integrates all relevant process steps with the transportation planning system.

The business background always concerns sending ordered goods to an external customer, while the transport is executed by an external carrier, and the goods are stored in warehouse. In this context, SAP TM is used for transportation planning, and SAP EWM for warehouse execution.

Known Restrictions

In a direct integration scenario, where SAP TM and SAP EWM behave as a common execution platform, SAP S/4HANA (or SAP ERP) is used to support the order integration on the SAP TM side, as well as the standard integration with SAP EWM.

In this context, we draw your attention to SAP Note 1984252, which describes the known supported functional scope and limitations of the direct integration.

In this section, we explain both delivery-based and order-based direct integration. For the delivery-based scenario, to make you familiar with the core functionality, we concentrate on both the explanation of the relevant warehouse activities and a documented process example with screenshots. For inbound processing, as well as order-based integration, we provide an overview and mention the main functional differences.

Outbound Planning with Warehouse Execution

According to the mentioned scenarios, a delivery-based or order-based planning process is used for outbound execution. Therefore, SAP TM sends freight order details to SAP EWM. Warehouse execution for outbound processes, such as picking, packing, staging, loading, and GI, takes place in SAP EWM. Given the seamless integration, SAP TM is updated with the actual dates, as well as discrepancies and quantity deviations.

SAP S/4HANA versus SAP ERP

The scenarios discussed here will work in all possible deployment scenarios:

- SAP TM and/or SAP EWM in SAP S/4HANA
- SAP TM and SAP EWM standalone in conjunction with a SAP S/4HANA system
- SAP TM and SAP EWM standalone in conjunction with a SAP ERP system

The following example, however, will be based on the latest technology and assume an execution scenario where both SAP EWM for SAP S/4HANA and SAP TM in SAP S/4HANA are used.

Delivery-Based Integration

The delivery-based integration scenario is an integrated warehousing and transportation process that sends ordered goods via an external carrier to external customers from a warehouse managed with SAP EWM. Transportation is planned in SAP TM, while warehouse activities are planned and executed in SAP EWM. This process is based on SAP S/4HANA SOs, and transportation requirements are based on SAP S/4HANA outbound deliveries.

Delivery processing in SAP S/4HANA involves grouping deliveries to pick, pack, and ship and then performing all the functions associated with the delivery process. Based on split criteria or combination indicators, you can group together entire orders or individual items or split orders into partial deliveries. As shown in Figure 13.13, outbound deliveries are created and scheduled in SAP S/4HANA and are the basis for transportation planning in SAP TM.

Because of the transportation planning in SAP TM, a freight order is created in SAP TM, which, as soon as the freight order is ready for loading, results in the creation of a TU in SAP EWM, together with the assignment of the relevant ODO.

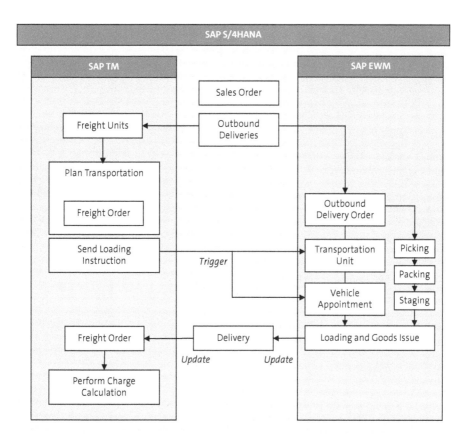

Figure 13.13 Delivery-Based Integration

Figure 13.13 depicts the flow of documents in the delivery-based execution using SAP EWM and SAP TM in conjunction in SAP S/4HANA.

Figure 13.14 shows an SAP ERP **Outbound Deliv. 800006718**. In this scenario, the item overview shows one line item as the transportation requirement. For its use in SAP TM, freight units are automatically built based on this information. SAP TM determines the smallest logistical unit to be transported through the transportation chain and regards this during its creation.

One or more delivery positions can create one or more freight units. At all times, the documents created in SAP TM can be seen in the delivery via the document flow in the **TM Status** tab of the delivery (see Figure 13.15).

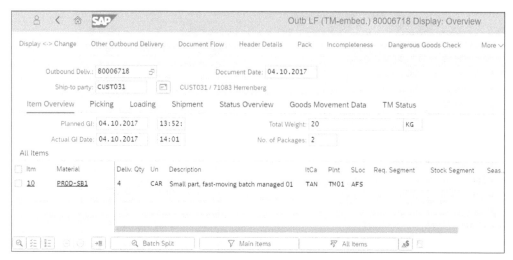

Figure 13.14 SAP ERP Delivery Line Item

Figure 13.15 SAP ERP Delivery Process Flow

During transportation planning, the freight units are assigned to freight orders. Figure 13.15 shows SAP S/4HANA delivery **80006718** with its current document flow. From here, you can also navigate to the individual documents by following the links.

In our example, freight unit **4100002850** was built. Transportation planning is executed based on this transportation requirement, and the freight unit is assigned to freight order **6100001651**.

Batch Split

Note that the freight unit has two positions. They reflect that SAP EWM determined that the materials are batch relevant and performed the picking of two different batches. The positions are split up in SAP TM after the batches have been determined in SAP EWM, and the message LoadingAppointmentNotification was triggered.

Figure 13.16 shows the **Stages** tab of the freight order and the **Source Location SP_0001**, which represents the corresponding SAP EWM warehouse where the outbound processing is executed.

Figure 13.16 SAP TM Freight Order Stages

The deliveries are visible both in SAP TM for transportation planning and execution and in SAP EWM for warehouse planning and execution. In SAP EWM, the delivery creates an ODO, which acts as the actual warehouse request and initiates the GI process in SAP EWM.

The outbound delivery 310000024500 contains data assumed from the preceding document and all necessary information to trigger the GI process and monitor it accordingly. From the perspective of warehouse management, the ODO represents a worklist that is completed only when the picked materials have been loaded and shipped. Figure 13.17 shows the ODO **310000024500** and a header reference to the **Vehicle 6100001651**. You can see that the order has been split into several ODO items. Two batches are relevant for warehouse processing.

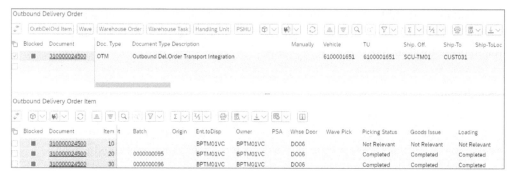

Figure 13.17 SAP EWM Outbound Delivery Order

After the generation of the ODO, SAP EWM begins all procedures required to supply the document with the necessary information and map the process in accordance with the settings in the system based on process-oriented or layout-oriented storage control. We describe the basics of SAP EWM storage control when we explain warehouse execution.

The ODO in SAP EWM is still blocked for processing. It's released as soon as the transportation planning process in SAP TM is completed, and SAP EWM is updated with the final planning results. Sending the loading instructions to SAP EWM creates a TU and automatically assigns the ODOs. With this assignment, the ODOs are unlocked und updated with the related carrier information from SAP TM.

Unlocked ODOs with TUs are now the basis for warehouse execution in SAP EWM. The SAP TM freight order now exists as a TU in SAP EWM. To easily identify the same object across all three systems, they all share the same document number.

Figure 13.18 shows TU **6100001651**, which has the same number as the SAP TM freight order (refer to Figure 13.16).

The SAP EWM TU has been referenced with its external key in the SAP EWM outbound delivery.

The warehouse-internal process starts when the deliveries are unblocked, and waves are created and released. When the ODOs are created, the system can automatically assign them to waves. This assignment to a picking wave is based on the shipping information, and an optional but useful step is to optimize the picking efficiency and to monitor and track the outbound process.

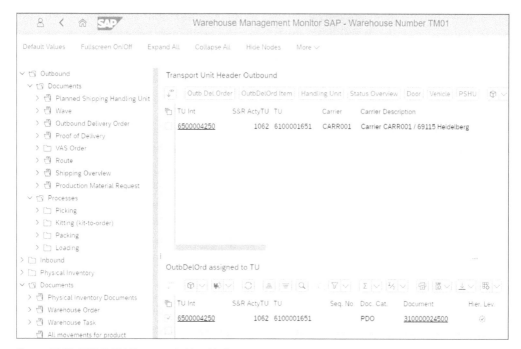

Figure 13.18 SAP EWM Transportation Unit

In this context, *wave management* groups a certain kind of warehouse request into a wave. Regardless of when a wave is to be released (i.e., the point in which warehouse tasks can be processed), wave management generates the necessary work packages in the form of warehouse orders and their corresponding warehouse tasks. The criteria for wave management can be kept in wave templates and can be based on shipping information.

To automatically allocate warehouse tasks to waves, you can use criteria from the delivery. Therefore, waves are created by combining warehouse request items based on common activity areas, routes, or materials in wave picks. The individual criteria and attributes for wave generation can be stored in the system as specifications and serve as the infrastructure for automatic or manual creation of waves.

Therefore, in operational practice, physical picking usually starts with grouping delivery items into waves. In doing so, SAP EWM can even take existing conveyor systems into account. Due to automated processing, this flexibility enables optimized grouping of the outgoing deliveries and drastically reducing picking times.

Wave management not only generates warehouse tasks, but also groups them into *warehouse orders*. Warehouse orders are executable work packages for warehouse employees that are generated according to the warehouse order generation rules stored in SAP EWM. The warehouse order contains the warehouse tasks or inventory items to be executed. In our case, these can be the tasks to pick the goods and move them to the staging area.

After the generation of the ODO, the system determines a warehouse process type and route and then conducts a rough estimate of the picking storage bin (source storage bin) based on a picking strategy. At the time, the staging area (destination storage bin) is determined using a *warehouse process type*. This parameter not only controls whether warehouse tasks should be immediately confirmed and which warehouse door should be determined but also the relevant steps in process-oriented storage control. Individual operational needs and spatial circumstances in the warehouse determine the processes in the warehouse, stock movements, and process steps to be performed. In real life, it's rare that the material flow is the same for all products and in all areas within a warehouse. Several people and resources are involved in the warehouse processes. Pallets might need to be deconsolidated in the GR area or consolidated in the GI area. SAP EWM offers storage control for flexible, tailor-made control of the material flow across several stations and to enable cross-resource stock movement through various stations.

The purpose of *storage control* is to map complex, multiple-level stock movements for put-away, removal, and internal warehouse transfer. Storage control is done in relation to the spatial circumstances along the lines of the predominant warehouse processes and the stock to be moved. Using storage control, SAP EWM can specify the put-away or removal route across several stations in a process-oriented or layout-oriented manner. This allows processes such as counting or deconsolidation in the GR area or packing in the GI area to be performed in an automated fashion. Storage control can be executed on multiple levels, enabling material flow via several interim storage bins. Stock movements are controlled via *storage processes*. Each process and all process steps in GR and GI are allocated to a storage process. The possible goods movement types and the direction of movement are assigned to a storage process via a warehouse process type and an activity.

The determination of the storage process depends especially on product and document information. The storage process is automatically selected by the system when the warehouse request is created, based on the document type, product, and delivery priority. If you use document characteristics and control indicators in the product master, the storage process can be controlled with great flexibility. For simple goods movements, the storage process itself can contain the storage type and bin from or to which a material is to be moved. For complex movements, it can contain the storage process or *process-oriented storage* control.

Process-oriented storage control allows you to map complex picking and put-away processes. The individual steps, such as staging or loading, or the execution of supplementary logistics services can be adjusted as desired and are allocated to a storage process in the system. The determined procedures and their activities are assumed by the HU to be picked or placed. The HU thus possesses the information regarding which process steps are necessary for picking or warehouse-internal stock movements. That is why process-oriented storage control works only with HUs.

Picking and moving the goods to the staging area is usually carried out using a *radio frequency* (RF) device. If RF is used, the warehouse worker logs on as a resource and takes an empty pallet or wire basket as a pick HU. After it's assigned to an RF queue, he or she receives the first pick task for execution and is prompted to create the pick HU for the warehouse order he or she is currently executing. After the HU is created, the system can automatically print the HU label, which contains both plain text descriptions and the HU number as a bar code.

The worker typically continues to the source bin and picks the requested product and quantity into the pick HU proposed by the system. To avoid mistakes, the source bin, product bar code, and pick HU are scanned before the picked quantity is entered. With the confirmation of the warehouse task, the worker proceeds with the next task. When the warehouse order has been executed, and the last task has been confirmed, process-oriented storage control can prompt the worker to move the pick HU to the staging area. In addition, if this has been foreseen in storage control, there might be additional, intermediate steps, such as shrink-wrapping or packaging.

SAP EWM generally allows one- and two-step picking. It also enables you to integrate the packaging process into picking. This procedure, called pick and pack, enables direct picking in a shipping unit. An expansion of this function is the pick, pack, and pass procedure, a one-step picking procedure with decentralized picking and static staging. Pick, pack, and pass allows the work to be passed from one resource or employee performing the work to another after part of the picking has taken place. The sequence of warehouse tasks for stock removal can be determined according to various criteria, such as the shortest path. SAP EWM and the corresponding SAP S/4HANA system are closely linked for the picking process. This allows picking specifications such as batches or batch characteristics to be considered.

When all warehouse tasks for stock removal are confirmed, the stock is removed from its source storage bin and moved to the destination storage bin. If a difference in quantity is detected in the process because the picked quantity deviates from the quantity to be picked, then another warehouse task can be created, or the quantity to be delivered is adjusted and diminished accordingly. When a second warehouse task is generated, stock removal isn't complete until the second warehouse task has also been confirmed. The warehouse worker drops the pick HU at the staging area, scans the staging bin bar code, and thus confirms this step in the system. With the last confirmation, SAP EWM prints a shipping HU (SHU) label to be attached to the pallet.

As soon as the materials have been picked and staged, the resulting HUs are loaded, and the GI can be posted. As mentioned previously, the system can also automatically determine the staging area and door for GI in advance.

From a process perspective, if Yard Management is used, the truck arrives at the checkpoint. It's identified by the external TU number, which also represents the freight order number in SAP TM. The truck can be automatically assigned to a warehouse door. Alternatively, the door assignment can be done manually be the checkpoint clerk or—in large yards—the shipping office.

After the truck has arrived at the warehouse and is docked to the door, the loading of the goods can begin. Loading is also supported by RF. Scanning the door starts the loading of the TU. The ship HU is loaded on the truck, its bar code is scanned, and the system automatically creates and confirms a corresponding warehouse task. Loading is confirmed as soon as all ship HUs have been loaded on the TU. When the loading is finished, delivery notes and the waybill can be printed, and the GI can be posted in SAP EWM based on the TU. When the GI is posted, SAP EWM sends confirmed execution results—the Lightweight Delivery Access Protocol (LDAP) notification—to SAP TM. At the same time, the SAP S/4HANA outbound delivery is also updated.

For the monitoring and processing of these tasks, a cockpit has been created in SAP EWM in addition to the well-known warehouse monitor, which has been used for the SAP EWM screenshots in this book so far.

As shown in Figure 13.19 the cockpit can show a list of TUs and their respective progress in the warehouse execution. Aside from getting an overview on the outgoing shipments, the monitor also allows for manually setting the statuses for **Loading**, **Arrival**, **Departure**, and **Goods Issue** and allows for manual processing steps, such as door and staging area assignments and seal changes. This functionality brings transparency to the TU processing and is a helpful tool for outbound execution processing in the context of an integrated scenario between SAP TM and SAP EWM.

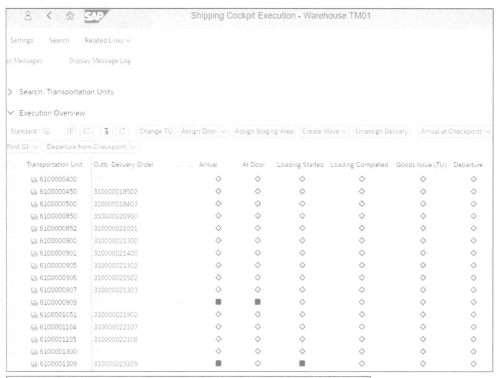

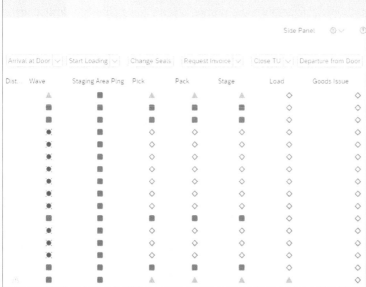

Figure 13.19 SAP EWM Shipping Cockpit Execution

If an SHU is missing, the ODO can be unassigned from the TU before posting goods use. It can be manually assigned to another TU or considered during the next transportation planning in SAP TM. Alternatively, the ODO can be split.

ODOs can be manually assigned to other TUs or considered during the next transportation planning in SAP TM. Freight units that could not be loaded to the TU in SAP EWM are automatically unassigned from the freight order and can be considered for the next transportation planning.

Integration Improvements for SAP EWM and SAP TM

With the introduction of SAP EWM 9.4 and SAP TM, the following process improvements were made (and thus relevant for this book). They became necessary as integrated execution demanded higher flexibility in the handling of changes throughout the process.

- **Inbound processing**
  SAP TM can send updates to vehicles or TUs and changes in delivery item assignments (added or removed items) to SAP EWM until the truck arrives at the checkpoint. SAP EWM in turn can communicate arrivals and departures at checkpoints and their respective reversals back to SAP TM.

- **Outbound processing**
  Vehicle or TU changes can be communicated from SAP TM to SAP EWM until arrival at checkpoint. Delivery item assignments can still be changed until loading completion. SAP EWM can communicate the arrival of a TU at a checkpoint and the reversal back to SAP TM.

- **Bidirectional**
  Seals that are, for example, used for containers can be updated bidirectionally between the systems.

When the carrier confirms the arrival of the truck at the customer site, the freight order is completely executed and confirmed.

During the outbound process execution, SAP TM is updated with all execution-relevant information and events.

As shown in Figure 13.20, the SAP EWM updates sent via the loading notification are used to set the respective event timings, allowing for full transparency on the actual status of the freight order. In addition, the actual loaded quantities and seals are updated in SAP TM to consider any deviations from the initial plan that might have occurred during warehouse execution.

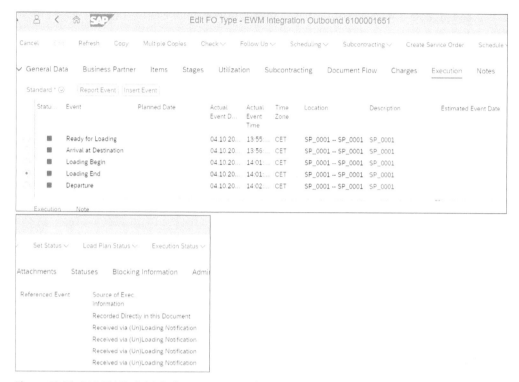

Figure 13.20 SAP TM Freight Order Event Reporting

Order-Based Integration

In addition to delivery-based integration, SAP EWM and SAP TM can also work together in an order-based process. In contrast to the previous scenario, the outbound delivery is now created because of freight unit–based delivery proposals and transportation planning in SAP TM. In the delivery-based scenario, inventory planning and logistics execution had priority over the transportation planning process in SAP TM, and deliveries were already created.

In the order-based scenario, SAP TM plans transportation based on SAP S/4HANA SOs and as a result proposes and creates deliveries based on the determined dates and quantities. Transportation planning results in the creation of freight orders, which are the basis for the delivery creation in SAP S/4HANA. In this context, SAP TM considers transportation constraints, such as resource availability and transportation durations. The created deliveries are usable by SAP EWM (see Figure 13.21). In SAP TM, the freight order can be the basis for tendering and carrier selection (refer to Chapter 7).

The process flow of the order-based integration is quite like the delivery-based integration planning, so we just focus on the main differences here.

The process starts with a SO and a planned delivery date. This automatically creates freight units. These are then the basis for transportation planning and optimization in SAP TM.

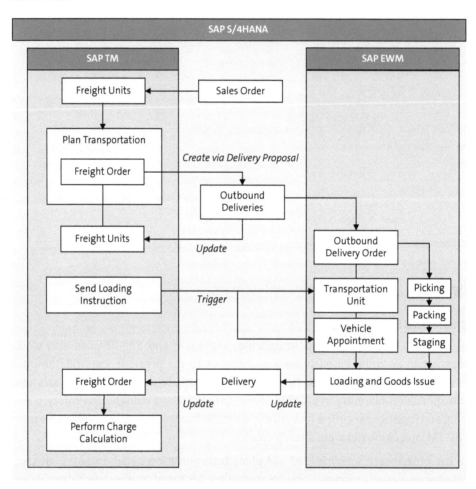

Figure 13.21 Order-Based Transportation and Warehouse Execution

The transportation planning in SAP TM is completed as soon as the transportation capacity of the freight orders has been fully planned and all relevant transportation requirements have been assigned. After the carrier has been assigned, SAP TM can trigger the creation of a SAP S/4HANA outbound delivery and communicate the freight order number to the selected carrier. These deliveries are based on the transportation planning results and therefore consider planning constraints, such as resource availability, distances, durations, and consolidation and dates. This step can be executed manually or automatically as a background job.

As soon as the delivery has been created, the document flow in SAP TM is updated to show all related documents to a freight unit and freight order.

In Figure 13.22, the document flow of a freight order in SAP TM is shown. **Sales Order 69659** was initially the basis for the **Freight Unit 4100000258**. After the creation of the **Outbound Delivery 80049967**, its number shows up in the document flow.

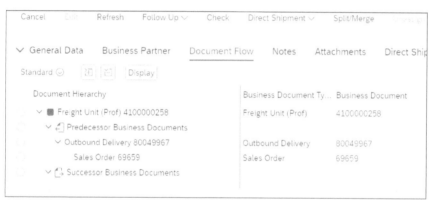

Figure 13.22 Document Flow: SAP TM with SO

When the deliveries have been created, they are visible in the SAP EWM environment for further processing as ODOs. The SAP S/4HANA delivery is created with the proposed delivery date from SAP TM.

If the SAP EWM ODOs haven't been assigned to a TU, these orders are locked for execution. When the transportation planning activities are finished, and the freight order status has been set to **Cargo Ready for Loading**, SAP TM sends a loading instruction to SAP EWM. This triggers the creation of a TU in SAP EWM.

In SAP EWM, the TUs are automatically assigned to the (locked) ODOs. With this assignment, the ODOs are unlocked and updated with the related carrier information from SAP TM. Unlocked ODOs, assigned to a TU, are now the basis for warehouse execution in SAP EWM. As in the previous scenario, goods are typically picked by waves, put directly into SHUs, staged, and finally loaded on a truck. Posting GI in SAP EWM immediately adjusts the inventory in SAP S/4HANA, updating the outbound deliveries and the freight order in SAP TM for a later freight cost settlement.

Inbound Planning with Warehouse Execution

In addition to outbound processing, the direct integration of SAP TM with SAP EWM also supports planning and execution for inbound processing. As has been mentioned for outbound, the planning process for inbound execution can be delivery-based or order-based. Therefore, SAP TM sends freight order details to SAP EWM. Warehouse execution for inbound—such as unloading and GR—takes place in SAP EWM. Given the seamless integration, SAP TM is updated with the actual dates and quantities.

Delivery-Based Integration

The process starts with a purchase order (PO) and follow-up inbound deliveries. In SAP EWM, the inbound delivery, which represents a warehouse request, and the starting point for subsequent activities in SAP EWM are created.

Because of the transportation planning in SAP TM, a freight order is created. As soon as the transportation planning activities are finished, and the freight order status has been set to **Cargo Ready for Unloading**, SAP TM automatically sends an unloading instruction to SAP EWM, triggering the creation of a TU.

The inbound delivery, now being assigned to the TU, contains all necessary information to trigger and monitor the goods delivery process in SAP EWM. This process typically continues with the truck arriving at the yard and unloading the cargo, and finally ends with put-away of the materials in the warehouse. During unloading, the goods are moved out of the transport unit from the door to a staging zone, consolidation zone, or work center for quality inspection, depending on operational needs. When Yard Management is used, the unloading process begins with the recording of the vehicle or TU at the control point. Put-away in the destination storage bin completes the GR process from a warehouse management perspective (see Figure 13.23).

After unloading, as soon as the warehouse worker has posted the GR, the SAP S/4HANA inbound delivery is automatically updated. In SAP TM, the relevant freight documents are updated accordingly.

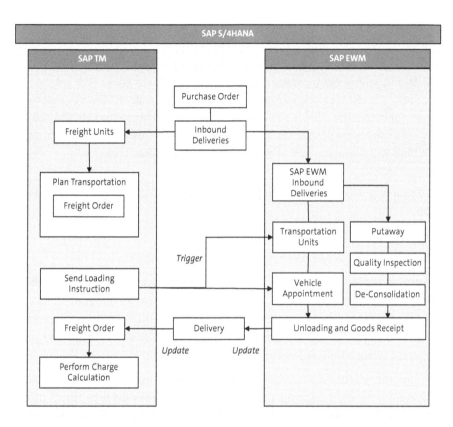

Figure 13.23 Delivery-Based Inbound Processing

Order-Based Integration

In the order-based scenario, SAP TM plans transportation based on SAP S/4HANA POs. These create freight units in SAP TM. The freight units are planned on freight orders, and subsequently SAP S/4HANA inbound deliveries are created.

Warehouse execution is like the order-based integration mentioned previously. After GR has been posted, the SAP TM documents will be updated with the actual dates and quantities.

We've now introduced the integration of SAP TM and SAP EWM for SAP S/4HANA. The changes in this area have been mainly of a technical nature, whereas the process remained nearly the same compared to the previous version of this book.

Integration If SAP EWM and SAP TM Aren't Embedded

Note that while not explicitly mentioned everywhere, the integration of SAP TM and SAP EWM also still works in nonembedded scenarios, where either SAP TM, SAP EWM, or both are installed side by side to an SAP S/4HANA system. This is especially important for customers already running SAP TM or SAP EWM side by side and contemplating a conversion of their SAP ERP system to SAP S/4HANA: the integration to both systems will still be possible after the core system has been converted.

In the next section, we introduce the integration with transit warehouses based on SAP EWM.

13.2.3 Integration with SAP EWM for Transit Warehouses

In the previous section, we introduced the core processes and functional building blocks of warehouse operations based on SAP EWM and gave an integrated process example based on standard integration scenarios with SAP TM. In this context, we explained the integration and warehouse-internal processes for inbound and outbound operations for a typical distribution center scenario.

Now let's turn our attention to integration with SAP EWM from a transit warehouse perspective. Globalization requires that products sometimes need to travel thousands of miles before they can reach a consumer. And in global transportation chains, numerous parties are connected in a supply chain and challenged to efficiently carry out logistics process going beyond transportation to involve handling, consolidation, rearrangement, staging, and other warehouse operations at intermediate locations. The general goal is to cover the physical distances and temporal periods between the location where the goods are produced and the location where they are needed efficiently.

SAP S/4HANA versus SAP ERP

Although SAP S/4HANA is our base system, the processes described in the following sections haven't been changed significantly since the preceding edition of this book. Air cargo security handling and seals have been introduced in later releases of SAP TM.

Transshipment Operations

Freight forwarders can use SAP TM together with SAP EWM to solve transportation problems for their customers and efficiently manage transshipment operations at intermediate locations. These operations typically include transportation, transshipping, and storage of products in an integrated, cross-system scenario. The integration is based on execution documents resulting from forwarding orders, and it can help you organize the cargo flow over the entire transportation chain and get transparency regarding warehouse-specific data.

Transportation processes move goods from one source to a destination and typically serve to alter the location of these goods and products. In this context, the means of transport is closely tied to commercial factors and the characteristics of the goods to be transported. To provide an efficient transport between two distant locations, diverse means of transport (e.g., trains, ships, trucks, or planes) are needed. The change in means of transport is called transshipping.

Therefore, a transshipment warehouse is used to store goods for a short period of time and generally only to transfer them to another means of transport. The focus is placed on movement processes. For this reason, the primary concern is generally not high storage capacity but rather high transshipping efficiency or high transshipping speed.

SAP EWM provides both the functionality to consolidate, separate, and sort goods to create the most efficient transport possible and the performance and capabilities to handle transshipment operations, seamlessly integrated with SAP TM.

Transshipments

In the previous section, we mentioned that SAP TM is used for transportation planning and execution along the complete transportation chain, while SAP EWM is used to manage the transit warehouses.

These transshipment locations serve as a bridge between the receipt and the dispatch of goods. From a transportation planning perspective, transshipment locations are transit warehouses in which goods are stored for a limited time and transshipped from one vehicle to another, while differences between receipt and dispatch can be addressed. As a rule, they are distribution centers, container freight stations, railway stations, gateways, or similar places where a change in transit carrier (e.g., from a truck to a plane) frequently takes place.

Integration of SAP TM and SAP EWM for Transit Warehousing

This section provides you with an overview of the main integration aspects of SAP TM with SAP EWM for transit warehousing by using an air freight scenario as an example.

Documentation

In the previous edition of this book, the documentation for the transshipment process between SAP TM and SAP EWM wasn't completed yet upon its release. The current process description can be found at *http://help.sap.com*. Search for "SAP S/4HANA", and select the link for product assistance. Follow the path **Enterprise Business Applications** • **Supply Chain** • **Transportation Management** • **Integration** • **Integration with SAP Extended Warehouse Management**.

As you'll learn next, the outbound integration from SAP TM to SAP EWM is based mainly on LDAP requests known from the direct integration. The structure of this message is very flexible and can contain information resulting from freight orders as well as freight bookings. Supporting different scenarios, it offers a flexible structure to send context-specific information to SAP EWM. This context is mainly specific to locations and transportation chains, and it varies mainly regarding the granularity and structure of line-item hierarchies and clear instructions reflecting how capacity and cargo items are nested in a specific business context.

The following sections provide you with only an overview of how this integration generally works and make you familiar with only some of the functional building blocks of transit warehousing.

In previous chapters, you've seen that freight documents in SAP TM use different item categories to define the goods to be transported, as well as the capacity to do so. From an integration perspective, with SAP EWM, we therefore need to distinguish between *cargo items* and *capacity items*. Both items can have a hierarchy where, for example, cargo items are normally assigned to capacity items (refer to Chapter 7, Section 7.2).

Capacity items are transportation resources, whereas cargo items are typically *package items* (PKG), *containers* (TUR), or the *products* (PRD) themselves. *Transportation resources* can be active or passive (refer to Chapter 3, Section 3.3). *Active vehicle resources* (AVR) are self-propelled and can drive by themselves (e.g., trucks), while *passive vehicle resources* (PVR) must be coupled to an AVR to move (e.g., trailers).

In SAP EWM, the warehouse-specific processes are based on business documents that are created using loading and unloading instructions that are sent from SAP TM. You can configure the warehouse layout according to the specific requirements of the transit warehousing process. For example, specific storage types are available, and a product master is no longer necessary. Further, the handling of cargo is done on the package level and not on the product level.

The integration itself starts in SAP TM. After a transportation planner finishes planning freight orders, for example, the execution of loading or unloading steps in a warehouse system can be triggered. SAP TM uses LDAP requests (loading appointments based on SAP Process Integration message TransportationOrderLoadingAppointmentRequest_IN) to integrate freight orders with SAP EWM. These requests are mapped to SAP EWM, finally creating documents, vehicles, TUs, and planned HUs for inbound and outbound processing. After the warehouse operations have been executed, SAP EWM communicates the loading or unloading results back to SAP TM. This LDAP notification is based on SAP Process Integration message TransportationOrderLoadingAppointmentNotification_OUT.

To illustrate the complete process, we'll use an air freight example for an end-to-end transshipment process as depicted in Figure 13.24.

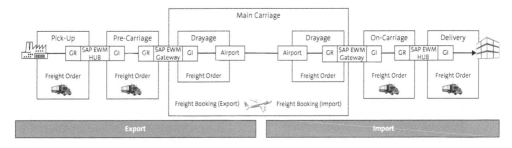

Figure 13.24 End-to-End Air Freight Transshipment

As Figure 13.24 shows and previously described, the goods pass several warehouse locations before they reach their destination. From a SAP TM perspective, the objects involved in the communication with SAP EWM are freight orders and freight bookings. In each warehouse along the transportation chain, a GR and a GI process take place. Information on incoming and outgoing trucks and planned goods to be transported is supplied by SAP TM.

Note

Although an air freight scenario serves as our example, the same procedures can be applied to ocean freight as well.

Within the next two sections, we'll discuss the inbound and outbound processes for one location in the transportation chain. We'll then proceed with an example to illustrate the process further.

Inbound Integration

In a transit warehouse, only packages are moved. Typically, the warehouse system knows the attributes of the package content, while the content itself doesn't correspond to a product master record. For SAP EWM, that means that this integration with SAP TM doesn't support product master records. The "content" attributes and characteristics are stored at the document level and received via an LDAP request or manually maintained in the receiving process.

The basis for the process is the creation of a forwarding order in SAP TM, where the intended route is either entered manually, via default route, or automatically determined by the system with the help of a transportation proposal.

Constraints and Functional Scope

The described functionality focuses on freight forwarders and is currently not foreseen for shippers, so the execution of this process always relies on forwarding orders as the base document.

Corresponding freight units are then planned on a freight order, which is the integration-relevant object. The messaging to SAP EWM is triggered based on the created freight order.

SAP TM sends an LDAP request (LoadingAppointmentRequest) to the destination, a SAP EWM location, after the *unload plan finalized* action is s triggered. The freight order includes at least packaging items (PKG) from a shipper (see Figure 13.25). SAP EWM then creates the corresponding TU, an inbound delivery for each freight order, a delivery item for each package item, and planned HUs for the corresponding item quantities.

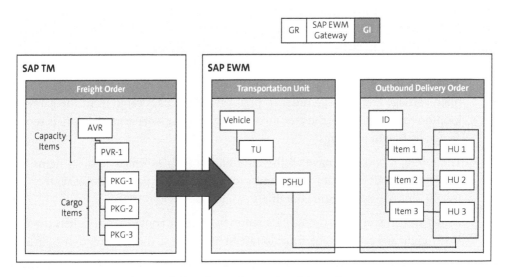

Figure 13.25 Integration in Transit Warehouse Processing: Inbound

13

In a standard SAP EWM inbound process, HU items are linked to delivery items, while a top HU is linked to the inbound delivery header. This reference is lost after the delivery is put away. As we mentioned earlier, a transit warehouse doesn't need product items and therefore can't link the HU to a delivery item. In order not to lose the reference to the inbound delivery after the delivery is put away, HUs in this integrated scenario have a permanent reference to the corresponding delivery item and won't lose it after put-away. The arrival of the truck, unloading, and GR is confirmed to SAP TM via the LoadingAppointmentNotification message, where it updates the freight order.

After the GR has been posted, the HUs change their status from **Planned** to **Existing**. Alternatively, if package items are already received in another transit location, SAP TM sends the exact HU identification to SAP EWM, together with the information of which HU is assigned to which vehicle resource. This typically happens in a second warehouse after the cargo is received at a previous transit location and the HU identification was sent to SAP TM via an LDAP notification. SAP TM can now send detailed information specifying which HU is nested in which PVR. In SAP EWM, these HUs are also created as planned HUs with the (existing) HU identification from SAP TM as an external HU identification.

For inbound processing in an entire transportation chain, the integration between SAP TM and SAP EWM supports both the initial receipt of cargo items at an entry location and their relationship to capacity items as soon as cargo is received at an intermediate location. Gateway locations are typically the last consolidation location before cargo is transported on the main carriage. From a system perspective, the main carriage and drayage order to physically hand over cargo from the gateway location to, for example, the ground handling agent at a departure airport, is represented by freight bookings.

These freight bookings have all the information such as which capacity items are expected in SAP EWM for outbound processing at the gateway location. For air freight, this typically means containers or *unit load devices* (ULDs).

For air freight scenarios, these ULDs represent specific containers or pallets used to load freight and cargo onboard an aircraft. In this context, the LDAP request from SAP TM contains mainly TUR items representing a container or ULD. Based on that information, SAP EWM creates either a TU for ocean freight or an HU for air freight.

Because the freight booking has no information about the vehicle bringing the container or ULD, it needs a second message to send these relevant freight order details to SAP EWM and create a corresponding TU for this drayage freight order. This order is used mainly to cover and document the short distance of the intermodal transport between the gateway and the means of transport itself.

Outbound Integration
Like the inbound integration, SAP TM also uses LDAP requests to send outbound-relevant information and trigger the warehouse execution for packing, staging, and loading in SAP EWM.

These requests are based on freight orders containing information about the freight (SHU) that is loaded onto a freight order, as well as freight bookings containing information about HUs and TUR items that need to be packed or nested. For the intermodal transport and to finally hand over ULDs (e.g., to a ground handling agent), SAP TM also uses drayage freight orders to specify which ULD is loaded onto which TU.

We've already mentioned that these LDAP requests contain both cargo items and capacity items. For outbound processing, that means SAP TM sends all relevant items, if needed in a hierarchy, to trigger the creation of planned HUs in SAP EWM and to specify which of these HUs will be loaded onto which TU (see Figure 13.26).

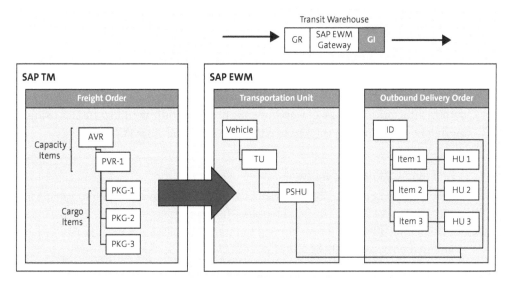

Figure 13.26 Integration in Transit Warehouse Processing: Outbound

The integration typically starts with the LDAP request (LoadingAppointmentRequest) containing freight order information specifying the AVR and PVR being used for loading outbound processing. In this context, SAP TM can send either rough information about cargo and capacity items or the exact hierarchy specifying which SHU must be packed in which TU.

In the case of freight bookings, as has been mentioned previously for the inbound integration, SAP TM sends a loading appointment request. If SAP EWM is provided with a HU container (PSHU), it packs the ULDs according to the provided PSHU. After completion, SAP EWM sends the LDAP notification (LoadingAppointmentNotification) to SAP TM. This notification is sent for each ULD and contains the actual HU, which is picked into the ULD. It updates the SAP TM freight booking and freight units with this information.

Alternatively, SAP TM can send less detailed information without clear instructions regarding which PKG items are nested under which TUR item. SAP EWM then creates the TU with a PSHU itself and reports the results back to SAP TM with a LoadingAppointmentNotification to update the freight booking and freight units.

To finally cover and document the short distance of the intermodal transport between the gateway to the place where the goods are to be loaded on the plane, SAP

TM also sends a message to communicate details of this drayage freight order to SAP EWM. This message creates a corresponding TU in SAP EWM and contains all ULDs that are loaded on a TU to transport the ULD to the airport.

Sample Air Freight Scenario

In the previous section, we explained the main characteristics and principles of the system integration for transit warehousing. In this section, we illustrate this using an air freight scenario from shipper to consignee (refer to Figure 13.24).

Air Freight Scenario Specifics

Note that we won't describe the specifics of how to execute an air freight scenario in this section. We'll rather focus on the steps that need to be performed to allow integration into SAP EWM for performing the transit warehousing process. For further information on air freight bookings, refer to Chapter 5, Section 5.4.2.

This sample scenario starts with a forwarding order (export) 1100009315 to ship goods from a shipper in Japan to a consignee in the United States.

Figure 13.27 shows the forwarding order for this air freight export scenario in SAP TM.

Display Air Freight - Forwarding Order Export 1100009315

| | Save | Cancel | Edit | | Copy | Other Copy Options | | Refresh | | Follow Up | | Check | Confirm | | Cancel Document | | Customs | | HAWB | Forwarding |

| | General Data | Business Partner | Locations and Dates/Times | Ordered Route | **Actual Route** | Nature of Goods |

Stage Overview

Source Gateway IATA Code:	NRT
Airport of Departure (IATA Code):	NRT
Cargo Cut-Off Date:	07.11.2018 15:30:00 JAPAN
Customs Documentation Cut-Off Date:	07.11.2018 00:00:00 JAPAN
Dangerous Goods Documentation Cut-Off Date:	06.11.2018 17:00:00 JAPAN
Documentation Cut-Off Date:	07.11.2018 00:00:00 JAPAN
VGM Cut-Off Date/Time Given by Carrier:	

| | Change Hierarchy: Item View | | Insert | Merge | | Route | Schedule | Capacity Document | Set OI Status | Determine Distance and Du |

Stage Description	Stage Type	Transportation Mode	Source Location	UN/L.. (Source)	IATA Code (Source)	City (Source)	
▼ Route			CUOAF-CU-02@Q8R...			Ota-ku	
Stage 1	01 (Pick-Up)	01 (Road)	CUOAF-CU-02@Q8R...			Ota-ku	
Stage 2	02 (Pre-Carriage)	01 (Road)	OAF-STA-JPTYO	JPTYO		Tokyo	
Stage 3	03 (Main Carriage)	05 (Air)	AIR-GW-JPNRT	JPNRT	NRT	Narita Airport	
Stage 4	04 (On-Carriage)	01 (Road)	AIR-GW-USLAX	USLAX	LAX	Irvine	
Stage 5	05 (Delivery)	01 (Road)	OAF-STA-USSAN	USSAN		San Diego	

Figure 13.27 Forwarding Order in SAP TM

For this scenario, it already contains all relevant stages (**Stage 1** to **Stage 5**), from picking up the cargo from the shipper and receiving it at the first transit warehouse location in Japan, the domestic pre-carriage to the departure airport, and the main carriage to the United States, with the on-carriage and final delivery to the consignee.

Let's walk through these stages:

1. **Pickup**

   For the first stage, a pickup freight order is created. Freight units are assigned to the respective freight order, and the cargo is picked up from the customer and brought to the SAP EWM hub.

   After the freight order has been set to **Ready for Transportation Execution**, and the **Load Plan Status** is set to **Unload Plan Finalized**, the LoadingAppointmentRequest is sent to SAP EWM.

   SAP EWM receives the LDAP request with the inbound transportation planning result from SAP TM. In this example, this message contains information about the truck bringing pallets from the shipper to the transit warehouse. HUs and TUs are created in SAP EWM.

   Figure 13.28 shows the freight order which is inbound to the warehouse and the items that are reported to SAP EWM for processing, in this case, six pallets. Changes can still be made on the forwarding order and resent to SAP EWM via the **Load Plan Finalized** status until the cargo is reported as **On Hand**.

Display AF – Pickup/Delivery Freight Order 300045314								
Save Cancel Edit Refresh Copy Multiple Copies Check Follow Up Scheduling Subcontracting Cre								
▾ General Data Business Partner **Items** Stages Utilization Subcontracting Document Fl◻								

All Items

▷I ▷I   Change Hierarchy   All Items   ⌄   Insert   Choose Item Types   Insert ▴   Create Service Order   A

Item Hierarchy	Qua...	Qua... UoM	Gross Weight	Gross Weight UoM	Gross Volu...	Gross Volu... UoM	FU or TU
▾ 🚚 Active Vehicle OAF-JP-TRUCK 1000000	6	EA	1,4	TO	6	M3	
▾ 📖 Air Freight - Forwarding Order Export 11000...	6	EA	1,4	TO	6	M3	
▾ 🗐 AF Freight Unit Type 4100004152	6	EA	1,4	TO	6	M3	4100004152
▪▪ Package 10 Electronic Components	6	EA	1,4	TO	6	M3	4100004152

Figure 13.28 Pickup Freight Order

After the truck arrives at the warehouse yard, SAP EWM starts sending updates to SAP TM. The truck is unloaded, and the six pallets are received as HUs and put away in the transit warehouse. SAP EWM posts the GR for the unloaded HUs and automatically determines a put-away bin.

Several LoadingAppointmentNotification messages are sent for the statuses **Arrival at Destination, Unloading End**, and **Departure**. Discrepancies that occur during the warehousing process, such as missing or damaged goods, are also part of the SAP EWM–SAP TM communication and can subsequently be addressed.

Documentation

For further detailed information on discrepancy handling, refer to *https://bit.ly/2Evi-wMl*. The discrepancy handling for transit warehousing is specifically described there.

---

2. **Pre-carriage**

   To transport the HUs to the export gateway, SAP TM sends the outbound transportation results to SAP EWM. In this context, the LDAP request contains all relevant information to move the cargo from a transit warehouse JPTYO to a next transit warehouse (refer to Figure 13.27). This outbound process represents Stage 2 in forwarding order 1100009315.

   For the second stage, another freight order is built, and the cargo assigned to it. From a SAP TM perspective, the only difference in the handling of the freight order is the setting of the status **Load Plan Finalized** instead of **Unload Plan Finalized**.

   The respective freight order is received in SAP EWM, and the TU with respective HUs and an ODO are created. Because the goods have already passed a SAP EWM location, the outbound HUs are automatically linked with their unique SAP EWM identifiers and referenced to forwarding order 1100002021.

   For loading activities and for the departure of the truck, SAP EWM updates SAP TM again with a LoadingAppointmentNotification message, based on which the statuses in SAP TM are updated.

   The same freight order is used to inform the gateway about the incoming goods via setting the status **Unload Plan Finalized**. Inbound handling happens once more, as is described in the previous explanation of the inbound process.

3. **Main carriage**

   According to the sample scenario, the truck finally arrives at the gateway location

JPNRT, where the cargo is unloaded and staged, before it departs for the main carriage from Japan to the United States. This step, Stage 3 in our air freight scenario (refer to Figure 13.27), requires an air freight booking.

Figure 13.29 shows the export air freight booking **400007868**. In the **Overview** tab, SAP TM shows the current state of the planned and executed warehouse steps, including the **Load Plan Status** and SAP EWM transmission status for each of the stages. In addition, in the **Capacity and Cargo** tab, the expected ULDs and their content is described. After the **Load Plan Finalized** status is set in the freight booking, the LoadingAppointmentRequest is sent to the SAP EWM system.

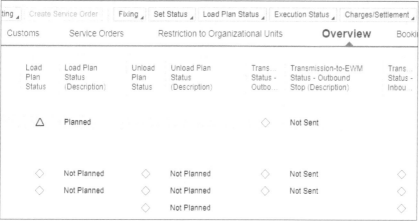

Figure 13.29 Air Freight Booking Overview

To prepare loading and double-check that the outbound quantities are staged, SAP EWM delivers its own transactions to supervise the receiving progress and prepare loading and unloading activities for freight bookings while monitoring the scheduled departure times.

After all HUs are loaded into the respective ULDs, the process is confirmed to SAP TM, and the corresponding freight booking and freight unit are updated.

For the last stage, a freight order for pickup is created from the freight booking **Cargo Management** tab, as shown in Figure 13.30. The transit warehouse process for this freight order is exactly like the one mentioned in the pre-carriage step.

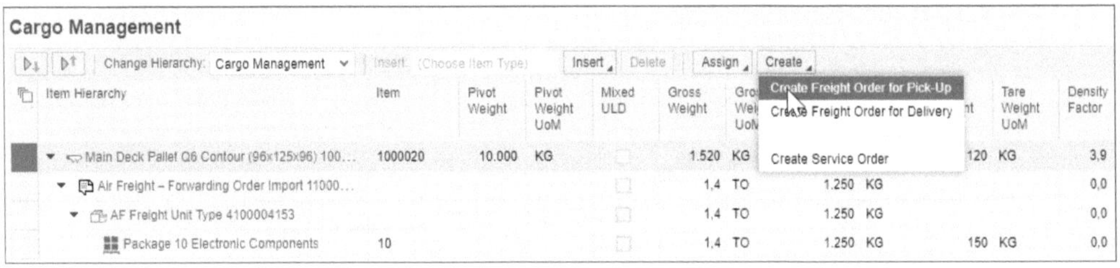

Cargo Management											
▷₁ ▷ᵀ Change Hierarchy: Cargo Management ∨ Insert (Choose Item Type) Insert ▴ Delete Assign ▴ Create ▴											
📁 Item Hierarchy	Item	Pivot Weight	Pivot Weight UoM	Mixed ULD	Gross Weight	Gro Wei UoN	Create Freight Order for Pick-Up	nt	Tare Weight UoM	Density Factor	
							Create Freight Order for Delivery				
▾ ◁▷ Main Deck Pallet Q6 Contour (96x125x96) 100...	1000020	10.000	KG	☐	1.520	KG	Create Service Order		120 KG	3.9	
▾ 📄 Air Freight – Forwarding Order Import 11000...				☐	1.4	TO		1.250 KG		0.0	
▾ 📄 AF Freight Unit Type 4100004153				☐	1.4	TO		1.250 KG		0.0	
▦ Package 10 Electronic Components	10			☐	1.4	TO		1.250 KG	150 KG	0.0	

Figure 13.30 Creation of Pickup Freight Order

After loading is completed, SAP EWM again sends the LDAP notification back to SAP TM containing the actual quantities that have been loaded into the truck. The truck finally covers the last mile and transports the ULD from the gateway to the place of loading. With the plane departing and the execution of the main carriage occurring, the freight booking is set to **Uplift Confirmed**, the export process ends, and the import process starts at the destination airport. Export freight booking and export forwarding order are copied into the respective inbound documents, and the process continues.

The completed document flow, recorded in the forwarding order in SAP TM, is depicted in Figure 13.31.

Figure 13.31 Document Flow of the Completed Air Freight Process

13.2.4   Warehouse Billing

Upon the creation of SAP TM there was a decision that a dedicated transportation management system would need a flexible and powerful charge management framework that allowed for the maintenance of rate structure across all modes of transport while considering the necessities of a very diverse methodology for the calculation of charges across the globe. Since its creation, Transportation Charge Management has evolved, and it still adds new capabilities with every release. Contrary to this, SAP EWM didn't have similar requirements upon its creation and hence no framework for charge calculation is embedded in the software.

With the trend of outsourcing warehouse-based activities and processes, cost calculation became a necessity to determine the value of services performed in a warehouse.

As an example, a LSP using SAP EWM regularly performs value-added services such as packaging and relabeling of goods for its customers. Both parties agreed that these services will be charged at the end of each month. The LSP uses its SAP EWM system to keep track of how often the respective actions were performed, to calculate the amount to be charged, and to trigger the billing process.

There are two process variants for warehouse billing depending on who performs the service in the warehouse and ultimately who runs the SAP system in the process:

- The LSP performs services for a customer. It measures how often the ordered actions have been performed and subsequently bills the customer for an amount that was calculated based on this data.

- The customer tracks services performed by an external party. These measurements are used to calculate the costs of the services performed. The amount is settled via self-billing.

  Billing and self-billing in both scenarios happen periodically.

Within this section, we'll give an overview of both variants. The overall Transportation Charge Management process on which the warehouse cost calculation depends is described in Chapter 10, Chapter 11, and Chapter 12 of this book, so we'll focus mainly on the integration aspects here. As usual, we'll look at the process from an SAP S/4HANA perspective; however, it will run the same way in a side-by side installation scenario.

Measurement of Services and Billing to Customer

This scenario fits the air freight situation we introduced in Section 13.2.3. The LSP will measure the services performed and bill the customer(s) periodically. The LSP is also accountable for providing proof on which basis the billing was performed if necessary.

At the start of the process depicted in Figure 13.32, a forwarding agreement is created in SAP TM. The line items of the linked calculation sheet represent the services that are to be measured. The calculation base for each item is quantity_val. A remark can be added to each charge line to clarify which measurement is expected as basis for the calculation of costs.

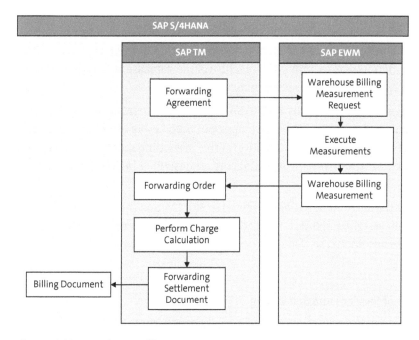

Figure 13.32 Warehouse Billing Process

Charge Management Master Data

For a reminder on how to create the respective Transportation Charge Management master data, refer to Chapter 10, Section 10.1 of this book. For the specifics of forwarding agreements, see Chapter 12, Section 12.1.1.

After the release of the agreement, a *warehouse billing measurement request* (WMBR) is created in SAP EWM. It serves as a starting point for the SAP EWM operations and is used to define which measurements are to be used to determine the cost of services performed. For changing the SAP TM forwarding agreement after this step, it must be set back into the **In Process** status. After its subsequent release, the changes will be reflected in SAP EWM. The periods in which the amounts will be settled and the warehouse measurements will be performed is maintained in the business partner master data as a factory calendar.

In SAP EWM, the received WMBR is reviewed by an expert who decides which SAP EWM measurement service is to be used to determine the correct amounts (20 predelivered services are available).

The service amounts are periodically calculated based on *snapshot tables* in SAP EWM. These snapshots are used to document the situation in the warehouse at distinct measurement points by providing a picture of the database at that time, as well as providing proof of the services performed when required.

The calculated amounts are finally sent to SAP TM in SAP S/4HANA, where they create a forwarding order. The warehouse charges can then be calculated based on this object. The subsequent steps are the creation of the forwarding settlement document and the billing in the SAP S/4HANA digital core, as described in Chapter 12, Section 12.3.

Note that after the agreement has been created in SAP TM, and the measurement services have been assigned in SAP EWM, the subsequent process steps occur periodically and can be automated so that no further user interaction is required to perform the billing.

Measurement of Services and Self-Billing

The process steps in the self-billing scenario don't change, but the objects used in the SAP TM system are different. In this process, the customer outsources work to an LSP. The customer runs the SAP EWM and SAP TM systems required to measure the services performed and, in the end, performs a self-billing with the LSP to settle the cost. The changed objects in SAP TM are listed as follows:

- At the beginning of the process, instead of a forwarding agreement, a freight agreement is created. For more details on freight agreements, refer to Chapter 10, Section 10.1.1.

- The document created to calculate the cost of the measured services is a service order in SAP TM.

- Consequently, the document that initiates the self-billing on the SAP TM side is the freight settlement document. For further details on the charge settlement process, refer to Chapter 11.

- In the last step, the PO and service entry sheet are created in the SAP S/4HANA digital core where accruals posting and self-billing are performed.

This concludes our brief description of the process variants for warehouse billing. We've discussed how costs for warehouse activities are calculated to perform either a self-billing to an LSP or to bill a customer periodically. For further information about this process, refer to *https://bit.ly/2EviwMI*.

13.3   SAP Transportation Resource Planning

SAP Transportation Resource Planning is a standalone solution, which allows you to manage equipment for transportation, generally addresses resources in terms of various characteristics:

- Passive inventory used for transportation, such as containers, railcars, or trailers, can be managed in depot locations. Availability requests for equipment types and instances can be answered as well.
- Shortages and surplus of inventory instances can be detected and flagged. Resource imbalances in the network can be discovered.
- Ingoing and outgoing inventory streams from transportation to and from depots can be registered and included in the inventory availability calculation.
- Repositioning in the network can be simulated, proposed, and made transparent in terms of related cost.

Based on these features, SAP Transportation Resource Planning provides for efficient management of equipment for transportation moving around in a LSP network. These moves can easily cause imbalances, which can lead to unavailability of transportation equipment and thus to the inability to accept and execute transportation orders.

An example happens every year in the months before Christmas: As the increased sales for Christmas gifts leads to very high container transportation volumes from China to Europe and America, the availability of empty containers in China goes down dramatically. If there is no process in place to move empty containers to China early enough before Christmas, there could be a shortage of goods and a drop of sales figures in the target markets.

In the following sections, we'll unpack SAP Transportation Resource Planning. We'll begin with the integration basics, before providing a tour of the available features and views, as well as your deployment options.

13.3.1   Integration Overview

SAP Transportation Resource Planning is software that has been built as a genuine SAP HANA solution. It runs standalone and can be tightly coupled with SAP TM, in which case, a deployment on the same SAP HANA database is possible. The direct integration of SAP Transportation Resource Planning into the shipment processes allows the following:

- Providing information on availability of equipment for order items or options to substitute at low costs with comparable equipment
- Registration of outgoing equipment and its requests as well as incoming equipment based on container units or freight orders and bookings

The main question in SAP Transportation Resource Planning is how to optimize the resource availability and usage for transportation processes. Detailed answers need to be given to the following questions:

- Is a resource of a specific type available (e.g., 40-foot dry container)?
- How can the supply of empty transportation resources be monitored?
- Can a company guarantee an available-to-promise (ATP) date?
- How can a company reliably forecast the supply and demand of resources?
- How can the repositioning of empty equipment be avoided and the utilization of a company's own resources be increased?
- How can a company reduce cost per resource?
- Is it more economical to buy or lease new resources?
- How can a company handle service recovery in exceptional cases?

Therefore, a system such as SAP Transportation Resource Planning will supply a proposal to realize the equipment provisioning and balancing: provide the right equipment at the right time at the right location with the minimum cost. Of course, there are some local and global challenges in equipment management and balancing:

- Impact of global decisions on the local balancing situation
- Impact of local evacuation decisions as a reaction to imbalance in terminals
- Uncertainty of supply and demand forecasts
- Decisions on empty versus laden moves as empty moves cost money, and laden moves make money but potentially increase the imbalance
- Reconciliation of high-level planning with terminal operation constraints

To achieve these goals, multiple functionalities in SAP S/4HANA are integrated with SAP Transportation Resource Planning. In Figure 13.33, you can see an overview of the interaction of the related components with SAP Transportation Resource Planning:

- Materials management (MM) for purchasing or leasing equipment
- Asset management for resource master as well as maintenance and repair activities
- SAP S/4HANA Finance covering financial processes
- SAP TM supporting operational processes
- SAP Event Management for event management
- SAP Transportation Resource Planning for equipment management

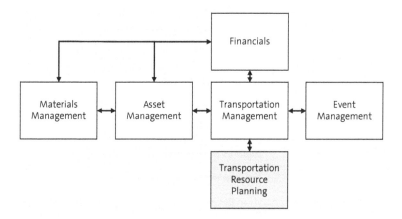

Figure 13.33 Component Interaction with SAP Transportation Resource Planning

SAP TM is the component that is directly interacting with SAP Transportation Resource Planning. There are multiple interfaces to exchange data and to integrate the process flow, which you can see in Figure 13.34. For detailed functional descriptions of the subcomponents, refer to Figure 1.8 in Chapter 1, Section 1.3.1. The figure here shows the same subcomponents and their integration into the SAP Transportation Resource Planning building blocks. The blocks with the light frame have optimization features in the resource planning process. Let's walk through these blocks:

- The components to secure capacity in SAP TM, which also hold relevant master data, are synchronized with resource and network master data on SAP Transportation Resource Planning.

- The customer order management triggers requests to determine resource and equipment availability for transports related to the orders.
- If resources are associated to orders, the corresponding equipment is requested and reserved in SAP Transportation Resource Planning.
- Resources used and arriving or leaving a location in SAP TM freight handling or assigned to tours in cargo management are synchronized with SAP Transportation Resource Planning equipment management.
- SAP Transportation Resource Planning equipment balancing creates moves and reservations in SAP TM to reposition resources in the network.

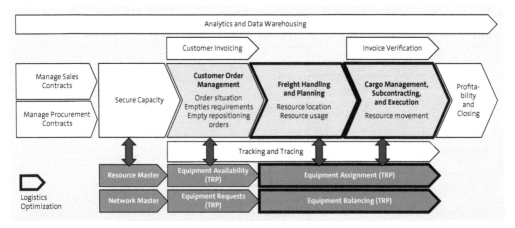

Figure 13.34 Integration of SAP Transportation Resource Planning Functionalities into the Transportation Management Process

The supply and demand optimization process in SAP Transportation Resource Planning can be run in different model definitions, which allows you to improve the equipment situation either on a global view for all resources or as a limited solution with a local scope or selected resource types. The optimization has a variety of input data, which you can see in Figure 13.35. This includes the inventory of equipment in the selected locations and on the transports to these destinations (depots, container yards, consignee locations), as well as bookings that require usage and assignment of certain equipment types or individual equipment.

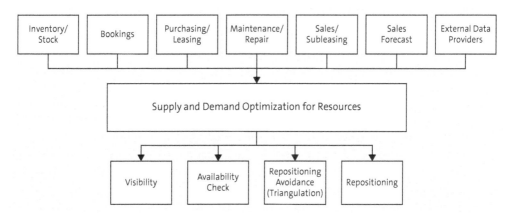

Figure 13.35 Supply and Demand Optimization and Input/Output Data

The equipment inventory for supply and demand optimization is influenced not only by the requested, planned, and ongoing transportation activities of types laden and empty but also by the entry of new resources into the network through procurement, leasing, or by temporary or long-term activities due to maintenance, repair, sales, scrapping, or subleasing. Concerning future calculations, further input information comes from sales forecasts of products to be shipped or logistics orders to be fulfilled. Last, but not least, external providers and their resources may influence the available resource pool.

13.3.2   Features

The supply and demand optimization are done through usage of an SAP HANA-based optimizer (MCNF), which addresses the tasks as a multicommodity network flow problem. This requires solving a network flow problem with multiple commodities (flow demands) between different source and sink nodes inside the given network and with the resources to be considered. Technically, a linear programming algorithm (SOPLEX) for capacity-restricted networks and a special graph algorithm for planning without capacity limitation are utilized. The target strategies of the optimization are avoidance of empty equipment repositioning, a maximum level of order fulfillment, and minimization of cost.

In terms of cost, the optimization model and algorithm handle multiple components:

- Handling cost for loading and unloading
- Transshipment cost for storage and related fixed cost for infrastructure
- Transportation cost for empty equipment delivery, pickup, triangulation, or repositioning, considering a company's own fleet, a third-party fleet, and intermodal cost

After running an optimization, the model output can be used to support the availability check of requested equipment, the development of a solution with lowest possible cost and least repositioning activities, a solution for empty pickup or return moves, and a cost-efficient repositioning strategy for the equipment that needs to be moved to other terminal locations.

Triangulation is a strategy used by carriers to reduce cost of positioning, repositioning, and storage, especially when they are short of equipment. You can see the principle in Figure 13.36.

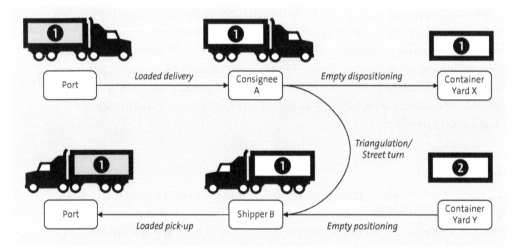

Figure 13.36 Triangulation of Containers

If a container ❶ of specific type (e.g., 40-foot high cube) arrives at a port, it's moved, for example, to a truck that does the loaded delivery to consignee A. After emptying the container, it would be usually dispositioned to a feasible container yard X based on lowest cost or highest demand. Another container of comparable type requested by shipper B would, for example, be empty positioned by another truck from container yard Y to load it and move it loaded to the port. The idea behind triangulation, also called "street turn," is to avoid the three activities (dispositioning, storage, and positioning) for the two units, and instead search for two business cases (arrival and departure), which can be consolidated, so that an empty container to be dispositioned can be immediately turned around and positioned empty at a consignee. In this case, unit ❶ never arrives in container yard X, and unit ❷ isn't moved out of yard Y.

13.3.3   Views

Users of SAP Transportation Resource Planning are usually in charge of managing the used and available equipment of a carrier or logistics company or managing the space and activities in a container depot or yard with the perspective of managing the available space best and satisfying incoming equipment demand.

For this purpose, SAP Transportation Resource Planning provides a variety of views, transactions, and optimization processes to allow users to manage their task best related to their corresponding authorization and scope responsibility.

In Figure 13.37, you can see the SAP Transportation Resource Planning home dashboard, which is the landing pare of a user if configured correspondingly. The home dashboard offers four tile categories (**Stock View**, **Supply and Demand**, **Alerts**, and **KPIs**), based on which several tiles can be personalized, added, or removed from the home dashboard:

- The **Alerts** tile allows you to monitor alerts related to some scheduled supply and demand or to KPIs.
- The **Supply and Demand** tile visualizes a forecast of a certain equipment situation related to a selected plan. You may get an overview on the balance or incoming, stored, and outgoing resources for a selected scope (equipment types and locations).
- The **Stock** tile shows you the equipment situation for selected resource types and locations.
- In the **KPI** tile, you can see a trend for typical equipment-related KPIs (e.g., idle rate or import/export balance).

In addition to the overview on the home dashboard, SAP Transportation Resource Planning offers you several work centers for aspects of resource planning: **RESOURCE VISIBILITY**, **SUPPLY AND DEMAND** (forecast), **KPI** for monitoring, **PICK-UP AND RETURN** for optimization of these processes, **RESOURCE BALANCING** for detection of critical inventory situations, and further administrative functions to maintain master data and settings.

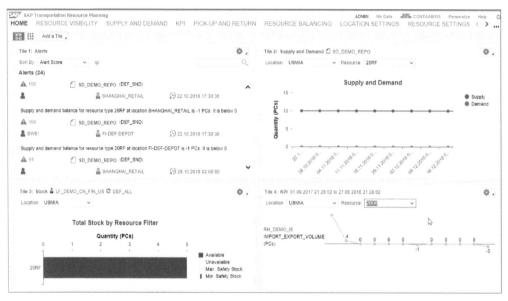

Figure 13.37 SAP Transportation Resource Planning Home Dashboard with Tiles

The detailed transactions in the work centers allow you to look at the SAP Transportation Resource Planning data in three different ways:

- **Table views**
  Provide a detailed listing of the facts with various characteristics listed for all selected elements.

- **Chart views**
  Give a visual overview of the facts in the form of KPIs, for example, a bar chart. In some cases, the presented figure is enhanced with additional information, such as the safety stock indicator when looking at the current inventory levels.

- **M views**
  Provide a geographic perspective on the data. On a zoomable and scrollable world map, the selected locations and resource types and the related data aspects are presented. Different indicators such as stock levels, empty or full status, and other aspects can be presented by geo-located, circular charts of different colors. Figure 13.38 shows an example of this form of data representation in SAP Transportation Resource Planning.

The **RESOURCE VISIBILITY** work center allows you to monitor the inventory situation for equipment within your selected locations. You can find resources by setting filter criteria and attributes and then determine the resource's relation to lease contracts. Moving stock inventories coming into selected locations can be displayed and analyzed with reference to the related booking orders or freight orders in SAP TM.

In the **SUPPLY AND DEMAND** work center, you can view the situation of your monitored locations concerning the available supply and requested demand. The system can visualize the data based on the plans defined. You can either work with it from a global or local perspective with relation to all requests and available resource types or with the goal to find a solution for critical equipment.

In Figure 13.38, you can see a map-based supply and demand visualization with a worldwide view related to **Plan SD_DEMO_PLAN** and a point in time. Locations that have a surplus of equipment are depicted in violet, and those with a deficit are red. The size of the circles indicates the quantity, dark colors show supply, and light colors tag demands. This kind of representation allows you to get a very fast overview of resource distribution and supply-demand matching.

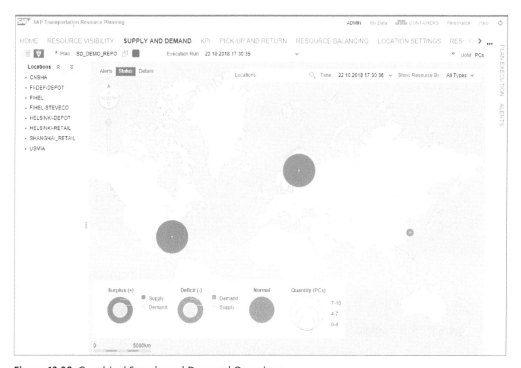

Figure 13.38 Graphical Supply and Demand Overview

For the **SUPPLY AND DEMAND** work center, an automatic scheduling of the plan providing a target equipment distribution is possible, which is indicated in the **Execution Run** time stamp field.

The **RESOURCE BALANCING** work center helps you detect critical situations of available and requested equipment and run simulations to optimize the resource balance in the corresponding part of your network. For a plan, multiple simulations are possible, out of which you may finally chose the one that provides the most sensible or cost-efficient result. In the **RESOURCE BALANCING** work center, different views are available:

- **Supply and Demand**

  Gives you a tabular representation of equipment and their types in a list of locations with an indication of supply and demand per combination (see Figure 13.39). Cells that lead to a deficit are displayed with an alert. In the example, the location **SHANGHAI_RETAIL** still has a deficit of containers, but other requests have been satisfied by running the **Balancing Simulation RB_DEMO_REPO2**.

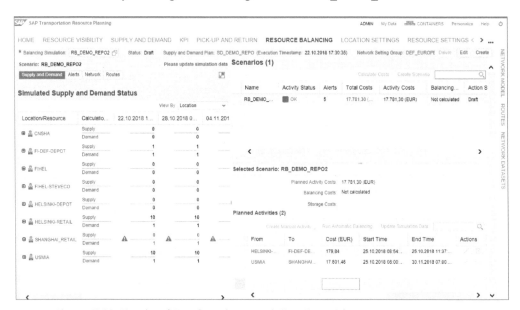

Figure 13.39 Simulated Supply and Demand Situation with Cost

- **Alerts**

  The **Alerts** view exposes the alerts in a resource balancing view.

■ **Network/Routes**

These views provide map displays that allow you to judge the resource balancing with an emphasis on its distribution within your services network or along typical repositioning routes.

The SAP Transportation Resource Planning **RESOURCE HISTORY** view provides you access to all events related to the resources managed by the system and gives you answers on resource state, usage, and current or previous locations.

13.3.4   Deployment

SAP Transportation Resource Planning can be operated as a standalone system without using SAP TM in an integrated mode. This is possible if, for example, a carrier, such as a container shipping line (CSL) is using its own developed legacy app to run transportation management but needs an extension for optimization of equipment. For this situation, several interfaces to exchange master data and transactional information are provided.

The more common deployment scenario, however, is to operate SAP Transportation Resource Planning in combination with SAP TM as shown previously in Figure 13.34. The interfaces to exchange master and operational data with SAP TM are predefined, and SAP TM operates as the leading system.

There are multiple work centers in SAP Transportation Resource Planning that allow you to view or maintain master data, for example, resource details or location information. This might also be helpful for mixed operations, where part of the equipment is provided based on your own pool and has master data records in the SAP TM resource master, and another part of the equipment flows into your own network as third-party or partner-owned resources, where your own SAP TM doesn't have an appropriate master record. In Figure 13.40, you can see a maintenance transaction for resource types that are used in the SAP Transportation Resource Planning scenario.

Besides the master data settings, SAP Transportation Resource Planning also provides maintenance activities in the **PLANS** work center, where you can set up the simulation plans or views for the supply, demand, movement, and optimization scenarios described earlier.

13

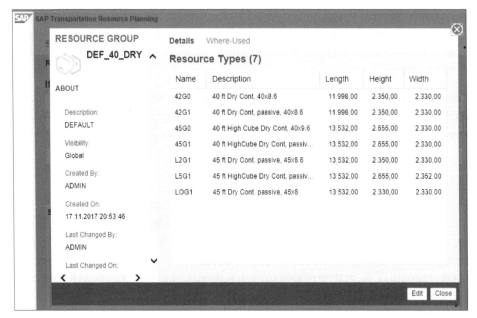

Figure 13.40 Equipment Definition

For companies owning and managing equipment or making heavy use of third-party resources, SAP Transportation Resource Planning is a valuable enhancement of the processes, which allows transportation processes to run smoother as typical road-blocks, such as equipment unavailability and high equipment sourcing cost, can be avoided or reduced.

13.4   SAP Yard Logistics

In this chapter, you learned about the importance of warehouse management systems, either as a tool to manage a shipper's/contract logistics provider's warehouse or as transit warehouse, which provides an interface between linked subprocesses in transportation, such as an air freight hub or ocean container freight station. If packages and TUs are handled in terms of arrival, departure, unloading and loading, or unpacking and packing, SAP EWM is a flexible tool to be integrated into the logistics chain. There are many cases, however, where larger facilities for receipt, storage and dispatch of TUs, means of transportation, or individual items must be managed. These type of facilities include, the following, for example:

- Container terminals that allow storage of loaded or empty containers, including cargo, handling of vehicles on the land side (truck, railway) and water side (ocean vessels, barges), and the related load transfer processes
- Rail terminals that provide storage of loaded or empty containers but also railcars, handling of truck on the road side and rail equipment on the rail ramp side, and the related load transfer processes
- Air freight ground handling stations that facilitate loading and unloading processes for air cargo, including provisioning of air cargo containers and pallets
- Automotive hubs that allow intermediate storage for vehicles unloaded from or to be loaded to roll-on/roll-off (Ro-Ro) car transporter vessels
- Bulk yards that allow intermediate storage and load transfer for bulky materials

SAP decided to add more specialized software called SAP Yard Logistics to the logistics portfolio, which makes use of SAP EWM but provides the functional scope for managing a variety of yards and tasks in the different industries that may use software to manage their yards Typical use cases are in the following industry areas where cargo items, trucks, trailers, railcars, vessels, cranes, reach stackers, and other handling devices need to be coordinated:

- **Automotive**
  Yards for finished vehicles.
- **Building materials and heavy industries**
  Construction material yards and machinery project yards for various factory projects.
- **Chemical and oil and gas industry**
  Bulk material yards.
- **Consumer products, wholesale, and retail distribution**
  Prepackaged distribution of goods.
- **Logistics industry**
  All mode-transferring yard facilities, such as truck-rail, truck/rail-ocean, truck-air terminals, to store and move cargo.

As in SAP EWM, the portfolio of functionality in SAP Yard Logistics helps to manage inbound, outbound, storage, loading, and unloading processes, but it introduces strong support for the corresponding business processes and functions in yards and terminals instead of a warehouse.

Let's take a closer look into SAP Yard Logistics, including its business processes, main features, UI, mobile options, and integration capabilities.

13.4.1 Business Processes

The business processes supported by SAP Yard Logistics include planning; check-in of cargo, TUs, vehicles, and drivers; execution of the necessary yard tasks and operations; and check-out. The specific functional implementations, of which many are based on SAP EWM foundation, allow companies to improve their yard management in the following ways:

- Reduce waiting times
- Increase speed of operation
- Save costs by tracking and minimizing operation times
- Avoid losing track of assets in the yard
- Use suitable tools for the required tasks instead of bending standard warehouse tools to somehow fit to a yard
- Reduce total cost of ownership for the system landscape
- Identify and remove bottlenecks

The business processes in SAP Yard Logistics offer a wide variety of functions, which you can see in Figure 13.41.

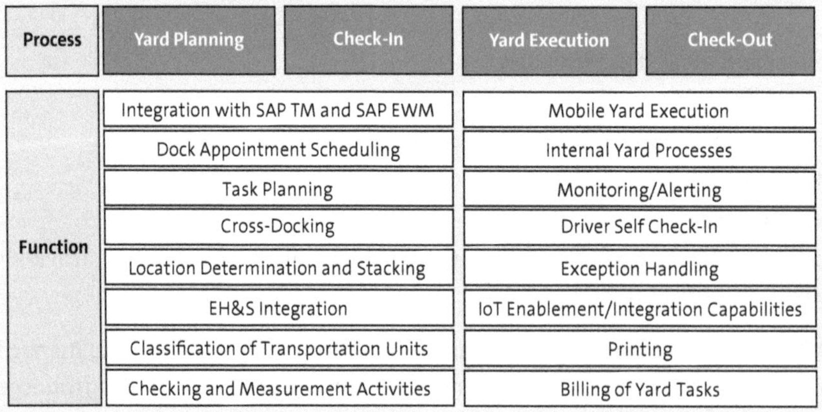

Process	Yard Planning	Check-In	Yard Execution	Check-Out
Function	Integration with SAP TM and SAP EWM		Mobile Yard Execution	
	Dock Appointment Scheduling		Internal Yard Processes	
	Task Planning		Monitoring/Alerting	
	Cross-Docking		Driver Self Check-In	
	Location Determination and Stacking		Exception Handling	
	EH&S Integration		IoT Enablement/Integration Capabilities	
	Classification of Transportation Units		Printing	
	Checking and Measurement Activities		Billing of Yard Tasks	

Figure 13.41 Business Processes and Functions in SAP Yard Logistics

13.4.2   Features

As previously mentioned, SAP EWM builds the foundation for many yard-specific functionalities and implementations. This is a great benefit, as many configuration and modeling approaches can be reused for yard logistics. In addition, yard-specific features that may not be flexible enough in standard SAP EWM have been enhanced to deal with the increased complexity of specific handling or processes in a yard. Some examples are as follows:

- Inventory and stacking management for containers in a container yard
- Specialized management of the mode-specific loading areas in yards, such as berths for ocean vessels or rail ramps in rail yards
- Integration of yard-specific technologies in the Internet of Things (IoT) and device-specific areas

To achieve smooth processing inside the yard, SAP Yard Logistics has been integrated with SAP TM, and yard-specific objects have been built on top of the SAP EWM foundation. In the master data area, main enhancements have been done for yard entities:

- The *yard number* and its characteristics are based on the SAP EWM warehouse number.
- *Yard tasks* are an enhancement of SAP EWM warehouse tasks.
- The *yard TU* is a progression of the SAP EWM transport unit.

The yard request and the yard order have been introduced as new objects, but these new objects make use of SAP EWM as a foundation for implementation to align functional principles and create synergies wherever possible.

13.4.3   User Interface

Along with the new master data and transactional business objects, SAP provides new UIs in SAPUI5 technology and the corresponding Floorplan Manager (FPM) configurations to allow integration into the SAP Fiori launchpad. Furthermore, many additional Open Data (OData) protocol services have been provided to allow the appropriate integration of yard-specific devices and IoT technology to control the yard processes with the degree of automation that is currently pushed into the logistics market by various vendors. In Figure 13.42, you can see an overview on SAP Yard Logistics and its reuse of SAP EWM.

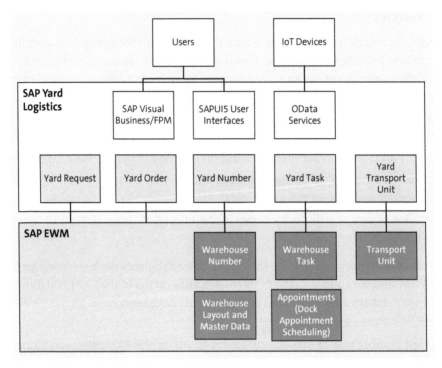

Figure 13.42 SAP Yard Logistics and SAP EWM

Because yards can be quite complex and large, the new UIs in SAP Yard Logistics put an emphasis on the visualization of the yard, its situation and entities, and ongoing and planned processes. Additionally, a variety of entity-specific functions can be triggered from the visualization level. In Figure 13.43, you can see some examples.

Following are some typical visualization, information retrieval and functional steps you can take in SAP Yard Logistics:

- View status information of yard and cargo entities and situations via color coding.
- Manage exceptions, for example, via functional breakdown.
- Lay out and visualize your own facilities via layout editor provided with SAP Yard Logistics.
- Create new tasks for containers, trucks, railcars, and other devices to change locations via drag and drop.
- Manage space in the yard, for example, in a container storage area.
- Block locations, such as gates or doors, for ingoing or outgoing movements.

- Retrieve detailed information about individual entities, such as, TUs located in the yard.
- Retrieve details about yard locations and their blocking status.

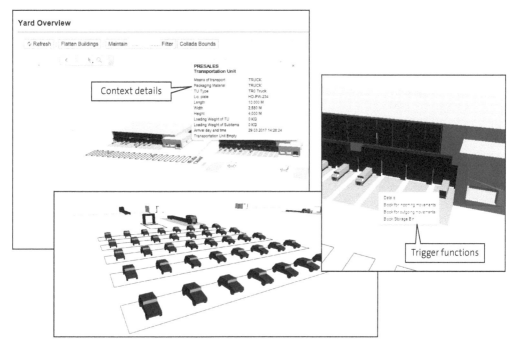

Figure 13.43 SAP Yard Logistics Visualization with Examples of Context Details and Functional Triggers

SAP Yard Logistics offers multiple roles for users to execute the required functions to manage a yard. Figure 13.44 gives you an overview of the typical tasks of a supervisor, hub manager, gate agent, driver, and operator.

Within SAP Yard Logistics, there are multiple areas that have to be configured, are used in transactional processing, or provide integration with the world outside of SAP Yard Logistics.

You must define multiple entities as master data before using SAP Yard Logistics. The setup has a similar structure to the one you find in SAP EWM but is more focused on the yard structure. A yard number represents the organizational unit of the yard. Storage types, storage sections, and storage bins allow you to hierarchically define the structure of the yard.

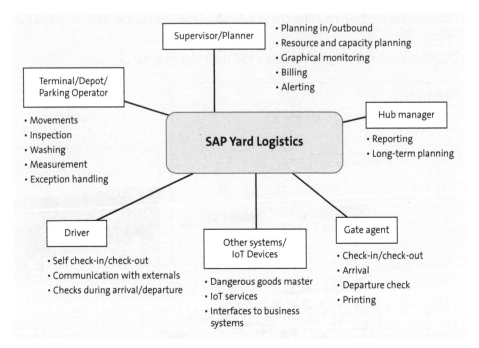

Figure 13.44 Role Overview in SAP Yard Logistics

With a graphical yard layout design tool, you can visualize the structure and entities of a yard. The graphical representation is available afterward in the transactional processing of yard status and yard activities.

13.4.4   Yard Logistics Objects

Yard requests are planning documents that provide you with information about structure and characteristics of TUs that move into, out of, or within a yard. A yard request may include a list of activities that are required to subsequently execute the move and its related work tasks. Yard requests can be manually generated, be a result of a transportation planning process, or be triggered externally via interfaces.

The purpose of a yard request is to identify the required workload of handling the TU and the properties that may influence the execution. Based on the yard requests in a system, a long-term workload plan can be defined. Yard requests contain information on the type of operations and the TU, on the direction of movement (inbound or outbound), on arrival or departure locations and time frames, and on material characteristics that may need specific handling.

Yard orders are short-term planning and execution documents for the yard. They contain comparable information as yard requests but focus on executing the related tasks and documenting the resulting information. Based on yard orders, the long-term plan for the yard may be revised. A yard order carries an execution status, which allows you to get an overview of the overall execution state of the order.

Based on yard orders, *yard tasks* can be created that reflect and control the activities to be done in the yard in terms of handling the TUs and the contents. Typical yard tasks are, for example, cleaning a unit, storing a unit in a storage section or bin, or moving a vehicle to a check-out area.

To manage the yard and the multitude of requests and orders, SAP Yard Logistics offers the yard cockpit as a central means of overlooking and controlling the various activities. The cockpit uses list-based as well as graphical tools to provide a best-fitting view to the yard, its units, orders, and activities. It also allows you to appropriately react to alerts coming up in the yard. In Figure 13.45, you can see an overview of the yard cockpit.

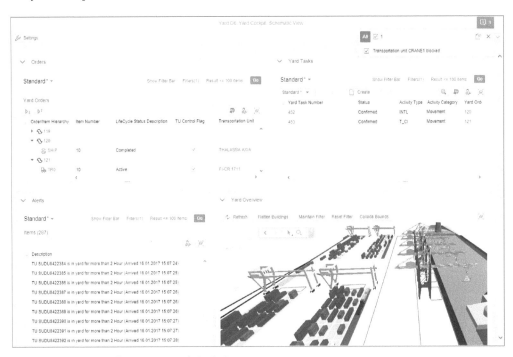

Figure 13.45 SAP Yard Logistics Yard Cockpit

The visual display of the yard and its objects allow you to select and trigger actions on the selected objects. Doing so, you can, for example, block locations or trigger and execute movements via drag-and-drop activities.

13.4.5   Mobile Options

As yards usually require many inbound and outbound activities with external parties, the availability of the self check-in function for drivers delivering TUs is a big benefit. Drivers can use SAP Fiori apps on their mobile devices, which allow check-in or check-out in their preferred language with a guided procedure through a definable set of questions. The answers will then automatically drive the changes to the related yard objects.

Many other transactions in SAP Yard Logistics can be executed as mobile transactions, which allow a high degree of freedom for the persons working in the yard. The mobile transactions can be run on a variety of devices, including mobile phones, tablets, or typical on-board units of forklifts or other handling devices. Figure 13.46 shows you a selection of such mobile devices.

Figure 13.46 Mobile Devices for Use with SAP Yard Logistics Transactions

13.4.6   Integration Capabilities

For external drivers, SAP Yard Logistics offers an integration to *dock appointment scheduling* (DAS), which can be used by external parties to arrange time slots and locations for a loading or unloading activity.

Similar to the SAP EWM warehouse billing described in Section 13.2.4, SAP Yard Logistics includes a billing capability that allows you to either sell yard services to a shipper or get billed by a service provider that supports you in handling certain yard activities. Contracts for yard billing are maintained in SAP TM, which subsequently also is used as the settlement tool.

In previous chapters, we already mentioned SAP Leonardo and its ability to integrate any kind of digital technology into SAP S/4HANA systems. This capability can be used very efficiently in SAP Yard Logistics to achieve a variety of benefits:

- Smart sensors allow you to monitor and control all assets in the yard using standard sensor integration.
- Check-in processes can be managed without manual interaction using gate automation technology.
- RFID technology can be applied and integrated to a variety of units.
- Smart filling allows scales, silos, and transportation assets to be connected to automatically control loading processes.
- Drone control can be used for inspection of remote areas of the yard.

13.5   SAP Logistics Business Network

The Collaboration Portal in SAP TM 9.6 has the goal of offering an access point for external parties (vendors, third-party logistics providers) to subcontracting processes in SAP TM. With the overall logistics and supply chain process moving into a public cloud, however, SAP likes to provide tools spanning a larger scope of logistics collaboration functions with a higher involvement of the participating parties. The functional scope to be provided may extend the reach of typical transportation-driven features.

As an alternative to the Collaboration Portal, SAP started to develop the SAP Logistics Business Network as a public cloud offering. It's planned to encompass the functionality of the SAP TM integrated Collaboration Portal, as well as to go beyond and integrate supply chain planning and tracking and tracing features in an overarching application so that end-to-end supply chain processes with many players can be handled in a public, integrated process. Where the SAP TM Collaboration Portal offers a shipper-owned or single LSP-owned infrastructure to communicate and collaborate with selected suppliers and carriers, the SAP Logistics Business Network offers a network-managed infrastructure, which is open for suppliers, partners with applications, and other network operators to provide and run an end-to-end infrastructure. In Figure 13.47, you can see the collaboration and integration vision of the SAP Logistics Business Network and the difference from the Collaboration Portal model. Not all functionality of the SAP Logistics Business Network will be available in the first releases.

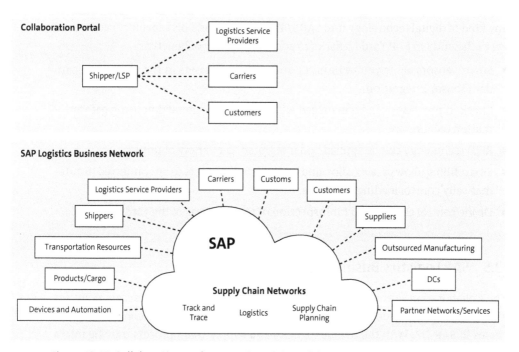

Figure 13.47 Collaboration and Integration Vision of the SAP Logistics Business Network

Projected Release

The first release of SAP Logistics Business Network is planned to be hosted on the cloud by SAP from Q1/2019. As of the time of writing (winter 2018), the SAP Logistics Business Network is in an incubation phase with selected customers.

Some aspects of the practical use of SAP Logistics Business Network in terms of using tendering functionality for SAP TM freight orders have already been described in Chapter 8. In this chapter, we'll give you a broader overview of the concepts and goals of SAP Logistics Business Network.

Implementations of business networks come with a variety of requirements. Typical collaboration models like those provided by the SAP TM Collaboration Portal usually have the following challenges:

- Peer-to-peer communication
- High collaboration and integration effort
- Siloed operations and visibility.

The SAP Logistics Business Network networking approach, however, promises benefits:

- Many-to-many communication
- Easy connectivity
- End-to-end process collaboration and visibility

In addition to the benefit of SAP systems, which, in many cases, already hosts order, logistics, and supply chain data, the integration of digital services (e.g., IoT, sensors, machine learning, and device data), can bring additional benefits in terms of handling design, planning, response, production, logistics, and operations processes via an SAP Logistics Business Network. The openness of the network also allows innovative, new services to integrate efficiently into the end-to-end process.

The SAP Logistics Business Network provides four functional areas:

- **Discover**
  The SAP Logistics Business Network allows you to identify and connect new business partners, find and use new business services, and investigate new business opportunities.

- **Connect**
  The network can be easily used from a company perspective as it's managed centrally, and onboarding a well as connectivity are provided by the operating party or the participants. There is an out-of-the-box integration with SAP systems and partner solutions, and managed integration services allow connectivity to various common standards (e.g., business-to-business [B2B]/EDI, devices, sensors).

- **Collaborate**

  The SAP Logistics Business Network provides a global, multimodal network that allows collaboration between all parties related to and authorized in viewing and managing data, content, and document sharing of a joint process. Comprehensive process and service coverage is intended to be provided in later releases.

- **Gain insight**

  Accessing the multitude of options through the network, embedded analytics and real-time shipment visibility can be provided beyond the traditional tools operated from a single-party perspective. The goal is to provide end-to-end visibility on intercompany processes.

An important factor of SAP Logistics Business Network in terms of openness and reach is the *network of networks* concept, which allows acceleration of innovation and flexibility by leveraging the established and new services of a variety of partners. SAP Logistics Business Network becomes a multinetwork by not only integrating its own services but also linking into subnetworks that are already up and running in logistics communities and, in many cases, concentrate on a subview of activities, for example, tracking and tracing for truck fleets. The collaboration of partners can be consolidated to the end-to-end management of logistics and shipment processes, which is projected as a goal of SAP Logistics Business Network. Figure 13.48 visualizes the network of networks architecture of SAP Logistics Business Network.

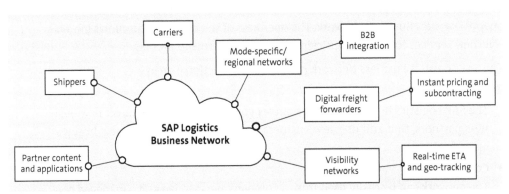

Figure 13.48 Network of Networks Architecture in SAP Logistics Business Network

In Figure 13.49, you can see a functional view of SAP Logistics Business Network, which also includes some envisioned features (italics, gray, and marked as **Planned**), which won't be available in the first phase.

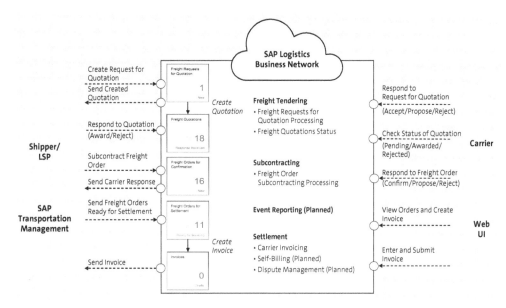

Figure 13.49 Functional and Envisioned View of SAP Logistics Business Network

From the functional perspective, the first version of SAP Logistics Business Network will provide the following selected core features of the Collaboration Portal:

- Request of a freight quotation (i.e., single freight order)
- Sending a quotation for a freight request with acceptance, price proposal, and rejection
- Exchange of quotation status information
- Receiving freight order information
- Responding to a freight order with confirmation, proposal, or rejection
- Viewing of freight orders
- Receipt of a vendor invoice

Further Collaboration Portal functions or other features, such as track and trace, support will be added subsequently. In Figure 13.50, you can see a list of freight orders for confirmation, which was transmitted from a SAP TM freight order tendering process to SAP Logistics Business Network.

Figure 13.50 List of Freight Orders for Confirmation in SAP Logistics Business Network

13.6   Blockchain in Logistics

The term *blockchain* received big hype in 2017 and 2018. There has been a lot of focus on providing and exchanging information between business partners and running intracompany and intercompany transactions in a safe, provable, and immutable way.

Starting mainly in the monetary sector with the introduction of electronic currencies such as Bitcoin, blockchain technology made its way into the logistics area, as the technology offers much more than just trading and storing money.

SAP is involved in the development of blockchain technologies and processes in various areas. These include processes directly hosted in logistics, as well as many other industries. In addition, blockchain technology allows improved logistics processes in areas where those processes don't directly have a relation to the actual transportation but provide additional safeguarding of the actual logistics process. Following are some examples for the use of blockchain technology in SAP logistics functionality and beyond:

- Creation and exchange of electronic bills of lading (B/L)
- Secured authorization procedures, for example, in signatures of transportation contracts
- Secured bidding processes for freight procurement
- Real-time payments
- Improvements in the drug supply chain security
- Trusted information on supply chain entities and means of transportation
- Distribute manufacturing for use of 3D printing

Behind the term blockchain, a couple of technologies are often mingled:

- **Blockchain**
  This is a protocol that enables decentralized, secure, direct, and digital transfer of information, values, responsibilities, and assets.
- **Distributed ledger**
  This is the consensus of replicated and digital data spread across multiple sites, countries, or institutions. There is no central administrator or storage facility for the related data.

Generally, a blockchain can be either permission-less or can require a permission. In the first case, the blockchain is open for everyone and allows reading and writing participation. The second type only allows access to a certain group of persons and strictly controls who owns an object, and who can read, write, overwrite, or append to an object. The permissioned blockchain is typically used for logistics processes.

Blockchain processes and use cases typically have one or more drivers that make the use of the new technology valuable:

- Participants have a need to share data in a secure way, for example, communication around a B/L for cargo handover and ownership.
- Multiple writers participate in a process and must change or enrich information with proof of authorship and immutability. For example, cargo in a supply needs to be handed over to the next parties, such as an inland trucker after an ocean import, and these parties need to join the information exchange and participate in the blockchain.
- A business requires trust because a large amount of money or credibility is at stake. Examples are payments against a delivery of a container full of goods or a fraudulent delivery note that can lead to a payment for nonexistent cargo.

- The information exchange and enhancement processes are disintermediated; that is, there is no central party that collects and distributes the information.
- The interaction of participants is transaction-based; that is, participation should drive a business process into the next step.

Looking at these use cases, logistics is an excellent playground for blockchain technology to improve trust, data integrity, immutability, and open and secure connectivity. In Figure 13.51, you can see an example of how insecure peer-to-peer communication with a variety of transmission methods (EDI, fax, email, etc.) can be replaced by blockchain technology that may improve and secure the end-to-end transactions and information flow in the whole logistics chain. The traditional peer-to-peer communication of the partners is implied by the thin, straight arrows. The replacement by blockchain is displayed as thick, dashed arrows.

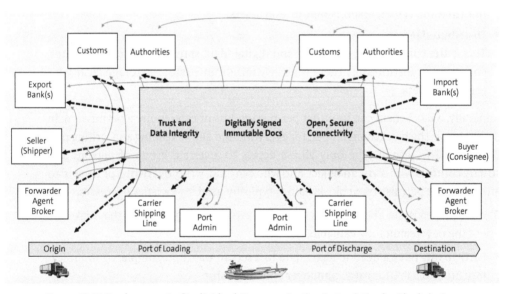

Figure 13.51 Replacement of Individual Communication in Logistics by Blockchain Technology

The necessity of blockchain usage in logistics is also underlined by the variety of standardization approaches that began in 2017 and beyond. An example is the *Blockchain in Transportation Alliance* (BiTA), which addresses the issues around smart contracts, freight payment, asset maintenance and ownership, equipment pools, and the transparency and chain of custody of freight.

SAP is developing blockchain technology as an important part of SAP Leonardo. Meanwhile, first products incorporating blockchain processes and many demo implementations have been done and shown around various blockchain use cases in logistics and other applications. In Figure 13.52, you can see an example screenshot from a SAP logistics blockchain demo where trading, shipping, and delivery issues are addressed. Multiple authorized parties in the process can access the information related to a shipment in the cloud, and, with proper rights, participants may amend the documents in a secure way.

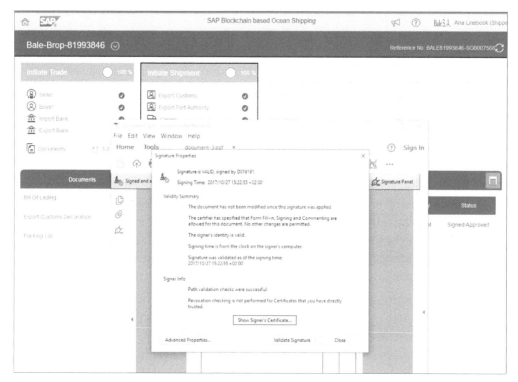

Figure 13.52 Example of Blockchain Usage from an SAP Demo on End-to-End Logistics

13.7 SAP Customer Relationship Management

For installation of SAP TM 9.6 on SAP Business Suite, an integration with SAP CRM is offered for both master data and transactions, which has been briefly introduced in Chapter 1. This functionality isn't available for SAP TM in SAP S/4HANA, as the connection to the classical SAP CRM isn't supported in the 1809 release with the SAP CRM add-on.

In SAP Business Suite installations of SAP TM 9.6, you can use a harmonized service product catalog across SAP TM and SAP CRM for the generation of opportunities in SAP CRM and a direct integration with forwarding agreement quotations. You also can execute various SAP TM transactions directly from SAP CRM. The forwarding quotation process allows you to analyze and price RFQs issued from your customers. You can use built-in analytics with the BCV to analyze demands and revenues. For successful deals, you can directly convert quotations into forwarding agreements.

It's a very common business practice for freight forwarders and carriers to have sales employees who work frequently with customers at the client site. Consequently, they rarely use backend applications other than an SAP CRM system, which supports the core sales business. With the integration of SAP TM into SAP CRM, you can fulfill this requirement, and a sales user doesn't need to navigate to a separate SAP TM system. You can use your standard SAP CRM functionalities, such as campaign management and prospect, lead, and opportunity generation, which are now fully integrated with contract quotations via the forwarding agreement quotations.

The actual integration starts with an opportunity. In an SAP CRM opportunity, you can choose a sales organization, business partner, and the newly introduced SAP TM service products that will be quoted. You can select a service in the opportunity item table by selecting **New • Product ID**. The service product ID is equal to and replicated from your service product ID in the service product catalog in SAP TM. As a result, your service offering is synchronized across the different systems.

After an opportunity is prepared (see Figure 13.53), you can create a forwarding agreement quotation by selecting **Create Follow-Up • TM FWA RFQ**. Before a new forwarding agreement RFQ is generated, you can choose between one and multiple service products that are priced in the agreement quotation. Eventually, a new forwarding agreement RFQ is created, and it contains all relevant fields from the opportunity, such as the business partner, sales organization, and SAP TM service products. Additional attributes from the service product catalog in SAP TM are supplemented in parallel (e.g., all service items that are part of a service product). You can now save the forwarding agreement RFQ, and it's available in SAP TM.

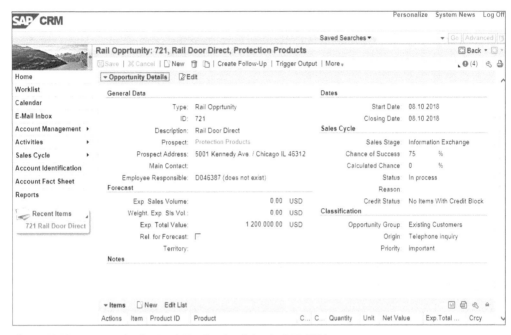

Figure 13.53 Opportunity for Logistics Service Sales in SAP CRM

To enable forwarding agreement quotations, you need to make a few settings in SAP TM and SAP CRM (Figure 13.54):

1. Create a forwarding agreement RFQ type in the SAP TM Customizing by following the menu path **Transportation Management · Master Data · Agreement RFQs · Define Forwarding Agreement RFQ Types**.

2. Set up the SAP CRM opportunity types and transaction types (this is mandatory). Navigate to **Customer Relationship Management · Transactions · Basic Settings · Define Transaction Types**.

3. Map your forwarding agreement types to the opportunity types that are contained in SAP CRM transaction types: **Customer Relationship Management · Transactions · Settings for Opportunities · Integration with SAP Transportation Management · Assign Forwarding Agreement Quotation Types to Transaction Types**.

Business Partners

To populate the business partner from the SAP CRM opportunity to the SAP TM forwarding agreement quotation, you must replicate the same business partner data from SAP ERP to both SAP CRM and SAP TM. In addition, you need to use the same organizational structure in both systems to retrieve the sales organization as specified in the opportunity.

Figure 13.54 Forwarding Agreement Quotation Created from SAP CRM Opportunity

Replicating the service product master data is a very important task in your integration with SAP CRM. The service products are available for the SAP CRM opportunity only after correct setup. It's important to note that the integration is limited to service products and doesn't include an entire service product catalog. Additional data, such as service items, are referenced only when you generate the forwarding agreement quotation from SAP CRM.

To achieve a proper integration, some configuration steps are required:

1. **Enable SAP TM item types**
   Activate the **Enable CRM** flag in the SAP TM Customizing, and mark SAP CRM as the mapping system by following the menu path **IMG • Transportation Management • Master Data • Agreements and Service Products • Define FWA and Service Product Item Types**.

2. **Perform initial and delta replication**

   Download the initial service product master from SAP TM via Transaction R3AS in SAP CRM, and choose the newly introduced load object **TM_SERVICE_PROD**. This new object specifies in which SAP CRM database tables the new information needs to be stored. In addition, you need to choose the source and destination sites that contain SAP TM and SAP CRM as the logical systems for the integration. After you execute the download program, your master data is initially replicated. Whenever you create, change, or delete a service product in SAP TM, this change is automatically populated to SAP CRM.

3. **Define the category and hierarchy**

   You must assign a category and hierarchy to the SAP TM service product. First, define a category and hierarchy in SAP CRM Customizing, and then assign the hierarchy and category to the product and service object in SAP CRM. You can find this setting in SAP CRM Customizing via the menu path **Cross-Application Components • SAP Product • Product Category • Assign Category Hierarchies to Applications**.

4. **Map hierarchies against service types**

   Map the SAP CRM hierarchies to your service items

In addition to the integration of the SAP CRM opportunity to the SAP TM forwarding agreement RFQ, you can launch other SAP TM functionalities directly from SAP CRM. This isn't a real data interface but a remote launch of an SAP TM transaction to avoid switching between systems. Figure 13.55 shows an example of an SAP CRM UI that is customized for a sales representative and depicts all the transactions that can be accessed directly from SAP CRM.

The integration to SAP CRM functions to support their sales force is an important factor for LSPs. In addition, the direct access of customers to certain functions of an LSP instance is a regularly requested feature (customer portal). These are typically functions such as the following:

- Request a quote for a shipment
- Retrieve rates for transportation scenarios
- Hand in electronic documents for previously placed orders

Based on this, it's a possible extension to see these functionalities in the future SAP portfolio, especially with the new CRM suite SAP C/4HANA.

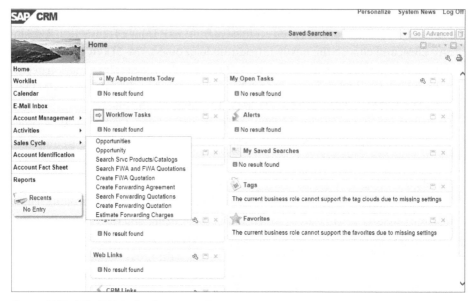

Figure 13.55 SAP CRM UI for Customer Contract Management

13.8 Summary

In this chapter, we explained both the prerequisites and content SAP provides to connect SAP TM to analytics functionality, to SAP EWM, and to SAP CRM. In the analytics section, we explained how an enterprise can use the various technologies provided by SAP either with SAP S/4HANA or classic SAP BW to create analytical reporting and retrieve analytics results used in SAP TM. The overview sections on SAP EWM gave you insight into the main warehouse use cases and integration scenarios for running your own or contract warehouse or using SAP EWM for a transit warehouse supporting SAP TM transportation processes.

The new components for SAP Transportation Resource Planning and SAP Yard Logistics allow you to extend the logistics functionality into equipment management and yard management areas. Concerning new collaboration technologies, we gave you information on the SAP Logistics Business Network, which will link a variety of networks together. Blockchain technology can make the communication considerably safer than traditional processes. Finally, we gave you an update on SAP CRM and its integration with SAP TM.

In the next chapter, we continue with the implementation best practices.

Chapter 14
Implementation Best Practices

For an integrated software suite like SAP Transportation Management, it's always helpful to get hints on where to start, what to do next, and what to consider in the overall implementation. By following best practices, you'll reach the goal more easily and safely.

As you've seen throughout this book, SAP Transportation Management (SAP TM) is a very comprehensive software suite. Its breadth and coverage are comparable with an enterprise system. It covers areas such as sales, procurement, planning, execution, the costing and settlement processes, configurations around the system, and connected components. From this perspective, it's important to know where to start with implementation, which steps are critical, and where you can find dependencies or characteristics that need to be considered to successfully get transportation processes up and running.

In this chapter, we give you an overview of the challenges involved with implementing SAP TM in large installations. We offer SAP TM configuration hints that fall into the following categories:

- Topics to be considered when business transformation projects are done related to SAP TM
- Moving from a SAP Business Suite installation of SAP TM to SAP TM in SAP S/4HANA
- Cross-functional influence of specific settings (i.e., settings that may influence various parts of the SAP TM functionality)
- General Customizing know-how
- Setup sequence
- System improvement dos and don'ts

We also provide an overview of the central control elements of the system to give insight on certain dependencies. Organizational setup, process coverage, and the complexity of the process steps and details can make implementing a transportation management system (TMS) quite a challenging process. This isn't unusual and is valid for all TMS setups that are targeted at managing the core business processes of a company.

14.1   Large Transportation Management System Installations

Typical situations in large or extra-large organizations dealing with transportation management, such as used for logistics service providers, occur due to the extreme organizational distribution and its networking requirements. We find these challenges at countrywide trucking companies, as well as in worldwide freight-forwarding or carrier organizations. It's also sometimes applicable for large manufacturing companies that have a worldwide network, especially if they take care of distribution on their own.

First, let's look at an LSP's company and network setup to better understand its challenges:

- Each LSP might be divided into many global, regional, and local organizational units with different responsibilities, its own profitability goals, and thousands of employees interacting in different roles with each other and external parties. A fictitious profile of a large, worldwide LSP may be, for example:
  - Operating 1,500+ stations in 150+ countries
  - Employing 10,000+ persons, of whom many may be users
  - Running multilevel organizational hierarchies
  - Serving 10,000+ customers with customer hierarchies (enterprise, companies, and then subsidiaries) assigned to one or multiple organizational units
- Global, regional, or local customers and subcontractors might have individually created contracts with corresponding pricing and service-level agreements (SLAs). It's very important that all of the employees in the logistics chain are—within their responsibility area—aware of the characteristics, commitments, and restrictions of the services sold.
- Support for many modes of transport might be creatively mixed. In regions and countries, the type of vehicles used can vary widely, from a motor bike in Africa to a 20,000-ton bulk train in Australia or a 20,000-container ocean vessel.
- LSPs need to identify, capture, and respond to many, often very individual, customer preferences.

- LSPs must adhere to legal, cargo, and country-related obligations and regulations to avoid penalties.
- It's important to be able to change the organizational or network structure setup when the business foundation changes and to introduce new services, products, or geographical regions into the business.

Figure 14.1 shows an example of this type of LSP organization.

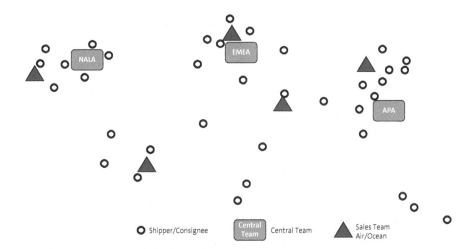

Figure 14.1 Example of a Worldwide LSP Organization and Network

In addition to the distribution of work tasks and workforce, individual teams must deal with many local legal settings in terms of handling cargo, local customs requirements, and local obligations to print or communicate. This needs to be reflected in the authorization and role settings of the users, menus, and worklist setup of the individual assigned roles.

Because LSPs are often still organized in a very regional way (i.e., different regions have profit center responsibility but must work together on customer orders), there is often the requirement to hide specific data from the eyes of the "competitive" internal organization. For example, the export organization only can view the invoice from an import group for an ocean shipment but should not be able to see the import group's price paid to the ocean carrier. This internal hiding requires very detailed authorization settings, which often may cause difficulties for IT departments in terms of data maintenance. Some LSPs already identified this as a disadvantage and cost driver and started increasing transparency. This often leads to restructuring of their organization as well as their financial and business processes to simplify the internal collaboration.

14.2   Customer Onboarding in SAP TM Installations

Customer onboarding is the process of setting up the requirements of a new customer in an LSP's existing system installation (e.g., SAP TM). In simple cases, onboarding just means a bit of master data maintenance. In more complex situations—for example, a new worldwide customer with custom-tailored logistics service requirements must be supported—configuration settings for the processes defined for a new customer must be fitted into the existing system. Setup must be done in a way that other, already-running customer processes aren't affected, and the LSP can manage the new customer with all its requirements. The following list gives you an overview of the various steps you must consider:

1. In the contracting phase, it's important to properly specify the customer's requirements, including the SLAs.

   Take the following steps to document and close the contract:

   - Document the customer-specific requirements.
   - Issue the contract.
   - Obtain internal approval of the contract.
   - Close the contract.
   - Initiate setup of the contract through the related IT and logistics departments.

2. During setup, you need to translate requirements into straightforward system settings. This chapter provides valuable hints about what to consider. Because setup sometimes increases complexity, keep an eye on the impacts of new settings on existing processes (e.g., if you're implementing a completely new air freight service that requires a new means of transport).

   Take the following steps to set up contract-specific settings:

   - Translate the contract to system-specific settings in Customizing, master data, and enhancements.
   - Implement settings.

- Implement coding and enhancements.
- Document settings, for example, in SAP Solution Manager.

3. During the test phase, existing processes should be thoroughly tested but also checked regarding impact and side effects with other, existing processes:

- Test settings with real customer data.
- Test influence of customer settings on other customers or regional or global settings (regression test).
- Release settings.

4. In the run phase, run customer orders with the following steps:

- Receive and process orders.
- Analyze SLAs.
- Execute contract reviews.

5. After the customer process is up and running, maintenance must be done because customer business changes, contract renewals, and requirements adjustments might affect system settings.

6. To update settings when required, follow these steps:

- Update, extend, or close new contracts.
- Identify existing settings.
- Retire unnecessary settings.
- Update or create new and changed settings.
- Retest new and existing scenarios.

14.3   Use of Central Control Elements in SAP TM Setup

In the previous chapters, we explained that SAP TM has many settings and configuration capabilities. You can influence these when creating scenarios and processes for transportation management. Most of these settings are straightforward in their setup and have a local or direct influence on the behavior and design of the system (e.g., limited to order management or invoicing). However, some very central control elements need special attention (note that the list isn't complete):

- Elements that can affect the behavior of multiple process steps. Changing a setting for a specific process purpose might unintentionally affect the behavior of quite different process steps, such as the following:

- Means of transport
- Equipment types and groups
- Freight unit building rules (FUBRs) and freight unit types
- Elements that are critical in terms of well-designed data structuring and long-term maintenance:
  - Charge calculation sheets and tariffs
  - Rate tables
- Elements that must be set up in a balanced way:
  - Transportation planning cost
  - Forwarding and freight order types
  - Resource types

Figure 14.2 presents an overview of selected Customizing elements and configuration settings that control the transportation management process.

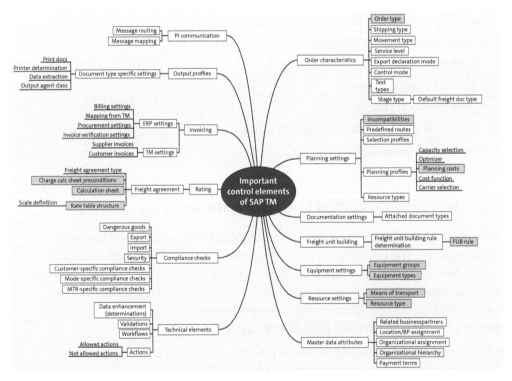

Figure 14.2 Some Control Elements of SAP TM

The control elements mentioned are marked in dark with white text. Some of the relations in the configuration are displayed by dashed arrows.

Let's consider some of these central control elements further.

14.3.1   Define Means of Transport

As a control element, means of transport is used in many ways. Because it's very central to transportation planning, cost calculation, and decision-making by conditions, it's very important to think hard about the required granularity and complexity of means of transport for planning, costing, and conditioning and to select a model that fits best into all three aspects.

The means of transport indicates a categorization of groups of resources that can be coarse or very fine, which makes it a bit tricky. Depending on the regional, country, or organization-specific requirement, you can define the means of transport according to different strategies, for example:

- **Truck, tractor, trailer (to build semitrailer truck)**
  This is a very coarse definition just to decide between a self-moving vehicle and a passive vehicle. For example, it might be sufficient for planning in *some* overall contexts but not granular enough for local decisions or costing purposes.
- **Large truck, small truck, tractor, large trailer, small trailer, and chassis**
  This is a definition of different self-moving vehicles, as well as passive vehicles with different characteristics and loading capabilities, but it's still valid on a general basis.
- **12-ton truck (Germany), 30-ton trailer (Germany), standard tractor (United States), 80,000-pound trailer (United States), and many more**
  This is the usual case for large LSPs, especially if the assets are owned by the LSP. If the fleet becomes very diverse due to national, regional, local, or subcontractor-specific regulations and capabilities, the definition of means of transport can become manifold, and you may end up with hundreds or thousands of means of transport.

If the definition of the means of transport is simply for controlling the planning, then the variety doesn't have a major impact. Otherwise, in many implementations, means of transport definitions are also used as input parameters for calculation of freight costs and prices or for other condition evaluations, such as determination of loading durations. In this case, the complexity is linked directly to the number of

14

definitions in planning. If you define many means of transport because it's practical for planning, you may create unnecessary complexity in cost calculation.

14.3.2   Structure Equipment Types and Groups

The situation described for means of transport is also valid for equipment types and groups: the more complex the definition of cargo aspects, the larger the impact on pricing definition and condition complexity.

Equipment type and group have an additional challenge. The equipment type is usually based directly on definitions of individual kinds of equipment, such as 20-foot standard container, 20-foot-high cube container, and 20-foot refrigerated container (reefer), which are assigned to the individual equipment master records for each unit (e.g., according to ISO 6346). The grouping can be used to determine which equipment types logically belong together. A grouping defined for cargo handling and movement purposes focused on use of space and compatibility of stowing doesn't need to be in line with a grouping focused on pricing. Table 14.1 shows some examples of cases in which the grouping criteria may lead to conflicts.

Grouping for Cargo Handling	Grouping for Pricing
Dry containers, high-cube containers, reefer containers, flatbed containers	20-footer dry (standard, ventilated, high-cube), 40-footer dry, and so on
By category (e.g., open railcars, closed railcars, bulk railcars)	By railcar size/length and maximum weight

Table 14.1 Equipment Grouping from the Cargo Handling and Pricing Perspective

For equipment grouping, you should therefore also create a well-defined set of equipment types and groups that meet all requirements up front.

14.3.3   Balance Freight Unit Complexity

Freight units are created using FUBRs. For the creation of a freight unit and the setup of the corresponding rule, you need to find a good balance between the flexibility of freight unit assignment and system performance and then choose the correct freight unit granularity.

If, for example, you want to ship three orders with general cargo (20 forwarding order items with 577 loose packages), you can use freight unit building (FUB) to create various results. Table 14.2 gives an overview of three of these options. If space utilization of vehicles up to the limit isn't the first goal, you may want to create fewer freight units because this creates the lowest workload for the employees and the system. You also have the option to split the freight unit as required and optimize space utilization selectively.

Strategy of FUB	Result of FUB	Consequence
Freight units per item	20 large freight units	■ Low flexibility in distributing freight units over trucks and utilizing available smaller remaining capacity ■ Simple dispatching and cargo management
Freight unit with maximum of 10 packages	58 medium-sized freight units	■ Compromise between increased flexibility to use small loading spaces and handling effort in cargo management ■ No direct control of which package goes into which freight unit
Freight unit per package	577 small-sized freight units	■ Best flexibility in using the remaining capacity of the truck, leading to the highest utilization results ■ High effort in cargo management; many objects on dispatching screens ■ Higher performance requirements due to many freight units

Table 14.2 Example Results and Consequences of FUB

14.3.4   Structure Charging Rules and Rates

When you're working with tariffs, charge calculation sheets, and rate tables, it's advisable to create templates for most of the pricing entities. This allows you to give guidance to the users who must set up forwarding and freight charge calculations. These templates should align with the company's pricing strategy. A standardized, company-wide strategy simplifies the price definition, negotiation, quoting, and contracting process. It also allows you to do price maintenance (e.g., uplift or rate increase) in a more straightforward way without giving up the flexibility of individual pricing.

Standardization means defining a set of rate table structures with sensible scales, a list of reused charge elements, and a set of template charge calculation sheets based on service products (e.g., air freight transatlantic or ocean freight standard). These are all reused to create customer-specific contracts that may then have individual prices but a structure that follows the template scheme.

14.3.5   Other Planning Configuration Settings

You may want to think twice about how simple or diverse you set up some other configuration elements. These settings should be well balanced among easy maintenance, process flexibility, and practical value, and you should answer some typical questions to help you to find the right solution:

- **Transportation planning costs in optimization**
  What factors drive decisions in transportation planning and optimization? Do you need to include virtual penalty costs for late deliveries or nondeliveries to get the best result, or is it sufficient to plan just by cost-driving factors, such as miles driven, space utilization, or vehicles used? The answers to these questions drive the complexity of cost models in optimization.

- **Forwarding and freight order types**
  How many order types do you need for your processes? Is an express order a separate order type, or is it simply modeled by characteristics such as the shipping type or a service product? We generally recommend that you reduce the number of order types to those that have a clear-cut focus (e.g., air freight order, ocean freight order, and perhaps a distinction between less than container load [LCL] and full container load [FCL]).

- **Resource types**
  Do you need separate resource instances for each vehicle that is used to transport cargo? In many cases, it may be sufficient to model resources just as a resource pool (e.g., 20 instances of a generic 40-ton truck resource instead of each truck resource as a separate instance). Distinct resources are required if you also need to maintain the resources. Mixed models are often suitable; with these, you might have instance-based models in your core regions or core business and pool-based models for regions where you don't have direct control.

14.3.6 Structure and Name Your Data Well

Before starting configuration, think about naming schemes for your configuration data. After the employees are familiar with these schemes, they can more easily find their way around a complex implementation project. Naming schemes such as the following should be applied for all settings:

- **Naming of forwarding order types**
  You can name the forwarding order type in a way to indicate the mode of transport and service (e.g., AF for air freight standard and OFL for ocean freight LCL).

- **Rate tables**
  You can include the scope, service, and customer significance in the naming. "BSF_ ASUS_C1234" could be a rate table applicable for basic sea freight (BSF) on a route from Asia to the United States (ASUS) with specific prices for customer 1234.

If you run multiple scenarios in a single client, it's helpful to segregate the settings by selecting consistent identification names, such as starting all air freight settings and purely air freight-related master data with "AF" and starting those for ocean freight with "OF". This can be beneficial in setting up consolidation settings, such as planning profiles, where you need to select other entities by referencing. By consistently segregating the name spaces for unit-specific settings, you can reduce the maintenance effort considerably.

14.4 Optimize the Sequence of SAP TM Configuration

You already understand the importance of having well-structured configuration data before going into a larger process implementation project. This is especially important if the configuration is done in a system where processes are already running and may be affected.

The following system setup sequence should give you a rough guideline, independent of whether you use SAP TM in SAP S/4HANA or SAP TM 9.6 (this isn't a complete list):

- **Set up basic systems settings**
  If you start in a new system, several prerequisite settings are required:
  - Set up logical system connections (cross-application).
  - Create an active version and model for SAP Supply Chain Management (SAP SCM) master data; otherwise, no master data can be maintained (SAP TM).

- Set up geo-location services (cross-application).

- Set up archiving, attachments, and Post Processing Framework (PPF) basics (cross-application).

■ **Set up basic SAP TM settings**
Basic SAP TM settings should be done in the beginning because they can be referenced in a later phase of configuration:

- Set up code lists (e.g., aircraft type codes).

- Set up fundamental types and categories after deciding on the granularity of the model (e.g., means of transport types, forwarding agreement item types, and charge element types).

■ **Set up business object configuration**
Business object configuration includes setting up the behavior of different object types used. If you use the order integration with SAP ERP in an SAP Business Suite implementation, the general layout of the process should already be done before you start SAP TM configuration (e.g., SAP ERP sales order (SO) types and their use in SAP TM). The same is relevant, if you use SAP S/4HANA and integrated SOs and deliveries:

- Define customer order types and order types used for SAP ERP integration (e.g., forwarding order types, forwarding quotation types, and order-based transportation requirement [OTR] and delivery-based transportation requirement [DTR] types) or corresponding SAP S/4HANA object types.

- Define planning and capacity object types (e.g., freight unit types and freight booking types).

- Define subcontracting order types (e.g., freight order types).

- Define agreement types (e.g., freight agreement types and forwarding agreement types).

■ **Set up processes and their configuration**
Process configuration defines the behavior of the system when it works with data and functions that span multiple business objects, create new information, or update existing information. Because some of the required setup may be heavily dependent on master data, you may need to make some refinements later or define some master data first:

- Set up the global service product catalog.

- Set up charge calculation rules (e.g., forwarding agreement determination, charge calculation sheet structures that reuse the charge element types, and rate tables).

- Set up planning rules (e.g., FUBRs, planning profiles, and incompatibilities).

■ **Define master data**

Master data can be set up in parallel with the process configuration:

- Business partner master data.

- Organizational model.

- Location and network master data (e.g., locations, schedules, and resources).

- Rate and tariff data.

■ **Set up integration with other systems such as SAP S/4 HANA (Billing), SAP Event Management, and SAP Global Trade Services (SAP GTS)**

- Set up system integration (remote function call [RFC], Core Interface Framework [CIF], enterprise services, etc.).

- Transmit master data.

■ **Set up ancillary services**

Ancillary services can be set up relatively late in the implementation process:

- Set up output or printing rules and printing forms.

- Integrate with the analytics system.

- Configure archiving integration and document management within the process (archiving itself has already been set up).

■ **Set up user interface (UI) configuration**

UI setup is done in SAP S/4HANA or SAP Business Client (SAP Business Suite):

- Set up menu structures, roles, launchpad, and tiles (as applicable).

- Set up worklist layouts based on the standard layout so that they meet their purpose and show valuable information.

- Set up transportation cockpit layouts.

- Adjust screen layouts with the Floorplan Manager (FPM).

- Give menu topics and fields recognizable names and adjust to country-, industry-, or customer-specific naming.

It's generally wise to run small tests during the configuration, so you can estimate the extent of design flaws in the whole setup. In some cases, you must go back to a previous step and complete or adjust the configuration (e.g., add a default output profile to an existing forwarding order type).

14.5   SAP TM Scenario Builder

In the previous sections, you read that a configuration of a scenario in SAP TM may contain a variety of settings, such as master data, Customizing, configuration, and transactional data. With traditional SAP tools, only a part of this data can be packaged in a way that a complete scenario can be defined, transferred to another system, or redeployed in a new system or client to retest and run existing scenarios.

However, the *Scenario Builder* introduced for SAP TM with releases SAP S/4HANA 1709 FPS 01, SAP TM 9.5 SP 01, and SAP TM 9.4 SP 05 allows you to create these complete scenarios. The SAP Fiori app is for nonproductive use and allows you to create test data for SAP TM with the goal of simplifying bundling and repeated creation of master data, transactional data, Customizing, and configuration for test and demo situations.

The Scenario Builder can be started in SAP S/4HANA via **Application Administration • Scenario Builder** (in SAP TM 9.6, use path **Application Administration • General Settings • Scenario Builder**). In Figure 14.3, you can see the Scenario Builder overview page.

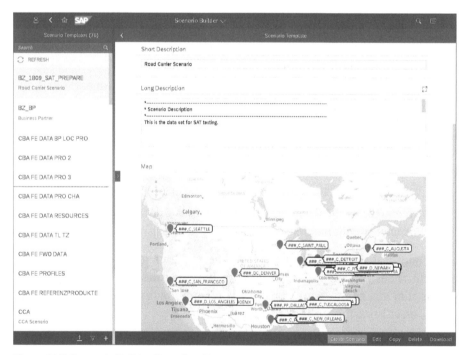

Figure 14.3 Scenario Builder Overview Page

After selecting a scenario or creating a new scenario, various aspects of the scenario can be edited, that is, the related master data, Customizing entries, configuration entities, or transactional objects can be added. In the current version, the following elements are available:

- Info
  - Short and long descriptions for the scenario
  - Map display that visualized the geographical elements of the scenario (see Figure 14.3)
- Master data, which is displayed in Figure 14.4
  - Transportation network: Locations, transportation zones, transshipment locations, schedules, and transportation lanes
  - Vehicle resources
  - General master data, such as business partners and their relations and materials

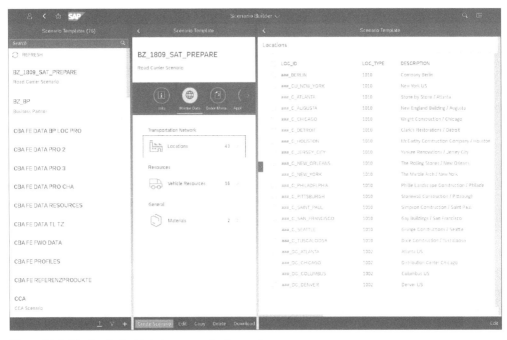

Figure 14.4 Master Data Maintenance of a Scenario

- Order management data for the use as templates
  - Forwarding orders
  - Transportation orders for road, rail, air, and ocean
- Administrative planning settings
  - FUB profiles
  - Planning profile elements and selection profiles
- Reporting variants
- Customizing data consolidated in business configuration sets

After a scenario is completely defined, it can be exported in an Excel-based table format per entity and bundled in a Zip archive, which allows system-independent copying of scenarios. Figure 14.5 shows such an export file.

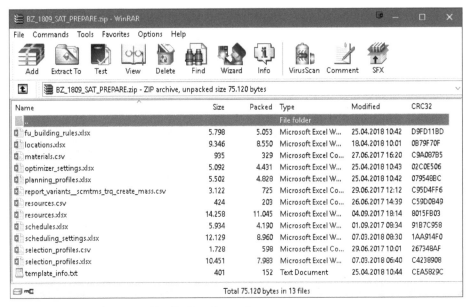

Figure 14.5 Example Export Zip File for a Scenario

The current version of Scenario Builder is mainly targeted to support reuse of order and planning scenarios. The charge management data is still missing. This however may be added in a later version or alternatively export and import via charge and contract objects can be an option.

14.6   Moving SAP TM from the SAP Business Suite to an SAP S/4HANA System

Using SAP TM in SAP S/4HANA or standalone brings a variety of benefits starting from the more than 400 simplifications available to the technical advantages, data integration, and embedded analytics benefits. If you want to implement SAP TM in SAP S/4HANA 1809, there are generally three different scenarios:

- **New implementation**
  Reengineering and process simplification-based implementation of innovative business processes using SAP Best Practice content on a new SAP S/4HANA platform with initial data load and retirement of an old landscape (legacy or third party). Looking at SAP TM, we've already discussed this scenario, as it's a new setup of a TMS.

- **System conversion**
  A complete technical in-place conversion of an existing SAP Business Suite system to SAP S/4HANA to adopt innovations. The main scenario for a SAP TM move is an existing SAP Business Suite installation that should be moved to an SAP S/4HANA platform, as addressed in this scenario.

- **Landscape transformation**
  Value-driven data migration to the new platform by consolidation of current multiple SAP Business Suite landscapes into one global SAP S/4HANA system or selective data migration based on legal entities. This scenario can be left out in our case, as it's primarily focused on a distributed SAP ERP landscape with multiple instances and provides a guideline to consolidate these. It's therefore not the typical goal for a SAP TM installation.

SAP provides a set of tools that supports the conversion or system migration from SAP ERP to SAP S/4HANA. However, the move of an SAP TM instance isn't fully automated yet and still needs manual activities for a complete move. An important tool for a system conversion is the *SAP S/4HANA migration cockpit*, which is the tool of choice available with an SAP S/4HANA installation. It's a ready-to-use solution offering a comprehensive set of preconfigured migration objects, such as customers, suppliers, as well as automated mapping between source data and SAP S/4HANA target values. The SAP S/4HANA migration cockpit can help bring the SAP ERP-based process foundation of an SAP TM implementation into the SAP S/4HANA world. In Figure 14.6, you can see the steps of a typical migration process with the preparation and realization phases.

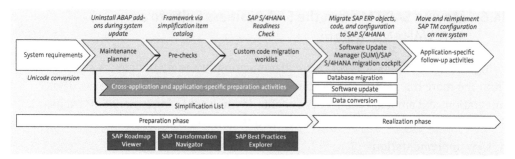

Figure 14.6 Typical Migration Process with Preparation and Realization Phases

The SAP S/4HANA migration cockpit, which is part of the realization phase, provides step-by-step guidance through the migration process with template files for each migration object and data validation to ensure high-data quality and consistency. It also supports mass data transfer with the help of a staging solution.

Data staging can be done either via files or staging tables. In future releases, a direct data transfer from other SAP systems is planned. For staging table usage, the following occurs when migrating data:

1. You choose an SAP or non-SAP system as the source system.
2. You access the SAP S/4HANA migration cockpit in the SAP S/4HANA instance.
3. Next, you create a database connection to the SAP HANA database and identify the objects that need to be migrated. After that, the staging tables are created.
4. The staging tables are filled by migration tools.
5. Finally, the staging table content is transferred into the SAP S/4HANA database.

For SAP S/4HANA 1809, 68 migration objects from the SAP ERP scope are predefined. You can find a detailed list in the SAP Help Portal at *https://help.sap.com* when you search for "SAP S/4HANA migration cockpit." Figure 14.7 shows the SAP Help page for the migration objects available in SAP S/4HANA 1809. Objects contained include customer and vendor data, finance and General Ledger (G/L) data, material and maintenance master data, pricing conditions (SAP ERP), sales and purchasing contracts, and many others.

Some migration steps that aren't yet part of the SAP S/4HANA migration cockpit can also be supported with additional software tools, such as the Scenario Builder or charge data export and import via Excel tables. However, a full migration is still a goal to be provided in future releases.

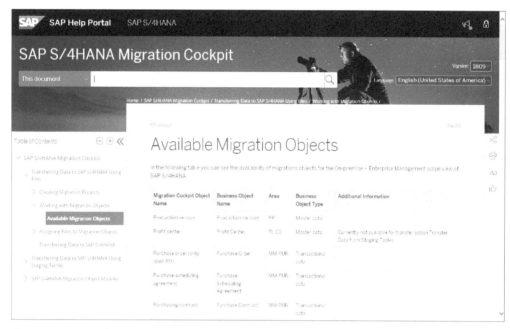

Figure 14.7 SAP Help for Available Migration Objects

14.7   Consider SAP TM's Strengths and Limitations

In this section, we offer some additional hints that can clarify both the capabilities and current limitations of SAP TM and its ecosystem:

- **Limit the network and plan to necessary elements and complexity**
  Because SAP TM has many means of defining a transportation network and using it for planning and routing, you might be tempted to set it up in a very detailed way—perhaps to define customer locations down to the dock door as part of the transportation network.

  Instead, we recommend that you keep the network as simple as possible so that the planning performance is good, and the definition of planning rules doesn't become overly complicated.

- **Be cautious when using SAP Fiori or Web Dynpro screens on the web**
  You can use SAP TM's Web Dynpro screens on the Internet. Some screens are prepared for this (e.g., the collaboration portal in SAP TM on SAP Business Suite, where

a carrier can place bids on tenders), but many of the SAP TM screens shouldn't be exposed to external access in this way. Of course, intracompany use on the web via a virtual private network is no problem, but don't try to expose a forwarding order entry screen as a customer portal screen for online ordering because the data security isn't targeted for external use. For example, by pressing (F4) while the cursor is in the **Business Partner** field, an external user can see a large list of customers that he isn't authorized to see. If SAP TM screens are reused for external web usage, you should create a new screen (also as a copy of an existing one) and adjust the layout, security, and authorization so that it meets the required standard.

- **Consider configuration versus personalization**
  Many tasks that are done during SAP TM setup are classified as configuration; they control the system for all users with the appropriate authorization (other users simply can't use a configured feature). In UI setup, some tasks can be classified as *personalization*, which means that the setup is made only for the user making the alterations. This is applicable to all nonadministrative activities in the UI adjustment (e.g., hiding fields) or worklist setup, where you change the selection criteria, queries, or layout and sequence of columns. If you need to provide changes to a larger group of users, do it with the administrative tools.

- **Create new worklist applications**
  Worklist applications can't be reused directly and adjusted to a different context. If, for example, you want to create a menu structure with different branches for order management (e.g., industrial customer orders and end customer orders) and reuse the forwarding order worklists in both menu branches, then adjustment of the worklist in one branch automatically leads to the same changes in the other branch. If you need to reuse a worklist, you must do the following to create a new personal object worklist (POWL) application (do this in the SAP GUI, not SAP Business Client):

  - Call Transaction FPB_MAINTAIN_HIER. Create a new POWL application as a copy of the one you want to reuse (e.g., the order management POWL SCMTMS_ POWL_OM).
  - Go to Transaction POWL_TYPER, and set the role assignment for the new POWL application.
  - Use Transaction POWL_QUERYR to define the role assignment details.
  - Finally, run report POWL_D01 using Transaction SE38 to reset the POWL caches.

14.8 Enhance SAP TM via SAP Innovative Business Solutions

Even though SAP TM is a very powerful tool, it's not always complete in terms of covering everything customers envision or require. Therefore, the SAP Innovative Business Solutions organization provides solutions for single customers or small groups of customers requiring deeper functionality in specific areas. Several *custom development projects* (CDP) have been created for SAP TM, including the following:

- **Validation Framework**
  BRF+ can be used to easily set up validation rules in order processing that gives users hints on how to check or complete an order.

- **Container shipping line (CSL) solutions**
  CSL is a complete suite of add-on applications that includes three separate packages: Lead-to-Agreement for CSL, Order-to-Cash for CSL, and Network and Operations for CSL, which allow an end-to-end operation for large ocean carriers on top of SAP TM.

- **Product Configurator**
  The Product Configurator allows the use of the Internet Pricing Configuration (IPC) capabilities in SAP TM contract creation and order management.

- **Resource planning Gantt chart**
  This Gantt chart is a scheduling board for vehicle and driver resources in the trucking business. It comes with a very practical "yard in–out view," allowing you to clearly see when certain resources are expected to come into a yard and which shipments still need assignment of resources to go out on time.

- **Incident Management integration**
  This integration among SAP Event Management, SAP Customer Relationship Management (SAP CRM), and SAP TM allows the handling of incidents by customer service in a very structured and auditable way.

Several other CDPs have been developed as well. SAP may decide to retrofit some of the CDPs in a future SAP TM release.

14.9 Summary

You've learned about the various functional areas and components of SAP TM, examined the technical foundation and other integrated SAP applications, and explored various scenarios. With these best practice tips, we conclude the journey through this book.

We hope to have achieved an overview of both SAP TM in SAP S/4HANA 1809 and SAP TM 9.6. In this chapter, you learned useful best practices for implementing SAP TM and innovative methods for making use of SAP's extensibility. You got insight into topics such as customer onboarding, specific things to take care of when implementing SAP TM, tools to migrate from an SAP Business Suite version of SAP TM to SAP TM in SAP S/4HANA, and also tools to transport business scenario content for SAP TM between different system instances.

We'll end with a final chapter reflecting on what we've learned and the future outlook for SAP TM.

Chapter 15
Summary and Outlook

Digitalization and competition from new players in the logistics market are two major challenges for today's logistics companies, but they also provide a chance for companies to increase the efficiency of their own processes. The SAP Transportation Management solution is an important building block to handle today's complexities.

Customer orientation, digitalization, and new players—either as competitors or potential partners—are the demanding trends characterizing required efforts to protect existing markets and grow into new channels, regions, or services. Many companies need to reorganize their value-added processes, paying special attention to the interfaces between the sales and procurement markets, which are increasing in importance. With the new digital platforms, the integration of corporate functions has become more important than ever before.

Based on availability, logistics has functionally mapped into the standard business software context. Accordingly, there is a great demand for transportation functionality, adaptability to digital data sources and capabilities, and ability to implement transportation management in complex supply chain systems with the know-how of a strong software provider and knowledgeable partners. Logistics has grown from a fifth wheel to an essential element of strategic corporate leadership.

The operational significance of logistics for many companies still lies in its rationalization potential. In general, a reduction of logistics costs should improve corporate success by achieving a competitive advantage. Surveys of businesses have demonstrated that, for the coming years, companies are still counting on a considerable cost reduction potential. On top of that, the digitalization strategies and new networking opportunities open plenty of opportunities but also pressure to adapt and stay flexible.

The scope of logistics in recent years has continually expanded. We now can include production planning or quality control systems into the end-to-end scope of logistics. In addition, significant investments are made in IT in areas such as supply chain management planning. In the future, this will lead to a decrease in administrative logistics costs (e.g., through shipment tracking, transport organization or Internet-based ordering). It not only affects efficiency but also the fulfillment of demands of customers, who expect better integration with all their supply chain partners and higher visibility and insight based on available digital data, big data evaluation, and intelligent technologies.

In highly competitive supply chain environments, outsourcing traditional core logistics processes, for example, is still a stable trend and a decisive means of cost cutting and competitive differentiation, especially among manufacturers and retailers. In this context, companies expect further savings by subcontracting logistics services and outsourcing these services to logistics service providers (LSPs). Even in LSP domains, outsourcing of pure logistics operations and higher focus on serving their customer's needs and increasing their loyalty with the LSPs offering are high priorities.

Operative logistics tasks, such as transport, storage, commissioning, and packaging, have already been outsourced to a high degree to external LSPs or carriers. Modern logistic solutions support all aspects of corporate and outsourced logistics, including warehousing and transportation, as well as a seamless integration with an organization or its customers' backend systems.

In today's fast-moving, modern society, it's vital for suppliers to have a fully integrated solution and to prevent silos from forming where insight is limited to only parts of a company or parts of a network. From the perspectives of both the shipper and the LSP, several logistics processes either include interfaces with customers or affect the customer. That is why logistics processes must be oriented toward customer needs and performed in a service-friendly manner. The new technologies offered by the cloud, secure and immutable communication, and collaboration open the door to the kind of network that is demanded today.

When the quality of competitors' products continues to become more comparable, competition takes place on the level of service performance, especially because, in most industries, there is hardly room to lower prices any more. Within these services, transportation as a direct or indirect service ranks high. Delivery perfection and flexibility, rapid returns processing, and high quality of customer service are characteristics with which a company can set itself apart from its competitors.

The commercial world is shrinking as modern communication channels give everyone the ability to share information. Many companies are beginning to think in terms of their global logistics operations rather than individual local goals. They want technology providers to deliver an integrated logistics and supply chain system that is capable of seamlessly delivering goods from one end of the globe to the other by integration of all relevant partners. In this context, transportation and logistics is a major growth area and a priority investment today. Logistics costs represent around 10% of a country's gross domestic product and have a major impact on a company's profitability, customer service level, and sustainability balance sheet. Supply chain, transportation, and warehouse managers are now under pressure to automate, transform, and optimize their business processes. The integration of new technologies, such as sensors, Internet of Things (IoT) devices, machine learning processes, or big data analytics, enriches this pressure, as traditional legacy systems often prove to be dead-ends in this new, fast-changing technology world.

In this context, transportation management solutions were initially developed to just plan and operate day-to-day local handling processes. Today, planned innovations for logistics focus on optimizing integrated supply chain execution processes and connecting them to the IoT. This will allow for the management of distribution hubs, as well as deeper integration of the manufacturing material flow with production warehouses. Overall, the SAP logistics strategy allows efficient and speedy fulfillment of customer demands. It breaks down the operational silos of separated responsibilities and allows greater focus on end-to-end business processes, enabling logistics managers to become network orchestrators who can create value for the end customer and stay in sync with the team.

Without sophisticated transportation systems, logistics could not bring its advantages into full play. Besides a good transport system, logistics activities could provide better logistics efficiency, reduce operation costs, promote service quality, and increase connectivity and insight. The improvement of transportation systems needs efforts from both customers and software vendors. SAP S/4HANA and SAP Leonardo are an ideal foundation to provide all these features to a company and its peers.

Looking ahead, transportation logistics will greatly magnify the inefficiencies of spending too much time on tactical or low-value tasks. Granted, international transportation can be far more complex than domestic shipping. It's not uncommon for global shipments to touch many intermediaries, each of whom has a distinct set of regulations, cultural beliefs, and IT capabilities. Nor is technology alone the answer; too many shippers have deployed transportation management software, only to have it fail and drive users back to their old, laborious duties. The most successful

15

global companies use strategies that allow for "acceptable tolerances" in their transportation networks. They rely on event management features of technology to alert operators when attention is needed for unusual situations. In addition, effective transportation management solutions and services should allow users to generate a real-time, global "control tower" view of their networks and drill down into the specifics of each shipment, such as purchase orders (POs), freight bills, stock-keeping units (SKUs), and so on.

Global instability and rapidly changing infrastructures in countries around the world call for dynamic routing approaches. The most efficient route in December may not be so in January. Bad weather, political instability, fuel prices, capacity, or any number of other factors can influence the outcome of a decision process. To account for all the variables, effective global transportation strategies will likely employ transportation management technology, processes, and expertise, which allow for real-time agility and risk mitigation

Following SAP's strategic mission to deliver the world's best logistics solution portfolio, SAP TM began a new era in the market for transportation management software. It became a best-in-class solution that supports integrated and connected supply chain execution processes with a vertical offering for shippers, freight forwarders, and carriers. In addition, with the integration into SAP S/4HANA, SAP TM has a bright future, which is open to the level of digitalization that today's companies need.

This book is intended to provide you with a comprehensive reference work and workbook for transportation management with SAP TM. Our experience as SAP TM architects, developers, and product managers offers you comprehensive insight into application-oriented process handling, operation, and the technical background of transportation management with SAP.

By matching logistics demands and capacities to short-term planning; optimizing processes and resources of the entire distribution network; providing responsiveness and flexibility through complete real-time visibility; and giving insight into plans, operations, and inventory—all based on a transportation management that is seamlessly connected to the business network—SAP's vision is to help companies achieve their supply chain execution excellence, increase transportation and logistics efficiency and productivity, reduce supply chain execution costs, and improve sustainability and compliance.

SAP will extend and improve its transportation management solution as part of SAP S/4 HANA with additional versions in the years ahead. This book points to functions of SAP TM 1809 and SAP TM 9.6, which enable a major step forward in terms of practical relevance, functionality, user friendliness, and an even tighter integration across SAP's supply chain execution platform.

Finally, we also want to recommend that you have a look for online information and books from Rheinwerk Publishing. We hope you've achieved what you desired with this book and found valuable answers to your questions. Most importantly, we hope we've sparked or encouraged your passion for transportation and logistics with SAP TM.

Thank you very much for your interest in our works,
Dr. Bernd Lauterbach, **Stefan Sauer**, **Dr. Jens Gottlieb**,
Dr. Christopher Sürie, and **Ulrich Benz**

15

Appendix A
Abbreviations

Abbreviation	Meaning
24/7	7 days, 24 hours; i.e. around the clock
2PL	Second-party logistic provider (carrier with own assets)
3PL	Third-party logistics provider (forwarder potentially without assets)
4PL	Fourth-party logistics provider (end-to-end service provider)
A2A	Application to application
ABAP	Advanced Business Application Programming
ABD	Agency business document
ACI	Advanced Commercial Information (Canada)
ACS	Air cargo security
ADR	European agreement concerning the international carriage of dangerous goods by road
AMS	Automated manifest system (US)
APO	SAP Advanced Planner and Optimizer
ASEAN	Association of Southeast Asian Nations
ATP	Available-to-promise
AWB	Air waybill
B2B	Business to business
B2C	Business to customer
BAdI	Business add-in
BC	SAP Business Client

Abbreviation	Meaning
BI	SAP BusinessObjects Business Intelligence
B/L	Bill of lading
BO	Business object
BoB	Best-of-breed
BOBJ	SAP BusinessObjects
BOPF	Business Objects Processing Framework
BPM	Business process management
BPM	Business partner
BRF+	Business Rules Framework plus
BRIM	SAP Billing and Revenue Innovation Management
BS	Business share
CASS	Cargo Account Settlement System
CC	Convergent charging
CCAD	Charge correction advice document
CDP	Custom development project
CEP	Courier, express, and parcel
CFR	Code of Federal Regulations
CFS	Container freight station
CI	Convergent invoicing
CIF	Core Interface Framework
CO-PA	SAP Controlling & Profitability Analysis
CRM	SAP Customer Relationship Management
CRUD	Create, read, update, delete
CSL	Container shipping line
CSR	Cargo sales report

Abbreviation	Meaning
CSR	Customer service representative
CSV	Comma-separated value (file type)
CU	Container unit
CVI	Customer vendor integration
DAD	Data access definition
DCM	Debit/credit memo
DD, D2D	Door to door
DDIC	Data Dictionary
DG	Dangerous goods
DGR	IATA Dangerous Goods Regulations
DRF	Data Replication Framework
DSD	Direct store delivery
DSO	Direct shipment option
DSO	DataStore object
DTR	Delivery-based transportation requirement
ECC	SAP ERP Core Component
EDI	Electronic data interchange
EFTA	European Free Trade Association
EH	Event handler
EHP	Enhancement pack
EHS	SAP Environment, Health, and Safety Management
EM	SAP Event Management
EMS	Event Management System
EP	SAP Enterprise Portal
ERP	SAP Enterprise Resource Planning

Abbreviation	Meaning
ERS	Evaluated receipt settlement/self-billing
ESOA	Enterprise service-oriented architecture
ESR	Enterprise services repository
EWM	SAP Extended Warehouse Management
FA	Freight agreement
FB	Freight booking
FBI	Floorplan Manager BOPF integration
FCC	SAP Financial Customer Care
FCL	Full container load
FEU	Forty-feet equivalent unit (container)
FI-AP	SAP ERP Financials – Accounts Payables
FI-AR	SAP ERP Financials – Accounts Receivables
FI-CA	SAP ERP Financials – Contract Accounting
FI-CO	SAP ERP Finance and Controlling
FO	Freight order
FPM	Floorplan Manager
FSCM	Financial Supply Chain Management
FSD	Freight settlement document
FTL	Full truck load
FU	Freight unit
FUB	Freight unit building
FUBR	Freight unit building rule
FWA	Forwarding agreement
FWAQ	Forwarding agreement quotation
FWO	Forwarding order

Abbreviation	Meaning
FWQ	Forwarding quotation
FWSD	Forwarding settlement document
GCR	General cargo rates
GFX	Global freight exchange (air freight)
GHF	Ground handling facility
GIS	Geographical Information System
GPS	Global Positioning System
GRC	SAP Governance, Risk, and Compliance
GTS	SAP Global Trade Services
GTT	SAP Global Track and Trace
GUI	Graphical user interface
GUIBB	Generic user interface building block
HANA	High Performance Analytic Appliance
HAWB	House airway bill
HEC	SAP HANA Enterprise Cloud
HBL	House bill of lading
HS code	Harmonized system code
IATA	International Air Transport Association
ICAO	International Civil Aviation Organization
ID	Identifier
IGS	Internal graphic server
IMDG	International Maritime Dangerous Goods Code
IMG	Implementation Guide
IMO	International Maritime Organization
ISF	Importer Security Filing

Abbreviation	Meaning
IT	Information technology
KPI	Key performance indicator (analytics)
LBN	SAP Logistics Business Network
LCL	Less than container load
LE	SAP ERP Logistics Execution
LSP	Logistics service provider
LTL	Less than truck load
LVD	Long-term vendor declaration
MAWB	Master air waybill
MBL	Master bill of lading
MDG	SAP Master Data Governance
MDM	SAP NetWeaver Master Data Management
MM	Materials Management (SAP ERP and SAP S/4HANA)
MRN	Movement reference number
NAFTA	North American Free Trade Agreement
NCTS	New Computerized Transit System
NOG	Nature of goods
NSC	Not secure
NW	SAP NetWeaver
NWBC	SAP NetWeaver Business Client
OTR	Order-based transportation requirement
P2P	Peer-to-peer tendering
PDF	Portable document format
PI	SAP NetWeaver Process Integration
PI	SAP Process Integration

Abbreviation	Meaning
PM	Plant maintenance
PO	Purchase order
POWL	Personal object worklist
PP, P2P	Port to port
PPF	Post-processing framework
PS&S	Product Safety and Stewardship
PU	Package unit
RCCF	Remote control and communication framework
RCS	Repeatable custom solution (SAP custom development)
REACH	Registration, Evaluation, and Authorization of Chemicals
REST	Representational State Transfer
RFC	Remote function call
RFID	Radio-frequency identification
RFQ	Request for quotation
RU	Railcar unit
SCAC	Standard Carrier Alpha Code
SCM	SAP Supply Chain Management
SCO	Secure for cargo aircraft
SCP	Supply chain platform
SCP	SAP Cloud Platform
SCR	Specialized commodity rates
SD	Sales and Distribution (SAP ERP and SAP S/4HANA)
SES	Service entry sheet
SFM	Strategic freight management
SFP	Strategic freight procurement

Abbreviation	Meaning
SFS	Strategic freight selling
SICF	Service Interface Component Framework
SLA	Service-level agreement
SLD	System landscape directory
SO	Sales order
SOA	Service-oriented architecture
SOP	Standard operating procedure
SPX	Secure for passenger aircraft
STO	Stock transfer order
TACT	The Air Cargo Tariff and Rules
TAL	Transportation allocations
TCCS	Transportation charge calculation sheet
TCM	Transportation charge management
TD	SAP Transportation and Distribution (Oil & Gas)
TEU	Twenty-foot equivalent unit
TM	SAP Transportation Management
TMS	Transportation Management System
TO	Transportation order
TOR	Transportation order (business object)
TP/VS	SAP APO transportation planning and vehicle scheduling
TRP	SAP Transportation Resource Planning
TRQ	Transportation requirement (business object)
TU	Transportation unit
UI	User interface
UIBB	User interface building block

Abbreviation	Meaning
ULD	Unit load device (container or pallet)
UN/LOCODE	United Nations Code for Trade and Transport Locations
URL	Uniform resource locator
VB	SAP Visual Business
VSR	Vehicle scheduling and routing
WD	Web Dynpro
WMS	Warehouse Management System
WSRM	SAP Web Service Reliable Messaging
XML	Extensible markup language
YL	SAP Yard Logistics

Appendix B
The Authors

Dr. Bernd Lauterbach is chief solution architect for SAP's industry business unit (IBU) Travel & Transportation (T&T) – Cargo&Logistics practice. He joined SAP in 1995 and works with carriers, forwarders, and other logistics companies to bring together LSP needs and SAP solution competence, in terms of customer requirements, business processes, target architectures, and software capabilities.

Before assuming his role in IBU T&T, Bernd worked for 13 years within SAP as a development/project manager, as well as a development architect in SAP TM, SAP Event Management, Auto ID Infrastructure, and SAP ERP transportation development projects.

Bernd studied and received a PhD in electrical engineering from University of Bremen, Germany. Before working with SAP, he spent several years doing satellite electronics, C++ and Occam parallel programming for image processing, assembler programming, GIS, and auto-routing systems.

Stefan Sauer has been with SAP since 2007. With the ramp-up of SAP Transportation Management 8.0 in 2010, he accompanied the success of the software product as an SAP TM consultant, being involved in implementation projects in retail, rail, and ocean freight industries and participating in customer engagements in other industries such as fashion, air freight, and manufacturing. Stefan supported projects both from a business process perspective by creating blueprints and implementation concepts, and from a technical perspective as the link between project and custom development. Furthermore, he worked as a trainer for SAP TM for both functional and technical training courses.

Stefan is now SAP's solution manager for the industry sector of ocean freight and port operations.

Dr. Jens Gottlieb received a PhD in computer science and has worked in supply chain software development at SAP SE in Walldorf, Germany, since 2000. He has written five books and more than 25 scientific publications in the areas of transportation management and heuristic optimization algorithms, and has edited six books.

Jens was the development architect for the vehicle scheduling and routing optimizer and the carrier selection optimizer, which are used in SAP TM, SAP APO-TPVS, and SAP MRS. He led development projects both in SAP TM and SAP APO-TPVS and served as development manager for SAP TM. Holding the position of chief product expert, Jens works as product owner for SAP TM, where he is responsible for transportation planning and network.

Dr. Christopher Sürie has worked for more than 15 years as a principal consultant in supply chain optimization and transportation management at SAP Deutschland SE & Co KG in Walldorf, Germany. In this position, he has been involved in numerous international customer projects, implementing both SAP APO and SAP TM and focusing on their planning capabilities and optimization engines in production and transportation. He worked as a solution architect in several SAP TM projects and taught numerous SAP TM customer trainings.

Before joining SAP, he worked in the department of production and supply chain management at Darmstadt University of Technology and completed his prize-winning PhD thesis in the area of production planning for process industries.

Ulrich Benz is an SAP supply chain management specialist with a focus on SAP Transportation Management. As a consultant, he has managed and supported multinational IT transformation projects, covering different industries, for the past 11 years. In his current role, he advises customers on how to realize their vision of an intelligent enterprise utilizing SAP software.

Index

G

- Configure embedded and decentralized EWM in SAP S/4HANA

- Get step-by-step instructions for implementing key warehouse processes, from goods issue to kitting

- Explore your options for integration and reporting on your warehouse

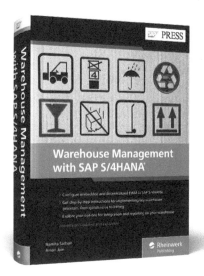

Namita Sachan, Aman Jain

Warehouse Management with SAP S/4HANA

Are you ready for warehouse management in SAP S/4HANA? With this implementation guide to EWM in SAP S/4HANA, lay the foundation by setting up organizational and warehouse structures. Then configure your master data and cross-process settings with step-by-step instructions. Finally, customize your core processes, from inbound and outbound deliveries to value-added services and cartonization. SAP S/4HANA is now ready for you!

909 pages, 2nd edition, pub. 02/2020
E-Book: $79.99 | **Print:** $89.95 | **Bundle:** $99.99

www.sap-press.com/5005

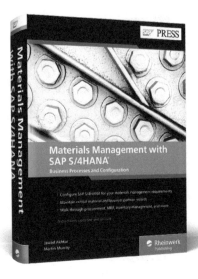

Interested in reading more?

Please visit our website for all new book
and e-book releases from SAP PRESS.

www.sap-press.com